ENCYCLOPEDIA OF COMPUTER SCIENCE AND TECHNOLOGY

VOLUME 28

ENCYCLOPEDIA OF COMPUTER SCIENCE AND TECHNOLOGY

EXECUTIVE EDITORS

Allen Kent   *James G. Williams*

UNIVERSITY OF PITTSBURGH
PITTSBURGH, PENNSYLVANIA

ADMINISTRATIVE EDITORS

Carolyn M. Hall   *Rosalind Kent*

PITTSBURGH, PENNSYLVANIA

VOLUME 28
SUPPLEMENT 13

 **CRC Press**
Taylor & Francis Group
Boca Raton London New York

CRC Press is an imprint of the
Taylor & Francis Group, an **informa** business

First published 1993 by Marcel Dekker, Inc.

Published 2021 by CRC Press
Taylor & Francis Group
6000 Broken Sound Parkway NW, Suite 300
Boca Raton, FL 33487-2742

© 1993 by Taylor & Francis Group, LLC
CRC Press is an imprint of Taylor & Francis Group, an Informa business

No claim to original U.S. Government works

ISBN 13: 978-0-8247-2281-4 (hbk)

Visit the Taylor & Francis Web site at
http://www.taylorandfrancis.com

and the CRC Press Web site at
http://www.crcpress.com

LIBRARY OF CONGRESS CATALOG CARD NUMBER: 74-29436

CONTENTS OF VOLUME 28

Contributors to Volume 28   *v*

AEROSPACE APPLICATIONS OF
    ARTIFICIAL INTELLIGENCE
    James R. Johnson   1

ARTIFICIAL INTELLIGENCE ON WALL STREET
    Roy S. Freedman   15

COMPUTER RELIABILITY
    J. J. Stiffler and Dhiraj K. Pradhan   27

CONTROL FUNCTIONS: MICROPROGRAMMING
    Michael J. Eager   33

DATA FLOW MODELING
    Mehdi T. Harandi   63

DATA REPAIR
    John B. Leber   89

DYNAMIC MEMORY
    V. Rajaraman   103

END-USER COMPUTING
    Kate M. Kaiser   123

HIGH-LEVEL SYNTHESIS
    Raul Camposano   129

INTELLIGENT COMPUTER-AIDED DESIGN
    David C. Brown   153

LARGE-SCALE NUMERICAL OPTIMIZATION:
    INTRODUCTION AND OVERVIEW
    Thomas F. Coleman   167

iii

LITERAL INTELLIGENCE OF COMPUTERS
    AND DOCUMENTS
Julian Warner   197

POSITRON EMISSION TOMOGRAPHY
Mongi Al Abidi and Paul Benjamin Davis   217

PROGRAM VERIFICATION
James H. Fetzer   237

RELIABLE DISTRIBUTED SYSTEMS
Tony P. Ng   255

STRUCTURED ANALYSIS
Paul T. Ward   277

STUDY OF GEOPHYSICAL PHENOMENA
    USING COMPUTERS
William Harbert   317

TECHNOLOGICAL SUBSTITUTIONS IN THE
    COMPUTER INDUSTRY
Theodore Modis   331

3-D IMAGING IN MEDICINE
Andreas Pommert, Michael Bomans, Martin Riemer,
Ulf Tiede, and Karl Heinz Höhne   341

TREE STRUCTURES
Yannis Manolopoulos   371

FINITE-STATE MACHINES (Errata)
Yishai A. Feldman   387

CONTRIBUTORS TO VOLUME 28

MONGI AL ABIDI, Department of Electrical and Computer Engineering, The University of Tennessee, Knoxville, Tennessee: *Positron Emission Tomography*

MICHAEL BOMANS, Institute of Mathematics and Computer Science in Medicine (IMDM), University Hospital Eppendorf, Hamburg, Germany: *3-D Imaging in Medicine*

DAVID C. BROWN, Professor, AI Research Group, Computer Science Department, Worcester Polytechnic Institute, Worcester, Massachusetts: *Intelligent Computer-Aided Design*

RAUL CAMPOSANO, Ph.D., Professor and Institute Director, University of Paderborn and GMD, System Design Institute, Saint Augustin, Germany: *High-Level Synthesis*

THOMAS F. COLEMAN, Professor, Computer Science Department, Cornell University, Ithaca, New York: *Large-Scale Numerical Optimization: Introduction and Overview*

PAUL BENJAMIN DAVIS, Department of Electrical and Computer Engineering, The University of Tennessee, Knoxville, Tennessee: *Positron Emission Tomography*

MICHAEL J. EAGER, Consultant, Eager Consulting, Campbell, California: *Control Functions: Microprogramming*

YISHAI A. FELDMAN, Ph.D., Institute of Computer Science, Tel Aviv University, Tel Aviv, Israel: *Finite-State Machines*

JAMES H. FETZER, Department of Philosophy, University of Minnesota, Duluth, Minnesota: *Program Verification*

ROY S. FREEDMAN, Ph.D.,   President and Chief Scientist, Inductive Solutions, Inc., New York, New York: *Artificial Intelligence on Wall Street*

MEHDI T. HARANDI,   Associate Professor and Director of Knowledge Based Programming Assistant Project, Department of Computer Science, University of Illinois at Urbana-Champaign, Urbana, Illinois: *Data Flow Modeling*

WILLIAM HARBERT,   Department of Geology and Planetary Science, University of Pittsburgh, Pittsburgh, Pennsylvania: *Study of Geophysical Phenomena Using Computers*

KARL HEINZ HÖHNE, Ph.D.,   Institute of Mathematics and Computer Science in Medicine (IMDM), University Hospital Eppendorf, Hamburg, Germany: *3-D Imaging in Medicine*

JAMES R. JOHNSON,   Midwestern Regional Manager, Netrologic, Inc., Dayton, Ohio: *Aerospace Applications of Artificial Intelligence*

KATE M. KAISER,   Associate Professor MIS, College of Business, Marquette University, Milwaukee, Wisconsin: *End-User Computing*

JOHN B. LEBER,   Leber Enterprises, Peoria, Illinois: *Data Repair*

YANNIS MANOLOPOULOS, Ph.D.,   Assistant Professor, Department of Electrical Engineering, Aristotle University of Thessaloniki, Thessaloniki, Greece: *Tree Structures*

THEODORE MODIS, Ph.D.,   Management Science Consultant, European Consulting Services, Digital Equipment Corporation International, Geneva, Switzerland: *Technological Substitutions in the Computer Industry*

TONY P. NG, Ph.D.,   Assistant Professor, Department of Computer Science, University of Illinois at Urbana-Champaign, Urbana, Illinois: *Reliable Distributed Systems*

ANDREAS POMMERT,   Institute of Mathematics and Computer Science in Medicine (IMDM), University Hospital Eppendorf, Hamburg, Germany: *3-D Imaging in Medicine*

DHIRAJ K. PRADHAN,   Professor of Electrical and Computer Engineering, University of Massachusetts, Amherst, Massachusetts: *Computer Reliability*

V. RAJARAMAN, Ph.D.,   Professor and Chairman of Supercomputer Education and Research Centre, Indian Institute of Science, Bangalore, India: *Dynamic Memory*

MARTIN RIEMER,   Institute of Mathematics and Computer Science in Medicine (IMDM), University Hospital Eppendorf, Hamburg, Germany: *3-D Imaging in Medicine*

J. J. STIFFLER,   Executive Vice President, Sequoia Systems, Inc., Marlborough, Massachusetts: *Computer Reliability*

ULF TIEDE,   Institute of Mathematics and Computer Science in Medicine (IMDM), University Hospital Eppendorf, Hamburg, Germany: *3-D Imaging in Medicine*

PAUL T. WARD, Ph.D.,   Principal Partner, Software Development Concepts, New York, New York: *Structured Analysis*

JULIAN WARNER,   Department of Information Management, School of Finance and Information, Queen's University of Belfast, Northern Ireland: *Literal Intelligence of Computers and Documents*

AEROSPACE APPLICATIONS OF ARTIFICIAL INTELLIGENCE

INTRODUCTION AND HISTORY

Recent Advent of AI to Aerospace

The emergence of artificial intelligence (AI) as a technology of significant benefit to aerospace was based upon the progression of technology in general. The theoretical roots of AI are founded in the work of biologists such as Lorente de Nó (1) in 1934 and McCullough and Pitts (2) in 1943, who established the function and connectivity of neurons. In 1949, Hebb (3) introduced an equation for machine learning that is, with a number of variations, still in wide use today. Early researchers such as Samuels (4) with his checker player and Widrow (5) with his adaptive noise cancellation techniques demonstrated interesting applications of this technology which excited the interests of others. In 1959 Rosenblatt (6) of Cornell University built a visual pattern recognition system known as the Perceptron. His claims caused excitement which resulted, during this period, in much work being done in government laboratories such as the Avionics Laboratory in Dayton, Ohio, where analog systems for aerospace applications were built. However, prior to the advent of powerful, inexpensive computers, there simply was no practical way to implement many of the types of algorithms and techniques that scientists devised. Nevertheless, Rosenblatt's invention generated enthusiastic research until Minsky and Papert (7) of the Massachusetts Institute of Technology proved that Rosenblatt's Perceptron was unable to learn nonlinear problems. A few researchers such as Grossberg (8) and Rummelhart and Ortony (9) continued their research during this period and made significant contributions to the mathematical representation of learning systems, but their results were then not widely read.

Neural Networks

In 1982 neural networks sprang back to prominence in the aerospace research community with the publication of Hopfield's (10) work in an exciting application of neural networks to optimization of the combinatorically complex Traveling Salesman Problem. The flurry of excitement that accompanied the publication of Hopfield's paper reignited many research efforts. Subsequently, spurred by the number of researchers active in the field, TRW's AI research center in San Diego provided the means to accelerate application development by virtue of its delivery of the first commercial neurocomputer in 1985. During the same period Geoffrey Hinton of Carnegie-Mellon University and David Rumelhart (11) of the University of California in San Diego contributed the back propagation architecture that is most widely used today.

Since 1982 artificial intelligence has forged an increasingly prominent role in high technology industry. This has been true especially in aerospace because of the extreme demands the operating regime, particularly those of an intense combat environment,

1

place on operational performance. The extreme requirements on system performance for many years have been exerting strong upward pressure on total system cost and system development time. Because of the spiraling costs in system development, manufacturers were seeking any means to reduce cost and development time while retaining performance. However, in order for AI to be a significant force in aerospace development, it was necessary for AI to clearly demonstrate that it could contribute toward meeting those military requirements.

The tremendous rebirth of AI research following Hopfield's report produced a number of AI application prototypes which demonstrated the capability of the new technology. Personal computers and large main frame computers were now accessible to individual researchers who were able to utilize these tools to demonstrate for their immediate employers first hand the value of the AI technology. The availability of high-performance computers was particularly important, for, in aerospace, the limitations imposed by hardware on the AI technology had been felt more keenly due to the fact that many of the practical problems were large, required real-time processing or involved safety issues. Because of these factors this industry does not insert new and untried techniques in actual aircraft until there is a chance for seasoning of the technology. In addition to the fact that AI hardware was not adequate, the industry had already invested heavily in other tools and techniques that resulted in an understandable reluctance to change.

Initial industry skepticism was offset by the fact that there are hard problems such as target identification for which conventional techniques have no good solution, but for which AI offers excellent approaches. Once it established credibility in the industry, AI soon had significant impact in reducing cost, vastly improving performance, and dramatically shortening development time. More powerful computers, powerful expert system shells and neural network development environments enabled many new applications that could only be dreamed of before the development of these tools. Dramatic strides in data representation and construction of very capable inference engines made expert systems practical and placed them in daily use in many corporations. Expert system shells and neural network software development environments have allowed developers to avoid building a new set of tools for every project and to build upon previously existing software they have developed.

Expert System Technology

Expert systems offer the ability to capture rules that can be expressed in words based upon the knowledge of experts. Neural networks allow the ability to capture rules based upon examples of input data and the desired matching output. Both of these approaches provide capabilities that were very difficult or impossible to achieve for the mathematical and heuristic approaches which were exclusively used prior to the invention of expert systems and neural networks, yet they are very different in concept. Expert systems were developed in the late 1970s by researchers such as Barr and Feigenbaum (12) to take a high level cognitive approach and deal with linguistic concepts and logic. Neural networks use a low-level data-driven approach and learn patterns from repeated exposure to examples. Together they form a set of complementary and very powerful problem-solving techniques. Neural networks may be used to detect patterns in raw or slightly preprocessed data, and the expert system can then be invoked to decide what to do about the detected pattern. Fuzzy sets are a middle ground recently gaining in popularity which fits between the two. They initially were developed by Zadeh (13) to handle data and situations that cannot be precisely quantified. Fuzzy sets use high level rules based on human experience in conjunction with fuzzy statistics to allow rules and desired operating characteristics to be expressed in linguistic terms as "good, small, fast, slower, etc." In this manner desired performance can be obtained using imprecise, noisy, raw data described in terms of human linguistic concepts. It shares expert system characteristics in that it does not extract rules from the data as neural nets do, but must be programmed with high-level rules compiled by an expert. It shares neural net characteristics in that it is much easier to develop than expert systems, easily handles noise in the raw data, and does not have to be explicitly programmed to handle every eventuality.

The high-level, top-down approach is characterized by expert systems and inferential reasoning systems such as Roger Shank's (14). Shank's approach uses reasoning under uncertainty and inference to deduce certain things that must be true about the data under consideration. The approach used by Shank and other inferential reasoning groups differs somewhat from the expert system approach in that they do not attempt to explicitly express all of the rules, but they are both similar in that both assume that if enough logical reasoning and human expressible knowledge about the domain can be brought to bear on a problem it can be solved.

Expert systems with their rule-based structure have become commonplace in the aerospace industry for operation of complex machinery such as satellite environmental control equipment and machining operations. They are particularly useful in developing user interfaces because the linguistic nature of expert systems allows a user to easily understand them. They also provide an audit trail in the logic such that users can query the expert system to understand why a decision was arrived at. In recent years pure expert systems have been giving way to knowledge-based systems. Knowledge-based systems incorporate sources of knowledge other than purely expert systems. Knowledge-based systems would utilize database analysis, algorithmic approaches, inferential reasoning, deduction, and various kinds of learning in addition to an expert's rules to analyze a problem.

TECHNOLOGY IMPLEMENTATIONS

Robotics

Artificial intelligence was begun in an effort to duplicate some of the things that humans do so easily but which have been exceedingly difficult or impossible to accomplish with machines. Robotics has been an obvious choice and one, at least in terms of robotic control, which requires the least amount of computational power. Vision, navigation, and speech are much more computationally expensive. Practical robots with autonomous navigation, vision and control are now rapidly finding their way into aerospace. The Japanese in particular have adopted the technology wholesale and have entire factories that are totally automated. In contrast, in the United States, a previous generation of industrial robots was largely abandoned due to a lack of human factor integration of robot design, resistance by labor unions, and the availability of cheap labor. In certain applications, however, they are the only practical way to get the job done. For example, in nuclear clean-up they perform tasks which would kill humans in a matter of minutes. They also perform boring, repetitive work with consistently high quality, such as parts and aircraft inspection.

Martin Marietta is designing an "astrobot" for assembling and servicing the planned U.S. space station. In 1992 NASA sent the robot on a shuttle flight for an in-orbit test. Carnegie-Mellon University is developing a six-legged robot that navigates by bouncing laser radar off surrounding objects and which will be used by NASA to explore Mars. Military robots are finding applications in roving reconnaissance vehicles, hazardous materials handling, and repairing runways cratered by bombs. Cyberworks of Orillia, Ontario is manufacturing a vacuum robot that is capable of maneuvering around equipment while it vacuums the floor. It can instantly analyze the layout of a room and set to work vacuuming. Transitions Research Corp. is developing Robot-Kent, an industrial grade floor scrubber, for use in heavy duty locations in aerospace and other industries.

During Operation Desert Storm, robotic reconnaissance vehicles flew round-the-clock missions to allow real-time imagry from the battle field. These robotic aircraft flew long endurance missions providing eye-in-the-sky reports on enemy positions and movements. Reports indicate that some battle field commanders used them as a real-time assistance in targeting tanks in tank battles. Because of the success of autonomous air vehicles (AAV) in the conflict, the military is planning to purchase more of them and make their use more endemic to the military theatre. The AAVs also are being used in civilian applications such as the *Perseus* high altitude (25 km) AAV designed by Aurora Flight Sciences of Manassas, Virginia, which will be used in long endurance data collection for environmental monitoring.

Process Control

This is one of the most beneficial applications of artificial intelligence because it allows easy control of nonlinear systems. This has been clearly demonstrated in neural network control of power systems where a neural net controller provided load balancing of generators for industrial power within .2 million voltage-ampere-reactance units per day which was 100 times better than the best that human operators could do manually. Netrologic of Dayton, Ohio has developed a controller for the Air Force using a neural network controller which responded to imagery of an aircraft to fly a refueling boom into a refueling receptacle during a simulated mid-air refueling without the aid of a boom operator. NASA has developed neural network controllers to provide remote feedback of forces experienced at the robot to telerobotic operators. The Defense Advanced Research Projects Agency has sponsored research to develop neural network-assisted control of magnetically levitated bearings for space and industrial applications. The National Science Foundation is sponsoring development of neural network control of machine tools for extremely precise machining of parts for strong and defect free construction of components. The Air Force has also developed a knowledge-based system to control autoclaves curing composites and is at use at San Antonio Air Logistics Center. This system has reduced curing time from 12 to 3 hours and produces as good or better parts than the older method.

Fuzzy logic is proving beneficial in aerospace applications as well as other industries. The Japanese have numerous commercial successes using fuzzy sets and the Americans are also beginning to use the technology in aerospace. Fuzzy logic is very useful for aerospace control applications because it allows limited natural language interaction with a controller and accommodates fuzzy concepts such as "hotter" or "faster." NASA is interested in the capabilities of the technology and has applied it to controlling space shuttle tether reel motor voltages for retrieving tethered satellites. The complex and nonlinear dynamics of tether systems make it hard to implement any system that will not result in the tether being wrapped around the space shuttle. However, a prototype system reduced errors in tether length by one-half to one-third and worked more smoothly than manual control throughout the mission, including satellite deployment to 20 km, station keeping while the tether was fully deployed, and retrieval.

Vision Systems

The development of vision systems pose the greatest challenge to both computers and image processing algorithms because of the high bandwidth and extremely high data rates required by image processors. This challenge is being handled by special-purpose high-speed imaging chips and parallel processing hardware running neural network algorithms. Synaptics (San Jose, CA) has developed an image processing chip based on Carver Meade's (15) replication of the human retina and has built parallel analog neural network pattern classifiers to accomplish optical character recognition thousands of times faster than present systems. Alan Waxman at MIT Lincoln Labs is developing a vision system for an autonomous robot which utilizes a special-purpose image computer and pipeline processing to handle the neural network parallel image processing algorithms pioneered by Grossberg (16). These systems are required for truly autonomous robots and for many military and space applications. LANDSAT and SPOT imagery, for example, continues to flood into the archives in terabyte quantities and provides data without information. The problem of translating data into information is acute in military target recognition systems, reconnaissance and security surveillance. Recent research has focused on reducing imagery to icons or concepts so that the quantity of data handled may be reduced. Advances are being made in locating specific items in a cluttered scene and reducing false alarms. Progress is still required in identifying the same object viewed from different and distorted perspectives. Commercial vision systems such as the one fielded by Excalibur Corp of Albuquerque, New Mexico are capable of learning the appearance of an object and can then identify it when it is rotated in the field of view. The military is developing optical computers that are capable of billions of operations a second to facilitate data handling for its many image processing applications from sonar and radar to infrared and laser imagery.

Natural Language

Natural Language is viewed as another channel available to humans in a hands/eyes busy environment and the most natural one for an operator. The military services have experimented with natural language for many years, but the cockpit is a difficult place to implement spoken inputs due to the high noise environment and stress induced changes to the pilot's tonality. Test flights with voice activated commands for handling radio communications, setting navigation waypoints, doing fuel management, and performing pre-arm functions on ordinance proved generally satisfactory though some system errors were encountered in failure to understand commands.

Current natural language understanding systems are in use in high technology air freight sorting and distribution centers such as those run by UPS and Federal Express. Commercial systems for personal computers are available which can understand 30 to 40 words a minute of discrete utterances. Rapid progress is being made in this area, with the military services soliciting research proposals in natural language speaker identification, automatic text processing, radio intelligence gathering, message processing, and speaker-independent key word recognition. The technology is being employed by Wesson International in their air traffic controller environment simulators to permit the controller to make voice inputs to simulated aircraft under their control and have the simulator respond to the voice commands as if it were an actual pilot. Other research is underway on automatic voice translation because of the need for pilots and controllers to communicate the air traffic control environment of whatever country they are in.

Rapid advances are being made in pen-based operating systems which allow users to write on a computer screen as if they were writing on paper. Grid, Go, NCR, and other companies have invested heavily in systems that recognize handwriting and can respond to the users' inputs. These systems are finding use in industrial settings and airborne delivery services such as UPS.

Monitoring and Diagnosis

Because of their pattern-recognizing capabilities neural networks have found use as monitoring systems. NASA developed a prototype system for test stand rocket engine monitoring to prevent catastrophic accidents on the test stand. This system was taught to monitor Space Shuttle Main Engine data to watch for excursions in the data. If anomalous values were detected, an alarm was sounded to allow engineers to shut down the test.

Other test devices are in use in the NASA launch preparation facilities to detect faults in circuit boards used in the shuttle launch system. These boards have hundreds of different configurations which must be checked, and if a faulty board is returned to service it will cause more problems at a later date. More than 80 test programs were developed for checking out the boards. Generation of the test programs was tedious and time consuming and took up most of the time of the engineers. To reduce costs in maintaining the boards, the Automatic Test Equipment Expert Aiding System expert system was created to assist in developing test programs. This expert system created a consolidated work environment with reference information, schematics, existing software reuseability advice, and automatic documentation of new software. The system had a dramatic effect on the time to produce test programs by demonstrating a 50 percent reduction of test generation time in actual practice.

To assist in maintaining computers at the Kennedy Space Center, the Computer Care Center Expert System was developed to analyze data about computers. This system employed 1st Class/HT, an inductive-based commercial ES tool which generates rules to look for similarities among a set of examples or cases. It also observes specialists at work, listens to telephone sessions between experts and customers and digests technical reference documents to extract repair advising rules. The system has improved computer repair customer technical support by 30 percent and has reduced file cabinets full of reference materials to a manageable, easily referenced on-line computer system.

The Smart Processing of Real Time Telemetry (SPORT) expert system has been developed to acquire data from NASA's Level IV Checkout facility. SPORT is a distributed system that acquires facility data, interprets it, and offers advice to engineers. It has allowed payload engineers to do things with the payloads that were impossible before the advent of SPORT.

The space shuttle launch operations include many other expert systems, including one called OPERA to track the configuration and status of all ground components to determine the cause of anomalies and to recommend fixes. An older diagnostic tool called LES was used to fix the shuttle life support and environmental control system. Other systems generate and monitor launch commit criteria, provide diagnostics for avionics packages, and assist with planning and scheduling.

In a somewhat different application, the FAA has contracted with SAIC of San Diego to design and build bomb detectors for major airports. While these detectors are somewhat large and expensive they have proved effective in a series of tests. Prototype systems have been installed at San Francisco and JFK airports and several systems have been sold to foreign airports including one to Saudi Arabia. The heart of the bomb detector is a neural network which looks for a characteristic signature in the emissions from luggage that results when the chemicals in an explosive are bombarded with high energy beams.

Manufacturing

In other applications neural networks are in use at GE Aircraft Engines in Cincinnati, Ohio, monitoring machine tool wear and indicating when the end of useful life has been reached. Many different wear indicator signals are monitored including vibration, spindle horse power, feed rate, and temperature of the cutting tool. GE has found that certain sensor signatures are 100 percent reliable indicators of broken tools and that other pattern detectors are only slightly less reliable in determining when tools should be changed. Qualitative Process Automation has been used by the Air Force Materials Laboratory to adaptively handle feedrate of the end milling process to produce the fastest possible cut while preventing shank and tooth overloads. Neural network and expert system methods have also been used to direct an automated laser welder by being able to detect the molten weld puddle through smoke and splatter and keep the beam on track along the seam. These systems are currently in use in naval ship yards to make seam welds tens of times faster and more reliably than humans. Other manufacturing applications of AI include optical character recognition such as is in use at GE to read the characters placed on parts during their fabrication to indicate their status and history. This OCR number recognition system has proved to be extremely accurate in actual use over a variety of handwriting styles.

The Air Force is also constructing a capability to rapidly fabricate parts to test form, fit, and function. The capability is being generated by a process known as stereolithography. The project is attempting to capture design methodology through developing a set of design primitives. Then in an object-oriented fashion the primitives can be assembled to compose whatever structure the designer desires. Once the design is in place, a CAD design drawing is transferred to a stereolithography machine and it generates a model directly from the part drawings. The part can be checked for form and fit and sometimes function directly from the laser-produced stereolithography process. The process requires extensive use of AI pattern recognition capabilities, knowledge-based reasoning, heuristic search techniques, and expert systems.

Decision Aiding

The FAA has done some research into constructing a controller's associate which would assist a controller to maintain safe operations and would flag his performance if he was overtired, stressed, or inattentive. The military services have begun to rely heavily on decision-aiding systems such as the Automated Airload Planning System, particularly during the war in the Persian Gulf. This system was used extensively during Desert Storm to factor in such parameters as the aircraft's expected flight envelope, enemy air defenses, and the amount of ordinance that the aircraft is expected to deliver so that more efficient loading of stores on an aircraft could be accomplished. Logistical support benefited from the supply and requisition support afforded by the Automated Container Offering System which was used to assist the Military Sealift Command in booking shipments of material to the Persian Gulf. The system helped booking personnel sort through the large volumes of shipping requests and schedule and rate information. Tactical situation assessment assistance was provided by the Single Army Battlefield Requirements Evaluator and the Tactical Operation Planning Support System which were used to plan tactical operations and to generate force readiness projections.

Modelling

Neural networks possess the ability to model data. This is proving to be very valuable in condensing large models to smaller ones with the same capability. An example is the Sandia National Laboratory's combustion model that runs on a Cray. This model determines what happens, for example, in the cylinder of an engine when the gasses in it are ignited. The model takes several hours of Cray time and must be run every time a user wants to change the initial conditions of the model. Consequently, it becomes very expensive to play what-if games in combustion research. Neural networks offer an avenue to use the data generated by cases already run on the Cray model and develop a neural network model of the combustion process based on that data. The result is a model of the combustion process that runs on a PC and can interpolate between data points that have not been previously explicitly calculated. Many other uses of the process are under investigation because the savings in computations can be substantial. The same technique has been used by Los Alamos National Laboratory to model and predict chaotic systems. Such capabilities have obvious uses in code breaking, predicting aerospace stock prices, fares and passenger-load break-even predictions, data compression, communication scheduling, and many other chaotic or quasi-unstable processes.

IN-DEPTH ILLUSTRATIONS OF AI IN AEROSPACE

Military/NASA Successes

Airbreathing: Pilot's Associate

The technologies that resulted from nearly two decades of research in AI now are having measurable success in projects such as the pilot's associate. The motivation for PA was the increasing complexity of the manned fighter and the Air Force's desire to have single-seat fighters. To achieve the goal; a safe and effective single-seat fighter in a complex, extremely fast-moving combat scenario; PA was developed to monitor aircraft status, control the information content on the pilot's displays, advise the pilot of the appropriate rules of engagement and doctrine, and recommend or implement optimal maneuvers and actions. Because of the Christmas tree effect where all the warning lights go off during an emergency, it sometimes is difficult to determine what really is wrong and what is important. The PA assists the pilot during these trying circumstances in locating emergency airfields, determining what emergency procedures would be appropriate, and generally trying to sort out the situation, stabilize it, and offload as much of the work load as it can. Because combat situations may change depending upon the threat, PA will plan and replan a mission profile to meet the dynamics of the moment and place the aircraft in the safest condition considering the mission requirements.

As a sort of corollary to PA, the Air Force has developed the Learning Pilot's Performance System. The system monitors the current status of the aircraft and the pilot's actions to maintain safe aircraft control. The LPPS monitors the pilot's control movements and learns from the pilot how he controls the aircraft and what his response parameters are. This has become important as the aircraft's performance capabilities have exceeded the pilot's physiological limitations. Because the newer aircraft can stand more G-forces than the pilot, G-induced loss of consciousness has become a problem and caused the loss of several aircraft. In cases such as this the LPPS becomes a life saver when it detects the pilot's cessation of meaningful inputs to aircraft control and intervenes to return the aircraft to safe and controlled flight.

Space: Real-Time Data System (RTDS)

RTDS is a rule-based expert system designed to assist NASA's integrated communications flight controllers such as the Johnson Space Center Mission Control and seven other spacecraft mission control centers. RTDS is designed to upgrade the 1970s technology which, basically, was a vast array of failure indicator lights and a strip chart recording which attempted to display the thousands of data points a second received from mission telemetry. Four systems have been created using RTDS to monitor Space Shuttle fuel cells, analyze the on-board computer system, configure the reaction control system, and manage the data recorders.

The space shuttle reaction control system directs a complex array of 38 jets operating in 18 different modes. These modes may be restricted for operational considerations to avoid fouling equipment or astronauts during extravehicular activities. At times certain thrusters or cluster controllers may be inoperative. The RTDS allows controllers to tell at a glance which cluster modes are good, which are sloppy, which incur high propellant use, and which result in loss of control. The expert system interprets incoming data in real time to give the operator current status and decision options. The expert system rules and knowledge base allow controllers to handle the many complexities caused by jet interactions and determine the status of the system in case of equipment failure. Controllers can manually fail jets and multiplexers to allow the system to tell them what would happen if these jets fail. By this method, controllers can detect weaknesses in the remaining control distribution and reallocate multiplexers among computers and can select alternative modes to allow for more robust vehicle control and to guard against consequences of additional equipment degradation.

RTDS has also been used to develop a data recorder expert system which allowed NASA to replace three operations personnel. Further development of RTDS is expected to allow for elimination of an additional two positions by 1993. The tool has also allowed NASA to develop its own expert systems without the use of expensive contractors and long software development cycles. The use of this high level tool allows programmers to work at conceptually higher levels where they enjoy higher productivity because they do not have to worry about many minute details of the system.

Commercial

Aircraft Manufacturing

The major aircraft companies have gradually incorporated AI techniques as the technology came of age until now every month several AI applications are fielded in both NASA and the commercial sector. A case in point is the successful implementation of a scheduler for an aircraft parts treatment process at the Lockheed plant in Marietta, Georgia. Three overhead cranes on a common track were used to move aircraft parts between 22 chemical tanks. Microprocessors were installed on each crane to control the position of the crane, the hoist, and grabs. A conventional software design handles most of the scheduling, but a major problem was encountered in selecting which crane would move a job from its current task to the next. Because of different dwell times for different parts in different tanks, scheduling the cranes was a typical traveling salesman problem with many possible choices, one optimal solution, and no cheap way to compute a solution. Lockheed decided to observe how the human operators decided which crane would be made available to start the next job and try to capture this expertise in a rule based system. After months of observing the operators, writing rules and refining results, a workable system with over 150 rules was produced. The system provided a crane scheduled part pickup time needed by the supervisor and a crane schedule the control system could implement. The system performed well and, because they had participated in its development, was extraordinarily well received by workers in the plant.

Aircraft Design: Northrup's CAMNet

Northrup recognized that its efforts to further contain costs by finding places to save materials, labor, and direct manufacturing expenses were realizing diminishing returns. Management turned its cost-cutting efforts to indirect cost areas such as manufacturing engineering. The result of this effort was a set of four expert systems known as CAMNet which helps manufacturing engineers in their process planning functions to reduce costs in the fabrication of detail parts.

The human generation of process plans inevitably incorporates the eccentricities of the individual designers. Since more than 20,000 parts go into the construction of an aircraft, there were many costly inconsistencies to remediate when building a new aircraft. CAMNet reduces these costs by producing consistent plans that represent a specific manufacturing philosophy.

The Expert System Planner (ESP) is the primary expert system within CAMNet and is an object-oriented, rule-based generative planning system. Since ESP produces process plans for extrusion and aluminum sheetmetal parts, it handles plans for the majority of Northrup's parts fabrication. ESP allows easy modification of its specifications which permits it to handle material such as steel, aluminum and titanium. It has the added advantage of retaining knowledge gained in the manufacturing process in its permanent database instead of allowing corporate experience to be atrophied by personnel departures.

ESP is augmented by the Tool Order Generator, the Time Standard Generator, and the Offsite System Planner. The Tool Order Generator parses ESP to generate requirements and the tool orders required to make parts designed under ESP. The Time Standard Generator insures that industrial time standards are applied to operations required to produce a part designed under ESP. The Offsite System Planner detects when a designed part will have to be produced elsewhere and alerts system planners to the requirements for offsite subcontractors and generates production plans.

Robotics

Japan Airlines (JAL) is developing automated, computer-linked maintenance systems to speed aircraft turnaround, eliminate defects and standardize repairs. Automation is reducing JAL's labor costs by reducing rework and eliminating monotonous component inspection and parts cleaning procedures. Robots are allowing the airline to recover and repair more parts. An engine maintenance facility is already handling about 95 percent of the parts during major engine overhaul using an automatic fluorescent penetrant inspection system. A five-robot system processes parts in racks that pass through the various robot stations that spray penetrant dye and developer solution and blow-drying air.

JAL's fan blade recovery system uses three robots to rebuild worn jet engine blades. These robots remove worn leading edges, insert titanium replacements, and secure them with electron beam welds. The robots then reshape the blades precisely to restore their function. Restoring the blades saves the airline about $11,000 per blade. Other robots automatically measure turbine blades and polish them, greatly reducing time to rebuild an engine. Another robot stop-drills and refinishes small cracks in compressor and turbine disks. Inspection robots are being installed which detect flaws in honeycomb material and inspect rivets for cracks in aircraft sheet metal.

Diagnostics

Neural networks are extremely well suited to diagnostics applications; they provide exceptional speed, fault tolerance, generalization, and the immediate adaptation capabilities that many existing diagnostics systems do not possess. Because of these qualities, neural networks hold the promise of solving difficult logistics problems such as: multiple fault diagnosis, prognostication, changing configurations and environments and inaccurate diagnosis attributable to incomplete or flawed rules. General Dynamics (San Diego, CA) developed an F-16 aircraft malfunction neural network diagnostic system which could select maintenance procedures to correct a malfunction from a description of the symptoms. Six months worth of fire control data were used to train a neural network to determine what maintenance action should be taken to correct a malfunction. The training data used were actual aircraft writeups which contained many incomplete and inaccurate entries. The algorithm used was an extension of Grossberg's ART1 algorithm because it allowed new information to be added to the database without retraining. When jointly considering both high and low confidence responses, the diagnostic system produced completely correct responses 74 percent of the time when operating with data that it has never seen before. If the new data are incorporated into the system, the system performance is 100 percent accurate. The tests show a diagnostic system's ability to operate with noisy data, operate reliably with test cases it has never encountered before, and to add additional cases to its database. These characteristics make this system a very powerful diagnostic system and show the remarkable powers of artificial intelligence in general.

CONCLUSIONS

The use of artificial intelligence in the form of expert systems, knowledge-based systems, neural networks, and fuzzy logic is becoming pervasive in aerospace and through out industry. Its ability to handle noise and uncertainty and to capture human knowledge, learning ability, and its reasoning capability make these systems an increasingly indispensable weapon in the technologist's toolkit. We are well on our way to seemingly intelligent machines that will possess the ability to interact with humans in human-like ways including understanding speech, translating into other languages, and recognizing objects, faces, and names. The technology offers great promise and, used wisely, will bring much benefit and comfort into our lives.

REFERENCES

1. Lorente de Nó, R., Cerebral Cortex: Architecture, Intracortical Connections, Motor Projections. In: *Physiology of the Nervous System*, 2nd ed. (J. F. Fulton, ed.) Oxford University Press, New York, 1943, pp. 274–301.
2. McCulloch, W. S., and Pitts, W. A., Logical Calculus of the Ideas Imminent in Nervous Activity, *Bull. Math. Biophys.* 5:115–133 (1943).
3. Hebb, D. O., *The Organization of Behavior*, Wiley, New York, 1949.
4. Samuels, A. L., Some Studies in Machine Learning Using the Game of Checkers. In: *Computers and Thought* (E. A. Feigenbaum, and J. Feldman, eds.), McGraw-Hill, New York, 1986, pp. 71–105.
5. Widrow, B., Adaptive Switching Circuits, *IRE WESCON Conv. Rec.* Part 4, 96–104, (1960).
6. Rosenblatt, F., Two theorems of Statistical Separability in the Perceptron. In: *Mechanisation of Thought Processes: Proceedings of a Symposium Held at the National Physical Laboratory*. November 1958, HM Stationary Office, London, 1958, Vol. I, pp. 421–456.
7. Minsky, M., and Papert, S., *Perceptrons*, MIT Press, Cambridge, MA, 1969.
8. Grossberg, S., Nonlinear Difference-Differential Equation in Prediction and Learning Theory, *Proc. Natl. Acad. Sci.*, 58:1329–1334 (1967).
9. Rumelhart, D. E., and Ortony, A., The Representation of Knowledge in Memory. In: *Schooling and the Acquisition of Knowledge*, (R. C. Anderson, R. J. Spiro, and W. E. Montague, eds.), Erlbaum, Hillsdale, NJ, 1977.
10. Hopfield, J. J., Neural Networks and Physical Systems with Emergent Computation Abilities. *Proc. Natl. Acad. Sci. (USA)*, 79:2554–2558 (1982).
11. Rumelhart, D., Hinton, G., and Williams, R., Learning Representations by Back-Propagating Errors, *Nature Col.*, Oct. 9, 1986, p. 323.
12. Barr, A., and Feigenbaum, E. A., *Handbook of Artificial Intelligence*, Vols. I–IV, Addison Wesley, Reading, MA, 1989.
13. Zadeh, L. A., Fuzzy Logic, *IEEE Comput.*, 21:89–93 (1988).
14. Shank, R., *Dynamic Memory: A Theory of Reminding and Learning in Computers and People*, Cambridge University Press, Cambridge, MA, 1982.
15. Meade, C., *Analog VLSI and Neural Systems*, Addison-Wesley Publishing Co., Reading, MA, 1988.
16. Grossberg, S., Cortical Dynamics of Three-Dimensional Form, Color, and Brightness Perception: I Monocular Theory, *Percept. Psychophys.*, 45(2):87–116, (1987).

BIBLIOGRAPHY

Aerospace America, published monthly by the American Institute of Aeronautics and Astronautics, Inc., Washington, DC.
Aerospace Applications of Artificial Intelligence 1985 (J. Johnson, ed.), Dayton SIGART, Dayton, OH, 1985, p. 365. (Also see AAAIC proceedings for 1986, 1987, 1988, 1989, and 1990.)
AI Expert, published monthly by Miller Freeman Publications, San Francisco, CA.
DARPA Neural Network Study. AFCEA International Press, Fairfax, VA 1988.

Greenwood, D., Automatic Perception for NASA Mission Planning and Flight Control: A Survey of Artificial Neural Systems. Final Report to Johnson Space Center, Houston, TX on contract NASA7 R-044-87 (July 1987).

Neural Networks, published bimonthly by Pergamon Press, Fairview Park, Elmsford, NY.

PC AI, published bimonthly by Knowledge Technology, Phoenix, AZ.

JAMES R. JOHNSON

ARTIFICIAL INTELLIGENCE ON WALL STREET

He cursed Theocritus and Homer, in Adam Smith was his diploma; our deep economist had got the gift of recognizing what a nation's wealth is, what augments it, and how a country lives, and why it needs no gold if a supply of simple product supplements it. His father failed to understand and took a mortgage on his land.

Alexander Pushkin, Eugene Onegin 1, VII
(1829), translated by Charles Johnston

"Wall Street" refers to the complex data-intensive, and international environment that supports the buying and selling of financial products and commodities. This environment evolved with the explosion of international trade that followed the discovery of the New World. Centralized financial "exchanges" appeared in Antwerp (1530), Hamburg (1558), London (the Royal Exchange in 1565), Amsterdam (1613), Japan (with the Mitsui family in 1673), and Vienna (1753). These financial centers helped organizations raise money for trade and investment, and redefined such concepts as ownership, risk, and trust in terms of financial products, including securities (stocks, bonds, and mortgages), currencies, and other instruments. In fact, the term "share" of stock seems to have been used first by the Dutch East India Company in 1609 when raising capital for their New Amsterdam enterprises (1).

New York City had an auction market that supported financial–product trading as early as 1725. This market initially supported the trading of commodities (wheat and tobacco) and later expanded to support the trading of Revolutionary War bonds and other securities. In 1792, several brokers separated from the auction market to form a new market specializing in securities. They initially met under a buttonwood tree at 68 Wall Street. This organization later became the New York Stock Exchange, an organization virtually synonymous with "Wall Street."

Market participants know that improved information technology provides competitive business advantages and improves the fairness of the market for all participants. A market is fair when all participants have access to the same information about products. In the nineteenth century, market information was publicly displayed on a large blackboard (called the "Big Board" at the New York Stock Exchange). Like blackboard expert system models, market participants would all look at the board and fire rules to determine their market activity. In the Wall Street environment, this blackboard model proved inadequate. As the number of products increased, the board quickly ran out of space. Moreover, information was not really public: It was public only to those market participants who had access to the board.

Public access to information (and increased market fairness) improved with the invention of the ticker, an electronic device that displays information on recent trades. The stock ticker was invented in 1867 by E. Calahan, a New York Stock Exchange employee, and later enhanced and modified by Thomas Edison.

Today, the relationship between improved information technology and market fairness and competition is still valid. The ticker still exists, and we can see the principal of disseminating and exploiting market knowledge at work in several deployed systems that use expert system and artificial intelligence techniques. Many Wall Street firms have developed systems that demonstrate how this technology supports the buying and selling of financial products and commodities in applications such as automated news understanding, credit assessment, risk management, market surveillance, auditing, and trading (2, 3). Many of these highly proprietary systems have been quietly deployed; others have been abandoned as incomplete prototypes.

An AI approach is motivated by situations where a cognitive model of human judgment performs better than an analytic model. Since human judgments are dynamic and often difficult to test in predictive situations, we expect the expert system approach will fail if the underlying cognitive model is inadequate.

Let's explore why some Wall Street AI applications are successful while others fail. If we first model the Wall Street problem domain from a knowledge-based perspective, we can represent the environment from both an object-oriented view and a process view. Both models demonstrate the complexity inherent in formally defining the Wall Street environment. This complexity prevents a complete, predictive, analytical model of the Wall Street environment.

AN OBJECT-ORIENTED VIEW

Object-oriented models seek to simultaneously specify objects together with the morphisms (rules and operations) defined on these objects. Objects send messages to other objects; object semantics are defined by the reception of messages.

Our object-oriented view of the Wall Street environment defines a complex set of competitive "worlds" that are highly distributed in space and time. Each world is an instantiation of markets, market participants, products, orders, news, and regulatory structures. Figure 1 shows a semantic network representation of some of the objects and messages in a world. The Products object represents assets (e.g., securities such as bonds and stocks), contracts (e.g., options to buy or sell as asset within a specified future time), or an index computed on an underlying product (e.g., an interest rate or an average price of a "basket" or set of securities).

Market participant objects buy and sell products by performing a set of actions that maximize an economic-objective function. Buy and sell transactions are recorded as orders. One way that market participants can maximize an economic-objective function is by firing the following rules:

> Buy low and sell high.
> Do it before anyone else.

If these actions are common to a set of market participants, then the only participants who can maximize their economic-objective functions are those who have a product knowledge advantage (so that they can effectively determine what is "high" and "low"), and those who have an order execution advantage (so that they do not wait to achieve these actions: waiting might change the price to a suboptimal level).

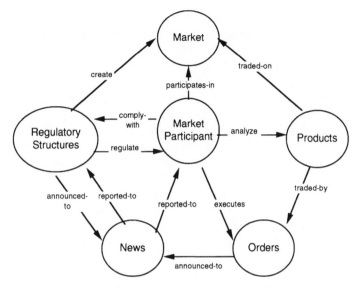

FIGURE 1   A semantic network representation of a Wall Street world.

Order objects indicate different timing and size parameters for trades. Many different types of orders exist that are based on the number of combinations for size (product quantity), side (buy or sell, long or short), price limits, time limits, and other constraints (including stop orders, orders on the opening or close, and "fire or kill" orders). Order execution has improved since the installation of telegraph communications more than 100 years ago, and continues to improve today in the context of global markets and 24-hour trading. Better order, billing, and clearance systems can handle large numbers of transactions. In this context, AI has been applied to financial telecommunication network management; funds transfer; and image, voice, and forms processing.

Product knowledge advantages have traditionally been acquired through efforts in fundamental and technical financial analysis. Fundamental analysis refers to evaluating a product with respect to deep knowledge about assets, risks, and classical financial ratios. Technical analysis refers to evaluating a product based on the shallow knowledge of price and volume trends. Trends can be statistical (based on so-called "moving averages") or nonstatistical (based on ad hoc theories).

One goal in the Wall Street environment is to discover product knowledge advantages for assessing prices. If all market participants have perfect information and the same execution capabilities, then, on the average, none will have any knowledge advantage over the other. In this ideal environment, the price of a product on a market converges to its "true price."

In the real Wall Street environment, deviations exist between true prices and market prices because not all traders have complete information. These deviations are further exaggerated by rumors, "good news," "bad news," panics, and crashes. The existence of the true price is a consequence of the so-called efficient-market hypothesis: an object's true price is its observed price if all traders act rationally, have perfect information about the object, and are all participating in the market. This hypothesis is usually accepted when all traders have access to identical telecommunication and information systems and when all information obtainable about an object is known to all participants. Consequently, in this rational and perfect information scenario, there is no profitable way to speculate. Knowledge advantages can result from acting on knowledge acquired from non-public information sources. Such insider trading—the use of proprietary or non-public "inside" information for financial gain—is illegal in many markets.

Regulatory structures objects prevent illegal knowledge advantages in the market so that trading remains fair and orderly. These regulations, or laws, exist at the government agency level, the market level, and the market participant compliance level. In some sense, regulatory structures define the market. In our model, regulatory structures monitor trading and can execute actions if they determine that the market is not fair or orderly. Regulatory actions include temporarily halting the trading of an object in a market, permanently preventing the trading of a market participant, or temporarily halting the trading of all products in a market. Other actions include levying financial fines and penalties for rule violations.

One of the more challenging applications of AI on Wall Street is the detection of (legal and illegal) knowledge advantages in trading and regulation. Such systems have been deployed to determine potential opportunities (risk assessment, underwriting, exposure), evaluate lost opportunities (auditing), and assess compliance with different regulatory structures.

Markets comply with different regulatory structures. The most regulated markets are exchanges. These are centralized markets registered with a government agency, such as the Securities and Exchange Commission. The least regulated are crossing markets, where buyers and sellers agree between themselves on an order. Orders that take place not on an exchange but within a system of brokers are said to take place on over-the-counter markets.

Different markets support different types of objects. Some are market makers (also known as dealers). Their regulated function is to help trade products quickly—so that the market is continuous—and to ensure that deviations between true prices and market prices are small—so that the market is liquid. Dealers provide market continuity and liquidity by keeping an inventory of the traded object.

Other market participants are brokers, whose regulated function is to represent traders in an order (for a commission) and to match buyers and sellers. Market makers who are simultaneously brokers and dealers are called specialists. Because of this dual role, specialists must comply with very strong market rules. For example, a specialist is prohibited from selling a product if its price declined on the previous executed order. This action of "selling on a down tick" is prohibited because it may affect the market by lowering the price even further—in a potentially destabilizing way—thus affecting market liquidity.

To complete the above object-oriented specification of the Wall Street environment, we need several interdependent markets. This linkage can be accomplished in several ways:

1. A product can be traded on several markets at once.
2. A product trading on one market can affect the trading of a different product on another market.
3. A market participant can participate on several markets at once.
4. Information might (or might not) reach all market participants.

The first type of linkage has been in existence for at least 100 years. This corresponds to the case where shares of Acme Corporation trade simultaneously on the New York and London exchanges.

The second type of linkage can be explicit or implicit. For example, market participants can trade contracts that give them the right to buy a product (the "underlying" product) at a particular price during a stated time period on an option market. With suitable statistical assumptions, we can show that the option's price is mathematically related to the underlying object's market price. A future is another example of a derivative object. It is a commitment to buy or sell an underlying product at a specific price during a stated time period. There can also be options on futures, futures on indexes ("indexed" futures), and so on.

The third type of linkage is seen in the practice of trading on multiple markets, either to take advantage of some arbitrage opportunities, or to manage risks by hedging. In general, only implicit relationships might exist between the prices of different products on different markets; precise mathematical models detailing explicit relationships can be inadequate for predicting prices. For example, a trader might believe that the price of yen depends on the price of gold, basing this belief on judgment and experience rather than any formal analytical econometric model.

The fourth type of linkage introduces the complexity of information flow. In general, not all market participants are totally connected to the information available in each market. In our model, the object used to disseminate information among market participants and regulatory structures is called news.

Figure 1 is a model of a single world. A more complete model of Wall Street would contain instances of the figure (which can be drawn in multiple layers), with inter- and intralayer messages linking the different markets, products, news, market participants, and regulatory structures in different layers.

Any casual model of the Wall Street environment must be incomplete. As market participants become aware of the different information flows affecting the environment, feedback from news causes the objects to change and evolve new products, new markets, new regulatory structures, and new market participants. Complete causal analytic models either do not exist or are too complex to justify short-term predictions. In this sense, the Wall Street environment behaves like a living organism.

A PROCESS VIEW

Process models emphasize information transformation. The Wall Street environment can be modeled in terms of a generic structure of processes that create and monitor events. Our model is a variation of the predict-detect-isolate-correct feedback loop discussed in the ISO network management model. Network management is another domain known for event complexity and AI applicability (4).

Figure 2 shows a procedural model of trading and regulation scenarios, which differ in their interpretations of an event. In trading, the goal is to discover events that represent a buy or sell opportunity; in regulation, the goal is to discover events that possibly indicate something unusual that must be investigated further for noncompliance.

Prediction refers to the determination that an event will occur in the future,and involves creating a model that can represent past experiences. In a market trading scenario,

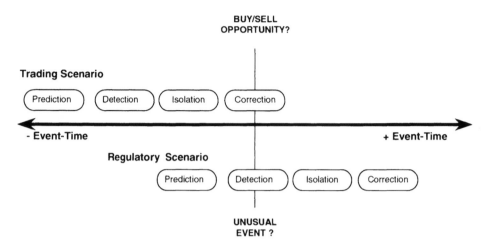

FIGURE 2   Trading and regulation scenarios.

the prediction process determines the likely signals that indicate buy or sell events. For example, a trading model might have a set of predictive rules based on price and volume movements, such as "If the 10-day moving price average crosses the price curve in a broadening bottom pattern, then signal a buy, otherwise hold."

The behavior of the market regulation scenario is similar. Here, the prediction process determines the likely signals that indicate that an unusual event has occurred. For example, a model might have a set of predictive rules that are also based on price and volume movements, such as "If the price of a product increases by 15 percent, it is likely that there was an unusual event about the product."

Detection (determining that an event has occurred) is concerned with discovering patterns. In a market trading scenario, the detection process determines that a buy or sell opportunity has occurred by firing the predictive rules on available data. In a market regulation scenario, the detection process determines that an unusual event has occurred. These rule firings trigger alarms, or alerts.

Isolation refers to the process of analyzing the event to determine event components or event participants. Given a pattern, isolation is concerned with discovering component patterns. For example, in a market trading scenario, the isolation process can analyze several rule firings (alarms) and extract the most likely subset of products to buy or sell. These objects might also involve derivative objects.

Correction refers to the enforcement of rules to adjust the predictive model. This process executes an action (such as producing a plan or explanation) that can change the world or the model. In a market trading scenario, one output of this process might be an actual trade order. In a market regulation scenario, an output might halt trading for a product, a participant, or the entire market. The correction process sometimes maintains a database of past actions and predictions that can be used to update the predictive model.

Figure 3 shows a basic Wall Street process model. Essentially, it is an expansion of Figure 2, showing the information flows between processes. In this diagram, we assume the efficient market hypothesis that all world knowledge (market and news) is available to each process.

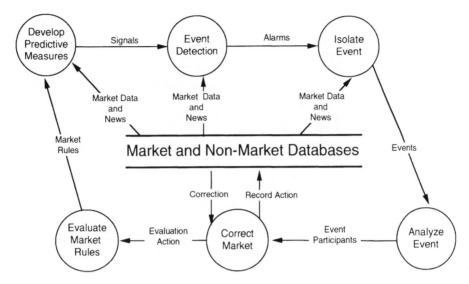

FIGURE 3   The Wall Street environment as a real-time process model.

Process models and object-oriented models are related. In some sense, all objects interact with their world by performing the predict-detect-isolate-correct loop. The process model helps form a local view of the world. Because of this local view, we can examine small domains to assess the applicability of different AI technologies.

Some Wall Street applications, such as credit screening, represent knowledge through standard, stable decision procedures. In these applications, deductive methods such as those based on production rules provide the easiest way to build predictive cognitive models, and probabilistic reasoning can be embedded in these models fairly easily. The predictive model is based on a rule-constrained search. Here, the predict-detect-isolate-correct loop corresponds to the steps (1) build the rule base; (2) fire rules on the global data structure; (3) fire rules on the detailed data structure; and (4) perform the recommended system action (and possibly create new rules). This last step is extremely important to many Wall Street applications, because it addresses the nonmonotonic behavior of the world—information acquired at a future time might be inconsistent with default assumptions. In deductive systems, such consistency is required.

Other Wall Street applications cannot represent knowledge by standard decision procedures. In these applications, it might be appropriate to build predictive cognitive models using nondeductive (or inductive) methods, which don't require logical consistency.

Case-based approaches are appropriate when the application requires the representation of actual experiences. In many applications, a database of exemplars must be created and maintained. The predictive model is based on searching for experiences that are "most similar" to the current situation, and adapting those experiences to fit the current situation. Here, the predict-detect-isolate-correct loop corresponds to the steps (1) build and index the case base; (2) find the most similar exemplars; (3) select the best exemplar and adapt it; and (4) perform the recommended system action (and possibly create new cases).

Machine learning techniques may be appropriate when a database of actual experiences exists and a standard decision procedure is assumed to exist. Here, part of the prediction process consists of inferring rules that can be used in a deductive predict-detect-isolate-correct loop.

Connectionist (neural network) approaches are appropriate when the application requires the representation of actual experiences in a "compiled form." These approaches are subsymbolic: they rely on numerical representations and computational models using linear and nonlinear discriminants. In some sense, a connectionist approach resembles analytic approaches, in that the output of the prediction process can be considered an analytic (statistical) model.

ANALYTIC VERSUS COGNITIVE MODELS

Many analytic models have been developed for the Wall Street environment in recent years. Several have been used successfully for decision-making and prediction, such as the well-known Capital Asset Pricing Model and the Black-Scholes model for options pricing (5).

In other domains, such as economic forecasting, even though some analytic models often outperform human decision-makers, the model outputs are not generally well accepted. Many analysts reject a model's conclusions, especially if they are presented with a binary choice between total acceptance and total rejection of the model's decision. Reasons for this include:

- Incomplete model theories: Models often contain incomplete theories as well as incomplete data.
- Incomplete model inputs: Even the best models occasionally produce decisions much worse than a human analyst would, because they do not include some important factors.
- Incomplete model outputs: The analyst's risk preference in dealing with uncertain outcomes might differ from that of the model. Conversely, the analyst's role is trivialized if the model makes all the decisions.
- Incomplete explanations: Models provide precision at the expense of intuition and common sense.

Some analysts try to compensate for these limitations and "tune" results by making heuristic adjustments to the model. Tuning produces a model forecast that is consistent with intuitive expectations, and maintains the detail and structure of the analytic model. However, tuned forecasts can easily be misused (6,7).

The Wall Street environment is rich enough to permit domains where human judgment performs better than analytic models. Consequently, a cognitive model of an analyst, implemented as an expert system, might perform better at predictive tasks then an analytic model. For example, it is difficult to build a formal analytic model for assessing whether an individual is a good loan risk. This problem domain relies on judgment and experience. On the other hand, several expert systems handle this type of screening application. Other Wall Street domains that have incomplete analytic models but rely on experience include auditing, clearing, compliance, and applications involving natural language processing (such as the parsing of news and market data).

On the other hand, cognitive models fail in domains where there is too much reliance on judgment. In these domains, judgments are dynamic and their representations are difficult to quantify and verify.

The fallibility of human judgment in many decision-making domains echoes the experience of several financial expert systems. Several kinds of representational failures occur in human analysts and the expert systems that model them.

These failures include:

- Anchoring: This is the tendency not to stray from an initial judgment even when confronted with conflicting evidence. People are reluctant to revise their opinions in light of experience. Similarly, expert systems have difficulty in revising default assumptions in nonmonotonic reasoning.
- Inconsistency: If a pair of alternatives is presented to a subject many times, successive presentations being well separated by other choices, the subject does not necessarily choose the same alternative each time. In expert systems, this is seen in the representation of fuzzy and probabilistic reasoning. In some of these systems, if proposition A has certainty p_A of occurring, then we might infer that the certainty of the proposition "A and not-A" has certain $p_A \times (1 - p_A)$.
- Selectivity: This involves using only a portion of the information available. Human analysts make poor decisions when they must take into account several attributes simultaneously. Decision makers might be aware of many different factors, but they seldom consider more than one or two at a time (6). One effect is that experts are often influenced by irrelevant information.
- Fallacy: This is the improper use of probabilistic reasoning. Common errors include conservatism (the failure to revise prior probabilities sufficiently when new information arises) and calibration (the discrepancy between subjective and objective probabilities).
- Representativeness: This involves focusing on how closely a hypothesis matches the most recent information while excluding generally available information.
- Autonomy versus collaboration: Decision makers are disinclined to surrender control over a decision to a single model, either a mathematical or a cognitive one.
- Availability of expertise: In some domains it is not possible to create a complete model for an expert system that will produce satisfactory results; there could be no experts with sufficient knowledge. The knowledge base required to anticipate all possible conditions and actions would be extremely large.
- Conflicting expertise: Different experts reason with different styles. They might have different operational styles (the information they require and in what order they prefer it) and different functional styles (preferred problem-solving strategies, such as top-down, bottom-up, and middle-out reasoning).

COLLABORATIVE SYSTEMS

Using analytic models, human judgment, and expert systems on Wall Street is not necessarily disjoint. We can improve the different models not only through integration, but by building collaborative models.

The desirability of developing techniques by which people and computers collaborate in making decisions has been recognized for some time. As early as 1961, Yntema and Torgerson questioned how to combine the speed of the computer with the "good sense" of the human user, without sacrificing too much of either (8). They proposed letting the machine make the decisions according to simple rules, but requiring analysts to monitor the results and change the machine's answer if they find the results too foolish.

Analytic models have become much more complex since 1961. However, all abstract models are only approximations: Optimization achieved with respect to the model is not the same as optimization with respect to the real Wall Street environment. Ultimately, only a person can judge if the discrepancy between the real Wall Street and the model is large or small.

The combination of analytic models, human judgment, and cognitive models leads to a new kind of intelligent tool. It is not so much an intelligent assistant as it is a collaborator. From an operational perspective, a collaborator should relieve an analyst of routine computation, data handling, and decision making. When requested, a collaborator should also explain is reasoning. In this regard, collaborators resemble apprentices and tutors in that they compare user behavior to expert behavior and try to minimize the difference by negotiation. The objective of the negotiating process is to influence the user's behavior, making it as rational as possible from the perspective of expert knowledge about the domain.

Lacy proposed an "artificial laboratory" of such tools (9), where the assistance provided to analysts falls into three categories; model developers and representers; model testers; and model refiners. Such tools could be used as collaborators in discovery (model creation) as well as in model use.

Figure 4 shows the relationships among analytic models, human judgment, and cognitive models. Apte and Dionne (10) and Dhar and Croker (11) discuss examples of knowledge-based collaboration between expert systems and analytic models for the Wall Street environment. Abelson et al. discuss other intelligent computational tools that assist in developing and representing analytic models (12). Freedman and Stuzin discuss knowledge-based tuning in the context of econometric models (7). Leinweber (2) and Schmerken (3) present examples of knowledge-based expert systems based on cognitive models of financial experts.

From an operational perspective, the two most challenging problems concerning the building of AI systems for Wall Street applications are feasibility—"Can it work?"— and validation—"Does it work?"

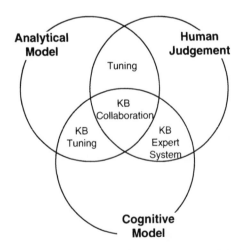

FIGURE 4   The relationship among analytic models, cognitive models, and human judgment.

The complexity of the Wall Street systems we've discussed, which are based on object-oriented and process-oriented models, mimics the complexity of the environment. We can reduce this complexity to understandable levels by using already existing and understandable system components. To do this, we can require standard definitions for user and data interfaces to permit the interoperability between expert system implementations of cognitive models, implementations of analytic models, and users.

Validation is as much a function of management and user commitment to the system as it is a function of system complexity. Even if complexity is well managed, no one will deploy a system that cannot demonstrate how it supports specific business and user goals.

Wall Street continues to be a challenging domain for innovative AI applications. Today, successful AI systems have the important operational property of being well integrated with other systems. Future Wall Street AI systems will continue to build on the advantages of system integration by demonstrating intelligent collaboration among components.

REFERENCES

1. Grun, B., *Timetables of History*, Simon and Schuster, New York, 1979.
2. Leinweber, D., Knowledge-Based Systems for Financial Applications, *IEEE Expert*, 3 (3): 18–31 (Fall 1988).
3. Schmerken, I., Wall Street's Elusive Goal: Computers that Think Like Pros, *Wall Street Comput. Rev.* 7 (9): 24–34 (June 1990).
4. Joseph, C., Sherzer, A., and Muralidhar, K. Knowledge-Based Fault Management for OSI Networks, *Proc. Third Intl. Conf. Industrial and Eng. Applications of Artificial Intelligence*, ACM, New York, 1990, pp. 61–69.
5. Miller, R. M., *Computer-Aided Financial Analysis*, Addison-Wesley, Reading, MA 1990.
6. Pindyck, R. S., and Rubinfeld, D. L., *Econometric Models and Economic Forecasts*, McGraw-Hill, New York, 1976.
7. Freedman, R. S., and Stuzin, G. J. A Knowledge-Based Methodology for Tuning Analytical Models, *IEEE Trans. Syst. Man, Cybernet.* 21 (2), 347–358 (March 1991).
8. Yntema, D. B., and Torgerson, W. S. Man–Computer Cooperation in Decisions Requiring Common Sense, *IRE Trans. Human Factors in Electronics*, Vol. HFE-2, 1961, pp. 20–26. Reprinted in Edwards, W., and Tversky, A., *Decision Making*, Penguin Books, New York, 1967.
9. Lacy, M., Artificial Laboratories, *AI Magazine*, 10 (2) 43–48 (1989).
10. Apte, C., and Dionne, R. Building Numerical Sensitivity Analysis Using a Knowledge-Based Approach, In: *Proc. IEEE Fourth Conf. Artificial Intelligence Applications*, Computer Soc. Press. Los Alamitos, CA, 1988, pp. 371–378.
11. Dhar, V. and Croker, A, Knowledge-Based Decision Support in Business: Issues and a Solution, *IEEE Expert*, 3 (1): 53–62 (Spring 1988).
12. Abelson, H., Eisenberg, M., Halfant, M., Katznelson, J., Sacks, E., Sussman, G. J., Wisdom, J., and Yip, K. Intelligence in Scientific Computing, *Comm. ACM*, 32 (5): 546–561 May 1989.

ROY S. FREEDMAN

COMPUTER RELIABILITY

Computer reliability is nearly as critical a concern as the concept of the computer itself. von Neumann, e.g., investigated techniques for constructing reliable computers from unreliable components and developed some key concepts used today in computers said to be fault tolerant.

Concern with computer reliability diminished for a time because of the dramatic increase in the reliability of component implements—first, with transistors and later, with integrated circuits (instead of the earlier relays and vacuum tubes). Recently, though, concern about reliability has revived for two principal reasons: (a) Computers have become increasingly powerful, hence increasingly complex and subject to increasing possibilities of system failure; (b) computer use to perform tasks essential to human commerce and even to human safety has markedly increased; the cost of a disruption in the performance of such tasks has increased correspondingly.

Computers sometimes are compared unfavorably with other electronic equipment such as television receivers. ("My television set has to be repaired on the average only once every 5 years. Why are all of these fault-tolerant features needed to make a computer with similar reliability?") The difference, of course, is that even simple computers may be tens of times more complex (measured, e.g., in terms of the respective sums of the failure rates of their components), and large computers may be hundreds or thousands of times more complex, than a standard television set. To the extent that such things as wear can be ignored in electronic equipment, the mean time between repairs is inversely proportional to complexity; the 5-year interval between television set repairs reduces to 6 months in small computers and a few hours to a few days in large systems.

The second reason for the renewed concern over computer reliability, the increasing responsibility assigned to computers, needs little elaboration. Computer malfunctions have caused delays in everything from bank transactions to space shuttle launches. The costs of such delays range from customer dissatisfaction to potential loss of human life. These trends toward increased dependence on computers and increased costs of their malfunctions can be expected to continue at least over the next decade.

The components of a computer system most generally prone to failure are the peripherals (line printers, terminals, actuators, etc.) where mechanical wear does play a role. The most serious failures, however, usually are those affecting the central computer itself. This is because a central computer failure effectively disables all peripherals and, in addition, may violate the integrity of the computer's database, thereby destroying the results of many hours of user effort. If a user's terminal fails, that user may be able to go to another terminal and continue to use the computer, an obvious impossibility if the central computer system fails. Moreover, a computer can be programmed to monitor its peripherals (e.g., actuators in an avionics control system or sensors in printers and disk drives) and to activate an alternate should a primary device be found to be defective, an option that is again obviously impossible if the failure disables the computer itself.

A particularly pesky class of computer failures is that which causes it to malfunction without producing obviously incorrect results. Many failures manifest themselves through a program "crash." A failure in the program counter, e.g., may cause the computer to fetch instructions from a portion of memory containing data and thereby to encounter an unexecutable "instruction." Many failures produce less dramatic effects, however, and may allow the computer to function apparently normally for extended periods, generating entirely invalid results. This latter class or "soft" failures are due frequently to transient events that cause a circuit to malfunction for a brief period, producing, e.g., erroneous arithmetic results and then resume normal operation.

Latent failures constitute another class of potentially troublesome failures, especially in fault-tolerant computers. Latent failures produce no apparent effects until coupled with a subsequent failure. A failure in an error-detecting decoder, for example, would be classed as a latent failure if it prevented the decoder from recognizing a later failure in the memory or on the bus it is supposedly monitoring. In highly fault-tolerant computers containing extensive fault-monitoring and fault-masking circuitry, latent faults may well constitute the most serious threat to system reliability, even when the latency interval (i.e., the interval between the occurrence of a failure and its detection) is short.

The difficulty in estimating the reliability of a computer system and the necessity to do so accurately both tend to increase significantly as more capacity for fault tolerance is designed into the computer. The difficulty increases because such factors as soft failures and latent failures that are relatively insignificant in non-fault-tolerant or minimally fault-tolerant computers are no longer so in computers designed to tolerate large numbers of failures. Such failures affect what is generally referred to as the fault coverage capability of a computer. The coverage probability (or, more tersely, the coverage) associated with a failure is defined as the probability that the failure is detected and isolated before it causes the system as a whole to malfunction (e.g., before it results in an erroneous output or loss of program integrity). In highly fault-tolerant computers containing extensive redundancy, coverage failures may well be considerably more likely than failures resulting from an exhaustion of hardware resources.

Accurate reliability estimation increases in importance with increased fault tolerance for two reasons: First, the fact that fault tolerance is to be designed into the system indicates that reliability is an important consideration. Because fault tolerance implies redundancy and redundancy implies increased cost, cost-effective design is possible only if the designer is able to estimate accurately the effect on reliability of the design option under consideration. Second, the more reliable the computer, the more expensive it is to estimate its reliability. Consider, e.g., the reliability of a flight-control avionics system designed to have a 10-hour mission failure probability of no more than 10^{-9}. Without some procedure for modeling the reliability of such a system, more than 10 million computer years of testing (e.g., 100,000 computers under test for 100 years) would be required to get even a minimum number of statistically significant failures.

Reliability estimation involves two generally distinct activities. First, it is necessary to estimate the failure rates of the various individual components comprising the system in question. Because the components are usually much less expensive than the system as a whole, it may be feasible to estimate their failure rates by testing large numbers of them. Constantly changing technologies and manufacturing procedures, however, make it prohibitively expensive to establish failure rates for all components in this manner. Consequently, mathematical models have been established to enable failure rates to be extrapolated both from data gathered from accelerated life-cycle tests (e.g., tests under elevated temperatures) and from data developed through tests of similar devices. MIL-HNBK-217* is a frequently used source of component failure rate information derived in this manner.

The second step in estimating the reliability of a computer system is to use these component failure rates to determine the overall system reliability. At its simplest, this merely entails adding up all the component failure rates, since, for non-fault-tolerant computers, a failure in any component is equivalent to a system failure. The problem becomes more complicated, however, when fault tolerance is introduced, as several component failures may be needed to project a system failure. Numerous computer programs have been developed to aid in this effort. One approach is to use fault-tree (or, conversely, success-path) techniques to establish all combinations of failures (all combinations of functioning components) that result in a failed operational system. Boeing Aircraft Corporation's FTREE computer program is one example of a reliability estimation program based on this technique. Another approach is to ask the user to describe the system in terms of standard redundant building blocks (e.g., dually or triply redundant configurations) and to use this information, combined, of course, with the component failure rates to estimate system reliability. The Jet Propulsion Laboratory's CARE (Computer-Aided Reliability Estimation) program is based on this notion.

These relatively straightforward combinatorial techniques are generally inadequate, however, for modeling highly fault-tolerant systems. As already noted, coverage failures tend to dominate in such systems. Combinatorial models tend either to ignore the possibility of a coverage failure or to treat the coverage probability as a constant independent both of time and of the operational state of the system. In general, coverage is a function of both of these parameters.

Markov-chain models have been used, in part, to overcome these combinatorial model limitations. Markov (or semi-Markov) models allow the use to represent the modeled system in terms of its operational states. A state is defined by the component failures that have been experienced and, depending on the extent to which coverage is being modeled, the coverage-related state (detected, undetected, intermittent, transient, etc.) of all of these failed components. Once transition rates between states are established, the probability that the system is in any specific state and, in particular, in any failed state, can be determined by relatively straightforward procedures. A number of reliability estimation computer programs have been developed to exploit this technique.

The major limitation to the Markov method is that the computational effort needed to determine the state-occupancy probabilities is a rapidly increasing function of the number of states used to model the system. And, unfortunately, the more accurately a system is to be modeled, the greater the number of descriptors required to characterize a defective component; hence, the greater the number of system states. This number can be enormous even for a relatively simple system. (If each failed component can be in any one of six coverage-related states, e.g., a system consisting of only four triply redundant components can occupy any one of 614,656 operational states.) One technique for circumventing this Markov-model limitation is called state aggregation. In effect, states are

---

*MIL-HDBK-217 *Reliability Prediction of Electronic Equipment*, published and periodically updated by Rome Air Development Center.

defined only by the number of failures present; the coverage-related states of these failed components influence the transition rates rather than the number of states. A separate coverage model is then used to determine these transition rates. The number of states that have to be considered is drastically reduced (from 614,656 in the example mentioned previously to 81) at the cost of less easily determined transition probabilities. The net reduction in computational effort can be dramatic, thereby making it possible to estimate the reliability of highly reliable complex systems without having to ignore or overly simplify the effects of coverage.

Computer reliability estimation techniques are all subject to one major criticism: The results obtained are no better than the data (component failure rates, coverage parameters, etc.) upon which they are based, and such data are notoriously difficult to establish. The drive for more accurate reliability estimation procedures can nevertheless be justified on at least two counts. First, confidence in the resulting estimate is increased in direct proportion to the extent to which the user is able to specify parameters that are intuitively meaningful or directly measureable (e.g., fault detector characteristics rather than coverage). Second, at the very least, the user can determine the sensitivity of the predicted reliability to these various parameters, thereby establishing the relative strengths and weaknesses of the design under investigation even if the input data are not available with sufficient accuracy to allow the absolute reliability of that design to be confidently estimated to four significant decimal digits.

Computer system reliability can be enhanced through the use of redundancy. Broadly, redundancy can be classified as hardware, software, and time redundancy. Hardware redundancy involves additional components performing related computations. For example, the early UNIVAC Computer (1951) had two central processing units that computed the results of a computation independently and then compared the results to verify correctness.

Software redundancy incorporates additional programs that check the correctness of computation, recomputing the result (sometimes by independently written software) if an error is found. The assumption is that any temporary malfunction of the hardware will not produce errors for both executions. Also when two independent programs have been designed to compute the same task, it is unlikely that both of them have the same ''bug.''

Also, quite effective against transient hardware failures is time redundancy. The Bell Relay Computer (1944), e.g., performed all calculations repeated numbers of times, comparing the results.

Early computers relied on ad hoc techniques for fault tolerance. Then, beginning in the mid-1960s, more systematic techniques for incorporating redundancy emerged. One early example of the systematic use of the various forms of hardware redundancy can be found in the Bell ESS telephone-switching computers. Here, a broad class of error-detecting/correcting techniques are employed in both hardware and software. More recently, from the mid-1970s, fault tolerance became a major concern of commercial design. Transaction processing is a representative area where fault tolerance has seen increasing application. In fact, several computers available on the market list fault tolerance as a major feature, including Tandem, Stratus, and Sequoia systems. All are designed to provide what is known as high availability.

Availability is an attribute that provides a measure of expected up time. Many applications such as those found in banking and airline reservation systems not only require that failures occur infrequently but also that they be repaired in a very short time (sometimes in milliseconds). Such short repair time demands that the repair be automatically executed by the computer itself. Most commercial fault-tolerant systems employ redundant units that replace a faulty unit as soon as an error is detected and the faulty unit is located. Such switchings are accomplished in real-time often without being visible to the user.

Fault-tolerant systems, generally, may be classified into three categories: (a) ultrareliable systems, (b) long-life systems, and (c) highly available systems.

Ultrareliable systems are those used in critical real-time applications. Avionic computers are one popular example, with their stringent reliability requirements over a short mission time. Usually, such systems are designed using massive redundancy. One of the early space shuttle computers employed four identical processing units, with an additional backup unit. A typical scheme employed here is a majority voter. That is, to tolerate a single unit failure, three identical units can be employed whose outputs are "voted" on. In the event that all three units do not produce the same output, but two out of the three do, then the output of the system corresponds to that produced by the pair in agreement. Shown in Figure 1, this configuration will tolerate any single failure, except one occurring in the voter itself. In general, such a voted scheme will tolerate m failures if $2m + 1$ identical units are employed.

Long-life systems, on the other hand, require that the system continue to be in operation for a long mission time, with a certain minimum level of performance assured. Spacecraft that explore outlying planets may have on-board computers that need to be functional for years. A key concern is that in the event of a failure, it is impossible to repair such systems manually; therefore, any repair has to be performed automatically.

Such systems may allow for graceful degradation after all the spare units have been exhausted. Instead of majority voted logic, what is known as dynamic redundancy would normally be employed. Spare units are provided that can be switched in when the primary units fail. The switching logic obviously has to work reliably for the system to work.

A typical metric that is used to evaluate long-life systems is the mean time to failure (MTTF). For ultrareliable systems, the MTTF is not meaningful and, in fact, may be less

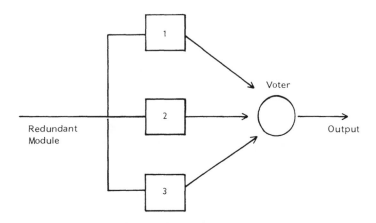

FIGURE 1 Triple modular redundancy.

than that of a long-life system. On the other hand, for a specific mission time, the reliability of an ultrareliable system may be much higher than that of the long-life system.

Finally, as mentioned earlier, for highly available systems it is important not only to have a long MTTF but a short repair time as well. The repair time can be measured in terms of mean time to repair. A fault-tolerant system that employs automatic fault recovery can effect repairs in a few seconds or even milliseconds. Repairs that involve manual replacement of the faulty unit may take hours, or even days. A highly available system attempts to minimize the likelihood of manual repairs.

J. J. STIFFLER

DHIRAJ K. PRADHAN

CONTROL FUNCTIONS: MICROPROGRAMMING

GENERAL DESCRIPTION

Microprogramming is a technique for controlling the low-level operation of a computer. It is most often used to direct the emulation of an instruction set architecture. The following discussion is in this context, although microprogramming has a wider range of applications.

The classic von Neumann computer consists of four components: (*a*) memory, (*b*) data processing unit, (*c*) input/output unit, and (*d*) the control unit, as shown in Figure 1. Data are transferred between the first three units (solid lines), with the control unit providing directions to the other three units, directing their detailed operation. The control unit translates the operation (or order) code of a machine instruction into the detailed sequence of operations necessary to perform the function requested by the operation code.

The earliest computers (and many modern high-performance computers) implement the control unit as discrete hardware, a portion of which is shown in Figure 2. The control unit consists of counters, gates, and decoders to generate the correct sequence of signals with the correct timing. The order code is decoded to select a set of AND gates in the AND array. The ring counter divides the clock into multiple phases (in this case, four), which step through the sequence of control points in order. The OR array combines the lines from each set of AND gates to drive the appropriate control lines. The AND and OR arrays were implemented with diode matrices in the early systems and are now often implemented using programmed logic arrays (PLAs).

Implementing more sophisticated instructions requires more phases and more gates, as does implementing larger instruction sets. Some computers have been designed with asynchronous control units to improve performance. Instead of using a clock and ring counter to sequence the control points, as each functional unit completes its

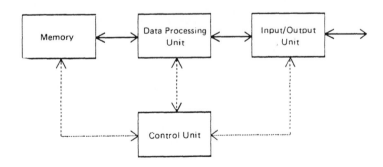

FIGURE 1   Classic computer structure.

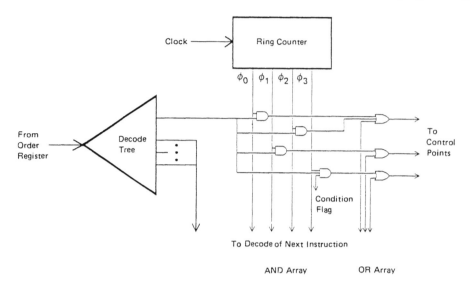

FIGURE 2   Hard-wired control unit.

operation, it initiates the operation of the next functional unit in sequence. Hardwired control units can and do become large and complex, especially when optimized for high performance.

A microprogrammed control unit is shown in Figure 3. The hardware to implement the microprogrammed control unit is comparatively simple to design and build. The detailed sequence of directions to the data processing unit is specified by the microinstructions contained in the control memory. The instruction to be read from control memory is selected by the microprogram sequencer. Data are loaded into the pipeline register from the control store (CS) (or control memory). The control points are driven by the state of bits in the pipeline register.

To a large degree, microprogramming is a technique that converts a very complex hardware design task into a much more tractable programming task.

Definition

Several different definitions have been proposed for microprogramming, but none has been universally accepted. This is the result of the breadth of application for microprogramming and the growth and change in the field. Microprogramming can be defined as follows:

1. A systematic and orderly approach to designing the control section of any computing system (1,2).
2. A technique for designing and implementing the control functions of a data processing system as a sequence of control signals (3).
3. A technique that imposes an interpreter between the hardware and the architectural level of a computer (4).
4. Programming special-purpose processors to achieve high performance, where the techniques used are similar to the above.

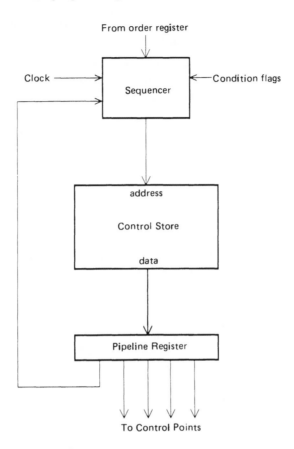

FIGURE 3 Microprogrammed control unit.

Related Fields

Several areas overlap with the field of microprogramming. Each contributes to the study and understanding of microprogramming. Some of these related areas are as follows:

Computer architecture—the design and structure of computers. To some degree, microprogramming can be viewed as one of the tools of the computer architect: one choice in the hardware/software trade-off. Microprogramming has also contributed to architecture, particularly in the area of reduced instruction set computers (RISCs) (discussed later in the text).

Verification—the automated proving of the correctness of programs. Because the correctness of the microprogram for a computer has a very large impact on the users of the computer (it defines the details of how the computer operates), it is important to show that the microcode is correct. Automated verification of microcode is more difficult than proving algorithms correct, because there are often multiple simultaneous operations, with complex timing requirements.

Hardware description—the specification of the implementation and architectural levels of a computer in a rigorous fashion. This is used in generating and verifying microprograms and developing tools (such as compilers or simulators).

Software development tools—compilers, linkers, simulators, and other tools used to ease the development of microprograms.

Some of the more complex problems in each of these areas is raised by microprogramming. For example, generating a machine language instruction for a computer, with one operation code, one register specification, and one memory location, is much simpler than generating a microinstruction, which may consist of many fields, controlling independent registers, memories, buses, arithmetic logic units (ALUs), and the sequencing of the microinstruction.

HISTORY

Development by Wilkes

Maurice Wilkes of the University of Manchester developed the basic concepts of microprogramming in 1951 (1,2). A time line with the highlights of microprogramming history is shown in Figure 4. Wilkes was considering methodologies for the design of the control section of electronic digital computers. Even at this early date in computing history (the same year as the introduction of the first commercial computer, the Univac I), Wilkes realized that the complexity of the control section was a drawback to development of comprehensive and flexible computers. The parts of the computer that were most reliable and simplest to maintain were those that had a simple logical structure.

He described the discrete operations of each machine order as a series of micro-orders or elementary operations, which are used to construct a microprogram. The microprogram to add the contents of registers A and B would be broken into a sequence of micro-orders, such as move a value from register A to the ALU; move a value from register B to the ALU; add the values; move the result to register A.

The design he proposed is shown in Figure 5. The order code is loaded into register II to select the initial microinstruction. This value is clocked into register I and is used to select one output line from the decode tree, which is an N to 2^N demultiplexer. Matrix A generates signals that are directed to the data processing unit of the computer, while matrix B generates the next microinstruction address. This address is loaded into register II. In this fashion, each microinstruction specifies its successor microinstruction.

To allow the sequence of microinstructions to be altered, based on the status of the data section, a two-way switch (the fork between matrix A and matrix B) is used to select between two successor instructions. The specific condition flag to be tested may be selected by control points specified by matrix A.

Although modern implementations of microprogramming take advantage of the advances of memory and register technology, they have the same basic components: a sequencer to select a microinstruction (similar to registers I and II, the decode tree, and the conditional flip-flop), and a memory for the microinstruction that may also control the next instruction address (similar to matrices A and B).

Rationale and Need

Wilkes realized that the design of high-speed memory and a simple sequencer was much easier than the design of large amounts of discrete hardware. Verifying that the correct sequence of operations was being performed was simpler when represented by values in memory than when embedded in the wire list for gates and ring counters.

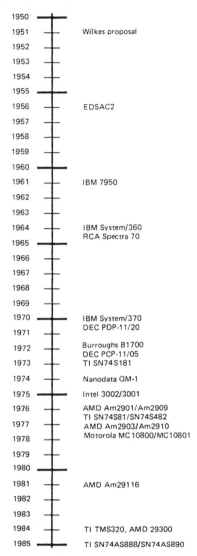

FIGURE 4   Microprogramming time line.

Simpler hardware results in easier maintenance. Diagnostics can be run that test substantial parts of the control section independent of the data section. If errors are found in the algorithms programmed in microcode, they can frequently be corrected by altering the microprogram without requiring hardware alterations.

For medium to large computers, the memory needed to implement a microprogrammed control unit is also less expensive than discrete hardware control systems. The net result is a simpler, less expensive, and more maintainable system.

On the other hand, there is a penalty: decreased performance. In microprogrammed design, the sequencer extracts the microinstruction from the memory, determines the next microinstruction address, and prepares to extract the next microinstruction. In a discrete

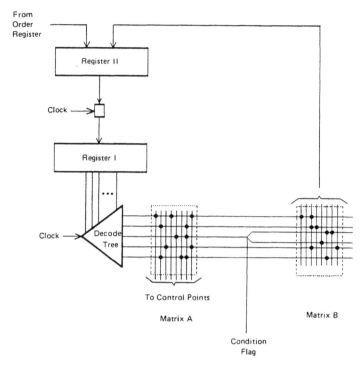

FIGURE 5   Wilkes' control unit.

controller design, the next set of operations can be started without the delay caused by the memory or next address computation.

The concept of microprogramming did not see widespread use for a decade after its inception (3). There was some interest at universities, especially in Europe. Wilkes developed the EDSAC 2 at Cambridge University in 1956 using a microprogrammed control unit. The memory technology available in the 1950s was very limited, and the machines were uncomplicated. Wilkes' design used diodes for his two matrices, which were expensive and difficult to modify. High-speed memory was expensive and its use was limited to internal registers in the early machines.

Introduction by IBM

International Business Machines (IBM) was the first major manufacturer to make use of microprogramming, first in the IBM 7950 (in 1961), and then very extensively in the IBM System/360 announced in 1964 (3). IBM wished to introduce not just one computer, but an entire series of compatible computers, with a range of costs and performances.

Using microprogramming, any program written for one of the System/360 computers would execute with the same results on any of the System/360 machines. Users could move to more powerful computers without the need for an extensive (and expensive) conversion.

IBM used microprogramming to address several other needs. One was to perform diagnostics on the hardware. Microprograms could be written that would test each of the components and locate defects. A second need was compatibility with previous machines. For example, by executing a different microprogram, a System/360 could be made to execute programs written for the IBM 1401.

Two of the computers in the System/360 series demonstrate the benefits of microprogramming. The System/360 Model 30, a low-end computer, consisted of an IBM 2030 central processing unit (CPU) with 64K 8-bit bytes of core memory, 64 bytes of local storage, 12 8-bit data registers, 2 16-bit address registers, 5 8-bit internal busses, and an 8-bit ALU. There were 4,032 microinstructions, each was 57 bits plus 3 parity bits wide, broken into nine fields. The CPU cycle time was 750 nanoseconds, although it took two cycles to access the local storage for register values (3,4).

The System/360 Model 50 was a mid-range computer. The 2050 CPU was built with the same technology but had 32-bit registers, buses, and ALU. The cycle time was 0.5 microsecond, and registers could be accessed in one cycle. There were 2,816 words, with 90-bit-wide microinstructions, split into 15 fields. It was possible to have simultaneous transfers through the main adder, through the auxiliary data path, and to or from local storage (3). The Model 50 was about 10 times the speed of the Model 30. Although there was substantial difference in price, performance, and the size of the programs that could be run on these two systems, they could both execute the same operating system, DOS/360, and run the same application programs.

As indicated above, the speed and cost of the memory used for the CS has major impact on the performance and cost of the resulting microprogrammed control unit. Several different technologies were used to implement the CS in the System/360 machines, ranging from capacitive (CCROS) and transformer (TROS) memories (1-microsecond access time) to the first high-speed (80-nanosecond access time) semiconductor memories on the Model 85, announced in 1968.

By varying the amount of hardware, a comprehensive series of compatible computers could be introduced with a performance range of 1:70, positioned at various prices, which contributed to IBM's market dominance.

Not all computers in the System 360 series were microprogrammed: The Model 70 contained a hard-wired control section. The Model 44 implemented the scientific portion of the System/360 instruction set in hardware.

Other Early Manufacturers

Several other manufacturers developed computer systems using microprogrammed processors. The RCA Spectra 70 series consisted of models 70/15, 70/25, 70/35, 70/45, 70/55, and 70/60. These computers were architecturally similar to the IBM/360, although they had different internal structures. The Spectra computers provided four sets of general-purpose registers compared with IBM's single set. The Spectra series was also designed with considerably less hardware then the IBM computers. The Spectra 70/45 had a single bus and a minimum of hardware registers, whereas the IBM 360/40 and 360/50 had multiple data buses and several internal registers. The Spectra series was optimized for the specific data operations of the architecture, whereas the IBM 360 series used more general microarchitectures.

The initial computer in Digital Equipment Corporation's PDP-11 series was the PDP-11/20. This computer, introduced in 1970, used a hard-wired control unit. All other processors in the PDP-11/20 series were constructed using microprogrammed control units (4). The PDP-11/20 had an average instruction time of 3.5 microseconds. The microprogrammed implementations had average instruction times ranging from 5.9 (LSI-11) to 0.9 microseconds (PDP-11/45).

Burroughs introduced the B1700 in 1972 as a flexible architecture machine. The hardware provided a 24-bit ALU and memory that could be accessed in 18-bit words. Additionally, mask registers allowed limiting ALU operations to smaller values, making the ALU appear as though it were 8 or 16 bits wide. By reloading the microprogram, the B1700 could have architectures that differ significantly, with one oriented to FORTRAN processing and another oriented to COBOL (5). The B1800, successor to the B1700, did not have a separate control store but stored microinstructions in the processor memory along with the users program and data.

Nanodata Corporation introduced the QM-1 in 1974. The QM-1 embodied several significant concepts, including that of a two-level control store, the lower level of which is often called a nanostore. The computer was designed to be an emulation machine, i.e., it was designed so that it would be relatively easy to program any architecture. Many of the bus connections were controlled by the microprogram. This resulted in a very flexible machine, although using this flexibility to full advantage was quite difficult. It received some use in universities and other research facilities.

Microprogrammable Components

In the mid-1970s several semiconductor companies introduced components oriented toward microprogramming. Texas Instruments (TI) introduced the SN74S181 4-bit ALU in 1972. This component could be cascaded with the aid of carry look-ahead circuitry to reconstruct an ALU of any desired length. The TI chip was soon followed by the introduction of bit-slice components by Intel (the 3002/3001 in 1975), Advanced Micro Devices (AMD) (AM2901/2909 in 1976, and Am2903/2910 in 1977), TI (SN74S481/482 in 1976), and Motorola (MC10800/10801 in 1977) (4). The bit-slice components (discussed in more detail below) integrated registers, look-ahead status, ALU, and control functions onto single integrated circuits in a fashion that allowed them to be combined to create processors for any desired word size. All were 4-bit slices, except the Intel parts, which were 2-bit slices.

Ten years of advances in semiconductor development have led to 8-bit slices (TI SN74AS888) or integrating four 2901s with look-ahead onto a single chip (Integrated Device Technologies, and others) to make a 16-bit processor. Another direction has been to create a single-chip microprogrammable processors oriented toward specific applications. Examples of these are the AMD Am29116, introduced in 1981, a 16-bit processor oriented toward graphics and controllers, and the TI TMS320, introduced in 1983, also 16-bits wide, oriented toward digital signal processing. Both contain ALU, registers, ALU control, and input/output (I/O) circuitry. The TMS320 also has a 16-bit multiplier and a program counter. The Am29116 executes an instruction every 100 nanoseconds, the TMS320 in 160 nanoseconds.

Recent developments diverge from the bit-slice approach. The latest components are functional units, such as ALUs, floating-point multipliers, program controllers, etc. In some sense, this trend represents a return to the functional orientation represented by the TI SN74181 in the mid-1970s. This can be explained by the advances in technology that have occurred since the introduction of bit-slice components. It is now possible to place many more gates on a single integrated circuit and also possible to provide more connections to the circuit. Many of the forces leading to the development of bit-slice components are much weaker than they were in the 1970s.

CONTROL UNIT DESIGN

Within the data processing unit of any computer, from the smallest to the largest, is a network of registers, buses, and functional units that manipulate data. This network is called the data path, and its operations are controlled by the control unit.

The operation of the data path is regulated by the state of certain signals, called control points. A control point may be a single line that controls the loading of a register, gating a register to a bus, clearing or incrementing a register, initiating a memory read or write, or any other component that manipulates data. Alternately, a control point may consist of several lines that are decoded to select a register, specify one of several possible ALU operations, or select from some other collection of related operations. In general, the control points are also controlled by the system clock, so that they take effect at a specific point in each clock cycle.

The function of the control unit is to direct the operations of the data path in the correct sequence. This sequence may be the interpretation of a machine language instruction or to cause a response to internal or external status lines, e.g., to service an I/O interrupt. Control is achieved by asserting the control signals in the correct sequence and at the correct time to cause the data path to execute a desired operation.

For example, in a simple data path, adding two registers and storing the results in a third register may involve a complex sequence of control signals. First, each of the registers is selected and gated through a data bus to the ALU input registers. The ALU is then instructed to add them. Finally, the result is gated onto the data bus, the destination register selected, and the result stored in the register.

A hard-wired control unit is implemented as a combinatorial circuit (sometimes called random logic or discrete control). A counter generates a series of clock pulses to sequence through operations. The set of conditions that must be met for each of the control points to be activated is computed and used to construct a network of AND and OR gates or encoded in a PLA. Because there may be many sequences (one for each instruction in the machine language) and a large number of conditions (interrupts, memory data ready, condition codes, etc.), the size of the encode matrix can be quite large.

A simple microprogrammed control unit (Fig. 3) consists of a sequencer, memory (the CS), and a pipeline register. Inputs to the sequencer include the state of the data path (such as carry out of the ALU, overflow state, zero value, etc.), external state (e.g., interrupt lines), and control from the current microinstruction. The sequencer generates the address of the next microinstruction. This instruction is read from the CS and loaded into the pipeline register at the start of a clock cycle. The output of the pipeline register is directed to the data path control points, as well as to the sequencer, to select the next microinstruction. CS may be implemented as read-only memory (ROM) or as writable memory, often termed writable control store (WCS).

MICROPROGRAMMED SEQUENCERS

The simplest form of sequencer is shown in Figure 6. This consists of the CS and a small amount of combination circuitry, which is used to test conditions. Each microinstruction contains the address of the next instruction. When a condition is tested, the condition bits are "ORed" with the next address to generate a multiway branch. The output of the control store is connected directly to the control points of the data path. Because each microinstruction specifies the address of the next instruction, it is called an *explicit address sequencer*.

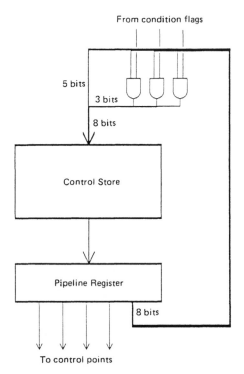

FIGURE 6   Explicit address sequencer.

Little hardware is required to implement this sequencer, but it has several disadvantages:

1. The address for each instruction must be encoded in every microinstruction and stored in the CS, which is usually high-speed memory and therefore quite expensive.
2. Even when a series of instructions is to be executed in sequential locations, each address must be stored. The bits in the microinstruction could be used more effectively.
3. The sequencer is slow. Each microinstruction must be obtained from the CS before the next microinstruction address can be determined.
4. Placing the microinstructions in CS is difficult because the destinations of branch targets are determined by the condition code bits. Instructions are scattered throughout the CS.

These disadvantages have led to features in microprogramming sequencers that improve code density, speed, and simplicity of use. These techniques include:

Pipelining—overlap execution within sequencer.
Command orientation—eliminate next address field.
Field encoding—reduce microinstruction width.
Residual control—remove infrequently used fields.
Multiple formats—select part of data path for control.

Multilevel control—select instructions actually used.

Paged control store—reduce number of address bits.

Each of these techniques may be applied independently or together to improve the performance or efficiency of the microcode.

Pipelining

The total time to execute an instruction with this simple sequencer is the sum of the access time for the CS, the time to generate the next instruction address, and the time required by the data path to complete its operations and return status. This timing can be improved by pipelining the sequencer. Pipelining is adding one or more registers in the address calculation or CS output paths to allow one or more of these functions to operate in parallel.

Adding a pipeline register on the output of the CS allows the access to the CS to be performed during the time that the data path performs its operation, rather than after. The control points are driven by the output of the pipeline register and remain stable. The CS can be read to obtain the next instruction without affecting the control points. This has the side effect of creating a branch delay of one cycle, i.e., of delaying decisions based on data path status by one cycle. If microinstruction I_1 is the instruction currently being executed, the status of the condition lines is that of the previous instruction I_0. This status from I_0, along with the address in I_1, is used to calculate the address of the next microinstruction, I_2. The instruction time for this sequencer is the greater data path time or the sum of the address computation and CS access time.

Adding a second register, this time between the sequencer and the CS, allows them to operate in parallel. In this case, while I_1 is executing, instruction I_2 is being fetched from the CS, and the address of I_3 is being computed by the sequencer using the status generated by I_0. This causes a branch delay of two cycles.

Command-Oriented Sequencer

There is little need to encode the next address of each instruction in every microinstruction. Because many instructions are executed one after another, if instructions are placed sequentially in memory, the most common operation of the sequencer is to increment the previous address. A command-oriented sequencer is controlled by a command field in the microinstruction. This field specifies how the sequencer is to determine the next address. Because this command field is usually 1–4 bits, there is a substantial savings in the memory required for each instruction. The bits that were previously occupied by the next address field can be used for other control lines. The field is now only needed when certain branches are to be taken.

Modern command-oriented sequencers provide many functions, including a loop counter, a subroutine call stack, and a circuitry to allow the next address to be specified externally. The AMD Am2910 is a common example, shown in Figure 7. It generates a 12-bit microinstruction address and requires a 4-bit instruction.

Each microinstruction contains a sequencer control field that specifies how the sequencer is to compute the next address. Some of the functions of the Am2910 are jump to zero, call, repeat, return, jump, and continue. Most of the instructions perform slightly different functions, depending on the state of the condition code input. They are conditional, so that a call, jump, return, or repeat is executed only when the condition flag is true.

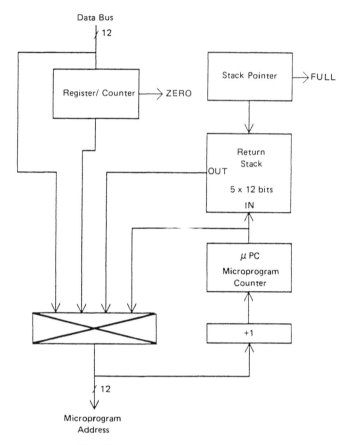

FIGURE 7   AMD Am2910 sequencer.

Degree of Encoding

When each of the control points is controlled by a bit in the microinstruction, the microinstruction is said to be unencoded or to use direct control. This allows complete control of the operation of the data path, but some of the control points may conflict when selected together. For example, gating two registers onto a single bus at the same time is unlikely to produce any reasonable result and may even cause damage to the hardware. There are certain combinations of control bits that have little or no value, such as gating a register onto a bus and not using the value on the bus.

The control lines that are mutually exclusive (such as selecting one of the registers to be gated to a common bus) may be combined using a 1-to-2^N decoder. For more complex relationships, a matrix of AND/OR gates may be used to generate the control lines based on a limited number of input selections.

This limited amount of encoding is done on almost all microprogrammed systems. The microinstruction contains the bits that are fed to the decoder, reducing the size of the control store. There is a small amount of time added to the data path by the delay time required for the decoders.

Several control lines may be controlled by a decoder (usually a PLA or ROM) to specify a small number of more complex operations. As an example, the AM2901 uses

3 bits to specify a value destination controlling two single bit shifters, storing into the register array, loading the Q register, and selecting the source for the output bus (Fig. 8). Because there are only eight possible choices, only the most valuable or common combination of operations are available. The reduction in microinstruction width and CS size is at the expense of increased delay due to the decoder and potential loss of parallelism and increased number of instructions.

As an extreme, all of the operations of the data path may be fully encoded into a single field of N bits, selecting 2^N functions to create a fully encoded microinstruction. This would be a "pure" vertical microinstruction. A fully decoded microinstruction is a pure horizontal microinstruction. Most microinstruction designs use a mixed approach with a number of independent fields encoding control points that are mutually exclusive.

Because there is a continuum from pure vertical to pure horizontal, microinstruction formats that are combinations of both have been called "diagonal." Although most people would agree that the Burroughs B1700 with a 16-bit microinstruction (1–8 fields) is a vertical architecture and the Nanodata QM-1 with a 144-bit microinstruction (over 60 fields) is horizontal, there is little agreement where the boundary between the two lies.

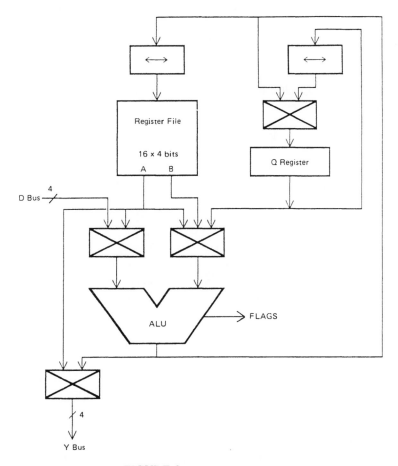

FIGURE 8   AMD Am2901 ALU.

Residual Control

Ofter there are control points that are set to the same state in many microinstructions. These might control the bus structure of the data path or the value of a mask. To reduce the size of the microinstruction, control bits that are altered infrequently may be moved from the microinstruction to a separate register. This register can then be loaded as needed under control of the microinstruction. The value loaded into the control register may come from a field in the microinstruction that can be used for other purposes in other instructions, such as the branch address for the sequencer or constant data.

Multiple Instruction Formats

Some machines may contain functional units that cannot operate simultaneously. For example, if a fixed-point and a floating-point ALU are both connected to the same input and output bases, only one may be operating at a given time. In this case, the same microinstruction bits may be used to control both ALUs, with a selector bit determining which is being commanded.

Additionally, when there are different sections of the data path that are infrequently used at the same time, these sections may be directed by the same microinstruction bits. This allows sharing of the microinstruction bits with several parts of the data path. One common example of this sharing is the use of a single field in the microinstruction for the microinstruction address for jumps, the data to be loaded into a control register for residual control, and constant data for data path operations.

The cost of the CS may be reduced by using multiple fields. Independent sections of the data path are controlled by the same bits in the microinstruction. This reduces the width at the cost of possibly increasing the number of microinstructions and reducing the performance of the computer.

This technique, also called bit steering, can be limited to using a single bit fields to select between two uses of the microinstruction fields, or it may use a format specification field to select between a number of different interpretations of the microinstruction. The Burroughs B1700, for example, uses a 4-bit field to select 1 of 16 instruction formats.

Multiple instruction formats are used more extensively in vertical architectures and less so in horizontal architectures. The multiple formats serve to reduce the width of the microinstruction, thus reducing the cost. The sequencer may also be simpler, and thus faster. This is at the expense of parallelism, because two parts of the data path that are controlled by different formats may not operate simultaneously. There is generally an increase in the number of instructions necessary to perform a given function as more formats are used.

Multiple-Level Control Store

When there are N control bits in the microinstruction, there are 2^N possible combinations. For even small numbers of N, there may be only a small fraction of the possible combinations of control bits actually used. Microinstructions with identical fields may appear many times in the CS.

Each unique microinstruction (or a large portion of the microinstruction) may be saved in a separate CS, often called a nanostore. The CS now contains an index into the nanostore, perhaps with additional fields specifying registers, etc.

This technique has been used in different ways. In the Nanodata QM-1 the nano-store contains up to 1,024 words, each of which consists of a 72-bit K field and four 72-bit T fields, for a total of 360 bits. The K field and one of the T fields control the data path on each cycle, with the T fields selected sequentially. The CS contains up to 32K 18-bit words, of which 10 bits select the nanoinstruction to be executed. In this way, the nanostore can be tailored to produce a vertical microarchitecture in a very flexible and general fashion.

In the Motorola M68000, semiconductor technology limited the number of bits of CS that could be stored on the chip. After the entire instruction set for the microprocessor was written in microcode, each unique microinstruction was placed in the nanostore and selected by a field in the CS. The 172 control points are controlled by 68 bits in the nanostore. The nanostore contains 280 discrete instructions. The CS is 17 bits wide by 640 instructions deep. Each instruction selects one of the nanoinstructions and specifies the sequencer operation. This two-level memory technique resulted in a reduction in the

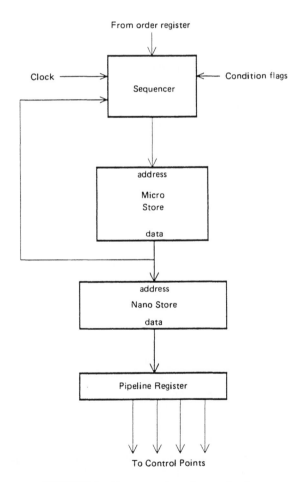

FIGURE 9   Nanoprogrammed control unit.

number of memory bits required from 43,520 bits in a single level store to the 30,480 in the two-level store (6,7).

Paged Control Store

Most branches within a microprogram are to nearby locations. This means that there is redundancy between the address of target instruction and the current address. To remove this redundancy from the CS and reduce the cost of large CSs, paging may be used. The high-order bits of the microinstruction address are saved in a register, and only the low-order bits are stored in the microinstruction.

For example, in a system with 64K words of CS, 16 bits are needed to address every location. The high-order 4 bits may be stored in a page register, leaving 12 bits for addresses in the microinstruction. Branches within a 16K-word page may be done without altering the page register value. Branches between pages are somewhat more difficult, requiring loading of the page register with a new value, as well as changing the address within the page. This technique could allow the use of a common component, such as the 12-bit-wide Am2910 sequencer, and avoid the design of a much more expensive 16 bit-wide sequencer.

MICROPROGRAMMABLE COMPONENTS

Several semiconductor manufacturers have designed integrated circuit components that are intended to be used in microprogrammed systems. These components fall into three categories: fucntional parts (which perform a single set of operations), bit-sliced parts (which perform several unrelated operations on a limited number of bits), and single chip processors. Additionally, there are components that are frequently used in the construction of microprogrammed systems but are not specifically directed toward this application. These include PALs (MMI ™), gate arrays, and semicustom and custom circuits.

Integrated circuit technology has been characterized by steady increases in the number of gates that may be placed on a chip and the number of pins that can connect with other chips. Early components had less than 35 gates and were packaged in a 14- or 16-pin dual in-line package (DIP). These components included registers, gates, flip-flop, decoders, multiplexers, counters, and binary adders. Although they were used to build microprogrammed systems, they are very low level components and were not targeted toward microprogramming.

Early Components

During the 1970s, as integrated circuit technology developed, it became possible to place a significant number of transistors on a single chip. Although it was possible to place all the gates for an ALU on a single chip, the packaging was inadequate to support transferring signals on and off the chip. A 16-bit ALU might require 60 or more external connections for three buses, flags, control lines, and power.

Several parts were introduced in the mid-1970s in 24-pin DIPS with about 45 gates, which oriented toward (but were not limited to) microprogramming. One of these parts is the TI SN74181 ALU/Function Generator. This component could perform 16 logical or arithmetic operations on two 4-bit values. Four control lines into the chip selected the operation to be performed. The SN74181 could be cascaded (with the use of a look-ahead carry generator chip) to construct an ALU of any desired length. About the same time, TI introduced the SN74S274 4 × 4-bit binary multiplier, in a 20-pin DIP. Sixteen of these could be used to construct a 16 × 16-bit multiplier, which would operate in 75 nanoseconds.

These components could be cascaded to create an ALU or multiplier of any desired size. Large registers could be constructed similarly by collections of memory chips. The many connections between the components and many multiplexers and gates make the construction of a CPU with these components complex and expensive.

There are gate density, power, and speed penalties in transferring data between the chip and external lines. The drivers for pins are large, taking away chip area that could be used for processing circuitry. They also take more power and are slower because they have to drive the capacitance of the external circuitry.

Bit-Slice Components

Bit-slice components were developed to address these problems. Because there are a large number of connections between the functional units, bit-slice components attempt to keep these within the chip. Instead of partitioning each of the functional blocks (ALU, registers, etc.) on individual chips, a bit-slice component takes a vertical slice, either 2 or 4 bits wide, of the entire CPU. Each bit-slice was connected to its neighbors to propagate the carry or shift bits. There are few interchip connections; most connections are internal to the chip. Many separate functions are integrated on one chip: registers, shifters, ALU, multiplexers, and control circuitry. This results in a significant reduction in the number of integrated circuits and interconnections.

In 1975, AMD introduced the 4-bit wide Am2901 (Fig. 8) in a 40-pin package which has become the most popular bit-slice processor. Intel introduced the 2-bit-wide 3002 in 1976 in a 28-pin package, but it did not achieve wide use, perhaps because twice as many 3002s were needed as 2901s to build the same size processor. TI introduced the 74LS481 4-bit slice, and Motorola introduced the MC10800 ECL 4-bit slice for high-speed applications. Most bit-slice components were part of a ''family'' of components, designed to interface easily and flexibly.

Sequencers have also been sliced, although this is less useful. AMD introduced the Am2909/2911/29811 set of 4-bit-wide sequencer parts, which could be cascaded to construct a sequencer of any desired size. Shortly after introducing this set, they introduced the Am2910, a 12-bit sequencer, which essentially consisted of three AM2911s and a AM29811 in a single 40-pin package. Because the AM2910 can address 4,096 words of CS, the AM2909/11 is used only in high-speed applications.

Since these first components were introduced in the mid-1970s, enhancements have been made in the performance of the chips, as well as extensions to the chip families. One enhancement has been to design the chip using emitter-coupled logic (ECL) internally, with transistor-transistor logic (TTL)-compatible input and output. Extensions to the chip families have included deeper return address stacks in the sequencers and functional extensions in the ALUs, such as binary-coded decimal (BCD) arithmetic.

In the mid-1980s, several companies introduced low-power complementary metal-oxide semiconductor (CMOS) versions of the 2901 and 2910. Developers of gate arrays have included the 2901 as a building block in their libraries to be used in constructing proprietary processors. As an outgrowth of the gate arrays, single integrated circuits containing four 2901s and supporting circuitry have been introduced to make a 16-bit microprogrammable processor.

In 1985, TI introduced the SN74AS888 8-bit processor slice in a 68-pin package. Architecturally, the 74AS888 is quite similar to the Am2901. It does provide a number of ALU operations to support divides, bit and byte operations, and data conversions.

Bit-slice components permit much simpler construction of a CPU, although they constrain the designer to using the internal design of the bit-slice components. The data path of a 16-bit ALU can be constructed with four Am2901s in 40-pin DIPs plus a few supporting components. Constructing a similar CPU from functional components in similar-size DIPs requires perhaps 30 components.

It is my view that bit slice was a development based on a disparity between the number of gates that could be built on a single integrated circuit and the number of pins. Although there will always be limitations on the connections to an integrated circuit, these limits are now about 144. Bit-slice design limited the flexibility of the computer architect by dictating the connections between functions within the bit slice. Future development will be directed toward components with greater functionality or toward special-purpose microprogrammed parts, rather than toward more bit-slice products. Because there is a substantial installed base of bit-slice systems and substantial experience, there will be continued improvements in the performance or packaging.

Functional Parts

Functional parts provide a single function in a single package for the designer to build microprogrammed processors with. In 1977, AMD introduced the AM2910, a 12-bit microprogram sequencer. This sequencer (Fig. 7) contains a five-level stack, incrementer, microprogram address register, a loop counter, and control logic that provides 16 different sequencing commands. This popular chip is an outgrowth of the AM2909/29811 bit-slice sequencer components.

During the late 1970s and early 1980s, TRW introduced a series of single chip multipliers in 10×10-bit, 12×12-bit, and 16×16-bit versions. The 16×16-bit component (TRW MPY-16J) was packaged in a 64-pin DIP and provided a product in under 50 nanoseconds.

During this period, attention was on the development of bit-slice components (described above), rather than on improved functional parts. The limitations on density, and especially pin-out, made the development of significant functional parts difficult. In the mid-1980s the cost-effectiveness of bit slice over functional parts shifted to favor functional parts.

In 1984, AMD introduced the Am29300 series of components. These are the Am29331 (16-bit microprogram sequencer), Am29332 (32-bit ALU), Am29333 (32-bit multiplier), Am29334 (four-port 64×18-bit register file), and Am29325 (32-bit floating-point processor).

In 1986, Analog Devices introduced the ADSP-1401, a 16-bit microprogram sequencer with multiple stack pointers and interrupt processing. Weitek introduced the WTL7136, a 32-bit sequencer with vectored interrupts and breakpoints.

Single-Chip Microprogrammed Processors

A third direction in microprogrammed components is the development of a complete processor on a single integrated circuit. These processors differ from the metal-oxide semiconductor (MOS) microprocessors, first introduced in the early 1970s, in that the programmer has extensive control over internal data paths and parallelism. They have been designed as either high-speed controllers (AMD Am29116) or as digital signal processors (TI TMS320 and Analog Devices ADSP-2100). None of these can be cascaded to construct larger processors, as can be done with bit-slice components.

The Am29116, introduced in 1982, is a 16-bit processor. It contains 32 words of RAM, an ALU that supports operations on two values with an optional mask, a barrel shifter, status registers, and an instruction decoder. A single 16-bit bus connects with other components. The bus is bidirectional and may both read and write in a single 100-nanosecond cycle. The instructions are encoded in 16 bits, generally in five fields. There are 14 different instruction formats. The sequencer and CS are external to the Am29116 and usually also control other components in addition to the processor. Most operations can be applied either on 16-bit words or 8-bit bytes. The AM29116 does not contain a multiplier; it is oriented toward high-speed controllers for disk or tape drives and toward graphics applications.

The TMS320, introduced in 1984, is a 16-bit processor designed for signal processing applications such as digital filtering, image processing, or telecommunications. It contains 544 words of RAM, divided into three blocks, one of which (256 words) can be used for either data or program, and it can access 128K of external memory. A 16×16-bit multiplier, 16-bit shifter, and 32-bit ALU provide a large number of data operations. Serial input and output ports are provided, as well as a 16-bit timer. A 16-bit sequencer built into the processor supports subroutines (four deep), looping, and interrupt processing. Each instruction is 16-bits wide and executes in 200 nanoseconds. The instructions are very highly encoded, allowing little parallelism within the processor.

The ADSP-2100, introduced in 1986, is similar to the TMS320 in that both contain an integrated sequencer, multiplier, and highly encoded instruction set. A 16-bit ALU, 16×16-bit multiplier, and 16-bit barrel shifter are connected in parallel and are somewhat more flexible than the TMS320. The 14-bit sequencer supports looping and subroutines (16 deep), as well as interrupt processing. Two data address generators are used to address external data. One of the data address generators supports bit-reversed addressing used with Fast Fourier Transforms. There are a limited number of registers dedicated to specific functions. Both data and instructions are stored external to the processor. Up to 16K instructions or 64K data may be addressed. A 16-entry instruction cache stores the most recently used instructions to speed up loops. Each instruction is 24 bits wide and executes in 125 nanoseconds.

MICROPROGRAM DEVELOPMENT TOOLS

While developing a microprogrammed system using bit-slice or functional integrated circuits, it is valuable to be able to see values on the various buses in the system, alter values in registers or memory, modify the CS, step through instructions singly, and stop at specific addresses or upon specified conditions. When debugging is complete, there is little or no need for the hardware to support these functions.

A hardware development system contains a writable control store (WCS), which is used in place of the target systems CS. The user can list and alter the contents of the WCS. Probes connected to selected buses or registers capture values within the target machine. The data on the probes may be stored in a trace memory, along with the sequence of instructions executed, or may be used to detect conditions and halt processing.

During the development of a microprogrammed microprocessor, a breadboard or mock-up of the circuitry is often constructed using functional integrated circuits. Although it is possible to add buses and registers to the circuitry to capture data, it is often easier to use a freestanding hardware development system.

Many of the facilities provided by a hardware development system are often designed into the target system when the incremental cost and effort is not great. For example, in the design of a mainframe CPU, an external processor is used to provide the interface to the user. Registers within the CPU can be read or written by the external processor to perform diagnostics or to assist in the debugging of microcode. This interface processor may also run the console and perform ongoing status monitoring.

ASSEMBLERS AND META-ASSEMBLERS

Each new microprogrammable system has a new and unique instruction set. This means that frequently there is a new assembler written for each machine. These assemblers are often very simple, with a fixed format requiring that the values for each field in the instruction be entered in order, either as numeric or symbolic values.

Meta-assemblers ease the burden of producing a new assembler. A meta-assembler accepts a description of the instruction format for a machine and constructs an assembler tailored to that processor. Because the assembler can be easily targeted to a new processor, these meta-assemblers are frequently described as retargetable assemblers. Several meta-assemblers have been described by Skordalakis (8).

The most common meta-assembler is AMDASM, which was developed by AMD in 1978 (9) to support programming the Am2900 chip set. Several derivative meta-assemblers have been developed which extend AMDASM to support macros or relocatable output. The definition file for a processor defines groups of related fields in the instruction and symbolic names for the values that may be placed in these fields. A portion of a definition file is shown in Figure 10a.

The assembly process accepts the names of the field groups and the values and constructs an instruction in the format specified in the definition. The address of the current instruction is maintained and may be used to define labels as in a conventional assembler. Several groups of fields may be "overlaid" to construct the instruction. A sample of the assembler input is shown in Figure 10b.

AMDASM does have some drawbacks: It is difficult to understand or create the definition files, the assembly language is not flexible, and it is quite easy to make the error of using a symbolic value in the wrong field. In 1983, AMD developed M29 as an advanced meta-assembler (10). M29 permitted clearer descriptions of processors and enhanced the assembly process. M29 also provides more error checking than AMDASM and supports macros and relocatable output. Portions of a definition file and assembly are shown in Figure 11, which correspond to the AMDASM versions. M29 has been released through Microtec Research as mcASM, which also markets an enhanced version of AMDASM. A derivative product named metaSTEP has been created by Step Engineering.

Compilers

Compilers and high-level languages were developed soon after the introduction of computers in the early 1950s. FORTRAN was introduced along with the IBM 704 in

```
;  Field equates for ALU inputs
;                                          R Source   S Source
AQ:      EQU      Q#Ø        ;                A          Q
AB:      EQU      Q#1        ;                A          B
ZQ:      EQU      Q#2        ;                Ø          Q
ZB:      EQU      Q#3        ;                Ø          B
ZA:      EQU      Q#4        ;                Ø          A
DA:      EQU      Q#5        ;                D          A
DQ:      EQU      Q#6        ;                D          Q
DZ:      EQU      Q#7        ;                D          Ø

;  Field equates for ALU function
;
ADD:     EQU      Q#Ø        ;             R plus S
SUBR:    EQU      Q#1        ;             S minus R
SUBS:    EQU      Q#2        ;             R minus S
OR:      EQU      Q#3        ;             R or S
AND:     EQU      Q#4        ;             R and S
NOTRS:   EQU      Q#5        ;             not R and S
EXOR:    EQU      Q#6        ;             R exclusive or S
EXNOR:   EQU      Q#7        ;             R exclusive nor S

;  Field equates for ALU destination and shifter control
;                                        Regs       Q-Reg     Y-Output
QREG:    EQU      Q#Ø        ;                        ALU->Q    ALU
NOP:     EQU      Q#1        ;                                  ALU
RAMA:    EQU      Q#2        ;          ALU->B                  A
RAMF:    EQU      Q#3        ;          ALU->B                  ALU
RAMQD:   EQU      Q#4        ;          ALU/2->B   Q/2->Q     ALU
RAMD:    EQU      Q#5        ;          ALU/2->B                ALU
RAMQU:   EQU      Q#6        ;          ALU*2->B   Q*2->Q     ALU
RAMU:    EQU      Q#7        ;          ALU*2->B                ALU

;  Definition of field positions
;
AM29Ø1:  DEF      4VH#Ø,4VH#Ø,3VQ#Ø,3VQ#Ø,3VQ#Ø,1VB#Ø
;                 Areg  Breg  Src   Op   Dest Carry
END
```

(a)   AMDASM Definition for AMD Am29Ø1

```
;  Assembly

ORG H#1ØØ
        AM29Ø1 Ø, 4, DZ, OR, RAMA        ; D -> R4
        AM29Ø1 5, 5, DZ, AND, RAMA       ; ZERO -> R5
        AM29Ø1 5, 5, AB, ADD, QREG , 1   ; 1 -> QREG
END
```

(b)   AMDASM Assembly

FIGURE 10   Sample AMDASM definition and assembly.

1957, with ALGOL following in 1958 and COBOL in 1960. Variations of these languages are still in widespread use. There are hundreds of high-level language compilers in current use.

Although microprogramming was developed in the early days of computer history, there are no common high-level languages or compilers available. There has been and continues to be promising research in this area.

```
Areg:    length (4), default (Ø);
Breg:    length (4), default (Ø);
Src:     length (3), default (Ø),( R Source    S Source   )
         values ( AQ : Ø,        (     A          Q       )
                  AB : 1,        (     A          B       )
                  ZQ : 2,        (     Ø          Q       )
                  ZB : 3,        (     Ø          B       )
                  ZA : 4,        (     Ø          A       )
                  DA : 5,        (     D          A       )
                  DQ : 6,        (     D          Q       )
                  DZ : 7);       (     D          Ø       )
Op:      length (3), default (Ø),
         values ( ADD  : Ø,      ( R plus S                )
                  SUBR : 1,      ( S minus R               )
                  SUBS : 2,      ( R minus S               )
                  OR   : 3,      ( R or S                  )
                  AND  : 4,      ( R and S                 )
                  NOTRS: 5,      ( not R and S             )
                  EXOR : 6,      ( R exclusive or S        )
                  EXNOR: 7);     ( R exclusive nor S       )
Dest:    length (3), default (Ø), (    Regs      Q-Reg    Y-Output )
         values ( QREG  : Ø,     (               ALU->Q     ALU    )
                  NOP   : 1,     (                          ALU    )
                  RAMA  : 2,     (    ALU->B                 A     )
                  RAMF  : 3,     (    ALU->B                ALU    )
                  RAMQD : 4,     (    ALU/2->B  Q/2->Q      ALU    )
                  RAMD  : 5,     (    ALU/2->B              ALU    )
                  RAMQU : 6,     (    ALU*2->B  Q*2->Q      ALU    )
                  RAMU  : 7);    (    ALU*2->B              ALU    )
Carry:   length (1), default (Ø);
```

                    (a) M29 definition for AMD Am29Ø1

```
{  Define macros for Am29Ø1   }
      macro  LOAD  &reg;
        BEGIN
          OUTPUT ("Breg = &reg, Src = DZ, Op = OR, Dest = RAMF");
        END
      macro  ZERO  &reg;
        BEGIN
          OUTPUT ("Breg = &reg, Src = DZ, Op = AND, Dest = RAMF");
        END

{  Assembly  }

      org H'1ØØ';

      LOAD 4;                    ( D -> R4    )
      ZERO 5;                    ( Zero -> R5 )
      Areg = 5, Breg = 5, Src = AB, Op = SUBR, Dest = QREG, Carry = 1;
                                 ( -1 -> Qreg  (no macro defined)   )

      end;
```

                         (b) M29 assembly

             FIGURE 11   Sample M29 definition and assembly.

   Several factors, both economic and technical, have made the development of compilers for microprogramming difficult. Much of the microcode written has been the
creation of instruction set interpreters. For example, all of the machines of IBM's System/
360 series, and its descendents, have substantially the same instruction set and architecture. The few hundreds of lines of microcode that implements this instruction set is

written once for each machine by the manufacturer. For such a small amount of microcode, the cost of developing a compiler is difficult to justify.

Compilers for languages such as FORTRAN sell many copies, allowing a reasonable per-piece cost and distributing the development cost over a large number of customers. Manufacturers of CPUs do not have the same economics: few copies of a microcode compiler might be sold, because there are few users who would be interested in re-microprogramming a CPU. The manufacturers have also been reluctant to allow users to generate their own microcode for fear of compromising the integrity of the microcode that gives the computer its personality.

Several manufacturers of minicomputers have introduced user-microprogrammable computers. There have been few users who have actively microcoded their computers, both due to the complexity of the microprogramming process and the limited application of user-written microcode. Because the size of the CS is small on these machines, the cost of developing a compiler has not been warranted. The market for microcode compilers has been very limited.

Microcode has several properties that make it difficult to generate using a compiler. At the architectural level of a computer, each instruction is conceptually discrete, performing a single function that completes before the next instruction begins. Computer architects go to great pains to design systems that can take advantage of the parallelism of the hardware and still produce the apparent discrete and independent execution of instructions. At the microcode level, the interactions between the different parts of the hardware are visible and must be taken into account. Often, data are transient and must be moved within a certain time. Microinstructions are interdependent: A microinstruction may use data placed on a bus by a previous instruction. This microinstruction may generate a result (perhaps by accessing memory) that may not be available for several cycles and must be moved within a limited period by some later microinstruction. During the time that this result is being developed, part of the hardware may be in use and must not be affected by subsequent microinstructions until its functioning is complete.

Horizontal microcode has several discrete micro-operations that are combined in a single microinstruction for simultaneous execution. These operations may be quite independent, e.g., computing the address of the next instruction to be executed in an instruction set interpreter while executing the current instruction. A compiler for microcode must generate instructions that perform several parallel functions at a time.

There is usually a very high premium on efficiency, both in speed and code size for microcode. If a sequence of microcode is executed each time that a CPU executes an instruction, e.g., to fetch the operation code from memory, any reduction in execution time greatly improves the performance of the CPU. Memory cost is proportional to the speed of the memory which, in turn, affects the speed of the microprogrammed system significantly. This mandates that the microcode be compact.

Several techniques have been developed to allow the generation of high-quality microcode. Trace scheduling (11) identifies the various resources of the hardware and the conflicting demands placed on them. The microprogram is considered a sequence of micro-operations that use these resources. Trace scheduling attempts to move the operations earlier or later in the sequence to allow them to be combined efficiently with other micro-operations into microinstructions. This movement of micro-operations is guaranteed not to alter the meaning of the microprogram.

Recently, the economic factors seem to be shifting. More computers are being developed with WCSs that are much larger than those in earlier machines. The cost of the memory used for the CS, although still significant, has decreased dramatically. Many are special-purpose machines, such as graphics or image processors, requiring many thousands of lines of microcode to perform very complex algorithms. These applications are less critical of the quality of the microcode generated by a compiler. The ability to write code faster and in a fashion more simple and easy to maintain outweighs the concern about code density or speed.

There has been considerable research in microcode compilers (12). The compilers developed may be described as low level or high level, and as machine dependent or machine independent. The low-level machine-dependent compilers (e.g., Strum or GMPL) have constructs that require explicit control of the machine resources and reference these resources explicitly. The low-level machine independent compilers (e.g., YALLL) also require explicit control but allow control of the binding of variables to machine resources. High-level machine dependent compilers (e.g., microTAL) manage more of the machine resources, relieving the programmer of the need to code looping constructs or memory accesses while still being closely bound to the specific architecture of the target hardware. The high-level machine-independent compilers provide features similar to those of convenient compilers: flexible constructs and hiding of the structure of the target machine. There are some compilers that fall into this last category (Micro-C or Marble), but there are significant problems with binding of machine resources to variables, resulting in programs that are not portable. An example of a program in Marble from Ref. *12* is shown in Figure 12.

```
/* Global declarations of bound resources */
type    bound x,y,z = bit 64;
        /* Assumption: registers named x,y,z */

function bound UF returns boolean;
        bound;
        /* Representing the flag.  Could also be
        declared as a bound
        data resource if more appropriate  */

procedure multiply (in A, B: bit 64; out C: bit 64);

var    mier: bound y;
        mcand: bound x;
        result: bound z;
begin
        mier := B;
        mcand := A;
        result := ((mier and <b>100...0) + mcand)
            and <b>100...0;
        mier := mier and<b>011...1;
        mcand := mcand and <b>011...1;
        while mier <> 0
        begin
            mier := mier rshift 1;
            if UF
            then result := result + mcand;
            mcand := mcand lshift 1;
        end;
        C := result
end; /* of procedure multiply */
```

FIGURE 12   Example program for Marble.

Simulators

Often microcode is developed at the same time as the hardware for a computer. This leads to the need to stimulate the operation of the hardware so that the correct operation of the microcode can be assured.

There are two types of simulations: behavioral and structural. The behavioral simulation attempts to act in the same fashion as the target hardware by modeling the features visible to the programmer. It makes no attempt to model features that the programmer does not have access to or control over, such as the internal operation of an ALU. A structural simulation attempts to model each component of the target machine, including both portions that can be controlled by the programmer and those that cannot. The timings and delays associated with the different components may be modeled.

There are advantages to both types, and some simulators have attempted to combine features of each. The behavioral simulation is faster than the structural simulation, because there is a higher level of abstraction. This makes it better for development of microcode, providing the hardware performs the functions modeled. The structural simulators can detect interactions and conflicts that were either unintended or unanticipated in the design of the hardware. As such, they are more widely used in the development of the hardware rather than the development of the microcode.

OTHER TOPICS

Verification

Verification is the process of assuring that the microcode actually does perform the function for which it was written. This is of particular interest in the development of microprograms because they are often encoded in ROM and may be difficult to alter. There is also the possibility of very adverse consequences of errors in the microcode, because it is usually very highly integrated with the architecture of the computer.

In general, verification depends on a formal description of the function to be performed by a portion of the microprogram and a description of the operation of each portion of the hardware. The verification then proceeds using theorem-proving methods to deduce that the function of the microcode is exactly that which was desired (13).

Hardware Description Languages

Both simulation and verification depend on the accurate and complete descriptions of the hardware of the target machine. As is the case with simulators, both behavioral and structural languages have been developed, and for similar reasons. The behavioral languages, such as ISPS (4), are best for simulation of microprograms. A section of a description is given in Figure 13.

Other hardware descriptions, such as S *A (14), give a detailed description of the operation of the hardware, including delay times through gates and the latencies in the hardware. These are more suitable to rigorous proofs of accuracy.

Direct Execution

The execution of a program on most computers involves several levels of translation: from the high-level source to an intermediate language, then to assembly language and,

```
AM2901 :=
  begin

**PC State**

R<3:0>,
S<3:0>,
F<3:0> := ALU<3:0>.             ! R inputs to ALU
Q<3:0>.                         ! S inputs to ALU
                                ! Output from ALU
                                ! Output from Q register

**Instruction.format**

I<8:0>,
  src<2:0>    := I<2:0>,        ! Instruction inputs
  op<2:0>     := I<5:3>,        ! Source operand field
  dest<2:0>   := I<8:6>.        ! Operation field
                                ! Destination operand field

**Implementation.Variables**

ALU<4:0>,                       ! ALU + carry output
c1amp<3:0>,                     ! Temporary for generating carry
macro z := |'1111|.             ! Tristate constant

**Instruction.Cycle**(us)

start(main) :=
  begin
  OE := OVR = fEQLO = Cn4 = 0;  ! Initialization
  P = G = 1 next
run :=
  begin                         ! Main instruction cycle
  source() next
  exec() next
  destination() run
  RESTART run
  end
  end

**Access.Computation**(us)

source :=
  begin                         ! Source calculation
  A.LATCH = RAM[A];
  B.LATCH = RAM[B] next
  DECODE src =>
    begin
    #0 := (R = A.LATCH; S = Q      ).
    #1 := (R = A.LATCH; S = B.LATCH).
    #2 := (R = 0;       S = Q      ).
    #3 := (R = 0;       S = B.LATCH).
    #4 := (R = 0;       S = A.LATCH).
    #5 := (R = D;       S = A.LATCH).
    #6 := (R = D;       S = Q      ).
    #7 := (R = D;       S = 0      ).
    end
  end.
end.

destination :=                  ! Destination calculation
  begin
  DECODE dest =>
    begin
    #0 = (Q = F; Y = F).
    #1 = (Y = F).
    #2 := (Y = RAM[A]; RAM[B] = F).
    #3 := (RAM[B] = F).
    #4 := (RAM[B] @ RAM0 = RAM3 @ F; Q @ Q0 = Q3 @ Q).
    #5 := (Y = ; RAM[B] @ RAM0 = RAM3 @ F).
    #6 := (Y = ; RAM[B] @ RAM0 = RAM3 @ F; Q3 @ Q = Q @ Q0).
    #7 := (Y = ; RAM3 @ RAM[B] = F @ RAM0).
    end
  end.

**Instruction.Execution**(us)

exec :=
  begin
  DECODE op =>
    begin
    #0 := (ALU = R + S;                                    ! R + S
           P = ((R or S) neq(us) '1111);
           G = g.compute(R, S);
           OVR = ALU<4> xor ALU<3>).
    #1 := (ALU = S - R;                                    ! S - R
           P = (((not R) or S) neq(us) '1111);
           G = g.compute((not R), S);
           OVR = ALU<4> xor ALU<3>).
    #2 := (ALU = R - S;                                    ! R - S
           P = (R or (not S) neq(us) '1111);
           G = g.compute(R, (not S));
           OVR = ALU<4> xor ALU<3>).
    #3 := (ALU = R or S;                                   ! R or S
           P = ((R or S) eq(us) '1111) next
           Cn4 = OVR = (not G) or Cn).
    #4 := (ALU = R and S;                                  ! R and S
           P = 0;
           Cn4 = OVR = (not G) or Cn).
    #5 := (ALU = (not R) and S;                            ! R and S
           P = 0;
           Cn4 = OVR = (not G) or Cn).
    #6 := (ALU = R xor S;                                  ! R xor S
           P = (((not R) and S) eq(us) '0000) next
           Cn4 = OVR = (not G) or Cn).
    #7 := (ALU = R eqv S;                                  ! R ecv S
           P = (((R and S) neq(us) .0000);
           G = no| g.compute(R, S);
           Cn4 = c67(R, S);
           OVR = ovr67(R, S))
    end next
    fEQLO = (F eqv '0000)
    end.

end            ! End of AM2901 description
```

FIGURE 13 Partial ISPS description of AMD Am2901.

finally, to machine instructions. The machine instructions are interpreted by the microprogram to produce the desired operations, resulting in another level of translation.

Several attempts have been made to eliminate one or more of these translations to improve performance. One approach has been the interpretation of the intermediate language by the microprogram or by the creation of a machine interface that is close to the high-level language being executed. Direct execution has been most effective with languages that are concise and have complex operations such as APL (15) and PROLOG (16).

Vertical Migration

There are certain functions in a computer system, usually within the operating system, that are executed very frequently. Examples of these functions are task dispatching or page fault management. The time spent performing these functions may be a significant percentage of the total system time.

Vertical migration (17) is the operation of moving all or part of these high-level functions into microcode. This has the potential benefit of improved performance at the expense of the CS. There is the added benefit of improved security, because certain features may now be hidden from the user.

This technique has been used quite effectively by IBM in the System Extensions to MVS on the System/370. Several new instructions were created to manage certain heavily used operating system functions such as page management and I/O command translation. For example, one of these new instructions replaced a number of instructions used to translate from virtual addresses to real addresses for I/O operations. The microinstructions implementing the new instruction execute at the speed of the microcode, which is much faster than the average instruction speed. Additionally, much of the overhead of fetching instructions from memory, decoding, and then executing them is avoided.

RISC Processors

RISC is an outgrowth of microprogramming that is characterized by a complete lack of microprogramming. A RISC is a computer with a simplified instruction set, which meets the following constraints (18):

1. Execute one instruction per cycle.
2. All instructions are the same size.
3. Access memory with load and store instructions only.
4. Support high-level languages.

RISC systems are characterized by simplicity and regularity in their design, which translates to improved performance. They are compared with complex instruction set computers (CISCs), which have instructions that generally take several cycles to execute and often come in various sizes. Several addressing modes may be supported.

CISCs are often implemented by microprogramming. To a great extent, vertical microprogrammed processors possess the first three characteristics listed above. RISC proponents claim that if the processor is designed to support high-level languages specifically, a compiler can generate code that operates directly on the hardware, bypassing a level of interpretation and its inefficiencies. The claim is that for the same cost, a RISC is simpler and therefore can be faster.

CISC instructions usually have more extensive or complex functions than those implemented on RISCs. For example, multiplication which is a single, multicycle instruction on a CISC, may be implemented as a series of add and shift instructions on a RISC. This increases the execution time on the RISC. Additionally, certain features of the RISC systems (such as very large register files) may obfuscate the benefit of simplified instruction sets.

Several companies have developed RISCs, including MIPS, Hewlett-Packard, IBM, and Ridge Computers. Sun Microsystems has introduced computers using their SPARC processor, derived from the Berkeley RISC processors developed by David A. Patterson (18). Certain computers have been described as RISCs when they have only one of the characteristics of the others. For example, a computer with the large overlapping register set similar to the RISC described in Ref. 18 has been described as a RISC, although it has a substantial amount of microcode, and instructions may take several cycles to execute.

REFERENCES

1. Wilkes, M. A., The Best Way to Design an Automatic Calculating Machine, presented at the Manchester University Computer Inaugural Conference, July 1951; reprinted in *Mallach and Sandak* Ref. 15.
2. Wilkes, M. A., and Stringer, J. B., Microprogramming and the Design of the Control Circuits in an Electronic Digital Computer, *Proc. Cambridge Phil. Soc.*, 49 (Part 2) 230–238 (April 1953); reprinted in Ref. 4.
3. Husson, S. S., *Microprogramming Principles and Practices*, Prentice-Hall, Englewood Cliffs, NJ, 1970.
4. Siewiorek, D. P., Bell, C. G., and Newell, A. (eds.), *Computer Structures: Principles and Examples*, McGraw-Hill, New York, 1982.
5. Myers, G. J., *Advances in Computer Architecture*, John Wiley and Sons, New York, 1978.
6. Stritter, S., and Tredennick, N., Microprogrammed Implementation of a Single Chip Microprocessor, *Proceedings of the Eleventh Annual Workshop on Microprogramming*, December 1978, pp. 8–16.
7. Nash, J., and Spak, M., Hardware and Software Tools for the Development of a Micro-Programmed Microprocessor, *Proceedings of the Twelfth Annual Workshop on Microprogramming*, November 1979, pp. 73–83.
8. Skordalakis, E., Meta-Assemblers, *IEEE Micro*, 6–16 (April 1983).
9. Powers, V. M., and Hernandez, J. H., Microprogram Assemblers for Bit-Slice Microprocessors, *Computer*, 11(7): 186–198 (July 1978).
10. Eager, M. J., M29—An Advanced Retargetable Microcode Assembler, *Proceedings of the Sixteenth Annual Workshop on Microprogramming*, October 1983, pp. 92–100.
11. Fisher, J. A., Trace Scheduling: A Technique for Global Microcode Compaction, *IEEE Trans. Comput.*, C–30(7): 478–490 (July 1981).
12. Davidson, S., Progress in High-Level Microprogramming, *IEEE Software*, 18–26 (July 1986).
13. Mueller, R. A., and Duda, M. R., Formal Methods of Microcode Verification and Synthesis, *IEEE Software*, 38–48 (July 1986).
14. Dasgupta, S., Hardware Description Languages in Microprogramming Systems, *Computer* 18(2): 67–76 (February 1985).
15. Hassitt, A., and Lyon, L. E., An APL Emulator on System/370, *IBM Syst. J.*, 15(4): 1976; reprinted in *Advances in Microprogramming* (E. Mallach and N. Sandak, eds.), Artec House, Dedham, MA, 1983.

16. Gee, J., Melvin, S. W., and Patt, Y. N., The Implementation of Prolog via VAX 8600 Microcode, *Proceedings of the Nineteenth Annual Workshop on Microprogramming*, October 1986, pp. 68–74.

17. Stockenberg, J., and van Dam, A., Vertical Migration for Performance Enhancement in Layered Hardware/Firmware/Software, *Computer*, 11(5):35–50 (May 1985).

18. Patterson, D. A., and Sequin, C. H., A VLSI RISC, *Computer*, 15(9):8–21 (September 1982).

19. Winner, R. I., Carter, E. M., Automated Vertical Migration to Dynamic Microcode: An Overview and Example, *IEEE Software*, July

MICHAEL J. EAGER

DATA FLOW MODELING

INTRODUCTION

Data flow modeling is a technique for specifying a system or program in terms of the types of data that flow through the system/program and transformations that process these data. Any such transformations can, in turn, be described by a more detailed data flow model that specifies the function of the transformation in terms of lower-level data flows and transformations. The diagrams used to document data flow models are called data flow diagrams (DFD).

Additional leveling in the data flow model can be used to represent design information. In fact, one may view a data flow transformation at one level to be the specification for the corresponding data flow submodel at the next lower level. Data flow-oriented design methods such as transform and transaction analysis are used to transform data flow models into structured designs.

The basic idea for representing the behavior of a system by a graph was first proposed by Martin and Estrin in 1967 (1). The same representation, which uses arrows to represent data and circles to represent transformations, is the basis of today's data flow diagrams. A similar flowgraph representation for modeling of mathematical systems was described by Whitehouse in 1973 (2). The notation has been refined since and adopted for systems analysis and design due to work by Myers (3), Ross (4), Yourdon (5), Constantine (6), and DeMarco (7). Recent studies by Kant and Newell (8) suggest that at least part of the conceptual level of system/program modeling occurs in a data flow context. The closeness to conceptual modeling makes data flow diagrams a powerful tool for system analysis and design.

WHAT IS DATA FLOW MODELING

All software systems deal with information (data), in essence transforming some types of information to other types. A system, in general *obtains* data, *processes* it through certain transformations, and *produces* output data as a result of the processing. To understand a software system, therefore, one has to understand the *domain of information* that the system has to deal with. To fully understand the domain of information we need to analyze and represent three aspects of data:

Information Flow

This aspect of information domain is a representative view of how different pieces of information move through a system, and the manner in which they are changed as they move. For example, in the system shown in Figure 1, two input data, D_1 and D_2 are

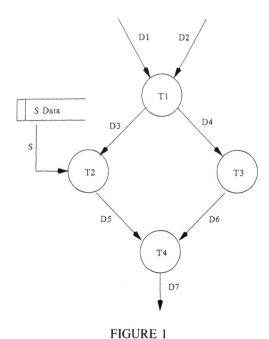

FIGURE 1

transformed by process T_1 into two new (types of) data, D_3 and D_4. D_3, together with information obtained from storage facility, is transformed into D_5 by process T_2. D_5 and the result of further processing of D_4 (D_6) are combined and transformed into the system's output, D_7. This view of the information domain represents major functions of the system (transformations) and the data that are passed from one function to another.

Information Structure

In this representation, the logical structure of data elements shows how data are viewed as aggregates, collections, tables, and so on. This view of the information domain also shows the relationships between different items of data within a single structure or between separate structures of data. For example, the representative structure of information used in a "Personnel Information" system shows that data needed for this system are organized into two substructures: employee records and department records. Each

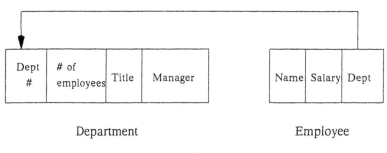

Department   Employee

FIGURE 2

substructure is an aggregate of certain items of information. Each employee record is related to a corresponding department record by a reference to the department number.

Information Content

Information content is concerned with the contents of each individual data item. The contents of a data structure and the classes of objects that an item of information represents are defined by this aspect. In the above example, the contents of employee records are names, a class of objects of alphabetic type, salaries, a class of objects which can have values in a specified range (the salary range), and department numbers.

Data flow modeling is a technique for analysis and representation of these three aspects of the "information domain" for a system or program. Analysis performed to understand and represent the requirements for a system is called a requirement specification. Analysis to identify and represent all functions of a system is considered a design model.

We can view a system/program at different levels of abstraction. At the most abstract level, the system can be viewed as a black box with a number of "data flows" entering it and some number of "data flows" leaving it. Data flows represent any form of data, such as a signal, a set of numbers, a file of records, or even a database. In this view, the black box transforms the set of input data flows into the set of output data flows. At a lower level of abstractions, a more detailed view of the system is presented by showing some components of the black box and data flows which run between these components. Various levels of abstraction can be produced in this manner.

Requirement specification is the process of describing the inside of the black box in terms of more and more detailed domain operations and intermediate data flows, as well as providing details that describe the input and output data flows more precisely. Structured analysis (7,9) has become a very popular tool in the analysis of information systems. It is based on these principles and uses data flow diagrams to represent the system model.

Data flow design can be viewed as a continuation of requirement analysis, in which further leveling (detailing) of the data flow model is carried on with the aim of discovering (or deciding) the details of the system's functions and the interfaces between these functions. The resulting data flow diagrams can be transformed into a structured design, representing the system's architecture, using the techniques of transform and transaction analysis (6,7). Alternatively, with advances in data flow architecture (10), data flow languages (11–13), and integrated reusable tool environments, a data flow model can be executed as a prototype or as the implementation of the ultimate system. These techniques suggest that data flow modeling may provide an integrated framework for some types of software development, based on a single unifying model, from requirement analysis through design to implementation.

DATA FLOW DIAGRAMS

A data flow diagram (DFD) represents the information flow of a system. The graph is composed mainly of directed arcs, representing data flows, and nodes (circles or rectangles), representing data transformations. Other symbols represent "external" sources or destinations of data flows and data stores, where data flows can be kept between transformations. Data flow diagrams usually are drawn from left to right and top to

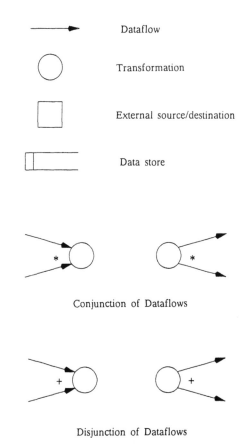

Dataflow

Transformation

External source/destination

Data store

Conjunction of Dataflows

Disjunction of Dataflows

FIGURE 3

bottom. The graph in Figure 1 is a simple DFD. Figure 3 illustrates a frequently used DFD symbology. The following sections describe in greater detail, each of these elements of data flow modeling.

Data Flows

The directed arcs of a DFD, called "data flows," represent data interfaces between components of a system, that is, system processes (also called data transformations, transformations for short) as well as external sources/destinations or data stores. Data flows can be thought of as pipelines which facilitate the flow of information between different processes.

The DFD of Figure 4 has five data flows. Two different data flows can interface the same two components, either in the same direction (i.e., "charge slip" and "credit slip"), or in opposing directions (i.e., "payment" and "monthly statement"). A data flow might represent a single piece of information (e.g., date in the above example), a continuous flow of information ("payment"), batches of data (e.g., "statement"), or information on demand (e.g., "customer info").

Two data flows might have identical structure and represent very similar data, but still be considered as two different data flows in a DFD. Such data flows differ in certain

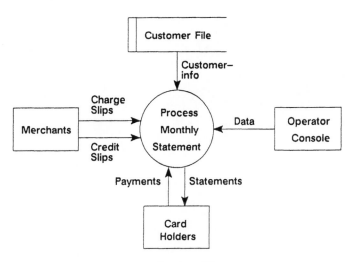

FIGURE 4

characteristics, such as their time of creation, the order of their component datum, or certain properties like being validated or reformatted. In Figure 5, "last month summary records" and "this month summary records" have identical composition (both represent records which summarize the volume and amount of sale for several products). The two data flows differ by their time stamps, which happens to be an important characteristic for the system under consideration (the comparison program). A data flow might have more than one source/destination. In this case, convergence or divergence of data flows happen (Fig. 6).

It should be noted that data flows do not represent flow of control or material flow, nor can they cause activation or deactivation of a process. In Figure 7, for example, if print-command is meant to activate the "form output" process, it is not a data flow and should not be included in the diagram.

Data Transformations (Processes)

These represent the processes that transform or manipulate data flows. Each "process" node shows some amount of work applied to a set of one or more input data flows (data flows that flow into the process) and would produce, as a result of this work, a set of one or more output data flows (data flows that flow out of the process). For example, the

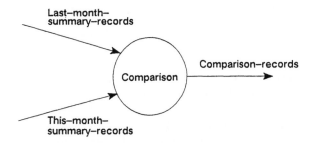

FIGURE 5

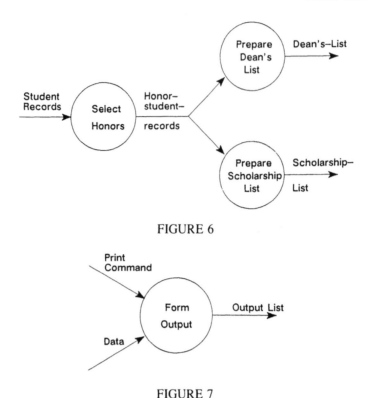

FIGURE 6

FIGURE 7

"process-monthly-statements" transformation in Figure 4 has five input data flows and one output data flow. Each data transformation of Figure 6 has one input and one output data flow.

Data transformations usually are shown by a circle or an oval bubble (in fact, DFDs are popularly known as bubble charts). In such systems as SADT, a data flow-oriented design tool, processes are shown by square bubbles.

Each "process" should be named uniquely. Therefore, if there are several "sorting" transformations in a DFD, they should not all be called, for instance, "Sort-Data." A good naming scheme would be to choose a name which represents the functionality of the "process" as well as its primary input data flows. For the above example, therefore, one should choose names such as "Sort-X," "Sort-Y," . . . , where X, Y, . . . are the names of the corresponding input data flows.

External Entities

External entities are representations of logical entities outside the system being modeled by a DFD that interface to the system as a source or destination of system's data flows. It is important to know that these entities can originate or consume data flows, but do not participate in the transformational process of the system. An external entity could represent people (customers, students, employees, etc.), organizations (accounting department, shipping office, etc.), machines (time card reader, bank teller, etc.), or any other type of physical/logical entities.

External entities that generate data flows are called "sources." Those that receive data flows are referred to as "sinks." It is possible for an external entity to be "source" of one data flow and "sink" of another data flow. The "cardholder" entity in Figure 4 is an example of this type of external entity.

Named boxes are used for representation of "external entities" in a DFD. In practice it is very common to exclude "external entities" from a data flow model, except when it is important to show a system's connection to its surrounding environment.

Data Stores

External entities are not the only source or destination of data flows. Data flows could be retrieved or stored in files, databases, or other means for storage of information. These storage mediums are represented in a DFD by "data stores" which are shown by narrow boxes with one side open. "Data stores" are also used to represent means for storing data between processes. Figure 8 shows two data stores. The "Customer-File" is used as the source for "Customer-Info," while the "Pending-Order" data store is used as a holding means between two processes. Note that "data stores" need not necessarily correspond to physical storage mediums. Data stores, whether acting as a source/destination or as a holding means, are part of the system being modeled and should always be included in the DFD.

Leveled Data Flow Diagrams

Whether data flow diagrams are used to model the requirements or the design of a system, there are two limitations to be dealt with. One is the size limitation of the mediums used to represent a data flow model. That is, there is a physical limit to the number of data transforms (bubbles) and data flows which can be fit into on standard sized paper or a computer terminal. A large data flow model, therefore, must be divided into segments

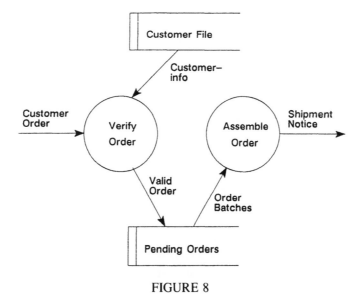

FIGURE 8

such that each segment can fit into one page. The second limitation is the degree of complexity of a data flow (or partition of) that can be handled comfortably by the designer as a whole, or can be comprehended with ease by others who deal with the design. These two limitations can be overcome by using a topdown refinement approach to data flow modeling. The data flow diagrams thus created are called "leveled data flow diagrams."

The method permits systematic partitioning of a system into smaller subsystems. The subsystems could be partitioned into sub-subsystems and so forth, until the units of the partition are small enough to fit in a page and at a level of complexity which can be comprehended as a whole. In this approach the entire data flow diagram will be divided as levels (or layers) of (sub)dataflows. The topmost level represents the most abstract view of the system. At this level, each data transform corresponds to a subsystem, with data flows showing the interfacing of these subsystems. At a lower level, major elements of each subsystem are shown as a more refined view (model) of that subsystem. If a data transform at this level is not detailed enough, a new level is created where that transform is shown with further detail. This could be done to whatever depth necessary. Figure 9 is a schematic view of parts of a leveled DFD. Note that data transforms 1, 2, and 4 of this diagram might also have levels of more detailed DFDs.

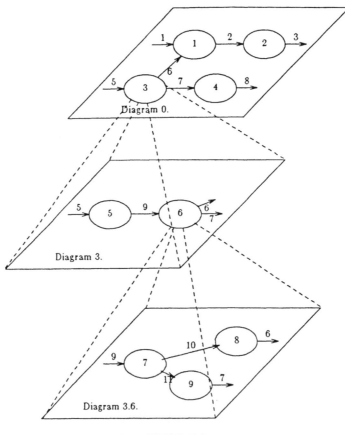

FIGURE 9

It is necessary that Input/Output data flows of a leveled DFD are consistent (balanced) between levels. In its most restrictive form the consistency rules states that:

> all input (output) dataflows of a sub-diagram should be the same as the input (output) dataflows of the higher-level process corresponding to the sub-diagram and vice-versa.

This rule can be relaxed whenever an input (output) data flow of a process is indeed a combination of two or more related data flows which are separated (refined) in the lower-level subdiagram of the process. For example, in the DFD of Figure 10, the data flow labeled "receipts," the input dataflow of the high-level transformation "process-receipts," is a combination of "deposit" and "withdrawal" receipts. In the refined sub-diagram of this transformation the combined data flow is separated into two data flows. The consistency rule can now be restated, incorporating this relaxation, as follows:

> the combined form of input (output) dataflows of a sub-diagram must match input (output) dataflows of the corresponding higher-level process, and vice-versa.

Lower-level subdiagrams, however, can have their own intermediate data flows and data stores which do not appear in a higher-level diagram. Such data stores (files) are considered local to the process represented by the subdiagram. Generally, a data store is introduced into a DFD at the level at which its inclusion is essential as either an interface between two processes or as an external source to a process of that level.

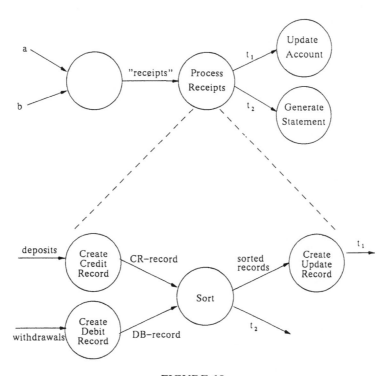

FIGURE 10

The Data Dictionary

A DFD represents only the "information flow" aspect of a system. For the requirement specification of a system to be complete, the DFD must be accompanied by an appropriate specification of the "information structure" and "information content" aspects of the system. In data flow modeling, these two aspects of system requirements are specified in a "data dictionary." The contents of a data dictionary can be categorized as follows:

Data elements   The smallest unit of data that cannot be decomposed further without losing its meaning

Data structures   Structures of data built from data elements and/or other smaller data structures

Data flows   Representing the data objects which are in "motion" from one part of the DFD to another

Data stores   Representing the data objects that are in "rest" waiting to be used by processes of the DFD

Process descriptions   Describing data transformations (or processes) of the DFD

External entities descriptions   Describing external entities of the DFD

Each category requires certain information to be recorded in the data dictionary. Data elements are represented by an identifier and a short description. The identifier might be composed of a main part and one or more qualifications. For example, DATE OF ORDER, DATE OF PURCHASE, and DATE OF PAYMENT are identifiers for three distinct data elements, all called DATE, which are further qualified as part of ORDER, PURCHASE, and PAYMENT structures (records), respectively. In addition, it is useful to describe other related information for a data element. Of particular importance are the type and range of values of the data item.

A "data structure" is specified by describing its component elements and its composite form. If one or more of the components are already described in the data dictionary, we only need refer to their identifiers. The description of the structure and of a data structure identifies the hierarchy, its components, and an indication of optional, alternative, or iterative elements. In Figure 11, PERSONAL-RECORD is a data structure com-

```
PERSON
    FIRST-NAME
    LAST-NAME
    ADDRESS
    EMPLOYMENT-CODE

    { either MONTHLY−SALARY }
    { of      HOURLY−WAGE   }  depending on EMPLOYMENT−CODE

JOB−HISTORY          (one or more times)
    JOB−CODE
    FROM−DATE
    TO−DATE
[NAME−OF−SPOUSE]
```

FIGURE 11

posed of six mandatory components (FIRST-NAME, LAST-NAME, ADDRESS, EMPLOYMENT-CODE, MONTHLY-SALARY OR HOURLY-WAGE and JOB-HISTORY), and one optional component (NAME-OF-SPOUSE). JOB-HISTORY itself is a (sub)structure and there can be one or more of it. The components in curly brackets represent alternatives.

A data flow is described by naming the data elements or data structures that pass along it. The data flow which carries PERSONAL-RECORD is simply named PERSONAL-RECORD. In addition, it is useful to record for each data flow its source and destinations, and an indication of the volume and frequency of each data structure passing along the data flow. Similarly, a data store is described in the data dictionary by the name of the data structure it holds and the source and destination of the data structure.

The description of a data transformation (process) component of a DFD should include the name of the process (the name or number used in the DFD), a short description of the functionality of the process, and a listing of the input/output data flows of the process. The description of the function performed by the process should be high level and very abstract.

In describing external entities, the data dictionary entry should include the name, associated data flows, and possibly references to where detailed information about the entity can be obtained.

A data dictionary indeed is a database of data. As with any database, it is important that contents of the dictionary can be accessed, individually and in combination, in a systematic and efficient way. The data dictionary is an important source of reference during detail analysis of a DFD and in the design stage which follows this analysis. The contents of a data dictionary are by no means fixed upon initial entry into the dictionary. As the DFD is being analyzed or in later design activities, we might need to enter new items into the dictionary, modify attributes or structures of certain elements, or even remove some elements from the dictionary. Since an entry in the dictionary is related to some other elements (e.g., a data flow entry relates to its source, destination, data structure), modification of one element might impact other related elements. Therefore, it is important that related elements of the dictionary be properly cross-referenced.

It is also important that the dictionary be complete and consistent. Incompleteness arises as the result of omission of an entry (e.g., a data flow is not defined) or the omission of an attribute of an entry (e.g., the source of a data flow is not defined). Inconsistency is introduced in a dictionary if conflicting information is entered. For example, if the source of a data flow "X" is defined to be the process "P," but "X" is not identified as the output data flow of P, we have conflicting information.

DATA FLOW-ORIENTED REQUIREMENT SPECIFICATION

Construction of a new computerized system begins with an analysis phase in which the problem to be solved and any related matters are studied and documented. The result of this analysis is represented by a "requirement specification," which states what the system, once developed, should deliver and in what manner.

To perform a successful analysis, an analyst needs methods and tools that help partition the problem into manageably small subproblems and facilitate documenting this partitioning in a systematic way. Data flow modeling and DFDs provide such an analysis method and tool. By representing the behavior of the intended system by a set of leveled DFDs, the analyst produces a comprehensive, highly maintainable, and easily understandable requirement specification.

System analysis involves the following activities:

Studying the "problem environment"   This involves identifying all entities (machines, organizations, people, etc.) involved with the intended system and their relationships. The result of this study can be documented by a physical data flow diagram (a diagram showing the physical flow of information).

Derivation of the equivalent "logical data flow" model   Once the physical DFD is produced, the analyst has to derive a corresponding system model showing only the logic of the problem. The logical data flow diagram represents a generalization of the system's functional behavior, while the physical DFD shows a specific implementation of this behavior. Figure 12 shows a small physical DFD and its corresponding logical DFD.

Refinement of the logical data flow model   This step produces the final requirement specification model from an initial logical model by a careful refinement/ enhancement of the initial model. The initial logical model represents the logic of the current system (of the system as envisioned by the user). The final logical model will represent the system to be built, as envisioned by the systems analyst.

The final logical DFD and the corresponding data dictionary specify the information domain of the system under analysis. This information is complemented with a functional description, usually using structured English, in which the detail functional behavior of each data transform (process) element of the logical DFD is described.

The requirement specification of a system is developed as a result of an iterative process of analysis and review. At each level of development of this document it is ab-

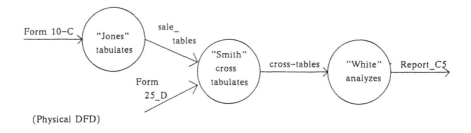

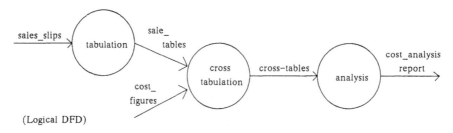

FIGURE 12

solutely essential to review and validate the specification before proceeding any further. A final validation process, using walk-through or other techniques, should be performed on the completed specification document. Without such careful review and validations, errors present in the requirement specification will propagate to the design and implementation of the system, where the cost of error repair is several degrees of magnitude more expensive than in the analysis phase.

Basic steps for validating a requirement specification are as follows:

Consistency Checking   The requirement specification must be shown to be consistent in all levels of detail. Inconsistencies result from conflicting definitions for data flows, processes, data objects, or other elements of the requirement specification.

Completeness Checking   The requirement specification must be shown to be complete by checking that all functions, data flows, constraints, or other elements of the specification are completely defined.

Conformity Checking   The requirements stated should be shown to be consistent and in conformance with the system goals and objectives. It is important to make sure that all system interfaces are properly specified and that all major functions of the system remain within the intended scope.

DATA FLOW-ORIENTED DESIGN

Refinement of a DFD into a sufficiently detailed structure becomes a representation of the system in terms of data that flow through it and the transformations which act upon these data. Furthermore, DFDs are a good starting point for the design of the modular structure of a system. Such a design technique is referred to as the "data flow-oriented" strategy.

The basic philosophy of this strategy is that the DFD of most common systems tend to have certain familiar patterns. These patterns are indicative of the overall "shape" of the system. By "shape" we mean the form of the modular hierarchy of the system. For example, the system represented by Figure 13a has a "tall" shape, while the shape of a system represented in Figure 13b is "fat." Most well-designed systems are "mosque" shape as represented in Figure 13c.

One common "pattern" is the case when a DFD is organized around a set of processing elements or "transforms" which obtain completely prepared input and produce "raw" output. This part of the DFD is called a transform center. The system or subsystem represented by that DFD is referred to as a transform-centered system. Removing the transform center from such a DFD leaves us with input and output data flows and transformations which prepare them. Figure 14 represents a schematic of such a DFD.

A second type of pattern commonly found in DFDs is the "transaction center" pattern. The elements of such a DFD are organized around a center which obtains some input data flow (called transaction) and dispatches them to different processing elements (transforms). This part of the DFD is called a "transaction center." A general case is shown in Figure 15.

The following two sections represent two design techniques, one for each of the above DFD patterns, by which we can derive a first draft of the modular structure of the corresponding system. It should be noted, however, that such designs are by no means

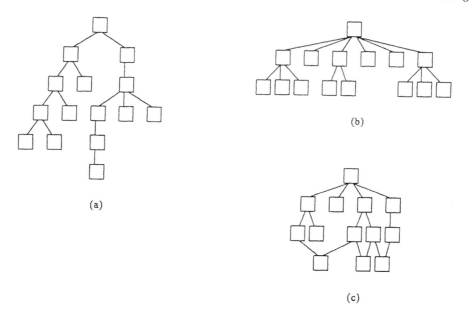

(a)

(b)

(c)

FIGURE 13

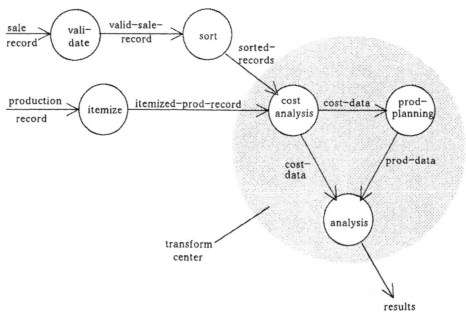

FIGURE 14

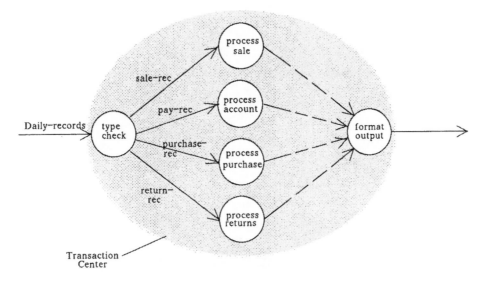

FIGURE 15

optimal. A careful study of the intermodular and intramodular relationships should be used to further refine and modify such designs.

Transform-Centered Design

Given a transform-centered DFD (or sub-DFD) we can derive the first draft of the modular structure of the system (or subsystem) represented by that DFD. The design can then be improved by observing and modifying those parts of the design which show a high degree of dependence between two modules or a low level of cohesion between components of one module.

The most important step in this strategy is to identify the boundary of the transform center of the DFD. To do this we must first find out the main input and output data flows of the system.

Any input to the DFD which is essential for the processing of the entire system, that is, without it the system cannot function, is a main input data flow. There are certain inputs to DFDs which are not essential to the major function of the system but are used by particular data transforms as constant values, formatting codes, data-oriented values. Such inputs should not be regarded as main input data flows. Similarly, main output data flows are those which one would normally expect as the main result of the processing.

Once the main input and output data flows are determined, we can identify the transform center of the DFD in the following way. Trace each main input data flow from its origin (entry to the DFD) toward the inside until you find a data transform whose output is no longer a refined form of that main input. In other words, find the first stage in which that main input is used for actual processing. Mark the point of entry to this data transform.

Similarly, trace each main output data flow from the point it exits the DFD inward until you find a data transform which produces the output in its first form. Mark the point of exit from this data transform. That part of the DFD which is bounded by the marked points is the transform center of the DFD. An input data flow entering the transform

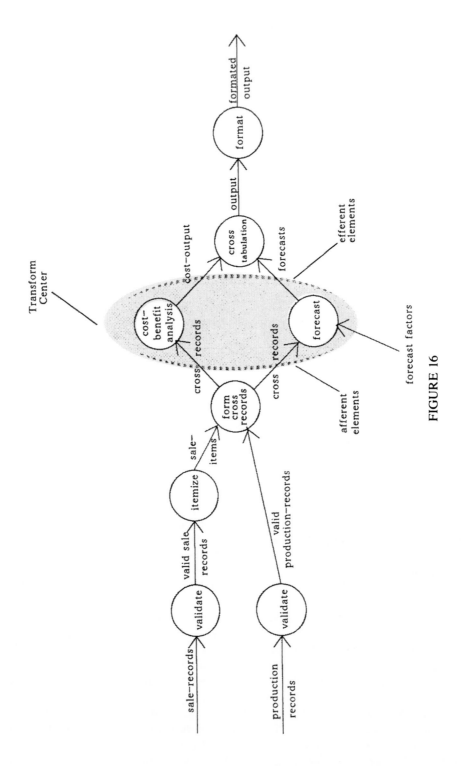

FIGURE 16

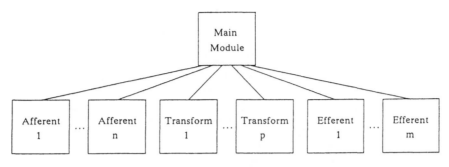

FIGURE 17

center is called an "afferent" data element of the system. An output data flow leaving the transform center is called an "efferent" data element of the system. Figure 16 shows a transform-centered DFD and its afferent and efferent data elements.

Once the transform center, afferent, and efferent data elements are identified, we can derive the first level of the modular hierarchy of the system as follows:

1. Introduce a top-level module as the main coordinator for the system (or subsystem).
2. For each afferent data element introduce a module, subordinate to the coordinator module, whose task will be to feed the coordinator the refined input represented by that afferent element. These are "afferent" modules.
3. For each data transform inside the transform center introduce a module, subordinate to the coordinator module, whose task is the transformation of its input data flows to its output data flows. These are called "transform" modules.
4. For each efferent data element introduce a module, subordinate to the coordinator module, whose task is to obtain and transfer the output data flow represented by that efferent data flow. These are "efferent" modules.

The result of this phase of design is a structure of the general form shown in Figure 17, which is called first-level factoring. The first-level factoring of the DFD of Figure 16 is shown in Figure 18. The design at this stage represents a top-level executive module, one or more modules which provide the "executive" module with completely prepared and ready to use data, one or more modules which get data and order from the executive module and return the result of their function to it, and finally one or more modules which obtain unedited output from the executive module.

The next step in the transform-centered design is to design the subordinates of each of the afferent, transform, and efferent modules introduced in the previous step. The hierarchy below an afferent module reflects the flow of the input data flow corresponding to that module. Starting from transform center and working toward the outside of the DFD, follow the trace of the afferent data element. For each transform bubble encountered, introduce a new level of hierarchy underneath the previous level. The first such level will be immediately below the afferent module being factored. If the transform bubble being considered represents a composition of two or more data elements, the factoring takes the format shown in Figure 19. In this case, for each data type (or a group of closely related data types) involved in the composition a module is created at the new level. If the combining activity is complex enough, another module is added to this level to perform

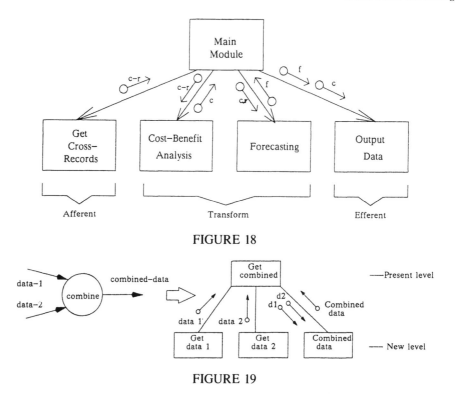

FIGURE 18

FIGURE 19

the composition task. Otherwise, the higher level module, GET-COMBINED in Figure 19, will be given the responsibility for the composition task.

If the transform bubble represents a refinement, analysis, or validation, then factoring is done as shown in Figure 20.

Modules at the lowest level of the afferent branches represent data access. Figure 21 shows the factoring of the afferent branch of our example.

The factoring of an efferent module is similar. Trace the output data flow from the center toward the outside of the DFD. For each bubble, introduce a new level. If the bubble represents a combination of two or more outputs, the factoring is as in Figure 22. If the bubble represents refinement, or further formatting of the output, it is factored as shown in Figure 23.

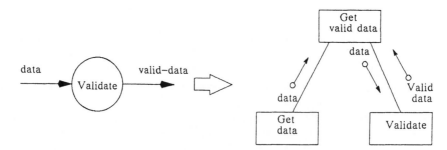

FIGURE 20

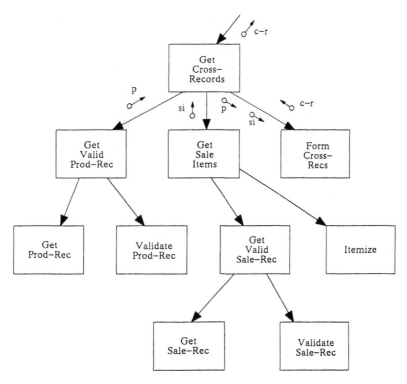

FIGURE 21

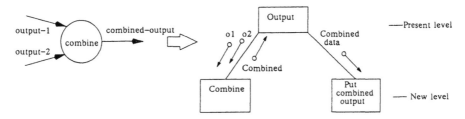

FIGURE 22

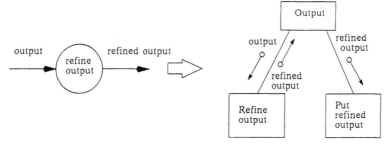

FIGURE 23

If the trace includes accessing new data as parameters to or for complementing the output, the factoring must include appropriate modules for this purpose. Figure 24 shows the factoring of the efferent branch of our example.

The factoring of transform modules requires a careful analysis of the function of that module. For each transform we must identify its subtransform and the basic functions from which they are composed. The basic functions form the lowest level modules. Subtransforms are represented by intermediate level modules.

The final step in this design methodology is to revise the trial design. This should be done based on a written specification of what each module does and how it interfaces with other modules. If a module represents a low level of cohesion or is very tightly coupled with other modules, that module and its immediate subordinates and superordinate must be re-examined to determine which of the following remedies might be used:

> Part or the entire module can be integrated into its superordinate and subordinates
> The module must be broken into a number of modules (at the same level)
> Part of the subordinate's duties should be moved to the module
> Part of the superordinate's duties should be moved to the module

Transaction-Centered Design

In many data processing applications, part or all of a system deals with processing transactions. In general, any element of a system, data or otherwise, which initiates some

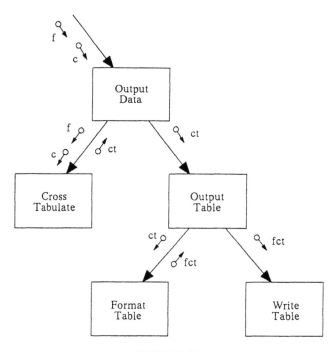

FIGURE 24

action is called a transaction. We are most interested in transactions which are data elements. Although almost all systems include some transactions, not all of them are transaction oriented. A system or part of a system is transaction centered if the DFD for the system (or subsystem) has the following structure

Input to the DFD are raw (most basic) transactions
Transactions may undergo stages of refinement
Refined transactions are analyzed or simply checked for their type
Transactions are dispatched according to their type for appropriate processing

Figure 25 illustrates a data flow diagram containing a transaction center. The objective of transaction analysis is to derive a modular structure for a given transaction center. In this modular structure the processing of each type of transaction forms a separate part of the modular hierarchy.

The transaction center contains the dispatching transformation and all the transaction processing transformations. The modular structure corresponding to such a center is composed of four major levels.

The topmost level corresponds to the entire processing and is represented by a single module whose task is to obtain transactions and dispatch them.
For each type of transaction which has independent processing there will be one module at the second level, the executive module for that type of transaction.
The next level of the hierarchy is composed of modules which represent major actions of the transaction processing. Each of these modules is connected to one or more of the second level modules which use the action represented by that module.
The lower levels belong to details of such actions.

Figure 26 shows the design of the system in Figure 25. Note that the modules at the third and fourth levels are designed using lower-levels DFDs corresponding to Process-Add, Process-Delete, and Process-Change transformations.

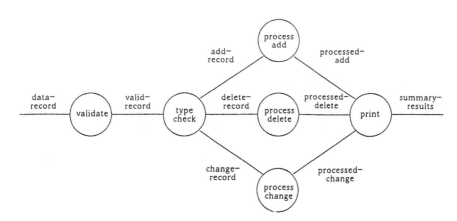

FIGURE 25

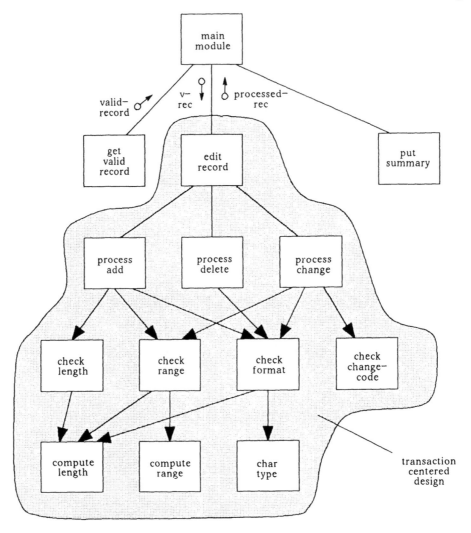

FIGURE 26

DATA FLOW-ORIENTED TOOLS

The process of requirement specification and design using data flow modeling can become cumbersome and error prone for large systems. Computer-aided tools can assist this process by providing clerical, organizational, and analysis assistance. The clerical assistance is provided through graphics editing, bookkeeping, and partitioning facilities. Organizational support is in the form of monitoring of the activities of requirement analysis or design, keeping track of incomplete or partially refined parts of the data flow model. Consistency and completeness can be checked if analysis support is provided by the tool. A large number of data flow modeling tools have been developed in recent years which incorporate some of these features in varying degrees. CASE 2000 (14) is such a system that assists the analyst in the creation and maintenance of data flow diagrams and the corresponding data dictionaries. This system also enables the analyst to verify the correctness, completeness, and consistency of the data flow model.

A number of other data flow-oriented tools provide a more complete environment for requirement analysis and system design, by extending the data flow modeling technique with some other features useful for requirement analysis.

The Structural Analysis and Design Technique, SADT (trademark of Softech Inc.), is such an environment (15). This data flow-oriented tool is used as a tool for software requirement specification and design. It uses a variation of DFDs called *actigrams* and *datagrams*, that model the relationships of information to system functions, allowing control information to be also included in the requirement specification. In addition, SADT provides facilities for specification of project control information. This tool is particularly useful for the analysis of real-time process control systems.

System Activity Modeling Method (SAMM) is another such tool which has been developed by the Boeing Company (16). Although the graphical notation of SAMM is not as rich as SADT, it has proved to be a useful tool for analysis and design and a communication medium between customer, analyst, user, and system designer. SAMM is based on modeling of activities and data flows, similar to modeling techniques used by engineers in manufacturing modeling. An important aspect of this system is the capability for showing feedbacks (backward data flows). An activity cell (a bubble or process) in this system has input-feedback and output-feedback data flows as well as the usual input/output data flows.

DATA FLOW LANGUAGES

Data flow languages provide features that facilitate high-level function-based descriptions of data flow models. These languages are designed for use on data flow computers. Data flow computers are composed of a (large) number of small processors, which cooperatively compute a single program represented by a data flow model. Computations associated with independent "processes" of a data flow model can occur in parallel.

VAL language, developed at MIT (13), is such a language. Programs written in VAL can be mapped into a data flow diagram in an easy and natural way. An important design principle of VAL is the provision of implicit concurrency. That is, operations that can be executed independently are not identified by any specific language notation. Being a "functional" language, VAL does not allow procedures (functions) to alter the program environment except by evaluating the result of a function from its input values. In this way, once the input values of a particular function are known, the execution of the function cannot influence the behavior of other functions ready to be executed. This means that if two operations do not depend on the results of each other, they can be executed concurrently. This is also true of the execution of a data flow model. Two "data transformations" which do not depend on each-other output data flows can be executed simultaneously. Figure 27 illustrates a simple VAL function, and the corresponding data flow diagram, for computation of (real) roots of a quadratic equation. As can be seen from the data flow model, if all inputs become available at once, operations Mult1, Computing ($A * C$), Mult2 ($A * 2$), Sq1 (b^2), and Neg1 can be executed in parallel. Similarly, operations Add1 and Sub2 can be performed simultaneously.

Another important design aspect of VAL is its support for creation of correct and efficient programs. The language, while LISP-like in nature, uses a conventional

```
function Roots( a, b, c : real  returns real, real )
    let
        twicea    := 2*a;
        delta     := Sqrt( b² – 4*a*c );
        root1     := ( –b + delta ) / twicea;
        root2     := ( –b – delta ) / twicea;
    in
        root1, root2
    endlet
endfun
```

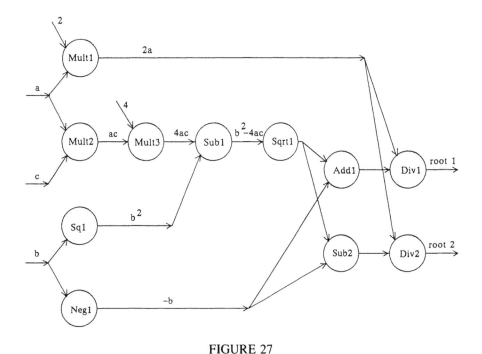

FIGURE 27

algebraic notation for expressions. Scope rules and type checking are rather limited in VAL, and are strictly enforced. To assist the identification of implicit concurrency, VAL allows functions and expressions with no side effect.

A fundamental concept in data flow languages such as VAL is the notion of values instead of variables. In conventional languages, variables represent memory cells and therefore changes in the values associated with variables signify "memory updating." In VAL no object can be modified. This concept is directly derived from the behavior of data flow models. As soon as an operator (process or data transformation in data flow terminology) evaluates a value and puts it in its output arc (as an output data flow), that value becomes available (without any change) to all operators which receive it as an input. That is not to say that the language does not provide identifier binding. Identifiers can be used to represent values. The identifier-value binding, however, remains in force for the entire scope of access of that identifier. Structured objects are viewed as a single value. Hence arrays and records, once bound to an identifier, cannot be changed. To modify a single element of an array one has to build a new array that has the same values in all positions except the particular position subject to change.

VAL and other data flow languages are designed in response to a need for more software-assisted computing power and more efficient use of computers. It is well understood that data flow models represent a highly parallel view of programs. Computer architectures that support execution of such models hence provide high-speed computing by effectively using the concurrency implicit in the model. VAL and other data flow languages give programmers the means by which they can express many forms of data flow-oriented concurrency. The language provides the important mapping of all concurrency implicit in a program into highly parallel data flow graphs.

REFERENCES

1. Martin, D., and Estrin, G., Models of Computations and Systems-Evaluations of Vertex Probabilities in Graph Models, *J. ACM*, 14(2): (1967).
2. Whitehouse, G. E., *System Analysis and Design Using Network Techniques*, Prentice-Hall, Englewood Cliffs, NJ, 1973.
3. Myers, G. J., *Reliable Software Through Composite Design*, Van Nostrand, New York, 1975.
4. Ross, D., Structured Analysis (SA): A Language for Communicating Ideas, *IEEE Trans. Software Eng.*, 3(1): 16–34 (1977).
5. Yourdon, E., *Techniques of Program Structure and Design*, Prentice-Hall, Englewood Cliffs, NJ, 1975.
6. Yourdon, E., and Constantine, L. L., *Structured Design: Fundamentals of a Discipline of Computer and Systems Design*, Prentice-Hall, Englewood Cliffs, NJ, 1973.
7. DeMarco, T., *Structured Analysis and System Specification*, Yourdon Inc., New York, 1978.
8. Kant, E., and Newell, A., *Problem Solving Techniques for the Design of Algorithms*, CMU-CS-82-145, Pittsburgh, PA, 1982.
9. Gane, C., and Sarson, T., *Structured Systems Analysis: Tools and Techniques*, Improved System Technologies, Inc., New York, 1977.
10. Dennis, J. B., Data Flow Supercomputers, *IEEE Comput.*, *13*(11): 48–56 (1980).
11. Acherman, W. B., Data Flow Languages, *IEEE Comput.*, 15(2): 15–25 (1982).
12. Hankin, C. L., and Glaser, H. W., The Data Flow Programming Language CAJOLE—An Informal Introduction, *SIGPLAN Notices*, 16(7): 35–44 (1981).
13. McGraw, J. R., The VAL Language: Description and Analysis, *ACM Trans. Progr. Lang. Sys.*, *4*(1): 44–82 (1982).
14. *SafeSpan: A PSL/PSA Bridge*, Nastec Corporation, Southfield, MI, 1986.
15. Ross, D., Applications and Extensions of SADT, *Computer*, *18*(4): 25–35 (1985).
16. SAMM (Systematic Activity Modeling Method) Primer, Boeing Computer Services, Seattle, WA, 1978.

MEHDI T. HARANDI

DATA REPAIR

OVERVIEW: DATA REPAIR NEEDS ARE INCREASING

As much as microcomputing was the trend in the 1980s, networking and connectivity are the trends of the 1990s. Data are being imported, exported, and migrated from format to format and platform to platform. The traditional domain of data verification was the data input application, with type, range, and integrity checks performed before data was allowed into systems. The trends in connectivity and user demands for shared data are giving rise to entirely new demands on a field of computing, that of data repair.

The traditional means of data verification is also changing, as distributed systems on multiple platforms increase the opportunities for data corruption. The mechanisms by which data enter computing systems presently include uploads and downloads from remote sites, scanned text converted with OCR programs (Optical Character Recognition), and is beginning to include handwritten data entry on special interface pads. Exclusive reliance on data entry verification systems simply isn't practical.

The changing nature of data use is also confounding data accuracy problems. Decision Support Systems (DSS), in many cases, require a method of dealing with imprecise information—and determining or detecting inaccurate information. As computing systems embrace the Enterprise Model, the range of information, and the domain of that information greatly expands.

Executive Information Systems (EIS) require information from systems traditionally separate. The use of EIS also greatly increases the potential damage of "bad" or inaccurate data, as business decisions are based not only on summary status reports of a static historical nature but also on real time "snap-shots" of present status and near term projections.

Electronic Data Interchange (EDI) will mean that in-house data will be supplied not only by remote sites and systems, but also by sources crossing corporate lines. DSS and EIS systems increase the importance of data accuracy, and distributed systems and EDI increase the difficulty of maintaining data verification and control.

TYPES OF DATA DAMAGE

Data Accuracy Versus Data Integrity

Data accuracy is not to be confused with data integrity. Data integrity is a familiar problem in computing, and the relational database is gaining wide acceptance in part because of its ability to include integrity constraints "built in." Data integrity falls within the domain of the database administrator or MIS department. Data accuracy is quite outside the strict domain of MIS.

An example of data integrity would be the requirement that all line items in a purchase order line item table have an associated purchase order in a purchase order table. This type of data integrity is called referential integrity, and deals with agreement between internal database structures. Since the purchase order record probably contains information on vendor, data, and other information common to all line items, if it is deleted the line items, while possibly accurate, are useless.

Data accuracy is quite simply the degree to which the information represented by the stored data reflects the real world. Accuracy does not deal solely with internal database structures. As systems become better and better at extracting information from data, the importance of data accuracy increases.

As systems increase in complexity and geographic scope, the likelihood of data errors also increases. These factors, together, dictate the development of a suit of techniques for data repair, and that is the subject of this article.

Data Typing Problems

Problems with data type are well known in the programming world. Real numbers do not fit readily into integer data spaces and so forth. These kinds of problems take on a new dimension as data are ported across both programs, or the software that accesses data, and platforms, the hardware and operating systems within which programs run.

For example, the relational database introduces a NULL data type—which still has a physical, and often proprietary, representation. Dates may be stored as an integer counting the number of days since a proprietary "0" day, or as character strings, or a combination of integers representing day/month/year. Each of these types of storage can pose data typing problems when moving information.

Data Format Problems

Even when data typing is not a problem, data format can be. Moving information, for example, from a word processing program into a database can appear to be impossible without manual data entry. The nature of the problem stems from the respective formats: a database is essentially columnar in nature and a word processing program is presentational in nature.

MECHANISMS FOR DATA REPAIR

Data Repair Mechanisms in Overview

Mechanisms for coping with problems of data repair often exceed the traditional domain of computing services. This is especially true with problems of data accuracy. Data accuracy is, by definition, external to the data and data system. As a measure of agreement between stored data and external "facts," measurement of data accuracy requires an external source of information to be compared with the information provided by the data. While that can sound obvious, it poses a definite problem for the attempt to automate data accuracy verification, and leads directly into the application of Artificial Intelligence (AI) techniques.

Mechanisms for coping with problems of data typing and data format are largely procedural. The common theme is understanding thoroughly both the logical and the physical needs involved. The logical needs are the dictates of the programs, both source and target . . . a database uses fields and a word processing program uses formatted text. The physical needs reflect how those logical needs must be met.

A theme which will recur throughout any discussion of data repair is the need to "ask the right question." If the initial question is "Can this be done?" all too often the foregone answer is "no." If the question is, instead, "How can this be done?" the answer may be remarkably simple. As the demands on data processing and data manipulation grow in both scope and domain, so must the range of solutions grow. What follows now is a sample of a generic data repair tool kit.

Data Accuracy Repair

Problems with data accuracy may require an approach which is based on techniques borrowed from artificial intelligence research. For example, mechanisms based on fuzzy set theory (1) can be implemented to deal with list consolidation when small inaccuracies exist in the data (2). This approach works with both small amounts of inaccurate data and also small amounts of unknown data.

The growing extent of "migrating data," data being ported from mainframe to micro, program to program, and operating system to operating system can increase the amount of both data format incompatibility and data damage—transmission or download induced errors. Both of these kinds of problems can frequently be dealt with by a procedurally processed "fix" if a sufficient understanding of the problems is used to design the repair.

Data Format Repair Overview

For problems of data format, a generic procedural program can easily accommodate changes from fixed length records, records where each value occupies a predefined data space, to delimited records, records where each value is marked by special characters. This approach can even work in situations where a conversion "cannot be done" such as from a formatted word processor document to either fixed or delimited records, as we shall see in the section on procedural repair.

DATABASE DEFINITIONS AND TOOLS (3)

Before looking in detail at mechanisms for data repair, database tools and terms must be briefly defined. The database arena presently is filled with marketing clouds and conflicting definitions. This survey of terms will therefore begin at the beginning. If 300 completed forms are thrown into a drawer in a haphazard manner, the drawer has DATA. If 300 completed forms are in a drawer sorted by any order at all, the drawer has a DATABASE. A database consists of ordered data. A software product which allows ordering of stored information in a database product.

All database products have at least one of two component parts, a data definition language (DDL) and a data manipulation language (DML). Both the DDL and DML may be simple as designing a picture of a form on screen, as in microcomputer low-end products, or as complex as structured query language (SQL) coding for a fully distributed relational database. Likewise, the physical data structure may be as simple as a sorted file of ASCII on disk or as complex as the proprietary black box structures of major relational DBMS vendors.

While historically three data models (a conceptual picture of data structure) have competed for industry acceptance, the hierarchical model, the network model, and the relational model, at present the relational model appears to be the de facto standard, so we will restrict discussions to products based on the relational model (4). More recently, a fourth model, the object-oriented model is emerging.

Three sets of terms are used almost interchangeably when discussing relational databases. Relation/file/table, tuple/record/row, and attribute/field/column all convey roughly the same meaning. The industry appears to be adopting as standard the choices table, record and attribute (although ANSI use Tables, Columns, and Rows) (5).

Very briefly, a table is a collection of records composed of attributes, where a record is a particular instantiation of the set of attributes. Whether or not null or "unknown" values are allowed and whether or not duplicate records are allowed are still areas of theoretical dissention (6,7). However, duplicate data do exist and some data are unknown, so for our purposes, we will not argue theory, but assume reality.

SQL is the *de facto* DML and DDL for relational database products. SQL as a DML is a set manipulation language designed to retrieve and manipulate sets of data. As a DML, it supports arithmetic operations, string comparisons, and pattern matching. Most vendor implementations (database products) support use of wildcard characteristics and substring operations. This then supports exact and partial matching.

However, this is insufficient to introduce "judgment" into database operations. When used in conjunction with a sufficiently robust database language, however, capability exists in today's products for "intelligent mail merges" and other data accuracy solutions.

DATA ACCURACY REPAIR—A "FUZZY APPROACH"

Sample Problem

At this point, consider two simple tables—the first a table of walk-in customers, and the second a table of a mailing list for advertising (Fig. 1). One common task is to merge the customer list into the mailing list. Of the names in Table B, three are matches to names in Table A, and two more are names which clearly are duplicate individuals without being duplicate records. Neither an exact match nor even a partial match is sufficient to identify "similar" records identifying the same individual.

A person skimming the lists can readily pick out names that are potential duplicates, even despite misspellings. This intuitive process can be simulated using concepts borrowed from fuzzy set theory.

A Fuzzy Join

In essence, a fuzzy join is accomplished by means of a fuzzy operator defined in the DBMS 4GL. This raises three questions: What is a join?; What is a fuzzy operator?; How does a fuzzy operator enable a fuzzy join?

For a relational database, a join is "The relational operation performed on two relations, A and B, producing relation C such that C contains the product of A and B, minus duplicate tuples and, optionally, minus duplicate attributes" (8).

A join is shown schematically in Figure 2, with duplicate attributes removed. As used above, the term product refers to Cartesian product. Although not explicitly stated,

Walk-in Customer Listing--Table A

Last Name	First Name	Address	Phone	Date
Smith	John	1201 AnyStreet	444-3333	04/04/88
Johnson	Mary	311 Twelfth Street	333-4444	04/05/88
Davidson	Henry	5121 First Ave.	555-8888	01/02/89
Abott	Louise	4129 Adams	666-7777	05/02/89
Johnson	Ed		777-8888	07/08/89
Turner	F.	Box 9149	111-7890	02/19/90
Metz	M.			03/12/90
Upjohn	Joseph	132 Main St.	222-9999	04/12/90
Clarke	Eugenia	2542 A Ave.	333-0000	04/12/90
Tyler	Frank	987 Ross Road		04/13/90
Adams	Samantha	8900 Thompson		04/14/90
Kelly	Tom	90 W. Wildwood	444-6754	04/14/90
Meyer	Mike		555-3456	04/14/90
Rogers	Sam	2343 Pinecrest	666-2345	04/15/90
Smith	Jason	121 Fourth St.	777-9876	04/16/90

Mailing List--Table B

Last Name	First Name	Address
Kelly	Tom	8900 Thompson
Gerber	Henry	3140 Seaside
Mets	Mike	1210 Sampson
Clarke	Eugenia	2542 A Ave.
Rogers	Sam	2343 Pinecrest
Turner	Francis	P.O. 9149

FIGURE 1.   Two sample tables to be merged. Reprinted by permission from Ref. 3.

implied in a join is condition involving an operator. This can be an equality operator, an inequality operator, or any supported operator which can produce a boolean value of true or false.

A fuzzy operator in the above example might be an operator "almost equal" signified by $F=>$. The SQL expression to implement a fuzzy join on A and B could then be expressed as

```
SELECT a last_name, a.first_name, a.address,
    b. last_name fblnam, b.first_name bnam, b.address *badd
FROM a,b
WHERE a.last_name F=>b.last_name AND
    a.address F=>b.last_name;
```

The above approach requires user-defined operators. In RDBMS (relational data base management system) products available today, operators are rigidly limited to those supplied by the vendor, and normally include equal, not equal, contains, exists, and a few other algebraic operators ($>$, $<$, $<=$, $>=$).

Key

A-1-1	A-2-1	A-3-1	A-4-1	A-5-1
A-1-2	A-2-2	A-3-2	A-4-2	A-5-2
A-1-3	A-2-3	A-3-3	A-4-3	A-5-3

Key

A-1-3	B-2-1	B-3-1
A-1-2	B-2-2	B-3-2
A-1-1	B-2-3	B-3-3

Table formed as Cartesian Product

```
A-1-1 A-2-1 A-3-1 A-4-1 A-5-1 A-1-3 B-2-1 B-3-1
A-1-2 A-2-2 A-3-2 A-4-2 A-5-2 A-1-3 B-2-1 B-3-1
A-1-3 A-2-3 A-3-3 A-4-3 A-5-3 A-1-3 B-2-1 B-3-1
A-1-1 A-2-1 A-3-1 A-4-1 A-5-1 A-1-2 B-2-2 B-3-2
A-1-2 A-2-2 A-3-2 A-4-2 A-5-2 A-1-2 B-2-2 B-3-2
A-1-3 A-2-3 A-3-3 A-4-3 A-5-3 A-1-2 B-2-2 B-3-2
A-1-1 A-2-1 A-3-1 A-4-1 A-5-1 A-1-1 B-2-3 B-3-3
A-1-2 A-2-2 A-3-2 A-4-2 A-5-2 A-1-1 B-2-3 B-3-3
A-1-3 A-2-3 A-3-3 A-4-3 A-5-3 A-1-1 B-2-3 B-3-3
```

Keys match

Keys match

Keys match

```
A-1-3 A-2-3 A-3-3 A-4-3 A-5-3 A-1-3 B-2-1 B-3-1
A-1-2 A-2-2 A-3-2 A-4-2 A-5-2 A-1-2 B-2-2 B-3-2
A-1-1 A-2-1 A-3-1 A-4-1 A-5-1 A-1-1 B-2-3 B-3-3
```

Table after Selection

```
A-1-3 A-2-3 A-3-3 A-4-3 A-5-3 B-2-1 B-3-1
A-1-2 A-2-2 A-3-2 A-4-2 A-5-2 B-2-2 B-3-2
A-1-1 A-2-1 A-3-1 A-4-1 A-5-1 B-2-3 B-3-3
```

Table after duplicate attributes removed

FIGURE 2.   Steps to a "Join." Reprinted by permission from Ref. 3.

A Fuzzy Attribute

A second approach is to define a fuzzy attribute. A fuzzy attribute is a number (most commonly between 0 and 1, inclusively) which represents a degree of something. This approach can work well where comparisons with other records in a table are not required to establish a value.

For example, a degree of credit standing could be established based on payment history and range between 0 and 1. Given a valid fuzzy attribute, a system can then make decisions based on a range, with statements which amount to "If credit is OK and loan is normal or less than approve loan."

A Working Fuzzy Solution

For the mail merge problem, a fuzzy attribute is difficult to construct. A simple arithmetic function, for instance, a letter value* letter position sum doesn't work, primarily because it fails to properly order the names. For a fuzzy attribute to function here, the letters and their relative position must be captured and expressed as a numerical value. If

```
Function Sameness(In string1; In string2; Out sameness);


                    For each letter in string1
          compare with letter in same position string2
                  If equal, add 1 to sameness.
                    For each letter in string1
      compare letter in position before and after in string2
                  If equal add 0.25 to sameness
            Divdide sameness by average length of strings
                        Return sameness
```

FIGURE 3.   Sameness function logic flow. Reprinted by permission from Ref. 3.

such an attribute were constructed, then a join based on numerical proximity could be done with an RDBMS product today.

Failing that, a fuzzy join, or a join accomplished by a fuzzy operator, can be done directly via a 4GL (fourth-generation language) and what amounts to sequential processing. In relational theory, a join is the end result of three operations: (1) a Cartesian product; (2) a selection; and (3) a projection. This is shown schematically in Figure 3.

In the inner workings of an RDBMS, joins may be done in a manner similar to the sequential process description which follows; the result of the first operation, the product of two sets or tables, has a number of rows which is the number of rows of the first table multiplied by the number of rows of the second. With large tables, disk space and access time can make a product operation prohibitively time consuming. To accomplish a join operation sequentially, we operate one record at a time, and form the product a row at a time, with selection and projection. In this fashion, the product table never truly exists.

Returning to the problem at hand, a fuzzy operator may now be defined to use in a fuzzy "join." The operator (sameness) has been detailed (2) but in essence consists of a value determined by comparing two strings (Figs. 3, 4). The sameness operator can be applied to records (Name, Address, City, and State) as well as fields (Name or Address or . . .) simply by summing the returns from each field and dividing by the number of fields. It is also quite easy to limit to an exact match (IF sameness < 1 THEN sameness = 0) for a particular field such as phone numbers, where intuitively, "close doesn't count."

Using frequency distribution analysis on a large set of sameness values, it was determined that sameness values above 0.55 were sufficient to alert an operator (2). By trial, this approach was found to work.

That is the bottom line. This approach was found to work! The approach draws on concepts from relational theory and fuzzy set theory. It is implemented procedurally

Sample Sameness Values

Stythoorn	Styfhoorn	0.89
Mets	Metz	0.75
Lauterbach	Lauterback	0.90

FIGURE 4.   Sample sameness values for "similar" strings. Reprinted by permission from Ref. *3*.

because present RDBMS products do not support user-defined operators and an adequate algorithm for a fuzzy attribute was not discovered.

The approach was found and implemented with today's products. It could easily be duplicated in any indexed flat file product with a sufficient programming language. It could be implemented on a text file with any general purpose programming language. The key here is the sameness algorithm, and the point is that it works.

There is synergy which happens when multiple disciplines work together. In the example above, old fashioned procedural sequential processing was the mechanism, relational theory the framework, and fuzzy set theory the direction. Without adequate understanding of any one of the three, this implementation would not be possible.

DATA TYPE ERRORS: A PROCEDURAL APPROACH

Data type errors can stem from keypunching errors, errors in data translation or downloading, or differences between the originating application and the destination application. For the sake of simplicity (and limiting scope) we will look at data typing errors and resolution in a data transfer using a fixed length ASCII file type.

In this type of transfer, data from one application is "dumped" to a file in which each record (or row in a table) occupies an exact and constant number of bytes or length. Each value in a record occupies an exact position within that length. This is a standard method for transfer and offers the most universal portability because it eliminates any need for common "separators" or symbols to designate the stop of one value and the start of another.

However, it does not deal with data type errors which may be introduced by differences in either internal data representation from one application to another or differences in tolerance to deviant values from one appliction to another.

In an information transfer with data typing problems, in the worst case the information cannot be loaded at its destination. In other cases, varying amounts of information are lost, or worse, incorrectly loaded (no information is always prferable to wrong information).

As an example, let us look at a "flat file" database table being loaded into a statistical analysis program. Drawing on a real example, the flat file product stored every value as a string of characters and keypunching had produced values incuding "?" and blanks to represent "unknown" in a field for which a meaningful answer included "1", "2", "3", "4" and a blank representing unknown.

```
Character
Positions      1         2         3         4         5         6
         12345678901234567890123456789012345678901234567890123456789012345678901234567890..
        +-----+----------+--+--+----+----+---+---+-----+
        |     |1John Smith|34| 2|    |1952|NO |3  | ... |
        |     |1Kim Frank |29| 1|1990|1951|YES|2  | ... |
        |     |?Unknown   |30| 3|1989|1953|?  |0  | ... |
        |     |0Tom Jones |25| 4|1990|1952|NO |1  | ... |
        |     |           |  | .|    |    |   |   |     |
        |     |           |  | .|    |    |   |   |     |
        +-----+----------+--+--+----+----+---+---+-----+
```

FIGURE 5.   Fixed length ASCII file with errors.

The statistical analysis program supported importing fixed length ASCII, but the import process aborted upon processing of a record with unexpected values (such as a "?"). The statistical analysis program also supported importation of text, but some responses were numerical in nature—meaning a four represented twice what a two did, so valid information would be lost to analysis if the data were imported as text.

Let us assume a sample record structure as shown in Figure 5. For example purposes, we can also assume fields 1,3,4,5,6, and 8 are expected to be numerical. As shown in Figure 5, the third record would abort the upload. Both question marks, while meaningful to the keyer, do not correctly identify an unknown, which is expected to be shown by a blank, as in the first record. If the record consists of hundreds of fields and there are tens or hundreds of thousands of records, a fix becomes definitely nontrivial.

Can we automate a fix? Or a much better question—how can we automate a fix? The answer is to borrow from standard programming process the technique of array processing, used routinely in programming but seldom in database applications. Any general purpose programming language like C, Pascal, or Fortran is able to read in a record as an indexed array of characters.

Knowing which fields are supposed to be only numbers or blanks makes the coding almost trivial. First, we construct a subroutine to check the validity of a string of characters as a number. Then we write a main program to read a record, and send the characters making up each numeric field to our "checker." Finally, we write a "fixer" to modify any unacceptable values. A sample program in Turbo Pascal is listed in Figure 6.

Once such a program is written, it should be kept in a "toolbox." Since the "checker" and "fixer" are modular, it can be a handy template for general purpose data repair. With very little effort, it can be adapted to fix case problems (including upper case for first letter in a word only), global data changes (wherever field # is "YES" set to "Y"), and any generic changes required or desired to a fixed length ASCII file.

Here again, the hardest part of the solution was determining the problem. Data cannot always be "sent back" to be fixed. By combining a basic understanding of databases, common sense, and fairly straightforward programming skills, problems stemming from data typing can generally be resolved.

Can problems which require "intelligence" be solved in a similar manner? One such problem can be a problem of data format. For example, let us say a company worked for well over a year developing a worldwide list of equipment in a word processor format.

All model numbers, specifications, and particulars were double and triple checked by field personnel, at great expense in time, effort, and patience (this example stems from a real story). The primary intended output was hard copy (printed pages), and a sample listing is shown in Figure 7.

As shown in Figure 7, the data structure is reflected in indentation and numerically designated sets and subsets. It is very easy to skim the list and understand the ordering and the type of information being presented. However, the structure of the text belies any kind of direct import into a formal database.

However, combining a knowledge of how a database would require data for import with the data structure reflected by formatting is sufficient to point at the answer. A sample data table is shown in Figure 8, along with a logic schematic to accomplish a conversion, reading in the text file and writing a file suitable for database import.

The basic idea is to duplicate the intuitive associations a person makes skimming the printed page. Every class, subclass, type, and item listed below a given category

```
program FILE_FIX;
uses crt;
{                  This procedure checks for errors in numeric fields
                   of a fixed length ASCII file--unknowns should be
                   blank (ASCII 32)   J. B. Leber -- 12/90          }
type
buf_type = string[255];

procedure fix_line(var buffer:buf_type;start_count,finish_count :integer);
var counter : integer;
begin
     for counter := start_count to finish_count do
     if ( (ord(buffer[counter]) > 57) OR      {if non numeric character}
          (ord(buffer[counter]) < 48)
        )
          THEN buffer[counter] := chr(32);      {replace with a space}
end;


procedure check_line(var buffer:buf_type);

begin                            {Numeric only fields}
   fix_line(buffer,1,6);         {field 1 from character 1 through 6}
   fix_line(buffer,19,40);       {fields 2,3,and 4}
   fix_line(buffer,49,49);       {field 9 }
end;

var
    buffer        :buf_type;
    line_num      :integer;
    infile :text;
    outfile:text;
    infilename:string[25];        {for variable file names if needed}
    outfilename:string[25];

begin
assign(infile,'in.txt');
assign(outfile,'outfile.txt');
reset(infile);                    {pointer to start of file}
rewrite(outfile);                 {empty file and move pointer to start of file}
line_num := 0;                    {initialize}
while not eof(infile) do begin
   readln(infile,buffer);              {read the original record}
   check_line(buffer);                 {check and fix}
   writeln(outfile,buffer);            {write the corrected record}
   line_num := line_num + 1;           {how many have we done?}
   gotoxy(20,10);write(line_num:5); {something to look at}
end;
close(infile);
close(outfile);
end.
```

FIGURE 6.   Generix fixed length ASCII ''File Fix'' program—written for Turbo Pascal by Borland International.

is assumed to be a member of that category. This type of unconscious assumption is programmable without difficulty if it is understood. The critical point is to identify why the structure is intuitively understandable, and duplicate that with programming logic.

Programming the logic shown in Figure 8 is a relatively straightforward task, and can begin with the general purpose toolbox program mentioned above. As shown it is a

```
1.0    Data Processing Resources

    1.1    Hardware

        1.1.1 Personal Computer Hardware

            1.1.1.1      80386 PC's

                         ABCD 386-Serial # 123456789.  Includes
                         130 Meg ESDI drive,Color VGA, 2 Meg Ram,
                         101 Keyboard

                         EFGH 386-Serial # 23456789.  Includes
                         40 Meg RLL drive, Color EGA, 1 Meg Ram,
                         w 101 Keyboard

            1.1.1.2      80286 PC's

                         Anybrand 286-Serial # 56789A.  Includes
                         40 Meg RLL drive, Monochrome VGA, 1 Meg
                         Ram, 101 Keyboard.
```

FIGURE 7.   Text file equipment listing.

Category	Class	Subclass	Type	Descriptions...>

```
Sample Table Structure
Category     Character 3
Class        Character 5
Subclass     Character 7
Type         Character 9
Item_Desc    Character 240
```

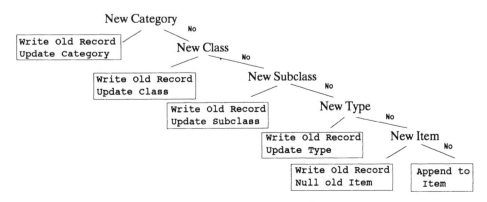

FIGURE 8.   Table structure and process logic flow.

very simple logic cascade. Note the ability for the program to remember the most recent "higher" categories and pad each record, much the same way a human being automatically carries higher topics down an outline.

It is also worth mentioning that the principle of marginal returns should be borrowed from economics and applied to this kind of work. That is, if 4 hours of a programmer's time eliminates 200 hours of keypunching time, it is a viable expense. When dealing with data repair projects, it is not uncommon to find that recovering the last 5 percent of data requires 50 percent of programmer time, which may translate to 8 hours of programmer time versus 8 hours of keypunching time, which is not likely to be economically favorable. In other words, it quite possibly is economically inefficient to attempt to accommodate every possible recovery condition with a program, particularly a program intended for a one time only use.

The common theme in all of the approaches discussed is to "Ask the right question." The first question should always be "How can we?" rather than "Can we?" A very good start is to examine how a person might perform the task and then program the logic. All too often quite feasible solutions to unusual questions are missed because the usual answers don't apply.

Computer technology and user expectations are both driving systems from being "report driven" to "data driven." To put it another way, data structure is becoming less a reflection of desired output and more a reflection of the data itself. As this trend increases, both the amount of information to be "migrated" and the importance of doing so correctly increase. Trends in data portability and distributed data only increase the need for abilities to repair data.

A great deal of typical data repair involves the application of some level of intelligence or decision-making ability. As seen above, that is feasible today using a generic programming language or database language. In the foreseeable future, the integration between "expert systems" and database products should make the task even easier.

However, even then, there will still be the requirement to "Ask the right question!"

REFERENCES

1. A. Kandel, *Fuzzy Mathematical Techniques with Applications*, Addison-Wesley, Reading, MA, 1986.
2. J. Leber, A Fuzzy Approach to Data Repair, *Database Progr. Des.*, *3*(1), 26–33 (January 1990).
3. J. Leber, Excerpted from Fuzzy Logic and Data Repair, presented at I.E.E.E. Committee on Artificial Intelligence and Expert Systems, Foothill College, Los Altos, CA, June 1990.
4. J. Leber, MicroComputer DBMS, Product Spotlight, *Computerworld*, *23*(25), 63–65 (June 19, 1989).
5. ANSI X3.135-(1986) Database language-SQL.
6. J. Celco, One Null, Two Null, Three Null, Four, DBA shoptalk, *Database Progr. Des.*, *2*(9), 19–21 (September 1989).
7. R. Kocharekar, Nulls in Relational Databases: Revisited, *ACM SIGMOD Rec.*, *18*(1), 68–73 (March 1989).
8. D. M. Kroenke and K. A. Dolan, *Database Processing: Fundamentals, Design, Implementation*, 3rd Edition, Science Research Associates, Inc., 1988.

BIBLIOGRAPHY

Caudill, M., Using Neural Nets: Fuzzy Decisions, *AI Expert*, *5*(4), 59–64, (April 1990).

Celco, J., One Null, Two Null, Three Null, Four, DBA Shoptalk, *Database Progr. Des.*, *2*(9), 19–21 (September).

Cox, E. and M. Goetz, Fuzzy Logic Clarified, In Depth, *Computerworld*, *25*(10), 69–71, (March 11, 1991).

Date, C. J., *An Introduction to Database Systems*, Vol. 1, 5th Ed., Addison-Wesley, Reading, MA, 1990.

*Kandel, A., *Fuzzy Mathematical Techniques with Applications*, Addison-Wesley, Reading, MA, 1986.

Kocharekar, R. Nulls in Relational Databases: Revisited, *ACM SIGMOD REC.*, *18*(1), 68–73 (March 1989).

Kroenke, D. M. and K. A. Dolan, *Database Processing*: *Fundamentals, Design, Implementation*, 3rd Edition, Science Research Associates, Inc., 1988.

Leber, J., A Fuzzy Approach to Data Repair, *Database Progr. Des.*, *3*(1), 26–33 (January 1990).

Leber, J., MicroComputer DBMS, Product Spotlight, *Computerworld*, *23*(25), 63–65 (June 19, 1989).

Liu, K., and R. Sunderraman, Indefinite and Maybe Information in Relational Databases, *ACM Transact. Database Syst.*, *15*(1), 1–39 (March 1990).

Pascal, F., *SQL and Relational Basics*, M&T Books, 1990.

Schwartz, T., Fuzzy Tools for Expert Systems, *AI Expert*, *6*(2), 34–41 (February 1991).

Fuzzy Contracts

I.E.E.E. Neural Networks Council-Jim Bezdek (904) 474-2784

International Journal of Approximate Reasoning (212) 989-5800

North American Fuzzy Information Processing Society-Secretary-Brian Schott (404) 651-4070

JOHN B. LEBER

---

*Extensive Bibliography for mathematical fuzzy set theory development.

DYNAMIC MEMORY

INTRODUCTION

One of the most important units of a digital computer is its main memory. Designers have realized that a very large, high-speed random access main memory is vital to a high performance computer. The decline in per bit cost of random access semiconductor memories has been more than counterbalanced by the insatiable appetite for larger and larger main memories. It is impossible to meet all of the storage requirements of a computer at reasonable cost using only random access semiconductor memories. Thus concurrent attempts have been made to reduce the cost and increase the size of such direct access storage devices as magnetic disks. Winchester disk technology has led to very high-capacity disk storage devices. Currently main memory size of 16 Mbytes and disk size of 400 Mbytes are the norm in desk-top high-performance work stations.

The basic reason for the variety of storage devices built into a computer is cost per byte of storage. Cost is inversely related to memory access time; the shorter the access time, the higher is the cost per byte. An approximate rule of thumb for cost and access time is:

$$\text{Cache memory cost per byte} = 10 \times \text{main memory cost/byte}$$
$$= 10^4 \times \text{Disk memory cost/byte}$$
$$\text{Cache memory access time} = 1/10 \text{ Main memory access time}$$
$$= 1/10^6 \text{ Disk memory access time}$$

We see a large gap in access time as well as cost between disk and main memory.

Dynamic memories that employ new storage technologies are useful to fill this wide gap in access time and cost between main memories and magnetic disks. Two main types of devices are used to construct dynamic memory: magnetic bubble memory and charge-coupled device (CCD) memory. Some attractive features of these technologies are nonvolatility, low power requirement, and high reliability. A memory cost/speed spectrum given by Pohm (1) is shown in Figure 1.

In magnetic disks, data items are stored in fixed locations on the surface of the disk and the surface rotates below a read/write head. Data items are read in the same order as they are stored on the disk surface. In contrast to this, devices used to construct dynamic memories require the continuous movement of data within the storage medium. In other words, the storage medium is static and the stored bits move. Cyclic access, that is, access of bits stored in contiguous cells requires simple interconnection of the basic cells. Cyclic access, however, is not the only allowed access. Appropriate cell interconnections facilitate achievement of random access to groups of bits. We will give a formal definition of dynamic memory later in this article and describe various cell interconnection methods.

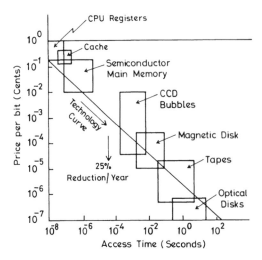

FIGURE 1   Memory cost/speed spectrum.

The term *dynamic memory* is interpreted by many computer scientists and most computer dictionaries as *dynamic random access memory* (DRAM). Our interpretation is different. We use this term to mean memories in which data bits move continuously within the storage medium. Due to this common assumption that dynamic memories are DRAMs, for the sake of completeness, we discuss briefly DRAMs below.

The principles of operation of charge-coupled devices (CCD) used in constructing dynamic memories, are presented and another important device, magnetic bubbles, is described briefly. Discussion of serial access in shift register memories defines what we mean by dynamic memory and various interconnections of cells and transformations to reduce access time are suggested. An associative dynamic memory is described in and its performance is analyzed. The subsequent section discusses buffered dynamic memories, and the article concludes with some thoughts on the future of dynamic memories.

DYNAMIC RANDOM ACCESS MEMORY

A random access memory (2) is one in which the time taken to read a stored data item (a byte or a word) is independent of where the data item is physically stored in the memory. Main memories of computers are random access memories (RAMs). Currently RAMs are fabricated using semiconductor memory cells in which each cell stores one bit. There are two types of cells: *static cells* and *dynamic cells*. A static cell is usually implemented using six metal-oxide semiconductor (MOS) transistors and stores one bit. A bit stored in a static cell is not destroyed when it is read. Such a readout is called a *nondestructive readout*. A bit stored in the cell remains intact as long as power is supplied.

A dynamic cell contains only one transistor and one capacitor as shown in Figure 2. The transistor T acts as a switch and the capacitor C stores a bit. If C is fully charged, the cell stores a 1 and if C is fully discharged, it stores a 0. The cell is connected to an address line and a data line as shown in Figure 2. To write a 1 into this cell a voltage V is applied to the data line and the address line. This switches on T and C gets charged. If the data line is 0 volts then C does not charge when T is switched. To read the contents

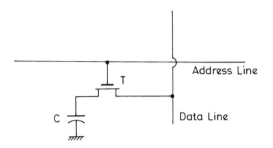

FIGURE 2   A single transistor DRAM cell.

of the cell the address line is connected to V volts. This turns on T. If the cell stores a 1 (i.e., if C is charged to voltage V) then the charge discharges on the delta line and is detected by a sense amplifier connected to it. If C is already discharged (i.e., the cell stores a 0) then no charge flows through the data line and the sense amplifier reads a 0. Notice that the data stored in a cell is destroyed when it is read. Thus the readout from a dynamic memory cell is *destructive*. The data must thus be restored after reading. The sense amplifier must also *refresh* the data stored in the cells by recharging the capacitor.

Even when the data in the cell is not read, it may be gradually lost due to the capacitor discharging through the transistor, as the transistor is not an ideal switch. Thus, all the memory cells in a dynamic RAM must be repeatedly read and restored. This process is called *memory refresh*. When the memory operates at 70°C it is necessary to refresh all the cells typically at two millisecond intervals (3). This is achieved by a *memory refresh cycle* activated by the system every two milliseconds. During this cycle all memory cells are refreshed simultaneously.

The main disadvantages of dynamic RAM are (1) the need to refresh periodically and (2) the need for the memory module to wait until a refresh cycle is completed before initiating a read or a write cycle. Thus a read or a write cycle initiated during refresh will take twice the normal time.

The main reasons for using dynamic cells to construct large semiconductor RAMS are:

1. The number of cells which can be integrated in a single chip is much higher compared with static RAMs. One megabit storage per chip has been achieved and next generation DRAMs will have 16 megabits per chip.
2. The power consumption per bit of dynamic RAM is much lower than that of static RAM. It is of the order of 0.005 mW per bit of dynamic RAM. This feature reduces the power requirements of the memory and consequently its cost. Further, the power consumption in standby mode is extremely low and thus the memory can be made nonvolatile with a low capacity backup power source.
3. The cost per bit of dynamic RAM is lower than static RAM. Even though a dynamic RAM needs more support circuitry for refresh, this cost is offset for large memories due to the low cost of each cell.

Dynamic RAM memory chips are marketed in a variety of sizes such as 64K × 1, 256K × 1, 1M × 1. Larger memories such as 4M × 32 are made up by interconnecting these chips with appropriate address decoders/transceivers, chip-enable logic, refresh circuits, and buffers. For details one may refer to text books (3,4). Normally around 4 Mbytes of dynamic RAMs are fabricated on a single printed circuit card of around 25 × 15 cm (in 1989). The number of bits per chip are dramatically increasing each year and multimegabit dynamic RAM chips will emerge.

CHARGE COUPLED DEVICES

Another important class of memories is *direct access memories*. Like RAMs, these memories are also addressable. Each address, however, stores a fairly large number of bits. Typically, 1 Kbits are stored in each address and once the contents of an address are accessed the stored bits are retrieved serially. Magnetic disks are direct access memories storing around a gigabyte (10^9 bytes) in each disk. The access time of disk memories depends on both the address from where the currently required data is to be retrieved and the address from where the immediately preceding data was retrieved. The time to access data from disks is of the order of 10 milliseconds.

Dynamic memories fabricated using charge-coupled devices (CCD) (5) are all electronic with no moving parts. The data bits move continuously in the medium. They are also addressable. These memories also store around 1 Kbits per address. These memories can be organized so that time to retrieve data from an address is of the order of 100 microseconds. The retrieval time can be made *independent of address*. In other words, special interconnection of memory cells allow *random access*. Once the contents of an address are retrieved the individual bits in the address are retrieved serially.

The capacity of such memories are of the order of 1 Mbytes which is much lower than that of disks. The cost per bit of storage is around 100 times that of disks and access time (1/100) that of the disk.

Data is stored in charge-coupled devices (CCDs) as electrical charges in potential wells which are formed at the surface of a semiconductor. These wells are created by fabricating a string of capacitors by oxidizing a low resistivity silicon wafer by a 10^{-5} cm thick oxide layer and placing metal electrodes over it. A p–n junction is used to introduce a charge underneath the first capacitor (under electrode A in Fig. 3). This capacitor has a voltage $-V$ applied to its electrode and a depletion layer is created below it, trapping the charge from the p–n junction. If a voltage $-2 V$ is applied to the electrode B of the next capacitor, a deeper depletion region is created and the charge from under A spills into this region. B is now taken to $-V$, pushing the charge under the next electrode C, which is taken to $-2 V$ and so on. Three electrodes forming a three-phase system are required for each bit location since the charges can move in either direction, and we need two electrodes to trap charge bundles between them and then move them in a controlled

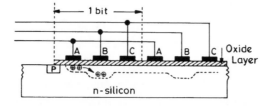

FIGURE 3   Cross-section of a CCD shift register.

fashion. In summary, this device functions as a shift register with a 1 being represented by a charge injection and 0 by no charge injection.

The primary advantage of this device is its ease of fabrication. There are, however, many problems in fabricating large memories using this idea. The three capacitances required per bit restrict the number of bits per chip. A more serious problem is the charge transfer efficiency from one bit location to the next. This limits the length of shift registers which can be fabricated using this technology. The other drawback of this memory is its volatility; when power is removed the information is lost.

MAGNETIC BUBBLE MEMORY

Magnetic bubble memory is a solid-state magnetic memory device. It was invented by Bobeck et al. (6), who found that tiny magnetic domains called bubbles could be created on a thin film of anisotropic magnetic material (such as garnets) by proper application of a magnetic field. These bubbles have two important properties: (1) once a bubble is created it is stable and nonvolatile and (2) a bubble can be moved in a controlled manner without being lost.

Using these two properties it is possible to build a nonvolatile memory. A two-dimensional array of positions is defined on a bubble memory chip. The presence of a bubble is interpreted as storing a 1 and the absence of bubble is interpreted as 0. In a bubble memory, bubbles move sequentially around a loop. It is analogous to a shift register. To read a bit one must wait till it appears below a read station on the chip. This sequential access can drastically increase access time. For instance, if a million bits are stored around a loop, and bubbles take say 200 nanoseconds to shift one bubble position, then the average access time to a bit $= 500,000 \times 200 = 100$ ms. This is too high. Thus bubble memories normally are organized into a system of loops known as major and minor loops (Fig. 4). When power is applied, a set of bubbles circulates endlessly around each loop. The transfer of data between the minor and major loop occurs simultaneously for all loops. Thus we can view the memory as consisting of W words of B bits each. The number of minor loops is B and there are W bubbles per minor loop. To read a stored

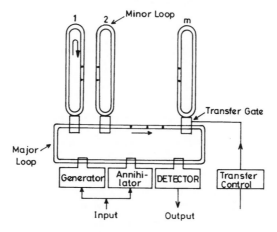

FIGURE 4   Magnetic bubble memory organization.

word, one bubble from each minor loop is copied on to the major loop. These B bubbles are read out serially from the major loop by a bubble detector. Thus if 1 Mbits are stored in 512 minor loops with 2048 bits per loop, the average time to transfer 512 bits to the major loop is 200×512 ns $= 204.8$ μs and the time to read this string of 512 bits $= 200 \times 512$ ns $= 102.4$ μs. Thus the total access time $= 307.2$ μs. This may be compared with 100 ms access time calculated earlier.

A B-bit data word is written into the bubble memory by feeding these bits serially to a bubble generator. The generator shifts these bits on to the major loop from which they are copied into the B minor loops.

Many functions such as shifting, address decoding, and even logic can be performed using the same bubble technology (7). All this logic can be placed on the chip to minimize interconnections. This is a distinct advantage of bubbles over other magnetic memory technologies. Bubble memory chips are small, lightweight, rugged, and nonvolatile. They are also becoming cheaper. This has led to some resurgence of interest in this technology (8). We have given a very brief description of bubble memories in this section. Those interested may refer to the comprehensive article by Chang (9).

SERIAL ACCESS IN ELECTRONIC SHIFT-REGISTER STORAGE

In this section we consider one simple way of organizing an electronic shift register of large capacity (bubbles or CCD) which gives multiple bit readout. Assume that each chip has 64 Kbits and we need a 1 Mbit memory with 16 bits to be read out as a word. Sixteen shift registers can be organized side by side and 16 bits (one bit from each register) shifted into a 16 bit I/O buffer in one shift interval. The access time to contiguous words thus equals only one shift interval (approximately 200 ns). The time to read a random word is, however, $32 \times 1024 \times 200$ ns $= 6.55$ ms which is very high. We can also organize this memory as 1 K registers of 1 Kbit each with 1 Kbit being accessed in one shift interval. In this case the average time to access 1 Kbit is 512×200 ns. Accessing 16 consecutive bits of a word from these 1 Kbits will take $(512 + 16) \times 200$ ns. Thus the total time is 1040×200 ns $= 0.208$ ms, which is considerably less than the previous organization. This speed up has been obtained at the expense of extra logic. This access time is the time to access a random word. Words following this are sequentially retrieved at 3.2 μs per word.

One would like to obtain faster access times if possible. This is indeed possible by using special interconnection networks to interconnect registers. We will discuss this in the next section.

DYNAMIC MEMORY INTERCONNECTIONS FOR FAST ACCESS

A dynamic memory is formally defined as an array of n cells. Each cell can hold a string of bits (a word). Only one cell in the array of cells can be used to read or write in the memory. This cell is called the window of the dynamic memory. The contents of cells within the array can be internally rearranged by applying a sequence of operations called *memory transformations*. A simple example of a dynamic memory, which we have considered so far, is a circular shift register. In a circular shift register the readout position is one bit or a group of consecutive bits at the I/O port (e.g., in bubble memory). The only memory transformation available in shift registers is a cyclic permutation of bits.

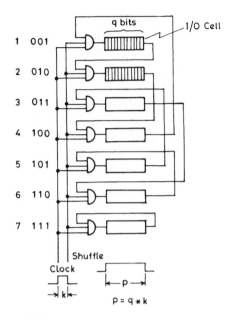

FIGURE 5   Depicting *Shuffle* transformation.

If only cyclic permutation is allowed, then the average time to bring the contents of a cell to the window in a n cell dynamic memory is $(n/2)p$ and the maximum time is $(n-1)p$, where p is the time for one permutation. Stone (10,11) and Aho and Ullman (12) pointed out that if more than one memory transformation is permitted, then the access time to any arbitrary cell can be dramatically reduced. Such transformations are possible by providing extra interconnections between cells. In figure 5 we depict an interconnection suggested by Stone (10), which allows a transformation called *shuffle*. A Shuffle transformation transfers the data in cell y to cell S(y) where $S(y)$ is given by

$$S(y) = \uparrow y$$

Where $\uparrow$ is an operator which left circular shifts the m bit binary address of y by 1 bit. For example, data in y = 010 is shifted to $S(y) = 100$. (Contents of cell 2 is sent to cell 4.) Table 1 gives how this transformation shifts data. Observe that applying m *shuffles* in a memory with $(2^m - 1)$ cells will bring the memory back to its initial state.

TABLE 1   *Shuffle* Transformation

Physical cell address	Contents of cell	Shuffle transformation	Cell contents after applying shuffle
1	425	C(1) ← C(4)	452
2	365	C(2) ← C(1)	425
3	876	C(3) ← C(5)	448
4	452	C(4) ← C(2)	365
5	448	C(5) ← C(6)	648
6	648	C(6) ← C(3)	876
7	562	C(7) ← C(7)	562

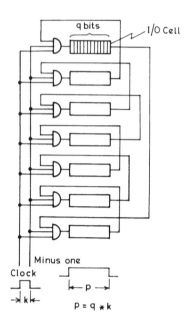

FIGURE 6   Depicting *Minus-One* transformation.

Another interconnection suggested by Aho and Ullman is a cyclic or *Minus-one* transformation shown in Figure 6. In this transformation data in cell y is transferred to $M(y)$ given by

$$M(y) = y \oplus (-1) \qquad y \neq 0$$

Where $\oplus$ denotes one's complement addition of m bit integers. This is equivalent to left circular shift of all the cells' contents by q bits where q is the number of bits per cell. Table 2 gives how this transformation shifts data.

Aho and Ullman (12) described a method of combining these two transformations in a memory with $(2^m - 1)$ cells. They showed that any cell can be retrieved on the average in $1.5\, m\, p$ units of time, and in the worst case in $(2m - 1)p$ units. These times are much smaller compared with those obtained if only circular permutation is allowed. For example, for n = 4096 cells the average time to access a cell in a shift register memory is 2048 p, whereas it is $(\log_2 4096 * 1.5)p = 18p$ units in Aho-Ullman memory. Besides fast access to any cell, this scheme also provides sequential access to neighboring addresses with one *minus one* transformation per access, after retrieving the first two data words. Data stored in the memory are stored in cells and have distinct logical addresses, namely, 1, 2, 3. . . . N and they are stored in this order in neighboring cells. To access a datum stored in a specified logical address, a sequence of *Shuffle* and *Minus-one* transformations are applied and eventually the data n with the desired logical address reaches the read/write port, that is, cell 1. The sequence of transformations is determined as follows. Let u be the logical address of the datum to be accessed and s be the logical address of the data currently available at the read/write port. We define the distance d between u and s as $d = u \oplus (-s)$. Let $d_{m-1}, d_{m-2}, \ldots, d_1, d_0)$ be the binary representation of d. Thus $d = d_{m-1}2^{m-1} + d_{m-2}2^{m-2} \ldots\ldots + d_1 2 + d_0$.

TABLE 2   *Minus-One* Transformation

Physical cell address	Contents of cell	*Minus-one* transformation	Cell contents after applying *Minus-one*
1	425	$C(1) \leftarrow C(2)$	365
2	365	$C(2) \leftarrow C(3)$	876
3	876	$C(3) \leftarrow C(4)$	452
4	452	$C(4) \leftarrow C(5)$	448
5	448	$C(5) \leftarrow C(6)$	648
6	648	$C(6) \leftarrow C(7)$	562
7	562	$C(7) \leftarrow C(1)$	425

The distance d determines the sequence of transformations required to bring the datum at the logical address u to the read/write port and place the memory in a cyclic shift of its initial state. This allows data with successive logical address to be accessed sequentially. The algorithm which achieves this is;

Algorithm: Aho-Ullman Random Access Algorithm

For $j = (m-1)$ *step*(-1) *until* 0 *do*
    begin {*Minus* d_j means *Minus-one* if $d_j = 1$
      and skip if $d_j = 0$}
    Shuffle;
    Minus d_j;
    end.

From the above algorithm we see that there will be m *Shuffles*, and assuming $d_j = 0$ or 1 with equal probability $(m/2)$ *minus-one* transformations. Thus the time to access the desired address is $(1.5\ m)$ steps. As the maximum ones in d cannot exceed $(m-1)$ the worst case time is $(2m-1)$ steps.

We illustrate how this algorithm works with an example given in Table 3. Assume that logical address $s - 110$ is in I/O cell and it is desired to retrieve contents of logical

TABLE 3   Random-Access of an Address in Aho-Ullman Memory $d = 100$

Physical cell address	Cell contents and logical address in parentheses	Transformations			
		$d_2 = 1$		$d_1 = 0$	$d_0 = 0$
		Shuffle	Minus-one	Shuffle	Shuffle
I/O cell 1	425 (6)	452 (2)	425 (6)	648 (4)	448 (3)
2	365 (7)	425 (6)	448 (3)	425 (6)	648 (4)
3	876 (1)	448 (3)	365 (7)	876 (1)	562 (5)
4	452 (2)	365 (7)	648 (4)	448 (3)	425 (6)
5	448 (3)	648 (4)	876 (1)	562 (5)	365 (7)
6	648 (4)	876 (1)	562 (5)	365 (7)	876 (1)
7	562 (5)	562 (5)	452 (2)	452 (2)	452 (2)

address $t = 011$. Then $d = t \oplus (-s) = 011 + 001 = 100$. As per the algorithm the transformations to be applied to the memory are:

Shuffle, Minus-one, Shuffle, Shuffle

This basic idea of interconnection transformation has been used in many ways. Another method of random access was earlier suggested by Stone (10), who defined besides the *Shuffle* transformation an *Exchange Shuffle* transformation. *Exchange* permutation is defined as

$$E = i + 1 \quad i \ even \qquad i \geq 0$$
$$\quad\ i - 1 \quad i \ odd \qquad i \leq 2^m - 1$$

Exchange-shuffle is obtained by first applying Exchange and then Shuffle permutation. This is shown in Table 4. Figure 7 depicts, for an 8 cell memory, how contents of cells shift after application of Shuffle and Exchange-Shuffle permutation. Stone suggested a dynamic memory with 2^m cells numbered from 0 to $(2^m - 1)$. The algorithm proposed by Stone to bring data with logical address u to I/O port which has data with logical address s is: Let $d = u + $ (2's complement of s) (ignore carry)

$$d = d_{m-1}d_{m-2} \ldots d_1d_0$$

Stone's Random Access Algorithm

Right circular shift d
For j $= (a-1)$ *step* (-1) *until* 0 *do*
    begin if $d_j = $ *then Shuffle*
      else Exchange Shuffle
    end

Average access time in this memory is worse than Aho-Ullman memory. Stone (11) later modified Aho-Ullman's memory by a change of labeling using *Shuffle* and *cyclic* transformations and slightly improved its performance.

Various other permutations such as rotate and use of number bases other than 2 to label locations have been reported. An extensive survey of these organizations and a performance analysis may be found in a tutorial article by Iyer and Sinclair (13). They also describe a dynamic memory with interleaved cells (14) which optimizes both random access and block access times.

TABLE 4   *Exchange-Shuffle* Transformation

Physical cell address	Contents of cell	Exchange-Shuffle transformation	Contents after exchange-shuffle
I/O Port 0	398	$C(0) \leftarrow C(1)$	425
1	425	$C(1) \leftarrow C(5)$	448
2	365	$C(2) \leftarrow C(0)$	398
3	876	$C(3) \leftarrow C(4)$	452
4	452	$C(4) \leftarrow C(3)$	876
5	448	$C(5) \leftarrow C(7)$	562
6	648	$C(6) \leftarrow C(2)$	365
7	562	$C(7) \leftarrow C(6)$	648

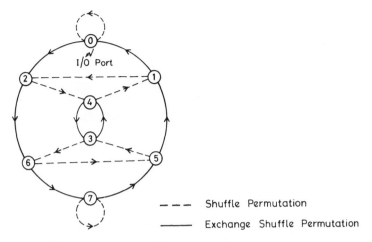

FIGURE 7   Illustrating *Shuffle* and *Exchange-Shuffle* transformation in an 8 cell memory.

ASSOCIATIVE DYNAMIC MEMORY

An associative memory is addressed by contents. In other words, given a search *key*, all data items containing this key are required to be retrieved. In some applications it is desirable to also retrieve a group of records with the first record in the group having a given key. To do this, an algorithm is required to search in the memory for a record with a given key at the lowest logical address and to retrieve sequentially a specified number of records following this. Such an algorithm was described by Stone (10), and an improved one by Om Vikas and Rajaraman (15). The algorithm assumes that the records are presorted (on key) and stored in a nondecreasing order in a memory of size $(2^m - 1)$. A binary search method (16) is employed to retrieve a record with a specified key.

The following Lemma establishes the address of the cell whose contents will be brought to cell 1 (i.e., the read/write port) of the memory. S is used as an abbreviation for *Shuffle* and M for *Minus-one*.

Lemma

Let the sequence of transformations applied to the memory be;

$$s\ t_1 t_2\ .\ .\ .\ t_p \qquad p \leqslant (m-1)$$

where each t_i is either S or MS. Then the contents of the cell

$$\underbrace{b_1 b_2\ .\ .\ .\ b_p\ 100\ .\ .\ .\ 0}_{m}$$

(where b_i is 1 if t_i is MS and b_i is 0 if t_i is S) will be brought to cell 1.

Proof

The proof is by induction on the length of memory transformation sequence. From the definitions of S and M given in the last section it is easy to verify that

$$SS\ (0100\ .\ .\ .\ 0) = 00\ .\ .\ .\ 01$$

and

$$SMS\ (1100\ .\ .\ .\ 0) = 00\ .\ .\ .\ 01$$

Let the lemma be true for

$$St_1t_2\ .\ .\ .\ t_p, \qquad p < (m-1)\ \text{(Induction hypothesis)}$$

hence

$$St_1t_2\ .\ .\ .\ t_p\underbrace{(b_1b_2\ .\ .\ .\ b_p\ 10\ .\ .\ .\ 0)}_{m-1} = \underbrace{000\ .\ .\ .\ 1}_{m-1}\ (p < m-1)$$

Let us now consider a sequence of transformations

$$\sigma = St_1t_2\ .\ .\ .\ t_{p+1}$$

Let B be defined as:

$$B = \underbrace{b_1b_2\ .\ .\ .\ b_pb_{p+1}\ 100\ .\ .\ .\ 0}_{m}$$

where $b_i = 0$ if t_i is S and 1 if t_i is MS. We are required to show that

$$\sigma\ (B) = \underbrace{00\ .\ .\ .\ 1}_{m}$$

Now

$$\begin{aligned}
\sigma\ (B) &= St_1t_2\ .\ .\ .\ t_{p+1}(b_1b_2\ .\ .\ .\ b_pb_{p+1}\ 100\ .\ .\ .\ 0) \\
&= t_1t_2\ .\ .\ .\ t_{p+1}(b_2\ .\ .\ .\ b_pb_{p+1}\ 100\ .\ .\ .\ b_1)
\end{aligned}$$

We have two cases

Case 1: $t_1 = S$

Then by definition of B, $b_1 = 0$
hence

$$\begin{aligned}
\therefore\ \sigma\ (B) &= St_2\ .\ .\ .\ t_{p+1}\ (b_2\ .\ .\ .\ b_pb_{p+1}100\ .\ .\ .\ 0) \\
&= 000\ .\ .\ .\ 01\ \text{(invoking the induction hypothesis)}
\end{aligned}$$

Case 2: $t_1 = $ MS

Then by definition of B, $b_1 = 1$
hence

$$\begin{aligned}
\therefore\ \sigma\ (B) &= MSt_2\ .\ .\ .\ t_{p+1}\ (b_2\ .\ .\ .\ b_pb_{p+1}100\ .\ .\ .\ 0) \\
&= St_2\ .\ .\ .\ t_{p+1}\ (b_2\ .\ .\ .\ b_pb_{p+1}100\ .\ .\ .\ 0) \\
&= 000\ .\ .\ .\ 01\ \text{(invoking the induction hypothesis)}
\end{aligned}$$

QED

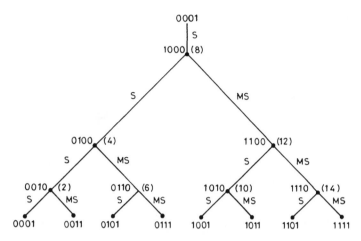

FIGURE 8   Binary search tree obtained using Lemma.

Using this lemma we observe that a judicious application of a sequence of S and MS transformations leads to the binary search tree of Figure 8. We interpret the tree as follows:

Take any node in the tree. The node is labeled with the address of the cell whose contents will reach cell 1 by applying the transformations indicated on the branches of the tree leading to this node from the root of the tree. For example, take the node labeled 0110. Then applying SSMS transformation to the memory will take the contents of location 0110 to cell 1.

This can be verified by observing that m = 4, $b_1 = 0$, $b_2 = 1$, p = 2. Thus the sequence SSMS applied to 0110 gives by lemma 1

$$SSMS\ (0110)\ =\ 0001$$

Search Algorithm

Let $R_1, R_2, \ldots, R_N$ be records whose keys $K_1, K_2, \ldots, K_N$ are in nondecreasing order so that $K_1 < K_2 \ldots < K_N$. Let Z be the key of the record in cell 1 and K be the key of the record to be retrieved. Let s be the m bit logical address of the record brought to cell 1 by a sequence of S and MS transformations. Let r be a flag which is set to 1 if the search for key succeeds before applying *m* S transformations. The value of s is derived using the lemma. The symbol $\oplus$ indicates one's complement addition of *m* bit numbers.

Algorithm for Binary Search in Aho-Ullman Memory

> *begin*
> > *If* Z = K *then write* ''No Search needed''
> > > *Else If* Z > K *then Write* ''Record not in memory''
> > > *Else If* Z < K *then Call* Search
> *end*
> *Search*:
> *begun*
> > r ← 0

Shuffle
$S \leftarrow 2^{m-1}$
For i = 1 *to* (m−1) *step* 1 *do*
begin
       If Z < K *then begin Minus-one*
                               Shuffle
                               $s \leftarrow \oplus \, 2^{m-i-1}$ *end*
      Else If Z = K *then begin Shuffle*
                          r ← 1
                          $s \leftarrow s \oplus (-2^{m-i-1})$ *end*
      Else If Z > K *then begin Shuffle*
                          $s \leftarrow s \oplus (-2^{m-i-1})$ *end*
   end
If r = 1 *and* Z ≠ K *then begin Minus-One*
                    $s \leftarrow s \oplus -1$ *end*
Else If r = 0 *and* Z ≠ K *then Write* "Search Fails"
end.

A proof of this algorithm is given elsewhere (15).

Initialization of Memory to Original State

After retrieving the record(s) with the desired key, the contents of the memory is to be placed back in the original sorted order with the record with the lowest key in cell 1. This is done by applying the Aho-Ullman algorithm as follows. At the termination of the search algorithm, the variable s contains the initial address of the record which is now in cell 1. We define the distance d as $1 \oplus (-s)$. Let $(d_m-1 d_m-2 \ldots d_1 d_0)$ be the binary representation of d. We use this with Aho-Ullman algorithm to initialize the memory to its original state.

Illustrative Example

Table 5 traces the search algorithm. The initial and subsequent contents of the memory are listed. We consider $m = 3$. Initially $r \leftarrow 0$. Search for 489 shows a successful match when i = 1; consequently, $r \leftarrow 1$ and $s \leftarrow 100$. To test for multiplicity of records containing the specified key, we examine records at addresses less than s, and hence apply an S transformation. At $i = 2$, $Z < K$ and hence M-S is applied. When we leave the loop $Z = K$, and $r = 1$. *Minus-one* transformation brings the most recently matched record (Key 489) to cell 1. Now the memory is ready for consecutive retrievals. The value of s is incremented by one for every subsequent retrieval. Initialization is carried out by knowing the binary representation of $d = 1 \oplus (-s)$. In our example, $d = 001 + (-100) = 100$. Thus the sequence of transformations (SM S S) places the memory in its initial state.

Estimating Mean Access Time

Every search, successful or unsuccessful, ends after m *Shuffle* transformations are applied to the initial memory state. If search is successful at the last state, no reordering is

TABLE 5   Searching in a Dynamic Memory

Physical contents with logical address in parenthesis	$Z < K$ Apply S	Contents	$i = 1$ $Z = K$ Apply S	Contents	$i = 2$ $Z < K$ Apply MS	Contents	$Z < K$ Apply M	Contents
1 150(1)	r = 0	489(4)	r = 1	200(2)	r = 1	305(3)	r = 1	489(4)
2 200(2)		150(1)		489(4)		489(4)		520(5)
3 305(3)		520(5)		520(6)		520(5)		520(6)
4 489(4)		200(2)		150(1)		520(6)		699(7)
5 520(5)		520(6)		305(3)		699(7)		150(1)
6 520(6)		305(3)		520(5)		150(1)		200(2)
7 699(7)		699(7)		699(7)		200(2)		305(3)
Initialization After Retrieval								
1 489(4)	Apply SM	489(4)	Apply S	200(2)	Apply S	150(1)		
2 520(5)		150(1)		489(4)		200(2)		
3 520(6)		520(5)		520(6)		305(3)		
4 699(7)		200(2)		150(1)		489(4)		
5 150(10		520(6)		305(3)		520(5)		
6 200(2)		305(3)		520(5)		520(6)		
7 305(3)		699(7)		699(7)		699(7)		

( ) denotes logical address of datum.

required. If it is successful at any stage but the last, a search for a possible match over lower addresses is required. If this search fails *Minus-one* transformation is applied.

To obtain the mean access time, we assume that each transformation is performed in unit time and the keys are uniformly distributed. For a dynamic memory of size $(2^m - 1)$, the average number of transformations, *Shuffle* and *Minus-one* are $1 + 1.5 (m-1)$ if the search succeeds at the $(m-1)^{th}$ step. It is $1 + 1.5 (m-1) + 1$ if the search succeeds at an earlier stage. Hence, the average number of transformations for a successful search is 1.5m, and for an unsuccessful search is $1 + 1.5(m-1)$.

For initialization, if $d = (000 \ldots 0)$ is detected, then no transformation is applied. The case $d = (11 \ldots 1)$ never occurs. The remaining values of d are equally likely. A 0 in the binary representation of d corresponds to the transformation S, and 1 to the transformation S followed by M. As 0 and 1 are equally probable, the average number of transformations for initialization is 1.5*m*.

Thus, it is concluded that the mean search time is 1.5m, the mean initialization time is 1.5m, and the worst case search time is $1 + 2(m-1) = 2m-1$.

It may be assumed that the mean interrequest time is sufficiently large compared with the mean initialization time so that a queue of requests does not build up. The initialization overhead is needed to bring the memory to its initial state so as to facilitate another binary search in the memory.

It is thus seen that if records in a dynamic memory of size $(2^m - 1)$ are stored in a nondecreasing order of their keys, then it is possible to retrieve a record with a given key using a binary search algorithm which is implemented by an appropriate sequence of application of *Shuffle* and *Minus-one Shuffle* transformations. The mean time to search and retrieve a record with a specified key is 1.5m. This time is identical to that needed to retrieve a record from a specified random address (12). After the search is over, it is necessary to spend an average of 1.5m steps to return the dynamic memory to its initial state, namely with the keys in nondecreasing order, to facilitate further search. This initialization may, however, be done between search requests.

BUFFERED DYNAMIC MEMORIES

Dynamic memories with cyclic permutations are inexpensive and are available as integrated circuits. Data is moved unidirectionally in such memories and we saw that for a n cell memory the average access time is $(n-1)/2$.

Stack Memory

Many applications in computer science require stacks, namely, last-in-first-out (LIFO) memories (17). It is possible to design a stack with unidirectional shift registers (18). As the shift register is unidirectional, it is required for a stack of size $(n+1)$ to shift circularly n times to make the last insertion available on top of the stack. For W bits/words, a stack may consist of W shift registers working in parallel. In a typical stack of size 2K words and speed 3 MHz, the retrieval rate cannot exceed 1.46 KHz, which is very slow.

It is possible to design stacks with a large unidirectional shift register (usr) connected to a small fast bidirectional shift register (bsr) to reduce the average delays in retrieval and insertion in the stack. The scheme used is described in Rajaraman and Vikas (18). In this scheme a word is written into both usr and bsr when initially bsr is empty. The bsr is made available after writing a word into it. The contents of usr, however, will be circularly shifted to make the recently inserted word available on its top. When bsr is full the bottom of bsr is transferred to usr and room on top of bsr is created by shifting its contents down. For retrieval, when bsr becomes empty, a word is transferred to the

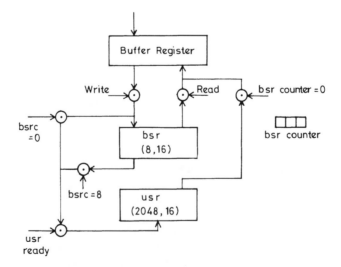

FIGURE 9 A stack using buffered dynamic memory.

buffer register from usr. If bsr is not empty then the word on top is shifted to the buffer. The organization is shown in Figure 9. Rajaraman and Vikas (18) have shown that for a usr of 2K words it is sufficient to use an 8-word bidirectional shift register for the composite system to behave like a 2K stack with 10% degradation in performance in most practical situations.

FIFO Memory

First-in-first-out (FIFO) serial storage is used in many areas of digital systems design. It serves as a reservoir when the retrieval rate is less than the average insertion rate over a large period of time.

A cyclic memory, like unidirectional dynamic MOS shift register, CCD, or bubble memory may be used to form a FIFO serial storage.

Insertion and retrieval request patterns to the storage are assumed to be independent random events. If insertion is made immediately after its arrival, holes will be created within SR, resulting in the problem of identification of first data entry and of garbage collection as data are scattered over the entire length of SR. A retrieval request could not be satisfied until first data entry is detected. Insertions made consecutively facilitates consecutive retrieval of data.

A scheme has been proposed (19) to realize a first-in-first-out (FIFO) storage consisting of a large size unidirectional cyclic memory and two small size high-speed buffer registers on input and output ends. Buffers on input and output ends facilitate fast insertion and retrieval, respectively. Insertion and retrieval requests can be entertained simultaneously.

In the proposed scheme m shift registers each of N-bits constitute a serial storage of N-words, m-bit/word. Figure 10 depicts the configuration of a single unidirectional dynamic shift register (SR) with two buffer registers, namely B_1 and B_2, on input and

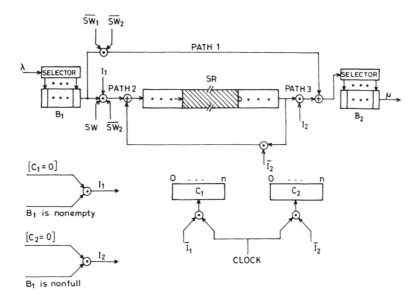

FIGURE 10 A FIFO memory using two buffers and a dynamic memory.

output ends. Buffer registers are parallel-in-serial-out (PISO) high-speed registers which enable the data to be stored in the rightmost vacant position. Selector unit is a combinatorial circuit to activate a switch in order to transfer a bit from SR into the corresponding buffer location. Counter C_1 indicates the distance of the tail, that is, last entry, of the chunk of information from the input port of SR. Counter C_2 indicates the distance of the head, that is, first entry of the chunk of information from the output port of SR. Distance is measured in terms of the number of circular shifts. Each shift clock increments the distance by one. Total size of the chunk of information can be obtained by the magnitude difference of C_1 and C_2.

Flipflop SW_1 is reset when SR becomes empty and set when B_2 becomes full, while SR is still empty, and remains set until SR becomes empty. Flipflop SW_2 is set when SR becomes full and remains reset otherwise. The FIFO memory operates as follows:

Let N be the size of SR and $1/T_S$ be its data transfer rate. As a request for insertion arrives, the occupancy of B_1 is found to be full and the request is rejected, otherwise an insertion is made into the rightmost vacant position of B_1. On the other hand, a request for retrieval is rejected if B_2 is found empty, otherwise retrieval is made from the rightmost end of B_2 followed by a single shift. Path 1 (see Fig. 10) is activated whenever SR becomes empty. Path 2 is activated whenever SW_1 is set and the tail of the chunk of information reaches the input port of SR. Data from B_1 is now transferred consecutively into SR until B_1 is left empty. Path 3 is activated whenever the head of the chunk of information reaches the output port of SR, and then data from SR are transferred into B_2 until B_2 gets full. Other data stored in SR keep recirculating.

Counter C_1 is incremented at every shift operation during the entire cycle except when path 2 remains activated. C_1 stops counting up during the period of consecutive transfers from B_1 into SR. It is to be noted that such a transfer was initiated when $C_1 = 0$, hence C_1 remains at zero during the path 2 activation period. Counter C_2 is incremented at every shift operation during the entire cycle, except when path 3 remains activated. C_2 remains at zero during the path 3 activation period.

The design of this FIFO entails finding optimal sizes of buffers and SR, given the insertion and retrieval request patterns and permissible fractional loss of information of the order of 0.001. The system is analyzed elsewhere (19) and it is shown that for an SR size of 2K words buffer sizes of 24 words are sufficient to ensure retrieval at buffer speed with no loss of information, provided the rate of service requests to the FIFO is less than 200 T_S where T_S is the basic clock used in the shift register.

CONCLUSIONS

The term dynamic memory is commonly interpreted to mean dynamic random access memory (DRAM). The primary reason for this interpretation is the almost universal use of DRAM as main memories of computers. Another important definition of dynamic memory is as a memory in which data bits continuously move and are serially accessed. Memories made using CCDs and magnetic bubbles fall into this class. These memories are also known as electronic cyclic memories. They have access speeds 100 times faster than magnetic disks but 100 times slower than DRAMs. Their cost per bit is 100 times lower than DRAMs and 100 times more than disks. Their capacity also lies between the capacities of DRAMs and disks. Thus they fill the gap between DRAM and disks in the cost/speed/size spectrum. This makes them attractive in some computer applications.

The primary disadvantage of currently available dynamic memories is their limited capacity. Most commercially available dynamic memory chips are serial access devices. It is possible to design and construct dynamic memories with random access to any cell in the memory by implementing in hardware memory transformations called *Shuffle* and *Minus-one* transformations. It is also possible to search a dynamic memory for a specified data in a time equal to the time taken to access at random a specified address. In other words associative memory can be efficiently built with a dynamic memory. We also saw that, by using small fast buffers, efficient memories with LIFO and FIFO disciplines can be built with dynamic memories. Thus these memories are quite versatile and inexpensive.

The main trend in the immediate past has been the increasing capacity of DRAM. However, of late the cost of DRAM has not been decreasing. There is no very fast, extremely cheap, and reliable new memory technology on the horizon. Thus hierarchy of memories will remain. Evolutionary improvements will take place in each of these technologies. New technologies replacing current technologies is rare, as several million dollars are required to evolve a totally new technology such as magnetic bubbles. Technologies which fill existing gaps in memory hierarchy are the ones which have good chance of success.

REFERENCES

1. Pohm, A. V., High Speed Memory Systems, *Computer*, 17(10), 162–171 (1984).
2. Feth, G. C., Memories: Smaller, Faster, Cheaper, *IEEE Spectrum*, 13(6), 36–43 (June 1976).
3. Liu, Y., and Gibson, G. A., *Micro Computer Systems: The 8086/8088 Family*, 2nd Ed., Prentice-Hall, Englewood Cliffs, NJ, 1986, pp. 434–442.
4. Rajaraman, V., and Radhakrishnan, T., *An Introduction to Digital Computer Design*, 3rd Ed., Prentice-Hall of India, New Delhi, 1987.
5. Panigrahi, G., Charge Coupled Device Memories for Computer Systems, *Computer*, 9(4), 33–41 (April 1976).
6. Bobeck, A. H., et al., Magnetic Bubbles—An Emerging New Memory Technology, *Proc. IEEE*, 63(8), 1176–1195 (August 1975).
7. Salzer, J. M., Bubble Memories—Where Do We Stand, *Computer*, 9(3), 36–41 (March 1976).
8. Mikhoff, N., Magnetic Bubble Memories Making a Come Back, *Computer Des.* (November 1984).
9. Chang, H., Memory Technology-Magnetic Bubble. In: *Encyclopedia of Computer Science & Technology*, Marcel Dekker, New York, 1978, Vol. 10, pp. 273–385.
10. Stone, H. S., Dynamic Memories with Enhanced Data Access, *IEEE Trans. Comput.*, C-21(4), 359–366 (April 1972).
11. Stone, H. S., Dynamic Memories with Fast Random and Sequential Access, *IEEE Trans. Comput.*, C-24(12), 1167–1174 (December 1975).
12. Aho, A. V., and Ullman, J. D., Dynamic Memories with Rapid Random and Sequential Access, *IEEE Trans. Comput.*, C-23(3), 272–276 (March 1974).
13. Iyer, B. R., and Sinclair, J. B., Comparison of Dynamic Memory Organizations: A Tutorial, *J. VLSI Comput. Sys.*, 1(3), 217–241 (1982).
14. Iyer, B. R., and Sinclair, J. B., Dynamic Memory Inter Connection for Rapid Access, *IEEE Trans. Comput.*, C-33(10), 923–927 (October 1984).
15. Vikas, O., and Rajaraman, V., Searching in a Dynamic Memory with Fast Sequential Access, *Comm.*, 25(7), 479–484 (July 1982).

16. Knuth, D. E., *The Art of Computer Programming*, Vol. 3, *Sorting and Searching*, Addison-Wesley, Reading MA, 1973.

17. Stone, H. S., et al., *Introduction to Computer Architecture*, 2nd Ed., Science Research Associates, Chicago, 1986, pp. 319–25.

18. Rajaraman, V., and Vikas, O., Buffered Stack Memory Organization, *Elec Lett.*, 11(14), 305–307 (July 1975).

19. Rajaraman, V. and Vikas, O., A First-In-First-Out Buffered Cyclic Memory, *Inform. Proc. Lett.*, 6(2), 63–68 (April 1977).

V. RAJARAMAN

END-USER COMPUTING

DEFINITION

End-user computing (EUC) is the activity of the white collar workforce, professionals and clericals, using standalone microcomputers or those connected to a multiuser system. Users may connect through a terminal to a mainframe or minicomputer or through a microcomputer on a local area network (LAN) with minimal and often no assistance from information systems professionals.

Office workers retrieve and update data from large corporate databases, process text with word processing packages, analyze data, design graphics presentations and program computers using fourth-generation languages which require relatively little training compared with the extensive training used to write programs in procedural languages. Every day white-collar workers transfer files, send electronic mail, schedule appointments, print professional presentation, and publish documents. Some have developed spreadsheets with sophisticated macro commands for specialized applications such as inventory control, budgeting, and sales order entry.

The dependence of business on computerization since the 1970s forces the majority of office workers to have self-sufficient computer skills. These may include using word processing packages, spreadsheets, graphics software, data management systems, communications packages, decision support systems, and expert systems. Although most use involves access to computers, other technologies peripheral to computers can supplement EUC. Users no longer can isolate reprographics and telecommunications from computer systems. The need to send information globally redefines computing. Integration of many technologies with computing equipment blurs the boundaries of what users and systems professionals responsibilities entail.

HISTORY AND CAUSES

There are four reasons that collectively account for the phenomenon of EUC:

1. The increase in the data processing backlog
2. The proliferation of microcomputers
3. Pervasive systems literacy among college graduates and professionals
4. User-friendly software

These conditions created an environment that challenged the traditional model of systems experts serving naive users. Users now can access and process information themselves.

DP Backlog

Mainframe and minicomputer use by the 1970s offered technical performance that promised answers to many information problems. Users wanted more. Systems professionals expertise and training had not met demand. Business managers knew that many projects could help them but found that their systems department could not implement them, in some cases, not for years. This backlog created negative relations for information systems departments. Management rushed some projects, reduced others in scope, and rejected some altogether in project planning and prioritization. Some users who had early home computers and knew how to program in BASIC decided to write their own programs rather than wait for their turn in the backlog.

Microcomputer Proliferation

In the late 1970s the hobby kits of microcomputers gave way to the commercially available Apple computer. First perceived as a toy for home use, Apple computers started showing up on office desks and soon on departmental budgets as "specialized typewriters." When IBM introduced its microcomputer, large corporate offices began buying them in quantity.

Systems Literacy

Before 1965 engineering college students were the only individuals who routinely used computers in their training. After 1965 many other disciplines required some form of computer use by students. As these professionals gained influence in their companies, they had no fear of technology and demanded more of it to support their work. From the mid-1980s, most business schools had set up microcomputer labs where they taught word processing, spreadsheets, and data management. Soon these skills became prerequisites for jobs in many levels of business.

Friendly Software

Advances in software and the decrease in the cost of mainframe hardware encouraged the development of fourth-generation languages (4GL). These languages had fewer rules or procedures than such high-level languages as COBOL and Fortran. Thus, they were called nonprocedural. With fewer rules to follow, the skill level necessary to write the codes was below that required by procedural languages. Office workers at any level could access mainframe data using 4GLs such as Focus or RAMIS. Some users were fairly proficient after a two-day workshop given that the nature of their access and needs was relatively unsophisticated. Most use of 4GL came from ad hoc queries which need not be institutionalized in production systems.

TYPES OF USERS

The term "end user" today is as appropriate as the term "horsepower." Users of computer systems used to receive hard copy reports usually produced at the end of a system's cycle. This end product was their only contact with the system. Today we use the term "end user" to include any contact with information systems.

In a white collar setting, most office workers are classified as clerical or professional. Clerical office workers use computers dedicated to word processing. Secretaries receive training for document retrieval, generation, and storage. Microcomputers as general-purpose processors have replaced dedicated machines on secretaries' desks and in some cases have replaced secretaries. One setting where significant clerical reduction has taken place is in law firms. Managers trained in microcomputer use often generate their own documents initially on the keyboard rather than give a longhand version to a secretary for recording.

Today clerical workers perform far more diverse tasks than merely substituting the typing function with word processing. Many secretaries maintain department budget information on spreadsheets, handle meetings on electronic calendars, and respond to electronic mail (E-mail) through a local area network (LAN). Other clerical tasks besides secretarial duties entail data entry. Before the advent of microcomputers, management information systems departments distributed the data entry function to user areas to make users more accountable. A sales department may have many sales order entry clerks who use terminals or microcomputers during their entire workday.

Lower and middle management levels in most organizations have created the image of "a computer on every desk." This one-to-one ratio has not been realized. In fact, several professionals may share a common area with several terminals and microcomputers. Management may spend most of their computing time accessing and analyzing data for budgets, sales projections, modeling trends, and using statistical packages. Top management has been slow to adopt technology on the desktop. Their special information needs (e.g., data external to the firm and summary information used in forecasting) have not been well served by information systems. Vendors now offer executive information systems (EIS) with some of this sophistication. As the generation of professionals who are comfortable using computers moves in to the executive suite, use by top management will increase.

Clerical users probably spend the major portion of their workday using computers. Professional workers may spend anywhere from 20 to 50 percent of their workdays in front of keyboards and screens. Firms have realized increased productivity (1). Some managers have complained that workers spend more time learning a system and using its nuances than focusing on its use for their work. The expectations of productivity increases and the ability to handle information differently increases pressure on both clerical and professional staff. Many workers insist that their workload has increased (2).

End-user computing allows many knowledge workers to work outside the office environment. Telecommuting presents options for worklife for handicapped workers, parents with preschool children, or families with a member who needs extra care. Other white collar workers prefer working at home for the concentration that is not possible in an office. Less reliance on computing professionals makes remote office work possible.

Collaborative work becomes more feasible with the ability to share files and send documents. Some coauthors need not see each other for months and produce an article or book. Groupware extends end-user computing to meetings. Group facilitators can conduct fact-to-face and dispersed meetings without the aid of systems staff. Electronic meetings can go on over time or synchronously.

PROBLEMS

The opportunities afforded by EUC do not come without a cost. Problems of security and data integrity surfaced early. The information systems department in most firms developed standards for computing that addressed these issues. For example, users must store diskettes in locked drawers away from dust. Transmitting information from a central database, updating it on a personal computer, and sending it back to replace the master data on a central mainframe generally requires authorization. Password protection, audit files, and limited access controls reduce security problems. Without enforcement or training in these areas, users can cause damage and duplicate work.

Data residing on personal computers should be consistent with that residing on a mainframe. This is referred to as data integrity. It has been a common problem for managers to present reports they generated on their personal computers that either do not agree with other managers or with central data. Organizations can maintain data integrity if users update their working data with the current central data.

THE IMPORTANCE OF INFRASTRUCTURE

The support given to end-user computing can vary across firms (3). Many office workers can take advantage of training classes. Help usually comes from fellow workers, often referred to as lead users (4). Some firms employ help desks or a staff dedicated to assisting end users.

In 1980 IBM Canada promoted the concept of an Information Center (IC) as a place where office workers could receive assistance for debugging, how to use mainframe data, and training. Most ICs would refuse to write programs but would help end users learn how to do it themselves. By 1990 the IC in some companies had disbanded because management felt that they had accomplished the training mission for early users. They continue to use outsourcing as a way to support that function. Those companies that have maintained an IC have charged it with broader duties such as troubleshooting, research and evaluation of new products, and developing and maintaining standards (5).

Although some would suspect that EUC has reduced the need for a systems department, they are mistaken. In fact, the backlog for MIS increased. The proficient end user became more demanding of technology and dangerously knowledgeable about new systems development. This phenomena did not reduce dependence on MIS. If anything, it created new job opportunities.

The IC staff comprises individuals with technical skills and good communication skills. A typical IC staff member may be a former elementary school teacher returning to the workforce after raising young children or after their children enter grade school. The career path for those in the IC raised questions. Some would matriculate to sales positions with vendors. Because IC staff had contact with people at all levels and departments in a company, they had significant exposure. This allowed them to seek positions in user departments as companies downsized ICs.

SUMMARY

The ability of nonsystems personnel to use computers extensively in their work without help from systems experts has revolutionized organizations. Easy access to information gives many people power. End-user computing has contributed to flattening organizational structure, enriching job opportunities, and causing chaos among other consequences. The 1980s experienced the growth of this phenomena. The 1990s must find ways to manage this change so that end-user computing contributes significantly to organizations rather than creates more problems.

SOURCES OF INFORMATION

Research journals which publish articles about this topic are *Communications of the Association for Computing Machinery*, *MIS Quarterly*, *Information and Management*, *Office*, *Technology*, *and People*, and *Information Systems Research*. Many publications carry articles focusing on office work or on microcomputers. Some examples of theses are: *PC World*, *PC Magazine*, *Computerworld*, *Datamation*, *Infosystems*, *IS Analyzer*, *MIS Week*, and *Information Center*.

REFERENCES

1. Zmuidzinas, M., Kling, R., and George, J., Desktop Computerization as a Continuing Process. In *Proceedings of the International Conference on Information Systems*, Association of Computing Machinery, New York, December 1990.
2. Kraut, R., Dumais, S., and S. Koch, Computerization, Productivity, and Quality of Work-life, *Commun. ACM*, 32(2): 220–238 (February 1989).
3. Leitheiser, R. L., and Wetherbe, J. C. Service Support Levels: An Organized Approach to End-User Computing, *MIS Q.*, 10(4): 337–349 (December 1986).
4. Lee, D. M. S., Usage Patterns and Sources of Assistance for Personal Computer Users, *MIS Qtrly*, 10(4): 313–325 (December 1986).
5. Huff, S. L., Munro, M. C., and Martin, B. H., Growth Stages of End-User Computing, *Commun. ACM*, 31(5): 542–551 (May 1988).

OTHER READINGS

Carr, H. H., *Managing End-User Computing*, Prentice-Hall, Englewood Cliffs, NJ, 1988.

Dunlop, C., and Kling R., *Computerization and Controversy: Value Conflicts and Social Choices*, Academic Press, New York, 1991.

Guimaraes, T., and Ramanujam, V. Personal Computing Trends and Problems: An Empirical Study, *MIS Qtrly*, 10(2): 179–187 (June 1986).

Panko, R. R., *End-User Computing: Management, Applications and Technology*, John Wiley and Sons, New York, 1988.

Rivard S., and Huff S. L., Factors of Success for End-User Computing, *Commun. ACM*, 31(5): 552–561 (May 1988).

Rockart, J. F., and Flannery, L. S., The Management of End-User Computing, *Commun. ACM*, 26(10): 776–784 (October 1983).

Toffler, A., *The Third Wave*, Bantam Books, New York, 1980.

Zuboff, S., *In the Age of the Smart Machine*, Basic Books, New York, 1988.

KATE M. KAISER

HIGH-LEVEL SYNTHESIS

INTRODUCTION

High-level synthesis (HLS) has been defined as "going from an algorithmic level specification of the behavior of a digital system to a register-transfer level structure that implements that behavior" (1). This definition contains the main aspects of HLS: It aims at transforming behavior into structure, it starts at a 'high level' or algorithmic level, and it usually is constrained to digital systems or even to synchronous digital systems. HLS bridges the gap between specifications, usually given as a program in a hardware description language (that may look very similar to a software program), and their implementation as a netlist of modules (such as ALUs, adders, gates, etc.).

The continuing trend toward shorter design turnaround times for increasingly complex circuits and the need for techniques that guarantee almost no design errors have made HLS almost a necessity. Automatic synthesis shortens the design cycle considerably, allowing a more thorough exploration of the design space. Furthermore, it is less error prone than manual design (correctness by construction). As the level of specification moves higher up, specifications become more concise, thus clearer, easier to understand and easier to change. Ultimately this results in increased design quality and in a reduction of design costs, which is essential in the design of large circuits and of circuits with a small production volume such as ASICs and PLDs.

The origins of HLS date back to the late 1960s. Friedman and Yang (2) already had addressed issues like automatic allocation of flip-flops (today called memory allocation) and sequence analysis (today called scheduling). Duley and Dietmeyer (3) built a system to translate DDL descriptions into logic. But these efforts were far from being practical. For example, Friedman and Yang (4) report results for an IBM 1800 computer synthesized automatically from an APL-like description; the synthesized version, however, used twice as many components as the manual design.

During the 1970s, HLS developed very rapidly. Although many basic algorithms originated during this period, HLS was still considered mainly an academic exercise. CMU developed the Expl system (5) in the early 1970s and the CMUDA system (6) later on. The latter was already a complete top down design system that addressed many of the relevant issues in HLS. In Europe, the MIMOLA system (7) has been developed since 1976. MIMOLA deals with data path and microcode synthesis. It was used later by Honeywell as part of their V-Synth (8) system. CADDY/DSL (9), which dates back to 1979, provided the basis for the synthesis system CALLAS (10) developed at Siemens.

Since the 1980s, the explosive amount of work on high-level synthesis has generated serious interest in industry. Besides the examples already cited, the continuing efforts of CMU led to the SAW system, which has been used by GM (11) and TI (12). Several industrial sites started their own efforts, among them IBM (13) and AT&T (14), and lately also NEC (15) and NTT (16). Research at universities continues to be strong;

some of the more prominent ongoing projects are those at CMU (17), the University of California at Irvine (18), the University of Southern California (19), Stanford University (20), the University of Karlsruhe (21), and Tsing Hua University (22).

Many other excellent research efforts could also be mentioned. HLS has also expanded to more specialized fields such as digital signal processing. The best known projects in this area are CATHEDRAL (23) developed at IMEC, which was used as the basis for the Philips Piramid system (24), and GE's FACE/PISYN system (25).

As already suggested, HLS is not a homogeneous field. Several specialized sub-disciplines have emerged. This article deals mostly with 'classical,' general-purpose HLS; meaning that the target architecture is largely unconstrained and all kinds of designs can be dealt with. General-purpose HLS has been used for such widely divergent applications as filters, processors, automotive electronics, implementation of small algorithms, etc. In contrast, there are more specialized disciplines such as pipeline synthesis, synthesis of digital signal processing applications, protocol and interface synthesis, asynchronous (self-timed, time-independent) system synthesis, synthesis of bussed architectures, etc. Target-specific synthesis systems tend to produce better results than general-purpose HLS, but for a smaller range of applications.

Multiple areas in high-level synthesis are well understood. The formidable task of HLS is divided into several steps.

- Compilation of the language into an internal representation and optimization of this representation, either at compile time or in a separate step. The internal representation usually consists of operations such as additions, logical operations, etc., and their dependencies.
- Assignment of all operations to a time slot (a control step in a microprogram, a state in a finite state machine). This step is called scheduling.
- Definition of the hardware structure and determination of which piece of hardware each operation will execute. This step is called allocation and binding.
- Partitioning the design into smaller units often increases the quality of the design, makes it easier to modify, and helps processing by other tools such as logic synthesis (since they may process smaller pieces at a time).

This article presents the main issues in HLS listed above. The next section deals with design representations and languages used in HLS, and the optimizations performed directly on high-level representations. Subsequent sections deal with the scheduling and allocation, the two central problems when converting a behavior into a structure. The most prominent algorithms are briefly revised. Partitioning, which is a key issue for the synthesis of large (practical) systems is covered next. Current issues and an outlook to further developments complete the report.

DESIGN REPRESENTATION

Design representations for digital circuits are often classified along two axes:

- The *domain*. Usually three different domains are distinguished, namely the behavioral (indicating function), the structural (indicating topology), and the physical (indicating geometry). A typical design is described in the behavioral domain by a program in a hardware description language, in the structural domain by a netlist, and in the physical domain by its layout.

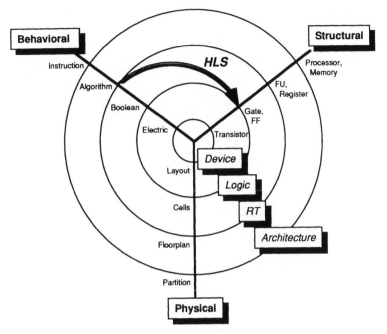

FIGURE 1   The Y-chart representing levels and domains.

- The *level*. Several levels are common in the representation of digital systems, among them the architectural level, the register-transfer (RT) level, the logic level, and the device level. Sometimes, too, an algorithmic level is distinguished between the architectural and RT levels. A level can be characterized by the elements used in its structural representation (the boxes in the netlist): processors, memories and busses at the architectural level, functional units (adders, ALUs) and registers at the register-transfer level, gates and flip-flops at the logic level, and transistors, resistors, and capacitors at the device level.
- Levels and domains can be summarized by the so called Y-chart (26) as shown in Figure 1. High-level synthesis is represented by the arrow in the Y-chart. The starting point is usually a specification in a hardware description language such as behavioral VHDL or Verilog. In the ideal case this is a pure functional specification, not containing any hints on how the specified functions are to be implemented. HLS converts this behavior into a structure at the RT level or at a lower level. Levels are often mixed; a design representation may as well contain adders and logic gates for example.

Languages and Compilation

Starting point for HLS is a specification in a hardware description language. Among the more popular languages discussed for behavioral specifications today are VHDL (27), Verilog (28), and UDL/I (29). It should be pointed out, however, that design by synthesis from HDLs in general and HLS in particular are emerging disciplines.

The self-explaining code fragment in behavioral VHDL given in Figure 2 represents the commonly used greatest common divisor (GCD) example. To the author's knowledge,

```
ENTITY gcd IS
  PORT
    (x, y:  IN   INTEGER;
     res :  OUT  INTEGER;
     start: IN BIT;
     ready: OUT BIT;
    )
END gcd;

ARCHITECTURE behavior OF gcd IS
BEGIN
  PROCESS
    VARIABLE xx, yy: INTEGER;

    WHILE (start /= '1')    -- wait for start
      LOOP
      END LOOP;
    ready <= '0';
    xx := x;                -- read inputs
    yy := y;
    WHILE (xx /= yy)        -- compute
      LOOP
        IF (xx > yy)
          THEN
            xx := xx - yy;
          ELSE
            yy := yy - xx;
        END IF;
      END LOOP;
    res   <= xx;            -- assign outputs
    ready <= '1';
  END PROCESS;
END behavior;
```

FIGURE 2   Behavioral VHDL code for the GCD example.

it appeared initially in Johnson (30) in the context of HLS. Such a specification is first compiled very much like a software program. The result of compilation is an internal representation of the behavior which is better suited to HLS than the original language.

Data and Control Flow Graphs

The most common design representation used for HLS is graphs (rather than syntax trees often used in compilers). Most representations are based on data flow and control flow graphs. The representation given in Figure 3 separates the data and the control flow for the GCD example. In both directed graphs the nodes represent the operations. The square nodes in the data flow graph represent input and output ports. In the control

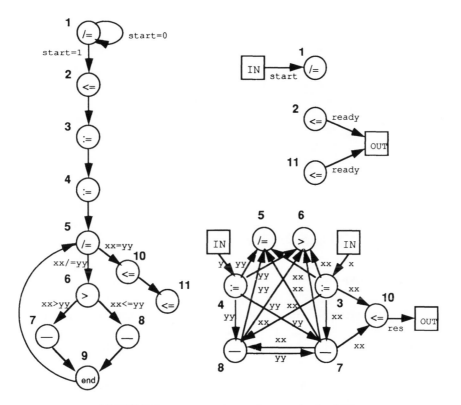

FIGURE 3   Control and data flow graphs for GCD.

flow graph, the edges represent the sequencing information, looping, and conditional branches, as given in the source code. Whenever an operation has more than one successor, only one of them is executed next, according to the condition attached to the edge. The edges in the data flow graph represent data dependencies (i.e., an operation uses the data produced by its predecessors).

Data and control flow often are represented in one simplified graph frequently called a flow graph or dependency graph. The dependency graph for GCD is given in Figure 4. The edges represent either a data dependency or an essential control dependency. Essential control dependencies are, for example, conditional branches and loops. For instance, operations 2, 3, and 4 have no data dependencies nor essential control dependencies and can be executed in parallel. The transitive closure and the cycles in the directed graph were omitted. The dependency graph captures less information than the data and the control flow graphs, but for many algorithms such a design representation suffices.

The above example is greatly simplified. Design representations for HLS have to deal also with many language issues such as data types and typing, data structures, arrays and indices, expressions rather than just operations, etc. Facilities to indicate hardware-specific elements such as multiplexers, three state buffers, memories, etc. must also be provided.

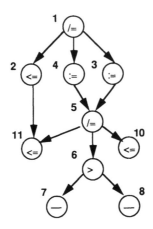

FIGURE 4   Dependency graph for the GCD.

High-Level Transformations

In HLS, up front optimizations (at compilation time) are often called high-level transformations. They are applied directly to the behavior represented by the data and control
flow graphs. Naturally, optimizations found in compilers (31) are used in HLS (e.g.,
dead code elimination, common subexpression elimination, constant propagation, loop
unrolling, etc.). Also hardware-specific transformations are used, such as

- Local transformations, e.g., substituting multiplication and division by a power
  of two by the appropriate shift, balancing of trees to increase potential parallelism, using commutativity of operations to reduce the number of inputs of
  multiplexers, etc. (32).
- The creation of concurrent processes which can run on independently synthesized, parallel hardware (33).
- Changing the number of levels in the flow graph to obtain faster hardware (e.g.,
  the FLAMEL system (34) is based on this and other transformations).

Transformations are very useful as they 'clean up' a design, making the tasks to come
more easy. Transformations are local and their result depends on the order in which they
are applied; completeness and consistency are difficult to assess.

SCHEDULING AND CONTROL GENERATION

Scheduling assigns each operation that appears in the behavioral specification to a time
slot called the control step. In synchronous systems, the control steps correspond to the
states of the controlling finite state machine or to one microinstruction. To define the
scheduling problem more precisely, it is necessary to introduce constraints and an objective function to maximize or minimize. The most typical constraints are

- The design area. Since at a high level it is difficult to measure area precisely,
  HLS often uses the 'amount of hardware' (e.g., the number of functional units,
  adders, registers, busses, etc.).
- The speed of the design. For a given function, the speed is determined by the
  cycle time and by the number of cycles required to complete the function. At a

high level the number of cycles can be counted exactly, but the cycle time is difficult to estimate. For complex designs with more than one function, defining performance is very complex. In a microprocessor, for instance, a function represents an instruction with a given addressing mode. Performance is defined as a weighted average of the execution time of all instructions. Time models used in HLS are simpler, often considering only factors such as fixed delays stored in a library, and chaining (executing operations with data dependencies in the same control step).

- The number and the type of ports (pins), and input/output constraints such as arrival times of signals. These constraints represent the interface protocol of the design.
- Constraints such as power, a given or derived floorplan, etc. sometimes are considered.

An objective function defines the measure to be maximized or minimized in a design. For example, a typical cost function to be minimized is AT^2, where A is the area and T is the delay.

Scheduling must find a valid schedule that meets all given constraints and minimizes or maximizes the objective function. For instance, scheduling may minimize the area for a given number of control steps and a given cycle time, or it may minimize only a cost function with no constraints. Much work on scheduling has been reported and many good algorithms exist.

Scheduling is an NP complete problem, so heuristics are used. In the sequel, several scheduling algorithms will be briefly described. They were classified into transformational algorithms, which start from a given schedule and use transformations to obtain other schedules, and constructive algorithms, which build a schedule directly from a specification. Several of the scheduling algorithms presented perform scheduling and allocation together. For the sake of clarity, it is mainly the scheduling aspects that we address.

Transformational Algorithms

A trivial schedule can be obtained by scheduling each operation in one control step, obtaining a maximally serial schedule. For example, the control graph given in Figure 3 can be interpreted as a finite state machine where each operation corresponds to a state. In the absence of constraints, another trivial way to schedule all operations is in a single control step, chaining all operations as necessary and obtaining a maximally parallel schedule. Both the maximally serial and parallel schedules have been used as the starting point for transformational scheduling.

Exhaustive Search

The Expl system (5) explored all possible schedules with a different degree of parallelism. The basic transformation used was the serial-parallel transformation shown in Figure 5.

If chaining is not allowed, only parallel operations can be scheduled in the same control step. The method exploits only potential parallelism. Davidson et al. (35) discuss exhaustive search using branch-and-bound techniques. Early efforts for scheduling using

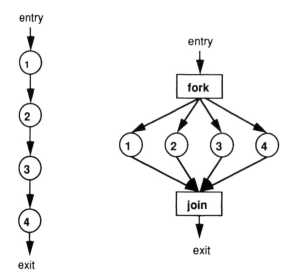

FIGURE 5   Series-parallel transformation.

integer linear programming (36) relied implicitly on this approach. Exhaustive search is not practical due to its large computational complexity, although it potentially achieves the optimal schedule.

Percolation Scheduling and State Splitting

The term percolation scheduling was introduced by Nicolau (37) for a technique of moving operations in a schedule whenever their dependencies and the constraints allow it. Thus, operations may 'percolate' through the schedule.

For example, starting with a serial schedule, operations can be moved to vacate control steps which can then be eliminated. Consider the control flow graph of Figure 3 interpreted as a finite-state machine representing a serial schedule. Operation 4 can be moved to the same state than operation 3 since there are no data dependencies and two ports for reading x and y in parallel are provided. Thus, one state can be eliminated.

Similar techniques have been widely used (e.g., 21,38–40). They yield good results, but the number of rules that define constraints and valid transformations may grow quite large. Also, the order in which operations percolate matters. Although a set of four basic transformations was proven to be complete with respect to the set of all possible local transformations that preserve dependencies in program trees (40), consistency and completeness of the set of transformations are difficult to prove.

An interesting note is that state splitting (rather than merging) has also been used. In the YSC (41), all operations are scheduled first in one state which is successively split, until all constraints are met. The transformations used for this purpose are proven to be behavior preserving (42).

Simulated Annealing

Simulated annealing (43) is a statistical hill-climbing technique which can be applied to different problems. It was first used for scheduling and allocation in Devadas and Newton (44). Simulated annealing defines a set of moves (e.g., operations may be moved to another control step if no constraint is violated). These moves are tried randomly and are applied whenever the design improves (the cost function decreases). To escape local minima, moves that worsen the design also are allowed with a certain probability. This probability decreases as the design evolves.

This algorithm yields good results, but it is expensive computationally, so that it is seldom used for scheduling in HLS. Another general optimization technique which has been applied to scheduling is self-organization (45), but it may be even more computationally intensive than simulated annealing.

Constructive Algorithms

Constructive algorithms obtain a schedule directly from the control flow, the data flow or the dependency graph.

List Scheduling

List scheduling (35) is based on the topological order of the operations. Operations in a dependency graph can be ordered, for example, using a depth-first search to obtain a so called as-soon-as-possible (ASAP) schedule. For the dependency graph of the GCD (Fig. 4) the ASAP schedule is given in Figure 6. For the sake of simplicity, no difference between data dependencies and control dependencies (such as conditional branches) is made, and no chaining is allowed (meaning that no two operations with a dependency can be scheduled in the same step). Clearly, an ASAP schedule is the shortest schedule under the above conditions.

Assume now that a constraint of only two input/output ports is imposed. Then, in step 2, only two operations can be scheduled. With no additional criteria, operations 2 and 3 may be scheduled in step 2, and operation 4 in step 3. In this case operation 5 must be delayed by one cycle, since it depends on operation 4, and all other operations have also to be delayed, resulting in a schedule with 6 steps. This could easily have been prevented by scheduling operations 3 and 4 in step 2, and operations 2 and 5 in step 3.

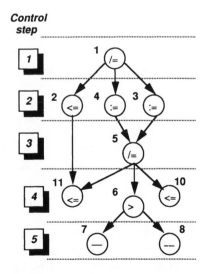

FIGURE 6   ASAP schedule for the GCD.

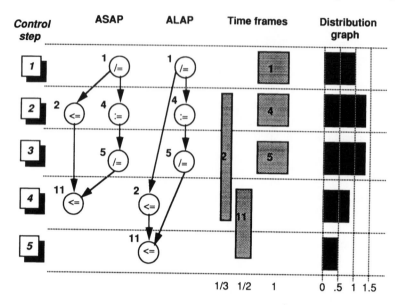

FIGURE 7   Force-directed scheduling for a part of GCD.

List scheduling overcomes precisely this shortcoming by providing an additional criteria whenever operations are sorted on the same topological level. The most frequently used criteria are the length of the longest path to the end (46,47), the longest path to a constraint (48), and the mobility or freedom (18,49). It is evident that operations with a longer path to the end should be scheduled earlier if the whole function is to be scheduled in the smallest number of control steps. Mobility or freedom is the difference among the ASAP and ALAP (as-late-as-possible) schedules. An ALAP schedule is also trivially obtained by topologically ordering the operations. For example, operation 2 would have been scheduled in step 4 in an ALAP schedule (Fig. 7), thus its mobility is $4 - 2 = 2$. An operation that cannot be moved and thus has the same ASAP and ALAP schedules has a mobility of 0. Evidently, operations with small mobilities should be scheduled first.

List scheduling yields quite good results; for microcode optimizations it works almost as good as branch and bound (35). Its time complexity is proportional to the size of the graph, thus it is often the choice for large scheduling problems.

Force-Directed Scheduling

Force-directed scheduling (50) can be seen as a list scheduling algorithm that uses a more complex criterion called force. This is explained using a fragment of GCD shown in Figure 7, which also includes the ASAP and ALAP schedules. Time frames are defined to have a length of ALAP − ASAP + 1 and a width of

$$\frac{1}{(ALAP - ASAP + 1)}$$

They represent the probabilities that an operation is scheduled in a particular control step. When all time frames for each control step are added to the distribution graph we can see how crowded a control step is. The aim is to schedule initial operations in control steps that are likely to be less crowded.

For each operation *j* and all control steps *k* it can be scheduled in, a force is defined as follows:

$$F^{jk} = \sum_{i \in CS} DG^i * \Delta^{ijk}$$

where *CS* is the set of all control steps, DG^i is the original value of the distribution graph at control step *i*, and Δ^{ijk} is the difference between the original value of the distribution graph at control step *i* and the new value after scheduling operation *j* in control step *k*.

For example, scheduling operation 11 in control step 4, produces a force $F^{11,4} = 0.83*0.5 - 0.5*0.5 = 0.17$, while scheduling the same operation in step 5 produces a force of $F^{11,5} = -0.83*0.5 + 0.5*0.5 = -0.17$. The algorithm selects the schedule with the smallest force, in this case operation 11 would be scheduled in step 5. Notice that the example does not allow chaining nor does it take into account that the edge between node 5 and 11 is a conditional dependency which arises from an IF statement (Fig. 3). Furthermore, operation 5 is forced into step 3 (Fig. 3).

Force-directed scheduling yields better results than list scheduling, but it is much more complex. It should be used whenever the number of control steps is not too large and/or the graphs are relatively small. Force-directed scheduling is used in Paulin and Knight (51) and Cloutier and Thomas (52).

Path-Based Scheduling

As opposed to the methods described so far which take advantage mainly of potential parallelism, path-based scheduling (53) deals mainly with mutual exclusion. It computes each path in the control flow graph, and then schedules each path independently, allowing a schedule of different length for each path. This proves essential for applications such as complex processors with instructions of different length (in number of cycles).

Path-based scheduling reduces the problem of computing a schedule for one path (with no conditional branches) to clique covering of an interval graph, or coloring of the dual graph (see also clique covering and coloring). Path-based scheduling also relies heavily on chaining.

For example, consider the path in GCD shown in Figure 8. The constraint is imposed, that no more than two ports should be used. The intervals represent the edges in the path where a new control step has to start. For example, the first interval indicates that operations 1, 2, and 3 cannot be scheduled in the same control step, since they all use ports and only two ports are available. A 'cut' that starts a new step must be introduced either between operations 1 and 2 or between operations 2 and 3. The problem of determining the minimum number of cuts is equivalent to finding a minimum clique cover for the generated interval graph. A node in the interval graph corresponds to an interval, and overlapping intervals are connected by an edge. Clique covering for interval graphs can be done in linear time. In the example, clearly only two cuts (yielding three states) are required. For instance, the graph can be covered with clique 1 and the trivial clique consisting only of interval 3. The corresponding cuts are between operations 2 and 3 (the intersection of intervals 1 and 2 represented by clique 1) and between operations 3, 4, 5, 10, or 11 (any point in interval 3). Many other optimal solutions exist.

Once a schedule is found in this way for each path, all schedules are overlapped using a similar technique. Unfortunately in this case the resulting graphs have no special property, and the problem becomes NP complete. But the graphs are sufficiently sparse

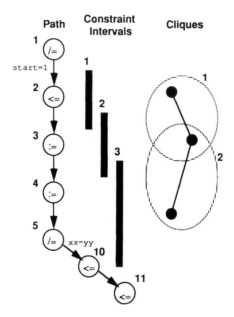

FIGURE 8   Scheduling of one path.

to compute exact solutions. Also, the number of paths may be exponential—in practice, however, the number of paths is a measure of the number of different functions a system performs and thus bounded.

Path-based scheduling gives excellent results for applications which are control intensive and have many conditional branches. Similar problems have also been addressed elsewhere (54,55).

Linear Programming

Scheduling and allocation can be formulated as integer linear programming problems which can be solved using standard techniques. Early efforts (36) showed the power of the method, but they proved impractical even for small designs. The method has been reintroduced with success for larger problems. Two of these approaches are discussed below. A formulation of memory port allocation as a 0-1 linear programming problem is given later.

Lee et al. (56) solve the problem of 'time-constrained' scheduling using an integer linear programming formulation (ILP). Time-constrained scheduling seeks the cheapest schedule, given a constraint on the maximum number of control steps. The solution space is drastically reduced by using ASAP and ALAP schedules to limit the possible solutions.

ILP can also be used to solve scheduling and allocation together. Gebotys and Elmasry (57) optimize a piecewise linear cost function using ILP. Significantly improved execution times are obtained using tight models which have a smaller set of solutions, and using facets more effectively. Hafer (58) uses a mixed integer linear programming (MILP) problem and reports significant improvements over previous approaches due to enhanced constraints, in particular the addition of minimum existence times for values and avoiding usage conflicts for components.

Control Generation

Once scheduling determines what operations are executed in each step and the sequence of control steps, a controller that sequences through the states as required can be built. To define all signals that the controller reads and generates, also the data path must be known. The controller has to interface with the data path as follows:

- Signals from the controller to the data path condition the function of elements in the data path. Examples are controlling the load of a register, selecting the input of a multiplexer, selecting the function of an ALU, etc.
- Signals from the data path to the controller carry conditions necessary to take decisions in the controller. Examples are the result of a comparison, a test for zero—the value of a given signal such as data-ready, etc.

Given all the above, the control can be specified as a finite state machine (FSM) and then can be synthesized with a PLA or with random logic. FSM synthesis has been studied since the early 1950s. It involves several subproblems such as state minimization (59) and state encoding (60). Some of the better known modern approaches are: for PLA-based FSMs, Ref. 61 and for random logic-based FSMs, Ref. 62.

Alternatively, a microsequencer may be used. Many different structures for micro-sequencers have been proposed and commercialized. Since the schedule is given, the main remaining problem is vertical microcode compaction (i.e., to minimize the width of the microprogram word, e.g., by sharing fields) (63).

ALLOCATION AND BINDING

The overall goal of *allocation* is the synthesis and optimization of the hardware necessary to perform the functions specified in the behavioral specification. This task has often been called *data–path* synthesis, since it essentially defines the data path. Other concepts closely related to allocation are binding and module assignment:

- Allocation usually refers to the ''allocation'' of the data-path as a whole
- Binding refers to the ''binding'' of specific operations in the behavioral speci-fication to specific pieces of hardware in the data path
- Module assignment has still a slightly different flavor: whenever an operation can be performed by different modules, e.g., an addition can be performed by an ALU, a fast adder or a slow adder, the task of ''assigning'' a particular mod-ule to the operation is called module assignment

All three tasks, however, are often performed together and called collectively, allocation or binding.

Allocation can be decomposed naturally into three parts: functional unit (FU) al-location, register allocation and interconnection allocation. Solving them separately sim-plifies allocation, but the solutions may be worse than solving them together. For example, functional unit allocation certainly has an effect on the communication structure.

As stated before, allocation and scheduling are very closely correlated. Indeed, many of the algorithms for scheduling studied in the previous sections solve allocation and scheduling together. For example, force-directed scheduling solves the problem of minimizing hardware for a given schedule length, path-based scheduling solves the problem of obtaining the shortest schedule for partially given hardware resources, and integer linear programming can schedule and allocate together minimizing any cost function.

Allocation having all goals in mind is extraordinarily complex even to formulate. For example, speed and size of the involved hardware has to be taken into account, interconnection has an influence on both speed and area, several alternative implementations of different speed and sizes usually are available for each operation, registers may or may not be grouped into single or multiport memories, etc. Several of these problems have been addressed within the context of different synthesis systems, but it is beyond the scope of this article to discuss all solutions, mostly ad hoc heuristics, in detail. This section is limited to an introduction of the main techniques used for allocations and of typical applications of these techniques in HLS systems.

Heuristic Techniques

Iterative techniques select one element (operation, variable, or interconnection) to be assigned at a time and assign them to either existing or newly allocated hardware. Usually the elements are selected in a greedy manner, by picking among the ones that generate the smallest additional cost (e.g., EMUCS) (46). Operations may also be assigned in the order they were scheduled, formulating all possible assignments as graph grammars (64) and then choosing the cheapest production rule for the given operation.

Rule-based systems choose where to assign the next operation according to design knowledge encoded in a set of rules. The DAA (65) uses such an approach for processor-like applications. In Cathedral II the allocator (66) uses DSP-specific rules (e.g., how to generate addressing schemes or how to implement iterations).

Yet another family of heuristic techniques is *branch and bound approaches*. A full search through all allocation possibilities would theoretically yield the optimal solution, but this is too complex. Splicer (67) uses branch and bound limited to given parts of the control/data flow graph. MIMOLA (68) uses branch and bound to allocate functional units, limiting the search to one control step at a time.

Heuristic approaches have the potential of solving FU, register and interconnection allocation together. They give reasonable results and are fast, specially if restricted to a given type of design (e.g., processors, DSP). Most allocation techniques include heuristics more or less extensively.

Graph-Based Techniques

Several approaches are based on graph algorithms. Most of these allocation schemes maximize hardware *sharing* based on the *clique covering* or *node coloring* formulation explained in Figure 9. A node represents an element to be allocated (e.g., an operation, a variable, or a bus). An edge in the conflict graph represents a conflict that prevents the elements it joins to share a hardware unit. For example, the lifetimes of the variables in the control flow graph shown on the left are the times between the generation and the last use of the variable. If lifetimes overlap, the values cannot be stored in the same register. For instance, value 1 overlaps with values 2, 3, and 6, but values 3 and 4 do not overlap because they are in different branches of a conditional branch (thus will never coexist). The compatibility graph is the dual of the conflict graph (i.e., an edge means that the elements are compatible and may share hardware units). Clearly, a minimal clique cov-

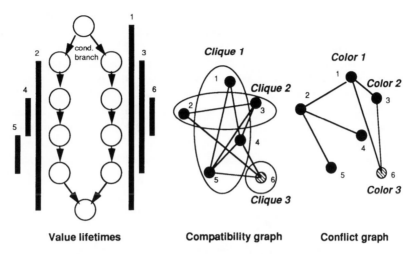

Value lifetimes	Compatibility graph	Conflict graph

FIGURE 9   Allocation using clique covering and node coloring.

ering of the compatibility graph will yield the smallest number of hardware units. This is equivalent to a minimal node coloring of the dual conflict graph. Clique covering (and node coloring) is NP complete in the general case.

The above formulation can be extended by adding weights to the edges in the compatibility graph representing the benefit of allocating both elements to the same hardware. In this case the problem of minimizing the hardware is equivalent to finding a maximal weight clique covering. Register allocation using graph coloring was already exercised (69). The first formulation of allocation as clique covering in HLS is due to Tseng and Siewiorek (70). He uses four weights to include interconnection costs in FU allocation. Operations have at most two inputs and one output. The weights represent none, 1, 2, or 3 common inputs and/or outputs and are used to guide a heuristic that solves the clique covering problem.

Many allocation approaches have used similar formulations, often solving the maximal weight clique covering using straightforward greedy heuristics such as selecting the edges in descending weight order or with a limited amount of backtracking. Other heuristics use a given lower bound n on the number of colors to eliminate all nodes with an outdegree smaller than $n - 1$ (which can be trivially colored). One such bound is the size of any clique in the conflict graph.

Some approaches solve the clique problem exactly (e.g., the YSC solves allocation of functional units exactly) (71), which can be done because the compatibility graph is reasonably small (all trivial operations such as logical operations are thrown out, leaving only comparisons and arithmetic operations). Since operations scheduled in different control steps do not conflict, the conflict graph for FU allocation may be very sparse. Alternatively, if only few operations may share hardware (in the extreme only operations of the same type), the compatibility graph is very sparse.

For certain graphs, node coloring and clique covering can be done efficiently in polynomial time (72). For example, *interval graphs* arise when allocation of registers or FUs is done on a straight piece of code with no conditional branches or loops. They can be colored in time $O(n*\log(n))$. REAL (73) solves register allocation in this case optimally.

Spaid (74) and Easy (75) in addition take advantage of *circular arc graphs* which in some cases can be colored in time $O(n^2)$, where n is the number of nodes in the graph. Easy (75) formulates the problem as a multicommodity network flow problem. Both Springer and Thomas (76) and Stock (75) give conditions when comparability graphs arise during allocation. Comparability graphs can be colored in polynomial time.

Formulating allocation as a graph problem is a powerful, global method that yields excellent results. However, it is difficult to formulate and solve all three allocation subproblems (operations, values, and interconnections) together. Furthermore, graph formulations deal mainly with sharing of hardware and it is difficult to adapt it to address problems such as selecting among different hardware modules, to take into account constraints on speed in the case of chaining, etc.

Linear Programming

Allocation and scheduling can be done together using integer linear programming, as discussed above. To illustrate the technique we include a simple formulation of multiport memory allocation as a 0-1 integer linear programming problem (77).

Let
x^i equal 1 if register i is included in memory M, else 0
m number of ports of M
c^{ik} equal 1 if register i is accessed in cycle k

Then, the problem of maximizing the number of registers that can be stored in memory M is formulated as the following problem.

$$\text{Allocate } x^i \text{ to maximize } \sum_i^{\text{registers}} x^i$$

$$\text{given the constraints } \quad \forall k: \sum_i^{\text{registers}} x^i * c^{ik} \le m$$

This 0-1 integer linear programming problem can be solved using a general algorithm (77).

PARTITIONING

In principle, partitioning a design into smaller pieces that are then processed in an independent manner, hides optimization possibilities. Thus, one would expect that an unpartitioned design has the potential to be superior to a partitioned one. In practice, however, both human designers and design tools have difficulties in processing large designs, thus a partitioned design has often better quality. If designs are too large to be designed as just one piece, partitioning is a necessity. Partitioning adds structure to a design. It is a difficult problem that has been addressed in detail (e.g., in the context of integrated circuit layout). This short review of partitioning in HLS gives an illustrative example.

During HLS, a design can be partitioned at different stages. APARTY (78) partitions the instruction set. BUD (47) partitions before scheduling and allocation to do a

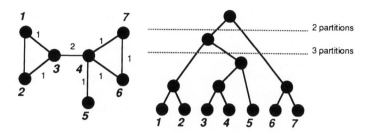

FIGURE 10 Hierarchical clustering.

preliminary allocation. The Olympus system (79) partitions after binding to have a better estimation of the hardware area and to be able to bind the latency of the partitioned implementation. The YSC (80) partitions after scheduling and allocation to generate smaller subproblems for logic synthesis.

Different algorithms have been applied to partitioning in HLS. Gupta and DeMicheli (79) use the Kernighan–Lin algorithm and simulated annealing. *Clustering* was pioneered in the context HLS (81) and later used by others (47,78,80). Hierarchical clustering (47) starts by computing the proximity of all pairs of operations. Proximity is a function based on the number of connections, the potential of sharing hardware and possibly the size. The operation pairs with the largest proximities are clustered and the process is then repeated until everything is clustered into one single piece.

Figure 10 shows an example. On the left, all operations (nodes) and their proximity (edges) with the value of the proximity (edge weights) is given. On the right, the clustering tree is shown. If the system is to be partitioned into two pieces, the clustering tree has to be sliced as indicated, generating the partitions (1,2,3,4,5) and (6,7). The better solution (1,2,3) and (4,5,6,7) was prevented due to the fact that first the two operations with proximity 2 are clustered. However, if three partitions are required, the solution is optimal for the given proximities.

CURRENT ISSUES AND OUTLOOK

While HLS is a rich and very active field of research, there are a number of areas were more development can be expected.

Despite the large amount of work on standardization, hardware description languages are still an issue. There is no single universally accepted standard (27–29). There are many open questions regarding the application of languages to design and to HLS in particular. For example, the application of different programming paradigms to HLS such as functional languages (21,30) and imperative languages (21,27) has been proposed. Some language constructs well suited for simulation, are quite difficult to synthesize (e.g., file types, dynamic memory allocation, etc.) (82).

Synthesis for a given interface specification is a key issue, but neither has interface specification been gracefully integrated into the functional specification, nor has interface synthesis been widely addressed in HLS. The situation with general constraints such as delay, area, power, etc. is similar. An issue often discussed in this context is technology constraints (e.g., the implications for HLS of an implementation with PGAs or with standard cells). Scheduling and allocation algorithms often allow inclusion of some constraints in a simplified way. The specific problem on how to deal with constraints and interface synthesis (sometimes called protocol synthesis) has been dealt with (48,83–85).

Besides the technical problems, there are many human factors regarding design specification that deserve more investigation. There is no widespread systematic experience on how to specify large designs using hardware description languages, and it is not even really clear what is needed. For example, is a purely textual form enough, or are parts of the design better entered graphically? What is specified better in the structural domain and what in the behavioral domain? Is perhaps even a natural language interface required? How automatic should synthesis systems be, what manual input should be allowed and how should user interaction be organized in general? There are very strong opinions but little systematic knowledge on these and other questions.

As designs become more complex, design process issues become more important. Similar to the development of large software systems with hundreds of programmers, hardware design faces large projects with hundreds of designers. HLS not only must be integrated into such a design process, but it must also address several specific technical issues. Design management in general, version control, design storage, databases, the design environment, support tools, frameworks, etc. become essential. Other specific system design issues of growing importance are system partitioning, early design estimation, the design trajectory (top-down, bottom-up, meet in the middle, or iterative in a closed design loop), redesign, and hardware/software codesign.

Integration with other tools at lower levels, also deserves more investigation. Decomposing synthesis into several independent steps requires a flow of information between the associated tools (86). For example, HLS must pass the design along with constraints to logic synthesis and must receive implementation information such as delays and sizes from logic synthesis. Issues such as the level of the interface among tools, the influence of the size and functionality of the partitions, testability aspects, the control scheme, the clock phases, etc. must be considered. Fortunately, the gap between HLS and lower level synthesis is being bridged. Integration of layout aspects into HLS has been addressed elsewhere (14,87). Logic synthesis and HLS are integrated in the YSC (71) and Olympus (20). Furthermore, the discipline of sequential synthesis (88) which includes finite-state machine synthesis and retiming is reducing the distance between HLS and logic synthesis.

The models used in HLS do not have as long a history as lower level models such as Boolean algebra and finite state machines. There is still a lack of general theory and precise semantics. Consequently, formal verification and design for testability are more difficult to formulate exactly and to solve than on lower levels. Much activity is ongoing in this field (89–93).

There also are multiple problems in core areas of HLS such as data path and control synthesis. Special architectures such as pipelined data paths (25,94,95), bit serial architectures (96,97), bussed architectures, and architectures with partitioned busses (98), etc. often allow synthetization of very competitive designs, but they require specialized synthesis techniques. The use of existing large components such as microprocessors in synthesis has been addressed only for a limited set of applications (99). Concurrency, necessary to obtain designs with higher speeds, not only requires specialized data paths (such as pipelines or arrays of processors), but also more complex controllers (consisting of more than one finite state machine) and synchronization techniques.

To allow a comparison of results, a benchmark suit was defined (100). But there are difficulties in the comparison and the assessment of HLS results. Some of them arise from the lack of acceptance of a standard hardware description language and from the lack of single accepted way to measure the results. Others stem from the very nature of high-level synthesis, which targets multiple objectives and uses hardware abstractions which are difficult to compare across systems.

Nevertheless, there is a good understanding of the main issues in high-level synthesis. The models used to formulate the problems are generally accepted. Good algorithms for scheduling and allocation exist. Several large designs synthesized by HLS tools have been reported. Since economic need is certain and the technical viability is proven, HLS techniques are already being integrated into commercial tools and in-house design systems of several companies.

REFERENCES

1. M. C. McFarland, A. C. Parker, and R. Camposano, The High-Level Synthesis of Digital Systems, *Proc. IEEE*, *78* (2), 301–318 (February 1990).
2. T. D. Friedman and S. C. Yang, Methods Used in an Automatic Logic Design Generator (ALERT), *IEEE Transact. Computers*, *C-18* (7), 593–614 (July 1969).
3. J. R. Duley and D. L. Dietmeyer, Translation of a DDL Digital System Specification to Boolean Equations, *IEEE Transact. Computers*, *C-18*, 305–313 (1969).
4. T. D. Friedman and S. C. Yang, Quality of Designs from an Automatic Logic Generator (ALERT), *Proc. 7th Design Automation Conference*, San Francisco, California, 1970, pp. 71–89.
5. M. Barbacci, *Automatic Exploration of the Design Space for Register Transfer (RT) Systems*, thesis, Department of Computer Science, Carnegie-Mellon University, November 1973.
6. S. W. Director, A. C. Parker, D. P. Siewiorek, and D. E. Thomas, A Design Methodology and Computer Aids for Digital VLSI Systems, *IEEE Trans. Circuits Sys.*, *VAS-28* (7), 634–645 (July 1981).
7. G. Zimmermann, *Eine Methode zum Entwurf von Digitalrechnern mit der Programmiersprache MIMOLA*, Informatik-Fachberichte, Vol. 5, Springer Verlag, Berlin, 1976.
8. S. J. Krolikoski, The V-SYNTH System, *Proc. COMPCON* Spring 88, San Francisco, February 1988, pp. 328–331.
9. R. Camposano and W. Rosenstiel, Algorithmische Synthese deterministischer (Petri-) Netze aus Ablaufbeschreibungen digitaler Systeme, Faculty of Computer Science, University of Karlsruhe, Bericht Nr. 22/80, 1980.
10. M. Koster, M. Geiger, and P. Duzy, ASIC Design Using the High-Level Synthesis System CALLAS: A Case Study, *Proc. ICCD'90*, Cambridge, MA, 1990, pp. 141–146.
11. D. E. Thomas and T. E. Fuhrman, Industrial Uses of the System Architect's Workbench. In: *High-Level VLSI Synthesis* (R. Camposano and W. Wolf, eds.), Kluwer Academic Publishers, Boston/Dordrecht/London, 1991, pp. 307–329.
12. R. Sarma, M. D. Dooley, N. C. Newman, and G. Hetherington, High-Level Synthesis: Technology Transfer to Industry. *Proc. 27th DAC*, Orlando, FL, June 1990, pp. 549–554.
13. R. Camposano, R. A. Bergamaschi, C. E. Haynes, M. Payer, and S. M. Wu, The IBM High-Level Synthesis System. In: *High-Level VLSI Synthesis* (R. Camposano and W. Wolf eds.), Kluwer Academic Publishers, Boston/Dordrecht/London, 1991, pp. 79–104.
14. M. C. McFarland and T. J. Kowalski, Incorporating Bottom-Up Design into Hardware Synthesis, *IEEE Transact. CAD*, *9* (9), 938–950 (September 1990).
15. K. Wakabayashi, Cyber: High-Level Synthesis Systems from Software into ASIC. In: *High-Level VLSI Synthesis* (R. Camposano and W. Wolf, eds.), Kluwer Academic Publishers, Boston/Dordrecht/London, 1991, pp. 127–151.
16. Y. Nakamura, K. Oguri, and A. Nagoya, Synthesis from Pure Behavioral Descriptions. In: *High-Level VLSI Synthesis* (R. Camposano and W. Wolf, eds.), Kluwer Academic Publishers, Boston/Dordrecht/London, 1991, pp. 205–229.

17. D. Thomas, E. Lagnese, R. Walker, J. Nestor, J. Rajan, and R. Blackburn, *Algorithmic and Register-Transfer Level Synthesis: The System Architect's Workbench*, Kluwer Academic Publishers, Boston/Dordrecht/London, 1990.

18. B. M. Pangrle and D. D. Gajski, Design Tools for Intelligent Silicon Compilation, *IEEE Transact. CAD*, 6 (6), 1098–1112 (November 1987).

19. J. Granacki, D. Knapp, and A. Parker, The ADAM Advanced Design AutoMation System: Overview, Planner and Natural Language Interface. In: *Proc. 22nd Design Automation Conference*, Las Vegas, June 1985, pp. 727–730.

20. D. C. Ku and G. De Micheli, Synthesis of ASICs with Hercules and Hebe. In: *High-Level Synthesis* (R. Camposano and W. Wolf, eds.), Kluwer Academic Publishers, Boston/Dordrecht/London, 1991, pp. 177–203.

21. R. Camposano and W. Rosenstiel, Synthesizing Circuits from Behavioral Descriptions, *IEEE Transact. CAD*, 8 (2), 171–180 (February 1989).

22. Y. C. Hsu, Y. L. Lin, High-Level Synthesis in the THEDA System. In: *High-Level VLSI Synthesis* (R. Camposano and W. Wolf, eds.), Kluwer Academic Publishers, Boston/Dordrecht/London, 1991, pp. 283–306.

23. J. Rabaey, H. DeMan, J. Vanhoff, G. Goossens, and F. Catthoor, Cathedral II: A Synthesis System for Multiprocessor DSP Systems. In: *Silicon Compilation* (D. Gajski ed.), Addison-Wesley, Reading, MA, 1988, pp. 311–360.

24. J. Huisken et al., Efficient Design of Systems on Silicon with PIRAMID, In: *Logic Architecture Synthesis for Silicon Compilers*, Elsevier, North-Holland, 1989, pp. 299–311.

25. A. E. Casavant, M. A. D'Abreu, M. Dragomirecky, D. A. Duff, J. R. Jasica, M. J. Hartman, K. S. Hwang, and W. D. Smith, A Synthesis Environment for Designing DSP Systems, *IEEE Design Test*, pp. 35–45 (April 1989).

26. D. Gajski and R. Kuhn, Guest's Editors Introduction: New VLSI Tools, *IEEE Computer*, 16 (12), 11–14 (1983).

27. *IEEE Standard VHDL Language Reference Manual*, Institute of Electrical and Electronics Engineers, Inc., New York, March 1988.

28. *Verilog-XL Reference Manual*, Cadence Design Systems, Lowell, MA, 1990.

29. O. Karatsu, VLSI Language Standardization Effort in Japan. In: *Proc. 26th Design Automation Conference*, Las Vegas, June 1989, pp. 50–55.

30. S. D. Johnson, *Synthesis of Digital Design from Recursion Equations*, MIT Press, Cambridge, MA, 1983.

31. A. V. Aho, R. Sethi, and D. D. Ullman, *Compilers: Principles, Techniques and Tools*, Addison-Wesley, Reading, MA, 1986.

32. W. Rosenstiel, Optimizations in High Level Synthesis, *Microprocessing Microprogramming*, 18, 543–549 (1986).

33. R. A. Walker and D. E. Thomas, Design Representation and Transformation in the System Architect's Workbench. In: *Proc. ICCAD'87*, Santa Clara, CA, November 1987, pp. 166–169.

34. H. Trickey, Flamel: A High-Level Hardware Compiler, *IEEE Transact. CAD*, 6 (2) 259–269 (March 1987).

35. S. Davidson, D. Landskov, B. D. Shriver, and P. W. Mallet, Some Experiments in Local Microcode Compaction for Horizontal Machines, *IEEE Transact. Computers*, C-30 (7) 460–477 (July 1981).

36. L. J. Hafer and A. C. Parker, A Formal Method for the Specification, Analysis and Design of Register-Transfer Level Digital Logic, *IEEE Transact. CAD*, 2 (1) 4–18 (January 1983).

37. A. Nicolau, *Percolation Scheduling: A Parallel Compilation Technique*, Department of Computer Science, Cornell University No TR 85-678, Ithaca, NY, May 1985.

38. Z. Peng, Synthesis of VLSI Systems with the CAMAD Design Aid, *Proc. 23rd Design Automation Conference*, ACM/IEEE, June 1986.

39. V. Berstis, The V Compiler: Automatic Hardware Design, *IEEE Des. Test. Comput.*, 8–17 (April 1989).
40. R. Potasaman, J. Lis, A. Nicolau, and D. Gajski, Percolation Based Synthesis, *Proc. 27rd Design Automation Conference*, June 1990, pp. 444–449.
41. R. Camposano, Structural Synthesis in the Yorktown Silicon Compiler. In: *Proc. VLSI'87* (C. H. Sequin ed.), North-Holland, Vancouver, 1988, pp. 61–72.
42. R. Camposano, Behavior-Preserving Transformations for High-Level Synthesis, In: *Proc. Workshop on Hardware Specification, Verification, and Synthesis: Mathematical Aspects* (M. Leeser and G. Brown eds.), Springer Verlag, Berlin, 1989.
43. S. Kirkpatrick, C. D. Gelatti, and M. P. Vecchi, Optimization by Simulated Annaling, *Science*, 220 (4958) (1983).
44. S. Devadas and A. R. Newton, Algorithms for Allocation in Data Path Synthesis, *IEEE Transact. CAD*, 8 (7), 768–781 (July 1989).
45. A. Hemani and A. Postula, A Neural Net Based Self Organising Scheduling Algorithm. In: *Proc. EDAC'90*, Glasgow, Scotland, March 1990, pp. 136–140.
46. C. Y. Hitchcock III and D. E. Thomas, A Method of Automated Data Path Synthesis. In: *Proc. 20th Design Automation Conference*, June 1983, pp. 484–489.
47. M. C. McFarland, Using Bottom-Up Design Techniques in the Synthesis of Digital Hardware from Abstract Behavioral Descriptions. In: *Proc. 23rd Design Automation Conference*, Las Vegas, June 1986, pp. 474–480.
48. J. A. Nestor and D. E. Thomas, Behavioral Synthesis with Interfaces. In *Proc. ICCAD'86*, Santa Clara, CA, November 1986, pp. 112–115.
49. A. C. Parker, J. Pizarro, and M. Mlinar, MAHA: A Program for Datapath Synthesis. In: *Proc. 23rd Design Automation Conference*, Las Vegas, June 1986, pp. 461–466.
50. P. G. Paulin and J. P. Knight, Force-Directed Scheduling in Automatic Data Path Synthesis. In: *Proc. 24th Design Automation Conference*, Miami Beach, FL, June 1987, pp. 195–202.
51. P. G. Paulin and J. P. Knight, Force-Directed Scheduling for the Behavioral Synthesis of ASIC's, *IEEE Transact. CAD*, 8 (6), 661–679 (June 1989).
52. R. Cloutier and D. Thomas, The Combination of Scheduling, Allocation and Mapping in a Single Algorithm. In: *Proc. 27th Design Automation Conference*, Orlando, FL, June 1990, pp. 71–76.
53. R. Camposano, Path-Based Scheduling for Synthesis, *IEEE Transact. CAD*, 10 (1) 85–93 (January 1990).
54. C. J. Tseng, R. S. Wei, S. G. Rothweiler, M. Tong, and A. K. Bose, Bridge: A Versatile Behavioral Synthesis System. In: *Proc. 25th ACM/IEEE Design Automation Conference*, Anaheim, CA, June 1988, pp. 415–420.
55. K. Wakabayashi and T. Yoshimura, A Resource Sharing Control Synthesis Method for Conditional Branches. In: *Proc. ICCAD'89*, Santa Clara, CA, November 1989, pp. 62–65.
56. J. Lee, Y. Hsu, and Y. Lin, A New Integer Linear Programming Formulation for the Scheduling Problem in Data-Path Synthesis. In *Proc. ICCAD'89*, Santa Clara, CA, November 1989.
57. C. H. Gebotys and M. I. Elmasry, Simultaneous Scheduling and Allocation for Cost Constrained Optimal Architectural Synthesis. In: *Proc. 28th ACM/IEEE Design Automation Conference*, San Francisco, CA, June 1991, pp. 2–7.
58. L. Hafer, Constraint Improvements for MILP-Based Hardware Synthesis. In: *Proc. 28th Design Automation Conference*, San Francisco, CA, June 1991, pp. 14–19.
59. M. C. Paul and S. H. Unger, Minimizing the Number of States in Incompletely Specified Sequential Circuits, *IRE Transact. Electron. Computers*, 356–357 (September 1959).
60. R. E. Stearns and J. Hartmanis, On the State Assignment Problem for Sequential Machines II, *IRE Transact. Electron. Computers*, 10, 593–604 (December 1961).

61. G. De Micheli, R. K. Brayton, and A. Sangiovanni-Vincentelli, Optimal State Assignment for Finite State Machines, *IEEE Transact. CAD*, *4* (3) (July 1985).

62. S. Devadas, A. R. Newton, and A. Sangiovanni-Vincentelli, MUSTANG. State Assignment of Finite State Machines Targeting Multi-Level Logic Implementations, *IEEE Transact. CAD*, *7* (12), 1290–1300 (December 1988).

63. A. W. Nagle and A. C. Parker, Algorithms for Multiple-Criteria Design of Micro-Programmed Control Hardware. In: *Proc. 18th DAC*, 1981, pp. 486–493.

64. E. F. Girczyc and J. P. Knight, An ADA to Standard Cell Hardware Compiler based on Graph Grammars and Scheduling, *Proc. ICCD'84*, October 1984.

65. T. J. Kowalski, *An Artificial Intelligence Approach to VLSI Design*, Kluwer, Boston, 1985.

66. G. Goossens, D. Lanneer, J. Vanhoof, J. Rabaey, J. van Meerbergen, and H. DeMan, Optimization-Based Synthesis of Multiprocessor Chips for Digital Signal Processing, with Cathedral-II. In: *Proc. International Workshop on Logic and Architecture Synthesis for Silicon Compilers*, Grenoble, May 1988.

67. B. M. Pangrle, Splicer: A Heuristic Approach to Connectivity Binding. *Proc. 25th Design Automation Conference*, July 1988.

68. P. Marwedel, A New Synthesis Algorithm for the MIMOLA Software System. In: *Proc. 23rd Design Automation Conference*, 1986, pp. 271–277.

69. G. J. Chaitin, M. A. Auslander, A. K. Chandra, J. Cocke, M. E. Hopkins, and P. W. Markstein, Register Allocation via Coloring, *J. Computer Languages*, *6* 47–57 (1981).

70. C. J. Tseng and D. P. Siewiorek. Automated Synthesis of Data Paths in Digital Systems, *IEEE Transact. CAD*, *5* (3) 379–395 (July 1986).

71. R. K. Brayton, R. Camposano, G. DeMicheli, R. H. J. M. Otten, and J. T. J. van Eijndhoven. The Yorktown Silicon Compiler System. In: *Silicon Compilation* (D. Gajski ed.), Addison-Wesley, Reading, MA, 1988.

72. M. C. Golumbic, *Algorithmic Graph Theory and Perfect Graphs*, Academic Press, New York, 1980.

73. F. J. Kurdahi and A. C. Parker, REAL: A Program for Register Allocation. In: *Proc. 24th Design Automation Conference*, ACM/IEEE, June 1987.

74. B. S. Haroun and M. I. Elmasry, Automatic Synthesis of a Multi-Bus Architecture for DSP. In: *Proc. ICCAD'88*, Santa Clara, CA, November 1988, pp. 44–47.

75. L. Stock, Architectural Synthesis and Optimization of Digital Systems, Ph.D. Thesis, University of Eindhoven, 1991.

76. D. L. Springer and D. E. Thomas, Exploiting the Special Structure of Conflict and Compatibility Graphs in High-Level Synthesis. In *Proc. ICCAD-90*, Santa Clara, CA, November 1990, pp. 254–257.

77. M. Balakrishnan, A. K. Majumdar, D. K. Banerji, and J. G. Linders, Allocation of Multi-Port Memories in Data Path Synthesis, *IEEE Transact. CAD*, *7* (4) 536–540 (April 1988).

78. E. D. Lagnese and D. E. Thomas, Architectural Partitioning for System Level Synthesis of Integrated Circuits, *IEEE Transact. CAD*, *10* (7) 847–860 (July 1991).

79. R. Gupta and G. DeMicheli, Partitioning of Functional Models of Synchronous Digital Systems. In: *IEEE Conference on Computer-Aided Design*, Santa Clara, CA, November 1990, pp. 216–219.

80. R. Camposano and R. K. Brayton, Partitioning Before Logic Synthesis. In: *Proc. of the ICCAD'87*, Santa Clara, CA, November 1987, pp. 237–246.

81. M. C. McFarland, Computer-Aided Partitioning of Behavioral Hardware Descriptions. In: *Proc. 20th DAC*, 1983, pp. 472–478.

82. R. Camposano, L. F. Saunders, and R. M. Tabet, High-Level Synthesis from VHDL, *IEEE Des. Test Computers*, March 1991.

83. R. Camposano and A. Kunzmann, Considering Timing Constraints in Synthesis from a Behavioral Description. In: *Proc. ICCD'86*, Port Chester, NY, October 1986, pp. 6–9.

84. G. Borriello, Combining Event and Data-Flow Graphs in Behavioral Synthesis. In: *Proc. ICCAD'88*, Santa Clara, CA, November 1988, pp. 56–59.

85. S. Hayati and A. Parker, Automatic Production of Controller Specifications from Control and Timing Behavioral Descriptions. In: *Proc. 26th Design Automation Conference*, Las Vegas, 1989, pp. 75–80.

86. R. Camposano and L. O. Trevillyan, The Integration of Logic Synthesis and High-Level Synthesis. In: *Proc. ISCAS'89*. IEEE, New York, 1989.

87. D. W. Knapp, Feedback-Driven Datapath Optimization in Fasolt. In: *Proc. ICCAD'90*, Santa Clara, CA, November 1990, pp. 300–303.

88. G. Borriello and A. Sangiovanni-Vincentelli, (eds.), Special Issue on HICCS'89—Sequential Logic Synthesis, *IEEE Transact. CAD*, *10* (1) (January 1991).

89. Ch.A. Papachristou, S. Chiu, and H. Harmanani, A Data Path Synthesis Method for Self-Testable Designs. In: *Proc. 28th ACM/IEEE DAC*, San Francisco, CA, June 1991, pp. 378–384.

90. C. Gebotys and M. Elmasri, VLSI Design Synthesis with Testability. In: *Proc. 25th Design Automation Conference*, June 1988, pp. 16–21.

91. J. R. Burch, E. M. Clarke, K. L. McMillan, and D. L. Dill, Sequential Circuit Verification Using Symbolic Model Checking. In: *Proc. 27th ACM/IEEE DAC*, Orlando, FL, June 1990, pp. 46–51.

92. A. Camilleri, M. Gordon, and T. Melham, *Hardware Verification Using Higher-Order Logic. From HDL Descriptions to Guaranteed Correct Circuit Designs.* (D. Borrione ed.), Elsevier, North-Holland, 1987, pp. 43–67.

93. F. Corella, R. Camposano, R. Bergamaschi, and M. Payer, Verification of Synchronous Sequential Circuits Obtained from Algorithmic Specifications. In: *Proc. CHDL'91*, Marseille, France, April 1991, pp. 209–227.

94. N. Park and A. C. Parker, SEHWA: A Program for Synthesis of Pipelines, *Proc. 23rd Design Automation Conference*, Las Vegas, June 1986, pp. 454–460.

95. C. C. Chu et al., Hyper, An Interactive Synthesis Environment for High-Performance Real Time Applications. In: *Proc. ICCD*, Cambridge, MA, October 1989, pp. 432–435.

96. P. Denyer and D. Renshaw, *VLSI Processing: A Bit Serial Approach*, Addison-Wesley, Reading, MA, 1985.

97. R. Hartley and J. Jasica, Behavioral to Structural Translation in a Bit-Serial Silicon Compiler, *IEEE Transact. CAD*, *7* (8), 877–886 (August 1988).

98. C. Ewering, Automatic High Level Synthesis of Partitioned Busses. In: *Proc. ICCAD'90*, Santa Clara, CA, November 1990, pp. 304–307.

99. W. P. Birmingham, A. P. Gupta, and D. P. Siewiorek, MICON: Automated Design of Computer Systems. In: *High-Level VLSI Synthesis* (R. Camposano and W. Wolf, eds.), Kluwer Academic Publishers, Boston/Dordrecht/London, 1991, pp. 307–329.

100. Benchmarks for the Fifth ACM/IEEE International Workshop on High-Level Synthesis, (Available through electronic mail at HLSW@ics.uci.edu), Buehlerhoehe, Germany, March 1991).

INTRODUCTORY BIBLIOGRAPHY

Books

Camposano, R. and W. Wolf, (ed.), *High-Level VLSI Synthesis*, Kluwer Academic Publishers, Boston/Dordrecht/London, 1991.

Gajski, D. (ed.) *Silicon Compilation*, Addison-Wesley, Reading, MA, 1988.

Thomas, D., E. Lagnese, R. Walker, J. Nestor, J. Rajan, and R. Blackburn, *Algorithmic and Register-Transfer Level Synthesis: The System Architect's Workbench*, Kluwer Academic Publishers, Boston/Dordrecht/London, 1990.

Walker, R. A. and R. Camposano, *A Survey of High-Level Synthesis Systems*, Kluwer Academic Publishers, Boston/Dordrecht/London, 1991.

Overview Articles

McFarland, M. C., A. C. Parker, and R. Camposano, Tutorial on High-Level Synthesis. In: *Proc. 25th DAC*, Anaheim, CA, June 1988, pp. 330–336.

McFarland, M. C., A. C. Parker, and R. Camposano, The High-Level Synthesis of Digital Systems. In: *Proc. IEEE*, 78 (2), 301–318 (February 1990).

R. Camposano, From Behavior to Structure: High-Level Synthesis, *IEEE Des. Test Computers*, 7 (5), 8–19 (October 1990).

RAUL CAMPOSANO

INTELLIGENT COMPUTER-AIDED DESIGN

INTRODUCTION

There are many activities that we refer to as design. We normally consider it to be "synthesis." However, a large design task can involve much "analysis" too. Design is an intelligent human activity requiring many skills and much knowledge. Design problems can be solved by individuals or by teams. They may take minutes or years to resolve. Design occurs in a wide variety of domains, ranging from the design of a Nuclear Power Plant to that of a mounting bracket, and from a computer to a ship. In this article we will focus on mechanical design. Given this enormous variety of problems and domains, it is important to try to define what is meant by design.

The general design process is often characterized as mapping *needs* to *function* to *structure*. It is carried out using many different types of reasoning and many different sources of knowledge. In general, design is the process of specifying a description of an artifact that satisfies a collection of constraints. These constraints may arise from a variety of sources.

Constraints may be imposed by the problem, the designer, the manufacturer, the user, or by natural laws. They reflect the desired function of the artifact, the available resources (e.g., money), the physical limitations of the materials (e.g., strength), the demands on the artifact from the environment in which it will be used (e.g., maintainability), the manufacturing processes required, general design criteria (e.g., simplicity), and the design process itself (1).

The term "constraint" usually means something which is either satisfied or not. For the definition above we need to extend the meaning to include "softer" restrictions such as preferences. In addition, there are usually special objectives to be met, such as to minimize cost, weight, or area. These act throughout the design process, and can be used for evaluation of the design. Not all these varied requirements need to be specified initially. It is a characteristic of many design problems that new constraints emerge as decisions are made.

REASONS FOR STUDY

Because design is an ill-structured activity requiring intelligence, it is a suitable topic of study for AI. Simon (2, p. 83) even goes far as to say that "the proper study of mankind is the science of design."

A fundamental hypothesis shared by most design researchers who use AI is that there are core reasoning mechanisms, and types of knowledge, that are common across domains (3). That is, although design problems in different domains require different domain knowledge, there are underlying similarities in the form of that knowledge and in the way it is used. Of course, different domains and different design problems will require a different mix. For example, designing a mechanism might require a lot of spatial reasoning in three dimensions, whereas designing a circuit would require very little.

Investigating that fundamental hypothesis will result in a better understanding of what design actually is. This should then allow us to build useful intelligent computer-aided design (IntCAD) systems to do or to support design activity. Systems can range from autonomous design tools, that when given requirements will produce designs, to design aids that interact with a human designer. Systems have been built for many different domains, such as VLSI, graphical interfaces, electronic circuits, protein purification processes, elevators, computers, air cylinders, aluminum alloys, construction sites, molecular genetics experiments, copier paper paths, and high-rise buildings (see Refs. 4–6 for discussion of most of these systems).

HISTORY

Computers have contributed to design for quite a while by providing analysis tools (e.g., the finite-element method), data bases (e.g., of drawings and components), and computer-aided drafting/drawing tools. The latter comes naturally to mind when CAD is mentioned, as such tools have been under development since the early 1960s. Their progress runs parallel to that of computer graphics (7).

Two-dimensional drafting tools, and 3-D display of objects as "wire-frames," were followed by raster displays. The capability to display a shaded image, along with developments in geometric modelling (8) allowed designers to consider objects on the screen as "real." They were able to concentrate on decisions about objects rather than about drawings. This is much closer to computer-aided *design*, as opposed to computer-aided *drafting*.

From its inception, CAD has gradually become concerned with representing increasing amounts about the objects being manipulated. Geometric information has moved from 2-D to 3-D, and from planar to curved surfaces. Information about surface finish and color has been added. Geometric and topological models specify the structural relationships between components. Descriptions of form features can be included. Application-specific information, such as material properties or manufacturing requirements is also useful.

Thus CAD representations have gradually been moving closer to being a knowledge representation, to include all aspects of knowledge about the designed object. Suitable additions would be precise part–whole relations (9), and the representation of function (10). Researchers are concerned with what needs to be represented to support IntCAD systems (11).

An additional type of information that has been added to CAD systems is the constraint. Constraints restrict the possible values of parameters. In 2-D, a constraint might be added to require that two lines be maintained at a certain angle. In 3-D, one could constrain two solids to always touch. When constraints are used, a single change can propagate through constraints to produce new values for many other parameters, effectively generating a whole new design. Thus, constraint satisfaction provides a parametric design capability (i.e., the system "designs" values for some parameters). Companies such as Cognition and ICAD were able to base commercial products on this idea. With these developments, CAD has gradually turned from being mainly concerned with object representation toward consideration of the design process (i.e., design process knowledge as opposed to design object knowledge).

As most designers can be considered to be experts, systems that design can be considered to be expert systems. Until quite recently, much of the expert systems research was concerned with diagnosis, and tools and techniques with which to build diagnostic systems. Now, design has become an important area to study, with a burgeoning literature. (3–6,12–22). Other books and papers can be found in Additional Reading.

Expert systems technology has allowed many new, practical applications. For example, in addition to systems that produce designs, systems can be built to check design decisions for conformance with standards or with company guidelines. Systems can be used to extract features, to select materials, to discover design flaws and suggest corrections, and to evaluate the manufacturability or constructability of the design.

ROLES FOR KNOWLEDGE-BASED REASONING IN DESIGN

These applications hint at the many roles that knowledge-based techniques and systems can play during design. Some of them are presented below. Each provides a particular function, and can be implemented in different ways using AI techniques.

Abstraction can be used to discover of which more general design the current design is an example. This might lead to a better understanding of which design plans or analysis methods to use.

Acquisition can request and integrate new design knowledge.

Analysis, which is often numerical, is needed to understand the properties (such as strength) of the design or of subcomponents.

Association allows related concepts to be discovered, and supports analogical reasoning.

Basic synthesis produces values for attributes, such as color or length, by calculation, or by decision.

Classification can be used to categorize the requirements or the current state of the design in order to decide what sort of method or analysis might be used.

Criticism compares a portion of the design against a standard, or some preferences, and points out the ways in which it is lacking. When design requirements are used this can be called "verification."

Decomposition divides a design problem into smaller more manageable subproblems.

Estimation can be used to produce design values which are roughly right, in order to discover more about the design problem.

Evaluation uses the results of analysis, or some aspects of the design, to provide an estimate of quality or the degree to which it meets some design goals (e.g., low cost).

Execution follows the instructions given in a design plan.

Extraction can be used to find features of the design that can be used for analysis or evaluation.

Generation of acceptable candidate values that can be used for the design might be done by "Constraint Satisfaction."

Guidance provides the designer with a methodology to be followed and can enforce it.

Learning can improve the resulting designs, or can improve the design process, making it more efficient (such as in "Knowledge Compilation") or more knowledgeable.

Memory allows a design history to be maintained that captures the intent or rationale of the designer. It can be used to remember successful methods or designs as cases for case-based reasoning.

Negotiation provides a way for a team of experts, or expert systems, to arrive at a design which is acceptable to all parties.

Note Making occurs when a designer makes a mental note at some early stage of the design to do or check something later during the design process (23). It might correspond to forming a new constraint.

Notification is used to communicate the consequences of a design decision in order to affect other portions of the design (as in "Constraint Propagation").

Optimization, usually numeric, can produce the best values for design attributes, relative to some criteria that can be evaluated.

Patching can be used to modify an existing design after flaws have been found in it.

Planning the design process, in order to design subcomponents in an appropriate order, for example, is a vital part of design in general.

Prediction is often needed to determine the consequences of a design decision. It might be done by "qualitative reasoning" or some other form of "knowledge-based simulation."

Presentation of information about the current state of the design, or about standards, for example, is important for assisting the human designer.

Recomposition takes finished designs for subcomponents and composes them into a component design.

Refinement occurs when a description (e.g., of a function) is mapped to a less abstract description (e.g., of a class of mechanisms).

Retraction allows previous design decisions to be discarded. This could be done using some form of "Backtracking."

Reuse, by "Analogy", or its weaker cousin "case-based reasoning," can save effort by reusing past methods or designs.

Selection is a major component of configuration. It can also be used to pick an appropriate plan or analysis method.

Simplification of the problem can be carried out by ignoring details, for example, by ignoring or "relaxing" less important constraints, or by noticing regularities. It might also be done by combining constraints (as in "Constraint Subsumption") (24).

Suggestions, generated after criticism, can provide information to guide the patching, or any other redesign activity.

APPROACHES TO DESIGN STUDY

The IntCAD research community now consists of CAD researchers, who use AI techniques to expand the capabilities of CAD systems; AI researchers, who study design knowledge and reasoning; engineers, who are eager to use smarter tools; and cognitive scientists, who study how designers think. Consequently, the literature on AI in design is spread quite widely.

Finger and Dixon (18,19), from a mechanical engineering point of view, describe design research as falling into several categories. These include: descriptive models, languages, representations, environments, and computer-based models. Descriptive models of the design process are concerned with the ''processes, strategies, and problem-solving methods designers use.'' These efforts include collecting protocols from designers, building cognitive models that could mimic the human designer, and collecting and analyzing design cases. Such studies have revealed, for example, the importance of drawing in design and the many roles, such as ''memory aid,'' that it plays (25). Languages and representations research includes the representation of form, of function and behavior, and of features. Work on environments attempts to build systems that aid the designer during the design process by providing an integrated set of tools. Computer-based models research is concerned with how the computer can design or assist with designing. AI-based design research is mostly associated with the languages, representations, and computer-based models categories.

TYPES OF DESIGN

In books and papers about design problem solving we find many terms for types of design, including: Preliminary, Conceptual, Functional, Innovative, Creative, Routine, Embodiment, Parametric, Detailed, Redesign, Non-Routine, and Configuration. However, there seems to be a general acceptance of the rough classification of design into routine, innovative, and creative, where each class has less known in advance by the designer. In routine design both the knowledge sources and the problem-solving strategies are known in advance. In innovative design, only the knowledge sources are known in advance. While in creative design neither are known.

For *routine* design, everything about the design process, including the knowledge needed, must be known in advance. This does not mean that either the specific design solution, or the pattern of use of the knowledge (i.e., the design trace) are completely known in advance. The underlying thesis is that design tasks become routine due to learning brought about by repetition of similar problem solving. That is, routineness is a direct reflection of experience. Routine designs are done more efficiently, and possibly with better results.

In fact, this three-class model is much too simple. The level of experience with a certain type of design can be reflected by a position on a Routine → Non-Routine axis—with ''very experienced'' at one end, and ''very inexperienced' '' at the other (see Brown in Ref. 26). An orthogonal Conceptual → Parametric axis can be used to show the abstractness of the decisions being made. Types of design are points in the space defined by the axes.

Conceptual design means that the kind of things being decided at that point in the design are abstract (i.e., conceptual). For example, that the design requirements can be satisfied by an object providing a particular function. In *parametric* design we mean that the things being decided are values for a prespecified set of attributes.

Another way of classifying design problems is to divide them into those that have subtask ordering decided a priori, those that know the dependencies in advance, but order them during the design, and those for which the dependencies between subtasks are both discovered and ordered during the design (27). We would expect routine problems to belong to the first type, and very nonroutine problems to belong to the third.

In Dixon's taxonomy of design problems (28), the levels are named *functional*, *phenomenological*, *embodiment*, *attribute*, and *parametric*, depending on whether function, physical principles, general class of solution, type of object, or parameter values are decided at that level. Clearly, these levels correspond to portions of the Conceptual → Parametric axis.

In general, design activity can start at any level of abstraction and finish at any more specific level. Usually, the larger the gap between the level of the specification and the desired level for the design, the harder the design process is. Dixon states that Conceptual design is often used to describe moving from the Function level to the Embodiment level. He considers preliminary design to be an extension of conceptual design to another level of specificity, i.e., to Artifact Type. Parametric design goes from artifact type level to the artifact instance level. As we move along the Conceptual → Parametric axis less structure needs to be decided during the design process.

In *configuration*, which is a restricted form of design, the components of the designed object can only come from a predefined set (29). They are selected and arranged together to satisfy some requirements. Each component describes the connections which it allows. It usually is not possible or practical to predetermine all possible configurations (30). Often, artifacts are configured according to a known functional architecture, and certain components can be predetermined as ''key.'' These assumptions help to prune the search for a configuration.

Depending on the complexity of the problem, the components may or may not need to have values provided for parameters. For example, a layout (or floor-planning) problem may just be concerned with spatial arrangement, but a resistor may need to be given a resistance value. Note that no new components are used, and a component's connectivity is not changed.

Rough design is an attempt to learn something additional about the design problem by deciding some aspects of the design and then evaluating that partial design. In a more routine design situation, ''those values on which much of the rest of the design depends'' are known by the designer and can be decided and checked first (17). Other senses of ''rough,'' other than ''incomplete,'' are ''abstract'' and ''approximate.'' Interval arithmetic may be able to contribute to approximate design (31). Abstract designs are hard to evaluate. However, Tong (24) suggests that information about ''potential bottlenecks with respect to some resource'' (such as the number of components needed) might be gathered by the formation and execution of abstract design plans.

Redesign problems are concerned with changing prior design decisions. This includes modifying an existing design in response to changing requirements, and making changes to decisions already made, during the design process, as a result of failing constraints (32–35). This can involve using suggestions about suitable changes, that are either prestored or generated by analyzing the situation. A record of the reasons for the prior design decisions (i.e., a design history) is also useful. A particular form of parametric redesign is *iterative redesign*, where an initial heuristically generated design is modified one parameter value at a time (36,37). After each modification an evaluation step leads to a suggestion about which parameter to change next and in which direction. This hill-climbing approach can be controlled by meta-knowledge to try to ensure that it keeps improving its solution and approaches a global optimum.

CHARACTERIZING THE DESIGN PROCESS

One goal of AI research in design is to try to characterize the design process in enough detail that systems can be built more easily, that design knowledge can be acquired more easily, and that design tools can be matched to design problems. At some level of abstraction, the description above of the possible roles for knowledge-based reasoning in design could be used to provide a vocabulary with which to describe design activity. The challenge is to fully describe each function, to characterize the knowledge each uses, to describe their inputs and outputs, to list their alternative implementations (using AI methods), and to discover distinctive patterns of use.

Many people would agree that the general flow of design can be characterized by *Requirements Formulation + Synthesis + Analysis + Evaluation*. There are very many similar models in the design literature. Unfortunately, this characterization is too abstract and does little to help us build computer models. For example, analysis could be done by many methods, such as quantitative simulation or qualitative simulation.

Tong (24) provides an analysis based on characterizing certain kinds of design as *incremental refinement*, where specifications can be converted to implementations (i.e., a design) "directly," via multiple refinements, possibly using "abstraction levels" and "decomposition," with details being provided by *constrained inference*, and corrections being provided by *debugging*.

Chandrasekaran (see Ref. 3, p. 59) attempts to characterize a large family of design tasks as: *Propose + Critique + Modify*. Each "subtask" can be carried out by different methods. For the Propose subtask he discussed *Decomposition + Solution Composition*, for recursively reducing the problem, and *Case Retrieval* and *Constraint Satisfaction* for solving the problems or subproblems.

In a similar proposal, McDermott (see Ref. 38, p. 225) argues that there are a set of methods "where each method defines the roles that the task-specific knowledge it requires must play and the forms in which that knowledge can be represented" [p. 228]. His *Propose + Revise* method first extends the design, then identifies constraint violations, suggests potential fixes, selects the least costly fix to try, tries the fix, identifies resulting constraint violations, if there are any it loops to select another fix, and if there are none it tidies up and loops to extend the design again, until it is completed. This is a method to achieve constraint satisfaction. He also suggests an *extrapolate-from-a-similar-case* method.

Balkany et al. (25) make a "knowledge-level" analysis and comparison of several design systems—that is, they attempt to isolate the behavior of each system from techniques used to implement that behavior. The systems are AIR-CYL (17), M1 (39), PRIDE (4a), VT (4b), and SightPlan (40). For each system, they characterize its action in terms of sequences of "mechanisms," such as *extend-design, find-constraints, test-constraints, suggest-fixes, select-fix, modify-design, find-constraint, test-constraints, propagate-changes, test-if-done*. This sequence, from the VT system, corresponds to McDermott's propose & revise method.

USING AI TECHNIQUES

In this section we discuss how some AI techniques might be used to implement functions that play roles in the building of design systems. We will refer to only some of the AI in design research, and have assumed that more information is available from other entries in this encyclopedia.

Knowledge Representation

In design, many types of knowledge can be used, not all of which can be alluded to here. Knowledge about things, knowledge about design requirements, and knowledge about processes are all useful. Knowledge about both the object being designed (e.g., 3.45 cm long), and general object knowledge (e.g., all #26 flanges have a 3:2 height-to-length ratio) needs to be represented. Frame representations are popular. The basic knowledge, about components concerns geometry and topology. Taxonomies of components and Part–Subpart descriptions need to be represented. Other information that needs to be stored are attributes such as color, hardness, material, and surface finish. Properties of material must be available. Features can relate to form and to function (41). Descriptions of function and behavior (10,42) are useful during conceptual design, for criticism (43), and for reasoning about mechanisms (44). Functional hierarchies are useful for reducing search during configuration (29,39).

Knowledge about the capabilities of processes are important if the design system needs to select an appropriate method. This can be as simple as picking a prestored plan, or as sophisticated as reasoning about which design method is most likely to be able to produce the desired result. Other knowledge can be about which decision should take priority (45), how to decompose a problem, or what tradeoffs might be made between conflicting goals (24).

Constraint Satisfaction

Constraints can be used to maintain consistency, prune search, and to record interactions between subproblems. They can express many things, including design heuristics, basic equations, material compatibility, and physical limits on components due to strength or manufacturing. Many constraints refer to parameters with numerical values (e.g., $L < 12$), but reference to symbols is possible (e.g., $M = $ one-of{Brass Steel Wood}). Adding constraints to the design as a result of making decisions is "constraint formulation." The creation of new constraints from old is "constraint subsumption." Decisions can be communicated by "constraint propagation," or by propagating acceptable values. Propagation enables a "least commitment" strategy. There are several approaches to "constraint satisfaction," that is, finding values that satisfy a set of constraints. Many problems can be solved using these methods (4c,45,46). In some design problems, variables and constraints emerge during the design (47). The use of constraints to handle large design problems has been criticized as being too computationally expensive, and not a good model of human problem-solving.

Search

In general, design cannot be completely modelled by a standard heuristic search, as evaluation functions are not always available, and as, at best, several search spaces are required—such as possible plans, possible configurations, and possible combinations of parameter values. In addition, not all problems have fully specified requirements that can act as goals or goal recognizers for a search. However, despite the often exploratory nature of conceptual design, much of design can be described as search.

The maintenance of consistency during the search for a design can be handled using Truth Maintenance methods. These are especially useful in situations where assumptions are made during the design. Chronological or dependency-directed backtracking can be used. Dependencies between design decisions can be explicitly recorded and used for backtracking, but they can also serve as a form of design history, for possible subsequent redesign or case-based reasoning. They can also serve as the basis for a truth maintenance system (TMS).

Learning

Some researchers, especially those interested in automatic generation of design tools, have used a learning mechanism with a simple search to learn problem decompositions, or with Generate & Test to improve the generator by moving knowledge from the Test back into the generator (see Ref. 48 for references to these and other systems). These are examples of *Knowledge Compilation* systems, which learn in order to increase efficiency (49,50). Other work on learning in design includes: the learning apprentice, LEAP, which learns design "refinement rules" by generalizing the user's input (see 48); the Designer-Soar system that learns to design algorithms (51); and Bridger, which learns to classify designs for reuse (52).

Case-Based Reasoning and Analogy

The use of previous designs or design plans can reduce the amount of search-time. Mostow (53) discusses the replaying of design plans, and compares some systems, including BOGART and ARGO (see Mostow et al. and Huhns and Acosta in Ref. 6), according to how cases are represented, stored, retrieved, and adapted. Case-based design is also discussed by Sycara et al. and by Goel (see both in Ref. 6). An engineering view of design history keeping can be found in (Chen et al. 54). Gero (see Ref. 3, p. 26) proposes that design cases and all other design knowledge be organized into Schema for efficient access during design.

Qualitative Reasoning

During the design process, qualitative reasoning techniques can be used to reason about space, flows—such as heat, fluid, or force—and, more generally, behavior. Required motions can determine shape (55), shape can be used to derive behavior (see Ref. 56, p. 597), and objects can be checked for fit (57). Innovative design is possible by mapping a network of qualitative interactions between quantities onto physical structures (58). In order to organize and move easily from one model of an object to another (e.g., from a heat flow model to a kinematic model) the use of a Metamodel (59) and a Graph of Models have been proposed (see Ref. 56 p. 546).

Blackboards

Blackboard-based architectures are useful for the integration of many sources of knowledge, such as in building design (5,60).

SAMPLE SYSTEMS

Most of the well-analyzed systems are fine for routine tasks. Besides systems already mentioned, XCON (30) and VEXED (24) deserve study. Some systems have been generalized to provide expert system shells. These include DSPL from AIR-CYL, EDESYN from HI-RISE (61), and EVEXED from VEXED. Other systems for less-routine design include, MOLGEN (45), DONTE (24), DESIGNER (62), EDISON (63) and AM (64).

RESEARCH ISSUES

In such a complex and poorly understood area as design, there are many research issues. In addition to basic work on representing features, function, and other aspects of design objects, it will be necessary to devise ways to integrate these types of knowledge, so that reasoning processes can use them fully. Languages are needed with which to express an expert's knowledge of design. Both learning (including knowledge compilation) and knowledge acquisition (38) for design systems are vital. The use of neural networks needs to be studied, for functions such as case classification or selection. More work is needed in creative design. This requires doing much more reasoning at "design time." Consequently, representing and reasoning about goals, dealing with alternative designs, reasoning about resources, analogy, problem decomposition, evaluation of partial designs, dynamic constraint satisfaction, functional reasoning, using multiple models, combining quantitative and qualitative reasoning, model-based reasoning, and reasoning about failure, all become major issues. Large design problems will require cooperative, and perhaps distributed, design problem-solvers, as well as negotiation (65).

RESEARCH CENTERS

Papers presenting overviews of the work at Carnegie-Mellon University, Rutgers University, the University of Sydney, Worcester Polytechnic Institute, the University of Illinois, Edinburgh University, North Carolina State University, and Wayne State University can be found in volumes edited by Gero (46,66). Other major centers include the University of Tokyo, the University of Massachusetts, MIT, the University of Michigan, and the Engineering Design Research Centers in the United Kingdom.

REFERENCES

1. T. Mitchell and J. Mostow, Artificial Intelligence and Design, Tutorial TP2 In: *Proc. The 6th Natl. Conf. on AI*, AAAI-87, Seattle, WA, July, 1987.
2. M. Simon, *The Sciences of the Artificial*, MIT Press, Cambridge, MA, 1969.
3. M. L. Maher and J. S. Gero, *AI Magazine*, Special issue on AI based design systems, AAAI, *11* (4) (Winter 1990).
4. (a) S. Mittel and Araya, in *Artificial Intelligence in Engineering Design*: Vol. I *Representation: Structure, Function and Constraints*; *Routine Design*, (C. Tong and D. Sriram, eds.), Academic Press, New York, 1991; (b) S. Marcus et al., *ibid*; (c) L. I. Steinberg, Ibid.
5. D. Sriram, in *Artificial Intelligence in Engineering Design* Vol. II: *Knowledge Acquisition*; *Commercial Systems*; *Integrated Environments*, (C. Tong and D. Sriram, eds.), Academic Press, New York, 1991.
6. D. Sriram and C. Tong (eds.), *Artificial Intelligence in Engineering Design*: Vol. II—*Models of Innovative Design*; *Reasoning About Physical Systems*; *Reasoning About Geometry*. Academic Press, New York, 1991.
7. J. D. Foley, A. van Dam, S. K. Feiner, and J. F. Hughes, *Computer Graphics: Principles and Practice*, 2nd ed., Addison-Wesley, Reading, MA, 1990.

8. M. Mantyla, *An Introduction to Solid Modelling*, Computer Science Press, Inc., New York, 1988.

9. M. E. Winston, R. Chaffin, and D. Herrmann, A Taxonomy of Part-Whole Relations, *Cognitive Sci.*, *11*, 417–444 (1987).

10. V. Sembugamoorthy and B. Chandrasekaran, Functional Representation of Devices and Compilation of Diagnostic Problem Solving Systems, *Experience, Memory and Reasoning* (J. Kolodner and C. Riesbeck, eds.), Erlbaum, Hillside, NJ, 1986, pp. 47–73.

11. F. Arbab, Features and Geometric Reasoning. *Intelligent CAD, II* (H. Yoshikawa and T. Holden, eds.), North-Holland, Amsterdam, 1990, pp. 45–65.

12. J. S. Gero (ed.), *Knowledge Engineering in Computer-Aided Design*, North-Holland, Amsterdam, 1985.

13. J. Mostow, Towards Better Models of the Design Process, *AI Magazine*, *6*(1), 44–57 (1985).

14. S. J. Hong (ed.), *IEEE Computer*, Special issue on Expert Systems in Engineering, *19*(7), 1986.

15. J. S. Gero (ed.), *Expert Systems in Computer-Aided Design*, North-Holland, Amsterdam, 1987.

16. M. D. Rychener (ed.), *Expert Systems for Engineering Design*, Academic Press, Inc., New York, 1988.

17. D. C. Brown and B. Chandrasekaran, *Design Problem Solving: Knowledge Structures and Control Strategies*. Research Notes in Artificial Intelligence Series, Morgan Kaufmann Publishers, Inc., San Francisco, 1989.

18. S. Finger and J. R. Dixon, A Review of Research in Mechanical Engineering Design, Part I: Descriptive, Prescriptive, and Computer-Based Models of Design, *Res. Eng. Des. 1*, 51–67 (1989).

19. S. Finger and J. R. Dixon, A Review of Research in Mechanical Engineering Design, Part II: Representations, Analysis, and Design for the Life Cycle, *Res. Eng. Des. 1*, 121–137 (1989).

20. R. D. Coyne, M. A. Rosenman, A. D. Radford, M. Balachandran, and J. S. Gero, *Knowledge-Based Design Systems*, Addison-Wesley, Reading, MA, 1990.

21. C. L. Dym and R. E. Levitt, *Knowledge-Based Systems in Engineering*, McGraw-Hill, Inc., New York, 1991.

22. M. Green (ed.), *Knowledge Aided Design*, Academic Press, New York, 1991.

23. B. Adelson and E. Soloway, The Role of Domain Experience in Software Design, *Transact. Software Eng. SE-11*(11), 1351–1360 (1985).

24. C. Tong, Toward an Engineering Science of Knowledge-Based Design, *AI Eng.*, *2*(3), 133–166 (1987).

25. D. G. Ullman, S. Wood, and D. Craig, The Importance of Drawings in the Mechanical Design Process, *Computers and Graphics*, *14*(2), 263–274 (1990).

26. M. Waldron and K. Waldron (eds.), *Mechanical Design: Theory and Methodology*, Springer-Verlag, New York, 1991.

27. A. Balkany, W. P. Birmingham, and I. D. Tommelein, A Knowledge-Level Analysis of Several Design Tools, *Artificial Intelligence in Design '91*, Butterworth-Heinemann Publishers, Edinburgh, 1991.

28. J. R. Dixon, M. R. Duffey, R. K. Irani, K. L. Meunier, and M. F. Orelup, A Proposed Taxonomy of Mechanical Design Problems. In: *Proc. ASME Computers in Engineering Conf.*, San Francisco, CA 1988, Vol. 1, pp. 41–46.

29. S. Mittal and F. Frayman, Towards a Generic Model of Configuration Tasks. In: *Proc. 11th Intl. Jnt. Conf. on AI*, IJCAI-89, Morgan Kaufmann Publishers, San Francisco, 1989, Vol. 2, pp. 1395–1401.

30. V. E. Barker and D. E. O'Connor, Expert Systems for Configuration at Digital: XCON and Beyond, *Commun. ACM*, *32* (3), 298–318 (March 1989).

31. D. Navinchandra and J. Rinderle, Interval Methods for Concurrent Evaluation of Design Constraints, *Proc. of the ASME Ann. Conf.*, Symposium on Concurrent Product and Process Design, 1989.

32. F. Daube and B. Hayes-Roth, A Case-Based Mechanical Redesign System. In: *Proc. 11th Int. Jnt. Conf. on AI*, IJCAI-89, Morgan Kaufmann, San Francisco, 1989, Vol. 2, pp. 1402–1407.

33. A. Goel and B. Chandrasekaran, Functional Representation of Designs and Redesign Problem Solving. In: *Proc. 11th Int. Jnt. Conf. on AI*, IJCAI-89, Morgan Kaufmann, San Francisco, 1989, Vol. 2, pp. 1388–1394.

34. D. C. Brown, Failure Handling in a Design Expert System, *Computer-Aided Design J.* Special edition (November 1985).

35. L. I. Steinberg and T. M. Mitchell, The Redesign System: A Knowledge-Based Approach to VLSI CAD, *IEEE Design & Test*, 45–54 (February 1985).

36. M. F. Orelup, J. R. Dixon, P. R. Cohen and M. K. Simmons, Dominic II: Meta-Level Control in Iterative Redesign. In: *Proc. 7th Natl. Conf. on AI*, AAAI, St. Paul, MN, Morgan Kaufmann, San Francisco, 1988, Vol. 1. pp. 25–30.

37. N. Ramachandran, A. Shah, and N. A. Langrana, Expert System Approach in Design of Mechanical Components, *Proc. ASME Int. Computers in Eng. Conf.*, San Francisco, CA, 1988, pp. 1–10.

38. S. Marcus (ed.), *Automating Knowledge Acquisition for Expert Systems*, Kluwer Academic Publishers, Dordrecht, 1988.

39. W. P. Birmingham, A. P. Gupta, and D. P. Siewiorek, The MICON System for Computer Design, *IEEE Micro*, 9(5), 61–67 (October 1989).

40. I. D. Tommelein, R. E. Levitt, B. Hayes-Roth, and T. Confrey, SightPlan Experiments: Alternative Strategies for Site Layout Design, *J. Computing Civil Eng.*, ASCE (January 1991).

41. J. R. Dixon, J. J. Cunningham, and M. K. Simmons, Research in Designing with Features, *Intelligent CAD, I* (H. Yoshikawa and D. Gossard eds.), North-Holland, Amsterdam, 1989, pp. 137–148.

42. K. T. Ulrich and W. P. Seering, Synthesis of Schematic Descriptions in Mechanical Design, *Res. Eng. Des.*, 1(1), 3 (1989).

43. K. Lai and W. R. D. Wilson, "FDL—A Language for Function Description and Rationalization in Mechanical Design, *Proc. Int. Computers in Eng. Conf.*, ASME, 1 87–94 (1987).

44. P. Pu and N. I. Badler, Design Knowledge Capturing for Device Behavior Reasoning, *Artificial Intelligence in Engineering: Design* (J. S. Gero ed.), Elsevier, New York, 1988, pp. 37–56.

45. M. Stefik, Planning with Constraints (MOLGEN: Part 1 and Part 2), *Artificial Intelligence*, 16(2) 111–169, 1980.

46. Bower and O'Grady in *Applications of AI in Engineering V, Design, Proc. 5th Int. Conf. on Applications of AI in Engineering*, (J. S. Gero ed.), Boston, MA, Computational Mechanics Publications & Springer-Verlag, New York, 1990.

47. S. Mittal and B. Falkenhainer, Dynamic Constraint Satisfaction Problems, *Proc. 8th Natl. Conf. on AI*, AAAI Press & MIT Press, Boston 1990, Vol. 1, pp. 25–32.

48. C. Tong, Knowledge-Based Design as an Engineering Science: the Rutgers AI/Design Project. In: *Applications of AI in Engineering V, Design* (J. S. Gero ed.), *Proc. 5th Int. Conf. on Appl. of AI in Eng.*, Boston, MA, Computational Mechanics Publications & Springer-Verlag, New York, 1990, pp. 297–319.

49. R. M. Keller, Applying Knowledge Compilation Techniques to Model-Based Reasoning, *IEEE Expert*, Special issue, *Knowledge Compilation: A Symposium* (A. K. Goel ed.), 6(2) (April 1991).

50. D. C. Brown, Compilation: The Hidden Dimension of Design Systems, *Intelligent CAD, III*, (H. Yoshikawa and F. Arbab, eds.) North-Holland, Amsterdam, 1991.

51. D. Steier and A. Newell, Integrating, Multiple Sources of Knowledge into Designer-Soar, an Automatic Algorithm Designer. In: *Proc. 7th Natl. Conf. on AI*, AAAI, St. Paul, MN, Morgan Kaufmann, San Francisco, 1988, Vol. 1, pp. 9–13.

52. Y. Reich, Design Knowledge Acquisition: Task Analysis and a Partial Implementation, *Knowledge Acquisition*, 1991.

53. J. Mostow, Design by Derivational Analogy: Issues in the Automated Replay of Design Plans. In: *Machine Learning: Paradigms and Methods*, MIT Press, Boston & Elsevier, New York, 1990, pp. 119–184.

54. A. Chen, B. McGinnis, and D. G. Ullman, Design History Knowledge Representation and its basic Computer Implementation, *Proc. 2nd ASME Int. Conf. on Design Theory and Methodology* (J. Rinderle, ed.), ASME, Chicago, 1990, DE-Vol. 27 pp. 175–184.

55. L. Joskowicz and S. Addanki, From Kinematics to Shape: An Approach to Innovative Design. In: *Proc. 7th Nat. Conf. on AI*, AAAI, St. Paul, MN, Morgan Kaufmann, San Francisco, 1988, pp. 347–352.

56. D. S. Weld and J. de Kleer (eds.), *Qualitative Reasoning About Physical Systems*, Morgan Kaufmann, San Francisco, 1990.

57. S. P. Carney and D. C. Brown, A Continued Investigation into Qualitative Reasoning about Shape and Fit, *(AI EDAM) J.*, *3*(2) 85–110, (November 1989).

58. B. Williams, Interaction-Based Invention: Designing Novel Devices from First Principles. In: *Proc. 8th Natl. Conf. on AI*, AAAI Press & MIT Press, Boston, *1* 349–356 (1990).

59. T. Tomiyama, T. Kiriyama, H. Takeda and D. Xue, Metamodel: A Key Intelligent CAD Systems, *Res. Eng. Des. 1*(1), 19–34 (1989).

60. Schmitt, in *Intelligent CAD II*, (H. Yoshikawa and T. Holden, eds.), North-Holland, Amsterdam, 1990.

61. M. L. Maher, HI-RISE: An Expert System for Preliminary Structural Design, *Expert Systems for Engineering Design* (M. D. Rychener, ed.), Academic Press, Inc., New York, 1988, pp. 37–52.

62. E. Kant, Understanding and Automating Algorithm Design, *IEEE Transact. Software Eng.*, *SE-11*(11) 1361–1374 (1985).

63. M. G. Dyer, M. Flowers and J. Hodges, EDISON: An Engineering Design Invention System Operating Naively, *AI in Eng.* 1(1), 36–44 (1986).

64. D. B. Lenat and J. S. Brown, Why AM and Eurisko Appear to Work, *Proc. Natl. Conf. on AI*, AAAI-83, Washington, DC, 1983, pp. 236–240.

65. K. Sycara, Negotiation in Design. In: *Computer Aided Cooperative Product Development* (D. Sriram, R. Logcher, and S. Fukuda eds.), Lecture Notes Series, Springer Verlag, New York, 1991.

66. J. S. Gero (ed.), *Artificial Intelligence in Design*, *Proc. 4th Int. Conf. on Applications of AI in Engineering*, Cambridge, England, Computational Mechanics Publications & Springer-Verlag, New York, 1989.

ADDITIONAL READING

Akman, V., P. J. W. ten Hagen, and P. J. Veerkamp, (eds.), *Intelligent CAD Systems II: Implementational Issues*. Springer-Verlag, New York, 1989.

Brown, D. C., M. Waldron, and H. Yoshikawa (eds.), *Intelligent Computer-Aided Design*, North-Holland, Amsterdam, 1992.

Bruns, G. R., and S. L. Gerhart, *Theories of Design: An Introduction to the Literature*, Technical Report STP-068-86, Microelectronics and Computer Technology Corporation (MCC), Austin, TX, 1986.

Finger, S., S. L. Newson, and W. R. Spillers (eds.), *Design Theory '88*, Springer-Verlag, New York, 1989.

Gero, J. S. and M. L. Maher (eds.), *Modelling Creativity and Knowledge-Based Design*, *Proc. Wkshp. on Modeling Creativity and Knowledge-Based Creative Design*, Lawrence Erlbaum, Hillsdale, NJ, 1991.

Goel, V. and P. Pirolli, Motivating the Notion of Generic Design within Information-Processing Theory: The Design Problem Space, *AI Magazine*, *10*(1) 19–36 (Spring 1989).

Huhns M. N. and R. Acosta, Argo: A System for Design by Analogy, *IEEE Expert*, 53–68 (Fall 1988).

Marcus, S., J. Stout, and J. McDermott, VT: An Expert Elevator Designer, *AI Magazine*, 9(1), 95–112 (1988).

ten Hagen, P. J. W. and T. Tomiyama (eds.), *Intelligent CAD Systems I: Theoretical and Methodological Aspects*, Springer-Verlag, New York, 1987.

H. Yoshikawa and F. Arbab (eds.), *Intelligent CAD, III*, North-Holland, Amsterdam, 1991.

H. Yoshikawa and D. Gossard (eds.), *Intelligent CAD*, I, North-Holland, Amsterdam, 1989.

Selected Conferences

International Conference on AI in Design.
International Conference on AI in Engineering, Computational Mechanics Institute.
International Computers in Engineering Conference, ASME.
International Conference on Design Theory & Methodology, ASME.
NSF Design & Manufacturing Systems Conference.
IFIP WG 5.2 Working Conferences.

Selected Journals

(*AIEDAM*), Academic Press.
AI in Engineering, Computational Mechanics Institute.
Research in Engineering Design, Springer International.

DAVID C. BROWN

LARGE-SCALE NUMERICAL OPTIMIZATION: INTRODUCTION AND OVERVIEW

INTRODUCTION

Large-scale optimization is concerned with the minimization (or maximization) of functions of large numbers of variables. Additional algebraic constraints may be imposed on some of the variables, or combinations of variables, in which case we are dealing with constrained optimization. It is difficult to give a precise definition of "large-scale": however, a pragmatic view is that a problem should be viewed as "large-scale," in a given computing environment, if it is economical to exploit structure. Structure can refer to sparsity (i.e., presence of many zeros in the various matrices), inherent parallelism, separability characteristics, and so on.

The purpose of this article is to give a personal introductory overview of the field, emphasizing methods, techniques, and practical concerns. We give theoretical issues a very brief treatment in this article. This is not meant to imply that theoretical issues are not important; indeed, every successful optimization method is supported, in part, by strong theoretical underpinnings. However, in the interest of brevity and breadth, we place theory in the background and instead highlight numerical and practical issues related to efficient computer implementation.

Research activity in the field is high; we hope this article will introduce the reader to some of the issues and trends. More details can be found in the proceedings of a recent workshop on this area (1). Some of the ideas are discussed at greater length elsewhere (2); background in optimization can be found in a number of optimization texts (3–7). Recent research developments are discussed in Fletcher (8) as well as in the handbook edited by Nemhauser, Rinnooy Kan, and Todd (9). Some parallel computing issues in optimization are discussed in other sources (10, 11).

The unconstrained minimization problem is usually stated as $\min_x f(x)$, where f is a real-valued function of n real variables $x = (x_1, x_2, \ldots, x_n)^T$. In this article we are primarily concerned with the case where f is smooth and differentiable* (usually twice continuously differentiable); however, many important large-scale optimization problems arise which do not satisfy these assumptions. For example, in some cases some of the variables (perhaps all) must attain integral values. Typically this makes the problem more difficult to solve and usually very costly. Wu (13) provides an example of such a problem and a parallel method of solution. Even without integrality constraints the general problem, minimize $f(x)$, can be very difficult to solve, especially if the global minimizer is

*We assume that the gradient of f, ∇f, can be computed. There are methods available that do not require the gradient (e.g., 12), but we do not discuss such methods here.

Example 1 [14,15].

This problem arises in several application areas including molecular chemistry, surveying, and satellite ranging. We will describe the problem in the parlance of molecular chemistry. It is required to locate, in 3-space, the positions of the atoms of a molecule given (incomplete) pairwise distance data. That is, let S be the set of index pairs corresponding to known distances, i.e., $(i, j) \in S$ if the distance between atom i and atom j, d_{ij}, is known. The cardinality of the set S, $|S|$, is usually much smaller than the number of all possible pairs, i.e., $|S| << \frac{n(n-1)}{2}$. The problem is to locate all atoms x_i, $i = 1, 2, ..., n$, in 3-space such that $\|x_i - x_j\| = d_{ij}$ for all $(i, j) \in S$. The dimension of the problem, n, is typically between several hundred to several thousand. The usual optimization formulation is

$$(1) \qquad \min \ f(x) = \sum_{(i,j) \in S} (\|x_i - x_j\|_2^2 - d_{ij}^2)^2.$$

FIGURE 1   The distance conformation problem.

required (i.e., a point x_* satisfying $f(x_*) \leq f(x)$, over all x). The distance conformation problem, in Example 1 (Fig. 1) is an example of such a problem.

There are several things to note about this problem. First, a point x is a global solution if and only if $f(x) = 0$; therefore, verifying* if a candidate solution is in fact a global solution is easy—this is not always the case in global optimization. Second, it is easy to see that the Hessian matrix, $\nabla^2 f(x)$, will be a sparse matrix if $|S| << \frac{n(n-1)}{2}$: variable x_i is related to variable x_j if and only if $(i, j) \in S$. The problem as stated actually yields a singular Hessian matrix, at any point—consider, for example, simple translations or rotations. Singular matrices can lead to numerical difficulties; however, in this case it is possible to overcome this difficulty by introducing a few simple constraints (to orient the molecule, arbitrarily, in space).

Notice that to satisfy the known information a global minimizer of (1) is required. However, locating a global minimizer of (1) is, in general, almost intractable. Indeed, even if it is known that the molecule is a one-dimensional structure (i.e., all the atoms form a single straight line), a very unlikely and simplified situation, the global minimization of (1) is still essentially intractable, in general. Hendrickson (15) shows that this one-dimensional problem is at least as hard as the "partition problem" which is known to be NP-complete (see Ref. 16 for an introduction to the theory of NP-completeness).

We are not concerned with global optimization techniques in this article. Currently, there is a lot of research activity in this area including development of parallel computational techniques (e.g., 17–20). It is a very important area. However, due to the extreme difficulty of this problem, it appears that domain-specific heuristics usually play an important role in the design of efficient computational techniques for large-scale global optimization problems.

We are primarily concerned with local minimization. In the unconstrained case this means finding a point x_* with the property that there is a neighborhood containing x_* such that f attains its lowest value, in this neighborhood, at x_*. More formally, we say that

---

*However, in practice the "known" distances may be contaminated with error in which case it may not be possible to realize $f(x) = 0$, for any x. This gives more credence to the optimization formulation (1).

Example 2 [22,23,24,25]. In this example one is interested in determining the distribution of radioactivity across a body cross-section. If a grid is placed across the body cross-section, dividing the cross-section into a number of squares, the quantity to be estimated is the level of radioactivity in each square, say x_i in square (or pixel) i. Assume the grid divides the cross-section into n pixels. To yield useful results, n must be very large – typically in the range [10,000 – 100,000]. So $x = (x_1, x_2, ..., x_n)^T$ is the vector to be determined. However, the quantity that can be measured experimentally is the level of activity along a number of straight lines that cut across the grid. Let there be m lines l_i each with measured radioactivity level y_i. Partition $l_i = (l_{i1}, l_{i2}, ..., l_{in})^T$ where l_{ij} denotes the length of intersection of the i-th line with the j-th pixel. It is proposed [25] to solve the following optimization problem to determine the vector x:

$$(2) \qquad \min_x \{ f(x) = x^T S x \ + \ \sum_{i=1}^m (l_i^T x - y_i \cdot ln(l_i^T x)) : \quad x \geq 0 \}$$

where S is a sparse symmetric positive semidefinite matrix (defined in Ref. [25]).

FIGURE 2   Image reconstruction.

x_* is a local minimizer if there exists a scalar $\delta > 0$ such that $f(x_*) \leq f(x)$ for all x satisfying $\| x - x_* \| < \delta$. Most optimization problems in science and engineering are adequately solved by local minimization. Moreover, global optimization problems are usually solved using a local minimization procedure as a subroutine, (e.g., 18,19,21).

The application areas where optimization is used are too numerous to enumerate; indeed, it is difficult to think of a significant branch of computational science where optimization is absent. Moreover, realistic models often lead to large-scale problems. To illustrate further, we consider two more examples, both from the biomedical research area. Both examples are merely sketched here to illustrate the nature of the optimization problem and its relationship to the application—to fully understand the derivation of the optimization problem the reader must refer to the sources cited.

Important things to note about Example 2 (Fig. 2) are: the objective function is nonlinear, there are lower bounds on the variables, the matrix S is large, very sparse, and with some block-structure (sparsity and block structure are both consequences of the grid design and "nearest-neighbor relationships").

A few things to note about Example 3 (Fig. 3): First, an evaluation of the objective function is very expensive—requiring a finite-element analysis, namely, the determination of the matrix K and the solution of (4). The calculation of the gradient (and even the Hessian matrix, if required) is possible and is not inordinately expensive provided it is done, with care, along with the finite-element analysis. If insufficient care is taken with the manner in which the function is evaluated the entire process will be unmanageably expensive. Sparse matrix technology will be required for the solution of y; unfortunately, it will not be required for computations involving the Hessian matrix—the Hessian matrix is dense. The reason for this is that each component of y typical depends on all the variables x, through Eq. (4).

This third example differs from the previous two in that sparsity and structure do not show up in the Hessian matrix, which is dense. Instead, sparsity and structure play an

Example 3 [26,27]. Broadly speaking this example falls into the subclass of optimization known as structural optimization. This type of problem arises when modelling structures of various kinds and is characterized by an objective function – the function to be minimized – of both dependent and independent variables. The dependent variables are themselves functions of the independent variables and can be determined only through the numerical solution to a system of partial differential equations. In this particular example of a structural optimization problem, the optimization process predicts how bone will "reconstruct" itself from a given starting position. The independent variables typically are bone density, bone thickness, and shape parameters. The objective function f is usually a combination of mass and strain energy. Before discretization the optimization problem is:

$$(3) \qquad\qquad \min_x \{f(y(x), x) : \ l \le x \le u\},$$

where f is a function combining mass and strain energy, and l, u are given vectors of lower and upper bounds respectively. The vector x represents the independent variables. The dependent variable y depends on x through a system of partial differential equations. Typically this problem is solved by first discretizing, dividing the bone to be modelled into a large number of "elements", and choosing finite vectors y and x. So, $y = y(x)$, and y is usually determined numerically, given x, by using finite element analysis. Amongst other things this involves forming and solving a very large sparse and positive-definite linear system of equations:

$$(4) \qquad\qquad\qquad K(x)y = F(x)$$

where $K(x)$, the "global stiffness" matrix, is positive definite for all x, and F is a vector-valued function.

FIGURE 3   The modelling of bone reconstruction.

important role in the evaluation of the function (and derivatives) and cannot be ignored here. Still, even with full attention paid to efficient function evaluations, the time spent to evaluate f (and derivatives) at a given point dominates all else. This fact—the extreme expense of evaluating the function—should play a determining role in the choice of optimization algorithm.

Many efficient and reliable algorithms have been developed for small-scale and medium-scale optimization: why are they not applicable to problems with many variables? The short answer is that they ignore structure usually present in large-scale problems; therefore, they are not as efficient as they need to be to solve such problems in reasonable time. For example, methods that by their nature cannot easily exploit sparsity cannot be applied to large-scale and sparse problems—computing time would be unmanageable. More subtly, perhaps, methods that consist of a large number of inexpensive but sequential or serial "major" iterations may be inappropriate for a large-scale problem in a parallel computing environment. (The major iterations cannot be overlapped; there is not enough work within each iteration to "crank up" a parallel supercomputer.) In this case, algorithms with fewer but more expensive major iterations may be much more suitable provided the computations within these major iterations can be done efficiently in parallel. As a final example, large-scale problems often consist of a sum of functions of simple form—second derivatives can often be obtained at relatively little extra expense beyond evaluation of the function and the gradient (and parallelism can be used). Therefore, an efficient approach to a large-scale problem may involve the calculation and use of second derivatives whereas this is usually not the case in the small-scale setting.

However, despite this apparent need for different approaches when optimization problems become large, it is important to realize there there is a common backbone to methods for large-scale and small-scale optimization. This is the Newton iteration. Practically all of optimization consists of variations on the Newton process: globalization strategies, approximation techniques, and efficient robust implementations.

UNCONSTRAINED MINIMIZATION

The problem is: minimize $f(x)$, where f is a twice continuously differentiable real-valued function of n real variables $x = (x_1, x_2, \ldots, x_n)^T$. We are interested in locating a local minimizer: i.e., find a point x_* such that there exists a scalar $\delta > 0$ with the property that $f(x_*) \leq f(x)$ for all x satisfying $\|x - x_*\| > \delta$.

There are two basic globalization strategies in unconstrained minimization: line search methods and trust-region methods. (By globalization strategy we refer to a method to ensure convergence to a local minimizer from a distant point. We do not refer to a method to find the global minimizer.)

In a line search method a direction of descent is determined, in other words, a direction s is determined satisfying $\nabla f(x_c)^T s < 0$, where x_c is the current point (i.e., the current approximation to the solution). Then, a one-dimensional approximate minimization is performed on the function $f(x_c + \alpha s)$, for $\alpha > 0$, to determine an acceptable α. Dennis and Schnabel (3) discuss this issue at fair length; in general, the current consensus is to terminate the line search process under fairly lenient conditions, and in each iteration to initially try $\alpha = 1$.

An alternative to a line search algorithm is a trust-region procedure. In this case a trial step s_* is determined by minimizing the local quadratic model of f, at x_c, subject to a restriction on the size of the solution, and possibly subject to s being in some specified subspace S:

$$\min_{s \in S} \left\{ \nabla f(x_c)^T s + \frac{1}{2} s^T H_c s : \|s\| \leq \Delta_c \right\}. \tag{5}$$

The matrix H_c is the current Hessian matrix $\nabla^2 f(x_c)$, or an approximation to it. In the full-blown trust-region problem S is the entire space R^n. However, in some recent and very promising work (mentioned in greater detail below) S is a two-dimensional subspace. The norm used in the constraint is usually the 2-norm; however, both the 1-norm and the ∞-norm have also been advocated. The solution to (5), s_*, is accepted and x is updated, $x = x_c + s_*$, if $f(x_c + s_*) < f(x_c)$. The trust region bound Δ_c is adjusted for the next iteration, according to various simple rules (e.g., 5,28,29), and the process iterates.

Which approach should one use, line search or trust-region? Which is better for large-scale optimization?

There is a place for both approaches in large-scale optimization. The line search strategy is clearly appropriate if a positive definite approximation to the true Hessian is being used (e.g., a quasi-Newton or secant method). A problem with special structure may also be appropriate for a line search method since a specialized line search procedure to exploit this structure may be possible—this is much harder to do in a trust-region approach.

A trust-region method is better suited to handle indefiniteness* and is most reasonable when the true Hessian (or an accurate approximation) is being used. Convergence properties are stronger for trust-region methods and they tend to outperform line search methods on difficult problems (e.g., problems that are very nonlinear with a lot of negative curvature). The mark against trust-region methods has been their linear algebra cost (and complexity) within each major iteration—experience suggests almost two Cholesky factorizations, on average, per iteration. However, Byrd and Schnabel (30) propose choosing S to be a two-dimensional subspace in which case the cost of the trust-region problem, once S is formed, is negligible (see also Ref. 31). The trick is how to choose S. Byrd and Schnabel (30) suggest to let S be the space spanned by the gradient and the Newton direction, if the Hessian is positive definite, and the space spanned by the gradient and a direction of negative curvature[†] otherwise. A negative curvature direction can be obtained using an "incomplete" Cholesky factorization and perhaps some further low-order computations. This approach is still in its early stages but seems most promising. Indeed, a combination of this reduced trust-region approach followed by a line search may capture the best of both worlds—this is a research question currently under investigation by the author.

In any event, trust-region or line search, it is important to obtain or approximate second-order information (i.e., the Hessian matrix) to get acceptable convergence properties. As we illustrate below, it is often reasonable in the large-scale setting to obtain analytic expressions for the second derivatives (see also the section on Automatic Differentiation). The extra computational cost beyond the cost of evaluating the function and the gradient is often acceptable—and the decrease in the number of iterations (over an approach that approximates the second derivatives) may be significant. However, an efficient Hessian computation can usually be computed only if intermediate quantities used in the evaluation of the function and the gradient are "reused." Therefore, the common practice of writing separate subroutines to evaluate the function, gradient, and the Hessian is not a good one in this context (Figure 4 illustrates the use of a single subroutine to evaluate $f(x)$, $\nabla f(x)$, and $\nabla^2 f(x)$ for the distance conformation problem).

Of course it is not always possible, desirable, or convenient to compute second derivatives. For example, the user may have had a function and gradient routine handed down (from generation to generation) and that's where he or she wants to begin, rather than returning to first principles. It may be the case that the problem is so large that even with sparsity it is not feasible to form and store the Hessian matrix—in this case, as we discuss briefly below, "product-form" approximations may be useful. In summary, there is a need for Hessian approximations and that's what we discuss next. Initially we focus on techniques that require storage of a sparse matrix; we follow this with a short discussion on possible alternatives suitable for very large problems.

---

*Note that H_c need not be positive-definite in (5).

[†]The vector s is a direction of negative curvature, with respect to a Hessian matrix H, if $s^T H s < 0$.

Sparse Secant Updates

One of the biggest success stories in optimization has been the development of quasi-Newton (or secant) methods for unconstrained minimization. Dennis and Schnabel (3) provide an excellent introduction to this area; the classic theoretical reference is Dennis and Moré (32). Unfortunately, the adaptation of this approach to the large-scale case, in which sparsity is a factor, has been less successful. (A possible exception is the use of secant updates in the context of a function f that is conveniently expressed in a partial separable manner—see below for more details.)

A secant method for multidimensional minimization requires that the user simply supply subroutines to evaluate f and the gradient of f, ∇f, at any given point x. An approximation $H(x)$ to the symmetric Hessian matrix, $\nabla^2 f(x)$, is maintained and updated at each iteration. The update requires the two pairs (x_c, x_+), $(\nabla f(x_c), \nabla f(x_+))$, and the current symmetric positive definite approximation H_c. The more successful updates require that the new approximation H_+ satisfy what is known as the secant (or quasi-Newton) equation:

$$H_+(x_+ - x_c) = \nabla f(x_+) - \nabla f(x_c).$$

The best updates also require that the approximation H_+ be positive-definite (and symmetric) and this can be ensured provided H_c is positive-definite and

$$s^T(\nabla f(x_+) - \nabla f(x_c)) > 0, \tag{7}$$

where $x_+ - x_c = \alpha s$ for some positive scalar α. A key point is this: condition (7) is consistent with approximate minimization of the function f along the line s starting at point x_c. This is crucial because it means that with an appropriate one-dimensional line search it is possible to obtain good decrease in the objective function f as well as ensure that a Hessian update (preserving the quasi-Newton Eq. (6), positive-definiteness, and symmetry) can be performed.

Many updating formulae have been suggested; however, the most successful to date (empirically) has been the BFGS (Broyden-Fletcher-Goldfarb-Shanno) update (see, e.g., Chap. 9 in Ref 3. The updated matrix H_+ is obtained from the current approximation, H_c, with a rank-2 update. (Alternatively, an update to a matrix approximating the inverse of the Hessian can be performed.) A computational attraction of this positive definite secant update is the low linear algebra cost to perform the update: the work is $O(n^2)$, which includes the time to compute the next search direction. This is obviously true if the inverse approximation is updated; achieving this bound with a numerically stable update to the Cholesky factors of the Hessian approximation is illustrated by others (3,7).

Unfortunately this success story does not carry over to the sparse setting. In the large-scale situation it is often the case that the Hessian matrix is sparse: i.e., most of the entries are zero for all values of x [Examples 1 (Fig. 1) and 2 (Fig. 2) illustrate this]. Typically, the sparsity pattern is either known or can be determined before the optimization process begins. Therefore, a worthwhile goal is to maintain an approximating matrix with the same sparsity pattern, allowing zeros to turn into nonzeros can dramatically increase computational costs to the extent that the overall expense of a single iteration is prohibitive. Unfortunately, the quest for a sparse, symmetric, positive-definite secant method has produced a grab-bag of heuristic techniques and strategies (e.g., 33–39), none of which possess the satisfying theoretical and computational underpinnings of the dense positive-definite secant updates suitable for small-scale problems. Coleman (2) summarizes this effort.

Sparse Finite Differences

Frustrations with the development of a successful sparse secant update has led to a search for alternatives and the generation of rather successful sparsity exploiting finite-differencing schemes.

To introduce this subject it is easiest to begin with the sparse finite-difference estimation of an unsymmetric Jacobian matrix. This arises in the common situation when trying to minimize a nonlinear least-squares function,

$$\min_x f(x) = \frac{1}{2}F(x)^T F(x) \tag{8}$$

where $F(x)$ is a vector-valued function: $F(x) = (f_1(x), f_2(x), \ldots, f_m(x))^T$ and each component function $f_i(x)$ is a real-valued function of the vector $x \in R^n$. Typically $m > n$. Hence, the function $F(x)$ maps $R^n \rightarrow R^m$ and has an m-by-n Jacobian matrix $J(x) = F'(x)$. Our objective is to estimate $J(x)$ using a subroutine to evaluate $F(x)$. By Taylor's theorem,

$$J(x)d = \frac{F(x + \gamma d) - F(x))}{\gamma} + O(\gamma) \tag{9}$$

where γ, the step size, is a positive quantity and d is an arbitrary vector of unit length. Therefore an approximation to the i-th column of the Jacobian matrix can be obtained with a subroutine to evaluate F, by choosing $d = e^i$ where e^i is the i-th column of the identity matrix. Clearly it is possible to obtain an approximation to the Jacobian matrix, at the current point x_c, using $n + 1$ function evaluations by estimating each column of J in turn.

Curtis, Powell, and Reid (40) were the first to point out that many fewer function evaluations may be enough to estimate a sparse matrix. For example, a tridiagonal matrix requires only three finite-differences. The general idea is to partition the columns of the Jacobian matrix J into groups of "structurally independent" columns. Two columns are structurally independent if their row indices corresponding to nonzeros are disjoint. Coleman and Moré (41,42) proposed graph-coloring heuristics to determine partitions with groups—each group corresponding to a function evaluation and a finite difference. The practical performance of this approach seems quite satisfactory requiring very few finite-differences (relative to n) on practical problems (41). Nevertheless, there is room for possible improvement in the situation when there are a few dense rows: the number of required finite-differences is bounded below by the maximum number of nonzeros in any row. In such a case what may be required is independent approximation of the dense rows (perhaps a secant approximation).

In the more general minimization context, $\min_x f(x)$, we are required to estimate the sparse matrix of second derivatives (the Hessian matrix) given a subroutine to evaluate $f(x)$. The unsymmetric approaches, described above, can be used here; however, usually it is better to use a method that also exploits the symmetry of the Hessian matrix. Appropriate column partitionings, allowing for the use of symmetry, are provided by various graph colorings (43–45) and once again the practical performance of this approach seems to be quite good, requiring few finite-differences relative to n, and taking near optimal advantage of symmetry.

In summary, the sparse finite-difference approach, given a subroutine to evaluate $\nabla f(x)$ in the general minimization case, and given a subroutine to evaluate $F(x)$ in the nonlinear least-square case, is often a viable approach for large-scale sparse problems. The number of evaluations usually is very small compared to n, the problem dimension. It is also true that the required finite-difference evaluations are totally independent tasks and so parallel computation of this aspect is easy. However, the efficient utilization of many processors, i.e., more than the number of required finite-differences, would require a parallel evaluation of $\nabla f(x)$. This situation is considered in the literature (46–48).

We do have three concerns. First, there is accuracy. While the accuracy in the Hessian approximation is much better than a quasi-Newton (or secant) method, choosing the appropriate step size, especially in the presence of noise, can be delicate. In this case automatic differentiation may (eventually) provide a more accurate alternative.* Second, while it is practically very useful to have matrix estimation methods that require the user to supply only a gradient subroutine, in some cases it may be more efficient to access the function and the gradient in a more fine-grained manner (e.g., component-wise), or perhaps as a sum of "small" functions (see following section). Finally, the estimated Hessian matrices will be symmetric but not, in general, positive-definite. Therefore solving for the Newton direction does not necessarily lead to a descent direction and so a negative-curvature method (discussed above) is appropriate.

Partial Separability

Many large-scale optimization problems are presented in a partially separable form:

$$f(x) = \sum_{i=1}^{n_e} f_i(x), \tag{10}$$

where each of the "element" functions f_i has a Hessian matrix of low rank relative to n. Considerable work has been done on the development of large-scale optimization methods designed especially to exploit this form: Philippe Toint, of the University of Namur, Belgium, has been the primary advocate of this approach (e.g., 50–53). Certainly this form leads to convenient design of subroutines to evaluate the gradient (and perhaps the Hessian). For example, in Figure 4, we consider the evaluation of the function, gradient, and Hessian in the distance conformation problem. To simplify we consider the special case when the molecule is restricted to lie in a straight line, namely the one-dimensional distance conformation problem.

Note that to evaluate the function alone requires $5 \cdot n_e$ operations (adds or multiplies), to evaluate the function and the gradient requires $9 \cdot n_e$ operations, and to evaluate the function, gradient, and Hessian requires $14 \cdot n_e$ operations. Therefore, in this case not only does partial separability lead to a convenient form for evaluating f and its first and second derivatives, it leads to an efficient method as well. Note that a single subroutine to evaluate the triple $(f, \nabla f, \nabla^2 f)$, or a leading subset of this triple, enhances efficiency: intermediate quantities can be reused.

If the element functions all depend on only a few variables—the usual case—then the full Hessian will be sparse and, if desired, can be formed to use in the calculation of

---

*It is interesting to note that the graph-coloring analogies used in the sparse finite-difference work are also applicable in the automatic differentiation setting (49).

{Determine function value}

For $k = 1 : n_e$ do   {n_e is the number of edges (elements)}

    Let $e_k = (i, j)$, $i > j$

    $t_k^1 = x_i - x_j$

enddo

$t^2 = t^1 . * t^1$ {pointwise multiplication}

$t^3 = t^2 - d . * d$ {pointwise multiplication, subtraction}

$f = (t^3)^T (t^3)$

{Determine gradient. Initially, $g = 0$.}

For $k = 1 : n_e$ do

    Let $e_k = (i, j), i > j$

    $g_i = g_i + 4t^3(k) \cdot t^1(k)$

    $g_j = g_j - 4t^3(k) \cdot t^1(k)$

enddo

{Determine Hessian. Initially, $H = 0$.}

For $k = 1 : n_e$ do

    Let $e_k = (i, j), i > j$

    $H(i, j) = H(i, j) - 8t^2(k) - 4t^3(k)$

    $H(j, i) = H(i, j)$

    $H(i, i) = H(i, i) + 8t^2(k) + 4t^3(k)$

    $H(j, j) = H(j, j) + 8t^2(k) + 4t^3(k)$

enddo

FIGURE 4   Evaluation of one-dimensional molecule function, gradient, and Hessian.

a search direction. However, the definition of partial separability implies that each element function has a symmetric low-rank Hessian matrix which does not necessarily imply dependence on only a few variables. Still, if there are only a few such global element functions (i.e., element functions that depend on many of the variables, then it may still be possible to proceed with a direct factorization method using sparsity. To illustrate, consider the following.

Let $H = H_0 + H_1$ where H_0 is sparse and H_1 is dense but is computed as $H_1 = UU^T$, where U is a t-by-n matrix with $t << n$, and rank$(U) = t$. A system of the form $Hs = r$ can be replaced with:

$$\begin{bmatrix} H_0 & U \\ U^T & -I \end{bmatrix} \begin{bmatrix} s \\ v \end{bmatrix} = \begin{bmatrix} r \\ 0 \end{bmatrix}. \tag{11}$$

Note that system (11) can be solved using a symmetric sparse factorization (e.g., 54). Of course if the true Hessian H is not positive-definite then we may wish to use a factorization of the matrix in (11) capable of revealing negative curvature with respect to the Hessian matrix H.

Instead of evaluating the Hessian matrix, it may be advantageous to estimate the elemental Hessian matrices, separately, using dense secant approximations. Each element function is of low rank and so a small dense approximation to each element Hessian is reasonable. (The elemental Hessian approximations can then be added together to form the full Hessian approximation as described above; alternatively, the elemental Hessian matrices can be used in an iterative way to solve for the next search direction, in which case they need not be collected together. A third possibility, in cases where sparsity prevails, is to integrate their summation with a sparse multi-frontal linear solver) (54). Unfortunately the elemental matrix approximations cannot be guaranteed to be positive-definite and so the positive-definite secant updates cannot be used. This had led to a serious investigation of alternative updates with the symmetric rank-1 update (SR1) being particularly popular (e.g., 55–57).

Exploiting the partial separable structure of many large-scale optimization problems is often an economic approach. However, this approach does not serve every need. We consider three limitations.

First, there are large-scale optimization problems that are not in a partially separable form but which can be solved using sparsity. Consider, for example, the following. Let f_1, f_2, and f_3 each be functions of many variables, each with sparse Hessian matrices. Assume that the sum of the Hessian matrices, $\Sigma_{i=1}^{3} \nabla^2 f_i$, is sparse. Now consider the problem: $\min f(x) = f_1(x) \cdot f_2(x) \cdot f_3(x)$. Clearly f is not in partially separable form. However, it turns out that the Hessian matrix of f can be written:

$$\nabla^2 f = \nabla^2 f_1 \cdot f_2 f_3 + \nabla^2 f_2 \cdot f_1 f_2 + \nabla^2 f_3 \cdot f_1 f_2 + U T U^T, \tag{12}$$

where $U = (\nabla f_1, \nabla f_2, \nabla f_3)$, and T is a symmetric 3×3 matrix,

$$T = \begin{bmatrix} 0 & f_3 & f_2 \\ f_3 & 0 & f_1 \\ f_2 & f_1 & 0 \end{bmatrix}. \tag{13}$$

Therefore, the Hessian is the sum of a sparse matrix and a symmetric low-rank matrix. The Newton step (for example) can be computed by using a technique similar to (11). Therefore, restriction to the partial separable form is not useful in this case.

Second, the optimization problem may be easily expressed in partially separable form, in principle, but perhaps it is not convenient for the user to do so. For example, the user may wish to begin with a given subroutine to evaluate the function and gradient.

Third, there is the case of global variables. A variable is global, with respect to a given partial separable formulation, if it appears in most of the element functions. If there are several such variables, and they are involved in significant common evaluations in most of the elements, then separate evaluation of element functions may be an inefficient way to evaluate the overall function or gradient.

In summary, the partial separable form arises frequently in large-scale optimization and it is often worthwhile exploiting this. However, it may not always be convenient to express a function in this form and so there will remain a need for optimization approaches that make fewer assumptions on the user-supplied subroutines.

Conjugate Gradient and Limited-Memory Secant Methods

For very large problems it may not even be feasible to store a sparse matrix approximation to the true Hessian matrix. In such cases conjugate gradient methods and limited-memory secant methods provide alternatives.

A number of nonlinear conjugate methods have been proposed (e.g., 58–65), and Fortran codes are publically available. Their great attraction, beyond simplicity, is their

---

Repeat

$$\beta_k = \frac{(y_{k-1})^T \nabla f(x_k)}{\|\nabla f(x_{k-1})\|^2} \quad \{y_{k-1} = \nabla f(x_k) - \nabla f(x_{k-1})\}$$

$$d_k = -\nabla f(x_k) + \beta_k d_{k-1}$$

$$x_{k+1} = x_k + \alpha_k d_k$$

FIGURE 5   The Polak-Ribière conjugate–gradient algorithm.

very small memory requirement—in their pure forms several dense vectors are required but no matrices. For example, consider the Polak-Ribière (62) algorithm in Figure 5.

A line search algorithm will determine α_k, the step length. Typical of conjugate gradient methods, this method is easy to program (given a line search routine) and requires little memory; only a handful of n-vectors.

Acceleration of convergence of these procedures can usually occur through the use of clever "restart" procedures and preconditioning strategies. Unfortunately, the skillful use of these techniques is very much an art requiring some experience with the problem at hand. Nocedal (66) has done some numerical experimentation and comparisons amongst several nonlinear conjugate gradient codes: he reports his results and gives tentative conclusions and advice.

An alternative to a nonlinear conjugate gradient method is a limited-memory secant method (e.g., 67–69). A limited-memory secant approximation does not update an explicit matrix approximation; instead, an initial sparse approximation to the inverse Hessian is saved (usually a diagonal matrix) along with a small collection of vectors representing the recent updates. This set is typically updated at each iteration by deleting vectors corresponding to old information and adding new. Note that since the density of the approximating matrix is not an issue—it is not formed explicitly—the very successful dense positive-definite secant update formulae can be used. Of course this is offset to some extent by the fact that only a small set of updates can be used. Nash and Nocedal (70) report on numerical experiments, comparing limited-memory quasi-Newton codes to (truncated) Newton methods.

Concluding Remarks on Unconstrained Problems

We conclude this section with a few remarks on the state of affairs with respect to the large-scale unconstrained optimization problem.

First, it is clear that there has been much progress in this area over the past 10 years. Work is continuing—and further research is definitely needed—but several alternatives are now available. Indeed, software packages especially tailored to the large-scale user are available (e.g., 50,71). Of course with a variety of methods comes the question: which to choose? Expect no clear definitive answer to this question for a long time, if ever. What we can offer are some (personal) guidelines.

The methods that are most robust and can achieve the greatest accuracy are the methods that compute second derivatives (or use finite-difference Hessian approximations) and that use sparse matrix factorizations with the ability to detect and use negative curvature. Computing second derivatives is feasible for many large-scale optimization problems. Such methods are particularly good for ill-conditioned problems and problems with much negative curvature. On the down side, the memory requirements may still be too much despite using sparsity, and some problems can be solved just as well with less effort. Methods that compute second derivatives (or use finite-differences) and use an iterative technique to solve the linearized problem (e.g., conjugate gradients [CG]), and that have the ability to deal reasonably with negative curvature, provide an alternative if the direct factorization is too expensive in space or time (e.g., 72,73). Of course the effectiveness of the CG iteration is problem dependent and may need preconditioning—a heuristic situation. In terms of overall reliability and robustness, the elemental secant methods follow the second-derivative methods (if the problem is expressed in the partially separable format) followed by the limited-memory secant and nonlinear conjugate gradient routines. [Of course this list can be read in reverse order: starting from the most inexpensive methods at the bottom (if they work!) to the most expensive at the top.]

The sparse secant updates, namely those that do not exploit the partially-separable structure, are too inconsistent in behavior to include in our list; however, they still provide a tool that can be useful on occasion.

A final remark: this list emphasizes the need for a computing environment that allows for experimentation within the large-scale optimization context. It is clear that the job of selecting a suitable approach to a large-scale optimization problem is not an easy one and is certainly not easily done without a trial-and-error process. This is very difficult to do today, without a major time investment, due to the lack of a flexible computing environment for large-scale optimization.

CONSTRAINED OPTIMIZATION

The general constrained optimization problem we consider is

$$\min_x \{f(x) : c(x) = 0, l \le x \le u\}, \tag{14}$$

where f is a twice continuously differentiable mapping from R^n to R^1, c is a twice continuously differentiable mapping from R^n to R^m, with $m < n$, and l, u are vectors of lower and upper bounds, respectively, $l \le u$. (For any i, if $l_i = -\infty$, then x_i is unbounded below; if $u_i = \infty$ then x_i is unbounded above.) The region defined by the constraints, $\{c(x) = 0, l \le x \le u\}$, is coined the feasible region; we denote this region $\mathcal{F}$. A problem may have no bounds on the variables, i.e., $u = \infty$, $l = -\infty$, in which case the optimization problem reduces to an equality-constrained problem: $\min_x\{f(x) : c(x) = 0\}$.

There are other formulations of the general problem. For example, a problem may include constraints of the form $c(x) \ge 0$; however, simple transformations such as the introduction of slack variables can yield the form given in (14) and so, for simplicity, we assume this formulation.

Again we restrict ourselves to methods for finding a local minimizer. In the constrained case this means we look to find x_* such that there exists a scalar $\delta > 0$, where δ, x_* satisfy:

$$f(x_*) \le f(x), \forall x \in \{x : \|x - x_*\| < \delta, x \in \mathcal{F}\}. \tag{15}$$

Most of the issues and concerns in unconstrained minimization carry over to the constrained case. For example, the two basic globalization strategies for unconstrained problems, line search and trust-region, have counterparts for constrained problems (though each has more complications in the presence of constraints).

In a certain sense constraints make a problem easier by restricting the domain of interest. However, constraints do complicate things in several ways.

First, handling constraints and exploiting sparsity are two objectives that can be difficult to achieve simultaneously. For example, a common approach to a problem with linear (or linearized) constraints is to determine a basis for the null space of the matrix corresponding to the linear (linearized) constraints and then work in the null space (e.g., 7). To illustrate, consider the problem, $\min_x\{f(x) : Ax = 0\}$. If the columns of the matrix Z form a basis for the null space of A, then a "reduced Newton system" is given by

$$(Z^T\nabla^2 fZ)\bar{s} = -Z^T\nabla f, \tag{16}$$

and the reduced Newton step is $s = Z\bar{s}$. This is a powerful methodology in constrained optimization. However, it is difficult to adapt to a large-scale problem with the additional hope of maintaining sparse matrices. There has been some successful work on understanding the problem of determining a sparse basis for the null space of a sparse matrix (74–76), i.e., finding a sparse matrix Z in (16); however, this is only part of the problem. A direct factorization method requires a representation of the reduced Hessian matrix, matrix $Z^T \nabla^2 fZ$ in (16), and if sparsity is also desired this is a difficult request to satisfy. Of course an iterative null space approach can be followed without explicitly forming $Z^T \nabla^2 fZ$; i.e., in (16) we need not form the matrix $Z^T \nabla^2 fZ$ but instead save the sparse matrices, Z, $\nabla^2 f$, and apply them, in sequence, to perform multiplication within an iterative solver. Nevertheless, the point is our options have been limited.

A second difficulty caused by the presence of constraints occurs when the constraints are nonlinear. The difficulty stems from the fact that most computational mathematics is linear; hence, a nonlinear manifold is usually difficult to follow. Algorithms that try to maintain feasibility, in the general nonlinearly constrained problem, can be very slow, expending much time trying to follow nonlinear boundaries. To see the usefulness of linearity, consider the nonlinear equality-constrained problem:

$$\min_z \{f(z): c(z) = 0\}. \tag{17}$$

In general it is difficult to restrict the iterates $\{z_k\}$ to be feasible, i.e., $c(z_k) = 0$, $k = 1, 2,\ldots$. However, if there is sufficient linearity then it is possible. For example, suppose the variables z can be partitioned $z = (y, x)$ such that $c(z) = 0$ can be equivalently written:

$$T(x) \cdot y + \tau(x) = 0, \tag{18}$$

where $T(x)$ is a nonsingular matrix for all x. Then, y appears in a linear role and can be "eliminated" via the equation:

$$y = -T(x)^{-1}\tau(x). \tag{19}$$

Therefore, problem (17) can be reduced to the following unconstrained problem:

$$\min_x f(y(x),x) \tag{20}$$

where x is the "independent" vector and y depends on x through (19). An algorithm for unconstrained minimization can be used to solve (20), and the nonlinear manifold, c(z) = 0, will be satisfied (implicitly) at every iteration. The key to the reduction of (17) to (20) is the linear role* played by the vector *y*.

An alternative to an algorithm that maintains feasibility is one that ignores it (except in the limit). This leads to two concerns. First, there is the question of how to force convergence from a distant point and what constitutes an improvement—hence the need for "merit" functions (and associated difficulties). Penalty and barrier functions are typical merit functions (see, e.g., Refs. 4–7). Second, in practical problems functions sometimes are not defined outside the feasible region; penalty or exterior methods clearly have difficulties in such cases.

A third difficulty due to the presence of constraints is specifically related to inequalities [in our formulation (14), this refers to finite bounds on the variables]. Inequalities give a combinatorial flavor to the problem which can cause some algorithms to require many iterations when the dimension is high. In addition, inequality constraints can increase the complexity of dealing with sparsity and can make the design of efficient parallel algorithms difficult.

There are two basic categories of algorithms for problems with inequalities. These are "active-set" algorithms and "passive-set" algorithms. (The first term is in common usage; the second is less common—we use it to refer to algorithms that are not "active-set"!) In each iteration of an active-set algorithm the inequality constraints are divided into two sets. The set of constraints currently satisfied exactly defines the active set $\mathcal{A}$: $\mathcal{A}(x) = \{i : x_i = l_i, \text{ or } x_i = u_i\}$. The complementary set, the set of constraints corresponding to variables not at their bounds, is the set of inactivities. In active-set algorithms, the determination of the "next-step" depends on these two sets.

In contrast, a "passive-set" algorithm does not permit variables to be at their bounds except in an asymptotic sense (i.e., in the limit as $k \rightarrow \infty$, where k is the iteration counter).

There are many examples of successful algorithms in both camps, active-set and passive-set. The simplex method for linear programming (e.g., 77), is the most prominent example in the active-set category; smooth penalty and barrier methods illustrate the passive-set approach. Note that an algorithm that is an active-set algorithm need not be restricted to a feasible-point algorithm (78).

Passive-set algorithms appear well-suited to large-scale problems: they typically require fewer iterations than many of their active-set counterparts and can be implemented using fixed data structures, which are very convenient for exploiting sparsity and parallelism. Some active-set algorithms are poorly suited to the large-scale setting; typically, those that restrict or inhibit change in the activity set from one iteration to the next do not fare well on large problems.[†] However, recently there has been considerable investigation into active-set methods that allow for significant change in the active set from one iteration to the next, and these methods do appear much more promising for large-scale problems.

In summary, the presence of constraints, despite decreasing the volume of the search space, tends to create more difficult problems (especially in the large-scale case

---

*Example 3 in the Introduction illustrates this type of "elimination."

[†]A glaring counter-example to this statement is the simplex method which restricts change in the activity set to a single variable each iteration. This strategy does not work well for more general (nonlinear) functions. Neither does it work well for some linear programming problems with special structure such as staircase problems.

when maintaining sparsity is important). Nevertheless, there has been significant progress lately, especially with respect to simple bound constraints and linear/quadratic programming. Our purpose here is to summarize and highlight some of the progress as well as attempt to give pointers to the future.

Minimization Subject to Bounds

Many optimization problems are constrained in a simple way:

$$\min_x \{f(x): l \leq x \leq u\}, \tag{21}$$

where $l \leq u$. This is sometimes referred to as a "box-constrained" problem.

Recently there has been considerable research effort on box-constrained problems, aimed at developing new algorithms, and refining old ones, especially with an eye toward large-scale sparse problems. Some of this work has been targeted specifically at the case where the objective function is quadratic. We will begin there.

Let $f(x) = g^T x + \frac{1}{2} x^T H x$, where H is a symmetric matrix; hence, our problem is:

$$\min_x \{g^T x + \frac{1}{2} x^T H x: l \leq x \leq u\}. \tag{22}$$

Clearly if the set of variables bound at the solution is known, that is, if $\mathcal{A}(x) = \mathcal{A}(x_*)$, and the tight variables are at their appropriate bounds, then a reduced Newton system will find the solution in a single step:

$$solve\ H_R s_R = -g_R, \quad update:\ x_R^+ = x_R + s_R, \tag{23}$$

where the subscript R denotes the "free" variables (i.e., those variables not at bounds). The matrix H_R consists of those rows and columns of H identified by the free variables. The idea behind the Moré and Toraldo algorithm (79), building on previous work by Dembo and Tulowitzki (80), and Bertsekas (81), is to mix steps that attempt to "guess" the active set at the solution with reduced Newton steps. The reduced Newton steps (23) are not solved for exactly: Moré and Toraldo propose a conjugate gradient "inner-iteration" for the inexact determination of this reduced Newton step. If a boundary is hit in the process then an efficient piecewise linear minimization is followed.

Therefore, the Moré-Toraldo algorithm is an active-set method with the ability to completely change the activity set in a single iteration. This is important for a large-scale problem. Coleman and Hulbert (82) suggest an alternative active-set algorithm in which they show how to compute and use direct sparse factorizations using the space required by the sparse Cholesky factor of a positive-definite matrix with the structure of the original matrix H.

Alternative strategies in the passive-set vein, also suitable for the large sparse case but currently restricted to the situation where H is positive-definite, have been suggested by Han, Pardalos, and Ye (83) and Coleman and Hulbert (84). These two approaches are entirely different: the Han-Pardalos-Ye method is an interior-point algorithm following the work of Ye (85); the Coleman-Hulbert algorithm is an exterior-point algorithm based on a Newton approach to the optimality conditions. However, the two methods are similar from the linear algebra point of view. Both methods require the repeated solution to a (short) sequence of positive-definite systems, all with the same structure as the original matrix **H**. Work on extending these approaches to problems with indefinite matrices, and to problems with linear constraints, is now continuing.

Adaptation of the methods mentioned above to problems with general nonlinear objective functions is under investigation. Other related methods, again especially targeted toward the large-scale case, have also been proposed recently (e.g., 55,56, 86–88).

What makes these newly proposed methods attractive for large-scale problems? First, they all try to avoid excessive number of iterations due to the combinatorial aspect of the problem (caused by the inequalities). Second, these methods pay some respect to the problem size by either considering iterative linear solvers or sparse direct factorizations. Finally, in several of the cases there has been some attention paid to the use of parallelism.

Linear Constraints (and Bounds)

Here we consider problems of the form:

$$\min_x \{f(x): Ax = b, 1 \leq x \leq u\}. \tag{24}$$

There has been recent research activity on this problem, especially in the case where f is a quadratic function. Again the basic approaches generally fall into two categories: active-set or passive-set. Many of the basic approaches used in the box-constrained case, discussed above, can be adapted to this more general situation. The algorithms for (24) are more complex, of course, due to the need to project onto the linear manifold $Ax = b$.

Three linear algebra situations play a prominent role in most of the proposed large-scale algorithms for problem (24). We will center our discussion around this aspect.

First, there is the weighted least-squares problem. This problem is central to virtually all of the new passive-set algorithms for linear programming* including interior-point, barrier, and exterior-point algorithms. There are several examples of work in this area (89–100). Several important related problems can also be efficiently solved using a sequence of weighted least-squares problems: linear l_1 estimation (101, 102); linear l_∞ estimation (103); the linear p-th-norm problem (104).

These various passive-set methods for linear programming have strikingly different computational and theoretical properties; however, from a linear algebra point of view they are quite similar. In particular, a sequence of least-squares problems of the form

$$D_k^{-1}A^T s_k \stackrel{\text{l.s.}}{=} -D_k g \tag{25}$$

must be solved; a primary aspect in which the algorithms differ is in the choice of diagonal weighting matrices D_k. These new passive-set algorithms have, in turn, increased interest in methods for solving a sequence of sparse least-squares problems including direct (sparse) factorization methods, parallel solvers, and iterative least-squares solvers (e.g., 47,48,105–107).

A second linear algebra problem arising in some of the new algorithms for large-scale problems with linear constraints, is the solution of reduced Newton systems of the

---

*Linear programming is a special case of (24) in which the objective function is linear: $f(x) = g^T x$.

form (16). In some cases this involves determining a basis Z for the null space of a matrix A such that the reduced Hessian matrix, $Z^T \nabla^2 f Z$, is sparse and can enjoy a sparse factorization. This works when the structure of $\nabla^2 f$ is very sparse and simple (108). However, this does not appear to be a promising avenue for general problems: construction of a sparse (or compactly represented) matrix Z and the design of an efficient iterative solver for (16) has more potential for general problems. Research issues include the development of efficient preconditioning strategies and how to deal with bounds on the variables (and perhaps changing activity sets).

The third linear algebra problem is the solution of sparse symmetric indefinite systems of the form:

$$\begin{bmatrix} H & A^T \\ A & -D \end{bmatrix} \begin{bmatrix} s \\ r \end{bmatrix} = \begin{bmatrix} -g \\ 0 \end{bmatrix}, \tag{26}$$

where D is a positive diagonal matrix (in some cases D is the identity, or a scaled identity matrix; in some cases D is the zero matrix). Note that the least-squares problem (25) can be solved using a system of the form (26). The reader can work out the details. Clearly any sparsity that was present in the original matrices **H** and **A** shows up in this augmented form (26), and that is the attraction of this approach. The dimension of the system is large, $m + n$, but this is often more than compensated for by the sparseness of the matrices. Unfortunately, the matrix in (26) is not positive definite; hence, the arsenal of techniques developed for sparse symmetric positive-definite systems is not applicable. Therefore, renewed interest is being shown in new and old techniques, direct and iterative, for solving sparse symmetric indefinite systems in general, and systems with the block structure evident in (26) (see Refs. 54,109,110). Beyond solving systems of the form (26), optimization has other concerns: determination (and use) of directions of negative curvature, guaranteeing descent properties, trust-region implementations, and the affect of the bound constraints (in active-set methods consideration must be given to the modification of a sparse factorization when the activity set changes) (e.g., 111).

The ease with which a large-scale optimization algorithm can be integrated with an appropriate parallel sparse linear solver, to produce an efficient overall procedure, will play an important role in determining the ultimate utility of proposed large-scale optimization algorithms in parallel computing environments. Certainly many of the new passive-set methods appear to be leading contenders since their interface with parallel linear solvers is exceedingly simple; just plug it in. In contrast, some other large-scale methods, such as the simplex method for linear programming, appear difficult to adapt to the parallel world. Certainly a simple interface with a "black-box" sparse linear solver would not produce an efficient overall procedure in this case.

Nonlinearly Constrained Problems

Effective procedures for problems with nonlinear constraints, even for the dense case, are still being heavily researched. Certainly the importance of sequential quadratic programming (SQP), in which a sequence of quadratic approximations is solved (perhaps approximately), is well-established (112–117). Therefore the work on large-scale quadratic programming,

$$\min_{s} \left\{ \nabla f(x_c)^T s + \frac{1}{2} s^T H_c s : As = 0, l_c \leq s \leq u_c \right\} \tag{27}$$

is directly relevant (111, 118). However, globalization strategies are still quite unsettled, with centers of gravity continually shifting from l_2-penalty functions, to l_1-penalty functions, to barrier functions, to augmented Lagrangian approaches, and around again. Despite this apparent thrashing, there is progress: for example, it is now clear that the l_2-penalty function can be used much more effectively than was thought possible just a few years ago. Some of the numerical difficulties caused by ill-conditioning can be overcome to a large degree (119,120).

Still, despite this uncertainty as to the best designs of overall methods, it is clear that the main linear algebra concerns are the same as for the linearly constrained problems discussed above (due to linearization), with increased emphasis on approximate solutions. So the progress on solving large linear systems of the form (26) is directly applicable.

CONCLUDING REMARKS

We have given the reader a quick personal tour of large-scale optimization. This field is enjoying a surge of research activity with several new trends; we have tried to capture some of them and explain some of the central concerns of large-scale optimization.

We conclude with a discussion of two developments, each with so much potential they may change the face of large-scale optimization altogether: they are automatic differentiation and parallelism.

Automatic Differentiation

Evaluation of the function, gradients, and possibly second-derivatives, often represents a significant portion of the overall computational cost of an optimization procedure. Moreover, hand-coding of derivative routines is an error-prone and tedious task; numerical approximations carry with them numerical errors. Automatic differentiation potentially offers an error-free, automatic, and efficient alternative. There still are some problems (summarized in our concluding paragraph in this section), but the recent flurry of research activity and related results (121–127) suggests great promise. The potential impact on large-scale optimization work is significant.

Automatic differentiation (AD) works like this. The user presents a description of the function to be minimized (and constraints) to the AD compiler. This is usually in the form of a Fortran or C program. The automatic compiler then produces a new program (usually in C or Fortran) that will evaluate the function and the gradient (and the Hessian if requested) at any point x in a single efficient routine. The code produced by the compiler is efficient: efficiency is achieved by calculating intermediate quantities in a good order and by saving and re-using intermediate quantities in the function, gradient, and Hessian calculations.

Automatic differentiation is distinct from symbolic differentiation. A symbolic differentiator will accept the same input as the automatic differentiator, but will produce code that represents the gradient (and Hessian if requested). The function evaluation routine is unchanged; it remains the user-written code. No account is made of efficient computation of the pair $\{f(x), \nabla f(x)\}$, or the triplet $\{f(x), \nabla f(x), \nabla^2 f(x)\}$. Intermediate quantities are not reused; typically, there is no bound on the accuracy of the resulting computations when the gradient (or Hessian) routines are used (in contrast to automatic differentiation).

The automatic differentiator can also reveal parallelism that can be used in the function, gradient, and Hessian evaluations. This is because the computational graph that is used in the AD compiler to determine the order of computation naturally exhibits the available parallelism as well. Researchers in automatic differentiation are already investigating this aspect.

The basic idea behind automatic differentiation is repeated application of the chain rule and saving intermediate quantities along the way. Indeed it has been argued (122) that instead of actually forming the Newton system it may be more efficient to solve a larger but sparser adjoint system that involves the intermediate quantities treated as temporary variables. This is similar to the techniques we used in (11), (12), and (13).

Still problems remain to be worked out. The first is a subtle one (and may not admit a solution). The code produced by the automatic differentiator is dependent on the form of the user-supplied function routine. Everything follows from this. However, different user-supplied encodings of the same function will yield different outputs from the AD compiler. It appears these outputs may differ widely and it is certainly not clear how to best encode the function originally.

Other problems: the space required by the automatic differentiation process (saving all those intermediate quantities!) may be quite substantial; the AD compiler itself is a large and complex code begging portability and ease-of-use issues; finally, can sparsity be fully and cleanly exploited? In our view these issues are extremely important for ultimate utility in the large-scale optimization context. Research activity is ongoing on these fronts and we can expect good progress in the next few years.

Parallel Computation

Parallel computation will soon play a major role in much of large-scale computational mathematics. Is optimization poised to effectively utilize this new and powerful technology? What are the research issues specifically relating parallel computation and large-scale optimization?

In order to see what role parallelism can play in large-scale optimization it is useful to both broaden and narrow our focus. On the broader scale it should be remembered that local minimization occurs in a context. This broader context often involves the solution of many independent minimizations that can be done in parallel. This easy coarse-grained parallelism yields very high parallel efficiency. Examples in this domain: global optimization typically involves the solution of many local disjoint minimization problems (18, 21); optimization problems with integrality constraints can be solved using various branch-and-bound techniques involving local nonlinear minimizations (13). In both these situations some communication and orchestration is required; however, the computational work in the local minimizations easily dominates communication/global orchestration costs by several orders of magnitude. These are important problem classes that typically yield many disjoint local minimization problems; however, the most common is probably the following. In many cases the objective function to be minimized is not really known precisely; often the form is known (or accepted), but there are several unknown parameters. These parameters are usually determined only after a lengthy trial-and-error period involving many independent minimizations—another perfect candidate for coarse-grained parallelism.

If we now sharpen the focus and look within an optimization procedure, we see the possibility of using parallelism* in both linear algebra computations and in the evaluation of function, gradients, and Hessians (46–48, 131–133). There are some subtleties here that have optimization implications and so we must examine this possibility more carefully.

First, it is clear that if the function and derivative evaluations dominate the computational costs then parallelism must begin there. A good example of this is the bone modelling problem we discussed in Example 3 (Fig. 3). In this example, on realistic problems, the finite-element analysis (i.e., the function evaluation) can take in excess of 90% of the serial computational time. Of course, the difficulty here is that this parallelization effort (organize the function evaluation to compute the function efficiently in parallel) falls into the hands of the user in general. General guidelines can be given but beyond that it will usually be up to the user. (It may be possible to design efficient parallel strategies for some very common function forms, e.g., partially separable functions. It may also be that automatic differentiation will save the day.)

Another issue is brought up by this bone reconstruction example. Despite the dominance of the overall computational cost by the function evaluation, it is incorrect to infer that the selection of the optimization routine is relatively unimportant. It is true that the computational cost of the linear algebra directly involved in the determination of a search direction may be (relatively) insignificant in this case; however, the choice of algorithm can dramatically influence the number of function evaluations and therefore a judicious choice can be most significant. For example, for a sufficiently large problem with inequalities some active-set methods will be a poor choice. Due to the combinatorial sensitivity of some active-set methods there may be a significant growth in the number of iterations—and therefore function evaluations—as the dimension grows. Passive-set methods, on the other hand, are more likely to require fewer (more expensive) iterations, and therefore fewer function evaluations. Moreover, in a parallel computing environment, it is difficult to effectively orchestrate the changing activity sets and corresponding matrix dimensions of an active-set method. Passive-set methods typically deal with a fixed dimension and fixed matrix structures and are therefore more likely to yield efficient parallelism. Finally, an algorithm that uses exact second derivatives may also significantly decrease the number of function evaluations. If the second derivatives can be computed efficiently, using parallelism, then this extra cost per iteration (over a method that uses only first derivatives) may be cost-effective.

To emphasize: The availability of a parallel computer should influence the choice of serial optimization algorithm to be used in a parallel computing environment. A serial algorithm that yields more work that can be effectively computed in parallel, perhaps at some increased serial cost per iteration, is to be preferred if the number of serial outer iterations decreases significantly.

---

*The literature on the parallel solution of problems with special structure is extensive (128–130), but falls outside the domain of this article.

Linear algebra considerations may also affect the choice of serial optimization algorithm used in a parallel computing environment. For example, in the serial world the unconstrained minimization of nonlinear functions is often performed by the positive definite secant update (BFGS). The modern choice is to update the Cholesky factor of the current approximation in a stable and efficient manner requiring $O(n^2)$ work. Therefore, the linear algebra involved per iteration is quite acceptable: $O(n^2)$ work for the Cholesky update, and $O(n^2)$ for the triangular solve. Unfortunately, this may not work well on a parallel machine. The difficulty is that known stable algorithms for these two steps exhibit limited parallelism. Couple this with the low-order of work required, within each iteration, and it is difficult to achieve good parallel efficiency (132, 133). It may be better to reconsider the methods for updating the inverse approximation in this case (131). The work is still $O(n^2)$, but the algorithms required exhibit much more parallelism. Of course, this option is not viable for sparse problems since the inverse of a sparse matrix is almost always dense (134).

Optimization problems with large dense matrices exist (e.g., Example 3, Fig. 3); for these we can expect to do well in the linear algebra arena, given the emphasis the linear algebra community has placed on developing high-performance dense linear algebra routines. However, most large-scale optimization algorithms do not exhibit large dense matrices. Much more common are large sparse matrices and large structured systems. Large-scale optimization needs effective high-performance algorithms for these classes of matrices.

Certainly there is considerable work on special structures as well as general sparse systems. However, these are difficult problems and progress is slow and more research work is needed.

Nevertheless, it is expected that reasonable success will be obtained in our ability to obtain high-performance parallel algorithms for standard factorizations of large sparse matrices and large matrices with a variety of standard structures. Therefore, serial optimization algorithms that plug into efficient parallel versions of standard linear algebra tasks, for example, the sparse QR-factorization will yield better overall performance than algorithms that use specialized low-order sparse matrix updating. We expect passive-set algorithms to ultimately yield better performance on parallel computers than active-set methods, for example.

In summary, numerical optimization and parallelism appear to intersect on two levels. At the high end, there is coarse-grained parallelism for problems that yield numerous disjoint local minimizations. This is typically easy parallelism to get, although research on effective orchestration, communication, load balancing is ongoing and still needed, and is very important. Obtaining parallelism for optimization at the low end, linear algebra (especially sparse and/or structured systems) and function and derivative calculations, is also ongoing and yields both fine-grained and medium-grained parallelism. The (local) optimization challenge consists of designing serial optimization algorithms that can effectively use the parallelized linear algebra and function evaluation subroutines.

It is interesting to note that we have said nothing about the design of general-purpose parallel local minimization algorithms per se. The parallelism we have discussed encircles the local minimization procedure or is internal to it, but the optimization algorithm itself remains serial; Typically some version of Newton's method (an inherently serial process). The general-purpose parallel optimization research to date has been largely concerned with the design and modification of serial algorithms that can effectively use parallelism at either of these two levels. Barring a breakthrough, say a truly parallel Newton process, this will continue to be the case.

ACKNOWLEDGMENTS

I extend thanks to a number of my Cornell colleagues for suggesting improvements to an earlier version of this paper. Specifically, I thank Moshe Braner, Shirish Chinchalkar, Yuying Li, Jianguo Liu, Michael Todd, Zhijun Wu, and Wei Yuan.

Research partially supported by the Applied Mathematical Sciences Research Program (KC-04-02) of the Office of Energy Research of the U.S. Department of Energy under grant DE-FG02-86ER25013.A000 and by the Computational Mathematics Program of the National Science Foundation under Grant DMS-8706133.

REFERENCES

1. T. F. Coleman and Y. Li, *Large-Scale Numerical Optimization*, SIAM, 1990.
2. T. F. Coleman, *Large Sparse Numerical Optimization*, Lecture Notes in Computer Science, Volume 165, Springer-Verlag, New York, 1984.
3. J. E. Dennis and R. B. Schnabel, *Numerical Methods for Unconstrained Optimization*, Prentice-Hall, Englewood Cliffs, NJ, 1983.
4. A. V. Fiacco and G. P. McCormick, *Nonlinear Programming: Sequential Unconstrained Minimization Techniques*, John Wiley and Sons, New York, 1968.
5. R. Fletcher, *Practical Methods of Optimization*, Second Edition, John Wiley and Sons, New York, 1987.
6. G. P. McCormick, *Nonlinear Programming. Theory, Algorithms, and Applications*, John Wiley and Sons, New York, 1983.
7. P. E. Gill, W. Murray, and M. H. Wright. *Practical Optimization*, Academic Press, New York, 1981.
8. R. Fletcher, Recent Developments in Methods for Nonlinear Programming, Technical Report NA/123, University of Dundee, 1990.
9. G. L. Nemhauser, A. H. G. Rinnooy Kan, and M. J. Todd, *Optimization*, Volume 1 *Handbooks in Operations Research and Management Science*, North-Holland, Amsterdam, 1989.
10. D. P. Bertsekas and J. N. Tsitsiklis, *Parallel and Distributed Computation*, Prentice-Hall, Englewood Cliffs, NJ, 1989.
11. S. A. Zenios, Parallel Optimization: Current Status and an Annotated Bibliography, *ORSA J. Computing*, *1*:20–43 (1989).
12. J. A. Nelder and R. Mead, A Simplex Method for Function Minimization, *Computer J.*, 7:308–313 (1965).
13. Z. Wu, A Subgradient Algorithm for Nonlinear Integer Programming and Its Parallel Implementation, Technical Report TR91-09, Dept. Math. Sci., Rice University, 1990.
14. B. A. Hendrickson, Conditions for Unique Graph Embeddings, Technical Report CS-88-950, Cornell University, 1988.
15. B. A. Hendrickson, The Molecule Problem: Determining conformation from pairwise distances, Ph.D. thesis, Department of Computer Science, Cornell University, 1991.
16. M. R. Garey and D. S. Johnson, *Computers and Intractability*. W. H. Freeman, San Francisco, 1979.
17. R. H. Byrd, C. L. Dert, A. H. G. Rinnooy Kan, and R. B. Schnabel, Concurrent Stochastic Methods for Global Optimization, *Math. Program.*, *46*(1):1–29 (1990).

18.   E. Eskow and R. B. Schnabel, Mathematical Modeling of a Parallel Global Optimization Algorithm, Technical Report CU-CS395-88, University of Colorado, Boulder, 1988.

19.   A. H. G. Rinnooy and G. T. Timmer, A Stochastic Approach to Global Optimization. In: *Numerical Optimization*, (P. Boggs, R. Byrd, and R. B. Schnabel, eds.) SIAM, New York, 1984, pp. 245–262.

20.   A. Torn and A. Zilinskas, Global Optimization.

21.   S. L. Smith. E. Eskow, and R. B. Schnabel, Adaptive, Asynchronous Stochastic Global Optimization Algorithms for Sequential and Parallel Computation. In: *Large-Scale Numerical Optimization* (T. F. Coleman and Y. Li, eds.) SIAM, New York, 1990, pp. 207–227.

22.   Y. Censor and G. T. Herman, On Some Optimization Techniques in Image Reconstruction from Projections, *Appl. Num. Math.*, *3*:365–391 (1987).

23.   G. T. Herman, *Image Reconstruction from Projections*: *The Fundamentals of Computerized Tomography*, Academic Press, New York, 1980.

24.   G. T. Herman, *Image Reconstruction from Projections*: *Implementation and Applications*, Springer, Berlin, 1979.

25.   G. T. Herman, D. Odhner, K. D. Toennies, and S. A. Zenios, A Parallelized Algorithm for Image Reconstruction from Noisy Projections. In *Large-Scale Numerical Optimization*, (T. F. Coleman and Y. Li, eds.) SIAM, New York, 1990, pp. 3–21.

26.   G. Subbarayan and D. L. Bartel, A Variational Model for Bone Construction/Reconstruction and Its Applications, Technical Report, Sibley School of Mechanical and Aerospace Engineering, 1989.

27.   G. Subbarayan and D. L. Bartel, VSAFE: A Program for Variational Sensitivity Analysis Using the Finite Element Discretization, Technical Report, Sibley School of Mechanical and Aerospace Engineering, Cornell University, 1989.

28.   D. M. Gay, Computing Optimal Locally Constrained Steps, *SIAM J. Sci. Stat. Computing*, *2*:186–197 (1981).

29.   J. J. Moré and D. C. Sorensen, Computing a Trust Region Step, *SIAM J. Sci. Stat. Computing*, *4*:553–572, 1983.

30.   R. H. Byrd and R. B. Schnabel, Approximate Solution of the Trust Region Problem by Minimization Over Two-Dimensional Subspaces, *Math. Program.*, *40*:247–263 (1988).

31.   G. A. Schultz, R. B. Schnabel, and R. H. Byrd, A Family of Trust-Region-Based Algorithms for Unconstrained Minimization with Strong Global Convergence Properties, *SIAM J. Numer. Analysis*, *22*(1):47–67 (1985).

32.   J. E. Dennis and J. J. Moré, Quasi-Newton Methods, Motivation and Theory, *SIAM Rev.*, *19*:46–89 (1977).

33.   M. J. D. Powell and Ph. L. Toint, A Note on Quasi-Newton Formulae for Sparse Second Derivative Matrices, *Math. Program.*, *20*:144–151 (1981).

34.   M. J. D. Powell and Ph. L. Toint, The Shanno-Toint Procedure for Updating Sparse Symmetric Matrices, *IMA J. Numer. Analysis*, *1*:403–413 (1981).

35.   D. F. Shanno, On the Variable Metric Methods for Sparse Hessians, *Math. Comp.*, *34*:499–514 (1980).

36.   D. C. Sorensen, An Example Concerning Quasi-Newton Estimation of a Sparse Hessian, *SIGNUM Newslett.*, *16*:8–10 (1981).

37.   Ph. L. Toint, On Sparse and Symmetric Updating Subject to a Linear Equation, *Math. Comp.*, *32*:839–851 (1977).

38.   Ph. L. Toint, A Note on Sparsity Exploiting Quasi-Newton Methods, *Math. Program.*, *21*:172–181 (1981).

39.   Ph. L. Toint, A Sparse Quasi-Newton Update Derived Variationally with a Non-diagonally Weighted Frobenius Norm, *Math. Comp.*, *37a*:425–434 (1981).

40.   A. Curtis, M. J. D. Powell, and J. Reid, On the Estimation of Sparse Jacobian Matrices, *J. Inst. Math. Appl.*, *13*:117–119 (1974).

41. T. F. Coleman and J. J. Moré, Estimation of Sparse Jacobian Matrices and Graph Coloring Problems, *SIAM J. Numer. Analysis*, *20*:187–209 (1983).

42. T. F. Coleman and J. J. Moré, Software for Estimating Sparse Jacobian Matrices, *ACM Transact. Math. Software*, *10*:329–345 (1984).

43. T. F. Coleman and J.-Y. Cai, The Cyclic Coloring Problem and Estimation of Sparse Hessian Matrices, *SIAM J. Appl. Math.*, *7*:221–235 (1986).

44. T. F. Coleman and J. J. Moré, Estimation of Sparse Hessian Matrices and Graph Coloring Problems, *Math. Program.*, *28*:243–270 (1984).

45. M. J. D. Powell and Ph. L. Toint, On the Estimation of Sparse Hessian Matrices, *SIAM J. Numer. Analysis*, *16*:1060–1074 (1979).

46. T. F. Coleman and P. E. Plassmann, Solution of Nonlinear Least-Squares Problems on a Multiprocessor. In: *Parallel Computing 1988, Shell Conference Proceedings* (G. A. van Zee and J. G. G. van de Vorst, eds.), Springer-Verlag, New York, 1989, p. 384.

47. T. F. Coleman and P. E. Plassmann, A Parallel Nonlinear Least-Squares Solver: Theoretical Analysis and Numerical Results, *SIAM J. Sci. Stat. Computing*.

48. P. E. Plassmann, Sparse Jacobian Estimation and Factorization on a Multiprocessor. In: *Large-Scale Numerical Optimization* (T. F. Coleman and Y. Li, eds.), SIAM, New York, 1990, pp. 152–179.

49. A. Griewank, The Chain Rule Revisited in Scientific Computing, Technical Report MCS-P227-0491, Argonne National Laboratory, 1991.

50. A. R. Conn, N. I. M. Gould, and Ph. L. Toint, An Introduction to the Structure of Large Scale Nonlinear Optimization Problems and the Lancelot Project. In: *Computing Methods in Applied Sciences and Engineering*, SIAM, New York, 1990, pp. 42–54.

51. A. Griewank and Ph. L. Toint, On the Unconstrained Optimization of Partially Separable Functions. In: *Nonlinear Optimization 1981* (M. J. D. Powell, ed.), Academic Press, New York, 1982, pp. 301–312.

52. A. Griewank and Ph. L. Toint, Partitioned Variable Metric Updates for Large Structured Optimization Problems, *Numerische Mathematik*, *39*:119–137 (1982).

53. A. Griewank and Ph. L. Toint, On the Existence of Convex Decompositions of Partially Separable Functions, *Math. Program.*, *28*:25–50 (1984).

54. I. S. Duff and J. K. Reid, The Multifrontal Solution of Indefinite Sparse Symmetric Linear Equations, *ACM Transact. Math. Software*, *9*:302–325 (1983).

55. A. R. Conn, N. I. M. Gould, and Ph. L. Toint, Global Convergence of a Class of Trust Region Algorithms for Optimization with Simple Bounds, *SIAM J. Numer. Analysis*, *25*:433–460 (1988).

56. A. R. Conn, N. I. M. Gould, and Ph. L. Toint, Testing a Class of Methods for Solving Minimization Problems with Simple Bounds on the Variables, *Math. Comput.*, *50*:399–430 (1988).

57. H. Khalfan, R. H. Byrd, and R. B. Schnabel, A Theoretical and Experimental Study of the Symmetric Rank One Update, Technical Report CU-CS-489-90, Dept. of Computer Science, University of Colorado, 1990.

58. A. Buckley and A. LeNir, QN-Like Variable Storage Conjugate Gradients, *Math. Program.*, *27*:155–175 (1983).

59. A. Buckley and A. LeNir, BBVSCG—A Variable Storage Algorithm for Function Minimization, *ACM Transact. Math. Software*, *11*(2):103–119 (1985).

60. R. Fletcher and C. M. Reeves, Function Minimization by Conjugate Gradients, *Computer J.*, *6*:163–168 (1964).

61. P. E. Gill and W. Murray, Conjugate-Gradient Methods for Large-Scale Nonlinear Optimization, Technical Report SOL79-15, Dept. Operations Research, Stanford University, 1979.

62. E. Polak and G. Ribière, Note sur la convergence de methodes de directions conjugées, *Rev. Francaise Informat. Recherche Operationelle*, *16*:35–43 (1960).

63. M. J. D. Powell, Nonconvex Minimization Calculations and the Conjugate Gradient Method. In: *Numerical Analysis Proceedings*, (D. F. Griffiths, ed.), Springer Verlag, New York, 1984.

64. D. F. Shanno, Conjugate-Gradient Methods with Inexact Searches, *Math. Oper. Res.*, *3*:244–256 (1978).

65. D. F. Shanno and K. H. Phua, Remark on Algorithm 500: Minimization of Unconstrained Multivariate Functions, *ACM Transact. Math. Software*, 6:618–622 (1980).

66. J. Nocedal, The Performance of Several Algorithms for Large Scale Unconstrained Optimization. In: *Large-Scale Numerical Optimization*, (T. F. Coleman and Y. Li, eds.), SIAM, New York, 1990, pp. 138–151.

67. R. Fletcher, Low Storage Methods for Unconstrained Optimization, Technical Report NA/117, University of Dundee, 1990.

68. D. C. Liu and J. Nocedal, On the Limited Memory BFGS Method for Large Scale Optimization, Technical Report, Dept. Electrical Engineering and Computer Science, Northwestern University, 1988.

69. J. Nocedal, Updating Quasi-Newton Matrices with Limited Storage, *Math. Comput.*, *35*:773–782 (1980).

70. S. G. Nash and J. Nocedal, A Numerical Study of the Limited Memory BFGS Method and the Truncated Newton Method for Large Scale Optimization, *SIAM J. Optimization*, *1*:358–372 (1991).

71. B. A. Murtaugh and M. A. Saunders, MINOS/Augmented User's Guide, Technical Report SOL-80-14, Stanford University, 1987.

72. S. G. Nash, Preconditioning of Truncated-Newton Methods, *SIAM J. Sci. Stat. Computing*, 6:599–616 (1985).

73. T. Steihaug, The Conjugate Gradient Methods and Trust Regions in Large Scale Optimization, *SIAM J. Numer. Analysis*, *20*:626–637 (1983).

74. T. F. Coleman and A. Pothen, The Null Space Problem I: Complexity, *SIAM J. Algebraic and Discrete Methods*, *7*:527–537 (1987).

75. T. F. Coleman and A. Pothen, The Null Space Problem II: Algorithms, *SIAM J. Algebraic and Discrete Methods*, *8*:544–563 (1987).

76. J. R. Gilbert and M. T. Heath, Computing a Sparse Basis for the Nullspace, *SIAM J. Algebraic and Discrete Methods*, *8*:446–459 (1987).

77. V. Chvátal, *Linear Programming*, W. H. Freeman and Company, San Francisco, 1980.

78. A. R. Conn, Linear Programming Via a Non-differentiable Penalty Function, *SIAM J. Numer. Analysis*, *13*:224–241 (1988).

79. J. J. Moré and G. Toraldo, Algorithms for Bound Constrained Quadratic Programming Problems, *Numerische Mathematik*, *55*:377–400 (1989).

80. R. S. Dembo and U. Tulowitzki, On the Minimization of Quadratic Functions Subject to Box Constraints, Technical Report B 71, Yale University, 1983.

81. D. P. Bertsekas, Projected Newton Methods for Optimization Problems with Simple Constraints, *SIAM J. Control and Optimization*, *20*(2):221–246 (1982).

82. T. F. Coleman and L. Hulbert, A Direct Active Set Algorithm for Large Sparse Quadratic Programs with Simple Bounds, *Math. Program.*, *45*:373–406 (1989).

83. C.-G. Han, P. M. Pardalos, and Y. Ye, Computational Aspects of an Interior Point Algorithm for Quadratic Programming Problems with Box Constraints. In: *Large-Scale Numerical Optimization*, (T. F. Coleman and Y. Li, eds.), SIAM, New York, 1990, pp. 92–112.

84. T. F. Coleman and L. Hulbert, A Globally and Superlinearly Convergent Algorithm for Convex Quadratic Programs with Simple Bounds, Technical Report TR 90-1092, Computer Science Dept., Cornell University, February 1990 (to appear in *SIAM J. Optimization*).

85. Y. Ye, On the Interior Algorithms for Nonconvex Quadratic Programming, Technical Report, Integrated Systems Inc., 1988.

86. J. J. Júdice and F. M. Pires, Direct Methods for Convex Quadratic Programs Subject to Box Constraints, Departamento de matemática, Universidade de Coimbra, 3000 Coimbra, Portugal, 1989.

87. P. Lotstedt, Solving the Minimal Least Squares Problem Subject to Bounds on the Variables, *BIT*, *24*:206–224 (1984).

88. E. K. Yang and J. W. Tolle, A Class of Methods for Solving Large Convex Quadratic Programs Subject to Box Constraints, Technical Report, Dept. of Operations Research, University of North Carolina, Chapel Hill, NC, 1988.

89. I. Adler, M. G. C. Resende, G. Veiga, and N. Karmarkar, An Implementation of Karmarkar's Algorithm for Linear Programming, *Math. Program.*, *44* (1989).

90. E. R. Barnes, A Variation on Karmarkar's Algorithm for Solving Linear Programming Problems, *Math. Program.*, *36*:174–182 (1986).

91. T. F. Coleman and Y. Li, A Quadratically-Convergent Algorithm for the Linear Programming Problem with Lower and Upper Bounds. In: *Large-Scale Numerical Optimization*, (T. F. Coleman and Y. Li, eds.), SIAM, New York, 1990, pp. 49–47. Proceedings of the Mathematical Sciences Institute workshop, October 1989, Cornell University.

92. D. M. Gay, A Variant of Karmarkar's Linear Programming Algorithm for Problems in Standard Form, *Math. Program.*, *37*:81–90 (1987).

93. P. E. Gill, W. Murray, M. A. Saunders, J. A. Tomlin, and M. H. Wright, On Projected Newton Barrier Methods for Linear Programming and an Equivalence to Karmarkar's Projective Method, *Math. Program.*, *36*:183–209 (1986).

94. N. Karmarkar, A New Polynomial-Time Algorithm for Linear Programming, *Combinatorica*, *4*:373–395 (1984).

95. I. J. Lustig, R. E. Marsten, and D. F. Shanno, The Primal-Dual Interior Point Method on the Cray Supercomputer. In: *Large-Scale Numerical Optimization*, (T. F. Coleman and Y. Li, eds.), SIAM, New York, 1990, pp. 70–80.

96. K. A. McShane, C. L. Monma, and D. F. Shanno, An Implementation of a Primal-Dual Interior Point Method for Linear Programming, *ORSA J. Computing*, *1*:70–83 (1989).

97. M. J. Todd, Recent Developments and New Directions in Linear Programming. In: *Mathematical Programming: Recent Developments and Applications*, (M. Iri and K. Tanabe, eds.), Kluwer Academic Publishers, Dordrecht, 1989, pp. 109–157.

98. M. J. Todd, Exploiting Special Structure in Karmarkar's Linear Programming Algorithm, *Math. Program.*, *41*:97–113 (1988).

99. R. J. Vanderbei, M. S. Meketon, and B. A. Freedman, A Modification of Karmarkar's Linear Programming Algorithm, *Algorithmica*, *1*:395–407 (1986).

100. Y. Ye, An $O(n^3 L)$ Potential Reduction Algorithm for Linear Programming, *Math. Program.*, *50*:239–258 (1991).

101. T. F. Coleman and Y. Li, A Global and Quadratic Affine Scaling Method for (Augmented) Linear l_1 Problems. In: *Proc. 1989 Dundee Conference on Numerical Analysis*, 1989.

102. T. F. Coleman and Y. Li, A Global and Quadratic Affine Scaling Method for Linear l_1 Problems, Technical Report 89-1026, Computer Science Dept., Cornell University, 1989 (to appear in *Math. Program.*).

103. T. F. Coleman and Y. Li, A Global and Quadratically-Convergent Method for Linear l_∞ Problems, Technical Report 90-1121, *SIAM J. Numer. Analy.*, *29*: 1166–1186 (1992).

104. Y. Li, A Globally Convergent Method for l_p Problems, Technical Report 91-1212, Computer Science Dept., Cornell University, 1991.

105. S. G. Kratzer, Massively Parallel Sparse-Matrix Computations, Technical Report, SRC-TR-90-008, Supercomputing Research Center, 1990.

106. U. Öreborn, A Direct Method for Sparse Nonnegative Least Squares Problems. Ph.D. thesis, Dept. of Mathematics, Linköping University, Linköping, Sweden, 1986.

107. P. E. Plassmann, The Parallel Solution of Nonlinear Least-Squares Problems, Ph.D. thesis, Center for Applied Mathematics, Cornell University, 1990.

108. S. S. Nielsen and S. A. Zenios, A Massively Parallel Algorithm for Nonlinear Stochastic Network Problems, Technical Report 90-09-08, Dept. of Decision Sciences, Wharton School, University of Pennsylvania, 1990.

109. I. S. Duff, N. I. M. Gould, J. K. Reid, J. A. Scott, and K. Turner, The Factorization of Sparse Symmetric Indefinite Matrices, *IMA J. Numer. Analy.*

110. P. E. Gill, W. Murray, M. A. Saunders, and M. H. Wright, A Schur-Complement Method for Sparse Quadratic Programming. In: *Reliable Numerical Computing* (M. G. Cox and S. J. Hammarling, eds.), Oxford University Press, New York, 1992.

111. N. I. M. Gould, An Algorithm for Large Scale Quadratic Programming, Technical Report 89-036, Computer Science and Systems Division, Harwell Laboratory, 1989.

112. T. F. Coleman, On Characterizations of Superlinear Convergence for Constrained Optimization. In: (E. L. Allgower and K. George, eds.), *Computational Solution of Nonlinear Systems of Equations*, Volume 26 *Lectures in Applied Mathematics*, American Mathematical Society, New York, 1990, pp. 113–134.

113. J. Stoer and R. A. Tapia, On the Characterization of Q-Superlinear Convergence of Quasi-Newton Methods for constrained Optimization, Technical Report 84-2, Dept. of Mathematical Sciences, Rice University, July 1984 (revised October 1986).

114. R. Fontecilla, T. Steihaug, and R. A. Tapia, A Convergence Theory for a Class of Quasi-Newton Methods for Constrained Optimization, *SIAM J. Numer. Analysis*, 24:1133–1151 (1987).

115. J. Goodman, Newton's Method for Constrained Optimization, *Math. Program.*, 33:162–171 (1985).

116. J. Nocedal and M. Overton, Projected Hessian Updating Algorithms for Nonlinearly Constrained Optimization, *SIAM J. Numer. Analysis*, 22:821–850 (1985).

117. R. A. Tapia, A Stable Approach to Newton's Method for Optimization Problems with Equality Constraints, *J. Optimization Theory Appl.*, 14:453–476 (1974).

118. P. E. Gill, W. Murray, M. A. Saunders, and M. H. Wright, A Schur Complement Method for Sparse Quadratic Programming. In: *Reliable Numerical Computation*, Clarendon Press, Oxford, 1990, pp. 113–138.

119. T. F. Coleman and C. Hempel, Computing a Trust Region Step for a Penalty Function, *SIAM J. Sci. Stat. Computing*, 11:180–201 (1990).

120. N. I. M. Gould, On the Accurate Determination of Search Directions for Simple Differentiable Penalty Functions, *I.M.A. J. Numer. Analysis*, 6:357–372 (1986).

121. A. Griewank, On Automatic Differentiation. In: *Mathematical Programming: Recent Developments and Applications*, (M. Iri and K. Tanabe, eds.), Kluwer Academic Publishers, Dordrecht, 1989, pp. 83–108.

122. A. Griewank, Direct Calculation of Newton Steps Without Accumulating Jacobians. In: *Large-Scale Numerical Optimization* (T. F. Coleman and Y. Li, eds.), SIAM, New York, 1990, pp. 115–137.

123. A. Griewank, D. Juedes, and J. Srinivasan, ADOL-C, A Package for the Automatic Differentiation of Algorithms Written in C/C^{++}, Technical Report MCSA-180-1190, Argonne National Laboratory, 1990.

124. M. Iri and K. Kubota, Methods of Fast Automatic Differentiation and Applications, Technical Report, Mathematical Engineering and Instrumentation Physics, University of Tokyo, 1988.

125. M. Iri, T. Tsuchiya, and M. Hoshi, Automatic Computation of Partial Derivatives and Rounding Error Estimates with Applications to Large-Scale Systems of Nonlinear Equations, *J. Comput. Appl. Math.*, 24:365–392 (1988).

126. K. V. Kim, J. Nesterov, V. A. Skokov, and B. V. Cherkasskii, An Efficient Algorithm for Computing Derivatives and Extremal Problems, *MATEKON*, 21:49–67 (1985).

127. G. L. Miller, V. Ramachandran, and E. Kaltofen, Efficient Parallel Evaluation of Straight-Line Code and Arithmetic Circuits, *SIAM J. Computing*, *17*:687–695 (1988).

128. E. D. Chajakis and S. A. Zenios, Synchronous and Asynchronous Implementations of Relaxation Algorithms for Nonlinear Network Optimization, Technical Report 89-10-07, Decision Sciences Dept., University of Pennsylvania, 1990.

129. S. A. Zenios and Y. Censor, Massively Parallel Row-Action Algorithms for Some Nonlinear Transportational Problems, Technical Report 89-09-10, Decision Sciences Dept., University of Pennsylvania, 1989.

130. S. A. Zenios, R. Qi, and E. D. Chajakis, A Comparative Study of Parallel Dual Coordinate Ascent Implementations for Nonlinear Network Optimization. In: *Large-Scale Numerical Optimization*, (T. F. Coleman and Y. Li, eds.), SIAM, New York, 1990, pp. 238–255.

131. R. Byrd, R. B. Schnabel, and G. Shultz, Parallel Quasi-Newton Methods for Unconstrained Optimization, Technical Report, Dept. of Computer Science, University of Colorado, 1988.

132. T. F. Coleman and G. Li, Solving Systems of Nonlinear Equations on a Message-Passing Multiprocessor, *SIAM J. Sci. Stat. Computing*, *11*:1116–1135 (1990).

133. G. Li and T. F. Coleman, A New Method for Solving Triangular Systems on a Distributed Memory Message-Passing Multiprocessor, *SIAM J. Sci. Stat. Computing*, *10*:382–396 (1989).

134. J. R. Gilbert, Predicting Structure in Sparse Matrix Computations, Technical Report CS-86-750, Cornell University, 1986.

BASIC READINGS FOR FURTHER STUDY

Bertsekas, D. P. and J. N. Tsitsiklis, *Parallel and Distributed Computation*, Prentice-Hall, Englewood Cliffs, NJ, 1989.

Coleman, T. F., *Large Sparse Numerical Optimization*, Volume 165, *Lecture Notes in Computer Science*, Springer-Verlag, New York, 1984.

Coleman, T. F. and Y. Li, *Large-Scale Numerical Optimization*, SIAM, New York, 1990.

Dennis, J. E. and J. J. Moré, Quasi-Newton Methods, Motivation and Theory, *SIAM Rev.*, *19*:46–89 (1977).

Dennis, J. E. and R. B. Schnabel, *Numerical Methods for Unconstrained Optimization*, Prentice-Hall, Englewood Cliffs, NJ, 1983.

Fiacco, A. V. and G. P. McCormick, *Nonlinear Programming: Sequential Unconstrained Minimization Techniques*, John Wiley and Sons, New York, 1968.

Gill, P. E., W. Murray, and M. H. Wright, *Practical Optimization*, Academic Press, New York, 1981.

McCormick, G. P., *Nonlinear Programming. Theory, Algorithms, and Applications*, John Wiley and Sons, New York, 1983.

Nemhauser, G. L., A. H. G. Rinnooy Kan, and M. J. Todd, *Optimization*, Vol. 1, *Handbooks in Operations Research and Management Science*, North-Holland, Amsterdam, 1989.

Zenios, S. A., Parallel Optimization: Current Status and an Annotated Bibliography, *ORSA J. Computing*, *1*:20–43 (1989).

THOMAS F. COLEMAN

LITERAL INTELLIGENCE OF COMPUTERS AND DOCUMENTS

INTRODUCTION

Speculations on the possibility of computers displaying intelligence are often traced to Alan Turing's paper, "Computing Machinery and Intelligence," first published in 1950 (1). It introduced a test for computer intelligence, subsequently known as the Turing test, which required the convincing simulation of human linguistic responses to questions. Claims for the literal intelligence of an appropriately programmed computer were refuted publicly in 1980 in an article by John Searle, "Minds, Brains and Programs." Even an adequate simulation of intelligence would still lack intentionality, "that feature of certain mental states by which they are directed at or about objects or states of affairs in the world" (2, pp.419–424). For Searle, then, it is a matter of definition that literal intelligence must involve a human act of interpretation, and I wish to endorse this position. Searle's refutation of claims for the intelligence of computers has been widely accepted (3). Claims for the possibility of the adequate simulation of intelligence by an appropriately programmed computer, as distinct from its literal presence, are now also increasingly, although not entirely, subdued (4,5).

Analogies between the computer and the human brain or mind have persisted (6). For example, on one important interpretation, cognitive science demands that "theories of the mind should be expressed in a form that can be modelled in a computer program," without recourse to intuition (7, p.52). A recent, and significant, contribution to linguistics, itself indebted to cognitive science, *Relevance: communication and cognition* models the mind, and comprehension of utterances, as a formal system or automation (8, p.94). Research into neural networks which, on one account (9), aims to simulate the parallel processing characteristic of human brain processes also rests on an extensive analogy between computational and human intellectual processes. Information science has been influenced by developments in cognitive science and artificial intelligence, for instance in conducting, and funding, research into expert systems (10) and neural networks (9).

More recent research has departed from an immediate analogy between the computer and the human brain or mind. A perspective which links computers directly with documents through writing and through the human faculty for constructing socially shared systems of signs has been established (11–13). From such a viewpoint, it can be shown that (1) claims for the literal intelligence of an appropriately programmed computer, in the tradition established by the Turing test, have rested on a similar basis to claims for the intelligence of a document, the production of depersonalized linguistic output, and (2) that claims for the intelligence of computers and documents are subject to an identical objection, that such linguistic output is made available without a prior act of comprehension by the artifact. Such a position would be tenable on purely logical grounds, but it is also supported by historical evidence.

In order to substantiate this, I wish first to review those contributions which have made writing, and the faculty for constructing systems of signs, into unifying principles for computers and documents; second, to place speculations for computer intelligence and the development of the Turing test in their intellectual and historical context; and, third, to turn to a complaint that documents offer only the appearance of intelligence, without its substance. This complaint, in Plato's *Phaedrus* (14), must also be seen in its historical context, the supplementing of oral communication by written language in Greece (15). My concern, then, is not with the disappointing results of attempts at simulation of human intelligence, but simply with showing that there are extensive similarities between claims for, and objections to, computer and documentary intelligence.

REVIEW: WRITING, DOCUMENTS, AND COMPUTERS

Spoken language can be regarded as one social sign system among others, such as written language, codes of gesture, symbolic rites and the like. Saussure in the *Course in General Linguistics*, first published in 1916, argued that "it is not spoken language which is natural to man, but the faculty of constructing a language, i.e. a system of distinct signs corresponding to distinct ideas" (16, p.10). The capacity for creating significant order invoked by Saussure has come to be known as the semiotic faculty. Linguistics has reiterated the proposition that there are no primitive spoken languages in that all discovered cultures have developed languages sufficient to meet their needs for communication. Recognition of spoken language as one among other social sign systems, and of a single faculty for constructing such systems, would seem to legitimate an extension of this proposition to other sign systems, including writing: that societies develop methods for storing and communicating information sufficient to meet their needs.

Written language has itself been partially disentangled from speech. Classic discussions of language tended to regard written language as a secondary system of signs, parasitic on speech. More recent research, partly aided by technical developments which have enabled the recording and inspection of utterances, have indicated extensive lexical and structural contrasts between written and spoken language. Neither the word nor the sentence have been satisfactorily isolated as features of utterance alone. Written language is visible not audible, extended in space not time, and linked to speech by coded correlation not resemblance. As a graphic form, written language has historical links and contemporary affinities with other codes of inscription without a simple correlate in utterance, such as musical or choreographic notation. Such contrasts seldom constitute absolute differences. Rather than insisting on written language as an independent system of signs, it may be more helpful to think of both spoken and written language as two contrasting ways of giving form to language.

Recognition of contrasts between written and spoken language, and of the affinities of written language with codes of inscription without a simple correlate in utterance, can lead to a subtle position which, however, continues to acknowledge links between written and spoken language. One form of writing draws on models in utterance for the purposes of graphic communication, but a connection to speech need not be made criterial to the recognition of writing. The boundaries between forms of writing connected with speech and those independent of it are uncertain mutable. Both spoken and written language can be enlarged. For instance, graphic signs conceivably independent of utterance, such as mathematical notations, can be given spoken substitutes for the purposes of discussion.

Determining the extent to which a form of writing is linked to utterance may be crucially dependent on the context available for interpretation.

A computer program can then be recognized as a written artifact which may have complex connections with written language. For information processing machines such as computers, ideas of energy and motion can be replaced by logical operations and logical events. The computer itself can be regarded as a universal information machine which is transformed into the particular information machine specified by a program. In contrast to pre-existing written analogues to programs, the logical operations specified by a program can now be executed by a working computer rather than simply, if even, indicated (11–13).

Sanction for the idea of a single faculty for constructing systems of signs, and for an interpretation of writing to include all forms of notation, can be derived from the historical development of copyright in the United Kingdom. The guiding principle which has informed the extension of copyright protection since c.1750 (17, p.60), that copyright should subsist in all works representing the product of a sufficient degree of intellectual skill or labor if so fixed so that they can be reproduced, invokes a faculty strongly analogous, although differently formulated, to the semiotic faculty. Cases heard in the 1880s allowed copyright to subsist in contractions developed as part of a system of shorthand and in ciphers compiled with the intention of enabling the elimination of errors in telegraphic transmissions. Such cases have been taken to establish that meaning in ordinary language, or human readability, was not criterial to the recognition of writing for the purposes of claims to intellectual property. The interpretation assigned to writing in copyright legislation was later brought into conformity with juridical precedent. The *Copyright, Designs and Patents Act 1988* required writing to be interpreted as "any form of notation or code, whether by hand or otherwise and regardless of the method by which, or medium in or on which, it is recorded" (18, ¶178). It also confirmed the assimilation of computer programs to copyright protection as "original . . . literary works" (18, ¶1–3), along with other written products of intellectual labor. In contrast, speech not rendered permanent by transcription or recording has never been protected. The sanction offered by United Kingdom copyright tends to be simultaneously qualified. Committees convened to review copyright have repeatedly expressed concern at difficulties in interpretation arising from the unusual meaning acquired by terms such as 'literary work.' Such reservations suggest that legislators have not unreservedly endorsed the concepts to which they have given public sanction (12).

A perspective which represents a marked departure from a direct analogy between the computer and human brain or mind has then been established. A text in written language and a computer program are equally products of the semiotic faculty for creating significant order. In particular, documents and computers are both linked to, and distinguished from, each other by the presence of writing. Written language is itself historically subsequent to speech as a product of the semiotic faculty, and computer programs can be regarded as a further development.

INTELLIGENCE OF COMPUTERS

Speculations on the possibility of computer intelligence were preceded by the construction of abstract models for the computational process. Turing's 1936 paper, "On Computable Numbers, with an Application to the *Entscheidungsproblem*," introduced the idea of universal logical computing machine, in connection with a mathematical proof

(19). Other, formally equivalent, descriptions of automata and of effective calculability were also made public in 1936, by lecture or written publication, by Church (20), and Post (21). A degree of intellectual convergence, together with complex patterns of direct reciprocal influence and mutual independence, has been detected (22). Turing's model of the computational process has since been subsequently widely adopted. In automata theory it is customary to evade real world problems over the definition of a computer and of a program by substituting the model of a universal Turing machine for the computer and a Turing machine for the program. Subsequent discussions of automata have reiterated the themes that a process is computable if, and only if, it is Turing machine computable and that modifications to Turing machines do not increase their computational power (11,13).

Turing's 1948 (23) and 1950 (1) papers followed the construction of universal logical computing machines, although part of these developments had occurred separately from the development of logic and automata theory (6, p.404, 24, p.292). They also introduced the possibility that computers could be programmed to perform tasks which would be called intelligent when performed by humans. Various games, including chess, the learning and translation of languages, cryptography, and mathematics were proposed as possible fields of endeavor. The idea of modification of the original parameters of a program was also introduced. This was called machine learning and an analogy between the computer and the brain was made explicit. Changes in the machine configuration were compared to the development of the originally unorganized cortex of the human infant (1,23). Research into neural networks (9) seems to represent a revival of interest in this approach (25). Perhaps because of the separate development of automata theory and working computers, discussions tend to leave it unclear whether neural networks can be assimilated to the Turing machine model (9,25).

The Turing test itself was introduced by "Computing Machinery and Intelligence." The test required the simulation of human linguistic responses to questions. Conditions were established which would make it impossible for the human enquirer to obtain sensory evidence as to whether the responses emanated from a person or a computer. For instance, answers were preferably to be typewritten rather than handwritten or spoken in order to remove personal traces from the linguistic output. If the questioner was deceived by the simulation, the Turing test would have been passed. Computers could then be credited with showing intelligent behavior. The production of depersonalized linguistic output was then to be taken as an adequate indicator of intelligence (1). Subsequent research in artificial intelligence, and speculations that computers might either be intelligent or made to exhibit intelligent behavior, have by no means confined themselves to attempting to meet the Turing test, although it has been influential (2,3). However, clarity and generality can be obtained by confining attention primarily to the Turing test, and I propose to do that here.

Connections can be made from the Turing test to Turing's personal situation. The particular deception considered by Turing, not necessarily followed in the subsequent development of the Turing test, involved a disguise of gender. First a man and a woman were to be hidden from the enquirer and to attempt to give replies which would mislead the questioner into believing that the man was the woman. Then, the man was to be replaced by a computer. If the computer was on deceptive as the man, it would be credited with showing comparable intelligence to the human it had replaced. It is tempting to make a connection with Turing's enforced disguise of his own sexuality (26).

Aspects of the Turing test simultaneously reveal links to Turing's autobiography and to the cultural temper of the time. The period from the development of the telephone and the phonograph in the 1870s is sometimes characterised as one of secondary orality, in contradistinction to the primary orality of societies without written language. In primarily oral societies, communication over space and time was strongly, although not necessarily exclusively, dependent on the memory of human intermediaries. Written language enabled the independent transmission of sophisticated messages to receivers distant in space and time. In turn, technical developments in audio, and then in audiovisual, media gave possibilities of distant temporal and spatial transmission to the sounds of utterance and then to the gestural accompaniments to verbal performances. Secondary orality tends to be marked by an interest in, or allusions to and echoes of, primary orality (13,27). The Turing test bears extensive similarities to a narrative developed in a primarily oral society, to the Greek myth of Teiresias (28). Teiresias was a Theban seer who was blind from his seventh year. Various causes for his blindness were alleged: one was that "he had revealed to mankind what they ought not to know" (29). Changes of sexuality are also involved. In one version of the story, Teiresias was originally a girl, but was changed into a boy by Apollo at the age of seven and then underwent several other transformations. An oracle was dedicated to Teiresias (29,30). Dialogue between questioner and responder at oracles allowed no direct sensory or visual contact between the questioner and responder and oracular voice might be disguised (31–34). The situation is therefore analogous to the removal from contact in the Turing test. For Homer, Teiresias was the only soul in Hades "whose understanding even death has not impaired" (35, p.168). While losing all other human qualities in exile from the world of the living, intelligence alone is retained. In the Turing test, the man is replaced by a machine which, although largely isolated from sensory and social contact, similarly keeps the capacity for intelligent response.

Connections between the Turing test and twentieth century logical and mathematical developments can be detected. In Turing's 1936 paper, it was shown that there could be no solution to the *Entscheidungsproblem* as no general procedure for determining whether a particular Turing machine would ever halt when presented with a set of data could be established (19). The halting problem for Turing machines shows similarities to other logical and mathematical themes of the period in its concern for the limitations of a formal system: to Russell's antimony connected with the class of all classes that are not members of themselves (36, p.60, 6, pp.100–101); and to Gödel's theorem that there exist well-formed sentences of a formal system whose truth or falsity cannot be decided on the basis of the axioms of that formal system (37). In another, rather neglected and unsympathetically received (38, pp.629–635, 39, p.49), interpretation of formal logic, in Wittgenstein's *Tractatus logico-philosophicus* (40), Russell's antinomy and Gödel's theorem could not be generated in the object language of a symbolic logic. Russell's antinomy is made to vanish on the grounds that a proposition cannot meaningfully take itself as an argument (40, p.57, 41, p.149). Contrary, although historically prior, to Gödel's theme, it is argued that: "A proposition cannot possibly assert of itself that it is true" (40, p.97). The halting problem for Turing machines seems to turn on the impossibility of finding a stable site outside an unbounded universe of discourse (19). The Turing test reverses this process. First the man, and then the computer, are taken outside the universe of discourse and it is left to those within that universe of discourse to determine its identity.

Historically, the Turing test can be traced back to Descartes. In the *Discourse on Method*, Descartes speculated that physically convincing automata could not deceive us into believing that they were men, for "they could never use words or other signs, composing them as we do to declare our thoughts to others." A machine could be made to emit words, but not "to arrange words in various ways to reply to the sense of everything that is said in its presence" (42, p.73–74). For Descartes, the capacity for intelligent discourse was the faculty which distinguishes man from beasts and machines. An analogous distinction had been made by Aristotle: animals had voice but only man, as a political animal, had speech (43, pp.59–60). The Turing test follows Descartes in implicitly making the faculty for arranging signs the distinguishing human characteristic. However, it requires that an automaton be made which will attain the capacity for dialectic response denied to it by Descartes. The idea that intelligence can be sustained with limited sensory and social contact also reveals an acceptance of the Cartesian dichotomy between mind and body and of Descartes' emphasis on the asocial, rational individual as the source of certainty (42).

A link to Descartes can also be detected in the assimilation of reasoning about human and social affairs to a mathematical or logical model, implied by the Turing test. Descartes had taken the "long chains of reasonings, quite simple and easy, which geometers are accustomed to using to teach their most difficult demonstrations" as a model for discovery and reasoning to be applied to all human knowledge (42, p.41). The subsequent development of symbolic logic, for instance by Leibniz (44, pp.275–276) and Boole (45), were, in part, further attempts to reduce all methods of reasoning to purely mechanical or formal procedures whose validity did not depend on the interpretation of the symbols used. Turing's 1936 paper finally gave a definition of a mechanical procedure sufficiently precise and intuitively plausible to be widely acceptable (19,46).

The attempt to assimilate discourse about human affairs, to a mathematical or logical model, is also comprehensible in its contemporary intellectual context. A. J. Ayer in his influential *Language, Truth and Logic*, saw no difference in kind between the maxims of science and those of common sense (47, p.65). In *The Mathematical Theory of Communication*, optimism was expressed that the model developed for the transmission of signals over telecommunication channels could be made to yield a sophisticated analysis of human communication: "entropy not only speaks the language of arithmetic; it also speaks the language of language" (48, p.28). Subsequent research did not bear out this optimism (49, pp.51–62). In linguistics, Chomsky's *Syntactic Structures*, influenced by automata studies, regarded a human speaker as essentially an automaton (50). Automata theory, and formal logic, is concerned primarily with the form of reasoning, not immediately with the interpretation of the primitive signs employed.

The idea that reasoning can be conducted without continuing reference to human interpretation of its content is also implicit in the idea of machine intelligence. An emphasis on the form, not the content of arguments, is present in Turing's intellectual context. In logic and mathematics, there had been a concern with the scope, and the limitations, of formal procedures not dependent on the meaning of symbols manipulated (19–22, 40,45). For bibliography, W. W. Greg had prescribed that the bibliographer should be "concerned with pieces of paper or parchment covered with certain written or printed signs . . . merely as arbitrary marks; their meaning is no business of his" (51, p.247). Shannon made an analogous methodological exclusion of the semantic aspects of communication from information theory in *The Mathematical Theory of Communication*, but used the term information to refer to sequences of symbols (48). A subtle criticism was later made of this choice of terms. The confusion generated between signals and information may not simply be a result of the misleading terminology. To some extent, at least, the confusion was the cause of the misleading terminology (52). In reducing information to signals, meaning is made an inherent property of messages and the human labor involved in their making and interpretation elided. The emphasis of *Syntactic Structures* was on the form, not the content, of linguistic communication, although this contrast tends to be rendered as one between syntax and semantics (50, pp.100–102). For Ryle in *The Concept of Mind*, which may have been a direct influence on Turing's 1950 paper (26, p.418), the "styles and procedures of people's activities *are* the way their minds work and not merely imperfect reflections of the postulated secret processes which were supposed to be the workings of minds" (53, p.57). Two levels which can be distinguished for analytical purposes, of expression and content, have been conflated with the expression given value in itself. An interest in the form, rather than with the content, of communication is, then, widely shared by Turing's intellectual context, although scarcely exclusive to it.

The shared emphasis on the form of communication, as well as the acceptance of the possibility of computer intelligence, can be partly explained by the bleakness of the Western political context of the early 1950s. The 1930s had witnessed the growth of Western intellectual optimism about the development of Soviet communism and also the development of fascism. Disillusion with Soviet communism had begun to grow with the news of the Moscow show trials of the late 1930s and with the Russo–German pact of 1941 (54, pp.136–138). *The God That Failed*, a collection of essays, was concerned to "study the state of mind of the Communist convert, and the atmosphere of the period— from 1917 to 1939–when conversion was so common" (55, p.7) testifies to the further loss of faith in this form of political progress. By the beginning of the Cold War, in the late 1940s, (56, pp.24–33), the brutality of Nazism had been recognized but hardly understood. Later public comments on Nazism and Japanese militarism, for instance those occasioned by Emperor Hirohito's visit to Britain in 1972, tend to characterize Nazism as an aberration, a kind of unmotivated evil, whereas Japan's militarism is seen as closely connected with its culture. It is an attitude which preserves contemporary Europeans, and Americans, from implication in the guilt of either: if Nazism was seen as a product of German culture, then other Europeans would, to some extent, be implicated by the culture and humanity they share with German; and Japanese militarism is kept safely distant by being perceived as a culturally specific development (57, pp.53–54). In the post-1945 political context, a stress on the form rather than the threatening and disturbing content of communication is comprehensible. Equally, the possibility of machine intelligence promises a source of authority which would free a politically troubled culture from the responsibility for choice.

The external signs of intelligence, or intelligent behavior, are implicitly equated with its inner presence by the development of the Turing test. Identifying intelligence with intelligent behavior has been regarded as radically behaviorist (58, pp.27–35). Turing's own position is subtle, although it lends itself to ambiguous interpretation. In "Computing machinery and intelligence," the question, Can a machine display intelligent behavior?, is advanced as an adequate, and clearer, substitute for the vague and difficult question, can a machine think? The subsequent development of speculations for computer intelligence, at least until Searle's intervention, tended to be less subtly qualified and to take the behavioral signs of intelligence as an unequivocal equivalent to intelligence (2).

One effect of substituting considerations of intelligent behavior for intelligence is partly to evade the difficult issue of what is meant by intelligence. In such circumstances, it is difficult to see why an obligation for definition should fall on critics, but some distinctions can be indicated. The Turing test implies, but does not state, that intelligence can be identified with the faculty for arranging signs and for producing written discourse. Even the name Teiresias can be rendered as he who delights in signs (30, vol. 2, p.409). From a semiotic perspective, intelligence and signification have been viewed as a single process (59, p.31). There is an unexpected concordance between the interpretation of human intelligence implied by the Turing test and one explicitly developed in semiotics. In contrast to the tendency to obscure the distinction which can be made between the behavioral signs of intelligence and its literal presence, it could be, and has been (2), made a matter of definition that literal intelligence can only reside in the human act of interpretation.

The stress on the form of reasoning and the elements of behaviorism in the Turing test were seized upon by Searle in his refutation of its adequacy as an indicator of literal intelligence. Computational operations on purely formally defined elements had no necessary connection with understanding. In an analogous distinction, computers were described as operating syntactically without a semantic content. Understanding and semantic content were subsumed under the more technical term, *intentionality*, the characteristic of mental states directed at objects or states of affairs in the world. For Searle, intentionality was essential to literal intelligence. Even an adequate simulation of intelligence would still lack his necessary quality (2). Searle's refutation of the adequacy of the Turing test as an indicator of literal intelligence has been generally accepted (3).

The growth, and collapse, of speculations for the literal intelligence of computers can also be understood in relation to the concept of a paradigm, the constellation of beliefs and assumptions held in common by a scientific community, developed by Kuhn in *The Structure of Scientific Revolutions* (60). Searle himself comments on the ideology of artificial intelligence. Its grip had made the implausible idea of literal computer intelligence plausible (2). Speculations for computer intelligence had developed partly within specialized, and, to some extent, enclosed, research communities. Destructive intervention came from outside those research communities, from a perspective free from some of the characteristics of their paradigms.

Speculations for computer intelligence may also have been stimulated, and partly protected, by the historical novelty of the technology. Other innovations in information technology have been associated with similar speculations. For instance, Lady Lovelace warned that Babbage's Analytical Engine had "no pretensions whatever to originate anything. It can do whatever we know how to order it to perform. It can follow analysis; but it has no power of anticipating any analytical relations or truths. Its province is to assist us in making available what we are already acquainted with" (61, p.58). Since 1950, and particularly from 1980 on, the date of Searle's intervention, computers have been increasingly incorporated into wider social life outside specialized research communities. Now that computers are familiar rather than mysterious objects, it is tempting to apply to claims for their literal intelligence a process of brutal persuasiveness analogous to Johnson's refutation of Berkeley's scepticism on the reality of the material world—"I never shall forget the alacrity with which Johnson answered, striking his foot with mighty force against a large stone, till he rebounded from it, 'I refute it *thus*' " (62, vol. 1, p.471)—and to flick a switch, without compunction, as we might close, although not burn, a book.

The discussion can now be summarized. (1) In the tradition established by the Turing test, claims for the literal intelligence, or other cognitive state, of computers rested on the production of depersonalized linguistic responses to questions. (2) Such claims foundered on the absence of intentionality, of a prior act of comprehension by the artifact. The growth, and collapse, of speculations for the literal intelligence of computers can be understood in terms of their intellectual and historical context, in relation to the continuing attempts to assimilate discourse about human affairs to a formal, logical model, and as a response to the bleakness of the post-1945 political context and to the novelty of the technology.

INTELLIGENCE OF DOCUMENTS

A feature of secondary orality is the attention given to earlier transitions in methods for communicating and storing information. The transition from primary orality in Greece has been a strong, but not exclusive focus of attention (15,27,63,64), with the *Phaedrus* (14) emerging as a crucial text, although not free from difficulties in interpretation (65). The *Phaedrus* must be placed in the context of the progressive supplementing of direct oral communication by written language removed from its producer.

The idea that documents could have been attributed intelligence may gain credibility from considering the depth of anxieties that can be associated with the introduction of written language. Bellerophon, in *The Iliad*, was given a message which he could not interpret and required the recipient to kill him. Bellerophon had been under the power of King Proetus. Queen Anteaia had falsely informed the king that Bellerophon had tried to rape her (66, pp.102–104):

> Rage filled the king
> over her slander, but being scrupulous
> he shrank from killing him. So into Lycia
> he sent him, charged to bear a deadly cipher,
> magical marks Proetus engraved and hid
> in folded tablets. He commanded him
> to show these to his father-in-law,
> thinking in this way he should meet his end.
>   . . .
> When he had read the deadly cipher, changing
> he gave his first command'

Bellerophon survived the series of trials imposed upon him. The episode is commonly taken as the only allusion to writing in Homer (64, p.15). Such an incident could be stigmatized as mythical, rather than historical, but this would be to import a value judgment foreign to its original context. A distinction between myth and history may not be made by cultures without written language (15, p.47). The development of history has been taken to depend on the possibility of written recording of testimony (67, p.3, 68, p.178). Etymologically, runes is cognate with 'roun,' a secret or mystery (69), and runes were credited with magical power. Those unable to interpret them were vulnerable to deception: In *Egil's saga*, a farmer's daughter had been ill and remedies had been tried (70, pp.190–191):

> I've had runes carved,' answered Thorfinn. 'A farmer's son from near by did it, but since then she's been even worse.' . . . Egil searched the bed where she had been lying and found a whale-bone there with runes carved on it. After he read them, he scraped them off and burnt them in the fire. . . . Then he made this verse:
>
> None should write runes
> Who can't read what he carves

A mystery mistaken
Can bring men to misery.
I saw cut on the curved bone
Ten secret characters,
These gave the young girl
Her grinding pain.'

Similar episodes, in which runes have magical powers, occur in other sagas. A more recent, historically documented, episode has been given fictional treatment. South American Indians carrying messages for a colonial power feared that the document would be
aware of their activities (70, p. 140):

Two Indians take the foreman's offering to Lima in two sacks. He has given them
a letter to deliver with the melons to Don Antonia Solar. 'If you eat any of the melons,'
he warns them, 'this letter will tell him about it.'

When they are a couple of leagues from the city of the kings, the Indians sit down
to rest in a ravine:

'How would this peculiar fruit taste?'
'Must be marvelous.'
'How about trying it? One melon, just one.'
'*The letter will sing*,' one of the Indians recalls.
They look at the letter and hate it. They look around
for a prison for it. They hide it behind a rock where
it can't see anything, and devour a melon in quick
bites . . . Then they pick up the letter, tuck it in
their clothing, throw the sacks over their shoulders,
and continue on their way.

A broadly political interpretation of such episodes is illuminating. Anxieties are associated not directly with the technology of writing itself, but with the power granted to those
who can interpret such message systems. A historically distant, although revealing, analogy with the role of a scientific paradigm in protecting claims for the literal intelligence
of computers can also be indicated: the scientific communities associated with artificial
intelligence were privileged interpreters of computational operations; intervention then
came from another paradigm and at a historical point where computers were being increasingly assimilated into wider social life.

Before considering the particular historical context of the *Phaedrus*, I wish to develop two distinctions between forms of writing: between writing which draws on verbal
models and writing which does not; and between forms of writing which are used primarily for transmission over time and those which are used for transmission over time and
space. Both these distinctions are relevant to a common dimension: the possibility of direct interrogation of the producer of a statement and of immediate acquaintance with its
social or spatial context. Writing which draws on verbal models can be used as a substitute for the presence of a live speaker, possibly open to questioning. If writing is transmitted over space as well as time, the opportunity for acquaintance with its original
context is liable to be diminished. The opportunity for questioning the producer of a statement, and for immediate knowledge of its context, has been called openness to direct
semantic ratification (27, p.47). It tends to be a highly consistent, although still not absolute, difference between written language and unrecorded speech (67, p.44). Everything connected with the study of writing is problematic (72, p.51) and distinctions made
are intended for analytical purposes and not as final, mutually exclusive, categories.

The distinction between forms of writing which have no necessary connection with utterance and forms which draw on verbal models for the purposes of graphic communication can be discovered in both historical and contemporary contrasts. A historical contrast would be between Egyptian hieroglyphics and syllabic or alphabetic written language. In one widely held interpretation, to which there are exceptions, Egyptian hieroglyphics are seen as coded marks standing directly for objects and having no necessary connection with utterance: 'hieroglyphic writing . . . pictures the facts it describes' (40, p.67). Syllabic or alphabetic written language can be regarded as development from pre-existing forms of writing but distinguished by the extent to which it draws on models in another sign system, in spoken language, for the purposes of graphic communication (64). A contemporary distinction between writing which draws on verbal models and writing possibly independent of spoken language can be found in the contrast between alphabetic written language and mathematical notations, the object-language of a symbolic logic or computer programming languages (12, 13). Such forms of writing can, under certain circumstances be read to utterance, but have no necessary connection with verbal models and are not directly intended as communicative substitutes for spoken language. There may be a loss of clarity when verbal substitutes are supplied for the purposes of discussion. For instance, the logical expression for material implication, '$p \rightarrow q$', can be given the verbal correlate, 'If p then q,' and is then more readily read to speech. Difficulties in interpretation have then tended to follow from the confusion generated between the definition of '$p \rightarrow q$' in formal logic, as equivalent to '$\sim p \vee q$,' and the meanings 'If p then q' can assume in wider discourse, where a necessary or causal connection between antecedent and consequent may be implied (73, p.84). The term 'writing' will be used to cover all forms of writing and 'written language' reserved for writing which has strong links with utterance.

The distinction which can be made between forms of writing intended for transmission over time alone and over both time and space can also be discerned in historical and contemporary contrasts. Egyptian hieroglyphs, for instance, have been found predominantly, although not exclusively, as monumental inscriptions (74, volume 1 p.29–34, 75, pp.33–36, 140, 151, 76, pp.12–16, 55, 85). Later, the contemporary, inscriptions, such as those found on gravestones, could be differentiated from documents. The interpretation of inscriptions can be crucially dependent on their spatial context: '*Si monumentum requiris, circumspice*' originally required the setting of St. Paul's cathedral to obtain its meaning as a testimony to Sir Christopher Wren. The term 'inscription' will be used for writing intended for preservation over time and 'document' for forms of writing transmitted over time and space.

Documents can be further distinguished into private and public forms, although this boundary is subject to historical change and to different interpretations. For instance, the scientific journal emerged from less public, although not fully private, scientific correspondence (77). In contemporary terms, it may be difficult to agree on a demarcation between private and public forms: at what point, for instance, does a report whose circulation is deliberately restricted become a public document? Committees convened to review United Kingdom copyright legislation, which requires legal deposit only for published documents, not for inscriptions or private correspondence, have found it difficult to define publication, although a criterion of transmission to a largely unknown audience distant in space and time has tended to be implicitly invoked (78, pp.25–26, 79, p.207). For instance, the Gregory committee of 1952 considered that works issued solely for the use of members of research associations were not to be regarded as publications for the purposes of legal deposit. Availability to the general public was to be the determining principle (78, pp. 25–26). Assertions in written language tend to be protected from the immediate questioning often possible with unrecorded speech. For published documents, as distinct from correspondence, the opportunity of immediate dialogue with the producer tends to be further greatly reduced. The degree of openness to semantic ratification, then, helps to differentiate private from public communication.

These distinctions, of written language from other forms of writing, between inscriptions and documents, and between public and private documents, can now be applied to the historical context of the *Phaedrus*. The common dimension on which they impinged, of semantic ratification, is also crucial to Plato's preference for oral dialectic over dissemination of thought by written language.

Both writing and written language existed in Plato's lifetime, 427–347 BC. The particular date for composition of the *Phaedrus* is disputed, although it tends to be regarded as an early dialogue (14,65, pp. 105–106). Forms of writing and graphic communication existed in the Ancient Mediterranean world before the introduction of alphabetic written language to Greek territories (72). For instance, in the legend of Theseus, who is usually dated to the generation before the Trojan war, tokens used to preserve information over time, and a binary code based on a contrast between a black and white sail for the transmission of a message over space, occur (13,80). The relation of such forms of writing and graphic communication to spoken language is not clear or agreed. The alphabet is often taken as an example of extreme cultural diffusion from its development as the North Semitic alphabet in the first half of the second millennium BC (15, p. 39, 64, pp. 31, 109, 120, 74, vol. 1, pp. 145–172). Evidence for alphabetic written language in the Greek mainland, islands and colonies from the mid-8th century BC has been found (72, p. 57). The *Phaedrus* then, can, be dated as some three centuries after the beginnings of a transition from predominantly, although not exclusively, oral to oral and written communication.

The main concern of the *Phaedrus* is with written language, although affinities between written language and other forms of writing are implied. A historical link is made in a myth which attributes the invention of writing to the Egyptian god Theuth along with 'number and calculation and geometry and astronomy' (14, p. 96). A contemporary analogy between written language and a graphic art is implied when figures in paintings are indicted of the same inability to respond to questioning as written words: 'writing involves a similar disadvantage to painting. The productions of paintings look like living beings, but if you ask them a question they maintain a solemn silence' (14, p. 97). In this passage, written language is also regarded as an imperfect substitute for a live speaker.

Both inscriptions and documents existed at the time of the *Phaedrus*. Many samples of early Greek writing which have survived are graffiti or other inscriptions (15, p. 42, 72, p. 58). However, the primary concern of the *Phaedrus* is with documents, not inscriptions, and with documents further divorced from their producer by public circulation: 'once a thing is committed to writing, it circulates equally among those who understand the subject and those who have no business with it; a writing cannot distinguish between suitable and unsuitable readers' (14, p. 97). A contrast can be made with the role written language can assume in societies at earlier stages of a transition from predominantly oral to oral and written linguistic communication, where the ability to interpret written language is confined to particular, often priestly, communities. In episodes, such as those of Bellerophon and Egil, power can be obtained by those with exclusive command of writing. Now that the ability to read is more widely shared, concern is expressed about the consequences of uncontrolled dissemination of thought by writing. Documents in written language would typically have been read aloud, perhaps by a slave (15, p.42). The immediate reader of a document would not, then, necessarily fully understand it, unless the slave were an Aesop. Attempts at direct semantic ratification would be liable to be frustrated with this form of spoken language. The practice of silent reading did not become widespread in Europe until printing from moveable type made it possible for documents to be reproduced with less labor than copying manuscripts involved (15, p. 42, 81).

A summary of distinctions established may be helpful here. Writing and written language, inscriptions and documents, all existed at the time of the *Phaedrus*. Its main, but not exclusive, concern is with documents in written language divorced from their producer by public circulation. Written language is supplementing, although not entirely displacing, oral communication.

Written and spoken language are extensively contrasted in the *Phaedrus*. Written language enables information to be retained over time without immediate reliance on the memory of a human intermediary. The use of writing can weaken personal memory: "those who acquire it will cease to exercise their memory and become forgetful; they will rely on writing to bring things to their remembrance by external signs instead of on their own internal resources" (14, p. 96). Writing is a "receipt for recollection, not memory" (14, p. 96), only acceptable as a prophylactic against the "forgetfulness of old age" (14, p. 99). Information acquired and preserved through written language is an imperfect substitute for the knowledge developed through personal dialectic. It will fill readers "with the conceit of wisdom instead of real wisdom" (14, p.97). The possibility of direct question and answer further differentiates spoken language, particularly dialogue, from written language. If a writing "is ill-treated or unfairly abused it always needs its parent to come to its rescue . . . it is quite incapable of defending or helping itself" (14, p.97). In contrast a personal speaker can be interrogated: "If any of them had knowledge of the truth when he wrote, and can defend what he has written by submitting to an interrogation on the subject . . . [he will] make it evident as soon as he speaks how comparatively inferior are his writings" (14, pp.101–102). Spoken language is, then, preferred to written language in the *Phaedrus*, particularly for the possibility of question and answer which it offers.

Forms of spoken language are also contrasted. Spoken discourse not delivered as part of a dialogue is subject to objections similar to those made to written language: "nothing worth serious attention has ever been written in prose or verse—or spoken for that matter, if by speaking one means the kind of recitation that aims merely at creating belief, without any attempt at instruction by question and answer" (14, p.101). *Recitation* may allude to orally performed poetry and here a trace of an objection to the content of linguistic communication, not just to its form of delivery, can be discerned. In the *Phaedrus* (14, pp. 36, 81–82), as in other Platonic dialogues, rational discourse which systematically assigns the objects of discussion to agreed definitions tends to be preferred to rhetoric (82) and poetry (83, pp. 130–153). For instance, poetry which encourages immorality by presenting gods and heroes whose conduct should be imitated by the young, as "no better than ordinary mortals" (83, p. 148), is excluded from the ideal state proposed in *The Republic*. Dialectic speech is valued above monologue for the possibility of mutual elucidation it holds, in a letter concerned with similar themes to the *Phaedrus*: "It is only when all these things, names and definitions, visual and other sensations, are rubbed together and subjected to tests in which questions and answers are exchanged in good faith and without malice that finally, when human capacity is stretched to its limit, a spark of understanding and intelligence flashes out and illuminates the subject at issue'' (14, p. 140). Within spoken language, then, dialogue between live speakers is preferred to rhetorical monologue. Dialogue holds the possibility of enlightenment which can only be derived from reciprocal question and answer. The feature of direct semantic ratification, which had caused written language to be seen only as an imperfect substitute for a speaker engaged in dialectic, also serves to discriminate valuable from less valued speech.

The issue of the attribution of intelligence to publicly circulated documents in written language can now be addressed. Written words seem to be intelligent: they ''appear to understand what they are saying'' (14, p. 97), or, in another translation, ''seem to talk to you as though they were intelligent'' (84, p. 154). Only intelligence, and not magical powers, for instance to cause or remove disease or to report a spoken conversation, is attributed to writing. The mystery associated with writing, plausibly connected with exclusivity of access to it, has diminished by the time of the *Phaedrus*.

A demystification of writing can also be detected in the qualification immediately imposed upon the intelligence of documents. Their appearance of intelligence which written words can have is betrayed by their incapacity to adapt themselves in response to questions. If written words are interrogated, neither they nor a reader delivering them without full comprehension, can exhibit the human capacity for dialectic response (14, p. 97):

> The productions of paintings look like living beings, but if you ask them a question they maintain a solemn silence. The same holds true of written words; you might suppose that they understand what they are saying, but if you ask them what they mean by anything they simply return the same answer over and over again.

The crux of this passage warrants reiteration in an alternative translation (84, p.158):

> written words . . . seem to talk to you as though they were intelligent, but if you question them anything about what they say, from a desire to be instructed, they go on telling you just the same thing for ever.

Written words are only 'a kind of shadow' of the 'living and animate speech of a man with knowledge' (14, p. 98). Documents, then, can give one behavioral sign of intelligence: they can be made to yield linguistic output. Yet their appearance of intelligence is deceptive and is betrayed by their incapacity to offer semantic ratification. They lack understanding of their linguistic output and cannot adapt it to new questions.

The extent of comparability between the concept of human intelligence implied by the *Phaedrus* and the Turing test is difficult to determine. The tendency to substitute considerations of intelligent behavior for intelligence in the development of the Turing test left the idea of intelligence poorly developed. Saussure's thesis that a linguistic term derives its meaning from its place in an indefinite network of slightly or greatly differing terms (16, pp. 113–116) would imply that the interpretation of crucial passages in the *Phaedrus* could only be further explored, and never finally explicated, by continuing to study them in relation to their co-existing semantic field. Nevertheless, a continuity and difference can be noted. For Plato and then for Descartes and Turing, intelligence is effectively equated with the faculty for arranging signs, in particular with the capacity for dialectic response. In the *Phaedrus*, and in Searle's critique of the claims for computers to intelligence, without human understanding, there can only be the appearance of intelligence, and not its literal presence.

The degree of scepticism about the value of written language in the *Phaedrus* contrasts with the fear revealed in the story of Bellerophon and can be taken as a sign of developing intellectual maturity with regard to writing. The views given in Platonic dialogues on the value of writing subsequently change: for instance, in the ideal state of the *The Republic*, laws are to be set down in writing for dissemination and preservation (65, p.105, 83). In Plato's time, writing is being progressively assimilated, both in historical actuality and in the political proposals of *The Republic*, into quotidian social life.

The argument of this section can now be summarized. The supplementing of predominantly oral communication by written language may lead to apprehensions about its effects, which can be plausibly connected with exclusivity of access to it. Such fears had partly diminished by the time of *Phaedrus*. Its main concern is with the contrast between the dissemination of thought by publicly circulated documents in written language and instruction by a live speaker engaged in dialogue. Written words can only offer the appearance of intelligence without the ability to explain themselves in response to questioning.

CONCLUSION

The perspective which links documents to computers through the presence of writing and through the human faculty for constructing systems of signs can then illuminate the issue of the literal intelligence of computers. Historical evidence supported a logically tenable position. Claims for the intelligence of computers and of documents in written language could be seen to rest on a similar basis: the production of depersonalized linguistic output at a distance in time and space from its original producer. Claims for the literal intelligence of computers and documents were subject to similar although differently formulated, objections: that linguistic responses were made available without intentionality or understanding.

Scepticism about the value of a new information technology would seem to be a sign of a movement toward intellectual maturity with regard to that technology. The measure of scepticism about the value of written language in the *Phaedrus* implies that its strangeness has been partly reduced by acquaintance and that it can be considered in relation to other forms of communication. Similarly, scepticism about the claims of computers to literal intelligence, and about the possibility of them being made to display intelligent behavior, seems to indicate that they too have been partly assimilated into wider social life outside specialized research communities and can be rationally evaluated in relation to other methods for storing, manipulating, and communicating information.

Signs of such a sceptical reaction, and then of considered evaluation, are beginning to emerge. Legal expert systems have been acerbically, and convincingly, criticized for presenting an excessively simplified version of the legal process (85,86): "there can be no algorithm which can be specified which can guide the system to decide what is honest and what is dishonest—the legal world, as lawyers know, is not that simple. Children and computer scientists might believe it to be, but that is a different matter" (86, p. 31). Apocalyptic prophecies of a transition to an information society, emblematized by the computer (87, p.509), are being supplemented by cautious reservations that "detailed empirical studies . . . suggest that there is no automatic effect from the technology itself" (88, p.117). It is now conceded that it is difficult to isolate those social and cultural changes which can be causally connected with changes in information technology, either in historical study or for prediction (72, p. 69). Where the effects of the introduction of new information technologies can be isolated, at least for analytical purposes, information appears to be a dependent rather than a primary variable. For instance, the "recent introduction of printing into nonliterate societies has seldom endorsed our traditional view of its efficacy as an agent of change'' (89, p. 52). A detailed study of information sources on the activities of an information-handling organization, of microform publishing by the British Library, which aimed to indicate the degree of autonomy which could be ascribed to information, found that the availability of information was determined largely by marketing interests and legal responsibilities. Only a limited autonomy could be legitimately ascribed to information, in that context (90, pp.161, 178). Scepticism carries destructive dangers of its own, but, followed by detailed analysis, it can create room for considered evaluation for considered evaluation of claims made for computers and their effects on societies.

Reviewing claims for the literal intelligence of computers is itself part of this evaluative process. Several interconnected factors seemed to have motivated belief in the possibility of computer intelligence. The anxieties associated with the historical novelty of the information technology are one plausible motivation. The tradition of logical analysis, associated, for instance, with Aristotle, Descartes, Leibniz, and Boole, which attempted to reduce discourse about human affairs to a logical or mechanical model, emerged as a further influence. The emphasis on expression and formal modelling of human discourse in post-war linguistics and information theory could itself be seen as extension of this logical tradition. It could also be understood in relation to the political context. Following the political traumas of the 1930s and 1940s, there appeared to be an unconscious search for an account of meaning which would concentrate only on expression and avoid having to face its disturbing content; for a model of human consciousness which would refer choice to a formal system or automaton; and for an external, oracular authority which could take responsibility for political decisions. With the collapse of claims for the literal intelligence of an appropriately programmed computer, and the decline of optimism in attaining a convincing simulation of intelligence, we are returned to a more sober world. We can consult the products of the semiotic faculty, whether in computer or documentary form, and confer meaning on signs by interpreting them, but can no longer hope for objective instruction or advice, from a site beyond humanity and dehumanized.

REFERENCES

1. Turing, A. M., Computing Machinery and Intelligence. In: *Minds and Machines* (Anderson, A. R. ed.), Prentice-Hall, Englewood Cliffs, NJ, 1964, pp.4–30. First published *Mind*, 69:433–460 (1950).
2. Searle, J. R., Minds, Brains and Programs, *Behav. Brain Sci.*, 3:417–457 (1980).
3. Motzkin, E., and Searle, J. R., Artificial Intelligence and the Chinese Room: An Exchange, *New York Rev. Books*, February 16, 1989, pp.44–45.
4. Michie, D., The Fifth Generation's Unbridged Gap. In *The Universal Turing Machine*: *A Half-Century Survey*, (Herken, R., ed.), Oxford University Press, Oxford, 1988, pp.467–489.
5. Churchland, P. M., and Churchland, P. S., Could a Machine Think? *Sci. Am.*, 262(1):26–31 (1990).
6. Penrose, R., *The Emperor's New Mind*: *Concerning Computers, Minds, and the Laws of Physics*, Oxford University Press, Oxford, 1989.
7. Johnson-Laird, P. N., *The Computer and the Mind*: *An Introduction to Cognitive Science*, Fontana, London, 1988.
8. Sperber, D., and Wilson, D., *Relevance*: *Communication and Cognition*, Basil Blackwell, Oxford, 1986.

9. Ford, N., From Information- to Knowledge-Management: The Role of Rule Induction and Neural Net Machine Learning Techniques in Knowledge Generation, *J. Inform. Sci.*, 15:299–304 (1989).

10. Walton, K., and Morris, A., Manpower Requirements and Availability in the Expert Systems Field (British Library Research Paper 65), British Library Research and Development Department, London, 1989.

11. Warner, J., Semiotics, Information Science, Documents and Computers, *J. Documen.*, 46:16–32 (1990).

12. Warner, J., Writing, Literary Work and Document in United Kingdom Copyright, *J. Inform. Sci.*, 16:279–289 (1990).

13. Warner, J., Writing, Programs, Computers and Logic. In: *Informatics 11: The Structuring of Information* (Proceedings of a Conference held by the Aslib Informatics Group and the Information Retrieval Group of the British Computer Society, University of York, March 1991), (Jones, K. P., ed.), Aslib, London, 1991, pp. 109–145.

14. Plato, *Phaedrus and the Seventh and Eighth Letters*. (Translated with an introduction by Walter Hamilton.) Penguin Books, Harmondsworth, 1973.

15. Goody, J., and Watt, I., The Consequences of Literacy. In: *Literacy in Traditional Societies* (Goody, J., ed.), Cambridge University Press, Cambridge, 1968, pp.27–68.

16. Saussure, F. De., *Course in General Linguistics* (Bally, C. and Sechehaye, A., eds., with the collaboration of A. Riedlinger; translated and annotated by Roy Harris), Duckworth, London, 1983.

17. Feather, J., Publishers and Politicians: The Remaking of the Law of Copyright 1775–1842. Part 1: Legal Deposit and the Battle of the Library Tax, *Publishing History*, 24:49–76 (1988).

18. *Copyright, Designs and Patents Act 1988*, c.48.

19. Turing, A. M., On Computable Numbers, with an Application to the *Entscheidungsproblem*, *Proc. London Math. Soc.*, 42:230–265 (1937).

20. Church, A., An Unsolvable Problem of Elementary Number Theory. In: *The Undecidable: Basic Papers on Undecidable Propositions, Unsolvable Problems and Computable Functions* (Davis, M., ed.), Raven Press, Hewlett, NY, 1965, pp.89–107. First published *Am. J. Math.*, 58:345–363 (1936).

21. Post, E. L., Finite Combinatory Processes. Formulation 1. In: *The Undecidable: Basic Papers on Undecidable Propositions, Unsolvable Problems and Computable Functions* (Davis, M., ed.), Raven Press, Hewlett, NY., 1965, pp.289–291. First published The *J. Symbol. Logic*, 1:103–105 (1936).

22. Gandy, R., The Confluence of Ideas in 1936. In: *The Universal Turing Machine: a Half-Century Survey*, (Hermen, R., ed.) Oxford University Press, Oxford, 1988, pp.55–111.

23. Turing, A. M., Intelligent Machinery. In: *Machine Intelligence 5* (Meltzer, B. and Michie, D., eds.), Edinburgh University Press, Edinburgh, 1969, pp.3–23. The editors state that this paper was submitted as a report to the National Physical Laboratory in 1948 but had not previously been published.

24. Wang, H., *From Mathematics to Philosophy*, Routledge & Kegan Paul, London, 1974.

25. Sloman, A., An Overview of Some Unsolved Problems in Artificial Intelligence. In: *Informatics 7: Intelligent Information Retrieval* (Proceedings of a conference held by the Aslib Informatics Group and the Information Retrieval Group of the British Computer Society, Cambridge 22–23 March 1983) (Jones, K. P., ed.), Aslib, London, 1983, pp.227–234.

26. Hodges, A., *Alan Turing: The Enigma*, Burnett Books in association with Hutchison Publishing Group, London, 1983.

27. Ong, W. J., *Orality and Literacy: The Technologizing of the Word*, Methuen, London and New York, 1982.

28. Artificial intelligence has subsequently shown elements of secondary orality, for instance in the practice of knowledge elicitation from experts and in its fondness for oracular names for projects. Teiresias would be more familiarly known as an expert system for diagnosing blood infections. See Aleksander, I., *Designing Intelligent Systems: An Introduction*, Kogan Page, London, 1984, p.132.

29. Teiresias, In: *Encyclopedia Britannica*, 11th edition, Cambridge University Press, Cambridge, 1911, vol. 26, p.508.

30. Graves, R., *The Greek Myths*, Penguin Books, London, 1960.

31. Aune, D. E., Oracles. In: *The Encyclopedia of Religion*, (Mircea, E., ed.), Macmillan, New York and Collier-Macmillan, London, 1987, Vol. 2, pp.80–87.

32. Bremmer, J., Delphi, Ibid, Vol. 4, pp.277–279.

33. Parke, H. W., and Wormell, D. E. W., *The Delphic Oracle*, Basil Blackwell, Oxford, 1956.

34. Price, S., Delphi and Divination. In: *Greek Religion and Society* (Easterling, P. E. and Muir, J. V., eds.), Cambridge University Press, Cambridge, 1985, pp.128–154.

35. Homer, *The Odyssey* (Translated by E. V. Rieu), Penguin Books, Harmondsworth, 1946.

36. Whitehead, A. N., and Russell, B., *Principia Mathematica to *56*, 2nd ed., Cambridge University Press, Cambridge, 1962.

37. Gödel, K., On formally undecidable propositions of Principia mathematica and related systems I. In: *The Undecidable: Basic Papers on Undecidable Propositions, Unsolvable Problems and Computable Functions* (Davis, M., ed.), Raven Press, Hewlett, NY., 1965, pp.5–38. First published in 1931 as Über formal unentscheidbare Sätze der Principia Mathematica und verwandter Systeme I, *Montashefte für Mathematik und Physik*, 38:173–198 (1931).

38. Kneale, W. K., and Kneale, M., *The Development of Logic*, Clarendon Press, Oxford, 1962.

39. Grayling, A. C., *Wittgenstein*, Oxford University Press, Oxford and New York, 1988.

40. Wittgenstein, L., *Tractatus Logico-Philosophicus*, Routledge and Kegan Paul, London, 1981. First published 1922.

41. Black, M., *A Companion to Wittgenstein's 'Tractatus'*, Cambridge University Press, Cambridge, 1964.

42. Descartes, R., *Discourse on Method and the Meditations* (Translated with an introduction by F. E. Sutcliffe), Penguin Books, London, 1968.

43. Aristotle, *The Politics* (Translated by T. A. Sinclair, Revised and re-presented by T. J. Saunders), Penguin Books, Harmondsworth, 1981.

44. Bochenski, I. M., *History of Formal Logic* (Translated and edited by I. Thomas), Notre Dame, IN, 1961.

45. Boole, G., *An Investigation of the Laws of Thought, on which are Founded the Mathematical Theories of Logic and Probabilities*, Walton and Maberly, London and Macmillan, Cambridge, 1854.

46. Gödel, K., Remarks Before the Princeton Bicentennial Conference on Problems in Mathematics. In: *The Undecidable: Basic Papers on Undecidable Propositions, Unsolvable Problems and Computable Functions*, (Davis, M., ed.), Raven Press, Hewlett, NY, 1965, pp.84–88.

47. Ayer, A. J., Language, Truth, and Logic, Penguin Books, Harmondsworth, 1971. First published Victor Gollancz, London 1936.

48. Shannon, C. E., and Weaver, W., *The Mathematical Theory of Communication*, University of Illinois Press, Urbana, 1949.

49. Fox, C. J., *Information and Misinformation: An Investigation of the Notions of Information, Misinformation, Informing and Misinforming*, Greenwood Press, London and Westport, CT, 1983.

50. Chomsky, N., *Syntactic Structures*, Mouton, The Hague, 1957.

51. Greg, W. W., Bibliography—An Apologia. In: *Collected Papers* (Maxwell, J. C., ed.), Clarendon Press, Oxford, 1966, pp.239–266. First published *Library*, xiii:113–143 (1932).

52. Bar-Hillel, Y. (ed.), An Examination of Information Theory. In: *Language and Information: Selected Essays on their Theory and Application*, Addison-Wesley, Reading, MA and Jerusalem Academic Press, Jerusalem, 1964, pp.275–297.

53. Ryle, G., *The Concept of Mind*, Penguin Books, Harmondsworth, 1988. First published by Hutchison 1949.

54. Warner, J., Liberalism and Marxism in the Work of George Orwell, D. Phil, Oxford University, 1983.

55. Crossman, R. (ed.), *The God that Failed: Six Studies in Communism*, Hamish Hamilton, London, 1950.

56. Hewison, R., *In Anger: British Culture in the Cold War* 1945–60, 2nd rev. ed., Methuen, London, 1981. First published by George Weidenfield and Nicholson, London, 1981.

57. Warner, J., Emperor Hirohito and the English Press: the Treatment of his State Visit to Britain in English National Daily Newspapers, MA Librarianship, University of Sheffield, 1984.

58. Harris, R., *The Language Machine*, Duckworth, London, 1987.

59. Eco, U., *A Theory of Semiotics*, Indiana University Press, London and Bloomington, IN, 1976.

60. Kuhn, T. S., *The Structure of Scientific Revolutions*, 2nd ed., University of Chicago Press, Chicago and London, 1970.

61. Bernstein, J., *The Analytical Engine: Computers—Past, Present and Future*, Secker & Warburg, London, 1965.

62. Hill, G. B. (ed.), *Boswell's Life of Johnson*, Revised and enlarged edition by L. F. Powell, Clarendon Press, Oxford, 1934.

63. Havelock, E. A., *The Literate Revolution in Greece and its Cultural Consequences*, Princeton University Press, Princeton, 1982.

64. Harris, R., *The Origin of Writing*, Duckworth, London, 1986.

65. Harris, R., How Does Writing Restructure Thought? *Language Commun.*, 9:99–106 (1989).

66. Homer, *The Iliad* (Translated by Robert Fitzgerald with an introduction by G. S. Kirk), Oxford University Press, Oxford, 1984.

67. Biber, D., *Variation Across Speech and Writing*, Cambridge University Press, Cambridge, 1988.

68. Herodotus, *The Histories* (Translated by Aubrey de Selincourt; revised, with an introduction and notes by A. R. Burn), Penguin Books, London, 1972.

69. *The Oxford English Dictionary*, 2nd ed. (Simpson, J. A. and Weiner, E. S. C., eds.), Clarendon Press, Oxford, 1989.

70. *Egil's Saga* (Translated with an introduction by H. Palsson and P. Edwards), Penguin Books, Harmondsworth, 1976.

71. Galeano, E., *Genesis* (Translated by C. Belfrage), Methuen, London, 1987.

72. Morpurgo Davies, A., Forms of Writing in the Ancient Mediterranean World. In: *The Written Word: Literacy in Transition (Wolfson College Lectures 1985)* (Baumann, G., ed.), Clarendon Press, Oxford, 1986.

73. Quine, W. V. O., *From a Logical Point of View: Logico-Philosophical Essays*, 2nd rev. ed., Harvard University Press, Cambridge, MA, 1964.

74. Diringer, D., *The Alphabet: A Key to the History of Mankind*, 3rd ed., rev., with the collaboration of R. Regensburger, Hutchison, London, 1968.

75. Gaur, A., *A History of Writing*, British Library, London, 1984.

76. Young, T., *An Account of Some Recent Discoveries in Hieroglyphical Literature and Egyptian Antiquities Including the Author's Original Alphabet, as Extended by Mr Champollion, with a Translation of Five Unpublished Greek and Egyptian Manuscripts*, John Murray, London, 1823.

77. Watson, L. E. et al., Sociology and information science. *J. Librar.*, 5:270–283 (1983).

78. Board of Trade, *Report of the Copyright Committee* (Cmnd 8662), HMSO, London, 1952.

79. *Copyright and Designs Law: Report of the Committee to Consider the Laws on Copyright and Designs. Chairman The Honourable Mr Justice Whitford* (Cmd 6732), HMSO, London, 1977.

80. Plutarch, Life of Theseus. In: *The Rise and Fall of Athens: Nine Greek Lives by Plutarch* (Translated with an introduction by I. Scott-Kilvert), Penguin Books, Harmondsworth, 1960, pp. 13–41.

81. Febvre, L., and Martin, H.-J., *The Coming of the Book: The Impact of Printing 1450–1800* (Translated by D. Gerard, Nowell-Smith, G. and Wootton, D. ed.), New Left Books, London, 1976.

82. Plato, *Gorgias* (Translated with an introduction by W. Hamilton), Penguin Books, Harmondsworth, 1960. Reprinted with revisions 1971.
83. *Plato, The Republic* 2nd ed., (Translated with an introduction by D. Lee), Penguin Books, London, 1987.
84. *Plato's Phaedrus* (Translated with an introduction and commentary by R. Hackforth), Cambridge University Press, Cambridge, 1952.
85. Leith, P., Fundamental Errors in Legal Logic Programming, *Comput. J.*, 29:545–552 (1986).
86. Leith, P., Legal Expert Systems: Misunderstanding the Legal Process, *Computers and Law*, 49:26–31 (1986).
87. Bell, D., The Social Framework of the Information Society. In: *The Microelectronics Revolution: The Complete Guide to the New Technology and Its Impact on Society* (Forester, T., ed.), Basil Blackwell, Oxford, 1980, pp.500–576.
88. Finnegan, R., Communication and Technology, *Lang. Commun.*, 9:107–127 (1989).
89. McKenzie, D. F., *Bibliography and the Sociology of Texts* (*The Panizzi Lectures 1985*), British Library, London, 1986.
90. Warner, J., British Library Microform Publications and Their Bibliographic Control, *J. Librar.*, 20:159–180 (1988).

BIBLIOGRAPHY

The following texts are of particular significance for the topics covered, or alluded to, in this article.

Intelligence of Computers

See Ref. 1, pp.4–30. (First published, *Mind*, 59:433–460 (1950)).
Ref. 2.

Automata

R. Herken (ed.), Ref. 4.

Writing

Ref. 14.
Ref. 64.

Writing and Computers

Ref. 89.
Ref. 12
Ref. 13.
J. Warner, *From Writing to Computers*, Routledge, London and New York, in press 1993.

JULIAN WARNER

POSITRON EMISSION TOMOGRAPHY

INTRODUCTION

Positron emission tomography (PET) is one of the newest components in the field of nuclear medicine. In contrast with the two relatively older techniques, computerized axial tomography (CAT) and nuclear magnetic resonance (NMR), PET truly has opened new avenues in both research and clinical ends of medicine by providing the means for precisely localizing and quantitatively assessing the biochemical processes underlying some of the most feared and hard-to-diagnose diseases.

Background

PET is the only imaging modality that provides doctors with early analytic and quantitative biochemical assessment and precise localization of pathology. Advances in medicine are demonstrating continuously that the earliest and most significant changes underlying most organs' diseases are those that disturb the biochemical processes governing the functions of those organs. Therapeutic procedures—chemotherapy, radiation therapy, and/or hormone therapy—for these disorders attempt to initiate, accelerate, remove, or block the chemical processes that have been disturbed by these diseases (1–3).

Until recently, inferences about the chemical status of an organ were achieved through chemical assays of blood, urine, cerebrospinal fluid, and/or biopsy procedures. In many cases, these tests do not provide a yes/no answer to many of the questions relating to the health of the targeted tissue. Since the emergence of PET, doctors and scientists have better tools to image in vivo and precisely quantify chemical processes in many organs. This has led to a significant increase in their capabilities in identifying and treating diseases. PET probes many organs for a wide variety of biological processes including metabolism, blood flow, organ perfusion, brain permeability, tumor drug levels, tissue pH, tissue lipid content, and tissue hematocrit (ratio of cells to plasma). Among the diseases that benefit from PET imaging directly and significantly are strokes, epilepsy, schizophrenia, brain tumors, dementia, and coronary artery diseases in general (4–6).

The use of PET imaging can be divided into three components.

Labeled Components

PET images are generated by injecting intravenously a tracer that radioactively decays in the patient's body, producing positrons. Each positron combines with an electron to produce two 511 keV (kiloelectron volt) gamma rays that are emitted 180° from each other. The detection of this radiation permits the imaging of the target tissue. Short-lived radioisotopes of such natural elements as carbon, nitrogen, and oxygen are used as labeling components.

217

Positron Tomograph

A tomograph is a circumferential array of radiation detectors placed around the patient's body to record the gamma rays emitted as a result of the positron annihilation process that depicts the tissue activity. The one-dimensional sinograms generated then are combined to reconstruct a two-dimensional image using the back-projection technique. The resulting image is an axial cross-section of the patient's body pictorially describing the targeted activity of the tissue.

Tracer Kinetic Models

The tracer kinetic models integrate (1) principles of the labeled compounds, (2) tissue radioassay of the camera, (3) mathematical models of reaction sequences occurring in the biochemical processes under study, and (4) analysis of the two-dimensional image to infer physiological measurements about the targeted tissue. It is worth noting that the quality of these quantitative measurements, hence the care given to patients, depends largely on the quality and the fidelity of the reconstructed image (1).

Unfortunately, the present PET technology does not provide the necessary image quality for such precise analytic and quantitative measurements. These issues can be addressed in conjunction with the disciplines of signal processing, image processing, and pattern recognition (7–9).

Motivation

In PET images, both boundary information as well as local pixel intensity are crucial for manual and/or automated feature tracing, extraction, and identification. The quality of such information is enhanced significantly by the reduction of random noise and artifacts in the image. PET images suffer from significantly high levels of radial noise present in the form of streaks caused by the inexactness of the models used in image reconstruction. An example is shown in Figure 1. This problem pertains to the quality of the tomography and the exactness of mathematical models used in signal conditioning, one-dimensional signal modeling and correction, and two-dimensional image modeling and reconstruction. Consequently, an image enhancement and restoration phase is necessary before PET data can be correctly interpreted.

The objective here is to model PET noise and remove it without altering dominant features in the image. The ultimate goal is to enhance these dominant features to allow for automatic computer interpretation and classification of PET images by developing techniques that take into consideration PET signal characteristics, data collection, and data reconstruction. The motivation of this work stems from the potential of PET imaging both in research and clinical activities. The primary benefits of PET include clear localization of regions of metabolism in the brain and the heart, quantitative permeability of brain tissue, and identification and sizing of heart infarcts. PET imaging also allows physicians to evaluate drugs by identifying and measuring regional metabolic changes resulting from drug therapy. PET's sensitivity detects early signs of disease. With CAT or conventional radiography, by the time a lesion is identifiable the damage to tissue is so advanced as to be irreparable. In PET images, the exact location and extent of the lesion are measured by detecting early biochemical changes and answering the fundamental question of whether or not the targeted tissue is active metabolically. With suitable interpretation of good quality PET images, doctors can assess the biochemical processes underlying the abnormality of an organ with a high degree of accuracy (2).

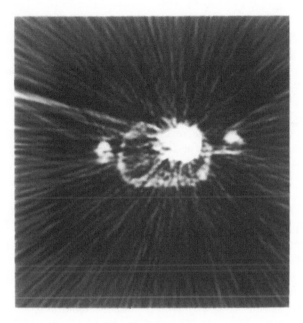

FIGURE 1   Axial cross-section of a patient's heart, generated by positron emission tomography, exhibiting severe radial noise.

Related Work

The artifacts that PET images exhibit are very detrimental to edge information. Edges are important for feature detection or identification in many image-processing applications including medical imagery. This is true for both ordinary visual examination of data as well as computer-assisted recognition. Because of the novelty of PET technology, the body of literature devoted to the area of noise modeling (10,11), image enhancement (12,13), or image interpretation and classification (7,14,15) as applied to PET imagry is limited. Some of the techniques developed for x-ray, CAT, or NMR imagery cannot be applied directly since PET images aim at a different spectrum of characteristics of the targeted tissue. In the paragraphs that follow, we offer a brief review of work that relates to the area of noise modeling in medical images in general and PET image enhancement in particular.

The noise and artifacts present in PET images manifests as spoke-like streaks starting at the boundaries of regions in the image that separate areas of significantly distinct intensities (hot spots), and ending at the edge of the image (see Fig. 1). Images that exhibit similar patterns of comparable attenuation generate artifacts that correlate highly. This phenomenon already has been noted in x-ray tomography in which "for typical thorax cross-sections, such streaks emanate mainly from the outside contour of the body, the outside boundary of the heart, and from dense regions such as the spine or contrast-infused heart chambers" (16). In image processing terms, all these regions share the common fact that they are all areas of high-intensity gradient.

These artifacts are eliminated significantly when the angular sampling is increased, which points toward an undersampling problem (17). A solution suggested by Garden and Robb consists of modeling the streak artifacts by averaging many reconstructions from different projections (16). This yielded a good understanding of the nature of the streak artifacts as reconstructed from few projections. Nonuniform sampling resulting from wobbling motion is yet another cause of noise in PET. The correction for this noise at the signal level introduces a secondary effect on the variance of the signal (18).

In characterizing noise distribution statistics due to emission and transmission (other sources of noise) in PET, Palmer noted that PET exhibits a relatively high level of noise in comparison with other imaging modalities; this is attributed to the limited counting statistics of the data (19). Averaging several scans to reduce noise (such as from transmission data) does not necessarily reduce noise levels because the data are statistically dependent. Furthermore, transmission images used for attenuation correction, for instance, vary significantly with the level of activity, which is in turn patient dependent as well as tracer dependent (19).

We propose a model for radial noise in PET images, then use it to devise a spectral filtering technique combined with rectangular-to-polar and polar-to-rectangular image mappings in order to filter radial noise. In the next section, we briefly review filtering techniques and image spectrum estimation. A model of radial noise then is developed. In the section on classical image filtering, we show how classical image filtering techniques cannot filter the artifacts from PET images without altering dominant features in the image significantly. The section on radial noise removal is devoted to experimental results illustrating the use of the newly proposed filtering technique and a comparison with classical filtering techniques. Summary and conclusions are given in the final section.

IMAGE FILTERING: A REVIEW

Before proceeding, we will review in brief the Fourier transform and its properties which will be used for image filtering as discussed in the next two sections (14). (Readers familiar with spectral image filtering may skip this section.)

Fourier transform is used to map an image into the frequency domain in which filtering sometimes is easier to perform. Let $f(x, y)$ be a continuous function of the real variables x and y. The Fourier transform of $f(x, y)$, denoted by $\mathcal{F}[f(x, y)] = F(u, v)$, is given by

$$F(u,v) = \int_{-\infty}^{+\infty} \int_{-\infty}^{+\infty} f(x,y) \exp[-j2\pi(ux + vy)] \, dx \, dy,$$

where (u, v) are the frequency domain coordinates. The inverse Fourier transform is given by

$$f(x,y) = \int_{-\infty}^{+\infty} \int_{-\infty}^{+\infty} F(u,v) \exp[j2\pi(ux + vy)] \, du \, dv.$$

The direct and inverse discrete Fourier transform for an $N \times N$ discrete image $f(x, y)$ defined for integer values of x and y are given by

$$F(u,v) = (1/N) \sum_{x=0}^{N-1} \sum_{y=0}^{N-1} f(x,y) \exp[-j2\pi(ux + vy)/N],$$

and

$$f(x,y) = (1/N) \sum_{u=0}^{N-1} \sum_{v=0}^{N-1} F(u,v) \exp[j2\pi(ux + vy)/N].$$

The Fourier transform of a real image is generally complex and can be represented in exponential form as

$$F(u,v) = |F(u,v)| \, e^{j\phi(u,v)}.$$

The spectrum and phase angle are given by

$$|F(u,v)| = [R^2(u,v) + I^2(u,v)]^{1/2},$$

$$\phi(u,v) = \tan^{-1}[I(u,v)/R(u,v)],$$

where $R(x, y)$ and $I(x, y)$ are the real and imaginary components of $F(u, v)$, respectively.

Typically, image filtering is performed by multiplying the Fourier transform $F(u, v)$ of a function $f(x, y)$ by a transfer function $H(u, v)$:

$$G(u,v) = H(u,v) \, F(u,v),$$

then computing the Fourier inverse of $G(u, v)$, $g(x, y)$, which is the filtered version of $f(x, y)$. This is illustrated diagrammatically in Figure 2. This filtering procedure is used for both x-y and ρ-θ image representations introduced in this article.

$$f(x,y) \xrightarrow{\mathscr{F}} F(u,v) \xrightarrow{\times H(u,v)} G(u,v) \xrightarrow{\mathscr{F}} g(x,y)$$

FIGURE 2   Spectral image filtering.

MODELING OF RADIAL NOISE

In this section, we model radial noise and study its effect on the frequency characteristics of a digital image. Both a theoretical presentation and a computer simulation of this effect are given.

The objective here is to show that, when presented in a rectangular form, radial noise does not map in a specific area of the Fourier domain, hence it is difficult to remove it by attenuating given components of the image spectrum without altering major features in the image significantly. To illustrate this, we graphically simulate radial noise as a set of bright rays emanating from the center of a dark image (Figure 3a). The Fourier spectrum of this noise is shown in Figure 3b. This shows clearly that radial noise does not map in a specific area of the Fourier spectrum, hence classical low-pass filtering techniques that usually rid an image of random noise would fail. To illustrate this, we apply a first-order, low-pass Butterworth filter with the following transfer function:

$$H_b(u,v) = \frac{1}{1 + [(u^2 + v^2)/R_b^2]^n}. \tag{1}$$

The cutoff frequency R_b is set to a variable fraction of the filtered-image radius $N/2$. The order of the filter n is set to 1 in this experiment. Figure 3c shows the filtered spectrum

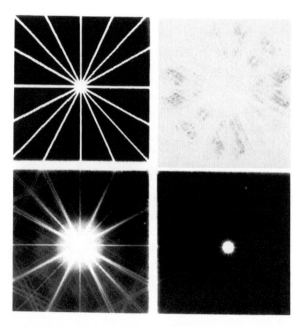

FIGURE 3   Radial noise filtering in a rectangular coordinate system: (*a*) simulated noise in the *x*-*y* space; (*b*) its Fourier spectrum in the *u*-*v* space; (*c*) low-pass filtered spectrum in the *u*-*v* space; (*d*) reconstructed filtered image in the *x*-*y* space.

for $R_b = N/20$; the resulting filtered image is shown in Figure 3*d*. The amount of filtered noise is limited for any reasonable cutoff frequency of the filter. As an alternative, we try to model this noise in a polar representation.

Assume a $2R \times 2R$ continuous image $f_1(x, y)$, defined for $-R < x < R$ and $-R < y < R$, is corrupted with an additive radial noise that results in an image $g_1(x, y)$.

$$g_1(x,y) = f_1(x,y) + n_1(x,y).$$

The function $g_1(x,y)$, is assumed to vanish outside a disk of radius R. If not, both $f_1(x,y)$ and $n_1(x, y)$ are multiplied by the unit step function $u(R^2 - x^2 - y^2)$.

Since the noise investigated here is radial, its properties are understood better in a polar coordinate system instead of a rectangular system. The rectangular-to-polar transformation in the *x*-*y* coordinate system is given by

$$\begin{cases} \rho = \sqrt{x^2 + y^2} \\ \theta = \tan^{-1}(y/x), \end{cases}$$

where

$$0 \le \rho < R$$

$$0 \le \theta < 2\pi$$

The inverse transformation, polar-to-rectangular, hence is given in the ρ-θ coordinate system by

$$\begin{cases} x = \rho \cos \theta \\ y = \rho \sin \theta. \end{cases}$$

As defined here, both the rectangular-to-polar and polar-to-rectangular transformations are one-to-one mappings. The resulting images from the rectangular-to-polar transformation are $f(\rho, \theta)$, $n(\rho, \theta)$, and $g(\rho, \theta)$. The objective here is to determine where the radial noise $n(\rho, \theta)$, maps in the frequency domain

$$\mathscr{F}[n(\rho,\theta)] = N(\omega, \phi).$$

In the x-y space, the radial noise can be modeled as a series of $(K + 1)$ delta functions emanating from the origin of the coordinate system along rays of length R at θ_0, $\theta_0 + \theta_1$, $\theta_0 + \theta_2$, . . . ,$\theta_0 + \theta_K$. The starting angle θ_0 is random; $\mathscr{S} = \{\theta_k\}$ is a series of increment angles of the delta functions. Though it is apparent from looking at the original image (Fig. 1), in general there seems to be some regularity in the noise spatial distribution in PET images. Next, we examine two radial-noise models with the following properties:

1. The starting angle θ_0 is random over the interval $[0, 2\pi[$; the series $\mathscr{S}$ is constant (i.e., $\mathscr{S} = \{\theta_k = \theta_s = \text{const}, k = 1, 2, \ldots ,K\}$) with the spacing angle θ_s within the interval $[0, 2\pi[$.
2. The starting angle θ_0 is random over the interval $[0, 2\pi[$; the series $\mathscr{S}$ is random but distributed uniformly over the interval $[0, 2\pi[$ (i.e., the probability distribution of θ_k, $p_{\theta_k}(\theta_k) = 0.5\pi^{-1}$).

In both cases, we show that the spectrum of the noise maps in a local and well-defined area of the image spectrum in the ω-ϕ system.

Model with θ_0 Random and $\mathscr{S}$ Constant

If the starting angle θ_0 is random and the spacing angle is constant, the radial noise may be modeled as a series of $(K + 1)$ delta functions emanating from the origin along rays of length R at θ_0, $\theta_0 + \theta_s$, $\theta_0 + 2\theta_s$, . . . ,$\theta_0 + K\theta_s$. The radial noise is defined as

$$n_1(x,y) = \sum_{k=0}^{K} \delta(\tan^{-1}(y/x) - \theta_0 - k\theta_s),$$

where

$$x^2 + y^2 < R^2$$

$$0 \le \theta_0 < 2\pi$$

$$0 < \theta_s < 2\pi - \theta_0$$

$$K = \lceil 2\pi/\theta_s \rceil - 1.$$

The function $\lceil z \rceil$ is equal to the largest integer greater than or equal to z. In polar representation, $n(\rho, \theta)$ is defined by

$$n(\rho,\theta) = \sum_{k=0}^{K} \delta (\theta - \theta_0 - k\theta_s),$$

with $0 \le \rho < R$ and $0 \le \theta < 2\pi$. The parameters θ_0, θ_s, and K are subject to the conditions mentioned earlier.

The Fourier transform of $n(\rho, \theta)$, $N(\omega, \phi)$ may be computed as

$$\mathcal{F}[N(\rho,\theta)] = N(\omega,\phi) = \int_{-\infty}^{+\infty} \int_{-\infty}^{+\infty} n(\rho,\theta) \exp[-j2\pi(\rho\omega + \theta\phi)] \, d\rho \, d\theta.$$

Since $n(\rho, \theta)$ is identically zero outside the intervals $[0, R[$ for ρ and $[0, 2\pi[$ for θ,

$$\mathcal{F}[n(\rho,\theta)] = \int_0^R \int_0^{2\pi} \sum_{k=0}^{K} \delta (\theta - \theta_0 - k\theta_s) \exp[-j2\pi(\rho\omega + \theta\phi)] \, d\theta \, d\rho$$

$$= \int_0^R \sum_{k=0}^{K} \exp[-j2\pi(\rho\omega + (\theta_0 + k\theta_s)\phi)] \, d\rho$$

$$= \frac{1}{-2\pi\omega} [e^{-j2\pi R\omega} - 1]e^{-j2\pi\theta_0\phi} \sum_{k=0}^{K} e^{-j2\pi k\theta_s\phi}.$$

If we let

$$\mathcal{F}[n(\rho,\theta)] = N(\omega,\phi) \, A \, N_\omega(\omega) \, N_\phi(\phi),$$

then

$$A = R,$$

$$N_\omega(\omega) = \frac{1}{-j2\pi R\omega} [e^{-j2\pi R\omega} - 1],$$

$$N_\phi(\phi) = e^{-j2\pi\theta_0\phi} \sum_{k=0}^{K} e^{-j2\pi k\theta_s\phi}.$$

The function $N_\phi(\phi)$ may be expressed as

$$N_\phi(\phi) = e^{-j2\pi\theta_0\phi} \sum_{k=0}^{K} e^{-j2\pi k\theta_s\phi} = e^{-j2\pi\theta_0\phi} \sum_{k=0}^{K} [e^{-j2\pi\theta_s\phi}]^k.$$

For $\phi = \theta_s^{-1}$,

$$N_\phi(\phi) = (K + 1)e^{-j2\pi\theta_0\phi},$$

hence,

$$|N_\omega(\omega)| = K + 1.$$

For $\phi \neq \theta_s^{-1}$,

$$N\phi(\phi) = e^{-j2\pi\theta_0\phi} \cdot \frac{1 - e^{-j2\pi(K+1)\theta_s\phi}}{1 - e^{-j2\pi g v_s\phi}},$$

hence

$$|N_\phi(\phi)| = (K + 1) \cdot \left| \frac{\sin\pi(K + 1)\theta_s\phi}{\pi(K + 1)\theta_s\phi} \right| \Big/ \left| \frac{\sin\pi\theta_s\phi}{\pi\theta_s\phi} \right|.$$

In both cases, within the range of ϕ as defined here, $|N_\phi(\phi)|$ is practically constant. The function $N_\omega(\omega)$, on the other hand, may be expressed as

$$N_\omega(\omega) = \frac{e^{-j2\pi R\omega} - 1}{-j2\rho R\omega},$$

hence

$$|N_\omega(\omega)| = \left| \frac{\sin \pi R\omega}{\pi R\omega} \right|.$$

Model with θ_0 Random and $\{\mathcal{S}\}$ Random

In the example of a random-noise model, the starting angle θ_0 is random and the spacing angle is random with a uniform probability distribution of the series $\mathcal{S}$ over $[0, 2\pi[$ for the angle θ_k (see Fig. 4).

The radial noise may be modeled as a series of $(K + 1)$ delta functions emanating from the origin of the coordinate system along rays of length R at θ_0, $\theta_0 + \theta_1$, $\theta_0 + \theta_2, \ldots, \theta_0 + \theta_K$. The mathematical derivations shown in the preceding section hold true if $k\theta_s$ is replaced by θ_k in all equations until the expression giving $N_\phi(\phi)$ is

$$N_\phi(\phi) = e^{-j2\pi\theta_0\phi} \sum_{k=0}^{K} [e^{-j2\pi\theta_k\phi}].$$

Since θ_k is uniform over $[0, 2\pi[$, $N_\phi(\phi)$ may be approximated by the expected value of the right-hand side of the preceding equation.

$$N_\phi(\phi) = e^{-j2\pi\theta_0\phi} E\left[\sum_{k=0}^{K} e^{-j2\pi\theta_k\phi} \right]$$

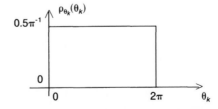

FIGURE 4 Ideal probability distribution of the spacing angle of the radial noise.

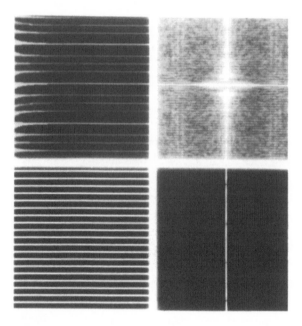

FIGURE 5   Radial noise filtering in a polar coordinate system: (*a*) simulated noise in *x-y* space converted into ρ-θ space; (*b*) its Fourier spectrum in the ω-φ space; (*c*) simulated noise in ρ-θ space; (*d*) its Fourier spectrum in the ω-φ space.

$$= \frac{1}{2\pi}(K + 1)e^{-j2\pi\theta_0\phi}[1 - e^{-j4\pi^2\phi}],$$

which is similar to the result found in the preceding model when $\phi = \theta_s^{-1}$. Hence,

$$N(\omega, \phi) = \frac{A}{2\pi}(K + 1)N_\omega(\omega)e^{-j2\pi\theta_0\phi}[1 - e^{-j4\pi^2\phi}].$$

Consequently, in both cases the magnitude of $N_\omega(\omega)$ behaves like $(\sin \omega)/\omega$, which achieves its maximum at $\omega = 0$ and decays rapidly as ω increases.

In summary,

$$|N(\omega,\phi)| \quad \alpha K \left| \frac{\sin \pi R\omega}{\pi R\omega} \right| \tag{2}$$

behaves like $(\sin \omega)/\omega$ running along and around the φ axis and is small for other values of ω and φ. Note that the strength of the power spectrum is directly proportional to the number of noise streaks in the image *K*. With the rectangular-to-polar mapping, the radial noise maps around the φ axis in the ω-φ polar image representation. This is illustrated easily by an experiment. The radial-noise pattern shown in Figure 3*a* is converted into the ρ-θ representation shown in Figure 5*a*. Its Fourier spectrum is shown in Figure 5*b*. Despite the inexact rectangular-to-polar mapping, the spectrum is concentrated on and around the φ axis. This also is true for noise that is simulated in the ρ-θ space (Fig. 5*c*) then converted into the ω-φ space (Fig. 5*d*). It is of note that most of the useful image data will map around the origin of the ω-φ space. Complete removal of the radial noise will wipe out the true image data. Hence, it is expected that a residual noise will be left around the origin in any filtering scheme.

CLASSICAL IMAGE FILTERING

Our objective in classical image filtering is to remove the radial noise without degrading the meaningful features in the image (such as the heart walls in a cardiac image). Though the true physical causes of noise in PET images are not known fully, it is reasonable to assume that classical spatial neighborhood averaging, spectral low-pass image filtering, and recursive noise removal techniques would increase the overall quality of a PET image without degrading some of its important features.

The Fourier spectrum of an image shows where the energy of an image is located in the frequency domain. Since noise often is associated with patterns that repeat frequently, usually it maps in the outer regions of a centered spectrum. The attenuation of these regions by low-pass filtering, for instance, removes the spatial noise if its content is indeed high in the outer regions of the spectrum image. For the sake of illustration, let us assume that the image to be filtered is simply the superimposition of an ideal image that is noise free and a noise image that would be the residual signal when we subtract the ideal image from the original image.

For the image shown in Figure 1, in order to remove the radial noise adequately with such classical low-pass Butterworth filtering, as that given in Eq. (1), the filter radius would have to be so small that most of the important information in the image would be lost. Using Eq. (1), several radii were tried. For large values of R_b, the energy content removed from the image is so limited that the overall aspect of the image is unchanged both for the ideal image and the noise image. On the other hand, for small values of R_b the amount of noise deleted is significant, but a significant amount of information in the ideal image is lost too. In this experiment, there seems to be no tradeoff region for R_b in which the amount of noise removed and edge content left are satisfactory. It is of note that these evaluations are purely subjective since the enhancement procedure is done for viewing and examination purposes. Two examples of this filtering operation for $R_b = R/10$ and $R_b = R/20$ are shown in Figure 6. (For a digital image the radius is $R = N/2$.)

To illustrate why this method has failed in removing radial noise, a Butterworth low-pass filter is applied to a simulated radial noise image (Fig 7a). The spectrum of this image is shown in Figure 7b. The spectrum after filtering for $R_b = R/20$ is shown in Figure 7c. The reconstructed noise image after filtering is shown in Figure 7d. We can see that the radial noise cannot be isolated easily in the spectrum of the image, hence its removal cannot be done successfully in a rectangular image representation.

RADIAL NOISE REMOVAL

In this section, we show some of the benefits of the mapping and the noise model developed in the section on modeling of radial noise. Using properties of this model, we devise a filtering procedure that rids the image of most of the radial noise. This procedure is summarized in Figure 8.

In order to remove the radial noise present in PET images efficiently, we have to characterize it spatially in the frequency domain. First, the image shown in Figure 1 is

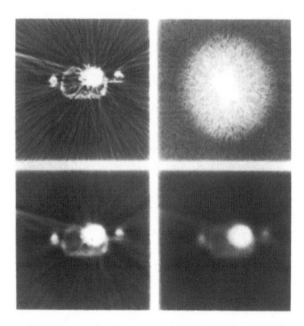

FIGURE 6   Low-pass filtering of a noisy PET image: (a) original image in the x-y space; (b) spectrum of the original image in the u-v space (note the low signal content in the outer region of the image); (c) filtered image in the x-y space for $R_b = R/10$; (d) filtered image in the x-y space for $R_b = R/20$.

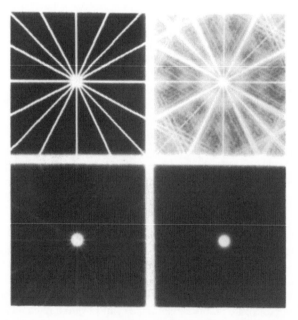

FIGURE 7   Low-pass filtering of simulated noise: (a) simulated-noise image in the x-y space; (b) spectrum of simulated noise in the u-v space; (c) filtered image in the x-y space for $R_b = R/10$; (d) filtered image in the x-y space for $R_b = R/20$.

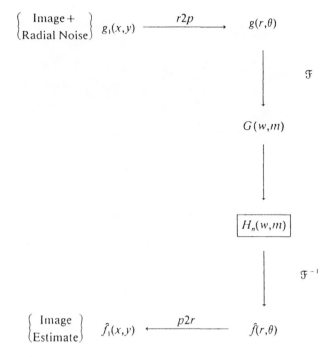

FIGURE 8 Summary of the mapping and filtering procedure.

converted from the x-y space into the ρ-θ space. The spectrum of both images then is computed. Figure 9 shows both images and their spectra.

Neither of the image spectra has distinct features from which the spectral component of the noise can be identified. To probe this issue further, we plot the power spectrum of the original image $f(x, y)$, $F(u, v)$ and the simulated noise $n(\rho, \theta)$ $N(\omega, \phi)$ in both domains (u-v and ω-ϕ spaces) as a function of $\sqrt{u^2 + v^2}$, $\sqrt{\omega^2 + \phi^2}$, $|\omega|$, and $|\phi|$, which is denoted briefly by r thereafter. This is summarized in Table 1 and Figure 10.

These plots are typical, in other words, the position of each curve does not vary significantly regardless of the real-image data and regardless of the simulated-noise data. From the analysis of these plots, we make the following remarks:

- For low values of the radius r, the power spectrum of the real PET image is higher than that of the simulated noise. The power spectra in percent for $r = 10 \simeq R/12$, are 51, 54, 64, and 83 for the real PET data versus 8, 8, 11, and 45 for the simulated noise data. This means that, on the average and toward small radii, the higher the noise the lower the image content.
- The image mapping from the x-y space raises the image content for the real data with higher increments than for the simulated data (for low values of r). This is clear by comparing Curve A to Curve B for the real data and Curve E to Curve F for the simulated data. This effect is masked significantly by the averaging effect inherent in the mapping from the x-y space into the ρ-θ space, which tends to "push" the image power spectrum toward the origin.

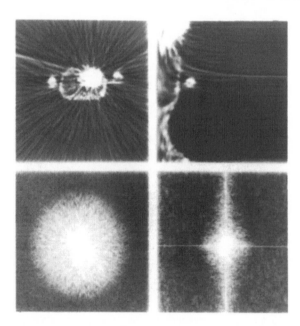

FIGURE 9   Image mapping: (*a*) noisy PET image in the *x-y* space; (*b*) converted image in the ρ-θ space; (*c*) image spectrum in the *u-v* space; (*d*) image spectrum in ω-ϕ space.

TABLE 1   Power Spectrum of Real Data and Simulated Noise as a Function of *r*

y Axis in %	$F_1(u, v)$	$F(\omega, \phi)$	$F(\omega, \phi)$	$F(\omega, \phi)$	$N_1(u, v)$	$N(\omega, \phi)$	$N(\omega, \phi)$	$N(\omega, \phi)$
*x*Axis in Pixels	$\sqrt{u^2 + v^2}$	$\sqrt{\omega^2 + \phi^2}$	$\mid \omega \mid$	$\mid \phi \mid$	$\sqrt{u^2 + v^2}$	$\sqrt{\omega^2 + \phi^2}$	$\mid \omega \mid$	$\mid \phi \mid$
r	*y*(A)	*y*(B)	*y*(C)	*y*(D)	*y*(E)	*y*(F)	*y*(G)	*y*(H)
0	0.0	0.0	0.0	0.0	0.0	0.0	0.0	0.0
1	2.6	4.2	11.4	18.3	0.4	0.5	5.2	15.6
2	9.8	11.9	21.1	30.3	1.3	1.2	5.7	24.3
4	26.9	27.1	39.1	53.4	2.8	3.1	7.6	34.1
8	47.7	45.1	57.0	77.2	6.2	6.6	10.2	42.9
10	50.5	53.6	64.4	83.4	7.9	8.1	11.3	45.4
20	69.7	80.3	82.6	94.6	14.9	29.6	36.6	55.2
40	87.3	90.3	90.2	97.9	27.9	52.6	57.2	70.1
80	99.4	95.6	96.0	98.8	53.8	79.5	82.3	87.4
100	99.7	97.5	98.1	99.2	66.0	88.6	91.3	93.4
140	99.9	99.7	100.0	100.0	93.0	99.0	100.0	100.0
180	100.0	100.0	100.0	100.0	100.0	100.0	100.0	100.0

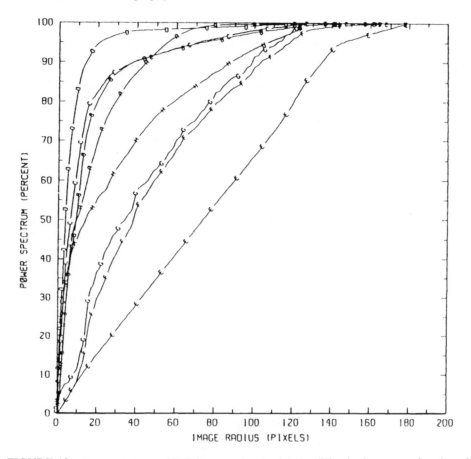

FIGURE 10 Power spectrum of PET image and a simulated radial noise image as a function of the image radii in the u-v and ω-ϕ spaces: (A) $F_1(u,v)$ as a function of $\sqrt{u^2 + v^2}$, (B) $F(\omega, \phi)$ as function of $\sqrt{\omega^2 + \phi^2}$ (C) $F(\omega, \phi)$ as a function of $|\omega|$, (D) $F(\omega, \phi)$ as a function of $|\phi|$, E: $N_1(u, v)$ as a function of $\sqrt{u^2 + v^2}$ (F) $N(\omega, \phi)$ as a function of $\sqrt{\omega^2 + \phi^2}$ (G) $N(\omega, \phi)$ as a function of $|\omega|$, (H) $N(\omega, \phi)$ as a function of $|\phi|$.

- By comparing Curves B and F (both in the ω-ϕ space), say for $r \leq 30$, we see that if filtered around this radius, 90% of the image is retained, in contrast to 20% of the noise content.
- By comparing the relative position of Curve G with respect to Curve F versus the Curve H to F, we see that the ω axis is more dominant than the ϕ axis. This is eminent in the surge in Curve H, particularly for small radii, which remains significantly higher not only to Curves E, F, and G but also higher than all other curves for small values of the radius r (see Table 1 also). This fact was verified theoretically in the section on the modeling of radial noise in which the noise was modeled by a series of impulses along rays, emanating from the origin, and running radially toward the edges of the image.

In summary, the image mapping and noise model proposed in the section on radial noise modeling show that the power spectrum of the noise (radial artifacts) present in

PET images that is spread randomly over the spectral domain in the rectangular representation of Figure 3 is mapped locally around the ϕ axis in the spectral representation of the image after the mapping above is applied in Figures 5 and 10. Using this fact, we designed a class of notch filters that attenuates the image spectral content along the ϕ axis and leaves the rest of the image untouched. Understandably, to preserve the noise-free image this filter cannot remove the image content around the origin. This will cause a residual radial noise to remain in the image. The residual noise can be controlled by the radius R_n, around the origin, which, for practical purposes, will be the only parameter to be selected in the notch filter

$$H_n(\omega, \phi) = [u(\omega^2 - R_n^2) - u(R_n^2 - \omega^2 - \phi^2)]^* \, G_\sigma \, (\omega, \phi). \tag{3}$$

The term $G_\sigma(\omega, \phi)$ is a Gaussian smoothing function (zero mean and σ^2 variance) used to avoid the ringing effects that often result from discontinuities in the filter transfer function. The degree of smoothing is controlled by the parameter σ^2 (14). A profile of a typical filter of this kind is shown in Figure 11. The filter radius R_n is set by selecting a percentage of the noise removed or a percentage of noise-free data to be left after filtering. The radius can be read simply from Table 1. it is worth emphasizing again that the performance of this filter is unchanged for a wide variety of images. This filter is applied to the PET image; the results are shown in Figures 9 and 12.

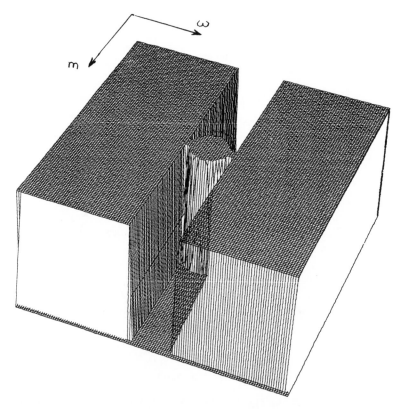

FIGURE 11   Profile of the notch filter used for radial-noise removal ($R_n = 10$; $\sigma^2 = 9$).

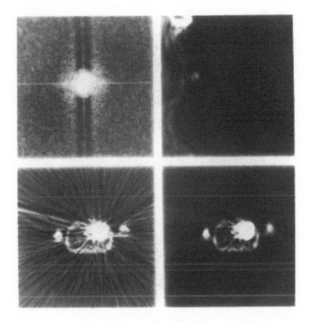

FIGURE 12   Notch filter: (*a*) filtered spectrum in the ω-φ space; (*b*) filtered spectrum in the *u-v* space; (*c*) original image in the *x-y* space; (*d*) filtered image.

Visual inspection and comparison between the original image and the filtered version reveal a significant reduction in artifact noise and an overall improvement in image quality. The artifacts have been removed without severe degradation of the edge information present in the image. This can be seen further by comparing the outcome of this filtering procedure against that obtained by classical noise-removal techniques based on spectral low-pass filtering. In Figure 13, we show the original PET image (Fig. 13*a*), the resulting filtered image using spectral low-pass filtering with a cutoff radius of $R_b = R/10$ (Fig. 13*b*), the resulting filtered image using spectral low-pass filtering with a cutoff radius of $R_b = R/20$ (Fig. 13*c*), and the resulting filtered image using the technique presented in the preceding section (Fig. 13*d*). As already mentioned, a reasonable tradeoff cutoff radius cannot be achieved. This can be seen easily in Figure 13*b* and *c*. However, using the transfer function of the notch filter given in Eq. (3), we were able to remove most of the artifacts without significant degradation of the dominant features of the image (20).

SUMMARY AND CONCLUSIONS

The quality of boundary information and local pixel intensity in PET images is enhanced significantly by the reduction of random noise and artifacts. Noise characteristics in PET do not allow for attenuation or elimination of these artifacts using simple filtering techniques. A method based on the spectral characteristics of the targeted noise and rectangular-to-polar and polar-to-rectangular mapping of the image data is developed and tested using synthetic and real data. Specifically, we model the noise streaks in PET images in both rectangular and polar domains and show, both analytically and through

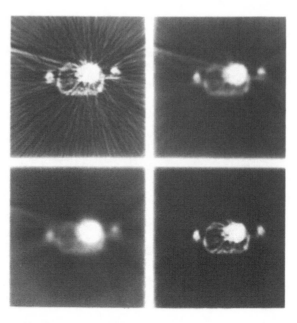

FIGURE 13 Notch filtering versus classical low-pass filtering: (*a*) original image; (*b*) noise removal by low-pass filtering ($R_b = R/10$); (*c*) noise removal by low-pass filtering ($R_b = R/20$); (*d*) noise removal by notch filter.

computer simulation, that it exhibits consistent mapping patterns. A class of filters is designed and applied successfully. Visual inspection of the filtered images shows clear enhancement over the original images.

Anticipated benefits from this noise-removal scheme are

- Increase in degree of success in the detection and identification of image features by an operator
- Increase in degree of success of automated feature detection and recognition
- Visualization improvement of tracked objects in dynamic images
- Real-time, artifact-free, three-dimensional display of vital organs

Future work will involve application of this technique to a large set of heart and brain images and the investigation of the statistical characteristics of this method and its degree of dependence on the noise level in the image data. The notch filter given in Eq. (3) is specified uniquely through the parameter R_n, which depends largely on the ratio of the ideal image data to the noise data. In this article, the radius R_n is selected by predefining the percentage of the data to be preserved; future work will address the automatic and optimal selection of this parameter as a function of some quantitative information extracted from the image itself.

REFERENCES

1. Phelps, M. E., and Mazziotta, J. C., Positron Emission Tomography: Human Brain Function and Biochemistry, *Science*, 228(4701):799–809 (May 1985).

2. Ter-Pogossian, M. M., Raichle, M. E., and Sobel, B. E., Positron-Emission Tomography, *Sci. Am.*, 243:170–181 (October 1980).

3. Sorenson, J. A., and Phelps, M. E., *Physics in Nuclear Medicine*, Grune & Stratton, Orlando, FL, 1987.

4. Phelps, M. E., Positron Computed Tomography for Studies of Myocardial and Cerebral Function, *Ann. Int. Med.*, 98(3):339–359 (March 1983).

5. Ballenot, J., and Freiherr, G., Cardiac PET Nears Routine Application, *Cardiology* (February 1987).

6. Wagner, H. N., Has the Time Arrived for Clinical PET Imaging? *Diag. Imaging* (November 1985).

7. Hall, E. L., *Computer Image Processing and Recognition*, Academic Press, New York, 1979.

8. Haykin, S., Justice, J., Owlsley, N. L., Yen, J. L., and Kak, A. C., *Array Signal Processing*, Prentice-Hall, Englewood Cliffs, NJ, 1985.

9. Jain, A. K., *Fundamentals of Digital Image Processing*, Prentice-Hall, Englewood Cliffs, NJ, 1989.

10. Chesler, D. A., Noise Power Spectrum in Time-of-Flight Tomography, in *Proc. Workshop on Time-of-Flight Tomography*, May 1982, pp. 113–116.

11. Vardi, Y., Shapp, L. A., and Kaufman, L., A Statistical Model for Positron Emission Tomography, *J. Am. Statist. Assoc.*, 80(389):8–38 (March 1985).

12. Derenzo, S. E., Fourier Deconvolution to Remove Positron Range Blurring in High-Resolution Tomography, *IEEE Trans. Nucl. Sci.* 565–569 (February 1986).

13. Hoffman, E. J., Positron-Emission Tomography: Role of Detection Systems in Quantification and Image Quality, *IEEE Trans. Nucl. Sci.*, 420–424 (February 1986).

14. Gonzalez, R. C., and Woods, R. E., *Digital Image Processing*, Addison-Wesley, Reading, MA, 1992.

15. Hwang, J. J., Regional Computed Tomography Image Enhancement, in *Proc. 5th Intl. Conf. on Pattern Recognition*, Miami Beach, FL, December 1980, pp. 412–418.

16. Garden, K. L., and Robb, R. A., 3-D Reconstruction of the Heart from Projections: A Practical Implementation of the McKinnon-Bates Algorithm, *IEEE Trans. Med. Imaging*, MI-5(4):233–239 (1986).

17. Smith, P. R., Peters, T. M., and Bates, R. H. T., Image Reconstruction from Finite Numbers of Projections, *J. Phys. Assoc.*, 6:361–382 (1973).

18. Alpert, N. M., Chesler, D. A., Correia, J. A., Ackerman, R. H., Chang, S. F. J. Y., Davis, S. M., Brownell, G. L., and Taveras, J. M., Estimation of the Local Statistical Noise in Emission Computed Tomography, *IEEE Trans. Med. Imaging*, MI-1(2):142–146 (1982).

19. Palmer, M. R., Noise Distribution Due to Emission and Transmission Statistics in Positron-Emission Tomography, *IEEE Trans. Nucl. Sci.*, 439–442 (February 1986).

20. Abidi, M. A., and Davis, P. B., Radial Noise Filtering in Positron Emission Tomography, *J. Optical Eng.*, 25(5):567–574 (May 1990).

MONGI AL ABIDI

PAUL BENJAMIN DAVIS

PROGRAM VERIFICATION

A fundamental issue in computer science is the extent to which purely formal methods are sufficient to secure the goals of the discipline. There are those, such as C. A. R. Hoare and Edsgar Dijkstra, who maintain that, in order to attain the standing of a science rather than that of a craft, computer science should model itself after mathematics. Others, including Richard DeMillo, Richard Lipton, and Alan Perlis, however, deny that the goals of the discipline can be gained by means of purely formal methods.

Much of the debate between adherents to these diverse positions has revolved about the extent to which purely formal methods can provide a guarantee of computer system performance. Yet the ramifications of this dispute extend beyond the boundaries of the discipline itself. The deeper question that lies beneath this controversy concern the paradigm most appropriate to computer science. This issue not only influences the way in which agencies disburse funding but also the way in which the public views this discipline.

Some of the most important issues that arise within this context concern questions of a philosophical character. These involve "ontic" (or ontological) questions about the kinds of thing computers and programs are as well as "epistemic" (or epistemological) questions about the kind of knowledge we can possess about things of these kinds. They also involve questions about crucial differences between "pure" and "applied" mathematics and whether the performance of a system when it executes a program can be guaranteed.

THE FORMAL APPROACH TO PROGRAM VERIFICATION

The phrase "program verification" occurs in two different senses, one of which is broad, the other narrow. In its broad sense, "program verification" refers to any methods, techniques, or procedures that can be employed for the purpose of assessing software reliability. These methods include testing programs by attempting to execute them and constructing prototypes of the systems on which they are intended to be run in an attempt to discover possible errors, mistakes, or "bugs" in those programs that need to be corrected.

In its narrow sense, "program verification" refers to specifically formal methods, techniques, or procedures that can be employed for the same purpose, especially to "proofs" of program correctness. This approach seeks to insure software reliability by utilizing the techniques of deductive logic and pure mathematics, where the lines that constitute the text of a program are subjected to formal scrutiny. Its attractive character has led to works by members of the community elaborating its virtues (1–3).

Thus, while program verification in its broad sense includes both formal and non-formal methods for evaluating reliability, in its narrow sense "program verification" is restricted to formal methods exclusively. The use of these methods tends to be driven by the desire to put computer science on a sound footing by means of greater reliance on mathematics in order to gain the ability to "define transformations upon strings of symbols that constitute a program, the result of which will enable us to predict how a given computer would behave when under the control of that program" (3, p. 1).

The conception of programming as a mathematical activity has been eloquently championed by Hoare, among others, as the following reflects (4, p. 576):

> Computer programming is an exact science in that all of the properties of a program and all of the consequences of executing it in any given environment can, in principle, be found out from the text of the program itself by means of purely deductive reasoning.

Thus, if this position is well-founded, programming ought to be viewed as a mathematical activity and computer science as a branch of mathematics. If it is not well-founded, however, some other paradigm may be required.

COMPUTER PROGRAMS AND FORMAL PROOFS OF CORRECTNESS

No doubt, the conception that underlies Hoare's position exerts an immense intuitive appeal. A computer $\mathbf{M}$, after all, can be viewed abstractly as a set of transformation functions T for effecting changes in its states S:

$$\mathbf{M} = \langle T, S \rangle \tag{1}$$

A program P in turn can be viewed as a function that transforms a computer from an initial state si to a final state sf when that program is executed E:

$$E\langle P, si \rangle = sf. \tag{2}$$

Eq. [2] thus represents a "special purpose" instance of a universal machine (1). [The account in this section follows that Beng et al. (3, in particular, Chaps. 2 and 3).]

Since every program is intended to effect a change of state from an initial state si before execution to a final one sf after execution, Hoare (4) introduced a notation that is equivalent to '$\{si\}\ P\ \{sf\}$,' where '$\{si\}$' denotes the state prior to and '$\{sf\}$' the state after the execution of program P (or, in general, to '$\{X\}\ P\ \{Y\}$', where 'X' describes some property satisfied by $\mathbf{M}$ prior to and 'Y' another property satisfied by $\mathbf{M}$ after the execution of P).

As Berg et al. explain (3, pp. 20–21), a distinction has to be drawn between *proofs of correctness* and *proofs of partial correctness*, where the difference depends upon whether or not the execution of program P terminates. When P terminates, then a formal proof that $E\langle P, si \rangle = sf$ becomes possible, where $E\langle P, si \rangle = sf$ if and only if $\vdash \{si\}\ P\ \{sf\}$ (i.e., if and only if $\{si\}\ P\ \{sf\}$ is syntactically derivable on the basis of the axioms defining $\mathbf{M}$).

Given a formal specification of the state transformations that are desired of a program P when it is executed in the general form $\{X\}\ P\ \{Y\}$, the aim of a (complete) correctness proof is to demonstrate $\vdash \{X\}\ P\ \{Y\}$, where:

$$\vdash \{X\}\ P\ \{Y\}$$

if and only if

$$(si)[\vdash X(si) \rightarrow \vdash (P \text{ terminates}) \quad \text{and} \vdash Y(E\langle P, si \rangle)].$$

(employing ". . . → __ " as the material condition "if . . . then __ " sign); and the aim of a (partial) correctness proof is to demonstrate $\vdash \{X\}\ P\ \{Y\}$ *if P terminates*, where termination is something that may or may not occur:

$$\vdash \{X\}\ P\ \{Y\}$$

if and only if

$$(si)[\vdash X(si) \text{ and } \vdash (P \text{ terminates}) \rightarrow \vdash Y(E\langle P,\ si\rangle)].$$

where the asterisk "*" attached to $\vdash \{X\}\ P\ \{Y\}$ indicates partial correctness. Proofs of correctness therefore are not precluded by the halting problem.

THE IMPLIED ANALOGY WITH PURE MATHEMATICS

One need not be a student of the history of mathematics to appreciate the implied analogy with pure mathematics. The model of formal proofs of program correctness immediately brings to mind Euclidean geometry with its formal proofs of geometrical theorems. Indeed, it is a plausible analogy to suppose that formal proofs of program correctness in computer science are precisely analogous to formal proofs of geometrical theorems in Euclid (Fig. 1).

Thus, by employing deductive reasoning that involves the application of formal rules of inference to the premises of an argument, various assertions could be shown to be valid formulae of Euclidean geometry (i.e., their status as theorems could be established). Analogously, by employing deductive reasoning that involves the application of formal rules of inference to the premises of an argument, various assertions might be shown to be valid formulae about computer programs (they could be theorems, too).

Indeed, the realization that programs can be viewed as functions from initial states (or "inputs") to final states (or "outputs"), as (1) and especially (2) above imply, provides an even more persuasive foundation for conceding the force of this comparison. For programs in computer science can be viewed as functions from inputs to outputs and rules of inference in mathematics can be viewed as functions from premises to conclusions (theorems) (Fig. 2).

As though these analogies were not convincing enough, the use of mathematical demonstrations seems to be warranted on the basis of at least two further benefits that accrue from adopting the mathematical paradigm. One is that the abstract characterization of computing machines represented by [1] and [2] attains a generality that transcends the special characteristics of specific machines. Another is that abstract characterizations also emphasize the propriety of adopting formal methods within formal domains. The use of deductive methodology thus appears appropriate [e. g., (3), p. 9].

	Mathematics	*Programming*
Objects of Inquiry:	Theorems	Programs
Method of Inquiry:	Proofs	Verifications

FIGURE 1   A plausible analogy.

	Mathematics	*Programming*
Domain:	Premises	Input
Function:	Rules of Inference	Programs
Range:	Theorems	Output

FIGURE 2   A more plausible analogy.

RECENT ADVOCATES OF PURELY FORMAL METHODS

Hoare is not alone in advocating the position that computer programming should model itself after mathematics. A fascinating illustration of a similar perspective has been advanced by William Wulf, who contends (5, p. 40):

> The *galling* thing about the generally poor quality of much current software is that there is no extrinsic reason for it; perfection is, in principle, possible. Unlike physical devices: (1) There are no natural laws limiting the tolerance to which a program can be manufactured; it can be built *exactly* as specified. (2) There is no Heisenberg uncertainty principle operative; once built, a program will behave exactly as prescribed. And (3) there is no friction or wear: the correctness and performance of a program will not decay with time. (original italics)

This concept of perfection in programming where, once built, a program will behave exactly as prescribed, could be called "Wulffian Perfectionism."

Similar views have been elaborated more recently by Dijkstra, among others, who has definite views on "the cruelty of really teaching computer science," especially when it is properly taught as a branch of mathematics (6, p. 1404):

> Finally, in order to drive home the message that this introductory programming course is primarily a course in formal mathematics, we see to it that the programming language in question has *not* been implemented on campus so that students are protected from the temptation to test their programs. (original italics)

Hoare (4), Wulf (5), and Dijkstra (6) thus represent several decades of commitment to formal methods by influential computer scientists.

It should come as no surprise, of course, that belief in formal methods tends to go hand in hand with the denigration of testing and prototyping. Consider recent remarks by J Strother Moore of Computational Logic, Inc., in support of the extension of formal methods to whole computer systems (7, p. 409):

> System verification grew out of dissatisfaction with program verification, in isolation. Why prove software correct if it is going to be run on unverified systems? In a verified system, one can make the following startling claim: *if the gates behave as formally modeled, then the system behaves as specified.* (italics added)

This claim is indeed "startling". (We shall explore later whether it is true.) And consider some recent messages sent out by Hal Render on USENET. On 17 January 1990, for example, Render transmitted the following claims (8):

> The process of proving a program correct should either indicate that there are no errors or should indicate that there are (and often what and where they are). Thus, *successful program proving methods should eliminate the need for testing.* In practice, things are not so straight-

forward, because verification is tough to do for many kinds of programs, and one still has to contend with erroneous specifications. (italics added)

Indeed, a commitment to formal methods tends to foster such an attitude.

Approximately two weeks later, Render returned to this theme in his response to a USENET critic, whom he dismissed with the following remarks (9):

> No one (except maybe you) thinks that "proving a program correct" means proving absolutely, positively that there is not a single (no, not even one) error in a program. Since the specification and the verifications can be in error, there is NO (not even one) way to infallibly prove a program correct. I know this, all informed proponents of verification know this, and you should know this (enough people have told you). (original emphasis; this was not directed toward me).

This position thus implies that only inadequate specifications, on the one hand, or mistaken reasoning, on the other, can generate program errors [compare (10)]. Taken together, there can be little doubt that passages such as these from Hoare, Wulf, Dijkstra, Moore, and Render, represent a coherent position. The question thus becomes whether it can be justified.

IS THE ANALOGY WITH MATHEMATICS PROPER?

Arguments by analogy compare two things (or kinds of things) with respect to certain properties, contending that, because they share certain properties in common and one of them has a certain additional property, the other has it too. When there are more differences than similarities or few but crucial differences or these arguments are taken to be conclusive, however, arguments by analogy can go astray. Some analogies are faulty. Perhaps programming and mathematics are very different kind of things.

There clearly is some foundation for a comparison between mathematics and programming, especially since mathematical theorems and computer programs are both syntactical entities that consist of sequences of lines. Computer programs seem to differ from mathematical theorems, however, insofar as they are intended to possess a semantical significance that mathematical theorems (within pure mathematics) lack a difference arising because programs, unlike theorems, are instructions for machines.

Indeed, a comparison between mathematical theorems and computer programs becomes more striking when scientific theories (classical mechanics, special relativity, quantum mechanics, and so forth) are considered as well. For scientific theories, like computer programs, have semantical significance that mathematical proofs do not possess. The lines that make up a program, like the sentences that make up a theory, after all, tend to stand for other things for the users of those programs and those theories.

The specific commands that constitute a program, for example, stand for corresponding operations by means of computing machines, while the generalizations that constitute a theory stand for lawful properties of the physical world. Yet even scientific theories do not possess the causal capabilities of computer programs, which can affect the performance of those machines when they are loaded and then executed. A more adequate comparison of their general features thus tends to assume the form of Figure 3.

The comparison that is reflected by Figure 3 suggests rather strongly that the differences between theorems and programs may outweigh their similarities. Whether a difference should make a difference in relation to an analogical argument, however, depends

	Mathematical Proofs:	Scientific Theories:	Computer Programs:
Syntactic Entities:	Yes	Yes	Yes
Semantic Significance:	No	Yes	Yes
Causal Capability:	No	No	Yes

FIGURE 3   A more general comparison

on how strongly it is weighted. If their existence as syntactical entities is all that matters, then computer programs, scientific theories, and mathematical theorems would appear to be exactly on a par. Why should such differences as these matter at all?

ARE OTHER IMPORTANT DIFFERENCES BEING OVERLOOKED?

The sections that follow are intended to explain why differences such as these are fundamental to understanding programming as an activity and computer science as a discipline. Before pursuing this objective, however, it should be observed that yet another difference has sometimes been supposed to be the fundamental difference between the construction of proofs in mathematics and the verification of programs in computing. This arises from a difference in dependence upon social processing in these disciplines.

DeMillo et al. (11), in particular, have suggested that the success of mathematics is crucially dependent upon a process of social interaction between various mathematicians. Without this social process, they contend, mathematics could not succeed. Because formal proofs of program correctness are complex and boring, however, they doubt there will ever be a process of similar social interaction between programmers. Such comparisons with mathematics thus depend upon a faulty analogy.

Even advocates of formal methods have been willing to acknowledge the significance of social processes within mathematical contexts. Some have accented the subjective character of mathematical proof procedure (1, p. 3)

> A mathematical proof is an agenda for a repeatable experiment, just as an experiment in a physics or chemistry laboratory. But the main subject in each experiment is another person instead of physical objects or material. *The intended result of the experiment is a subjective conviction on the part of the other person that a given logical hypothesis leads to a given logical conclusion.* . . . A successful experiment ends in a subjective conviction by a listener or reader that the hypothesis implies the conclusion. (italics added)

While they concede that subjective conviction provides no guarantee of the validity of a proof or the truth of a theorem, Linger et al. maintain that this process of social interaction is essential to producing mathematical products (1).

Since even advocates of formal methods apparently are willing to grant this premise of DeMillo, Lipton, and Perlis' position, the extent to which mathematics is comparable to programming evidently depends on the extent to which programs are like theorems, especially with respect to features that might affect their accessibility to social processing. While these arguments have been highly influential, there are reasons to believe that social interaction should be far more important to mathematics than to programming.

ARE SUBJECTIVE "PROOFS" THE ONLY AVAILABLE EVIDENCE?

The ground on which Linger et al. stake their claim to the importance of proof procedures (within programming as well as within mathematics)—in spite of their subjectivity—is the absence of procedural alternatives (1, p. 4):

> Why bother with mathematics at all, if it only leads to subjective conviction? *Because that is the only kind of reasoned conviction possible*, and because the principal experimental subject who examines your program proofs is yourself! Mathematics provides language and procedure for your own peace of mind. (italics added)

Although this position may initially appear very plausible, it fails to take into account other features that may distinguish programs and theorems.

After all, if computer programs possess a semantical significance and a causal capability that mathematical theorems lack, then there would appear to be opportunities for their evaluation of kinds other than social processing. Scientific theories (such as classical mechanics, special relativity, etc.) are suggestive illustrations, because (almost) no one would want to maintain that their acceptability is exclusively a matter of subjective conviction. Science relies upon observations and experiments.

If scientific theories are viewed as conjectures, then observation and experimentation afford nature opportunities for their refutation. The results of these observations and experiments are not mere matters of subjective conviction. There thus appear to be other methods for evaluating scientific theories that go beyond those available for evaluating proofs of theorems in mathematics. If that is the case, however, then there would appear to be kinds of "reasoned conviction" besides mathematical proofs.

If computer programs possess causal capability as well as semantical significance, then there should also be means for evaluating their correctness going beyond those available for scientific theories. Prototyping and testing offer opportunities for further types of experiments that arise from attempting to execute programs by machine: these are prospects over which we have (almost) complete control. But this indicates yet another kind of "reasoned conviction" going beyond social processing alone.

ARE FORMAL PROOFS OF PROGRAM CORRECTNESS NECESSARY?

If these reflections are well-founded, then the position of Linger et al. (1), which suggests that mathematical proofs of program correctness are indispensable, appears to be very difficult to sustain. If those who advocate formal methods for evaluating programs want to insist upon the primacy of this methodology, they need to find better ground for their position. And, indeed, that support appears to arise from at least two quite different directions, one of which is ontic, the other epistemic.

The ontic defense consists in characterizing "programs" as abstract objects to which physical machines have to conform. Consider Dijkstra (6, p. 140):

> What is a program? Several answers are possible. We can view the program as what turns the general-purpose computer into a special-purpose symbol manipulator, and it does so without the need to change a single wire. . . . I prefer to describe it the other way around. The program is an abstract symbol manipulator which can be turned into a concrete one by

supplying a computer to it. After all, *it is no longer the purpose of programs to instruct our machines: these days, it is the purpose of machines to execute our programs.* (italics added)

One of the attractions of this approach, no doubt, is its strong intimation that programming only involves reference to purely abstract machines.

The identification of "programs" with abstract symbol manipulators, however, warrants further contemplation. While "computers" are characterized sometimes as physical symbol systems—e.g., by Alan Newell and Herbert Simon (12)—"programs" are typically supposed to provide instructions that are executed by machine. By his tacit transformation of "programs" from instructions into machines, Dijkstra thereby distorts the traditional distinction between "programs" and "computers."

The epistemic defense consists in maintaining that formal methods provide the only access route to the kind of knowledge that is required. The maxim that "testing can be used to show the presence of bugs, but never to show their absence" has been promoted by Dijkstra and others (13). This position seems to conform to Sir Karl Popper's conception of scientific methodology as a deductive domain, where scientific hypotheses can possibly be shown to be false but never can be shown to be true.

The epistemic defense, however, appears to be far weaker than the ontic defense, not least because it almost certainly cannot be justified. A successful compilation supports the inference that certain kinds of bugs are absent, just as a successful execution supports the inference that certain other kinds of bugs are absent. Even the conception of conjectures and (attempted) refutations, after all, must take into account the positive significance of *unsuccessful* attempted refutations as well as the negative significance of *successful* attempted refutations [cf. (14), especially Chap. 7].

PROGRAMS AS ABSTRACT ENTITIES AND AS EXECUTABLE CODE

The principal defense of the primacy of formal methods in evaluating computer programs, therefore, appears to depend upon the adequacy of the conception of *programs* as "abstract symbol manipulators." Dijkstra offers several alternative accounts that reinforce the ontic defense (6, p. 1403). Thus

> . . . Another way of saying the same thing is the following one. A programming language, with its formal syntax and with the proof rules that define its semantics, is a formal system for which program execution provides only a model. It is well-known that formal systems should be dealt with in their own right and not in terms of a specific model. And, again, the corollary is that *we should reason about programs without even mentioning their possible "behaviors."* (italics added)

Observe in particular that Dijkstra translates a claim about formal systems into a claim about computer programs without justifying this identification.

Dijkstra further obscures the distinction between "programs" as abstract objects and "programs" as executable entities by asserting the benefits of working with the definition of a set rather than with its specific members (6, p. 1403):

> . . . the statement that a given program meets a certain specification amounts to a statement about *all* computations that could take place under control of that given program. And since this set of computations is defined by the given program, our recent moral says: deal with all computations possible under control of a given program by ignoring them and working with

the program. *We must learn to work with program texts while (temporarily) ignoring that they admit the interpretation of executable code.* (italics added)

The differences between sets and programs, however, are such that there are several good reasons to doubt that even this position can be justified.

Consider, for example, that sets are completely extensional entities, in the sense that two sets are the same when, and only when, they have the same members. The set {x, y, z}, for example, is the same as the set {x, x, y, z, z}, precisely because they have all and only the same elements. Programs, by comparison, are quite different, because two iterations of the same command qualifies as two commands, even if two iterations of the same element qualify as one member of the corresponding set. The principles that govern extensional entities do not govern causal relations.

Thus, although Dijkstra wants to view programs as "abstract symbol manipulators," he thereby obfuscates fundamental differences between things of two different kinds. "Programs" understood as *abstract entities* (to which individual concrete machines must conform) and "programs" as *executable code* (that causally interact with physical machines) have enormously different properties. Indeed, their differences are sufficiently great as to bring into doubt the adequacy of the mathematical analogy.

THE AMBIGUITY OF "PROGRAM VERIFICATION"

Part of the seductive appeal of formal methods within this context, I surmise, arises from a widespread reliance upon abstract models. These include abstract models that represent the *program specification*, which is the problem to be solved. (A program is shown to be "correct" when it is shown to satisfy its specification.) They also include abstract models that represent the *programming language*, which is a tool used in solving such a problem. (Pascal, LISP, and other high-level languages simulate the behavior of abstract machines rather than describe those of target machines.)

Enormous benefits accrue from the use of these abstract models. The construction of programs in Pascal, LISP, and so forth, for example, is far easier than the composition of programs in assembly language, where there is a one-to-one correspondence between program instructions and machine behavior. And, as was observed earlier, the abstract characterization of computing machines attains a generality that transcends the special characteristics of specific machines. But there is the correlated risk of mistaking properties of the abstract models for properties of the machines themselves.

Some machines, for example, have 8-bit words, while others have 16-bit (32-bit, . . .) words. And while register size makes no difference with respect to many operations, it can affect others [cf., (15) and (16) for some clear examples]. The capacity to represent real numbers by numerals, obviously, depends upon the characteristics of specific machines. While it is clearly possible to construct abstract models that successfully model specific machines, these abstract models no longer possess inherent generality.

The formal approach to program verification thus appears to trade upon an equivocation. While it is indeed possible to construct a formal proof of program correctness with respect to an abstract model of a machine, the significance of that proof depends upon the features of that model. When the model is an abstract model that does not represent a specific physical machine (the axioms of which can be given as stipulations), a formal proof of correctness can then guarantee that a program will perform as specified (unless mistakes have been made in its construction). Otherwise, it cannot.

DISAMBIGUATING "PROGRAM VERIFICATION"

The differences at stake here can be made explicit by using the term "PROGRAM" to refer to the operations that can be executed by an abstract machine for which there is no physical counterpart and by using the term "program" to refer to the operations that may be executed by an abstract machine for which there is some physical counterpart. It should then become apparent that, although the properties of abstract machines with no physical counterpart can be stipulated by definition, those of abstract machines with physical counterparts have to be discovered by investigation.

This difference can be illustrated by means of rules of inference such as Hoare has introduced. Consider, for example, the following illustrations:

Consequence 1   If $'\{X\} \ P \ \{Y\}'$ and $'Y \Rightarrow Z'$, then infer $'\{X\} \ P \ \{Z\}'$
Consequence 2   If $'X \Rightarrow Y'$ and $'\{Y\} \ P \ \{Z\}'$, then infer $'\{X\} \ P \ \{Z\}'$
Conjunction: If $'\{X\} \ P \ \{Y\}'$ and $'\{X\} \ P \ \{Y\}'$, then infer $'\{X \ \& \ X\} \ P \ \{Y \ \& \ Y\}'$,

(employing "$\ldots \Rightarrow \_$" as the semantical entailment "if . . . then __ " sign) [See examples, e.g., (17), p. 118]. *Consequence 1* asserts that, if a line of the form $'\{X\} \ P \ \{Y\}'$ is true and $'Y \Rightarrow Z'$ is true, then a line of the form $'\{X\} \ P \ \{Z\}'$ will also be true, necessarily. And likewise for *Consequence 2*, etc.

The problem that arises here is how it is possible to know when a line of the form $'\{X\} \ P \ \{Y\}'$ is true. Even on the assumption that semantic entailments of the form $'Y \Rightarrow Z'$ are knowable *a priori* (on the basis of grammar and vocabulary), does not provide any foundation for ascertaining the truth of lines that describe the state of the machine **M** before and after the execution of program *P*. There appear to be only two alternatives. If **M** is an abstract machine with no physical counterpart, axioms such as $'\{X\} \ P \ \{Y\}'$ can be true of **M** as a matter of stipulation, but not if **M** has a counterpart.

When **M** is an abstract machine with a physical counterpart, then the axioms that are true of **M** are only knowable *a posteriori* (on the basis of observation and experiment). But this means that two different kinds of "program verification" are possible, only one of which can be conclusive:

(D1) (Conclusive) *absolute verification* can guarantee the behavior of an abstract machine, because its axioms are true by definition.
(D2) (Inconclusive) *relative verification* cannot guarantee the behavior of a counterpart, because its axioms are not definitional truths.

Verifications that are conclusive are only significant for abstract machines, while those that are significant for physical machines are never conclusive.

THE DISTINCTION BETWEEN "PURE" AND "APPLIED" MATHEMATICS

The difference that have been uncovered here are parallel to those between "pure" and "applied" mathematics, where theorems of applied mathematics, unlike those of pure mathematics, run the risk of observational and experimental disconfirmation. A theorem about the natural numbers, say,

$$2 + 2 = 4 \qquad\qquad\qquad\qquad\qquad\qquad\qquad\qquad [a]$$

for example, cannot possibly be false within the context of that theory, since it follows from axioms that are true by definition. The application of those same numerical relations to physical phenomena, however, might be false.

Sometimes the results of mathematical descriptions of physical phenomena are surprising, indeed. Consider, for example, the following sentence:

2 *units of water* + 2 *units of alcohol* = 4 *units of mixture*.　　　　　　[*b*]

This certainly sounds plausible. Yet it turns out that, as an effect of their atomic structure, molecules of water and molecules of alcohol have the capacity to partially occupy the same volume when the are mixed together. This apparently true sentence, therefore, turns out to be empirically false.

Other examples afford equally interesting illustrations of the problem we have discovered. What truth-value should be assigned to these claims:

(c) 2 drops of water + 2 drops of water = 4 drops of water?
(d) 2 lumps of plutonium + 2 lumps of plutonium = 4 lumps of plutonium?
(e) 2 gaggle of geese + 2 gaggle of geese = 4 gaggle of geese?

Even if the assumed behavior of abstract machines can be known with deductive certainty, the real behavior of physical things can only be known with the empirical uncertainty that accompanies scientific investigations.

But surely this is something that we ought to have expected all along. The example of Euclidean geometry affords an instructive illustration; for, when "points" are locations without extension and "lines" are the shortest distances between them, their relations can be ascertained deductively on the basis of the axioms that define them. But as soon as "lines" are identified with the paths of light rays in space and "points" with their intersection, these relations can only be discovered empirically by means of observation and experimentation. (Space even turns out to be non-Euclidean!)

WHAT ABOUT HOARE'S "FOUR BASIC PRINCIPLES"?

From this point of view, certain contentions whose truth-values may have been unclear tend to become obvious. When Hoare maintains that (4, p. 576),

> Computer programming is an exact science in that all of the properties of a program and all of the consequences of executing it in any given environment can, in principle, be found out from the text of the program itself by means of purely deductive reasoning.

it should be apparent by now that, while this may be true for PROGRAMS on abstract machines, it certainly is false for programs on physical machines.

Similarly, when Dijkstra asserts that, "We must learn to work with program texts while (temporarily) ignoring that they admit the interpretation of executable code" (6, p. 1403), it ought to be generally agreed that, while this attitude appears to be appropriate for PROGRAMS whose properties can be known by deduction and with certainty, it is not appropriate for programs whose properties can only be known by experience and with uncertainty. Indeed, it should be apparent that the very idea of the mathematical paradigm for computer science trades on ambiguity.

Consider the "Four Principles" of Hoare (18), which can be viewed as defining the "mathematical paradigm" in application to this discipline:

1. Computers are mathematical machines
2. Computer programs are mathematical expressions
3. A programming language is a mathematical theory
4. Programming is a mathematical activity

Clearly, the structures and entities that satisfy these relations (as Hoare intended them to be understood) are PROGRAMS and abstract machines.

As soon as attention turns to programs and physical machines, it is evident that the proper comparison is with applied mathematics instead:

1. Computers are *applied* mathematical machines
2. Computer programs are *applied* mathematical expressions
3. A programming language is an *applied* mathematical theory
4. Programming is an *applied* mathematical activity

To the extent to which computer science can properly be entertained as a mathematical discipline, it qualifies as an applied rather than a pure one.

ANOTHER ARGUMENT FOR THE SAME CONCLUSION

The differences between PROGRAMS and programs that have been elaborated here, however, never would have come to light had we failed to appreciate the differences between mathematical theorems, scientific theories, and computer programs. Advocates of formal methods in computer science tend to overlook these differences, especially because they are drawn toward the position "that the meaning or the semantics of a program are precisely equivalent to what the program causes a machine to do" (3, p. 9). [A related discussion of "procedural semantics," can be found in Foder (19).] But a crucial equivocation arises at exactly this juncture.

The difference between the positions outlined by Hoare (4) and by Fetzer (20) can be formulated to address this point by distinguishing "programs-as-texts" (unloaded), which consist of sequences of lines, from "programs-as-causes" (loaded), which affect machine performance. Formal verification invariably involves the application of deductive techniques to programs-as-texts, where it does not even make sense to talk about the application of techniques of deduction to programs-as-causes. (Even a fine discussion by Barwise commits this mistake [21, p. 848]).

Hoare and I both assume (*) that programs-as-causes are represented by programs-as-texts, except that Hoare contends that verifying a program-as-text guarantees what will happen when a program-as-cause is executed, which I deny. Otherwise, in contending that even a successful verification of a program is never enough to guarantee what will happen when that program is executed, I would have simply changed the subject. In that case, we would not have joined issues and we might both be right.

Indeed, a key difference between Hoare's position and my own can be formulated in terms of different versions of thesis (*). For Hoare maintains,

(*') that programs-as-causes are *appropriately* represented by programs-as-texts;

while I assert that all he is entitled to assume is the strikingly weaker thesis,

(*") that programs-as-causes are *supposed-to-be* appropriately represented by program-as-texts.

For one of the major points I have sought to convey is that there might be two different ways in which this supposition could be grounded, namely: (a) when the program-as-text concerns an abstract machine for which there is no physical counterpart (where this relation can be true by definition); or, (b) when the program-as-text concerns an abstract machine for which there is a physical counterpart (where this relation must be empirically justified). Hoare's position—which, I believe, is tacitly adopted by the vast majority of those favoring the verificationist position—clearly overlooks this distinction.

ARE THERE OTHER ALTERNATIVE POSITIONS?

In their reflections on this debate as it has been carried in the pages of *Communications of the ACM*, John Dobson and Brian Randell (22) raise an important question, namely: Why do many proponents of formal methods in computer science deny that they hold the position that I have attacked? There may be more than one answer to this question, of course, since some of them may simply hold inconsistent positions (perhaps by persisting in the belief that purely formal methods *are* capable of providing guarantees concerning what would happen if a program were executed by a machine).

The situation is also complicated by differences regarding the ultimate importance of social processing as an aspect of computer methodology. If issues concerning social processing that DeMillo (11), and others have addressed are left aside, however, then the views of Avra Cohn (23) on behalf of provers of PROGRAMS and Glenford Myers (24) on behalf of testers of programs contribute to defining some of the most important alternative positions. The flow chart in Figure 4 is intended as a summary of the debate's central course without exhausting its details.

Thus, Cohn maintains that formal proofs of correctness, even those that involve entire computer systems, cannot possibly guarantee the performance of any real system, even when verified programs are being executed (23, pp. 131–132).

> Ideally, one would like to prove that a chip such as Viper correctly implements its intended behavior under all circumstances; we could then claim that the chip's behavior was predictable and correct. In reality, neither an actual *device* nor an *intention* is an object to which logical reasoning can be applied. . . . In short, verification involves a pair of *models* that bear an uncheckable and possibly imperfect relation to the intended design and to the actual device. (original italics)

Indeed, as she hastens to point out, these points "are not merely philosophical quibbles": errors were located even in the models assumed for Viper!

Strictly speaking, however, although specification models and machine models are *deductively* "uncheckable," they are not therefore *inductively* "uncheckable" as well, where "induction" relies upon the kinds of observation and experimentation that computer systems permit. It would therefore be a mistake to assume that the relationship between a specification and the world, on the one hand, or an abstract machine and a counterpart, on the other, are matters about which only subjective opinion is possible. Empirical evidence can even support reasoned convictions about models!

While Cohn disavows responsibility for what happens when a system executes a program, Myers embraces a Popperian conception of testing in which primary emphasis is placed upon the discovery of remaining errors. In his view, "*Testing is the process of executing a program with the intent of finding errors*" (124, especially p. 5). Yet it is no

Hoare (4): purely deductive methods
+
content about performance
=
branch of pure mathematics.
↓

Fetzer (20): you cannot have both purely
deductive methods + content
about performance = Hoare's
position cannot be justified.
↓

Dobson and Randell (22): but many others
deny that the view I attack is
their view. I agree that these
alternative views are available:

↙   ↘

Cohn (23): keep the purely   Myers (24): keep the empirical
deductive methods +   content + give up the
give up the empirical   purely deductive methods
content = still a branch   = now a branch of applied
of pure mathematics.   mathematics.
(Proving PROGRAMS)   (Testing programs)

FIGURE 4.   The program verification debate.

more necessary to suppose that testing can only discover errors than it is to suppose that formal proofs of programs can only establish their absence. These are two widely held but unjustifiable beliefs that qualify as myths of computer science.

WULFFIAN PERFECTIONISM CANNOT BE SUSTAINED

It should be obvious by now that Wulffian Perfectionism, which maintains that, once written, a program will execute exactly as prescribed, cannot possibly be correct. The problems with which it cannot cope even extend to those of the Intel 80486 microprocessor, which turned out to have a (potentially fatal) flaw. When certain instructions were executed in one sequence, they executed properly, yet in another sequence, they failed to execute properly (25, p. 39). Although this specific case was corrected, it is impossible to know which other cases remain to be discovered.

It also should be obvious that Moore's optimism in asserting that, if the gates behave as formally modeled, the system behaves as specified, is unwarranted even for the case of fully verified systems (7, p. 409). The verification of an abstract model, even in relation to an entire computer system, cannot guarantee system performance even if the gates behave as formally modeled, unless there is no more to that system than the gates themselves! Moreover, unless gate performance can be guaranteed, this claim amounts to a promissory note that can never be cashed in.

And it should also be obvious that the conception of computer science as a branch of pure mathematics cannot be sustained. The proper conception is that of computer science as a branch of applied mathematics, where even that position may not go far enough in acknowledging the limitations imposed by physical devices. Remarks like these from Hamilton Richards (26, p. viii),

> . . . the conversion of programming from a craft into a mathematical discipline requires an unorthodox type of mathematics in which the traditional distinction between "pure" and "applied" need not appear.

should be recognized as nonsense. They are both misleading and untrue.

Perhaps the resolution of these difficulties is to concede a point made by David Parnas in response to Dijkstra's piece on teaching programming (27, p. 1405):

> There is no engineering profession in which testing and mathematical validation are viewed as alternatives. It is universally accepted that they are complementary and that both are required.

Similar views are endorsed by Berg et al. (3, p. 124), and by others, including Goodenough and Gerhard (28) and Gerhard and Yelowitz (29). Computer science, after all, has both theoretical and experimental dimensions, where both formal methods and empirical procedures have a place.

WHAT POSITIONS SHOULD BE DISTINGUISHED?

As I have elsewhere emphasized (30), some of the issues at stake here involve questions of logic, others matters of methodology, and others issues of verifiability, which can be summarized here. In relation to questions of logic, for example, two positions are in dispute:

Positions of LOGIC:

(T1) Formal proofs of program correctness can provide an absolute, conclusive guarantee of program performance

(T2) Formal proofs of program correctness can provide only relative, inconclusive evidence concerning program performance

The purpose of Fetzer (20) was to establish that (T1) is false but that (T2) is true. I find it difficult to believe that anyone familiar with the course of this debate could continue to disagree. These theses are separate from three other positions that arise in relation to questions of methodology:

Positions of METHODOLOGY

(T3) Formal proofs of program correctness should be the exclusive methodology for assessing software reliability

(T4) Formal proofs of program correctness should be the principal methodology for assessing software reliability

(T5) Formal proofs of program correctness should be one among various methodologies for assessing software reliability

I maintain (T3) is false and, at the ACM Computer Science Conference 90, I argued further that (T4) is false; however, I have no doubt that (T5) is true. My opponents on that occasion—David Gries and Mark Ardis—did not choose to defend the merits of (T4). And in relation to verification in the broad sense:

Positions on VERIFICATION

(T6) Program verifications always require formal proofs of correctness
(T7) Program verifications always require proof sketches of correctness
(T8) Program verifications always require the use of deductive reasoning

I maintain that (T6) is clearly false and that (T8) is clearly true, but that the truth-value of (T7) is subject to debate. Much appears to hang on whether such proof sketches have to be written down, could be merely thought through, or whatever. If the former, (T7) becomes closer to (T6); if the latter, (T7) becomes closer to (T8). Charlie Martin believes "hand proofs" may be a suitable standard (30). However, these matters may ultimately be resolved, (T1) through (T8) seem to reflect the principal distinctions that must be drawn to understand the range of issues at stake.

WHAT IS THE APPROPRIATE ATTITUDE TO ADOPT?

To admit that formal methods have a place in computer science is not to grant that they have the capacity to guarantee program performance. If Berg et al. and others have appreciated the situation any more clearly than the Hoares, the Wulfs, the Dijkstras, the Moores, the Renders, and the Richards of the world, they are certainly to be commended. But it does not follow that Hoare, Wulf, Dijkstra, Moore, Render, Richards, and their followers do not hold inadequate positions. The views they offer cannot be justified.

If the entire debate has brought into the foreground some indefensible assumptions that have been made by some influential figures in the field, then it will have been entirely worthwhile. It should be obvious by now that pure mathematics provides an unsuitable paradigm for computer science. At the very least, the discipline appears to have some characteristics that are more akin to those that distinguish empirical sciences and others indicating that it ought to be viewed as an engineering discipline instead.

Although the issues that have been addressed here concern questions of ontology and of epistemology, the most important implications of this debate are ethical. The greater the seriousness of the consequences that would ensue from making a mistake, the greater our obligation to insure that it is not made. This suggests that the role for prototyping and testing increases dramatically as life-critical tasks come into play [compare (31)]. We can afford to run a system that has only been formally assessed if the consequences of mistakes are relatively minor but not when they are serious.

Formal proofs of program correctness provide one variety of assurance that a system will perform properly. Testing supplies another. Constructing prototypes yields a third. When we deal with abstract models, formal methods are available. When we want to know whether or not a physical system will perform as it is intended, however, there are no alternatives to prototyping and testing. The program verification debate has implications that are practical and ethical as well as theoretical and philosophical. And the future of our species may depend upon how well we understand them.

ACKNOWLEDGMENT

This article is adapted from Ref. 33 with permission of Kluwer Academic Publishers.

REFERENCES

1. Linger, R. C., Mills, H., and Witt, B. *Structured Programming: Theory and Practice*. Addison-Wesley, Reading, MA, 1979.
2. Gries, D. (ed.), *Programming Methodology*, Springer-Verlag, New York, 1979.
3. Berg, H. K., Boebert, W. E., Fronta, W. R., and Moher, T. G., *Formal Methods of Program Verification and Specification*, Prentice-Hall, Englewood Cliffs, NJ, 1982.
4. Hoare, C. A. R., An Axiomatic Basis for Computer Programming, *Commun. ACM*, 12: 576–580, (1969).
5. Wulf, W. A. Introduction to Part I: Comments on 'Current Practice', In: *Research Directions in Software Technology* P. Wegner, ed. MIT Press, Cambridge, MA, 1979, pp. 39–43.
6. Dijkstra, E. W., On the Cruelty of Really Teaching Computing Science, *Commun. ACM* 32: 1398–1404 (1989).
7. Moore, J. S., System Verification, *J. Autom. Reasoning* 5: 409–410 (1989).
8. Render, H., Article 755 (comp.software.eng), USENET, 20:01:00 GMT (January 17, 1990).
9. Render, H., Article 1413 (comp.software.eng), USENET, 01:31:30 GMT (February 1, 1990).
10. Smith B. C., The Limits of Correctness, *Comput. Soc.*, 14 (4): 18–28 (Winter 1985).
11. DeMillo, R., Lipton, R., and Perlis, A., Social Processes and Proofs of Theorems and Programs, *Commun. ACM*, 22: 271–280 (1979).
12. Newell, A., and Simon, H., Computer Science as Empirical Inquiry: Symbols and Search, *Commun. ACM*, 19: 113–126 (1976).
13. Dijkstra, E. W., Notes on Structured Programming. In: *Structured Programming* (O. Dahl et al., eds.) Academic Press, New York, 1972.
14. Fetzer, J. H., *Scientific Knowledge*. D. Reidel, Dordrecht, The Netherlands, 1981.
15. Tompkins, H., Verifying Feature—Bugs, *Commun. ACM*, 32: 1130–1131 (1989).
16. Garland, D., Technical Correspondence Letter (1990), unpublished.
17. Marcotty, M., and Ledgard, H., *Programming Language Landscape: Syntax/Semantics/Implementations*, 2nd ed., Science Research Associates, Chicago, IL, 1989.
18. Hoare, C. A. R., Mathematics of Programming, *BYTE* 115–149 (August, 1986).
19. Fodor, J., Tom Swift and his Procedural Grandmother, *Cognition*, 6: 229–247 (1978).
20. Fetzer, J. H., Program Verification: The Very Idea, *Commun. ACM*, 31: 1048–1063 (1988).
21. Barwise, J., Mathematical Proofs of Computer System Correctness, *Notices AMS*, 36: 844–851 (1989).
22. Dobson, J., and Randell, B. Viewpoint, *Commun. ACM*, 32: 420–422 (1989).
23. Cohn, A., The Notion of Proof in Hardware Verification, *J. Automat. Reasoning*, 5: 127–139 (1989).
24. Myers, G. J., *The Art of Software Testing*, John Wiley & Sons, New York, 1979.
25. Markoff, J., Top-of-Line Intel Chip is Flawed, *The New York Times* (Friday, October 27, 1989) pp. 25, 39.
26. Richards, H., Foreword. In: *Formal Development of Programs and Proofs* (E. W. Dijkstra, ed.), Addison-Wesley, Reading, MA, 1990, pp. vii-ix.
27. Parnas, D., Colleagues Respond to Dijkstra's Comments, *Commun. ACM*, 32: 1405–1406 (1989).

28. Goodenough, J., and Gerhart, S., Toward a Theory of Test Data Selection, *IEEE Transact. Software Eng.*, **1**: 156–173 (1975).
29. Gerhard, S., and Yelowitz, L., Observations of Fallibility in Applications of Modern Programming Methodologies, *IEEE Transact. Software Eng.*, **2**: 195–207 (1976).
30. Fetzer, J. H., and Martin, C. R. The Very Idea, Indeed! *Nat. Biomedical Simulation Resource*, Technical Report No. 1990-2.
31. Blum, B., Formalism and Prototyping in the Software Process, *Inform. Decision Technol.*, **15**: 327–341 (1989).
32. Colburn, T., Program Verification, Defeasible Reasoning, and Two Views of Computer Science, *Minds Machines*, **1**: 97–116 (1991).
33. Fetzer, J. H., Philosophical Aspects of Program Verification, *Minds Machines*, **1**: 197–216 (1991).
34. Nelson, D., Deductive Program Verification: A Practicioner's Perspective, *Minds Machines*, **2**: (1992).
35. Colburn, T., Fetzer, J. H., and Rankin, T. C., (eds.), *Program Verification: Fundamental Issues in Computer Science*, Kluwer Academic Publishers, Dordrecht, the Netherlands, 1993.

ADDITIONAL SUGGESTED READINGS

For further reading, valuable introductions to formal methods in computer science are provided in Ref. 1–3. The most recent discussions of the issues involved in their use to guarantee program performances are found in Refs. 32–34. A forthcoming anthology devoted to this subject (35) will reprint many of the most important papers cited here, including (4, 10, 11, 18, 20, 23, 31–33), and other papers that are relevant to this subject.

JAMES H. FETZER

RELIABLE DISTRIBUTED SYSTEMS

INTRODUCTION

With increasing dependence on computer systems on all aspects of our lives, we cannot overemphasize the importance of system reliability. Reliability has long been recognized as one of the potential benefits of a distributed system. The inherent redundancy and physical distribution of a distributed system allow reliability to be implemented naturally. In this article we present an overview of *reliable systems*. We will define the terminology in the rest of this section before describing the characteristics of reliable distributed systems and the techniques used to implement them.

What Is a Distributed System?

Distributed processing is a relatively new field, and so far there is no consensus on a precise definition. Intuitively, a distributed system is a collection of autonomous computer systems cooperating to achieve certain tasks. For example, it may be a collection of file servers providing file service to its users, or it may be a collection of databases providing the image of a single uniform database. In order to allow coordination and exchange of information, these computer systems are interconnected by a computer network. The emphasis on autonomy includes tightly coupled multiprocessors, where individual processors cannot survive independently without the rest of the system, as candidates of distributed systems. For similar reasons, the addition of specialized processors to a centralized system for input/output or arithmetic purposes does not create a distributed system.

The potential benefits of a distributed system are many. In general, they include reduced hardware costs, reliability, extensibility, modularity, increased performance, and local control of resources. In order to realize these benefits, a distributed system needs more than simple hardware decentralization. Enslow (1) defines a system as distributed if its hardware, control, and data are all decentralized. In this definition multiple computers co-operate rather than engage in a master-slave relationship, and the information stored in the system should be partitioned or replicated among the individual computers. In this article, we will refer to individual computers in a distributed system as *nodes*, each of which possess its own processor and memory.

Terminology

Failures, Reliability, and Availability

Using the definitions in Anderson and Lee (2), a *failure* of system occurs when "the behavior of the system first deviates from that required by its specification." A *specification* may specify the desired functional relationship between inputs and outputs or other aspects of system behavior (e.g., response times). Given a precise and complete specification, the *reliability* of a system "can be characterized by a function $R(t)$ which expresses the probability that the system will conform to its specification throughout a period of duration t."

A more specific form of reliability is the *availability* of a service, which can be defined as the probability that a system will be able to provide the service upon request. Availability of different services in a system may be different. For example, a banking database may provide high debit/credit transaction availability, but availability for services that require (accurate) account balances may be relatively low. When failures occur, a system may provide a limited set of services instead of shutting down completely. This is especially true in a distributed system in which complete failures of all components are highly unlikely.

Errors and Faults

In order to classify the causes of failures, one may decompose a system into multiple components. We can define an internal system state of a system as the external states of its components, and an *error* as an internal system state that differs from a valid state. In the absence of corrective actions by the system, the erroneous state eventually will lead to a system failure. By treating a component as a system itself, we can define a failure and an error of a component similarly. If an error of a system is caused by an error of one of its components, the component error is called a *component fault* in the system and the component is said to be faulty.

Fault Intolerance and Fault Tolerance

Two complementary approaches to achieving reliability have been proposed: *fault intolerance* (fault prevention) and *fault tolerance*. The former advocates using technologies that minimize the introduction of faults during the design and construction phases of a system. For example, the use of reliable hardware components, extensive testing, program verification, and other software engineering techniques are possible ways in which faults can be minimized. However, given the absence (or the costs) of totally fault-free components, fault tolerance has been proposed as a necessary supplement to achieve high reliability. Despite the existence of faults, a fault-tolerant system provides high reliability, which is achieved invariably with the use of some form of replication.

In general, the process of providing fault tolerance consists of *error detection, damage confinement and assessment, error recovery*, and *fault treatment*. Error detection is the first step taken in a fault-tolerant system to prevent an erroneous state from leading to a failure of the entire system. It may involve using timing checks or redundancy in the system to detect errors. During damage confinement, a system tries to prevent existing component errors from spreading to other parts of the system. For example, a damaged file should be made inaccessible so that its contents will not be used in future computations until the error is repaired. During error recovery, the system state should be repaired so that normal operation can proceed. Error recovery is the focus of most of the research in the area of fault-tolerant systems and will be one of the main topics covered in this article. In addition to error recovery, the cause of the error has to be identified to allow for fault diagnosis. During the fault treatment phase, a fault-tolerant system may decide to repair the faulty component identified, or reconfigure so that the faulty component can be removed.

The order in which these steps are taken varies. In fact, some of these steps may be omitted. For example, in a system that employs Triple Modular Redundancy (TMR), a component is replicated three times and the output of the components are compared by a voter to determine the majority. In its simplest form, TMR does not involve any error detection, error recovery, or fault treatment. At most, it can be viewed as a technique for damage confinement, in that an error in one of the components is marked and prevented from propagating beyond the voter.

Discussing all aspects of fault tolerance is beyond the scope of this article. Instead, we focus on aspects of fault tolerance that interact with the nature of distributed systems. Readers can find a more comprehensive treatment of fault-tolerance issues in Anderson and Lee (2). The techniques used to implement a fault-tolerant network also are not covered in this article. Most networks are organized as multiple layers of network protocols, each building upon its lower layer. For example, a data link layer protocol may be used to send packets across a data link reliably. A network layer above is responsible for sending packets across a network which may consist of sending the packet across many data links. In general, each layer provides a certain degree of fault tolerance. For example, a data link layer may use error-detecting and error-correcting codes to encode the information transmitted. When an error is detected, retransmission can be used for error recovery. In the network layer, timeouts can be used to detect errors and retransmission can be used for recovery. A detailed treatment of the layering of network protocols and their fault tolerance can be found in Stallings (3) and Tanenbaum (4). The subject of computing the reliability of a network is covered in Colbourn (5).

RELIABILITY IN DISTRIBUTED SYSTEMS

Providing fault tolerance in a distributed system shares some of the problems in a centralized system. On the other hand, the characteristics of a distributed system introduce new problems and new opportunities for improving reliability, some of which are enumerated in this section.

Size of a Distributed System

Given the autonomous nature of the components in a distributed system, partial failures are more likely than total failures. In a large distributed system, it may even be unlikely to find all the components operating simultaneously. The possibility of partial failures creates a consistency problem. If several nodes are cooperating on a computation, one of them may fail to complete its portion because of a failure, while the others either complete their portions or are suspended because of a failure to communicate with the failed node.

A similar consistency problem exists to a certain degree in a centralized system. When a computation on a centralized system is interrupted by a failure, it may only be partially completed. When the centralized system is restarted, the computation can be either undone or completed. In a distributed system, undoing a computation becomes more complex because the portion on the failed node as well as any related portions on other nodes must be undone. Furthermore, it is possible that the other nodes are unaware of the failure. They may have allowed the results of their computation to be used for other purposes, not realizing that the computation eventually will be undone.

The prevalence of partial failures also affects the choice of error recovery algorithms. When failures may occur frequently in a large distributed system, each of which affecting only a small number of components, it is desirable to have error recovery involve only the failed components, or at least localized in a small number of components. Localized error recovery avoids interrupting the entire distributed system, which may be serving the computation needs of a large number of users. It also limits indirectly the amount of wasted work due to a failure. On the other hand, localized error recovery constrains the choice of error recovery algorithms.

Failure Modes

The existence of a computer network in a distributed system introduces the possibility of communications failures. For example, the contents of a message exchanged over a network may be garbled due to line noises, two messages exchanged between the same sender and receiver may be reordered because of the different network routes taken by the messages, a message may be lost due to full message buffers or overworked CPUs and in attempting to recover a possibly lost message, the message may be resent and duplicates are received as a result. Finally, two nodes may not be able to communicate simply because a communication link is severed. Failures due to severed communication links dividing a distributed system into disconnected groups of nodes are termed *network partitionings*, and the disconnected groups of nodes are called *network partitions*. Although improvements to communication protocols and redundant communication links can be added, their costs may render a totally reliable network prohibitively expensive.

Among the different forms of communication failures, network partitionings can be one of the most difficult to handle. For example, consider a distributed database that replicates its files to increase availability. When a network partitioning develops, a naive algorithm may allow users to continue to access information stored in a replicated file as long as one of the replicas is accessible. Such an algorithm runs the risk of providing obsolete data. When a file replica is updated and the updates are prevented from propagating beyond a network partition, the file replicas in other network partitions are left with obsolete data. Worse, if updates are allowed in more than one network partition, the contents of different replicas may start to diverge, with the updates from different network partitions incompatible to one another.

The possibility of network partitionings also makes handling other forms of failure more difficult. Suppose two nodes n_1 and n_2 in a distributed system are cooperating in a distributed computation, and n_1 cannot communicate with n_2. In general, it is not possible for n_1 to tell whether there is a network partitioning, or n_2 has failed (and stops executing), or simply n_2 is executing slowly. Given a lack of global information, an error recovery algorithm has to allow all three possibilities. Thus even if n_2 has indeed failed, this knowledge may not be used by any error recovery initiated by n_1. Obviously, the lack of global information also complicates fault treatment.

On the other hand, the physical separation of the nodes in a distributed system provides a natural barrier for damage confinement should failures occur. For example, power failures and other natural catastrophes may cause some but not all of the nodes to fail. The separation can be utilized to guard against other classes of failures. For example, given that all communication is conducted through messages sent through the network, checksums and other more sophisticated communication protocols can be employed to guard against contamination by failed nodes.

Decentralized Control

Another characteristic of a distributed system is the lack of global control. It is difficult and expensive to maintain information about the global state of a distributed system when information about the global state must be transmitted across an unreliable network possibly with a significant delay.

The lack of global control complicates error detection, error recovery, and fault treatment. For example, different nodes in a distributed system may have different ideas of what failures have occurred, in which order, and for how long. Either the operating nodes must agree on the sequence of failures or the difference in opinion should not cause error recovery and fault treatment to fail.

FAILURE MODELS IN RELIABLE DISTRIBUTED SYSTEMS

In order to provide effective fault tolerance, one must decide on the class of anticipated faults and design the algorithms accordingly. In this section, we present some of the commonly used fault classifications.

Hardware and Software Faults

In the context of a distributed system, hardware consists of nodes (computers) and networks. Errors in these components are called hardware faults. In general, software faults are due to bugs in programs and are unanticipated individually. Obviously, software faults are difficult do diagnose and human intervention is required to remove the fault. It is difficult also to recover from a failure caused by a software fault, since duplication of hardware does not increase reliability when the same software is executed on all the hardware components. We also will include certain anticipated faults as software faults. For example, a system may fail because its software enters into a deadlocked state, or because certain software resources are exhausted. Resetting the system or some of its components usually is sufficient to recover from these failures.

Fail-Stop Processors and Byzantine Faults

Air-conditioning shutdowns, power outages, and chip failures are among the many possible reasons that a node may fail. Node failures can be further abstracted to present an idealized picture: a failed node stops executing before it sends out erroneous messages. Thus from the point of view of other nodes, the failed node simply stops executing the moment it fails. These idealized nodes are called *fail-stop processors* and can be approximated using existing hardware (6).

A less restrictive model is to allow *Byzantine faults* (7). In this model, a failed node may behave arbitrarily, which includes stopping its execution, or continuing to send possibly erroneous messages to other nodes in the system. Because of their general nature, Byzantine faults can also be used to model malicious behavior, such as when a node in a distributed system has been subverted by an enemy.

Reliable and Unreliable Networks

Among current research on reliable distributed systems, the assumed reliability of a communication network varies significantly. An unreliable network may have network partitionings, lost, reordered, duplicated, and garbled messages. At the other end of the spectrum, a reliable network delivers a message after a bounded delay without duplication or corruption of content. Two messages between the same sender and receiver are delivered in the same order they are sent.

Synchronous and Asynchronous Systems

Some of the research work in reliable distributed systems assumes that the distributed systems are *synchronous*. A synchronous system guarantees that the local clocks in individual nodes are synchronized and differ by at most some small period ε. However, a *timing fault* can cause the guarantee to be violated (8). The concept of timing faults can be extended to include assumptions that a message would be delivered in a certain time bound, or a computation would be finished by a certain deadline. *Asynchronous* systems do not make any assumptions about timing behaviors.

Transient and Permanent Faults

Faults can be classified by their durations. A *transient* fault disappears from the system a short time after it appears. A transient fault may also recur, in which case it is referred to as an *intermittent* fault. A fault that exists for a long time (beyond some threshold) is called a *permanent* fault. In general, a distributed system cannot tolerate permanent network partitionings, with the network being the only medium for communication

TAXONOMY OF CURRENT TECHNIQUES AND RESEARCH

Current techniques and research on reliable distributed systems can be classified into the following categories:

> Data consistency
> Data availability
> Process resilience
> Software fault tolerance
> Reliable protocols

Each of these categories is described briefly below and expanded in later sections. Frequently, we explain the concepts in the context of a database system consisting of a collection of data objects, where many of these techniques are pioneered. However, most, if not all, of the ideas are equally applicable in other types of distributed systems, such as a distributed operating system or a programming environment that supports distributed computing.

Data Consistency

When a transaction in a centralized database is interrupted by a failure or chose to abort voluntarily, the database may be left in an inconsistent state, with only part of the updates in the transaction completed. The classic example is that of a transaction transferring money from one account to another. If a failure occurs in the middle of the transactions, the database may be left in a state in which money has been withdrawn but not yet deposited. In order to preserve consistency despite failures, traditionally a database system uses a *concurrency control algorithm* and *recovery algorithm* (9) to guarantee that transactions are executed *atomically*. In other words, either all the updates in a transaction are performed or they have no effects at all, and concurrent transactions *appear* to execute serially. Incidentally, atomicity is also a useful damage confinement technique, since a failed transaction's effects cannot be observed by other transactions.

A distributed database system faces the same consistency problems as a centralized database. The concurrency control and recovery algorithms used in a centralized database can often be employed without any significant changes. Distributed database systems face an additional problem, however, when a transaction is distributed and accesses data objects from multiple nodes. When node failures and communication failures prevent the completion of a transaction the nodes participating in a distributed transaction must reach an agreement on the transaction's status in order to preserve atomicity. Using the previous money transfer example, if two nodes are used to store the two bank accounts, both should agree whether the transfer transaction has been committed or aborted. The agreement protocols used in this context are commonly called *commit protocols*. They are discussed in more detail later in this article.

Data Availability

Agreement protocols and recovery algorithms allow a distributed database to preserve consistency despite failures. However, failures may prevent the successful completion of transactions. If a node storing a data object has failed or become inaccessible due to communication failures, transactions accessing the data object would not be able to complete. A limited solution is to carefully select the storage location of a data object so that it is within close proximity to the nodes that may initiate any transaction accessing it. A more general solution is to replicate the data objects and store the replicas in multiple nodes. Data replication has the effect of increasing the availability of services (transactions) that access the replicated data objects.

In order to prevent the contents of different data replicas from diverging permanently, a *replica control algorithm* has to be used. Replica control algorithms can be classified into *optimistic* and *pessimistic* techniques. An optimistic algorithm allows each network partition to update the replicas of a data object accessible within the partition. It is optimistic in the sense that it expects concurrent updates to not happen most of the time. However, if multiple replicas in different network partitions are indeed updated independently, an optimistic algorithm has to provide a resolution protocol to resolve the possibly conflicting updates when the network partitioning disappeared. On the other hand, a pessimistic replica control algorithm allows a replicated data object to be updated in at most one network partition. Such an algorithm is more desirable when a resolution protocol is infeasible or too expensive. Voting techniques (10) are probably the most popular pessimistic algorithm. Pessimistic and optimistic algorithms are discussed in another paragraph.

Process Resilience

Replicating data objects increases their availability. However, failures may still cause a system to enter into an erroneous state and force the offending transactions to abort. For example, the node on which a transaction is executing may have failed, or a transaction may be deadlocked with another, each waiting for the other to release resources that it needs to acquire. A simple form of error recovery is to abort the offending transaction(s), and rely on a recovery algorithm to return the database to a consistent state. This approach is unsatisfactory mainly because aborting a transaction causes all previous work to be wasted. More general fault tolerance techniques have been explored and used. In general, they can be classified into *backward error recovery*, *forward error recovery*, and *process replication*. These techniques are applicable to atomic transactions as well as any general computations. Each of these techniques can be used to increase the resilience of a computation so that the computation can be completed despite being interrupted by failures.

In backward recovery, the state of a failed system is reset to a previous state. If the previous state can be certified to be valid, then errors caused by the fault are removed. A ''system'' may be either hardware or software, ranging from a collection of a distributed system, the unit of recovery considered is often a process, in which case the resetting involves restarting the process using a previously saved snapshot of its state. The unit of recovery may also be a node, in which case the resetting involves restarting all processes running on the node. Backward recovery is a powerful technique because it requires little damage assessment and handles a large class of failures. After an error is detected, the entire erroneous state can be discarded unless it is needed for fault diagnosis.

In forward recovery, an erroneous state is manipulated to produce a valid error-free new state. In this sense, all error recovery techniques can be regarded as either backward or forward recovery. An example of a forward recovery technique is an exception handler that supplies zeros as answers when arithmetic underflow exceptions are detected. Although forward recovery can be relatively efficient, it is highly application-specific and depends on an accurate prediction of the types and locations of errors. Because of its dependency on application characteristics, we will not cover the subject of implementing forward recovery in distributed systems further.

Instead of saving snapshots of a process' state, replication (and hence resilience) of a process' state can also be achieved by executing the same program in multiple nodes. We termed this approach *process replication* (11–13). It can be viewed as an application of the TMR technique implemented in software.

Software Fault Tolerance

The fault tolerance techniques discussed in the previous section are geared toward handling hardware faults. At most, they can handle transient software faults that disappear after the system software is reset to a certain state. If a (permanent) software fault is encountered, then regardless of how many times the execution of a process is repeated on different hardware units, the same fault would cause failures to recur. The recovery block approach (14) and N-version programming (15) have been proposed in order to deal with (permanent) software faults. Both require the use of redundant versions of software, but differ in their order of execution. N-version programming executes all redundant versions concurrently while the recovery block approach tries one version after another.

Reliable Protocols

Researchers working on reliable distributed systems have also studied fault-tolerant versions of commonly used protocols and algorithms. Frequently, these protocols and algorithms are part of a larger implementation of a fault tolerant system, like ones described in previous sections. In this article, we will describe several proposed reliable broadcast protocols, fault-tolerant mutual exclusion algorithms, and reliable agreement protocols. A broadcast protocol guarantees that all recipients will eventually receive a copy. A mutual exclusion algorithm can be used to synchronize access to a shared resource by eliminating concurrency in *critical regions*. A fault-tolerant version should guarantee mutual exclusion as well as eventual progress (the resource will be accessed). An agreement protocol can be used by a group of ''agents'' to reach a consensus. A reliable version guarantees that all agents reach the same conclusion quickly despite failures.

AVAILABILITY ENHANCEMENT

Availability enhancement techniques have been studied exclusively in the context of database systems. The need for availability enhancement is understandable given that the data objects are the most crucial resources of a database system. Their correctness and availability directly affects the usefulness of the database. In this section, we will describe some of the replica control algorithms designed to increase availability.

In the work on data replications, one of the most commonly used correctness criteria is called *one-copy serializability* (16). A replica control algorithm is said to preserve serializability if the transactions in the database appear to have executed serially. It preserves one-copy serializability if the transactions appear to have executed serially in a nonreplicated database. In other words, any replication of the database should be transparent to its users. Intuitively, in order to preserve one-copy serializability, a replica control algorithm has to prevent two transactions from accessing two disjoint groups of replicas, one reading one group without knowing that the other has updated another group. This scenario may happen when the two transactions are executing in two network partitions, each accessing the replicas in their own respective partitions, or when the nodes on which two replicas reside fail in such a manner that each was able to process one transaction and not the other.

Pessimistic Data Replication

Two algorithms are described in this section. The first is called the *available copies* algorithm. It provides high availability but does not tolerate communication failures. The second is called *voting* or *quorum consensus*. It tolerates both node and communication failures. Voting is perhaps the most popular data replication technique and a large number of extensions have been proposed to improve its performance. It has been shown to be the optimal pessimistic algorithm if communication failure rates are negligible (17). In general, pessimistic algorithms have the advantage that they do not require any error detection, damage assessment, or error recovery. When a transient failure arrives, it may cause some of the replicas to become unavailable, but normal transaction processing may proceed as long as there are enough available replicas. When the failure disappears eventually, no effort is required to reintegrate the affected replicas if the algorithm tolerates outdated replicas. Otherwise, a simple copy from any up-to-date replica to the affected replicas is sufficient.

Available Copies Algorithm

In the available copies algorithm (18,19), a read access to a replicated data object o is translated into a read access to one of the replicas of o, and write access to o is translated into write accesses to *all available* replicas of *o*. A replica becomes unavailable when the node on which it resides fails. The available copy algorithm obviously provides high availability to read transactions, since any available replica would be able to satisfy a read access. It can also reduce the average cost of communication when the closest replica can be used. Write accesses incur higher costs because all replicas that are available have to be written. The algorithm also provides high availability to write transactions because it is highly unlikely that all replicas are unavailable. Intuitively, the available copies algorithm preserves one-copy serializability for two reasons. First, it preserves serializability using standard concurrency control algorithms (9). Second, given serializability and that each update transaction updates all available replicas, any existing replica must consequently have identical contents. It does not tolerate communication failures because there is no provision in the algorithm to prevent two transactions in two network partitions from accessing their (disjoint) sets of available replicas.

Voting Algorithms

Basic Voting Algorithm: In order to deal with communication failures, a voting algorithm assigns a non-negative vote to each replica of a replicated data object. In addition, a read quorum and a write quorum of votes are selected such that their sum exceeds the total votes assigned to the replicas. During each access, enough replicas must be accessed so that the votes of the accessed replicas reach a quorum. The quorum used depends on the type of access being performed. For example, if a data object has five replicas, each replica is assigned one vote, and the read and write quorums are set to be two and four votes, respectively, then a read transaction must access at least two replicas and a write transaction must access at least four replicas.

A write transaction may not be able to access all replicas because of failures. Consequently, some replicas may be less up to date than others. Voting algorithms solve this problem by attaching a version number or a timestamp to each replica. A read transaction can use the timestamps to determine the most up-to-date replica among the ones it can access. Write transactions have to attach new unique timestamps to the replicas they write.

Given that the sum of the two quorums exceeds the total number of votes, a voting algorithm guarantees that any read transaction and any write transaction would access at least one common replica. Intuitively, one-copy serializability is preserved for two reasons. First, serializability is preserved using standard concurrency control algorithms. Second, given serializability and that read and write transactions access at least one common replica, that one replica can be regarded by a read transaction as the "true" replica containing the effects of all previous updates.

Extensions to Voting: Because of its insistence on a predetermined quorum, a voting algorithm tolerates communication and node failures. For example, if a network partitions such that one partition contains three replicas and another partition contains two, then in our previous vote assignment example, both partitions would be able to process read transactions on the replicated data object, but none would allow any update transactions. On the other hand, if the network partitions into four replicas on one side and one replica on the other, then the first partition would be able to process any type of transaction but the second partition cannot access the object at all.

The voting algorithm described in this section was proposed by Gifford (10). It is a generalization of the majority consensus algorithm (20,21). A large number of extensions have been proposed to improve the basic voting algorithm described above. Several authors have described voting algorithms in which the quorum can be adjusted dynamically (22–26). For example, if one of the five replicas in our previous example failed, then the failed vote can be shifted to a new replica, or to one of the original replicas. The vote assigned to the original replicas can also be changed. Dynamic vote assignment prevents the availability of a replicated object from deteriorating rapidly in a succession of failures. How to choose the optimal vote assignment is discussed in Tong and Kain (27).

A criticism of voting techniques is the large number of replicas required (at least three). A discussion on how to reduce the storage requirement while preserving the advantages of replication is provided elsewhere (28, 29). The cost of accessing multiple replicas can also be reduced using the algorithm described in Ref. 30. According to this algorithm, each replica keeps track of which other replicas belong to the same network partition in data structure called a *view*. A read access would be directed to one replica in the partition, provided that the partition has a read quorum. The overhead of voting is shifted from read access to view maintenance, which is performed only when failures arrive or disappear.

Optimistic Data Replication

In a voting algorithm, only network partitions with a quorum are allowed to access a data object. In the worse case, no network partition may have a quorum. Optimistic algorithms assume that conflicting updates rarely occur; consequently, each network partition is allowed to proceed on the assumption that it is the only partition accessing the data object. When the network is repaired eventually, conflicting transactions are determined and a resolution protocol is used to resolve the conflicts. Optimistic algorithms provide higher availability than pessimistic algorithms, at the expense of increased complexity and cost during recovery.

Two different types of resolution protocols have been proposed. In Davidson (31), some of the conflicting transactions are undone so that the transactions left would preserve one-copy serializability. Davidson (31) also describes a backout strategy that attempts to minimize the total backout cost by choosing the appropriate transactions to be undone. Undoing is not always possible when the backout involves actions outside the distributed system. For example, suppose a data object is used to represent a bank account and cash is distributed when the balance is debited. If the object is replicated and updates are performed independently on the account replicas, the same amount of money in the account may be withdrawn twice and undoing requires getting cash back from the user.

In Parker et al. (32), an automatic conflict detection scheme is proposed for a replicated file system. However, resolving the conflict is the responsibility of the applications. For example, if a replicated file is used to store electronic mail messages for a user, different pieces of new mail have been added to the file replicas during a network partition. Upon its detection, the inconsistency can be resolved by creating a file that includes all the new mail added in all the file replicas.

ERROR RECOVERY

After an error is detected, the amount of error recovery provided by a system can vary significantly. A common form of recovery provided by database systems aims at restoring data consistency. Ongoing transactions affected by the failure are aborted and their effects are undone. In this section, we focus on recovery techniques in which a computation affected by a failure can preserve part of its work. In order to allow a computation to be restarted from some point other than its beginning, the state of the computation should be recoverable after a failure. We will describe backward recovery and process replication techniques, respectively. If these techniques are used to recover from hardware or transient software failures (e.g., deadlocks), the same software can be used to resume normal execution after error recovery. We will describe attempts to tolerate software faults by replicating software.

Backward Recovery

Backward recovery attempts to restart a computation from one of its previous valid states. Backward recovery can be further classified by how the state of a computation is saved and restored. A computation state may be restored by starting with the current state and applying some form of undo operation. Alternatively, a computation may save a snapshot of its state periodically, and reloading one of these snapshots would restore the computation to the state at the snapshot. The former requires an application to supply application-dependent undo operations; it also assumes that the current state has not been corrupted to an extent that the undoing would be unsuccessful. For these reasons, it is more common to implement backward recovery by saving snapshots of the state of a computation. The snapshots are called *checkpoints* and the process of taking a checkpoint is called *checkpointing*.

A Consistent Checkpoint: In a distributed system, the state of a computation consists of the states of a collection of communicating but independent *processes*. The processes are independent in the sense that each may be executing at its own pace, and is synchronized with other processes only through sending and receiving messages. However, the checkpoint of a computation is not necessarily equal to the sum of the process checkpoints. For example, suppose a process p_1 takes a checkpoint c_1 and then sends a message m to p_2, which takes a checkpoint c_2 after receiving m. The checkpoints c_1 and c_2 are not *consistent* because they do not agree on which messages have been sent: the state of p_1 at c_1 corresponds to one in which m has not been sent, but the state of p_2 at c_2 corresponds to one in which m has been sent. If p_1 and p_2 are restarted at c_1 and c_2, respectively, p_1 may resend m, causing the message to be received and processed twice by p_2, or p_1 may follow an entirely different execution path in which m never is sent to p_2. These scenarios often are not acceptable. For example, m may be a message that instructs p_2 to withdraw money from a bank account.

Synchronous and Asynchronous Checkpointing: Checkpointing algorithms can be divided into *synchronous checkpointing* and *asynchronous checkpointing*. Synchronous checkpointing is studied in Refs. 33–36 and asynchronous checkpointing in Refs. 37–42. Synchronous checkpointing, is performed globally. During checkpointing, the communicating processes coordinate to guarantee that the local checkpoints by the individual processes are globally consistent. In asynchronous checkpointing, each process is allowed to checkpoint at its own pace. During recovery, a globally consistent checkpoint is constructed by choosing the appropriate local checkpoints.

The main advantages of synchronous checkpointing are simplified recovery and a bounded amount of *rollback*, where rollback is defined as the amount of work performed between the checkpoints from which a computation is restarted and the time of failure. In synchronous checkpointing, a computation can be rolled back to the last global checkpoint when a failure occurs. Asynchronous checkpointing allows the frequency of checkpointing to be determined locally. For example, a process can choose an idle period to checkpoint, or it can choose to checkpoint less frequently because it perceives itself to be relatively reliable. There is also no overhead needed to coordinate any global checkpointing until recovery is required. The main disadvantage of asynchronous checkpointing is the possibility of *cascading rollback*, which is also called the *domino effect*. In order to guarantee consistency, a process that failed and rolled back to its last checkpoint may cause other processes that may be executing on machines that have not failed to be rolled back also. The rollback of the latter processes may in turn require yet more rollback to maintain consistency. This domino effect may eventually cause some processes to roll back mpore than one checkpoint interval's worth of work.

A special class of synchronous checkpointing can be called *pessimistic checkpointing* (43). Pessimistic checkpointing requires that the sender of every message to complete a checkpoint atomically with sending the message. Consequently, the sender's state at the moment of a completed checkpoint is consistent with the state of the receiver. Compared with other synchronous checkpointing techniques, pessimistic checkpointing has the advantage that only failed processes have to be rolled back to their last checkpoints. On the other hand, pessimistic checkpointing requires a checkpoint each time a message is sent.

Where and What to Save a Checkpoint: Checkpoints of a process can be saved either on disk storage that survives transient node failures, or stable storage that survives single media failures (44), or the volatile memory of nodes that have failure characteristics independent from those of the checkpointing process (e.g., the hardware does not share the same power source).

In order to save the state of a process, a checkpoint should contain some form of program counter to determine the locus from which the process should be restarted. It should also contain a copy of the working storage of the process, such as the values of the variables. A checkpoint can be generated by application code, which can determine precisely the amount of information needed to restart a process. More commonly, it can be initiated by an external agent, such as the operating system. In this case, a checkpoint consists of the entire range of volatile memory used by the process. This alternative allows checkpointing to be application-independent and application-transparent. The checkpointing capability provided by the external agent can be used in any application without any modification of the application. How to optimize the process of saving process states is described in Ref. 45.

Process Replication

In contrast to checkpointing, the state of a process can be replicated by multiple nodes performing the same computation concurrently. Circus (16) is an example of this approach. Procedures are replicated as a troupe and the replicas are called the troupe members. When a troupe t_1 calls another troupe t_2, every member of t_2 will receive calls from every member of t_1. With calls replicated, each member of t_2 has to make sure that the procedure is performed exactly once. Each member in t_1 will receive multiple replies too, so it is responsible for gathering and selecting the appropriate response. Circus' approach requires the procedure to be deterministic so that the state of the members of t_2 will remain consistent.

Some systems described (12,13) solve the problem of nondeterministic computation by committing only one replica of a replicated computation. Each replica of a computation keeps its own version of data and causes other replicas and their data to be discarded when it commits.

SOFTWARE FAULT TOLERANCE

In order to provide tolerance against software faults, redundant software has to be provided. The redundant software should be programmed using the same system specification, but by different programming teams, and when possible, using different algorithms, to reduce common faults. Two different approaches to incorporate the redundant software have been proposed.

Recovery Blocks

In the recovery block approach (24) the redundant software, called a *recovery block*, is arranged into a *primary module* and one or more *alternate modules*. The primary module is first executed and an *acceptance test* provided by the application is used for error detection afterwards. If an error is detected, backward error recovery is used to roll back the updates performed by the primary module and the first alternate module is executed. The cycle of an acceptance test, rollback, and retry with another alternative module is repeated until one of the modules passes the acceptance test, or if all the alternate modules are exhausted. In the latter case, the entire recovery block is considered failed.

N-Version Programming

In N-version programming (15), the redundant software is arranged into multiple versions of the same program. The multiple versions are executed concurrently. Afterward, the results of the different versions are compared by a voter. The majority will be passed on by the voter, masking erroneous results returned by faulty versions. This proposal (15) emphasizes the use of different algorithms. Other articles have suggested the utility of using different specification languages (46) or different programming languages (47).

Recovery blocks and N-version programming both entail the overhead of programming the redundant software. In addition, recovery blocks have to provide acceptance tests and the voter in N-version programming can be nontrivial. Recovery blocks use backward recovery to undo the effects of faulty modules. N-version programming has to isolate the effects of concurrent versions. Using these techniques in a distributed system has a few advantages. In a distributed system, the use of redundant software can be combined with redundant hardware to achieve tolerance against software and hardware faults. In addition, in a distributed system with relatively abundant processing power, the overhead of executing multiple versions of software concurrently in the N-version programming approach is significantly mitigated.

RELIABLE PROTOCOLS

In this section we describe some of the commonly used distributed protocols and efforts in making them fault tolerant. We will briefly describe broadcast protocols, agreement protocols, and mutual exclusion protocols. Broadcast protocols are useful in the implementation of replicated data. For example, a broadcast protocol may be used to propagate updates to the replicated data. An agreement protocol can be used by a distributed system to determine which components have failed and should be left out in a new configuration. A special class of agreement protocols called *commit protocols* can be used by a distributed database to determine whether a transaction is committed or aborted. A mutual exclusion protocol can be used in a distributed system to synchronize access to shared resources. We will limit our discussion to fault-tolerant versions of these protocols.

Reliable Broadcast Protocols

Reliable broadcast protocols can be classified depending on whether they use information on the network topology to reduce the amount of message traffic. For example, several authors (6, 48–51) describe broadcast protocols that arrange the recipients into spanning trees along which broadcast messages are propagated. When the design objective of the protocols is to minimize message traffic, the spanning tree chosen tends to mirror the topology of the underlying network.

Others (8, 52) describe flooding protocols for broadcasting messages. A node participating in a flooding protocol propagates each message it receives through all available communication links except the one from which it receives the message. An advantage of flooding is speed. If two nodes are connected by a physical path, flooding guarantees that a message received by one node will be received by the other. One of the flooding protocols described by Christian et al. handle Byzantine faults.

Probabilistic algorithms are proposed (53). In those algorithms a node propagates messages to a few other randomly chosen nodes. In order to avoid missing some nodes permanently, each node also periodically compares its internal state with randomly chosen partners.

Other broadcast algorithms require the sender to communicate directly with the recipients (54–57). Some of them also guarantee that messages from all senders are received in the same order in the recipients. For example, the ordered broadcast protocol (54) requires a sender to communicate with its recipients in two phases. In the first phase, the message is sent to all recipients and information about what *other* messages have been received by the recipients is returned to the sender. In the second phase, the sender uses the information on other messages to determine a ranking of the message it sent. The recipients are informed of that ranking, and use it to order the messages received.

Mutual Exclusion Protocols

Fault-tolerant mutual exclusion protocols have been proposed (58–62). Most of these algorithms are *token-based*, which means that a token is passed between the nodes requesting mutual exclusion. Only the node possessing the token is allowed to enter into the critical region. If failures cause the token to be lost, a recovery algorithm is used to regenerate the token.

Voting algorithms (10) can be considered a class of fault-tolerant mutual exclusion algorithms. Each node initiating an update on a replicated data object must guarantee that it is the only one doing so.

Agreement Protocols

A special class of agreement protocols called *commit protocols* has been studied in the context of distributed database systems. The most commonly used commit protocol is the two-phase commit protocol (9,63). In the two-phase commit protocol, a coordinating node uses the first place to inform the rest of the participating nodes that a transaction is about to be committed. The participating nodes would prepare for the commitment by saving updates made by the transaction into stable storage, and inform the coordinator that they are ready to commit. If the coordinator finds out that all participants are ready to commit, it will save a *commit record* in its stable storage, and inform all participants that the transaction has been committed in the second phase. Upon learning that the transaction is committed, the participants would incorporate the previously saved updates into the permanent database state. Any failure before the preparation of the participants or before the writing of the commit record in the coordinator will cause the transaction to be aborted. The use of stable storage allows the coordinator or the participants to finish the commit protocol correctly after a (transient) failure.

The participants of the two-phase commit protocol may be blocked from finishing the protocol if the coordinator fails after the first place. They have to wait until the stable storage of the coordinator is accessible to determine whether the coordinator has written a commit record. The two-phase commit protocol is extended (64,65) to reduce the probability of blocking and the number of messages required. The two-phase commit protocol and some of its variations have been used in several distributed databases, including R* (66) Sirius-Delta (67), and Prime's distributed database system (68).

Another form of agreement protocols called *election protocols* are considered elsewhere (69,70). A fault-tolerant election protocol can be used to determine a coordinator in a distributed application in the presence of failures. Agreement protocols that tolerate Byzantine faults are considered elsewhere (7,71,72).

EXAMPLES OF RELIABLE DISTRIBUTED SYSTEMS

The fault-tolerant described in this article have been implemented on many experimental and production systems. We focus on a few representative production systems in this section, but our list is by no means complete.

Tandem

The Tandem-16 computing system is a distributed system consisting of fault tolerant nodes. Each node can have multiple processing modules and other duplicated hardware components (e.g., power source, disk, memory, bus, I/O channel) (73). The duplication allows each node to survive any single hardware failure. In addition, multiple nodes may be connected by a fiber optic network. The Tandem NonStop* operating system (43) allows each process to be executed as a *process pair*. A process pair consists of a primary process that checkpoints to a backup process. The primary and the backup execute on different processing modules. The backup will take over after the primary has failed. Consistency of the processes is guaranteed by pessimistic checkpointing. The operating system guarantees that messages sent to a process pair are directed to the backup after a failure of the primary.

Auragen

A Auragen 4000 series consists of basic processing units called *clusters* that are connected by a dual intercluster bus. All peripherals are dual-ported and connected to two

---

*NonStop is a trademark of the Tandem Corporation.

clusters. In addition, disks are connected in pairs to allow the implementation of mirrored files. The Auros[†] operating system (74) allows processes to communicate by sending messages. In order to provide process resilience, a process can be replicated with a primary and a backup.

A primary process checkpoints its state periodically to its backup. If the primary fails, the backup is started using the last checkpoint state. In order to ensure process consistency, the operating system guarantees that the backup will receive all messages that arrive after the last checkpoint, and if those messages have been received by the primary, the backup will follow an identical execution path but the messages will not re-sent. These guarantees are implemented by the operating system and the hardware by guaranteeing that each message sent is received by the sender's backup, the receiver, and the receiver's backup atomically. Using the saved messages, a backup can reconstruct the state of the primary by reprocessing the messages received, and suppress the messages that were already sent.

Stratus

The Stratus systems (75) consist of multiple processing modulus, each of which is a multiprocessor itself. Error detection is implemented by having two copies of each hardware component operating synchronously on the same board, and comparing their outputs. In addition, each board also runs in duplex with another board, so that if an error is detected on one board, the other can continue execution interruption. The relative low cost of off-the-shelf hardware components makes this approach cost-effective. In contrast to the normally quiescent backups in Tandem and Auragen systems, each program on a Stratus system is actually executed on four processors.

Locus

Locus (76) is a distributed version of Unix.[‡] Locus provides network transparency so that users need not be aware of the physical locations of various resources in the system. Locus provides fault tolerance in two different ways, both of which concerns the file system. First, an atomic commitment facility is provided for file updates. Atomic commitment ensures that either all or none of a file's updates are made. Locus also provides automatic file replication, with the degree of replication controlled by the user. The replica control algorithm used by Locus is relatively simple. A primary replica is chosen among the replicas of a file. During a network partition, only the partition with the primary replica is allowed to update the file. Other partitions are allowed to read the file only. When two network partitions are merged, the outdated file replicas are brought up to date.

SUMMARY AND FUTURE OUTLOOK

We have described several techniques that can be used to implement a reliable distributed system. These techniques can be categorized by the types of faults that they are designed

---

[†]Auros is a trademark of the Auragen Systems Corporation.

[‡]Unix is a trademark of AT&T Bell Laboratories.

to handle and the degree of fault tolerance they provide. In a distributed system, a recovery algorithm and a commit protocol can be used to maintain data consistency. A wide range of hardware and software faults can be tolerated by aborting transactions affected by a failure. The recovery algorithm and the commit protocol guarantee that changes made by an aborted transaction are undone in every node in the distributed system. The failure is tolerated at the expense of aborting affected transactions.

Data replication techniques improve reliability by making data objects highly available despite failures. Consequently, a computation is more likely to be able to complete despite failures of the network of the nodes containing data objects. Data replication techniques can be classified as either optimistic or pessimistic.

The state of a process can be made resilient to failures using error recovery and replication techniques. These techniques can be classified into forward recovery, backward recovery, and process replication. Checkpointing is a backward recovery technique that saves snapshots of the state of a process. Alternatively, the same process can be executed concurrently on multiple nodes so that each node possesses a copy of its state.

In order to tolerate software faults, redundant software has to be provided. Using recovery blocks, the multiple versions of software are executed sequentially and their results tested with an acceptance test. In the N-version programming approach, all versions are executed concurrently and their results compared by a voter.

Researchers have also identified commonly used protocols in a distributed system. Examples of these protocols include broadcast, mutual exclusion, and agreement protocols. The reliability of a distributed system can be increased using fault-tolerant versions of these protocols.

Several aspects of reliable distributed systems merit further research and development. In general, there is a lack of performance analysis and experimental studies. These studies would identify not only the overhead and merits of existing algorithms, the experience of implementing and using a reliable distributed system would also help reveal deficiencies and suggest avenues for further research.

Given that fault tolerance introduces significant complexity in a system, there is need to study the appropriate structuring techniques for a fault-tolerant system. Like other complex systems, the use of software engineering techniques in a reliable distributed system would be beneficial. In particular, a reliable distributed system should be structured such that it is highly adaptive while individual nodes remain autonomous.

A special type of reliable distributed systems is the topic of much current research. Many of the applications that require high reliability are also real-time systems. Computations in a real-time system must be completed before deadlines. The study of real-time fault tolerance raises new questions on what types of fault tolerance are needed in a real-time system, and how to provide them without missing the deadlines in such a system.

Despite the large amount of research performed, the experience of using and implementing reliable distributed systems remains limited. The lack of experience is due partly to the cost of providing fault tolerance. Users have to be convinced that the benefits of reliability justify the overhead. With our increasing dependence on computer systems, the potential inconvenience and cost of suffering a failure are steadily increasing. Thus we can expect reliability to play a more crucial role in a system design. With the advance of VLSI technologies and the decrease in cost of redundant hardware, the growing importance of reliability will be matched with improving cost-effectiveness of fault tolerant systems.

ACKNOWLEDGMENTS

The author thanks Jane W. S. Liu for her suggestions, corrections, and comments on an earlier draft of this article. They improved both the technical content and the clarity of the presentation.

REFERENCES

1. P. H. Enslow, What is a 'Distributed System'? *IEEE Computer*, *11*(1), 13–21 (January 1978).
2. T. Anderson and P. A. Lee, *Fault Tolerance: Principles and Practice*, Prentice Hall International, Englewood Cliffs, NJ, 1981.
3. W. Stallings, *Data and Computer Communications*, second edition, Macmillan, New York, 1988.
4. A. S. Tanenbaum, *Computer Networks*, second edition, Prentice Hall, Englewood Cliffs, NJ, 1988.
5. C. J. Colbourn, *The Combinatorics of Network Reliability*, Oxford University Press, Oxford, 1987.
6. R. D. Schlichting and F. B. Schneider, Fail-Stop Processors: An Approach to Designing Fault-Tolerant Computing Systems, *ACM Transact. Computer Syst.*, *1*(3) (1983).
7. L. Lamport, R. Shostak, and M. Pease, The Byzantine Generals Problem, *ACM Transact. Prog. Lang. Sys.*, *4*(3), 382–401 (July 1982).
8. F. Cristian, H. Aghili, and R. Strong, Atomic Broadcast: From Simple Message Diffusion to Byzantine Agreement, in *Proceedings of the Fifteenth Symposium on Fault-Tolerant Computing*, IEEE, New York, 1985, pp. 200–206.
9. J. N. Gray, Notes on Data Base Operating Systems, in *Operating Systems: An Advanced Course, Lecture Notes in Computer Science*, *60*, 393–481, (1978).
10. D. K. Gifford, Weighted Voting for Replicated Data, in *Proceedings of the Seventh Symposium on Operating Systems Principles*, ACM SIGOPS (December 1979).
11. E. C. Cooper, Replicated Distributed Programs, in *Proceedings of the Tenth Symposium on Operating Systems Principles*, ACM SIGOPS (December 1979).
12. T. P. Ng and S. B. Shi, Replicated Transactions, in *Proceedings of the Ninth International Conference on Distributed Computing Systems*, IEEE, New York, 1989, pp. 474–480.
13. M. Ahamad, P. Dasgupta, R. LeBlanc, and C. T. Wilkes, Fault Tolerant Computing in Object Based Distributed Operating Systems, in *Proceedings of the Sixth Symposium on Reliable Distributed Systems*, IEEE, Chicago, 1987, pp. 15–125.
14. J. J. Horning et al., A Program Structure for Error Detection and Recovery, in *Lecture Notes in Computer Science*, *16*, 171–187, (1974).
15. L. Chen and A. Avizienis, N-version Programming: A Fault-Tolerant Approach to Reliability of Software Operation, in *Proceeding of the Eighth Symposium on Fault-Tolerant Computing*, New York, 1978, pp. 3–9.
16. R. Attar, P. A. Bernstein, and N. Goodman, Site Initialization, Recovery and Backup in a Distributed Database System, *IEEE Transact. Software Eng.*, *SE-10*(6), 645–650 (November 1984).
17. M. Obradovic and P. Berman, Voting as the Optimal Static Pessimistic Scheme for Managing Replicated Data, in *Proceedings of the Ninth Symposium of Reliable Distributed Systems*, IEEE, New York, 1990, pp. 126–135.
18. P. A. Bernstein and N. Goodman, An Algorithm for Concurrency Control and Recovery in Replicated Distributed Databases, *ACM Transact. Database Sys.*, *9*(4), 596–615 (December 1984).
19. N. Goodman et al., A Recovery Algorithm for a Distributed Database System, in *Proceedings of ACM SIGACT-SIGMOD Symposium on Principles of Database Systems*, ACM, New York, 1983, pp. 8–15.

20. C. A. Ellis, Consistency and Correctness of Duplicate Database Systems, *Operating Syst. Rev.*, *11*, (1977).

21. R. T. Thomas, A Majority Consensus Approach to Concurrency Control for Multiple Copy Databases, *ACM Transact. Database Syst.*, *4*(2), 180–209 (June 1979).

22. D. L. Eager and K. C. Sevcik, Achieving Robustness in Distributed Database Systems, *ACM Transact. Database Sys. 8*(3), 354–381 (September 1983).

23. D. Davcev and W. A. Burkhard, Consistency and Recovery Control for Replicated Files, in *Proceedings of the Tenth Symposium on Operating Systems Principles*, ACM, New York, 1985, pp. 87–96.

24. D. Barbara, H. Garcia-Molina, and A. Spauster, Policies for Dynamic Vote Reassignment, in *Proceedings of the Sixth International Conference on Distributed Computing Systems*, IEEE, New York, 1986, pp. 37–44.

25. M. P. Herlihy, Dynamic Quorum Adjustments for Partitioned Data, *ACM Transact. Database Syst.*, *12*(2), 170–194 (June 1987).

26. S. Jajodia and D. Mutchler, Dynamic Voting, in *Proceedings of ACM/SIGMOD International Conference on Management of Data*, ACM/SIGMOD, New York, 1987, pp. 227–238.

27. Z. Tong, and R. Y. Kain, Vote Assignment in Weighted Voting Mechanism, in *Proceedings of the Seventh Symposium on Reliable Distributed Systems*, New York, 1988, pp. 22–31.

28. J. Paris, Voting with Witness: A Consistency Scheme for Replicated Files, in *Proceedings of the Sixth International Conference on Distributed Computing Systems*, New York, 1986, pp. 606–612.

29. D. Agrawal and A. E. Abbadi, Reducing Storage for Quorum Consensus Algorithms, in *Proceedings of the International Conference on Very Large Data Bases*, ACM, New York, 1988, pp. 419–430.

30. A. El Abbadi and S. Toueg, Availability in Partitioned Replicated Databases, in *Proceedings of ACM SIGACT-SIGMOD Symposium on Principles of Database Systems*, ACM, New York, 1986, pp. 240–251.

31. S. B. Davidson, Optimism and Consistency in Partitioned Distributed Database Systems, *ACM Transact. Database Sys.*, *9*(3), 456–481 (September 1984).

32. D. S. Parker et al., Detection of Mutual Inconsistency in Distributed Systems, in *Proceedings of the Fifth Berkeley Workshop on Distributed Data Management and Computer Networks*, IEEE, New York, 1981, pp. 172–183.

33. G. Barigazzi and L. Strigini, Application Transparent Setting of Recovery Points, in *Proceedings of the Thirteenth Symposium on Fault-Tolerant Computing*, IEEE, New York, 1983, pp. 48–55.

34. R. Koo and S. Toueg, Checkpointing and Rollback-Recovery for Distributed Systems, *IEEE Transact. Software Eng.*, *SE-13*(1), 23–31 (January 1987).

35. P. Leu and B. Bhargava, Concurrent Robust Checkpointing and Recovery in Distributed Systems, in *Proceedings of Fourth International Conference on Data Engineering*, IEEE, New York, 1988.

36. Y. Tamir and C. H. Sequin, Error Recovery in Multicomputers Using Global Checkpoints, in *Proceedings of the Thirteenth International Conference on Parallel Processing*, IEEE, New York, 1984.

37. V. Hadzilacos, An Algorithm for Minimizing Rollback Cost, in *Proceedings of ACM SIGACT-SIGMOD Symposium on Principles of Database Systems*, ACM, New York, 1982.

38. K. H. Kim, Programmer-Transparent Coordination of Recovering Concurrent Processes: Philosophy and Rules for Efficient Implementation, *IEEE Transact. Software Eng.*, *SE-14*(6), 810–821 (June 1988).

39. T. P. Ng, A Commit Protocol for Checkpointing Transactions, in *Proceedings of the Seventh Symposium on Reliable Distributed Systems*, IEEE, New York, 1988, pp. 22–31.

40. D. L. Russel, State Restoration in Systems of Communicating Processes, *IEEE Transact. Software Eng.*, *SE-6*(2), 183–194 (March 1980).

41. R. Strom and S. Yemini, Optimistic Recovery in Distributed Systems, *ACM Transact. Computer Syst.*, *3*(3), 204–226 (February 1985).
42. W. G. Wood, A Decentralized Recovery Control Protocol, in *Proceedings of Eleventh Conference on Fault-Tolerant Computing*, IEEE, New York, 1981.
43. J. F. Barlett, A NonStop Kernel, in *Proceedings of the Eighth Symposium on Operating Systems Principles*, ACM, New York, 1981, pp. 22–29.
44. B. Lampson, Atomic Transactions, in *Distributed Systems: Architecture and Implementation, Lecture Notes in Computer Science, V. 100*, Springer-Verlag, New York, 1988, Chap. 11.
45. M. M. Theimer, K. A. Lantz, and D. R. Cheriton, Preemptable Remote Execution Facilities for the V-System, in *Proceedings of the Tenth Symposium on Operating Systems Principles*, ACM, New York, 1985, pp. 2–12.
46. J. P. J. Kelly and A. Avizienis, A Specification-Oriented Multiversion Software Experiment, in *Proceedings of the Thirteenth Symposium on Fault-Tolerant Computing*, IEEE, New York, 1983.
47. A. Avizienis, and J. P. J. Kelly, Fault-Tolerance by Design Diversity: Concepts and Experiments. *IEEE Computer*, *17*(8), (August 1984).
48. H. Garcia-Molina and B. Kogan, Reliable Broadcast in Networks and Nonprogrammable Servers, in *Proceedings of the Eighth International Conference on Distributed Computing Systems*, IEEE, New York, 1988, pp. 428–437.
49. H. Garcia-Molina and B. Kogan, An Implementation of Reliable Broadcast Using an Unreliable Multicast Facility, in *Proceedings of the Seventh Symposium on Reliable Distributed Systems*, IEEE, New York, 1988, pp. 101–111.
50. T. P. Ng, Propagating Updates in a Highly Replicated Database, in *Proceedings of Sixth International Conference on Data Engineering*, IEEE, New York, 1990, pp. 529–536.
51. A. Segall and B. Awerbuch, "A Reliable Broadcast Protocol," *IEEE Transact. Comm.* COM-31(7), 896–901 (1983).
52. E. C. Rosen, "The Update Protocol of Arpanet's New Routing Algorithm," *Computer Networks*, *4*(1), 11–19 (1980).
53. A. Demers et al., Epidemic Algorithms for Replicated Database Management, in *Proceedings of Sixth Symposium on Principles of Distributed Computing*, ACM, New York, 1987, pp. 1–12.
54. K. P. Birman and T. A. Joseph, Reliable Communication in the Presence of Failures, *ACM Transact. Computer Syst.* 5(1), 47–76 (February 1987).
55. J. M. Change and N. F. Maxemchuk, Reliable Broadcast Protocols, *ACM Transact. Computer Syst.*, *2*(3), 251–273 (August 1984).
56. S. W. Luan and V. D. Gligor, A Fault-Tolerant Protocol for Atomic Broadcast, in *Proceedings of the Seventh Symposium on Reliable Distributed Systems*, IEEE, New York, 1988, pp. 117–126.
57. S. Navaratnam, S. Chanson, and G. Neufeld, Reliable Group Communication in Distributed Systems, in *Proceedings of the Eighth International Conference on Distributed Computing Systems*, IEEE, New York, 1988, pp. 439–446.
58. Y. I. Chang, M. Singhal, and M. T. Liu, A Fault Tolerant Algorithm for Distributed Mutual Exclusion, in *Proceedings of the Ninth Symposium on Reliable Distributed Systems*, IEEE, New York, 1990, pp. 146–154.
59. G. LeLann, Algorithms for Distributed Data Sharing Systems Which Use Tickets, in *Proceedings of the Third Berkeley Workshop on Distributed Data Management and Computer Networks*, IEEE, New York, 1978, 259–272.
60. S. Nishio, K. F. Li, and E. G. Manning, A Resilient Mutual Exclusion Algorithm for Computer Networks, *IEEE Transact. Parallel Distrib. Sys*, (3):344–355 (July 1990).
61. K. Raymond, A Tree-Based Algorithm for Distributed Mutual Exclusion, *ACM Transact. Computer Sys.*, *7*(1), 61–77 (February 1989).

62. M. Singhal, A Heuristically-Aided Algorithm for Mutual Exclusion in Distributed Systems, *IEEE Transact. Computers*, *C-38*(5), 651–662 (May 1989).

63. B. Lampson and H. Sturgis, Crash Recovery in a Distributed Data Storage System, Technical Report, Computer Science Laboratory, Xerox Palo Alto Research Center, 1979.

64. D. Skeen, Non-Blocking Commit Protocols, in *Proceedings of ACM/SIGMOD International Conference on Management of Data*, ACM/SIGMOD, New York, 1982, pp. 133–147.

65. C. Mohan and B. Lindsay, Efficient Commit Protocols for the Tree of Processes Model of Distributed Transactions, *Operating Sys. Rev.*, *19*(2), 40–52 (April 1985).

66. R. Williams et al., R.*: An Overview of the Architecture, in *Proceedings of Second International Conference on Databases: Improving Usability and Responsiveness*, ACM, New York, 1982.

67. G. LeLann, Error Recovery, in *Distributed Systems: Architecture and Implementation, Lecture Notes in Computer Science*, Vol. 100, Springer-Verlag, New York, 1980, Chap. 15.

68. D. J. Dubourdieu, Implementation of Distributed Transactions, in *Proceedings of the Sixth Berkeley Workshop on Distributed Data Management and Computer Networks*, ACM/IEEE, New York, pp. 81–94.

69. J. L. Kim and G. Belford, A Robust, Distributed Election Protocol, in *Proceedings of the Seventh Symposium on Reliable Distributed Systems*, IEEE, New York, 1988, pp. 54–60.

70. H. Garcia-Molina, Elections in a Distributed Computing System, *IEEE Transact. Computers*, *C-31*(1), 48–59 (January 1982).

71. D. Dolev and H. R. Strong, Authenticated Algorithms for Byzantine Agreement, *SIAM J. Computing*, *12*(4), 656–665 (November 1983).

72. K. J. Perry and S. Toueg, Distributed Agreement in the Presence of Processor and Communication Faults, *IEEE Transact. Software Eng.*, *SE-14*(3), 477–482 (March 1988).

73. J. A. Katzman, A Fault-Tolerant Computing System, in *Proceedings of the Eleventh Conference on System Sciences*, IEEE, New York, 1978, pp. 85–102.

74. A. Borg, J. Baumbach, and S. Glazer, A Message System Supporting Fault Tolerance, in *Proceedings of the Ninth Symposium on Operating Systems Principles*, ACM, New York, 1983, pp. 90–99.

75. D. Wilson, *The STRATUS Computer System*, Collins, 1985, pp. 208–231.

76. G. J. Popek and B. J. Walker, *The LOCUS Distributed System Architecture*, MIT Press, Boston, 1985.

TONY P. NG

STRUCTURED ANALYSIS

GENERAL INTRODUCTION

This article deals with: the evolution of structured analysis (SA) from its origins in the early 1960s to the publication of Tom DeMarco's book *Structured Analysis and System Specification* in January 1978; with the characteristics of the mainstream SA techniques as taught and practiced in the late 1970s and early 1980s; and finally with more recent developments, including real-time extensions of SA and recent attempts to combine SA with object-oriented development. I intend not only to outline the technical evolution of the discipline, but also to provide some sense of the people and the organizations that made this evolution possible.

Note that the narrow focus of this article does not allow for discussion of much of the work on software development that occurred in the 1960s and 1970s. I have given, for example, only the most rudimentary explanation of structured design, and have included this information only for the light it throws on the development of one version of structured analysis. Similarly, I have not included details of the many contributions made to development methods by academics such as Dijkstra, Parnas, and Teichroew, or by practitioners outside the academic establishment such as Jackson and Alford.

I don't mean to imply that SA is of more value than the methods developed by these other people and their organizations. However, there is a unique technical character to SA. *It is the only approach that proposed the building of an abstract, graphics-oriented, data flow-based model of the underlying computational requirement as a first step in systems development.* SA has also had a much greater influence on systems development practice than any other development method. It is certainly the most widely used of any technique explicitly targeted at *requirements definition*. It is also the parent of the methods embodied in nearly all of today's graphics-based CASE products.

Structured analysis developed not as a single discipline, but as two quite distinct ones. Each approach came to be strongly identified with a commercial organization: Yourdon, Inc., on the one hand, and SofTech, Inc., on the other. The fact that both approaches carry the same name is misleading. In fact, the adoption by Yourdon, Inc. of the name "structured analysis" for its requirements definition approach in the mid-1970s very nearly resulted in a lawsuit brought by SofTech. Whatever the merits of the nomenclature dispute, and despite the basic similarity mentioned above, the fact is that the two approaches differed significantly both in their technical details and in the working style of their advocates.

SofTech's method for systems development ultimately came to be called the Structured Analysis and Design Technique, hereafter referred to as SADT. Technically, SADT had very high aspirations. It was evolved as an abstract approach for modeling a system and its environment from a priori considerations, completely independent of any implementation details. It aimed for a carefully defined and theoretically justified intellectual unity.

In contrast, Yourdon's version of SA evolved "bottom-up" from widely used software design methods. It was intended to provide practical, down-to-earth, easy-to-comprehend assistance to the average systems developer. It tended to justify itself in terms of intuitiveness and of pragmatic usefulness rather than in terms of theory. This difference in intellectual character was at least partly due to the fact that SADT had essentially a single creator, Douglas Ross, with an overriding concern for theoretical unity, while Yourdon SA was an eclectic collection of ideas from a group of practical-minded creators that included Larry Constantine, Trish Sarson, Chris Gane, Tom DeMarco, and Ed Yourdon.

In terms of working style, Yourdon SA was, from its inception, public in character, aiming to reach a wide audience by a variety of media. Ultimately, a large Yourdon User Group held yearly public meetings at which the nature of SA was subject to intense scrutiny and debate. In contrast, SADT was closely held, propriety in nature, and intended to be applied by carefully selected clients under the close supervision of SofTech consultants. Even when a portion of the technique was, with misgivings, ultimately placed in the public domain, a number of significant technical details were held back.

THE EARLY YEARS

Introduction

The substantial differences between the two styles of SA makes it all the more interesting that they arose at essentially the same time in the same place. From the early 1960s, the Boston area was a beehive of software development activity, centered around both academic institutions (principally MIT) and around companies like Bolt, Beranek, and Newman that performed sponsored research. Digital computers had begun their rapid transition from laboratory curiosity and military secret to business tool early in the previous decade. By the early 1960s, computers were an established part of the economic infrastructure, and the possibilities for their vastly expanded use via time sharing and on-line access were exciting both intellectually and economically.

Larry Constantine and Ed Yourdon entered this highly charged atmosphere as freshman at MIT in 1961; Yourdon was a math major and Constantine a biology major. In those years, a college student interested in computers did not need to look far for non-academic work opportunities. Local companies such as Digital Equipment Corporation were actively seeking part-time and summer programmers. Yourdon worked for DEC on a part-time basis throughout his undergraduate years. To characterize his work contributions by describing him as a part-time student-employee seriously misstates the actual situation. Yourdon had substantial responsibilities—for example, he wrote the math library and the PAL-3 assembler for the DEC PDP-5 computer; PAL-3 was to have a major impact a few years later as a component of the system software for DEC's famous PDP-8. By the time of his graduation in 1965, he was an experienced assembly language programmer with substantial system software experience.

Constantine's college career was even more radically affected by software development work. He left MIT in the spring of his sophomore year to begin working for C.E.I.R., a Washington, DC area firm providing software development services to businesses and to the Defense Department. Constantine functioned both as a programmer and as a teacher of programming methods. He returned to MIT in 1965 and graduated in 1967. However, his completion of undergraduate formalities was somewhat of an anticlimax. In addition to ongoing work on commercial systems development projects, he had continued to teach, and had begun to publish in the area of systems design. By the time of his graduation, Constantine had developed and published the structure chart notation (1) and was an adjunct faculty member at the Wharton School in Philadelphia.

While Yourdon and Constantine were young Turks in the early 1960s, Douglas Ross was already a member of the establishment. A mathematician by training, Ross had come to MIT's Computing Applications Laboratory in 1954, earning a master's degree in engineering and completing the academic work for a doctorate in mathematics. Much of his research work focused on computer-aided manufacturing (CAM). His pioneering work in CAM included the development of the APT programming language (2). APT allows a programmer to describe a manufactured part, then uses the description to generate instructions for making the part for a numerically controlled machine tool. Ross's research interests also included the broader aspects of computation. He developed the AED language, a forerunner of PL/I, and the possessor of features, such as pointers and dynamic allocation, that were considerably ahead of their time (3). By the early 1960s Ross was a well-established and highly respected language developer and theorist (4).

In this intellectually fertile climate, Ross and Constantine (Yourdon's major role was to come much later) were poised to develop the ideas and the organizations that led to both versions of structured analysis.

An Organizational Role Model for Yourdon, Inc.

In 1966, Constantine founded the Information and Systems Institute. This was not simply another consulting and sponsored research firm; it was inspired by a particular vision of productive intellectual activity. The Institute was to operate in many ways like an academic department of a university; its functions were to teach, perform research, and publish, with the intellectual fruits of its labors very much in the public domain. However, the Institute was a private business, and thus free from the strictures imposed by conventional academic institutions.

The sources of Constantine's vision are to be found both in the cultural climate of the 1960s and in the flourishing of the various disciplines involved in software development. On the one hand, the typical 1960s unhappiness with ''the establishment'' in all its forms led to the formation of a plethora of organizations set up in opposition to, or as alternatives to, conventional organizations. The Information and Systems Institute was certainly formed in this spirit.

On the other hand, quite independently of the cultural climate, the proliferation of systems development as a human activity had reached a crisis point. New ideas and new avenues of inquiry were overwhelming and ultimately bypassing the conventional channels of academic research and publication. More and more, systems development practitioners were feeling that ''the action'' was to be found, not in academic departments of mathematics and engineering, but in industry and among small groups of independent entrepreneurs. The Institute was meant to be a nucleus for such activity.

The Information and Systems Institute never was the large-scale commercial success that SofTech, Inc., and, to a lesser extent, Yourdon, Inc. were to be. However, it exerted a lasting influence. Ed Yourdon taught for the institute in the late 1960s, and was encouraged by Constantine to publish his ideas. Ultimately, after Yourdon, Inc. was founded in 1974, these experiences, as well as the occasional physical presence of Constantine, were to ensure that the Institute was Yourdon, Inc.'s spiritual forerunner.

The Conceptual Basis of Yourdon SA

The seminal idea that led to Yourdon SA was conceived by Constantine in 1967 while he was teaching a class on structured design (SD).

A structured design is described by a structure chart (5), a graphic description of a collection of program modules, as illustrated by Figure 1—the pseudocode in the PROCESS_PAYROLL box is not part of the notation, but is intended to clarify the topology of the chart. A structure chart has somewhat the same basic character as a flowchart. The boxes represent chunks of processing work, and the arrows connecting the boxes represent the "flow of control." In other words, one reads a structure chart by assuming the role of the computer, and following the arrows to simulate the sequence in which the processing is performed.

However, there are two critical differences between structure charts and flowcharts. First, while each box on a flowchart represents a chunk of processing which must be completed before the next chunk is begun, a box on a structure chart may include multiple chunks which are performed at different times. The arrow connecting two boxes represents not simply a *transfer* of control but an *exchange* (transfer and return) of control. This permits a module to contain a collection of elements related by criteria (e.g., coordination of a particular level of a computation) other than strict position in the processing sequence. Secondly, the small arrows paralleling the large ones represent data which is exchanged in conjunction with the exchange of control. In other words, a structure chart describes the flow of data as well as the flow of control.

Although reading a structure chart that someone else has created is fairly straightforward, creating one from scratch (i.e., developing a modular design) is definitely not straightforward. One approach—the approach that Constantine was teaching his class— is to use functional decomposition. The computation to be performed is first conceived as a single module. This module is then divided into pieces, and each piece is assigned to a second-level module. The original module does not disappear, but its role changes from performing the computation work to coordinating the second-level modules that perform the work. Each second-level module is then divided up in a similar way, and the task is repeated until the lowest-level modules are sufficiently small.

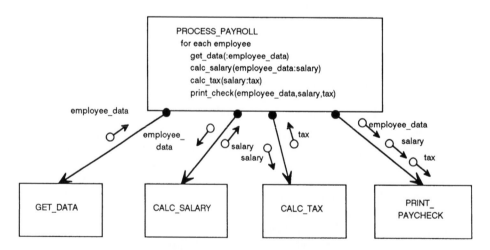

FIGURE 1   A structure chart.

Constantine's class was having difficulty building structure charts by functional decomposition. He happened to have with him a 1967 *JACM* article by Martin and Estrin (6), describing a theoretical model of a computation called a program graph (Fig. 2). Other than the substitution of circles for boxes, a program graph looks superficially similar to a structure chart, but is read quite differently. Each circle represents, not *instructions for a processor* that "visits" the circle, but *a processor with a standing set of instructions*. The arrows represent not *flow of control* but *flow of data*. One reads a program graph by playing the role of the data, which arrives at a particular circle, is operated on according to the standing instructions associated with the circle, and is then passed in a different form to the next circle.

Constantine suggested that his students build a program graph (he ultimately came to refer to it as a data flow graph) to describe the basic requirement for the computation, and then convert the program graph into a structure chart by adding flow of control. (The fully-worked-out procedure for doing this is referred to as "transform analysis", and includes a number of details that are omitted here.) On the surface, the suggestion was merely to use a program graph as a (possibly disposable) visualization aid, to ease the labor of building a structure chart by separating data flow from control flow. However, notice that the suggestion can be rephrased as follows: *As a prelude to creating a design, represent the basic computational requirement for the system to be designed in more abstract terms, namely in terms of data flow*. The use of the data flow graph as the basis of analysis was not to be further developed for almost a decade, and was to require augmentation by a number of other basic ideas, but the germ of Yourdon-style SA is already present here.

The Early Years of SofTech, Inc.

Douglas Ross, John Brackett, and Jorge Rodriquez, all from MIT, founded SofTech Inc., in Waltham, Massachusetts in 1969. Brackett had been an early user of Ross's AED language while a postdoctoral research associate, and had played an active role in the development of MIT's time-sharing system as a member of project MAC. Rodriquez had made extensive use of program graphs as part of his doctoral research for Jack Dennis on models of computation.

Although distinguished by the intellectual eminence of Ross, SofTech was in most respects a conventional firm whose purpose was to build custom software for large

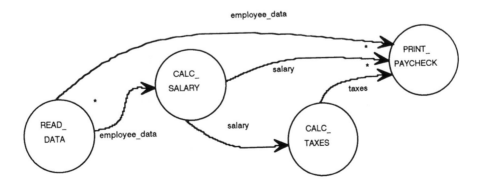

FIGURE 2   A program graph.

organizations. SofTech had no aspirations to be a private version of an academic department, nor to place its intellectual resources in the public domain. To the contrary, SofTech considered its systems development methods proprietary, and from the start attempted to avoid disclosure of many of the details of its approaches. SofTech's clients were required to pay a substantial license fee for access to its systems development technologies, which were designated as trade secrets.

Ross initially had aspirations to bring along some of his MIT research sponsors as SofTech clients. However, this was not to be the case, and a client list had to be built up slowly and painfully. This was accomplished by business savvy and by the technical acumen of the consulting staff, and by the early 1970s SofTech had a number of research contracts.

One such contract, from the Air Force, built on Ross's experience with CAM. It was aimed at creating a generic model for CAM, the AFCAM Master Plan, that would, it was hoped, be adopted by aerospace companies who did manufacturing under Air Force contracts. It was in the course of this work, during what he describes as a "frenzied" six-week period of activity in 1973, that the Ross evolved the basics of SADT. (SofTech's later involvement with the Air Force was to result in a version of the SADT approach which was placed in the public domain with SofTech's permission but to Ross's intense personal dissatisfaction.)

The Conceptual Basis of SADT

From the late 1950s Ross had been attempting to develop a comprehensive way of modeling systems. In a 1961 paper, he had described a development approach based on a unit called the plex (4), which integrated process, data, and control in a comprehensive way. The plex idea influenced the design of AED and later of PL/I. Ross was well aware of the modeling notations proposed by Martin and Estrin and by Larry Constantine, and had ongoing though casual interactions with Constantine through the late 1960s. However, he did not consider these notations adequate, because of their lack of ability to express constraints on system behavior and structure, and he continued to pursue his vision of a more comprehensive model.

The pursuit was to bear fruit finally in 1973, in the course of the AFCAM work mentioned earlier. Combining his plex idea with a CAM-related model developed by S. Hori and called the activity cell (7), Ross evolved the concept of the SA box (8), the activity version of which is illustrated in Figure 3. Note that the direction from which an arrow enters or leaves indicates whether it is input, output, mechanism, or control.

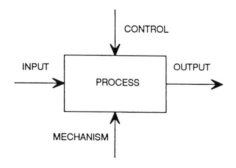

FIGURE 3   The activity version of the SA box.

A network model can be created by stringing together SA activity boxes in a fashion similar to the program graph of Figure 2, with one SA box providing an output which becomes the input to another SA box. In fact, an SA box without its "control" and "mechanism" arrows can be interpreted as one unit of a program graph. However, the presence of the control and mechanism arrows makes a network of SA boxes different in character from a program graph.

Both the program graph and the structure chart, in fact, have quite limited ability to represent control. Notice that in the structure chart (Fig. 1) data flow is slaved to the exchange of control—in other words, data can move from module to module only while one module is transferring control to another. In the program graph, transfer of control disappears, and the exertion of control is slaved to the flow of data—one circle can only control another by passing it the data it needs to produce an output. In the network of SA activity boxes, transfer of control also does not exist. However, control of one box by another can now be exerted *independently* of the flow of data. In other words, the output arrow of one SA box can become the control arrow of another, indicating not that control is transferred but that the first box exerts control on the second.

Since Figure 2 is a program graph, the only way to control PRINT_PAYCHECKS is to supply it with its inputs, and thus the fact that PRINT_PAYCHECKS might operate periodically can't be directly represented. An SA activity box version of Figure 2, therefore, might contain an additional CONTROL_PAYROLL_SCHEDULE activity whose output, labeled PRINT_CHECKS, is the control input to PRINT_PAYCHECKS. Control arrows allow for a much richer set of possible connections on a single diagram than is provided by a program graph or by a structure chart, while mechanism arrows permit referencing an activity to a model of an underlying resource, such as a language or a piece of hardware, that provides an implementation for the activity.

The SA box in Figure 3 also has a dual version, represented by Figure 4. Here, the box represents a data object rather than a unit of activity, the input arrow represents a data-creating activity, and the output arrow represents a data accessing activity. The control and mechanism arrows have meanings similar to those of Figure 3. For example, a data-type SA box might represent payroll data, the input arrow the creation of the data, the output arrow the use of the data in a report, the control arrow the control of data creation or access, and the mechanism arrow the a reference to the physical storage scheme. Data-type SA boxes can also be formed into a network, creating a data-oriented rather than an activity-oriented view of the subject matter.

Both types of SA boxes can also be arranged hierarchically, by representing a higher-level SA box by a diagram containing a network of lower-level boxes with the same net inputs and outputs.

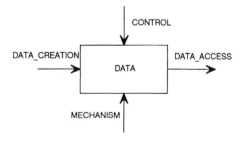

FIGURE 4   The data version of the SA box.

Data and activity hierarchies can be cross-referenced with "ties." Multiple activity hierarchies could be created, each representing either a view of the system or a mechanism used in implementing the system. Activity hierarchies can also be cross-referenced.

The creation of hierarchies of SA-box networks, augmented by substantial additional notational and diagramming conventions, is the heart of the SADT technique, SofTech's version of SA (9–11). The technique is, to a very large extent, the intellectual creation of Ross; the only people who had a slightly more than peripheral influence on its initial development were Clare(nce) Feldmann and Ralph Bravoco, Ross's SofTech co-workers on the AFCAM project. Bravoco describes his and Feldman's role as "translating" Ross's ideas into terms ordinary humans could understand. As the technique was translated into practice, Ross had other able collaborators on SADT-related work, including co-founders Brackett and Rodriquez, Melvin Dickover, Sterling Eanes, Al Irvine, David Marca, Clement McGowan, and Kenneth Schoman. However, these men served rather as able elaborators and appliers of Ross's ideas than as co-creators of SADT.

SADT in the Mid-1970s

The aftermath of the AFCAM project was a disappointment to the Air Force; individual aerospace contractors had their own ideas about CAM, and resisted using the AFCAM master plan. However, the project was a great success for SofTech, leaving the organization with the SADT technique as its proprietary property. Bravoco was sent to Europe and began applying the technique to a number of ITT telecommunications projects in 1974 and 1975 (12). (The "SADT" name was invented by Don Combelic of ITT during this time period.) The results were quite positive; in a number of cases, multilingual project teams were able to use the SADT diagrams to communicate effectively about the evolving systems. These positive results, of course, derived both from the intrinsic power of SADT and from SofTech's characteristic tight monitoring and control of the use of its techniques. During these years Bravoco and his SofTech colleagues in Europe developed case studies and other training methods that substantially enhanced the usability of SADT.

By the middle of the decade, SADT's European success had spread back to the United States, and SofTech began to sell SADT licenses, at $50,000 each, to U.S. Companies. One of the licensees was Banker's Trust in New York City, an organization that soon would have a role to play in the development of Yourdon SA.

The SADT techniques as used in practice fell somewhat short of Ross's idea of a comprehensive modeling approach. For one thing, the data version of the SA box was hard for systems developers to comprehend and was not much used in practice. The mechanism arrow was also not well understood and not too effective as a component of SADT models. In practice, therefore, many SADT modelers were building hierarchies of program graph networks in which control flow and data flow could be independently represented—clearly a powerful and useable notation, if somewhat weaker than Ross's vision of the technique's potential.

The Air Force re-entered SofTech's world in 1976. Spurred by a Defense Department directive to standardize CAM among defense contractors, the USAF had come out on top of an interservice scramble to determine who would sponsor the project, which was called ICAM. SofTech, with a large team of co-bidders consisting of the original users of the APT language, won the bid for the initial stage of creating a "reformalized" CAM architecture.

Using SADT as the vehicle for describing the detailed ICAM architecture was an obvious possibility. However, the contract bidding for the second stage of the reformalization caused problems for SofTech. The Request for Proposal stipulated that the methodology to be used must be in the public domain—SofTech's many co-contractors could not be required to buy SADT licenses to participate in the architecture modeling. Thus, to bid SADT as the ICAM methodology, SofTech would therefore need to agree to place it, or some part of it, in the public domain. The economics of the situation were compelling. SADT was a success, but licenses were not being sold in large numbers, and it would take a lot of licenses to make up the several million dollars per year in revenue that the ICAM contract would provide. The SofTech executive committee, led by president and CEO Brackett, decided to go ahead with the bid, and SofTech ultimately won it. Douglas Ross was very unhappy with placing SADT in the public domain. Nevertheless, in 1977 Bravoco and his colleagues began developing the subset of SADT, called IDEF0 (13), that was to become a very influential development technique, both among defense contractors and in other development areas as well.

The Founding of Yourdon, Inc.

Through the late 1960s and early 1970s, Ed Yourdon had continued to teach and to practice systems development, principally as a contractor to systems development training and consulting companies. In the process he had become a recognized authority on design and programming methods; his first book, *Real-Time Systems Design*, was published in 1967 by Larry Constantine's Information and Systems Press (14), followed by two other books on design published by Prentice-Hall in the mid-1970s (15). In 1974 Yourdon and his wife, Toni Nash, founded Yourdon, Inc. in New York City.

Yourdon, Inc., like Constantine's Institute, had aspirations to teach and to publish; Yourdon Press was an early component of the organization. The company also had a strong evangelical streak. Yourdon, for years immersed in a vigorously active intellectual community, had been shocked and then galvanized by the fact that the population of average systems developers were "great unwashed masses," desperately ignorant of even the most basic development techniques. Yourdon, Inc., had a mission to remedy this situation. So, starting in 1974, Yourdon and his early colleagues went on the road, teaching structured programming, and slightly later a Constantine-developed course on SD.

The Creation of Yourdon SA

Ed Yourdon was aware at the time that SofTech was having success with a graphics-based analysis method, and of course he was familiar with Constantine's data flow graphs. In the fall of 1975, he developed a new course on performing requirements analysis using data flow graphs (Yourdon's remembrance is that the course included hierarchical decomposition of the diagrams as well) and taught it for the first time at MONY. The results, to put it mildly, were not encouraging. The students were actively unhappy with the course, and MONY's management suggested partway through the course that Yourdon stop teaching and go home.

Back at the office, Yourdon asked Trish Sarson, a systems development consultant on his staff, and her husband Chris Gane, who at that time was the marketing manager at Yourdon, Inc., to think about extending the original Constantine data flow graph notation into a more effective analysis technique. Gane and Sarson were convinced that the key to the expansion was a more detailed representation of the *data* within the model.

During the winter and spring of 1975–1976, they extended the data flow graph by adding two new symbols, a *file* (ultimately to be called a data store) to represent stored data, and a *terminator* to represent a source or destination of data outside the scope of the model. The expanded graphic, renamed a data flow diagram (DFD) (it also came to be referred to as a "bubble chart"), is illustrated in Figure 5.

Gane and Sarson also developed a data dictionary to support the graphic model, consisting of a set of file cards with indented, hierarchical descriptions of the contents of the data flows and files. In mid-1976, Gane developed, and he and his colleague Victor Weinburg began teaching, a two-day course based on this expanded technique. Although Ed Yourdon did not literally invent any of the extensions of the Constantine data flow graph, his clear perceptions of the shortcomings of unaided data flow graphs as an analysis technique lay behind the development.

Meanwhile, Tom DeMarco was working on an SADT project at Banker's Trust. Although not a member of the Boston systems-development "mafia", DeMarco's career paralleled those of Yourdon and Constantine. Graduating in Engineering from Cornell in 1963, he done important early work at Bell Laboratories on digital telephone switching systems, and had worked as a systems developer and development manager in Europe and the United States in the late 1960s and early 1970s.

DeMarco joined Yourdon as a contract design instructor in 1976 and soon began teaching Gane's SA course. His SADT experience led him to an immediate appreciation of the potential of the DFD and data dictionary as analysis techniques. He felt that the presence of the data store made the data flow diagram much more intuitive than the SADT activity diagram. (An SA activity box can encapsulate data and thus serve as a data storage mechanism; however, such SA boxes are not distinguished graphically from SA boxes that represent pure processing.) But DeMarco was "shocked" to discover that Yourdon, Gane, and Sarson proposed to create analysis models that lacked control flows! This is fascinating, given DeMarco's subsequent strong identification with the maxim "Thou shalt not depict control on DFDs." DeMarco was persuaded by the simplicity of the Yourdon, Inc. approach (16), and in 1977 began writing a five day course combining SA with (structure-chart-based) SD. This course, called the Structured Analysis and Design Workshop (SADW) became Yourdon's all-time best selling seminar.

In SADW, DeMarco had to solve the problem of making a well-organized transition from data flow modeling to structure chart modeling. In the course of doing this, he conceived the idea of building a sequence of data flow models, the first representing the implementation details of a current system, and the succeeding ones representing suc-

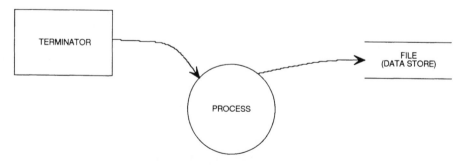

FIGURE 5   The Yourdon SA data flow diagram.

cessively the underlying logic of the current system, the revised logic of the new system, and finally, the physical architecture of the new system. This last data flow model was partitioned so as to make the transition to structure charts, via Constantine's transform analysis procedure, as simple as possible. SADW also included a formal textual notation for the data dictionary, based on Backus-Naur form (BNF).

While this was happening, Gane, unhappy with his financial compensation, left Yourdon, Inc. in 1977, followed soon after by his wife. Gane and Sarson holed up in their Manhattan apartment and began a marathon writing session that began on April 1 and ended with the publication of their book *Structured Systems Analysis: Tools and Techniques* (17) in July. This was the first publication of any kind on Yourdon SA, and ironically it was published under the aegis of a competing organization, Gane and Sarson's recently founded Improved System Technologies.

Meanwhile, Weinburg had signed a book contract with Yourdon Press to produce a book on SA, and work was underway on the manuscript, which incorporated data flow diagrams into a rather traditional systems analysis framework. In the fall of 1977, DeMarco proposed that he also write an SA book, and that it be gotten into print as soon as possible. Wendy Eakin, the director of Yourdon Press, rejected the idea of trying to rush through the DeMarco book because it would have drained resources needed to honor the prior commitment to Weinburg's book.

DeMarco, with the backing of Ed Yourdon and Toni Nash, decided to circumvent Yourdon Press. DeMarco began writing in the fall of 1977. Toni Nash edited DeMarco's copy, and ran off chapters on Yourdon, Inc.'s typesetting machinery as fast as they were written. DeMarco's book described the four-model sequence and the BNF notation that he had included in the SADW course and that were not included in Gane and Sarson's book. The book also recommended using the package of data flow diagrams and associated textual descriptions as an actual deliverable. In other words, the SA model was to *be* the specification rather than serving as an analytical prelude to a narrative specification.

Weinburg's book *Structured Analysis* (18) was published by Yourdon Press in 1978. It was to have much less impact than DeMarco's *Structured Analysis and System Specification* (19) which was published by Yourdon, Inc. (not by Yourdon Press) in March 1978. The early days of SA were over.

THE MAINSTREAM TECHNIQUES

Introduction

In this section, I will discuss the characteristics of the "mainstream" SA techniques as they were taught and as they were actually used from the late 1970s through the mid-1980s. In practice, using SA meant the building of hierarchical, process-oriented models of proposed systems. Although both SADT and Yourdon SA incorporated data modeling techniques, these had much less influence on systems development practice than did the process modeling techniques. The data modeling aspects of SA, along with such later developments as the real-time extensions to Yourdon SA, SA-oriented CASE products, and the integration of SA with object-oriented techniques, will be discussed in the final section of this article.

I will also discuss in this section the fortunes and the character of SofTech and Yourdon Inc. from the late 1970s through the mid 1980s. There were some similarities between the two organizations; for example, both were plagued with SA competition from ex-employees in the 1980s. However, SofTech and Yourdon for the most part remained as dramatically different as two organizations in the same general line of business could possibly be.

The Introduction of SA as a Product

Conventional wisdom dictates that before the proponents of a new professional technique recommend it to the profession at large, it needs a sound technical foundation, and there ought to be some empirical evidence of useability—someone needs to have applied the technique successfully to a non-trivial problem. The technical foundation requirement can be met by the process of peer review common to the physical and social sciences and to engineering. In other words, the proposed technique can be examined for theoretical shortcomings by experts in the field who have no vested interest in the technique and thus can credibly act in an adversarial role. The empirical evidence requirement can be met by one or (preferably) more carefully evaluated pilot projects, involving a group of professionals well aware of the experimental nature of the technique, and prepared to accept the risks of failure or extensive rework. It can be argued that extensive piloting can obviate the technical review requirement, and that an extensive history of successful use constitutes a de facto peer review. However, it is always possible that the pilot projects are too selective, and that a technical review can uncover potential problems in applying the technique to a full range of problems.

As mentioned in the first part of this article, Yourdon SA proponents relied heavily on the intuitiveness of their approach, and were relatively unconcerned with conventional criteria as they introduced the technique. The Yourdon SA extensions to Constantine's data flow graph that created the DFD—the data store and the terminator—were invented by Gane and Sarson in early 1976. Gane and Sarson started a book advocating the use of the revised notation little more than a year later, and the book was in print in July 1977 (17). Although there was a limited base of successful user experience with the new notation, nothing like a carefully supervised and evaluated pilot project was carried out. Moreover, there was no peer review of the manuscript, and in fact there is no practical way such a review *could* have been done effectively on a book-length document that was written and rushed into print over a period of five months.

In defense of Gane and Sarson, it can be argued that they were advocating a fairly modest extension to Constantine's data flow graph technique, and that the data flow graph as a prelude to detailed design had a long history of successful use. However, this modest extension, in the case of the data store, introduced technical inconsistencies. (The interested reader will find a more detailed technical appraisal of both Yourdon SA and SADT below.) Fortunately, the inconsistencies did not present insuperable difficulties to the practitioner, but Gane and Sarson clearly were relying on their intuitions, rather than on any solid base of evidence, in recommending the technique to their readers.

The DeMarco variant of Yourdon SA, at first glance, seems to have been more cautiously introduced. DeMarco had the benefit of about six more months of user experience with DFDs before he began writing his book (19), and a number of people read and commented on the manuscript while it was in preparation. The reviewers, however, were all employees of Yourdon, Inc. or of Deltak (producers of videotape courses on Yourdon SA), and thus were not in a position to perform an independent peer review, nor did they have a reasonable amount of time for a thorough review. Furthermore, DeMarco recommended to his readers a much more radical departure from conventional practice than did

Gane and Sarson—he advocated the creation of a sequence of *four* data flow models, beginning with a model of the current implementation, as a prelude to detailed design. DeMarco had only "limited" experience with the four-model sequence at the time of publication, and has admitted that the book's treatment of the topic was a mistake. There was no problem in asserting that data flow diagrams could be used to model a current implementation; this is clearly possible and often useful. The problem was that the DeMarco book strongly implied that a *complete* model of the current implementation should *always* be created as a preliminary systems development product. This implication has led many developers into the "current physical tarpit"—a diversion of the development process into time-consuming and unproductive modeling of current implementation details. As in the case of Gane and Sarson, DeMarco was relying heavily on his intuition that the technique would work. The fact that the book was rushed into print within about six months, with limited actual experience of the technique, precluded any possibility that this faulty emphasis would be caught and eliminated.

Despite the problems with the four-model sequence, Yourdon SA has, in fact, validated the intuitions of Gane, Sarson, and DeMarco and has been successful in practice. However, the original technique was advocated with very little regard for conventional channels of approval.

SADT rates much better than Yourdon SA with respect to the caution with which it was introduced. The technique was extensively piloted on a number of large projects for about two years in the mid-1970s, with the cooperation of a client (ITT) well aware of the status of the technique (12). Although there were some omissions that caused its practitioners problems, SADT had conclusively proven itself to be workable in practice. (Again, the reader is referred to the subsection on representational completeness and consistency below for more technical details.)

On the surface, SADT also fares well in terms of peer review, but this is a bit misleading. It is true that two articles referring to SADT appeared in a peer-reviewed journal (10,20). Both articles contain much sound discussion of requirements definition practice and of abstract model-building techniques. However, neither article provides more than sketchy details about the actual use of the SADT notation to model proposed systems. In fact, such details could not have been presented even in principle, since they were trade secrets! In short, neither article contains enough detail to permit a comprehensive technical peer review of SADT per se.

Note that this is not an argument against the technical soundness of SADT—it *is* technically sound—nor does it imply any misrepresentation. However, in this case, SofTech's desire to keep its techniques proprietary was in direct conflict with the requirements for effective peer review, and thus that the 1977 articles, while they may demonstrate the technical soundness of Ross's modeling theories, do not demonstrate the technical soundness of SADT.

In general, the available documentation (in the public domain) on SADT was scattered among a number of journal articles, a situation that prevailed until 1988 (11), and that made even the non-proprietary aspects of SADT somewhat inaccessible to technical review.

The Effectiveness of SA

Is SA effective? In other words, is the use of SA improving the ability of developers to build high-quality systems? To be answerable, such questions must be rephrased in relative terms. Is SA more effective than other requirements definition techniques? Is Yourdon SA more effective, or less effective, than SADT?

It is too early to answer these questions in a definitive way, because, although there have been successful applications of both SADT and Yourdon SA, there is not yet a large enough base of developers seriously using either version of SA, or for that matter *any* organized requirements definition technique. The general reason for this lack of use is the difficulty of technology transfer, with respect to development techniques, in systems development organizations. More specifically, in the case of SA and other graphics-based techniques, it was not until the mid-1980s that effective support for building graphic models, in the form of Computer-Aided Software Engineering (CASE) tools, became available. It may be possible to judge conclusively the effectiveness of SA in five or ten years, but the judgment cannot be made today.

Nevertheless, it is possible to draw some tentative conclusions, of a more limited nature, that *relate* to the relative effectiveness of Yourdon SA versus SADT:

1. Technology transfer for SADT was much more effective than it was for Yourdon SA. The penetration of Yourdon SA was both much broader and much shallower than the penetration of SADT. In other words, many more people learned Yourdon SA than learned SADT, but most of them didn't learn it very well. In contrast, the relatively small number of people who learned SADT learned it thoroughly.

    An organization that wanted to "buy in" to SADT was required to purchase an expensive ($50,000) license, and to agree to close supervision of its development process by SofTech's consultants. SADT training included a strong focus on techniques for quality assurance of the SADT model, and in fact these techniques, rather than the notation, constituted the real trade secret of SADT.

    In sharp contrast, an organization could send a developer to a week-long Yourdon public seminar for under a thousand dollars, and in fact could buy a detailed book on Yourdon SA for about twenty five dollars. The Yourdon books and seminars focused much more heavily on model building than on quality assurance— Yourdon did, in fact, provide books and seminars on quality assurance of SA models, but didn't emphasize the connection in the way SofTech did. This public availability guaranteed that Yourdon SA became much better known than SADT, but also guaranteed that many potential practitioners had only a superficial understanding of the technique.

2. SADT was much more complex, and thus harder to learn, than Yourdon SA. The SADT notation had a fair number of detailed drawing conventions, reflecting its heritage in the automation of the manufacturing process. An SADT model, in fact, is very much like a blueprint in overall appearance. SADT also had a number of variations in its basic symbology to reflect the nuances of interprocess communication. The notational richness of SADT was a mixed blessing. For an experienced analyst, the richness could be effectively harnessed for purposes of communication with other experienced analysts. However, non-analysts could find SADT models forbiddingly complex. [Ralph Bravoco, faced with the inclusion of non-analysts like manufacturing engineers in the modeling phases of the ICAM project, felt compelled to invent simpler descriptive techniques that could be used by non-analysts and then translated into SADT models. (ICAM is discussed in elsewhere in this article).]

    The Yourdon SA notation, on the other hand, used only a few symbols and had only a few drawing conventions. Its basics could be taught in a few minutes to nearly anyone. This made Yourdon DFDs very useful for creating informal, sketchy descriptions of a proposed system that were understandable to end users. This ease of use, however, was not necessarily an advantage for serious model building. It was certainly possible to build a detailed Yourdon SA model of a complex system, but it was not nearly so easy as it appeared at first glance.

3. SADT worked better for real-time systems than Yourdon SA. The initial projects on which SADT proved itself were, in fact, real-time telephony systems. DeMarco had a real-time background, and expected the Yourdon SA technique to be used mostly in the real-time area. However, Yourdon SA was used mostly for business systems, and real-time developers found it of quite limited usefulness. The reason for the greater effectiveness of SADT in the real-time arena was simply that it allowed the independent depiction of control flow and data flow—a critical feature for many real-time systems. (This issue is discussed in more detail below.)

4. Serious Yourdon SA practitioners doing business systems development probably found the technique roughly as useful as SADT business systems developers found their technique. The inability of Yourdon SA to portray control flow was much less of a problem for business systems, where control flow usually could be portrayed as being coincident with data flow. Furthermore, not all Yourdon SA practitioners learned the technique superficially. Organizations that took the initiative to combine Yourdon SA training with extensive follow-up consulting were especially successful in building data-flow-based requirements definition models.

The Flourishing of SofTech, Inc.

Turning from the SA technique to the organizations that promulgated it, the history of SofTech is one of virtually uninterrupted success. The organization grew steadily from the mid 1970s through the mid 1980s, reaching annual revenues of about fifteen million dollars by the early 1980s and about forty million dollars by the mid-1980s. SofTech became a publicly traded company in 1981, largely on the strength of its operating system being selected by IBM as one of three supported by the initial IBM PC. SofTech was also consistently profitable during this time period, its only loss being a planned one taken in conjunction with the formation of its microprocessor division in 1979–1980.

Although SofTech has been a very successful company, SADT has played only a minor role in that success, and that role from the early 1980s has further diminished. At its peak in the late 1970s, SADT generated revenue of only about one million dollars a year. About fifteen SofTech employees provided SADT training and consulting. Since these employees were also assigned to other SofTech projects, the company had the equivalent of perhaps seven to nine full-time SADT instructor/consultants, less than one fourth of Yourdon, Inc.'s instructor/consultant force at the height of its economic success in the early 1980s.

The reason for the relatively minor role of SADT is that SofTech's purpose had never been to promulgate its use as an end in itself. SofTech aimed to form long-term relationships with large clients, to create custom software for these clients, and to assist these clients directly in developing software. SADT was only one of SofTech's proprietary technologies, all of which were considered simply means to the end of forming client relationships. The ICAM project, for example, which was discussed earlier, aimed to help the participants implement CAM, and only secondarily involved the use of a subset of SADT. As another example, SofTech devoted a large portion of its resources to the development of compiler technology; the company was one of the competitors for the design of Ada, and developed the first Ada compiler.

The ICAM project was also the cause of a further diminution of the importance of SADT. As a condition of its participation in ICAM, SofTech had had to agree to place a subset of SADT, called IDEF0 (13), in the public domain. Although it omitted the notation and techniques based on the data version of the SA box, IDEF0 shared much of its content with SADT. SofTech provided IDEF0 training to the ICAM consortium companies, and when the ICAM final report describing IDEF0 was issued in 1981, SofTech began providing IDEF0 training, with no licensing requirement, to any client willing to pay the price of the training. This created a problem with respect to SADT. The portion of SADT which overlapped IDEF0 could no longer be treated as a trade secret, and continuing to sell SADT licences would have meant dividing the SADT training materials into trade-secret and non-trade-secret portions. This was considered impractical, and SofTech ceased to sell SADT licenses and to regard SADT as a trade secret in the early 1980s.

To add insult to injury, the publication of the IDEF0 materials and the removal of SADT from the trade secret category meant that ex-SofTech employees could, and did, become competitors of SofTech in providing SADT and IDEF0 training and consulting. As the 1980s progressed, SADT became a product that SofTech provided to clients on request but ceased to market aggressively.

The Flourishing and Faltering of Yourdon Inc.

Through 1982, the story of Yourdon, Inc. is also a success story. It had grown steadily from its founding in 1974, reaching annual revenues of nearly ten million dollars in the early 1980s, and had been consistently profitable. Toward the end of this period, Yourdon had an instructional staff, counting both contractors and employees, of about forty people.

Yourdon, Inc.'s income was nearly all from SA and structured design (SD) training and book sales, with a relatively small amount from follow-up consulting. The primary profit producer was the public seminar. The break-even point for a standard week-long public seminar was about six students, with additional registrations being almost pure profit. During the late 1970s and the early 1980s, Yourdon was routinely running public seminars with double or even triple this attendance.

Yourdon's dependence on training income was not the result of deliberate management policy but of lack of success in diversifying. Ed Yourdon was committed to making Yourdon, Inc. a much larger organization, and saw the production of software as a vehicle for growth. In the late 1970s and early 1980s, Yourdon, Inc. was awarded contracts to produce C compilers for various clients. These projects failed to produce acceptable products, and were later described by Ed Yourdon as "disasters." Yourdon, Inc.'s ventures into the software area not only were unprofitable, but also absorbed profits from the training business. It is a testimony to the strength of the training operation that the company, despite these problems, remained profitable over this time period.

Yourdon, Inc.'s attempts to diversify did not have the full support of the management team. In particular, opposition came from Tom Lister, who had begun as an instructor and was soon managing the instructor staff, which had previously reported to Bill Plauger. Lister argued that Yourdon should reinvest its profits in development of the instructor staff and in research on development methods rather than in software ventures. This difference in philosophy between Yourdon and Lister was to have very serious consequences for the company a few years later, as will be seen shortly.

The Yourdon success story began to falter in late 1982. From 1983 until the sale of the company to DeVry, Inc. in 1986, revenue growth stalled, and small profits alternated with small losses. The symptoms of the problem were very obvious. From 1983 to 1986, both the ratio of public seminars to in-house seminars, and the average attendance at public seminars, declined.

There was no single cause of Yourdon's financial problems. The novelty value of SA, and thus the willingness of companies to send "scouts" to public seminars, certainly declined as the 1980s progressed. In addition, competition for Yourdon SA training and consulting business steadily increased. (As mentioned earlier, Yourdon, Inc. had competition from the beginning; the first book on Yourdon SA, by Gane and Sarson, was issued by a competing organization they had formed in 1977.) Since Yourdon SA was in the public domain, anyone was free to create training materials, short of an actual copyright violation, and to become a competitor of Yourdon, Inc. in providing Yourdon SA training and consulting. Former employees and contractors continually became competitors, a problem that SofTech eventually experienced but that had plagued Yourdon, Inc. from much earlier. Finally, a management change in 1982, which will be discussed later in this article, almost certainly contributed to Yourdon's problems.

Yourdon As a Maverick Organization

Yourdon, Inc. was, in many respects, a maverick organization. It retained much of the flavor of the 1960s, as befits its heritage as the successor of Larry Constantine's Institute. (Constantine, for his part, continued to provide a maverick role model. He left the systems development field in the mid 1970s, became a family therapist, wrote several highly regarded behavioral science texts, and has only recently once again become a software development consultant.) Yourdon instructors for the most part considered themselves not as employees but as members of an intellectual community, united by their commitment to SA and their evangelical zeal to bring effective systems development techniques to the "great unwashed masses." The fact that teaching SA produced profits for Yourdon, and paid their salaries, was a pleasant but somewhat incidental aftereffect of the intellectual adventure in which they were engaged. Yourdon instructors were highly individualistic, and in fact, by normal corporate standards, were utterly unmanageable. A few vignettes will serve to illustrate the character of Yourdon, Inc. in the late 1970s and the early 1980s:

> In the summer of 1980, a Yourdon instructor recruitment ad appeared in *ComputerWorld*. It included the question: In how many languages can you say "Holiday Inn"?. It also asked the identity of Bohm and Jacopini (authors of an important early paper on structured programming theory) and offered the suggestion that they were members of an Italian bobsled team.

> One of Yourdon's Bay Area instructors was the third of his family line, bearing the same name as his father and his grandfather. To demonstrate his lack of continuity with his father's generation and its values, he rejected his name except for the suffix, and insisted on referring to himself, and being referred to, as III (pronounced "three"). III was very unorthodox in

his appearance and overall lifestyle. He would typically cause some consternation when he appeared at a bank or insurance company to teach a Yourdon seminar, but his personality and his teaching skills soon won people over.

Yourdon instructor meetings were held once a year at "Galactic Headquarters" in New York City. The meetings were basically intellectual love feasts. The instructors would spend their days in joyous technical arguments (referred to as "N-way shoutdowns") which would continue through dinner and turn boozy and philosophical as the evening progressed. As a diversion from technical discussions, they would occasionally spend an hour or two hurling good-natured abuse at management. As the 1980s progressed, the abuse continued, but did not remain good natured. As Yourdon's problems intensified, instructor meetings were postponed or cancelled. Although the motivation was largely financial, some instructors expressed the solemn conviction that management was trying to prevent all the instructors from gathering to forestall a mutiny!

The Yourdon User Group

The Yourdon User Group (YUG) was founded in November 1978 to provide a forum for SA practitioners to meet each other and the Yourdon instructor staff. The annual YUG meetings featured SA "success stories," and reports on advances in SA theory by staff and sometimes by practitioners.

The YUG meetings soon became a problem for Yourdon's management. The attendees wanted to hear from well-known Yourdon instructors, who, as time progressed, were more and more likely to be ex-Yourdon instructors turned competitors, who attended the meetings to lure away Yourdon clients.

The membership took matters into its own hands in 1984, voting overwhelmingly to disaffiliate from Yourdon and to become an independent organization called the Structured Development Forum. The SDF has remained active and has continued to hold periodic meetings.

Yourdon, Inc. Becomes a Conventional Business

In 1982, Ed Yourdon decided to retire from day-to-day management of Yourdon's affairs and to appoint a successor as president of the company. The logical candidates were Lister, who was Executive Vice-President for Professional Services (in effect, he was the instructor-in-chief), and Herb Morrow, who was Executive Vice-President for Sales and Marketing. However, the earlier disputes between Yourdon and Lister sealed the outcome. Morrow was appointed as president in September 1982, an event which a large part of the instructor staff regarded as a disaster for the company.

Whatever their individual differences with Morrow, there was an overriding cultural factor which virtually guaranteed this reaction by the instructors. *Morrow was not a member of the SA intellectual community*. He had never served as an instructor, and had neither training nor experience in systems development methods. The instructors simply did not trust him, either by background or by sympathies, to be a faithful custodian of the SA discipline.

The accession of Morrow marked the beginning of Yourdon's transition to a much more conventional, business-oriented organization. It also marked the beginning of a steady erosion of technical talent. The most prominent group of defectors included DeMarco, Lister, Steve McMenamin and John Palmer (co-authors of an important SA technical advance which will be described in a later section), and James and Suzanne

Robertson, who had been co-heads of the instructor staff following Lister. In April of 1983, the group founded the Atlantic Systems Guild in New York City.

The Guild was a conscious attempt to recover the lost spirit of Yourdon, Inc. Since the members felt that Ed Yourdon's desire to enlarge the company was the root of its subsequent problems (DeMarco felt that management "ate the seed corn"), a guiding principle was to be that the organization remain a fixed size. True to its Constantine–Yourdon heritage, the Guild soon grew a publishing arm, Dorset House Publishing, run by ex-Yourdon Press director (and Lister's wife) Wendy Eakin. Although legally a separate entity, Dorset House has shared the Guild's Manhattan's premises since 1986.

There is no way to prove that Yourdon would have done better under Lister's management than it did under Morrow's. However, it seems more than coincidence that Yourdon's policy with respect to training during its profitable years was set by instructor-managers (Yourdon, Plauger, and Lister), and that its years of problems were under a more conventional manager. Certainly, there are many ex-Yourdon instructors for whom the earlier years have a touch of Camelot.

A Technical Evaluation of Yourdon SA and SADT

The process modeling aspects of Yourdon SA and SADT will be compared based on three criteria; representational completeness and consistency, complexity control mechanisms, and operational semantics.

Representational Completeness and Consistency

Both SADT and Yourdon SA are representationally incomplete. However, the incompleteness is of a very different character. The activity version SADT provides a set of representations for the schematic level of a process-oriented requirements definition model—it is possible to represent processes, inputs and outputs of processes, control of one process by another, and mechanisms by which processes are implemented. (See the early part of this article for an explanation and illustration of the SADT activity model.) However, there is no explicit mechanism for defining stored data within a process model, nor for defining the primitives of the process model, namely the data structures of inputs and outputs and the logic of lowest-level processes. These were deliberate omissions. Ross had provided a dual SADT data model with an explicit representation of data objects, which together with the activity model provided, he felt, a complete schematic representation of requirements. Also, he felt that SADT was compatible with a variety of existing languages for defining primitives. However, the omissions left SADT practitioners, who were generally unwilling to build SADT data models and didn't see how they could be used to represent stored data, scrambling to find effective mechanisms for representing data storage, data structure, and process logic. Some of these practitioners, in fact, adopted the Yourdon SA mechanisms of "data dictionaries" and "minispecifications" for describing data structure and process logic, respectively.

Like SADT, Yourdon SA provides a set of process model representations. Unlike SADT, the process model provides for the representation of stored data within a DFD. However, including a stored data symbol in the process model introduces an inconsistency in the representation of data flows. Data flows are used both to represent interprocess data connections and to represent data connections between processes and data stores. Since a data store is a passive collection of persistent data items, it cannot produce and consume data in the same way that a process does. The problem is solved, for flows from

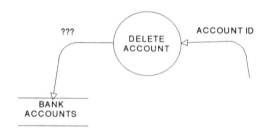

FIGURE 6   A flow definition problem.

a store into a process, by specifying that the flow represents the *net* flow of data from storage as selected by the process. However, there is no simple solution of this kind for data flows from a process to storage. Consider Figure 6, which shows a process that deletes individual bank accounts from a stored collection of bank accounts. The flow from the process to the store cannot be said to *contain* the data that is deleted without violating the basic idea of the flow as a data pipeline. Nor can the flow be omitted without causing consistency-checking problems in the model. This inconsistency was never satisfactorily resolved by Yourdon SA.*

The DeMarco version of Yourdon SA also provided a specific textual syntax for data structure, and both DeMarco and Gane and Sarson described specific tabular and pseudocode conventions for representing process logic, making Yourdon SA in this sense more complete than SADT. However, neither DeMarco nor Gane and Sarson provided for representing control flow or mechanism as connections to or from a DFD process, and in fact representation of these aspects of a system was specifically prohibited, a prohibition rooted in the nature of Constantine's data flow graph. In the case of the "mechanism arrow," it can be argued that the omission was legitimate, since the description of mechanisms should not be part of a requirements definition. (However, the situation is really not quite this simple, as discussed in the section on complexity control mechanisms below.) The argument for omission of control flows is much more dubious. Aside from the simple assertion that the graphic SA model should represent the problem solely from the point of view of the data, DeMarco's argument for omission of control flows is that they are "procedural," presumably meaning that they introduce arbitrary, implementation-dependent details. Consider, however, Figure 7, and assume that all the data needed for producing paychecks is present in the data store, but that the supervisor must okay the actual production. The flow from the Supervisor to the Produce Paychecks process thus contains no data and is illegal in Yourdon SA terms.[†] However, it is not clear why the existence of a cause-and-effect relationship between the supervisor and the paycheck production process is any more "procedural," i.e., any less of a requirement, than

---

*A possible resolution lies in combining Yourdon SA and SADT ideas. The arrows connecting the process to the data store can be considered to be data creation (or modification) and data accessing *activities* associated with the *process*. It is still possible to associate data structures with these activity arrows; the data structures represent the targets of the activities rather than inputs and outputs from the data store.

[†]SADT would show the supervisor's OK as a control input (also referred to as a dominant constraint) to the process box. Actually, the rules for producing paychecks also act as a dominant constraint on the process and could likewise be shown as a control input. However, Ross's SA modeling rules provide for omitting "obvious" inputs such as this.

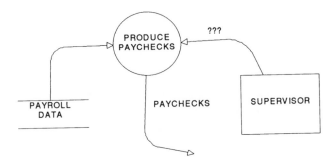

FIGURE 7   A problem in depicting control.

the data structure of a paycheck or the logic by which paychecks are produced. True, the program graph that was the basis of the Yourdon DFD can represent any *computation* in purely data flow terms, but a *system* requirement is not always reducible to a *computational* requirement.

In summary, both SADT and Yourdon SA are representationally incomplete in different ways. The incompleteness of SADT seems to stem from the difficulties of reducing theory to practice, while the incompleteness (and, in one case, the inconsistency) of Yourdon SA seems the result of the pitfalls of assembling a method in a pragmatic, bottom-up fashion.

Complexity Control Mechanisms

Yourdon SA and SADT both provide hierarchical decomposition as a complexity control strategy—any portion of a proposed system can be represented as a single process at one level of the hierarchy, and then decomposed into a network of processes at the next lower level. (Gane and Sarson limit this decomposition to a single level.) SADT also provides two additional complexity control strategies (21,22), both relying on the building of multiple, interrelated hierarchies.

The first SADT complexity control strategy involves the creation of multiple *views* of the system. This strategy could be used to synthesize requirements information gathered from users with different perspectives on a proposed system. In Figure 8, two interrelated views are shown. View X depicts the system as being composed of functions A, B, and C, while View Y depicts the system as being composed of functions C, D, and E. The decomposition of each function is shown only once, which is accomplishing by cross-referencing function C from View Y to View X. The overall requirement is for a system with functions A, B, C, D, and E, in other words, for the union of the two models.

The second complexity control strategy involves creation of additional hierarchical models, parts of which represent *mechanisms* for the implementation of parts of the original requirements model. As mentioned above, it could be argued that mechanisms are part of the design process and have no part in requirements definition. However, consider the following scenario: an application is to be developed that will run on a network of newly developed machines, machines that currently have operating systems but no other systems software. Implementing the system will thus require development not only of the application software but also of an interprocessor data communication system. From the point of view of the application problem, the creation of the data communication system is a design issue. However, the development of this system, from an internal point of

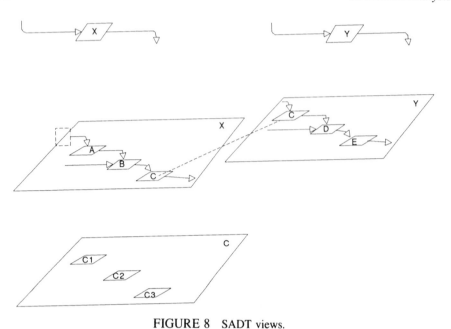

FIGURE 8   SADT views.

view, involves a requirements definition activity. Although software design is often described as the elaboration or refinement of a requirements definition model, it is clearly wrong in this case to "refine" the application by incorporating data communications components. One alternative is to model the overall system as two interrelated SADT requirements definition hierarchies, as illustrated by Figure 9. Each use of part of a model as a mechanism is shown as a mechanism arrow imbedded in the "using" model. These arrows do not really describe implementation details—they simply cross-reference the various requirements models needed for the total implementation.

Although SADT thus provided three complexity control strategies to Yourdon SA's one, the advantages were somewhat neutralized in practice by the lack of automated support for the model building process. It was difficult to manage the development of even a *single* hierarchy of diagrams on a manual basis. The problems of managing multiple

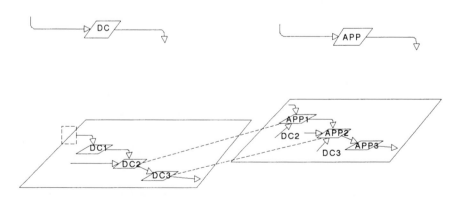

FIGURE 9   SADT mechanism hierarchies.

interrelated hierarchies ensured that multiple views were avoided by many SADT practitioners, and that mechanism hierarchies were little used.

Operational Semantics

The definition of an *operational semantics* for a modeling notation permits a model to be interpreted as a *machine* for producing outputs from inputs. In the case of a data flow model that "has state," that is, that incorporates stored data, an operational semantics necessarily introduces the concept of time, since stored data must be present before it can be used and thus the flow of data within the model must be time sequenced.

Published descriptions of both SADT and Yourdon SA disavowed an operational semantics as being inconsistent with the abstract, requirements definition character of the respective models. Strictly speaking, in fact, the term "data flow diagram" as applied to the Yourdon SA graphic model is somewhat inappropriate, since it implies the existence of an operational semantics which was never really defined. For both versions of SA, it is more appropriate to say that processes are required or constrained to consume certain inputs and to produce certain outputs than to say that data "flows." (SofTech actually did some research on an operational semantics for SADT in the late 1970s. However, SofTech felt that implementing an operational semantics would have required more automated support of the development process than was available at the time, and never incorporated the research results into SADT.) The absence of an operational semantics caused problems on two fronts. First, requirements for real-time systems often involve not only control flow, which SADT could handle although Yourdon SA could not, but explicit time sequencing of activities, which neither Yourdon SA nor SADT could handle. Second, an opportunity for model validation was missed, since an operational semantics need not imply a commitment to implement a system according to the operational interpretation of the requirements model. The operational interpretation can, instead, be used as a *quality control* strategy. In other words, developers can "play through" a requirements model, using scenarios, to detect requirements definition problems.

SA practitioners, in fact, often did "play through" models, using their own versions of an operational semantics. However, the lack of an official operational semantics could cause problems. For example, practitioners of Yourdon SA vehemently disagreed as to whether data flows represented continuously available data, or data that was provided at discrete intervals.

LATER EXTENSIONS

Introduction

In this section, I will discuss the divergence of SA from its sources. This involves both the spinoff of organizations from SofTech and Yourdon, Inc., and also various extensions of the "mainstream" SA techniques discussed earlier. The extensions developed as SA was joined to, or absorbed, other methods to produce hybrids with significant differences from the original technique.

In the case of SADT, the most significant extension involved the joining of the activity (process) modeling approach with an entity-relationship based data modeling technique, to form the IDEF techniques. There were a number of other hybrid methods, but these were not widely disseminated among systems developers and thus had very limited influence on practice.

In the case of Yourdon, there were several important extensions. Yourdon SA was joined with an entity–relationship-based modeling technique, with a technique for building process models based on stimulus–response analysis, and with a technique for using state machines to describe the real-time dynamics of a system. Most recently, a number of hybrid techniques merging Yourdon SA with object-oriented development have been put forward.

Finally, I will briefly discuss the emergence of Computer-Aided Software Engineering (CASE) products to support SA.

Spinoff Organizations

Pride of place in this category must go to Chris Gane and Trish Sarson's Improved Systems Technologies (IST). IST was founded in 1977, early in the lifetime of SA; its founders were co-creators of the Yourdon variant of SA, and authored the first publication on the subject; and IST became a relatively large and successful company.

Chris Gane was raised and educated in England. He took a Master's degree in Physics at Cambridge, and worked for IBM in London until emigrating to New York in 1973. Like Constantine, Yourdon, and DeMarco he did time as an independent consultant before joining Yourdon's fledgling organization in 1975. Trish Sarson is also an emigrant from Britain. Her degree in Zoology was from London University, and she also worked for IBM London, moved to New York, and joined Yourdon in 1975.

Gane and Sarson's role in the creation of Yourdon SA, and the differences between their approach and that of DeMarco were described earlier. After founding IST and publishing their book, they began selling SA seminars in the fall of 1977. The business was a quick success; when acquired by McDonnell-Douglas in 1981, IST had about a dozen instructors and a half-dozen sales representatives.

The fact that Yourdon SA was in the public domain meant that, in addition to IST, there were many other spinoffs. A fairly constant stream of Yourdon employees and contractors left the fold in the late 1970s and early 1980s to go into the training and consulting field on their own behalf. In most cases, what these entrepreneurs taught was identical to, or involved fairly minor (and generally unpublished) revisions of, Yourdon SA, and their organizations remained sole proprietorships or small companies.

With the accession of Herb Morrow to Yourdon's presidency in 1982, the rate of attrition increased. The deserters included DeMarco and several other well-known Yourdon employees who founded the Atlantic Systems Guild in 1983. These matters were discussed in detail in an earlier section.

Another important spinoff from Yourdon, Inc., involved, not consulting and training, but software products to support SA. Cadre Technologies, Inc. was founded in 1983 by a group that included ex-Yourdon design instructor Lou Mazzuchelli. Cadre was to become an important organization in the area of CASE with its Teamwork™ product. It should also be noted that Ed Yourdon himself severed his connections with the company when it was sold to DeVry, Inc. in 1986.

Turning to SofTech, it is important to remember that many SADT details were trade secrets until the early 1980s. This fact severely limited the possibilities for SofTech employees, in the earlier years, to form spinoff consulting and training organizations. However, with the emergence of the IDEF methods, created by the U.S. Air Force-sponsored ICAM project, in 1981, and the "declassification" of SADT, employees began leaving SofTech, the Air Force, and the other ICAM contractors, and going into competition.

As in the case of Yourdon, Inc., most of these spinoffs resulted in proprietorships or small consulting-and-training firms providing SADT or IDEF services. For example, Dennis Wisnosky, who was the ICAM project manager for the Air Force, founded Wizdom Systems, which provides IDEF products and services. In some cases, ICAM contractors other than SofTech began offering training and consulting, as was the case for D. Appleton & Co. (DACOM), a principal developer of the IDEF data modeling technique. SofTech also directly spawned a CASE spinoff; Al Irvine left in 1984 to found a company, Eclectic Solutions, that markets an SADT CASE tool.

The Growth of Data Modeling

"Data modeling" is sometimes used in a generic sense, to describe any model of the "things" involved in a systems development problem. "Data modeling" is also used in opposition to "information modeling" to describe building a model of physical data organization as opposed to a model of the significance of the data. I use "data modeling" here in the first, generic, sense.

To describe the organization of a database, a designer must indicate which collections of data (often called files or segments) will be included, and also which navigation paths (e.g., "keys" in one file that point to records in another file) exist between the collections. An important method for producing an optimal organization of this type is referred to as *normalization*; it was part of a comprehensive approach to data structure and access developed by E. F. Codd of IBM in the late 1960s (23).

Some database designers voiced the complaint that the normalization procedure focused too much on the mathematical structure and properties of data rather than its significance. These dissenters favored a modeling procedure that has a rather different starting point, although it can be made compatible in its final form with the Codd approach. Rather than starting with detailed data structures, it identifies *entities*—that is, types of things about which data is to be kept—and *relationships*—that is, real-world associations among the entities. An influential graphic version of this entity–relationship (ER) model was introduced by Peter Chen in 1976 (24).

In parallel with these developments in data modeling, an important technological change was occurring in the late 1960s and early 1970s. With the proliferation of disk storage technology, and the emergence of software products called database management systems, the importance of databases to many organizations grew dramatically. Information, or more precisely, information in rapidly accessible, machine-readable form, began to be regarded as a corporate resource. Stored data was seen as having characteristics much less variable than the characteristics of the processing systems that upgraded and used the data. Rather than designing data storage to meet the requirements of a processing system, it became conceivable to design processing systems to meet the requirements of enterprise-level databases. The information requirements for these databases could be explored by *data analysts* and expressed using entity–relationship modeling.

These ideas about the increased importance of data modeling were fostered by the needs of corporate data analysts, but were not restricted to such applications. It was a relatively small step from thinking of an entity as *something about which data must be stored* to thinking of an entity as *something important to the system under development*. In other words, an entity–relationship model can be thought of as a perfectly general requirements definition tool.

Data Modeling Extensions: IDEF1 and IDEF1X

As a condition of being the prime contractor on the U.S. Air Force (USAF) ICAM architecture project, SofTech was required to provide a public-domain systems development method to be called IDEF (ICAM definition). IDEF was to be based on SofTech's proprietary SADT technique, and was to become a model-building standard for the project. (The ICAM project was discussed earlier) SofTech was reluctant to put *any* of SADT in the public domain; putting *all* of SADT in the public domain was a special problem, because it would result in the loss of SofTech's ability to sell SADT licenses.

Fortunately for SofTech, the USAF handily solved the problem by deciding that it didn't *want* all of SADT. In particular, the notation and techniques based on the data version of the SA box, along with the adjunct to the SADT activity model that modeled dynamics (time sequencing), were rejected. The activity modeling subset of SADT was renamed IDEF0; the data and dynamics components of IDEF were developed by other ICAM contractors, and were called IDEF1 and IDEF2, respectively. IDEF1 was replaced in 1985 by an extended version called IDEF1X (25,26).

As discussed earlier, the data version of the SA box used boxes to represent data objects (or, more plainly, "things") relevant to the system being modeled, and arrows to represent activities associated with these data objects. For example, consider Figure 10, showing the data objects Customer, Product_Type, and Order, and some of the associated activities. The interconnection can be interpreted as follows: The activity that creates an order involves access to a customer and a product type. Models of this type are perfectly well-defined. However, most systems developers found them counterintuitive and hard to use.

The USAF, and the other ICAM contractors, favored a data modeling technique based on entities and relationships over the SADT data model. Hughes Aircraft and DACOM therefore collaborated to produce IDEF1 in the late 1970s. Figure 11 shows the IDEF1 version of Figure 10. The graphic differences are minimal, but the interpretation of the connections between the boxes is quite different. For example the connection between Customer and Order can be interpreted as follows: A customer places zero or more orders (the diamond means "zero or more"). Similarly, the other connection can be read as: A product type fills zero or more orders. Despite the fact that relationships may carry activity-like names, activities do not appear explicitly in an IDEF1 model; rather, the relationships describe *associations* that are the result of the activities. The attributes (items

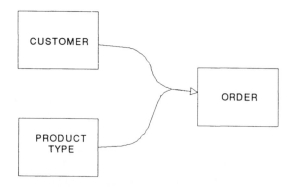

FIGURE 10   A partial SADT data model.

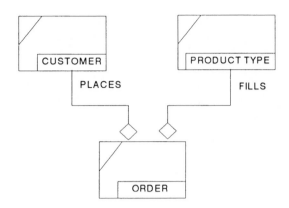

FIGURE 11   An IDEF1 data model.

of data) associated with each entity are also part of a complete IDEF1 model; for example, the customer name, address, and phone number might be attributes of Customer.

At least some members of the ICAM project team, no doubt influenced by the origins of data modeling, initially regarded IDEF1 as a technique to be used for the *design* phase of systems development. However, it gradually became clear that IDEF1 could also be used for requirements definition. Although it was perhaps more acceptable than the data modeling component of SADT, systems analysts (as opposed to data analysts) never accepted IDEF1 as a requirements definition technique to the extent that they accepted IDEF0.

Data Modeling Extensions: Yourdon SA and Data Modeling

Yourdon, Inc. was aware that the potential clientele for its training and consulting services included data analysts as well as software developers. Matt Flavin therefore was added to the Yourdon staff in 1980 to create seminars in the area of data modeling and related topics. Flavin had been working since the early 1970s as a teacher and consultant in database administration. The Yourdon, Inc. database seminars, especially Flavin's seminar called Information Modeling, were quite successful, though never as popular as the SA and SD seminars; about a half dozen instructors taught database seminars at the height of Yourdon's success. Flavin's monograph *Fundamental Concepts of Information Modeling* was published by Yourdon Press in 1981 (27). (Matt Flavin died in 1984.)

Flavin viewed ER modeling as a full-fledged requirements definition technique. Flavin's data model was an extension of Chen's, and is illustrated in Figure 12. The diamond is borrowed from the Chen model and, rather than a labeled line, is used to represent a relationship. The arrowhead pointing toward Order indicates that orders are dependent—creating an order requires a pre-existent customer and product type. (IDEF1 has no direct way to represent such a dependency, but the later extension, IDEF1X, would represent it by modifying Figure 11 to show Order as a box with rounded corners.)

Although Yourdon, Inc.'s database seminars were intended for a different audience than the SA seminars, the subject of ER modeling as a potential addition to SA soon engaged the attention of Yourdon staff members, who began actively investigating the possible links between an ER model and a data flow model.

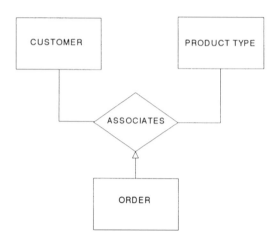

FIGURE 12   Chen/Flavin data model.

It should be noted that both the DeMarco and the Gane and Sarson variants of Yourdon SA had incorporated data modeling techniques from the beginning. However, these techniques were subordinate to the techniques for building process models. They were ways of reorganizing the stored data within an already-built data flow diagram, based on the requirements of the processes for access to stored data, and making use of Codd's normalization techniques.

The ER diagramming techniques potentially provided a data model that was not subordinate to the process model, and that provided an independent perspective on requirements. An independently constructed ER model could provide a framework for partitioning data stores so that they corresponded to data objects (entities)—this partitioning could be *imposed* as a data flow diagram was being constructed, as an alternative to *deriving* an optimal data store organization from process model details. The exact nature of the relationship between the ER model and the data flow model was the subject of much controversy within Yourdon, Inc. At one extreme, Flavin stated on occasion that ER modeling made data flow modeling unnecessary. At the other extreme, SA traditionalists doubted the relevance of ER modeling to system or software (as opposed to database) requirements modeling.

A middle-of-the-road camp ultimately prevailed. The Flavin ER model began to be introduced into SA seminars, not with the same emphasis given to the data flow diagram, but as an independent, complementary requirements definition model. It appeared in Real-Time SA seminars written during 1981–1983; in an end-user oriented SA seminar written in 1983; and finally in the mainstream Yourdon SA curriculum in 1985. However, as in the case of IDEF0, many systems analysts were resistant to the idea of an independent, requirements-level data model.

Event Modeling Extensions: Essential Systems Analysis

John Palmer graduated from Cornell as an economist in 1976, and worked as a systems analyst for a bank holding company until 1978. In that year he was persuaded to join Yourdon, Inc. by Steve McMenamin. McMenamin had studied engineering at Cornell, and had been a staff member at both MIT and Cornell. In 1977 he attended a seminar taught by Ed Yourdon and was promptly recruited as a Yourdon instructor.

McMenamin and Palmer were among the first teachers of the new five-day SA seminar written by DeMarco and also taught his older SADW (SA/SD combination) seminar. They both soon became absorbed by the problem of *logicalization*. This refers to the transition between the first two stages of the DeMarco four-model sequence, that is, between a model of the current implementation and a model of its underlying logic. DeMarco's approach did not provide detailed guidelines for making this transition, and McMenamin and Palmer set out to remedy this shortcoming. Their efforts led first to their rewriting of SADW to include a more detailed logicalization procedure, then to their creation of a specialized logicalization seminar called Advanced Structured Analysis, and finally, in 1984, to the appearance of their book *Essential Systems Analysis* (28) published by Yourdon Press.

McMenamin and Palmer came to realize that the problem of logicalization was intimately tied to an identification of the properties of physical models (descriptions of implementations) and of logical models (descriptions of the underlying requirements). This distinction was commonplace in systems development. However, the distinction was typically made by giving examples, or by saying that physical models described the "how" while logical models described the "what," rather than by a precise delineation of the differences.

McMenamin and Palmer ultimately created a detailed theory of the properties of an *essential* (logical) model to support their logicalization procedure. An essential model is an idealized requirements model, with its details restricted to those required by a hypothetical *perfect implementation technology*. The processes within this model are *responses to events* (stimuli) arising in the system's environment, and the data stores are representations of system-related entities. (McMenamin and Palmer accepted Flavin's concept of the identification of entities as an independent modeling activity, although they put little emphasis on techniques for such identification.)

McMenamin and Palmer's event–response modeling was incorporated into the version of the Yourdon real-time SA seminar developed in 1983, and into the 1985 version of the main Yourdon SA curriculum.

One major effect of the introduction of these ideas is that they sounded the death knell to the concept that Yourdon SA was a *top-down* model building approach. Modeling by top-down decomposition involves breaking a single process into a small number of subprocesses, breaking each subprocess into a small number of sub-subprocesses, and so on. SADT had always advocated top-down decomposition as a model-building technique, as had the Gane and Sarson SA approach. However, the DeMarco version of SA, while not neglecting top-down decomposition, actually placed more emphasis on model building examples that began at an intermediate level of detail. Nevertheless, the Yourdon SA community professed a strong allegiance to the "top-down" principle. This was probably due to a failure to differentiate the top-down *organization* of a completed SA model, which was a natural outcome of the hierarchical character of the data flow diagram, from the actual *procedure* for building a data flow model, which could just as well start at the middle or at the bottom of the hierarchy and work upward. In any case, McMenamin and Palmer's approach asserted that a logical SA model was fundamentally a network of responses rather than a hierarchy of functions, and this idea caused a good deal of controversy before it was ultimately accepted.

State Modeling Extensions: Yourdon Real-Time SA

"Real time" has been used in a variety of senses. I use it here as a synonym of the less-familiar term "reactive" which was introduced by David Harel and Amir Pneuli. A reactive system is one that maintains an ongoing interaction with its environment, accepting inputs and producing outputs as it runs, and changing its behavior dynamically as it receives inputs. In contrast, a traditional batch-oriented business system begins running with all its inputs initially present, and its behavior is deterministic from that point on. The Yourdon staff members principally involved in the real-time extensions of Yourdon SA were Ira Morrow, Steve Mellor, and Paul Ward.

Morrow held masters degrees in theoretical chemistry (Indiana University 1974) and in computer science (Columbia 1978). He had served in the Peace Corps in Ethiopia, worked for NASA on commercialization of space-program technology, and from 1976 to 1978 was a systems developer for a Wall Street firm. Morrow's Wall Street experience left him aghast at the lack of professional discipline among the "great unwashed masses" of systems developers, a realization that had come upon Ed Yourdon under similar circumstances a number of years before. It is thus not surprising that, having discovered some Yourdon Press books, he soon joined the Yourdon, Inc. instructor corps. He initially taught SD seminars, and occasionally SA seminars. Morrow had learned data modeling theory at Columbia, and had designed databases on Wall Street. He was thus a perfect candidate for the database seminars, and had begun teaching these as well subsequent to Matt Flavin's arrival in 1980.

Mellor had graduated with a degree in computer science from the University of Essex in England in 1974. He had subsequently worked for CERN in Geneva on compiler technology and on accelerator control systems. He emigrated to the United States in 1977, joined the staff at Lawrence Berkeley Laboratories, and soon became head of the software tools group. In this capacity, he provided assistance to a number of systems development projects, among them a project, headed by Sally Shlaer, to build a control system for the electric power to the BART subway tracks. Shlaer and Mellor attempted to use data flow diagrams to model the system, but were unsuccessful. They ultimately decided that the key to modeling the system was to understand the data, and used data modeling techniques heavily. Mellor joined Yourdon, Inc. in late 1980. He was recruited by former college roommate and current Yourdon instructor Meilir Page-Jones.

Ward had received a doctorate in physical chemistry from Cornell in 1971. Subsequently, he had run the computer facility at the Cornell Chemistry Department in 1972 and 1973, focusing mainly on real-time data acquisition from laboratory instruments. He had then worked for eight years as an analyst, project manager, and data base administrator for a manufacturing division of Borg-Warner. Ward was recruited to the Yourdon instructor force in 1980. He had been hired as a database instructor, but had initially begun teaching SADW and the five-day DeMarco SA course instead, and a bit later had worked with Morrow on a consulting assignment involving ER modeling, and with Mellor on a real-time consulting project.

The involvement of Morrow in real-time SA began because, as mentioned, Yourdon SA was not nearly as satisfactory to real-time systems developers as to business systems developers. As a result, some aerospace and industrial clients, encouraged by various instructors, pressured Yourdon, Inc.'s management to modify the seminars to better accommodate real-time development. The company rather reluctantly yielded to this pressure; in late 1980 Ira Morrow was assigned to create a real-time version of the five-day SA seminar. Morrow's modifications to the SA course reflected his general convictions about the appropriate way to do SA modeling, as well as his charter to accommodate real-time development. He included the use of ER modeling as a complement to data flow modeling, and dropped the DeMarco four-model sequence (Modeling was to begin with a logical model, not a physical one). In terms of specifically "real-time" modifications, Morrow introduced the substantial use of *state transition diagrams** in conjunction with data flow diagrams.

State diagrams are useful because a real-time system typically undergoes qualitative changes in behavior as it interacts with its environment. For example, a chemical process control system might manipulate valves while a reaction vessel is filling, then manipulate a heater to maintain a steady rise in temperature once the vessel is full. Figure 13 is a partial state transition diagram that can be thought of either as representing the behavior of the vessel and its contents, or as representing the *tracking* of this behavior by the control system. The rectangles represent *states*, the arrow represents a *transition* between states, and the label on the arrow indicates what caused the transition.

The connection between a state transition diagram and its associated data flow diagram is that different processes are active during different states. For example, if Figures 13 and 14 are used together to represent a control system, the Manipulate Valve process is active in the Filling Tank state and the Control Heating process is active in the Heating Contents state. Although different in details, this combination of diagrams has an effect similar to that of the SADT activity model with its control flow, since the control of processes can be represented independently of the inputs and outputs of the processes.

Morrow taught his new course to a number of real-time clients during 1981 and 1982, and it was generally well-received. However, Morrow became very frustrated, because excessive road work left no time to make urgently needed modifications to the course. The situation came to a head in the fall of 1982 with Morrow's abrupt resignation. With no staff instructor who was prepared to teach the real-time SA course, Morrow finally was persuaded to return to teach once more so that his designated replacement, Paul Ward, could observe the procedure. However, scheduling problems intervened;

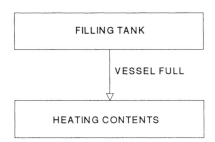

FIGURE 13   A state transition diagram.

---

*There is a version of the SADT data model that is a close relative of the state transition diagram. In this variation, the boxes represent "state of things" rather than "things," and the arrows represent activities associated with the changes of state. This version, however, was not used by many SADT modelers, and never entered the SADT mainstream. Note that the activity, data, and state versions of SADT all use the same graphic notation, a property aptly described by Clement McGowan as "fixed syntax, variable semantics."

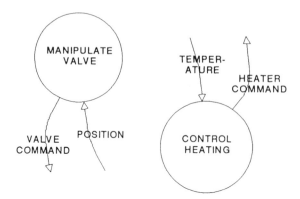

FIGURE 14   Processes controlled by states.

Ward was also logging heavy road time, and he was only able to watch the last two days of the course before taking over.

Ward was scheduled to begin teaching real-time SA only days after observing the last two days of Morrow's final seminar. On the Sunday night before the seminar began, he decided that he was not happy with Morrow's version. He spent the next five days rewriting chapters during the night, photocopying his handwritten lecture notes in the early morning, and teaching during the day.

Ward's modifications included the introduction of McMenamin and Palmer's event–response modeling. He also devised an explicit way to connect a state transition diagram and its associated data flow diagram; no such connection had existed in the Morrow version. Ward represented the state transition diagram as a special *control process* on the data flow diagram; the inputs to this process were the events that caused state changes, and the outputs were control flows that enabled and disabled processes in response to the state changes. Figure 15 is a modification of Figure 14 to show a control process and its associated control flows—the dashed circle represents, in condensed fashion, the state diagram of Figure 13. (The method also requires additional annotations of the state diagram, not shown here, to represent the processes that are controlled.)

With Ward's extensions, the independent representation of control flow, which had always existed in SADT but had been dropped from Yourdon SA, now reappeared. However, Yourdon Inc.'s real-time SA differed from SADT in that the production of control flows was restricted to special processes within which control logic was centralized; no such restriction existed in SADT. The Yourdon version also had a specific mechanism, the state diagram, to describe the logic which resulted in the production of control flows. Ward taught his course successfully a few times, but the handwritten course notes were incomplete and generally an embarrassment, and he urgently requested time off the road to produce a cleaned-up version. Yourdon's management, perhaps fearing a repeat of the Morrow episode, provided time starting in early 1983 for Ward and Mellor to create an integrated set of real-time SA–SD courses.

In 1980, at the same time that Morrow had been assigned to write a real-time SA seminar, Mellor had been assigned to create a real-time version of the five-day SD seminar. His initial version, like Morrow's SA seminar, incorporated the substantial use of state transition diagrams. He taught his initial version a number of times in 1981 and 1982 before teaming with Ward in early 1983 to create the new integrated real-time curricu-

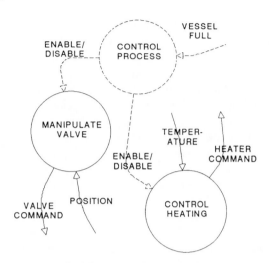

FIGURE 15   Ward's real-time DFD modification.

lum. Ward and Mellor were agreed on the use of data modeling* and of state diagrams for SA, and successfully reconciled their approaches into a series of Yourdon, Inc. seminars that were first taught in early 1984, and into a book, *Structured Development for Real-Time Systems*, published in 1985 by Yourdon Press (29,30).

State Modeling Extensions: Hatley Real-Time SA

Derek Hatley graduated as an electrical engineer in 1960 from Hatfield Technical College in England. He emigrated to the United States in 1966, and received a Masters Degree, also in EE, from Rochester Institute of Technology, in 1970. Hatley worked in the areas of optical character recognition, navigation and communications systems, and computer keyboard manufacture, before joining Lear-Siegler (now a division of Smiths Industries) in 1974. Lear-Siegler produced avionics systems; its principal customer was Boeing. In 1983 Lear-Siegler contracted with Boeing to produce a flight management control system for one of the Boeing 737 models. Hatley was assigned to a special project team that had the task of improving the communication of requirements between the two companies, which had previously been done mostly in the form of narrative text.

As was true for many real-time systems developers, Hatley saw the usefulness of Yourdon SA for requirements definition, but also its deficiencies for representing control requirements. He attended a Yourdon, Inc. real-time SA seminar in September 1983, taught by contract instructor Kate Bulman. The seminar materials described the use of state models in conjunction with data flow models, but apparently did not include Ward's recently invented integration of the two models. Hatley was dissatisfied with the notation, and proceeded, in late 1983, to invent his own way of integrating state and data flow models.

---

*Real-time developers are even better known than business system developers for looking at the world exclusively in terms of processes. Thus it is odd that Morrow, Ward, and Mellor all combined real-time and data modeling experience, and that ER modeling appeared in the *real-time* Yourdon SA seminars before it appeared in the business-oriented seminars.

Rather than embedding a state machine within a data flow diagram, Hatley invented a hierarchy of control flow diagrams that *paralleled* the DeMarco data flow diagram hierarchy. Each control flow diagram showed the interface to a piece of control logic that controlled the processes on the corresponding data flow diagram. The control logic itself could be shown as a state transition diagram, as one of a variety of state-oriented tabular forms, as a simplified table that connected control inputs to control outputs independently of sequence, or as some combination of these. A Hatley version of the example of Figure 14 is shown in Figure 16, with the data flow diagram on the left and the control flow diagram on the right; the control logic is given by Figure 13. (As in the Ward case, additional annotations of the state diagram are required.)

Hatley's real-time SA method was used on the Boeing 737 project, with positive results. Imtiaz Pirbhai, who had worked on the Boeing side of the project, left Boeing, and began teaching seminars that combined Hatley's SA method with a complementary approach to high-level design that Pirbhai had developed. Hatley published a paper on his SA technique in 1984 (31), and a book by Hatley and Pirbhai, *Strategies for Real-Time System Specification*, was published by Dorset House Publishing in 1988 (32) (Pirbhai died in August 1992).

State Modeling Extensions: Statecharts and Activity Charts

Any discussion of SA and state modeling must mention the work of David Harel, Professor of Computer Science at the Weizmann Institute of Science in Rehovot, Israel. Like the Ward-Mellor and Hatley notations, the Harel statechart/activity chart notation (33) involves the use of a state model, represented by a special process, to control the other processes on a data flow diagram. The statechart notation is much more comprehensive and powerful than either the Ward-Mellor or the Hatley state notation. However, Harel's work is not exactly part of the SA story. Rather than setting out to extend SA by adding state modeling, he set out to create a powerful state modeling notation, to which he later added a data flow model.

Harel's invention of statecharts occurred during 1983, while he was working as a consultant to Israel Aircraft Industries on the avionics system for the Lavi fighter aircraft. He and his colleagues later extended the notation to include data flow (activity chart) and modular design (module chart) components, and the combined notation was incorporated into a CASE product called Statemate™ (34) developed by Ad-Cad, Ltd. and marketed by i-Logix.

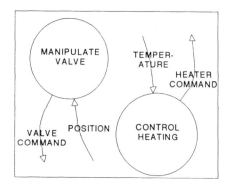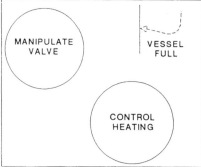

FIGURE 16   Hatley's real-time DFD modification.

Object Oriented Extensions

"Object-oriented" (OO) is a term which originally was applied to a family of programming languages that share a particular set of structural features. Specifically, these languages allow the programmer to create and use software structures called *objects*, which are sets of data values encapsulated by operations. The data within an object can be accessed or modified only by sending a *message* that invokes an operation belonging to the object; the invocation of an operation is similar in some respects to calling a subroutine. Objects are created by stamping out copies from a sort of template called a *class*, which defines the properties (the encapsulated data and the operations) of a set of objects. Class definitions can be arranged in hierarchies; subclasses *inherit* the properties of superclasses, and add properties of their own.

Imagine, for example, writing the code for a toy banking system in an object-oriented language. We define a class ACCOUNT, which contains the variables ACCOUNT_HOLDER and BALANCE, and contains the operations DEPOSIT and WITHDRAW. We can then create any number of ACCOUNT objects, named, say, ACCOUNT_1001, ACCOUNT_1002, and so on. Each of these objects has its own ACCOUNT_HOLDER and BALANCE values, and (at least in principle) its own copy of the DEPOSIT and WITHDRAW operations. To record the deposit of $1000 into account 1001, we send a message containing the value '1000' and the operation name DEPOSIT to the object ACCOUNT_1001, whereupon the operation increases the value of BALANCE appropriately.

If the system requires interest-bearing accounts, we can create a subclass of ACCOUNT called INTEREST_BEARING_ACCOUNT. Since the subclass inherits the properties of the original (super)class, we need only to define an additional operation APPLY_INTEREST, which, when invoked, uses a message containing an interest rate to modify the value of BALANCE.

During the 1980s, OO properties were incorporated into notations for building systems development models, at first design models, and, more recently, requirements definition models. The original set of OO design methods, for example, the earlier methods of Grady Booch (35) and Ed Seidowitz (36) (although not their later ones), were created under the assumption that requirements definition was to be done using SA, and that the SA models were then to be converted into OO designs.

A variety of OO requirements definition methods has recently been proposed. One subset of these methods, of special interest here, has come from modifications of SA notations and approaches to incorporate OO properties, and has been developed by people who were members of the SA community and who left to form their own organizations. The developers include Shlaer and Mellor of Project Technology, Inc. (37,38), Ward of Software Development Concepts (39,40), Peter Coad (of Object International, Inc.) and Yourdon (41,42), and Meilir Page-Jones and Steven Weiss of Wayland Systems (43). All of these people except Shlaer are former Yourdon instructors.

Space does not permit the examination of these methods in detail. However, it is useful to examine the characteristics of the methods as a group, from the point of view of how they evolved from Yourdon SA. This is especially interesting in the light of claims the SA is radically different from OO in its basic premises.

The case for the radical difference between SA and OO methods has some merit if one considers the *original* SA methods, which produced models dominated by process-oriented partitionings with no relationship to the classes that organize an object-oriented model. However, the case is weaker if the extensions of SA described earlier in this article are considered. A rigid classification scheme does not take the evolution and intermixing of methods into account, and merits the criticism of Stephen Jay Gould that "Parochial taxonomies are a curse of intellectual life."

The key to the connection between SA and OO methods is the data model and the organization, if any, that it imposes on the process model. In the original Yourdon SA methods of the late 1970s, the data model was subordinate to the process model, and served to reorganize the stored data within an already-created process model. When entity-relationship modeling was incorporated in the early and mid 1980s, the data model was independent of the process model, and imposed a stored data structure on the process model. In the recent object-oriented extensions, the data model dominates; it imposes its structure not only on the stored data within the process model, but on the processes as well, and requires that each process be associated with a single entity (i.e., a single class). This is, in essence, the requirement of encapsulation.

SA and CASE

In the late 1970s, SofTech was involved in the development of two different graphics-based CASE products, to support IDEF0 and SADT, respectively. SofTech developed the first of these products under the ICAM architecture contract. It ran on CDC Cybernet equipment and provided high-resolution, interactive graphic support of IDEF0 model building. However, creating even a single diagram consumed an unacceptable amount of storage, and the product was ultimately abandoned as being impractical.

The second product was developed with SofTech's assistance by Kongsberg VapenFabrik in Norway. It ran under the Unix operating system and provided a significant amount of support for SADT, including some automated quality assurance functions. The graphics interface, however, left much to be desired; to view a diagram in detail, for example, the user had to examine fragments spread over four distinct display areas. The product was used to some extent within Kongsberg but clearly was not viable as a commercial product.

In both of these cases, SofTech's ambitions to provide automated requirements definition support led the capabilities of the available technology by several years. By the early 1980s, effective support for the kind of interactive graphics required by CASE was becoming available. However, by that point in time, SofTech had decided that it was not in the CASE business, and left the field to others.

Yourdon, Inc.'s involvement in CASE began in 1982. In the summer of that year, instructor Lou Mazzuchelli approached Ed Yourdon with an ambitious proposal to build a CASE product on a 32-bit personal workstation to support SA and SD. Mazzuchelli would be the manager of the project and would help to raise the necessary venture capital. Yourdon rejected the proposal as being impractical, whereupon Mazzuchelli quit the company, found colleagues and venture capital, and founded Cadre Technologies. Cadre successfully developed the product Mazzuchelli had envisioned, and began marketing it under the trademark of Teamwork in 1984.

Meanwhile, Ed Yourdon had embarked on a CASE effort with much more modest financing requirements. Apple's Lisa computer was released in mid-1982. The Lisa was intermediate in power between a PC and a 32-bit engineering workstation, and boasted a sophisticated user interface later to be made famous by the MacIntosh. Yourdon and Apple promptly agreed to produce a CASE prototype on the Lisa. Yourdon's contribution was to station two employees, Gary Austin and Gail Arens, in Cupertino, California to work with two members of Apple's development staff.

By 1983, the team had produced a rather impressive prototype. Unfortunately, by 1983 Apple had concluded that the Lisa was a commercial failure and was prepared to abandon it. Despite Ed Yourdon's personal intercession with Steve Jobs, Apple would not agree to sustain the Lisa, nor provide support for transferring the prototype to the early members of the MacIntosh family. The project died.

This setback cost Yourdon, Inc. precious time in entering the case market. A PC-based Yourdon CASE product, the Analyst/Designer Toolkit, was ultimately developed by a joint venture company formed between Yourdon, Inc. and Cadware, Inc. Yourdon began marketing the product in 1985, and it enjoyed a modest commercial success.

Meanwhile, beginning in 1984, a number of other CASE products supporting SA had been introduced. From this point, the details are part of the story of CASE rather than the story of SA.

ACKNOWLEDGMENTS

I thank John Brackett, Ralph Bravoco, Larry Constantine, Tom DeMarco, Wendy Eakin, Chris Gane, David Harel, Derek Hatley, Tom Lister, Clement McGowan, Steve Mellor, Ira Morrow, Toni Nash, John Palmer, Douglas Ross, Wayne Stevens, Dennis Wisnosky, and Ed Yourdon for generously contributing their time and their memories in helping me prepare this article.

REFERENCES

1. Barnett, T., and Constantine, L. (eds.), *Proceedings of the National Symposium on Modular Programming*, Information and Systems Institute, Cambridge, MA, 1968. Although references to structure charts occurred in earlier publications, this contains the first published picture of one. Note that the *Proceedings* were also published by Constantine's Institute.
2. Ross, D. T., Origins of the APT Language for Automatically Programmed Tools. In *History of Programming Languages* (Wexelblat, R. L., ed.) Academic Press, New York, 1981.
3. Ross, D. T., *Introduction to Software Engineering with the AED-0 Language*, MIT Electronic Systems Laboratory Report No. ESL-R-405, Cambridge, MA, 1969.
4. Ross, D. T., A Generalized Technique for Symbol Manipulation and Numerical Calculation, *Commun. ACM* 4:147–150 (March 1961). The original article on plex theory.
5. Stevens, W., Myers, G., and Constantine, L., Structured Design. *IBM Sys. J.*, 13 (2):115–139 (1974). A detailed description of Constantine's structured design technique, and one of the most often cited articles in the history of systems development.
6. Martin, D., and Estrin, G., Models of Computations and Systems—Evaluations of Vertex Probabilities in Graphical Models of Computations, *J. ACM*, 14 (2):28 ff (April 1967). The article on program graphs on which Constantine based his data flow graphs.
7. Hori, S., Human-Directed Activity Cell Model, *CAM-I Long Range Planning Report*, Arlington, TX, CAM-I, Inc., 1972. The graphic basis of the SA box.
8. Air Force Materials Laboratory, *Air Force Computer-Aided Manufacturing (AFCAM) Master Plan*, Vol. II, app. A, and Vol. III, Report AFML-TR-74-104, AFSC, Wright-Patterson AFB, OH, July 1974. The first published reference to SofTech's SA technique.
9. Ross, D. T., and Brackett, J., An Approach to Structured Analysis, *Computer Decisions*, 6 (9):40–44 (September 1976). The first description of SADT in a periodical publication and a frequently cited article.

10. Ross, D. T., Structured Analysis (SA): A Language for Communicating Ideas, *IEEE Transact. Software Eng.*, SE-3 (1):16–34 (January 1977). An abstract discussion of SA modeling with few specific details about SADT.

11. Marca, D., and McGowan, C. *SADT: Structured Analysis and Design Technique*, McGraw-Hill, New York, 1988. Note that this book was published long after the time period described in this article as a direct result of SofTech's insistence on keeping its techniques proprietary.

12. Combelic, D., User Experience with New Software Methods (SADT), *Proceedings NCC*, 47:631–633 (1978). ITT's perspective on SADT.

13. U.S. Air Force, Integrated Computer-Aided Manufacturing (ICAM) Function Modeling Manual (IDEF0), Prime Contract F33615-78-C-5158. USAF Materials Laboratory, Wright-Patterson AFB, 1981.

14. Yourdon, E. (ed.), *Real-Time Systems Design*, Information and Systems Press, Cambridge, MA; 1967. Ed Yourdon's first book, published by Constantine's company.

15. Yourdon, E., *Techniques of Program Structure and Design*, Prentice Hall, Englewood Cliffs, NJ, 1975. An excellent description of the state of the practice in systems design in the early 1970s.

16. DeMarco, T., Structured Analysis: The Beginnings of a New Discipline, Preface to Delskof and Lange's *Structuret Analyse*, Tekniske Forlag, Copenhagen; 1989. A historical reflection on the origins of Yourdon SA. Copies of the preface are available from Tom DeMarco, Atlantic Systems Guild, 353 West 12th Street, New York, NY 10014.

17. Gane, C., and Sarson, T. *Structured Systems Analysis: Tools and Techniques*, Improved Systems Technologies, New York; 1977 (republished by Prentice Hall in 1979).

18. Weinburg, V., *Structured Analysis*, Yourdon Press, New York, 1978.

19. DeMarco, T., *Structured Analysis and System Specification*, Yourdon, Inc., New York, 1978 (now available from Yourdon Press/Prentice Hall, Englewood Cliffs, NJ).

20. Ross, D. T., and Schoman, K. E., Structured Analysis for Requirements Definition, *IEEE Transact. Software Eng.*, SE-3(1):6–15 (January 1977).

21. Brackett, J., and McGowan, C. Applying SADT to Large System Problems, *Proceedings of the Conference on Life Cycle Management*, August 1977, pp. 539–551. This provides some details on the SADT multiple model concept.

22. Dickover, M., McGowan, C., and Ross, D. T., Software Design Using SADT, *Proceedings of the ACM Annual Conference*, October 1977, pp. 125–133. This also provides some information about SADT multiple models.

23. Codd, E. F., A Relational Model of Data for Large Data Banks, *Commun. ACM*, 13:6 (June 1970).

24. Chen, P. P., The Entity-Relationship Model—Toward a Unified View of Data, *ACM Transact. Database Sys.*, 1(1):9–36 (March 1976).

25. U.S. Air Force, Information Modeling Manual: IDEF1—Extended (IDEF1X), ICAM Project Priority 6201, Subcontract #013-078846, Prime Contract F33615-80-C-5155, USAF Materials Laboratory, Wright-Patterson AFB; 1985.

26. Bruce, T. A., *Designing Quality Databases with IDEF1X Information Models*, Dorset House Publishing, New York, 1991.

27. Flavin, M., *Fundamental Concepts of Information Modeling*, Yourdon Press, New York, 1981.

28. McMenamin, S. M., and Palmer, J. F., *Essential Systems Analysis*, Prentice-Hall, Englewood Cliffs, NJ, 1984.

29. Ward, P. T., and Mellor, S. J., *Structured Development for Real-Time Systems*, Prentice Hall, Englewood Cliffs, NJ, 1985.

30. Ward, P. T., The Transformation Schema: An Extension of the Data Flow Diagram to Represent Control and Timing, *IEEE Transact. Software Eng.*, SE-12 (2):198–210 (February 1986).

31. Hatley, D. J., The Use of Structured Methods in the Development of Large Software-Based Avionics Systems, AIAA/IEEE 6th Digital Avionics Systems Conference, Baltimore, MD, December 1984.

32. Hatley, D. J., and Pirbhai, I. A., *Strategies for Real-Time System Specification*, Dorset House Publishing, New York, 1988.

33. Harel, D., Statecharts: A Visual Formalism for Complex Systems. In *Science of Computer Programming 8*, North-Holland, Amsterdam, 1987, pp. 231–274.

34. Harel, D., et al., Statemate: A Working Environment for the Development of Complex Reactive Systems, Proceedings: 10th International Conference on Software Engineering, Singapore, April 1988.

35. Booch, G., Object-Oriented Development. *IEEE Transact. Software Eng.*, SE-12(2):211–221, (February 1986).

36. NASA Goddard Space Flight Center, *General Object-Oriented Software Development*, SEL-86-002, August 1986.

37. Shlaer, S., and Mellor, S. J., *Object-Oriented Systems Analysis: Modeling the World in Data*, Prentice Hall, Englewood Cliffs, NJ, 1988.

38. Shlaer, S., and Mellor S. J., *Object Lifecycles: Modeling the World in States*, Prentice Hall, Englewood Cliffs, NJ, 1992.

39. Ward, P. T., How to Integrate Object Orientation with Structured Analysis and Design, *IEEE Software*, 6(2):74–82 (March 1989).

40. Ward, P. T., *Principles of Object-Oriented Development*, Dorset House Publishing, New York, in press.

41. Coad, P., and Yourdon, E., *Object-Oriented Analysis*, Prentice Hall, Englewood Cliffs, NJ, 1991.

42. Coad, P., and Yourdon E., *Object-Oriented Design*, Prentice Hall, Englewood Cliffs, NJ, 1991.

43. Page-Jones, M., and Weiss, S., Synthesis: An Object-Oriented Analysis and Design Method, *Am. Programmer*, 2:7–8 (1989).

PAUL T. WARD

STUDY OF GEOPHYSICAL PHENOMENA USING COMPUTERS

There are more things in heaven and earth, Horatio,
Than are dreamt of in your philosophy.

Hamlet, William Shakespeare (1564–1616)

Then at the balance let's be mute,
    We never can adjust it;
What's done we partly may compute,
    But know not what's resisted.

Robert Burns (1759–1796)

INTRODUCTION

Geophysics is defined as the physics of the earth including meteorology, hydrology, oceanography, seismology, volcanology, geomagnetism, radioactivity, and geodesy. The study of geophysics is firmly tied to geology, the study of the composition and structure of the earth. Using the membership of the American Geophysical Union as an estimate, in 1989, approximately 26,000 individuals were actively working in geophysics in the United States. Among the natural sciences, earth sciences such as geophysics and geology are inherently visual. The study of landforms involves explaining the origin of three-dimensional land surfaces; the paradigm of plate tectonics is based upon an extremely dynamic view of the Earth, in which crustal plates on the surface of the spherical planet move about through time and interact with one another; and most geological models require maps (often dynamic ones, in which time is a significant variable) and animations for proper understanding.

Over the past 30 years there has been a revolution taking place in the sciences of geology and geophysics. The introduction of the paradigm of plate tectonics has produced an abrupt advance of understanding in the geological sciences.

The plate tectonic paradigm states simply that the earth's surface consists of a series of rigid plates that move horizontally with respect to each other. Geologic structures, such as mountain chains, the evolution of life, distribution of natural resources, and many other subjects are all influenced by this motion. In order to develop the plate tectonic paradigm to a state in which it could be accepted by scientists, a large and diverse body of data had to be collected. Happily cooperation, on an international scale, in collecting geophysical data and declassification of major data sets, such as worldwide underwater bathymetry, coincided with the development of computer systems during the 1960s that could store and analyze massive data sets. Both the earth sciences and computer hardware and software have coevolved during the last quarter century.

The author presents a brief outline of a few of the major focuses of geophysical research, including earth structure, seismology, present-day plate motion as measured from satellite or other accurate means, and climate modelling. Several trends are emerging in the use of computers in geophysical research. These include, but are not limited to, the distribution of "massive" datasets in large number at low cost via Compact Disc-Read Only Memory (CD-ROM) media, development of File Transfer Protocol (FTP) archive sites at which large amounts of data, software, and application tools are available via anonymous log-in, remote serving of workstations over the Internet computer network, allowing direct access to compiled software and massive datasets, and a redistribution of computer resources that significantly decentralizes and distributes them. Figure 1 shows the distributed computing environment of the University of California at Berkeley Network. This computing environment is typical of the type being developed and maintained in corporations and in university departments doing research in geophysics.

In addition, future directions of the use of computers in geophysics are suggested by "blue sky" work on distributing data inclusive, interactive earth science journals on CD-ROM, and placing portions of the World Data Center geophysical data bases on-line.

COEVOLUTION AND TIME SCALES

It is interesting to consider the interconnected evolution, or coevolution, of computer hardware, software, and the developments of plate tectonics during the past quarter century. Evolution, in the sense Darwin used the term, is simply descent with modification. The process of evolution has a direction and is non-cyclical, as is the evolution of computer hardware and operating systems. The development of plate tectonics, which revolutionized the earth sciences was greatly facilitated by computers. Computer resources were required to make detailed plate tectonic reconstructions of continents, to model magnetic anomalies collected over the world's oceans and to model the complex circulation patterns in the earth's mantle and forces that cause the horizontal motion of plates.

It is useful to apply the time scale of geology to the past thirty years of computer hardware development. I think of the 1950s as a Precambrian era of computer hardware development, a time when computer hardware such as we are familiar with did not exist. The early to mid 1970s represent the Paleozoic era of computer hardware; computers now began to take on the appearance that most of us can identify. The Mesozoic era (literally meaning middle life), corresponds to the late 1970s early 1980s during which intermediate architectures that led to today's hardware were developed, and the late 1980s, the Cenozoic era of computer hardware, during which forms of computer hardware that are familiar today developed.

From the 1960s to today, computer systems evolved from mainframes, highly centralized units such as the IBM 650, 7090, and 360/50, to hardware such as the PDP 1/6/10/11 or Burroughs 5000 to workstations such as the SUN 3/60, and finally to massively parallel centralized computers such as the Connection Machine and powerful stand-alone, networked workstations such as the SUN SPARC series. Simultaneously with computer hardware, operating systems were evolving. Using the UNIX computer operating system as an example, the development of Versions 6-Versions 32 in Bell Labs to the AT&T Systems 5.1 to 5.3, to the Berkeley System Distributions 3 to 4.3, significantly improved the ability of workers to utilize computer hardware.

Today, in general, the UNIX computer operating system (OS), built on the foundation of forking processes, time-sharing, generalized and easily redirected input and output and the ability to simply write shell programs, has become the standard computer

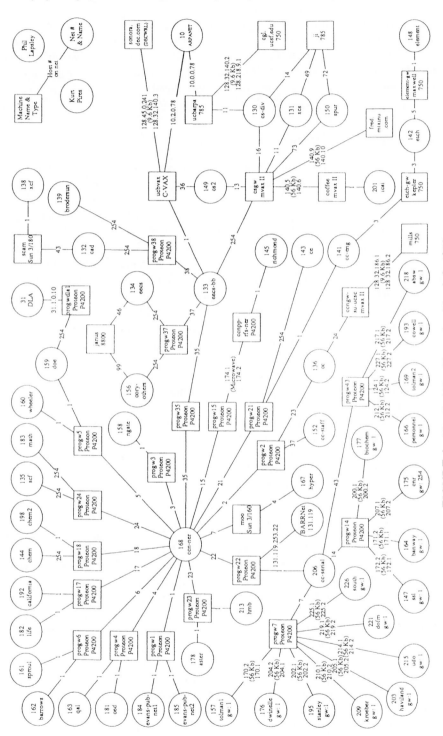

FIGURE 1   The Berkeley Network—March 9, 1989.

operating system on which most cutting-edge work in geophysics is being completed. The most commonly used graphical user interface (GUI) is the X window system developed at MIT, PostScript has developed into the principal page descriptor language, and C, C++, FROTRAN 77, and RatFor (Rational FORTRAN) are the principal computer languages in which application software is being developed.

GEOPHYSICAL APPLICATIONS

By dollar amount, the foremost use of computers in geophysical work is related to prospecting for an estimated 1.3 trillion barrels of undiscovered hydrocarbons using seismological methods. Reflection, refraction, and tomographic methods are routinely used by the petroleum industry to image geological structures related to the location, geometry, trapping structures, reservoir geometry, and distribution of hydrocarbons beneath the earth's surface. Determination of each of these parameters is critical to successfully locating economically sound accumulations of petroleum and natural gas. The importance of accurate determination of hydrocarbon resources is central given that the average cost of a single, potentially dry or worthless, oil or gas well is now about 5 million dollars.

In 1988, 45 Cray Research computers were being used in the petroleum industry. The most common applications for computerized study were complex signal analyses of reflection seismic data. Reflection seismology [see (1), (2) for details about the theory and practice of geophysical data processing related to hydrocarbon exploration] is based on the recording of seismic disturbances after they have propagated through the earth. Arrays of geophones, devices sensitive to vertical, or planar horizontal disturbances, are laid out and a series of seismic sources are recorded. This process can use impulsive seismic energy sources such as dynamite on land, air-guns underwater, or longer time duration energy sources such as a vibration. Propagation of seismic energy through the earth can involve reflection of seismic waves off impedance boundaries, refraction, and dispersion and distortion of fronts caused by complex reflection geometry, horizontal, vertical, or heterogeneous variations of seismic velocity and other factors.

Generally the data from each group or array of geophones are sorted into common midpoint gathers (CMP, groups of data that share the same midpoint between receiver and seismic source); these gathers are then processed and combined, or stacked, into a single trace of time versus displacement that represents the acoustic impedance geometry beneath the common midpoint. The resulting data is a cross section of the earth having dimensions of distance horizontally and time vertically. Often many closely spaced lines of seismic data are collected into a three-dimensional cube of seismic data. These data must be processed in three dimensions so that the resulting sections are an accurate representation of the earth's subsurface. In addition, once this data cube has been processed it is possible to generate an image of earth structure along any profile, independent of the geometry of the original survey.

Computers are used to perform velocity analysis from seismic data, to apply complex signal processing such as deconvolution of the seismic source wavelet, and to apply deconvolution of multiple reflections and migration to obtain the clearest possible image of geological structure. In addition, large amplitude signals or ground roll and air waves must be digitally filtered out of the data, and near-surface travel-time anomalies that are caused by the relatively slow seismic velocity of soil when compared with solid rock must be calculated and corrected. After extensive computer analysis, excellent quality acoustic images can be obtained to significant depths. In addition to these applications, computer resources are used to simulate reservoirs and determine how best to optimize hydrocarbon field-wide production.

In both exploration for hydrocarbons and scientific studies of the earth's crust, the number of receivers and/or sources has been exponentially increasing during the past 50 years. In industry, recording up to 1000 channels of data may be stacked to increase the signal-to-noise ratio of the resulting seismic trace. Today up to 20,000 kilobytes per multichannel seismic record may be produced compared with 200 kb of data per multichannel seismic record during the mid-1970s. The tremendous increase in the amount of data collected during these studies has only been made possible by the rapid development of computer hardware and software that allow timely reduction of these increasingly massive data sets.

Techniques used in the exploration of hydrocarbons to acoustically image geological structure are also used in studies of the large-scale crustal structure of the earth's crust and to construct detailed models of the seismic velocity structure of the mantle. These studies use natural earthquake or artificial impulsive energy sources and large-offset receivers. Simultaneous inversion of all data, plotted as distance between seismic source and receiver versus travel time of seismic waves, has been completed to determine a best-fitting velocity structure for the earth's mantle. These large tomographic calculations show a surprising variation in seismic velocity with depth. Both horizontal and vertical heterogeneity in velocity have been documented using worldwide massive datasets. These data support the model of complex circulation within the mantle (3). This circulation may be responsible for the horizontal motion of lithosphere plates that make up the earth's surface. Before the application of modern computers to this geophysical problem, no such inversion was possible.

The development of a system of global positioning satellites (GPS), very long baseline interferometry (VLBI), and satellite laser ranging (SLR) technologies, that can be used to measure horizontal crustal movement, have led to an unprecedented increase in the accurate knowledge of present-day lithosphere plate motions (4). Potential accuracies of 5 mm in positioning are possible using GPS. However, variations in the GPS system introduced by the Department of Defense (DOD) seriously degrade this accuracy for non-classified civilian users. These data can be collected and distributed rapidly via computer networks, they are easily reduced to significant and very accurate estimates of horizontal motion and deformation. Ethical questions have been raised regarding such rapid dissemination of data given that funding for many university programs are made on the basis of competitive grants (4).

A DELUGE OF DATA: CD-ROM USE IN GEOPHYSICS

During the last five years there has been a permanent change in the availability and cost of massive data sets useful in geophysics. The technological component is the CD-ROM, a robust medium that can record about 650 Megabytes (Mbytes) of data and be produced at an approximate cost of approximately $2.00 per disc. Before CD-ROM, massive data-sets were almost impossible to obtain and difficult to work with. Generally, these data were confined to government agencies that generated the data, or the largest universities. After the development of CD-ROM any researcher with an inexpensive CD-ROM drive can make use of these data. CD-ROM media have come to be heavily relied upon in the earth sciences and a commitment to releasing publicly financed datasets on CD-ROM has been shown by many government agencies. This open and unselfish commitment is well stated in the following;

> We believe that the ability to distribute data and information to researches and scientists by CD-ROM is a breakthrough. Our hope is that it will enable you and your colleagues to perform your research more effectively and economically
>
> John A. Knauss
> Under Secretary for Oceans and Atmospheres
> National Ocean and Atmospheric Agency (NOAA)

Directory of U.S. Marine CD-ROMS by NOAA published recently is available from the U.S. Department of Commerce. Twenty-one sets of CD-ROMS are grouped by subject in this directory. The subjects for which data are available include climatic, such as worldwide hourly precipitation, and a wide variety of images, such as high-resolution side-scan sonar pictures of the sea floor, NIMBUS-7 images of the earth, and detailed bathymetry. A representative example of one of these sets available on CD-ROM is the "World WeatherDisc: Climate Data for the Planet Earth." This single CD-ROM includes seventeen meteorological data sets, some beginning in the 1700s, and gives detailed records of temperature, precipitation, heating/cooling degree days, freeze occurrence, drought, soil moisture, wind, sunshine, lightning, tornados, and thunderstorms.

CD-ROMS have been used heavily in archiving seismological data. Seismology is the study of earthquakes and the structure of the earth as constrained by the observation of seismic energy. The United States Geological Survey (USGS) and the National Earthquake Information Center (NEIC) have begun to release massive amounts of seismological data on CD-ROM. The information falls into one of three categories, hypocenter-associated data, a global hypocenter database, and a continuing earthquake digital record database. Included in the global database CD-ROM are seven worldwide and twelve regional earthquake catalogs. For each earthquake, if available, this CD-ROM includes the data, origin time, location, depth, up to four magnitude estimates, intensity, cultural effects such as damage and casualties, fault plane movement and tensor solutions and related seismic phenomena such as tsunamis. Some of the regional earthquake catalogs included are for Europe between 2100 BC and 1982, Iberia/Spain 880 BC to 1980, China, 1177 BC to 1976, and the Soviet Union between 2100 BC and 1977. The continuing digital data set consists of all of the digital records from the worldwide seismic station network for each earthquake with surface wave-defined magnitude greater than 5.3, for volumes 1 through 8, and surface wave-defined magnitude greater or equal to 4.9 for volume 9 and future volumes.

CD-ROMS also offer the opportunity to combine a large amount of data from a single experiment. For example NASA recently completed the Geological Remote Sensing Field Experiment (GRSFE), generating a massive geophysical dataset. This experiment took place over three months during 1989 in the southern Mojave Desert, Death Valley, and the Lunar Crater volcanic field in Nevada. More than 5 Gbytes of data from this single geophysical experiment have been collected into 9 CD-ROMS and distributed widely.

Geographical information systems (GIS) are increasingly used in geophysics. This type of application and database combines information about land use, land cover, soil and rock type, cultural, hydrological and topographical data with interactive workstation-based display and analysis capabilities. Generally satellite imagery is central to this type of application, as in the GRSFE.

In addition, the USGS has initiated a pilot program of releasing Side Looking Airborne Radar (SLAR) images of selected regions on CD-ROM. SLAR data yields detailed records of the reflection of radar waves off the earth's surface. The images appear similar to a shaded, high-resolution, high-altitude photograph. The technology is such that SLAR effectively images through vegetation and can be collected regardless of weather or lighting conditions. Because surface topography and geological structure are often closely related, these images often are important in deducing the geological structure of a region. Presently four discs are available. Regions imaged (some images have about 10 meter pixel resolution) include selected regions of Alaska, Arkansas, Washington, Oregon, California, and Nevada. While approximately one third of the United States has been imaged using SLAR technology, only during the last few years have digital images become available.

An obvious application of CD-ROM technology is the archiving of LANDSAT satellite images. NASA has archived all interplanetary images on CD-ROM and recently released all Magellan Synthetic Aperature Radar (SAR) images of Venus on CD-ROM. Other than the pilot projects mentioned above, GRSFE and the SLAR program, no such release of LANDSAT images is planned. Although such data would be very valuable to a wide variety of geophysical and geological investigations, copyright protections associated with the "privatization" of the LANDSAT satellite make widespread distribution of these satellite images impossible. Privatization meant transfer of ownership of the LANDSAT satellite and of a significant data archive to a private corporation, the EOSAT corporation, which is jointly controlled by the General Electric Corporation and Hughes Aircraft Corporation. Since privatization, the price of a satellite image collected by the LANDSAT satellite, for which the public paid the cost of design, launch, and application development, has increased from a minimal cost to more than $6,000 per full scene.

At the University of Pittsburgh Department of Geology and Planetary Sciences this shift in data availability is well represented. A few years ago we had relatively small amounts of geophysical data available, while today we have all NASA interplanetary images (approximately 6.6 gigabytes of images available), all Magellan synthetic aperature radar (SAR) images (approximately 9.0 gigabytes), all National Earthquake Center (NEC) earthquake location and parameter data (about 5.6 gigabytes), digital topographic data for the entire world surface and oceans, including higher resolution data sets for North America, the United States, and Australia (about 300 megabytes), and approximately 2.1 gigabytes of a variety of remote-sensing data such as LANDSAT TM, MSS, SPOT, AVHRR, SLAR, and SAR data from selected regions.

GEOPHYSICAL FTP ARCHIVE SITES

The wide availability of inexpensive massive datasets in geophysics is a new event. In addition, very large Internet storage sites that are publicly available using the UNIX ftp command, the user interface to the ARPANET standard file transfer protocol (FTP), have recently been created. One of the largest is the NASA Climate Data System (NCDS).

The NCDS is an interactive data management system that incorporates data access using the Common Data Format (CDF), and graphics using the National Space Science Data Center System (NSSDC). This site is accessible via anonymous FTP access at no

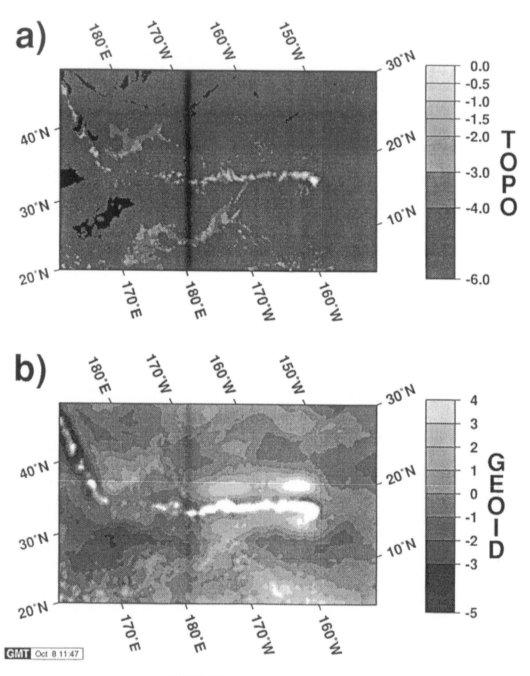

FIGURE 2   Hawaiian Topo and Geoid

charge. Data that are available fall into five broad categories: solar activity and irradiance (7 massive data sets are available), clouds and radiation (15 massive data sets), global climatologies and oceanographic data (21 massive data sets), atmospheric composition (10 massive data sets), and miscellaneous (3 massive data sets). Typical data sets, their duration and sizes, remotely available from any node on the INTERNET computer network, include 1.1 gigabytes (Gbytes) of global measurements of aerosols, ozone, humidity, nitrogen dioxide, 18-day global coverage, and 4 years of data, 11 Gbytes of global estimates of clouds, optical depth, ozone, pressure, reflectance, temperature, and 98.9 Gbytes of global measurements of clouds, radiance, twice daily imaging, 24 kilometer global resolution, 6 years of data. These data, easily available with software and graphical support, available via FTP are a new development made possible only by the coevolution of computer hardware, software, network connectivity, and geophysics.

High-quality, thoroughly tested application software is a key and central element to modern science. Previous exchange of software, when software was exchanged, was via mailed disk or magnetic tape. This was a slow and inefficient process that discouraged the exchange of useful computer code and led to duplication of applications. In geophysics the most obvious sign of this duplication is the general lack of common data formats for geophysics data. Recently, however, this situation has begun to change. A large collection of Generic Mapping Tools (GMT) have been placed on an FTP archive site Kiawe.soest.hawaii.edu (128.171.151.16). This code, described by Wessel and Smith (5), was developed at the Lamont-Doherty Geological Observatory of Columbia University (Lamont-Doherty). It consists of a large number of display and analysis applications that use simple ASCII or netCDF (network Common Data Format, available from unidata.ucar.edu, 128.117.140.3) files as input and output. Using ASCII was chosen as an option because these files can be manipulated simply using standard UNIX commands such as *sed* and *awk*. The output of all graphics is in PostScript, including support for 24-bit color output. All subroutines use or accept piped input, self document when a command name is typed without parameters, and the complete archive file includes excellent manual pages. In addition, examples and a user's manual are provided with the software. Figure 2 was created using the GMT graphics tools and shows digital topography near Hawaii and the topography of an equipotential gravitational surface called a geoid in the same region. Figure 3 shows deflection of Geosat sea surface slope track measurements, related to distortions of the sea surface sensed by satellite altimeter which are caused by underwater bathymetry in the southern Pacific ocean. Computer analysis and visualization of these data sets allows rapid and effective analysis.

Numerous smaller FTP sites in which geophysically useful applications or data are stored are appearing on INTERNET. Additional graphics software, the VPLOT system, developed in the Geophysics Department of Stanford University, and a large collection of geographical continental, river system, political, and glacier outlines are available from hanauma.stanford.edu (36.51.0.16). Access to the World Database of paleomagnetic data that constrains the motion of tectonic plates is available from earth.eps.pitt.edu (130.49.3.1). Detailed information describing earthquakes in southern California, including PostScript figures that show faults, earthquake locations, and magnitudes are available on a weekly basis from dix.gps.caltect.edu (131.215.65.1). Figure 4 shows a weekly plot of the location and size of earthquakes that occurred in southern California between December 26, 1991 and January 1, 1992. These plots are available along with a detailed ASCII listing of earthquake location and size.

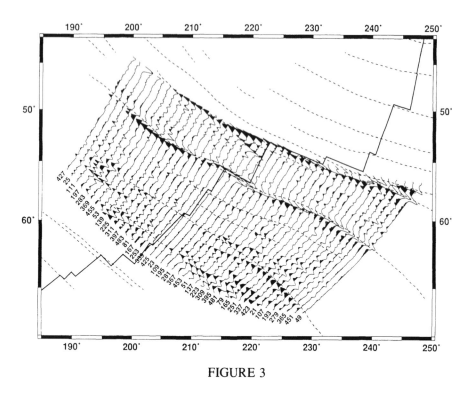

FIGURE 3

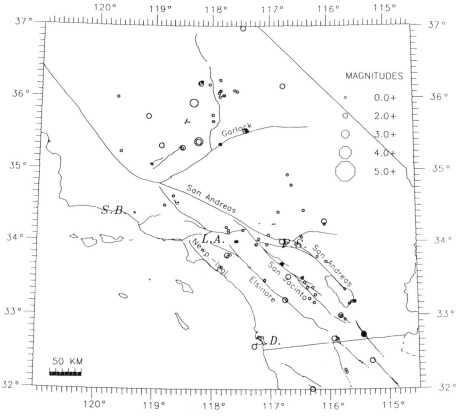

FIGURE 4   December 26, 1991–January 1, 1992. Preliminary Epicenters and Magnitudes.

CUTTING EDGE: REMOTE SERVING IN GEOPHYSICS

CD-ROMs are a tremendous advance over the previous situation, marked by either a lack of data sharing, or the mailing of tapes and disks. However, ordering and delivery can be relatively slow in that these media too must be delivered via the mail and often application software to complete detailed analysis of the datasets are not included with the disks themselves. A notable exception to this rule is the availability from anonymous FTP of software required to use the NEIC earthquake CD-ROM data set. From anonymous FTP the entire Seismic Analysis Code (SAC) and cartographic display programs for seismic data (MAP), developed in cooperation with the Lawrence Livermore National Laboratory are available. This availability of CD-ROM massive datasets and complete packages of application software is not the norm. In addition, for many users it is impossible to free 20 or 40 Mbytes of disk space for compiling of computer code. The coevolution of GUIs such as X and OpenLook, the latter developed by SUN Microsystems, and the increasingly large and varied data sets which are routinely used in geophysical investigations have led to a major innovation, remote serving of GUI–based analysis tools and remote analysis of massive datasets. This work has been pioneered in geophysical applications by William Menke and his colleagues at Lamont-Doherty (6).

At Lamont-Doherty a remote viewer-server system based on a Geographical Database Browser (GB or GeoBase, source code available from lamont.ldgo.columbia.edu, 129.236.10.30) has been developed. The network capabilities designed into workstation graphical user interfaces allows graphical data browsing to be remotely served by any of six publicly available computers at Lamont-Doherty. The remote servers display information such as magnetic anomalies, gravity anomalies, and selected earthquake data on practically any workstation connected to INTERNET. Even a simple X-terminal could be remotely served and access these massive on-line databases. The strengths and advantages of this system over simply ordering CD-ROM are that the data are made available without the delays inherent in mail; standard, tested, and compiled software tools are available with the massive data sets; and the remotely served X-devices are much less expensive than the servers themselves.

Data sets available for remote serving/viewing using GB include geodetic, seismological, gravity, magnetic, marine heat flow, and geological. Significant data contributions to this archive have been made by Lamont-Doherty, Oregon State University, NOAA, NEIC, and the National Center for Earthquake Engineering (NCEER). A list of remote-serving computers is maintained on chaos.ldgo.columbia.edu (129.236.10.20) and given in Menke et al., (6). Network-wide remote serving and viewing of massive data sets represent a significant advance toward openness and cooperation in geophysical research. Previously, significant delays occurred in obtaining even simple magnetic anomaly data. With remote viewing/serving, these data and accompanying sophisticated analysis programs are available instantly and at any time via remotely served workstations. A similar philosophy of openness and data availability was used to design the Global Land Information System, presently being implemented by the EROS Data Center of the USGS. From glis.cr.usgs.gov (192.41.204.54), users will be able to browse and actually view on-line satellite images, such as Advanced Very High Resolution Radiometer (AVHRR) images, check directories using browsing tools and check inventories and user guides remotely.

BEYOND CUTTING EDGE: INTERACTIVE
CD-ROM EARTH SCIENCE JOURNALS

A new journal from the USGS includes sections describing Global Change, Arctic Environment, Physical Oceanography, Resource Development, Sociology/Anthropology, Policy, and Bibliography. Such a journal is entirely new in concept in that it is completely contained on a CD-ROM and all raw data described, including satellite images, detailed bathymetry and sociological data are included in the journal and easily accessed and saved digitally. Denise A. Wiltshire and Payson Stevens of the USGS have developed this trial CD-ROM interactive journal (contact USGS, Information Systems Division, 703-648-7300). In my opinion the ArcticData Interactive journal suggests computer trends beyond the cutting edge, or using the phrase of Bill Joy, "Blue Sky" trends.

The ArcticData Interactive (ADI) CD-ROM is a scientific journal entirely contained on a CD-ROM. It may be viewed on an Apple Macintosh computer environment using HyperCard 2.0, or an MS/DOS environment using Windows 3.0 or later. At its minimum this electronic journal can be a simple computer version of a static text journal. One can read articles, look at figures, and review references as one would scroll through any long electronic document. However, a wide variety of very powerful tools are provided on the CD-ROM. Because ADI is viewed in a graphical user interface, icons, pull-down menus, hot-text and full-text search and retrieval provide a highly intuitive path to obtaining information. For example, the table of contents of the "journal" appears as an orientation map. By clicking on the "overview" label in the introduction a verbal overview of the entire project is given. Clicking, that is, moving the mouse pointer over an object on the screen and pressing the mouse button once, on the name of an article takes you directly to that article with a new table of contents naming the various sections of that article. Clicking a color icon that appears at the level of this local table of contents plays a short animation of dissolving color images relating to the contents of the article and ending with a short images text abstract.

When reading articles in the journal the reader has a variety of icons that allow him or her to quit, print either the entire article or only the page shown, and select the raw data that are being discussed or presented in the article. By clicking on a data icon, relevant data are displayed. These may include numeric data, for example, Bowhead whale harvests, tabular data relating to glacial movement in southeastern Alaska, or digital imagery such that, for example, one can access directly the raster images of selected glaciers of southeastern Alaska. Many of the raster images are in color or high resolution grey scale. One can also save to disk a single article or data set, search the entire disk or a single article for key words, and easily and quickly display all figures or tables relating to a certain article. In addition the Arctic Environmental Data Directory (AEDD), a listing of more than 300 references related to Arctic research, is included on the CD-ROM. This highly innovative and original work was funded by the Interagency Arctic Research Policy Committee and the Interagency Working Group on Data Management for Global Change.

CONCLUSION

The last few years have seen a fundamental change in the availability of massive data sets in geophysics. Large amounts of data are being made available quickly and at low cost via

CD-ROM media. In addition, large data archives are being developed in the INTERNET computer network. Interactive remote serving and viewing of massive geophysical datasets also is being developed. Distribution of data is so rapid that ethical questions regarding the speed with which data should be widely distributed are being raised in the scientific community. With respect to computer hardware, distributed networks of workstations are increasingly important. These workstations are generally UNIX OS based and running or compatible with the X GUI.

ACKNOWLEDGMENTS

I thank Victor Schmidt and the editor and staff of ECST for carefully reading and improving this manuscript.

REFERENCES

1. Claerbout, J. F., *Fundamentals of Geophysical Data Processing, With Applications to Petroleum Prospecting*, McGraw-Hill, New York 1976, 274 pp..
2. Claerbout, J. F., *Imaging the Earth's Interior*, Blackwell Scientific Publications, London, 1985.
3. Masters, T. G., *Rev. Geophys.* (Suppl) 671–679, (1991).
4. Lisowski, M., *Rev. Geophys.* (Suppl) 162–171, (1991).
5. Wessel, P., and Smith, W. H. F., EOS, *Transact. Am. Geophysical Union*, 72:441 (1991).
6. Menke, W., Friberg, P., Lerner-Lam, A., Simpson, D., Bookbinder, R., and Karner, G. EOS, *Transact. Am. Geophysical Union*, 72: 409 (1991).

WILLIAM HARBERT

TECHNOLOGICAL SUBSTITUTIONS IN THE COMPUTER INDUSTRY

INTRODUCTION

In 1971 J. C. Fisher and R. H. Pry published an article entitled "A Simple Substitution Model of Technological Change"(1) which became a classic. Their thesis was that man has few basic needs to satisfy: food, shelter, clothing, transportation, communication, etc., and that technological evolution consists of replacing the old ways of satisfaction with new ones. The advancements of technology may seem *evolutionary* or *revolutionary* depending on the time scale of the substitution. Regardless of the pace of change, however, the end result usually is to satisfy an ongoing need or perform an existing function differently than before. The need or the function itself rarely undergoes a radical change.

For such substitutions Fisher and Pry put forward a model based on natural competition. Its basic premise is that the percentage rate of substitution of new for old is proportionate to the amount of the old still left to be substituted. The model is inspired by biological populations which grow in proportion to the extent of the ecological niche still unoccupied (2). There are many examples of industrial one-to-one substitutions which corroborate their model.

It was not until several years later that Marchetti and Nakicenovic generalized the Fisher and Pry model to describe the multicompetitor market (3). Their first celebrated example was the substitution among primary energy sources. They considered the successive transitions from wood to coal to oil to gas to nuclear energy. The adapted model was able to handle the evolution of the "market" shares of all energy types simultaneously competing for society's favor.

In Digital we adopted this methodology to better understand the substitution among our products. We built user-friendly flexible software tools to facilitate nurturing scenarios deep into the future. As product life cycles decreased (less differentiated models), we found ourselves having to deal with *families* of products and computer *generations* rather than individual systems.

What is described in detail below is technological substitutions between Digital's older PDP products and the subsequent VAXes. This is done by market segment and the focus is on the low end, the microcomputers. What we learn are valuable guidelines concerning how to deal with what we are now facing: the rising new technology of RISC products (Reduced Instruction Set Computing).

THE LOGISTIC SUBSTITUTION MODEL

In the heart of the Fisher–Pry model one finds natural growth under competition described as:

The rate of growth at any given time is proportional to both the amount of growth already achieved and the amount of growth remaining.

What is presupposed is a final ceiling on the amount of growth, a niche with a finite capacity. This law was first formulated for species populations by Verhulst in the equation (4):

$$\frac{dP(t)}{dt} = \alpha \, P(t) \, [M - P(t)]$$

[1]

where $P(T)$ is the population at time t, and M and α are constants. The solution of this equation is the S-shaped logistic function:

$$P(t) = \frac{M}{1 + e^{-\alpha(t-t_o)}}$$

[2]

The value of M determines the level of the final ceiling, the niche capacity, and the constant t_o locates the process in time (see Fig. 1a).

For fractional one-to-one substitutions, M is defined equal to one (i.e., 100% of the niche), the market share for the new competitor is f, and for the old one it is $(1 - f)$ with

$$f = \frac{P(t)}{M}$$

Equation (2) can then be cast in the form:

$$\ln \frac{f}{(1-f)} = \alpha(t-t_o)$$

[3]

This expression amounts to a mathematical transformation which makes S-curves look like straight lines (Fig. 1b). It is a particularly convenient representation because plotting the ratio of the number of the new to the number of the old reveals the nature of the process. If the points fall on a straight line, it is a *logistic* growth process and represents a *natural* substitution. The scale on the left in Figure 1b (logarithmic) represents the ratio *new/old*. The one on the right (logistic) shows the market shares in percent.

There are several advantages to looking at substitutions in relative terms. One is that there is no longer a dependence on M which, after all may not be constant throughout the process [M was required to be constant in order to solve Eq. (1).] Another advantage is the capability of distinguishing and identifying competitive advantages. External factors, such as seasonality, political crises, and the general economic climate no longer have an impact. The rate of substitution in relative terms reflects purely the "genetic" characteristics which make the new competitor better fit for survival then the old one.

To handle the general case where more than two competitors are simultaneously present in a market, Marchetti and Nakicenovic decided to let the trajectories of fractional shares undergo three distinct phases: growth, saturation, and decline. The growth phase is the logistic substitution described by Eq. (3) which now stops before becoming complete. It is followed by the saturation phase during which the rate of growth progressively slows and, finally, ceases altogether. In the ensuing phase of decline the market share trajectory becomes logistic once again, but this time the competitor is losing ground to a newcomer.

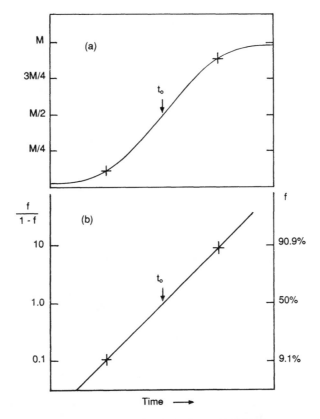

FIGURE 1   Graph (a) plots the function of Eq. (2). Most deviations occur outside the segment delimited by the crosses. Graph (b) shows the transformation from S-shaped curves to straight lines. The scale on the left relates to the ratio "new"/"old," while the scale on the right reveals the values of the fractional share f.

It is imposed that only one competitor is in the saturating phase at any time. Its share is calculated as 100% minus the shares of all other contemporaries, each of which traces out a growing or a declining logistic trajectory. Competitors enter the saturating phase in chronological order and the overall market picture in a semi-log graph takes on the profile of a mountainous landscape. Marchetti's oldest and most favorite example (Fig. 2) is on primary energy substitution worldwide. Such a figure was first published by Marchetti in 1977 (5), he wrote then:

> I started from the somehow iconoclastic hypothesis that the different primary energy sources are commodities competing for a market, like different brands of soap . . . so that the rules of the game may after-all be the same.

The model gave a surprisingly good description over a historical window of more than 100 years. An updated graph (Fig. 2) published some time later (6), reveal that over the last century, wood, coal, natural gas, and nuclear energy have been the main protagonists in supplying the world with energy. More than one energy source has been present at any time, but the leading role has passed from one to the other. Wind and water power provide an amount of energy which represents less than 1% of the total and is not shown in

Percentage of all energy

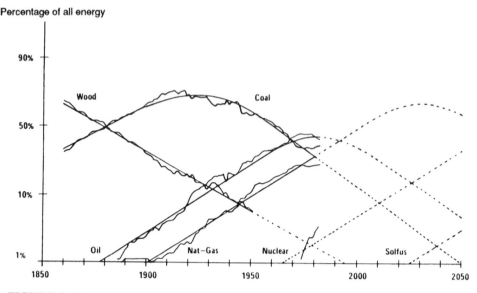

FIGURE 2   Data and substitution model description for the shares of different primary energies consumed worldwide. For nuclear, the dotted straight line is not a fit, but a trajectory suggested by analogy. The futuristic source labeled Solfus may involve solar energy and/or thermonuclear fusion. Adapted from Marchetti and Nakicenovic (6).

the figure, because the simple logistic model breaks down for very small and very large percentages (see next section.)

It becomes evident from this picture that a century-long history of an energy source can be described quite well—smooth lines—with only two constants, those required to define a straight line. The "destiny" of an energy source seems to be cast during its early "childhood," as soon as the two constants describing the straight line can be determined.

The saturating competitor is normally the oldest among the ones who are still growing. Usually it is the one with the largest share, has practically reached maximum penetration, and is expected soon to start declining. The trajectory traces out a curved transition between the end of the growth phase and the beginning of the decline phase. For an industrial product, this phase often corresponds to the maturity phase of the life cycle. It is when competition is keenest. The product has done well, it has attained a dominant position in the market niche, and all other products are trying to chip away on its gains.

The model requires that *one and only one* competitor is in the saturating phase at a given time. This condition is necessary in order to produce a workable model, but it well approximates what happens in a typical multicompetitor arena such as the Olympic Games. Many exceptional athletes all run for the first position, but there is always only one front runner. According to this model, products phasing in and phasing out do not compete with one another; they all compete against the product which is dominating the market.

The predictive power of the logistic substitution model rests with the fact that niches in nature do not remain partially filled (or emptied) for natural reasons. Once a natural process becomes well-established (i.e., it goes beyond the level of infant mortality) its continuation to completion is assured. The market share trajectories of the various competitors can be forecasted (as well as *back*casted.) To be able to construct the future picture one needs the introduction date for each future contender. This can be specified as the time when a significant market share—a few percent—is achieved. The rate of growth (the slope of the straight line) must not change from one contender to the next. The only condition which can perturb this evolution is an "unnatural" phenomenon defined here as something of unprecedented nature; a phenomenon that never took place during the historical period.

LIMITATIONS OF THE MODEL

At the extremities of the substitution process deviations from the logistic growth pattern have been observed. As the substitution approaches completion (above 90%) the trajectory pattern breaks into random fluctuations. Similar fluctuations have been observed during the early phases, below the 10% substitution level. These deviations have been explained in terms of states of chaos, which are encountered when the logistic function is put into a discrete form. Discretization becomes essential in order to analyze data via computer programs which employ iterative techniques, but it can be justified theoretically as well, because populations are discrete quantities after all.

Studying the chaotic behavior at the extremities of logistic growth provides explanations for various phenomena mentioned in the literature, such as "infant mortality," "precursors," "early catching-up effect," and "hunting for the optimum equilibrium level"(7). The main message concerning product substitutions is that a flag of caution must be raised below the 10% and above the 90% level. During product introductions the share trajectory may grow faster than naturally (catching-up effect). Alternatively, a young product which has not yet commanded 10% of its market niche, may not necessarily survive (infant mortality).

In the examples treated below we will see accelerated substitution rates during product introduction. Erratic fluctuations around the 95% level will also be witnessed.

APPLICATIONS IN THE LOW END OF THE COMPUTER RANGE

Here we will analyze technological substitutions among Digital's computer products. Four examples from the low end—microcomputers—are treated in detail. The market is defined as all computer sales of Digital Equipment Corporation in Europe. The data come from Digital's database on order history. For each transaction the price reflects the particular configuration of the system sold. Consequently, systems with different book prices show price distributions which often overlap. Market niches are defined in terms of price bands in which different computer models compete for customers' money. The transitions are in general from the PDP family of products (old technology) to the VAX ones (new technology), but the conclusions drawn can be applied to more recent technology shifts, such as from VAX to RISC.

In Figure 3 we see computer products in the price range $20 to 50K. The first VAX was introduced in the late 1970s, but its average-configuration price was around $350K. Smaller VAX models with lower prices only became available in the early 1980s; this propelled them into competing with the popular PDPs. The substitution started with a

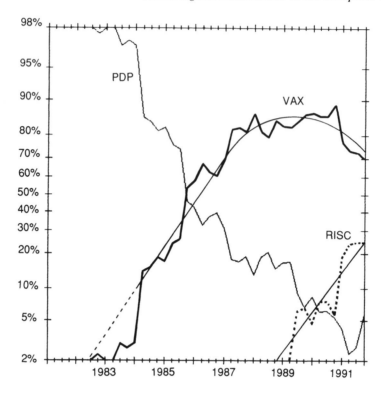

FISCAL YEAR

FIGURE 3   Substitution of PDP by VAX products. The market niche is defined as system configurations sold at a price between $20 and 50K. The recent entry of RISC products is also shown. The irregular lines are the actual data, while the thin smooth lines represent the model descriptions.

rather rapid rhythm, but for the most part (10–85%) it proceeded at a slower rate closely following a logistic trajectory (straight line.) It took 11 trimesters for the VAX share to go from 20% to 80%. The model (smooth thin lines) describes well what happened everywhere except during the early 10%, a deviation which can be understood in terms of the discussion of the previous section. The theoretical logistic trajectory starts at $t = -\infty$. When the product finally arrives, a steep early rise can be interpreted as "catching up" for the time lost.

Now again, 8 years later, a new transition is starting from VAX to RISC products and a similar picture starts to unfold.

Figure 4 shows the price range $10–20K. This price band is narrower than the previous one, but the sales volume in it is not smaller because volume increases as price decreases (8). Again the model offers an excellent description of the process. There are differences and similarities when comparing with the previous figure:

> The PDP to VAX transition now is more rapid. Along the straight line it takes only six trimesters to go from 20 to 80%. The mid point (50%) occurs two years later.

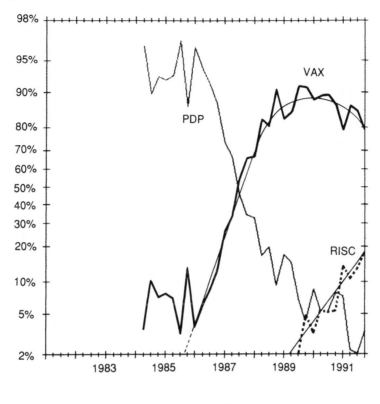

FISCAL YEAR

FIGURE 4   Substitution of PDP by VAX products. The market niche is defined as system configurations sold at a price between $10 and 20K. The recent entry of RISC products also is shown. The irregular lines are the actual data, while the thin smooth lines represent the model descriptions.

Again there are deviations below 10% and above 90%, but there is no more significant catching up effect (after all the new technology had already entered this niche two years ago.) There is no evidence that the rate of the VAX to RISC transition has changed.

These observations are reinforced in Figure 5, the lowest price band, for systems with an average-configuration price of less than $10K. The substitution PDP to VAX proceeds even faster (3.4 trimesters to go from 20 to 80%; the mid point is even later, and again no catching-up effect to speak off, only the usual fluctuations above 90%. Once more there is no significant change for VAX to RISC.

One may conclude that a progressive increase in the rate of substitution is correlated with time *and* with a decreasing price. However, correlation does not necessarily imply causality. Are these relationships, in fact, causal?

To answer this question we must consider the issue of software compatibility. PDP software applications did not run on VAXes. Consequently, a user had to rewrite an application before it could be used with the new technology. This is the reason for which later products diffused faster. Their penetration rate was positively influenced by the availability of more software packages.

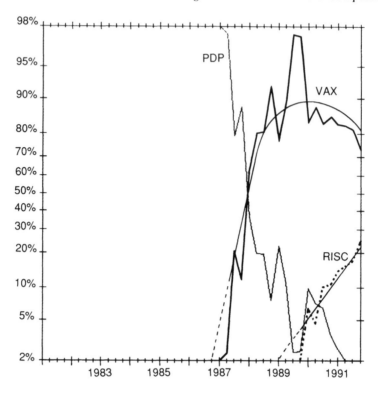

FISCAL YEAR

FIGURE 5 Substitution of PDP by VAX products. The market niche is defined as system configurations sold with a price below $10K. The recent entry of RISC products is also shown. The irregular lines are the actual data while the thin smooth lines represent the model descriptions.

There is evidence in support of this conclusion:

1. The newer technology, RISC, which is as different from VAX as VAX was from PDP (in the sense that there is again software incompatibility), proceeds with the same slow rate in all three price bands examined. This rate is very similar to that of the very early PDP to VAX substitution (1985).
2. *Compatible* computer models substitute each other rapidly even at a higher price. Figure 6 shows a microniche where MicroVAX II substituted the VAX 11/750 in a price-overlapping range ($50–180K). The substitution goes from 20 to 80% in 3.5 quarters just as it finally did for PDP to VAX (1987).
3. At Digital we have observed much larger systems (minis and superminis) also go through the bulk of a substitution process over one year as long as there was compatibility of software. (VAX to VAX).

Attention must be drawn to the fact that compatibility must not be restricted to software. Software was the main factor in the examples mentioned earlier. However, compatibility of peripherals, storage devices, and other installations all influence the rate of substitution in a similar way.

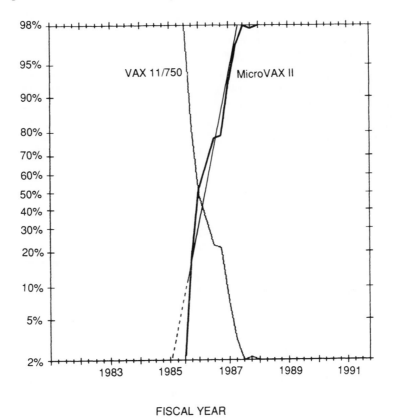

FISCAL YEAR

FIGURE 6   Substitution of the VAX 11/750 by MicroVAX II. The market niche is defined as all configurations of these two computer models sold at a price between $50 and 180K. The irregular lines are the actual data while the thin straight line represents the model description.

CONCLUSIONS

The major part of a competitive substitution between products, families of products, and computer technologies is well described by a *logistic-growth* process. Contrary to what one may intuitively expect, the rate of such a substitution does not depend on the price of the transaction. All new-technology computer models which have penetrated the market niche to 10% have proved their competitive advantage and will continue diffusing with comparable rates. Their diffusion will be hampered only by the degree of incompatibility with the previous technology. The replacement of PDPs by VAXes took around three years before it reached the substitution rates later observed among VAX products themselves.

Compatibility among computers mostly concerns software, but peripherals and other accessories can play a similar role. Under full compatibility, a new technology which becomes established (one which survives infant mortality) will pass from a 20% market share to an 80% one in less than one year. This transition can be up to three times slower for incompatible products.

During the early phases the substitution rates are different. The fully compatible idealized transition requires one trimester to pass from 10 to 20%, but also one trimester to pass from 5 to 10%. Moreover, there are deviations to be expected. An accelerated growth rate may be witnessed as a catching up effect, or erratic fluctuations may appear similar to those seen when approaching the ceiling (above 90%).

Despite these uncertainties the logistic substitution model can be used to understand the competitive dynamics. It can also be used to forecast market shares, but this was not done in Figures 3 to 6 as it fell outside the scope of this article. Such forecasts must be supplemented with added value from marketers, thus becoming a company's internal affair. What must be emphasized here is that this methodology conceived by Fisher and Pry and generalized by Marchetti and Nakicenovic is unquestionably a valuable one.

REFERENCES

1. Fisher, J. C., and Pry, R. H., A Simple Substitution Model of Technological Change, *Technol. Forecast. Soc. Change*, *3*: 1971, pp. 75–88.
2. A special form of Pearl's law; cf. Raymond Pearl, *The Biology of Population Growth*, New York: Alfred A. Knopf, 1925, as cited by Fisher and Pry, ref. *1*.
3. Nakicenovic, N., Software Package for the Logistic Substitution Model, *RR-79-12*, IIASA, Laxenburg, Austria, 1979.
4. Verhulst, P.-F., Notice sur la loi que la population suit dans son accroissement, *Corres. Mathématique et Physique*, *10*: 113–121 (1838).
5. Marchetti, C., Primary Energy Substitution Models: On the Interaction Between Energy and Society, *Technolog. Forecast. Soc. Change*, *10*: 345–356 (1977).
6. Marchetti, C., Infrastructures for Movement, *Technol. Forecast. Soc. Change*, *32* (4): 373–393 (1987); and Nakicenovic, N., Growth to Limits, Long Waves and the Dynamics of Technology, doctoral dissertation an der Sozial-und Wirtschaftswissenschaftlichen Fakultat, Universitat Wien, 1984.
7. Modis, T., and Debecker, A., Chaos-Like States Can Be Expected Before and After Logistic Growth, to appear in *Technolog. Forecast. Soc. Change*, 41(2): 111–120 (1992).
8. Bagwell, P., and Modis, T., Price Elasticity and Market Trends in the Computer Industry, *J. Mktg., Rev.* (submitted for publication).

THEODORE MODIS

3-D IMAGING IN MEDICINE

INTRODUCTION

Objectives

Medical imaging technology has experienced a dramatic change over the past two decades. Previously, x-ray radiography was the only method available capable of depicting organs as superimposed shadows on photographic film. These images suffered from poor contrast and—even more important—gave no information about the depth of an object. With the advent of modern computers, such new *tomographic* imaging modalities as computed tomography (CT) and magnetic resonance imaging (MRI) were developed which could deliver cross-sectional images of a patient's anatomy (*tomography*, from greek: τομη cut, γραφειν to record). These images depict, with unprecedented precision, various organs free of overlays (Fig. 1). Even the three-dimensional (3-D) structure of organs can be recorded if a sequence of parallel cross-sections is taken.

In current practice, the individual cross-sectional images of a tomographic study are visually inspected in order to establish a diagnosis. This procedure is suitable for typical radiological investigations like the detection of a tumor. For many clinical tasks (e.g., surgical planning), however, it is necessary to understand complex and often disordered 3-D structures. Experience has shown that a "mental reconstruction" of objects from cross-sectional images is extremely difficult and strongly depends on the observer's training and imagination. For these cases, it is certainly desirable to present the human body as a surgeon or an anatomist would see it.

The aim of 3-D imaging in medicine is to create precise and realistic views of objects from medical volume data. The resulting images, although, of course, they are two-dimensional, are often called 3-D images or *3-D reconstructions*, to distinguish them from 2-D cross-sections or conventional radiographic images. The first attempts date back to the late 1970s (1–3), with the first clinical applications reported on visualization of bone from CT in craniofacial surgery and orthopedics, (4–7). Methods and applications have since been extended to other subjects and imaging modalities. Recently, the same principles have also been applied to sampled and simulated data from other domains, such as fluid dynamics, geology, and meteorology. As a general expression, the term *volume visualization* is now widely accepted (8).

Related Fields

Three-dimensional imaging has its roots in three other fields of computer science, which are image processing, computer vision, and computer graphics, respectively. *Image processing* deals with any image-to-image transformations, such as filters or geometric

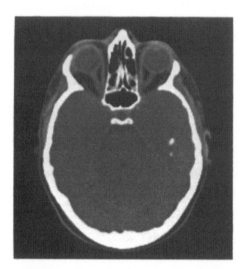 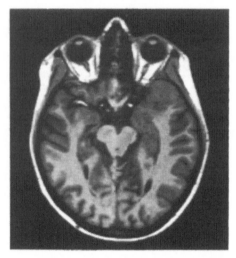

FIGURE 1   Tomographic images of a head. (Left) X-ray computed tomography (CT). (Right) magnetic resonance imaging (MRI). These modalities show widely complementary aspects of the anatomy.

transformations (9). Most steps in 3-D imaging can therefore be considered as special image processing methods.

Computer vision, also known as *image understanding*, is the construction of symbolic descriptions from input images (10,11). In 3-D imaging, the more low-level functions of image segmentation and interpretation are used in order to identify different parts of a volume which may be displayed or removed. They have to be strictly distinguished from higher level functions such as automatic detection of lesions or even computer aided diagnosis, which are investigated in *artificial intelligence* (12).

Computer graphics provides methods to synthesize images from numerical descriptions (13,14). These techniques were originally developed for realistic display of human-defined objects, such as models from *computer-aided design* (CAD). Objects in 3-D space usually are represented by infinitely thin surface patches such as triangles or higher order curves. Contributions of computer graphics to 3-D imaging include data structures, projection techniques, and shading models.

Basic Readings

Three-dimensional imaging in medicine is a rapidly evolving field. Basic readings comprise both textbooks on related areas (e.g., 9–14), and a number of research papers. A collection of major contributions from 1975–1990 is found in the excellent tutorial by Kaufman (8).

The current state of the art is presented in some conference proceedings (15–19) and special journal issues (20–22). Periodic updates are provided at conferences such as *SIGGRAPH* (published in *Computer Graphics*), *Visualization in Biomedical Computing*, *Computer Assisted Radiology*, and in such journals as *IEEE Transactions on Medical Imaging*, *IEEE Computer Graphics and Applications*, *Journal of Computer Assisted Tomography*, and *CVGIP: Graphical Models and Image Processing*.

IMAGING MODALITIES

Medical imaging technology is based on various physical phenomena, such as x-ray attenuation in computed tomography (CT) (23, 24), relaxation of magnetized hydrogen nuclei in magnetic resonance imaging (MRI) (25), sound reflections in ultrasonography (US) (26,27), or radioactive decay of injected markers in positron emission tomography (PET) and single photon emission computed tomography (SPECT) (28). The resulting images show widely complementary aspects of a patient's anatomy (structure) and physiology (function). CT is especially suitable to image high-density objects such as bone; MRI, in contrast, is very sensitive to variations in soft tissue (Fig. 1). Compared with these, US offers a rather low image quality, the depicted structures are mainly borders between different organs. PET and SPECT visualize the metabolism inside a patient.

All these imaging modalities are fully computerized and deliver the images already in digital form as a matrix of currently typical 128^2 to 1024^2 picture elements. The *intensity* of a picture element or *pixel* represents the physical property, measured in a small rectangular volume element or *voxel* in 3-D space. In CT and MRI, intensity resolution is typically 12 bits, equivalent to 4096 different gray values. This exceeds by far the abilities of a human observer who can distinguish at most between 100 different intensity levels.

For 3-D imaging, it is important whether different tissue types can be automatically identified. In CT, major classes such as background, soft tissue, and bone show characteristic intensity ranges. At their borders, however, the so-called *partial volume effect* occurs where two or more tissues are present within one voxel. The resulting intermediate intensity value indicates the percentages of the different materials.

In contrast to CT, the intensity ranges of different tissue types in MRI images typically overlap or are even identical. However, MRI can generate multiparameter images of the same anatomy, which somewhat compensates for this problem. Each parameter shows a different aspect, such as proton density or various relaxation times (so-called T_1- and T_2-weighted images). The recent introduction of MR angiography (MRA) emphasizes flow effects and thus is especially suitable to visualize blood vessels.

METHODS

Overview

We present a rather detailed description of 3-D imaging methodology. An overview is shown in Figure 2. After acquisition of a series of parallel cross-sections, the data usually undergo some preprocessing for data conversion and image filtering. From this point, one of several paths may be followed.

The dotted line in Figure 2 represents an early approach where an object is reconstructed from its contours on the cross-sectional images. This method is shortly reviewed later. All other methods, represented by the solid line, start from a contiguous *data volume*. If required, equal spacing in all three directions can be achieved by interpolation. Like a 2-D image, a 3-D volume can be filtered to improve image quality.

The next step is to identify the different objects represented in the data volume so that they can be removed or selected for visualization. This task breaks down into segmentation and interpretation. The simplest way is to binarize the data with an intensity threshold (e.g., to distinguish bone from other tissues in CT). Especially for MRI data,

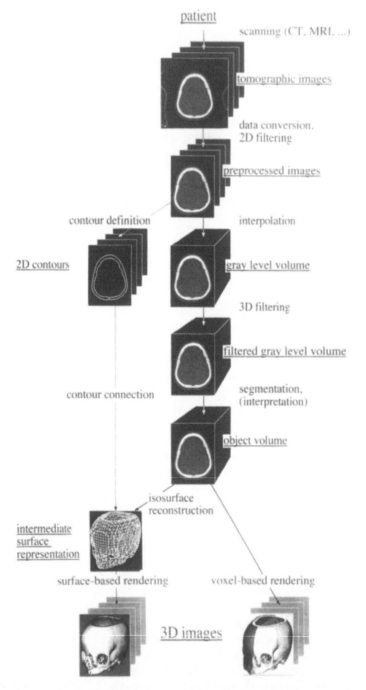

FIGURE 2   General sketch of the 3D imaging pipeline. Individual processing steps may be left out, combined, or reversed in order by a particular method.

however, more sophisticated segmentation methods are required. This field is still subject to basic research, the major focuses of which are presented below.

At this point, there is a choice to be made as to which *rendering* technique is to be used. The more traditional surface-based methods first create an intermediate surface representation of the object to be shown. It may then be rendered with any standard computer graphics method. More recently, voxel-based methods have been developed which create a 3-D view directly from the volume data. These methods use the full gray level information to render surfaces, cuts, or transparent and semitransparent volumes. Both surface- and voxel-based methods have their merits; the decision which one should be taken for a particular application depends both on the available memory and computing power and on the visualization goals.

The next two sections discuss some extensions to the 3-D imaging pipeline presented so far. The objective of multimodality matching is to register data volumes from different sources. Manipulation of volume data is used (e.g., for surgical simulation systems). Finally, we take a look at the accuracy of the resulting 3-D images, and some hard- and software considerations for implementing a 3-D imaging system.

Preprocessing

Data Conversion

The usual first step in the 3-D processing pipeline after image acquisition is data conversion. Besides a change of the data format which may be required, this involves a number of measures for data reduction to save storage space and processing time.

Three-dimensional imaging usually deals with huge amounts of data. A typical CT study consisting of 80 cross-sections with 512×512 pixels requires 40 megabytes of memory. Furthermore, if an explicit interpolation step is performed, the size of the data may be multiplied. Some common techniques for data reduction are

- Cutting: a region of interest is chosen; other parts (e.g., outside the body) of the images are cut.
- Reduced spatial resolution: matrix size is reduced (e.g., by averaging from 512^2 to 256^2 pixels).
- Reduced intensity resolution (e.g., from 16 to 8 bit): an intensity window is chosen which represents most of the contrast in the images. This is done usually on the basis of a *histogram* which shows the distribution of the gray values.

The latter two points will generally cause some loss of information, they should therefore be used with care.

Filtering

Another important aspect of preprocessing is image *filtering* (9). This is a rather general term for all kinds of image processing routines which are used to smooth or enhance the information contents of an image. A typical example is to improve the signal-to-noise ratio, especially in MRI and US images. Well-known *noise filters* are average, median, and Gaussian filters. These filters however tend to smooth out small details as well. Better results are obtained with *anisotropic diffusion* methods (29). Other filter types are applied to emphasize special aspects of an image (e.g., to enhance edges).

Filters can be designed to work on 1-D lines, 2-D images, 3-D volumes, or higher dimensional data. In principle, a 1-D filter can also be applied to the individual rows or columns of a 2-D image. In general, however, results are better if an image is filtered with a 2-D filter and a volume with a 3-D filter.

Interpolation

At this point, the data are still a stack of 2-D images. If stacked atop each other, a contiguous *gray level volume* is obtained. The resulting data structure is an orthogonal 3-D array of voxels, each representing an intensity value. It is called the *voxel model*.

Many algorithms for 3-D imaging are working on *isotropic* volumes where the sampling density is equal in all three dimensions. In practice, however, only very few data sets have this property. CT images are often taken with considerable and varying spacing between the cross-sections so that the resolution in the image plane is much better than perpendicular to it. In these cases, the missing information has to be reconstructed in an *interpolation* step. A very simple method is image replication (6). Better results are obtained with linear interpolation of the intensities between adjacent images. Higher order functions such as splines may be used as well (30). An alternative approach are shape-based methods (31); these are however wasting most of the original gray level information.

Data Structures

Among the number of different data structures for volume data, the most important are

- *Binary voxel model*: Voxel values are either 1 (object) or 0 (no object). This very simple model is not currently used in many situations. In order to reduce storage requirements, binary volumes may be recursively subdivided into homogeneous subvolumes; the resulting data structure is called an *octree* (32).
- *Gray level voxel model*: Each voxel holds an intensity information.
- *Generalized voxel model*: Besides a gray value, each voxel contains further information such as an object membership label (''this voxel belongs to brain''), material percentages (''this voxel contains 60% bone''), or data from other sources (e.g., MRI and PET). This data structure is the basis for many advanced applications (33).

Object Definition

A gray level volume usually represents a large number of different organs. To display a particular one, we thus have to decide which parts of the data we want to use or ignore. In an ideal case, selection would be done with a command like ''show only the brain.'' This requires, however, that the computer knows which parts of the volume (or, more precisely, which voxels) constitute the brain and which do not. This information is also needed for morphometric measurements of distances, angles, and volumes.

The aim of *object definition* is to establish relationships between voxels and meaningful (anatomical) terms. This task breaks down into segmentation and interpretation. The result is an *object volume* which may be organized using the generalized voxel model.

Segmentation

The first step toward object definition is to partition the gray level volume into different regions which are homogeneous with respect to some formal criteria and corresponding to real anatomical objects. This process is called *segmentation* (10).

A very simple but nevertheless important example which is used throughout the next sections is to specify a certain intensity range with lower and upper *threshold values*. A voxel belongs to the selected class if and only if its intensity value is within the specified range. Thresholding is a common method to select bone or soft tissues in CT. It is often performed during the rendering process itself so that no explicit segmentation step is required.

A drawback of any binary decisions (e.g., thresholding) is that small objects which take only a small fraction of a voxel and cases of uncertainty cannot be handled properly. To model these cases, *fuzzy* segmentation techniques have been developed. Here, a set of probabilities is assigned to every voxel, indicating the evidence for different materials. For CT data, Drebin et al. use a maximum likelihood classifier which calculates material percentages from a priori known distributions, according to Bayes' rule (34). Fuzzy segmentation is closely related to the so-called volume rendering methods discussed later.

The segmentation task gets much more complicated if different organs with similar gray level characteristics are to be distinguished. Advanced segmentation methods for these cases are still subject to basic research, the major directions are presented in a subsequent section.

Interpretation

Segmentation delivers a set of regions in a data volume, but in many cases it is not clear which anatomical objects they represent. If required, an *interpretation* step can be performed in which the various regions are *identified* and *labeled* with meaningful terms such as ''white matter'' or ''ventricle.'' This can be done interactively or with an automatic system. For simple applications such as visualization of bone from CT, interpretation is usually left out.

Surface-Based Rendering

The first techniques for volume visualization which evolved in the late 1970s were strongly based on conventional computer graphics methods. The key idea of these so-called *surface-based* methods is to extract an *intermediate surface description* of the relevant objects from the volume data. Only this information is then used for rendering.

A clear advantage of surface-based methods is the possibly very high data reduction from volume to surface representations. This affects both memory requirements and computing times. Views from different angles can thus quickly be generated. Computing times can be further reduced if the surface representations are based on common data structures such as triangle meshes which are supported by computer graphics workstations. Another advantage in this case is that standard computer graphics software can be used.

On the other hand, the *surface reconstruction* step throws away most of the valuable information on the cross-sectional images (35). Once the surface representation is created, there is no way to get back to the original intensity values. Even simple cuts

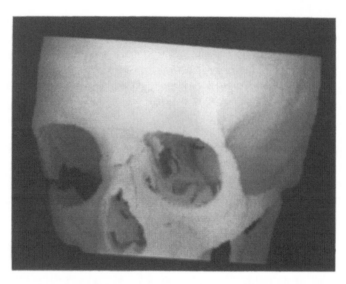

FIGURE 3   3D image of the skull of an accident victim produced from CT scans using the cuberille model (courtesy of G. T. Herman, Dept. of Radiology, University of Pennsylvania).

cannot be done because there is no information about the interior of an object. Furthermore, every change of surface definition criteria requires recalculation of the whole data
structure.

The following subsections focus on methods of how to reconstruct surface descriptions from tomographic images. The subsequent rendering is largely based on standard
computer graphics methods, thus the review is a short divergence.

Surface Reconstruction from Contours

In 1975, Keppel presented an algorithm to reconstruct a surface representation from a
stack of planar contours (36). This method has since been modified by several other authors (2,37–39). In a first step, a set of object contours is defined on every tomographic
image (Fig. 2, dotted line). This may be done interactively or with an edge detecting
operator. In a second step, the contours from adjacent cross-sections are connected to
form a 3-D structure. If triangles are used as surface elements, this process is called
triangulation.

The crucial step with this method is to connect properly the different contours. Especially for medical data, shapes are often extremely complex and vary greatly from one
cross-section to the next. With general solutions lacking, contour connection is based on
heuristic rules; it is questionable, however, whether they will apply in every case. Therefore, methods for surface reconstruction from 2-D contours are not used to any great extent in practice today.

Surface Reconstruction from Volumes

In contrast to contour connection, surface reconstruction from volumes is a true 3-D operation. Given a certain intensity value, its goal is to create an *isosurface*, representing
all points where this intensity is found in the original gray level volume. Alternatively,
the surface can be defined using object membership labels.

The first method to be widely used in clinical practice was developed by Herman and co-workers (3,4,40–42). It is known as the *cuberille model* (Fig. 3). The gray level volume is first binarized with an intensity threshold. Then, a list of square voxel faces is created which denote the border between voxels in- and outside the object, using a surface tracking algorithm. It can be shown that the resulting surfaces are always well-defined and closed.

A surface description created with this algorithm is quite simple in the sense that all faces are of the same size and shape, with only six different orientations. Of course, this is only a rough approximation of the actual object form. The resulting 3-D images thus miss a lot of fine details.

More recently, newer methods have been described which utilize the full gray level information. The *marching cubes* algorithm developed by Lorensen and Cline considers a basic cube of $2\times2\times2$ contiguous voxels in the data volume (43,44). Depending on whether one or more of these voxels are inside the object (i.e., above a threshold value), a surface representation of up to four triangles is placed within the cube. The exact location of the triangles is found by linear interpolation of the intensities at the voxel vertices. The result is a highly detailed surface representation with subvoxel resolution. Surface orientations are calculated from gray level gradients. Some erroneous details of the algorithm are discussed elsewhere (45,46).

Applied to clinical data, the marching cubes algorithm typically creates hundreds of thousands of triangles. Most of these triangles are so small that they hardly contribute to the final 3-D image. A somewhat simplified approach developed by the same group uses points instead of triangles (44). This *dividing cube* method subdivides a group of $2\times2\times2$ contiguous voxels into smaller cubes, whereby the intensities are interpolated. The surface description is made from the cubes that approximate the threshold value. As with the marching cubes algorithm, surface orientations are calculated from gray level gradients.

Shading

After the surface representation has been created with one of the above described methods, it is mapped to a raster image display to make the final 3-D image. This so-called *rasterization* step breaks down into the subtasks of scan conversion, hidden surface removal, and shading (13). Scan conversion and hidden surface removal are standard problems of computer graphics and will thus not be covered here. For surface shading, however, a number of nonstandard methods are used. A more detailed survey of shading methods for 3-D imaging can be found elsewhere (47).

In general, shading is the realistic display of an object, based on position, orientation, and characteristics of its surface and the light sources illuminating it (13,48). The reflective properties of a surface are described with an illumination model such as the Phong model, which uses a combination of ambient light, diffuse (such as chalk) and specular (such as polished metal) reflections. A key input to these models is the local surface orientation, described by a *normal vector* perpendicular to the surface.

In principle, the surfaces created with the cuberille method can be shaded with any of the methods developed in computer graphics. Due to the low dynamic range of only six different surface orientations, however, the images appear more or less jagged. An alternative approach is to use the information in the so-called z-buffer. This 2-D array describes the local depth of a scene (i.e., the distance between image plane and object surface). In *distance shading*, the intensity of a pixel is a function only of the corresponding value in the z-buffer (6,49). A more realistic impression is obtained if the z-buffer is used to estimate the local surface normal vectors. This *distance gradient shading* method was first used by Gordon and Reynolds (50), a number of variations have since been published (41,47,51). Still, image quality is low, as compared with other methods.

The original marching cubes algorithm calculates the surface normal vectors from the gray level gradients in the data volume. This method was first used for voxel-based surface rendering. Alternatively, the surface normal vectors of the created triangles can be taken. Both versions deliver highly detailed images, where the latter variation shows some staircase artifacts. Images produced with both methods are compared elsewhere (51,52).

Voxel-Based Rendering

In voxel-based rendering, images are created directly from the volume data. No intermediate surface representations are needed. After some early experiments by Oswald et al. (53), Tuy and Tuy (54), and Lenz et al. (55), voxel-based rendering of gray level volumes evolved in the second half of the 1980s and has since gained an enormous popularity. Compared with surface-based methods, the major advantage is that all gray level information which has originally been acquired is kept during the rendering process. As shown by Höhne et al. (56–58), this makes it an ideal technique for interactive data exploration. Threshold values and other parameters which are not clear from the beginning can interactively be changed. Furthermore, voxel-based rendering allows a combined display of different aspects such as opaque and semi-transparent surfaces, cuts, and maximum intensity projections.

A current drawback of voxel-based techniques is that the large amount of data which have to be handled does not allow real-time applications on present day computers. With dedicated hardware, however, rendering times are already down to less than a second. With computing power further increasing, this problem will be overcome in a few years.

Projection Techniques

In voxel-based rendering, we basically have the choice between two scanning strategies: pixel by pixel (image order) or voxel by voxel (volume order). These strategies correspond to the image and object order rasterization algorithms used in computer graphics (13).

Image order strategies scan the data volume on rays along the view direction (54,55). These methods are commonly known as *ray casting*:

FOR each pixel on image plane DO
    FOR each sampling point on associated ray DO
        compute contribution to pixel

The principle is illustrated in Figure 4. Ray casting can be considered as a nonrecursive variant of the ray tracing methods used in computer graphics. Along the ray, visibility of surfaces and objects is easily determined. After an opaque surface has been found, the ray can stop.

Ray casting is a very flexible and intuitive scanning strategy. Integration of opaque, semitransparent, and transparent rendering methods is comparatively easy. Furthermore, image order scanning can be used to render both voxel and polygon data at the same time (59,60). All images presented in this section were rendered with a ray casting technique.

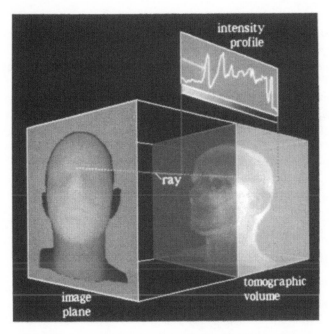

FIGURE 4   Principle of ray casting for volume visualization.

On the other hand, performance of ray casting algorithms is limited both by high memory (random access to the input volume) and computing (interpolation for oblique rays) requirements.

A strategy to reduce computation times is to prerotate the whole volume so that the rays for a given view angle scan along the lines of the array (34,57). Even if several images are rendered from this view, interpolation is thus required only once. A different technique for speed-up is to start with a coarse sampling density to generate a view quickly. If the user does not specify any changes, sampling density is adaptively refined to full resolution (61).

Volume order strategies scan the input volume along lines or columns of the 3-D array, projecting a chosen aspect onto the image plane in the direction of view:

FOR each sampling point in volume DO
    FOR each pixel projected onto DO
        compute contribution to pixel

The volume can either be traversed in back-to-front (BTF) order (62) from the voxel with maximal to the voxel with minimal distance to the image plane, or vice versa in front-to-back (FTB) order (50,53). In both cases, several voxels may be projected to the same pixel. If an opaque surface is to be shown, the visible parts thus have to be determined. In BTF, pixel values are simply overwritten so that only the visible surface appears. In FTB, pixels which have already been written are protected using a z-buffer.

Scanning the input data as they are stored, these techniques are reasonably fast even on computers with small main memory, and especially suitable to be parallelized. So far, ray casting algorithms still offer a higher flexibility in combining different display techniques. However, volume rendering techniques working in volume order have already been developed (63).

Surfaces

Using one of the described projection methods, the visible surface of an object can be determined with a threshold or an object membership label. For shading, any of the methods developed for the cuberille model, such as distance or distance gradient shading, can be applied.

As shown by Höhne and Bernstein (64) and independently by Barillot et al. (65), a much more realistic and detailed presentation is obtained if the gray level information present in the data is taken into account. As a consequence of the tomographic acquisition process, the gray levels in the 3-D neighborhood of a surface voxel are representing the relative proportions of different materials inside these voxels. The resulting gray level gradients can thus be used to calculate the surface inclinations. The simplest variant is to calculate the components of a gradient G for a surface voxel at (i,j,k) from the gray levels g of its six neighbors along the main axes as

$$G_x = g(i + 1,j,k) - g(i - 1,j,k)$$
$$G_y = g(i,j + 1,k) - g(i,j - 1,k)$$
$$G_z = g(i,j,k + 1) - g(i,j,k - 1)$$

Normalization of G yields the surface normal (66). The gray level gradient may also be calculated from all 26 neighbors in a $3 \times 3 \times 3$ neighborhood, weighted according to their distance from the surface voxel (66, 67). Aliasing patterns are thus almost eliminated.

In case of very small objects like thin bones, the gray level gradient does not correspond to the actual surface inclination any more. Pommert et al. proposed an adaptive gray level gradient method which chooses only 3–6 meaningful neighbors (51,52,68). The basic idea is to maximize the gradient magnitude. This algorithm gives smooth images even for thin objects.

Cut Planes

Once a surface view is available, a very simple and effective method to visualize interior structures is cutting. If the original intensity values are mapped onto the cut plane, they can be better understood in their anatomical context (56–58). A special case is selective cutting, where certain objects are excluded (Fig. 5).

Integral and Maximum Intensity Projection

A different way to look into an object is to integrate over the intensity values along the viewing ray. If applied to the whole data volume, this is a step back to the old x-ray projection technique (55,56). If applied in a selective way, it is nevertheless helpful in special cases (51,57).

For small bright objects such as vessels from MR angiography, maximum intensity projection is a suitable display technique. Along each ray through the data volume, the maximum gray value is determined and projected onto the image plane (69). The advantage of this method is that neither segmentation nor shading are needed, which may fail for very small vessels. But there are also some drawbacks: as light reflection is totally ignored, maximum intensity projection does not give a realistic 3-D impression. Spatial perception can be improved by rotating the object or by a combined presentation with other surfaces or cut planes (58).

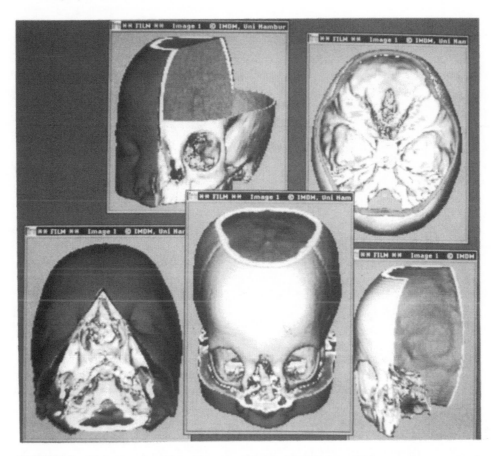

FIGURE 5 3D image of a child with a congenital facial cleft from CT (ray casting, gray level gradient shading). Soft tissues and bone were detected with threshold values and rendered as opaque surfaces. Cuts are visualizing the original intensity values.

Volume Rendering

Volume rendering is the visualization equivalent to fuzzy segmentation. These methods were first described in 1988 by Drebin et al. (34), Levoy (70), Sabella (71), and Upson and Keeler (72), and since modified by various groups (58,63,73–75). A commonly assumed underlying model is that of a colored, semitransparent gel with suspended reflective particles (76). Illumination rays are partly reflected and change color while travelling through the volume. Each voxel is assigned a color and an opacity. This opacity is a product of an "object weighting function" and a "gradient weighting function." The object weighting function is usually dependent of the gray value, but it can also be the result of a more sophisticated fuzzy segmentation algorithm. The gradient weighting function emphasizes surfaces for 3-D display. All voxels are shaded, using the gray level gradient method. The shaded values along a viewing ray are weighted and summed up. A somewhat simplified basic equation is given as follows (frontal illumination):

I intensity of reflected light
p index of sampling point on ray (0 . . . maximum depth of scene)

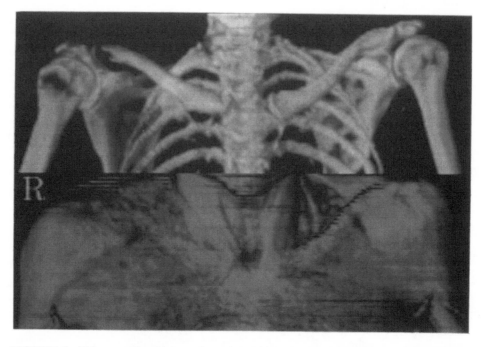

FIGURE 6   Volume-rendered image of a patient with a recurrent lymphoma in right supraclav-
icular and cervical region from CT. (Top) bone enhanced. (Bottom) soft tissue enhanced (figure by
E. K. Fishman, Dept. of Radiology, Johns Hopkins University. Reprinted with permission from
Ref. 17, p. 439).

l	fraction of incoming light	$(0 \ldots 1)$
α	local opacity	$(0 \ldots 1)$
ς	local shading component	

$$I(p,l) = \alpha(p) \cdot l \cdot \varsigma(p) + (1 - \alpha(p)) \cdot I(p + 1, l \cdot (1 - \alpha(p))$$

The total reflected intensity as displayed on the 3-D image is given as I (0,1).

Since binary decisions are avoided in volume rendering, the resulting images are
very smooth and show a lot of fine details (Fig. 6). Another important advantage is that
even coarsely defined objects can be rendered with acceptable quality. The 12-week-old
fetus shown in Figure 7 was rendered from rather noisy ultrasonography data for which
a binary segmentation proved worthless. Other examples can be found (51).

On the other hand, the more or less transparent images produced with volume
rendering methods are often hard to understand such that their clinical use is limited
(51, 52). Spatial perception can however be improved by rotating the object. Another
serious problem is the large number of parameters which have to be specified to define
the weighting functions. A good mapping is difficult to find, and even small variations
can completely change the image. Finally, volume rendering is comparably slow because
weighting and shading operations are performed for many voxels on each ray. If certain
values such as gradients are precalculated, a substantial speed-up can be achieved at the
cost of higher memory requirements (34).

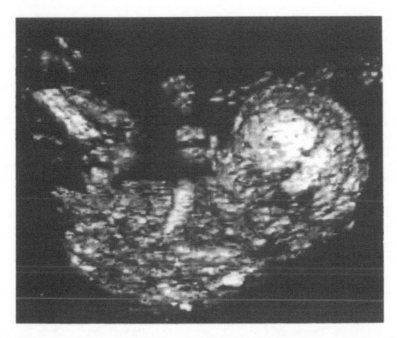

FIGURE 7 Volume-rendered image of a 12-week-old in vivo fetus from ultrasonography. Even though the data are rather noisy, the image shows some surprisingly fine details such as legs (left), arms (center), and the head with mandible, nose and some sutures (right).

Advanced Segmentation Methods

For all 3-D images shown so far, the interesting regions were selected with a threshold or a fuzzy classification. Unfortunately, these simple segmentation methods are not suitable if different structures have overlapping or even identical gray level ranges. This situation is a frequent occurrence for soft tissues from CT and MRI.

Several advanced segmentation methods for 3-D medical data are being developed at present. The major directions of research are presented in the following subsections. Division into three classes—point-, edge-, and region-based methods—roughly follows that in Ref. 10. The described methods have been tested, often successfully, on a number of cases; experience has shown, however, that they should be used with extreme care.

Point-Based Segmentation

Point-based segmentation methods classify a voxel depending solely on its intensity, no matter where it is located. A simple example is thresholding, which can be applied to single- or multiparameter data, such as T_1- and T_2-weighted images in MRI. In the latter case, individual threshold values are used for every parameter.

To somewhat generalize this concept, voxels in an *n*-parameter data set can be considered as *n*-dimensional vectors in an *n*-dimensional *feature space*. In *pattern recognition* (77), the feature space is partitioned into arbitrarily shaped subspaces, representing different tissue classes or organs. This is called the *training phase*: in supervised training, the partition is derived from feature vectors which are known to represent particular tissues (78–81). In unsupervised training, the partition is automatically generated (81). In the subsequent *test phase*, a voxel is classified according to the position of its feature vector in the partitioned feature space.

Pattern recognition methods have been successfully applied to considerable numbers of two- or three-parametric MRI data volumes of head (78,79,81) and chest (80). Quite frequently, however, isolated voxels or small regions are incorrectly classified (e.g., subcutaneous fat in the same class as white matter). To eliminate these errors, a connected component analysis is often applied (see region-based segmentation).

A closely related method based on recent *neural network* methodology has been developed by Kohonen (82). Instead of an *n*-dimensional feature space, a so-called *topological map* of *m* × *m* *n*-dimensional vectors is used. During the training phase, the map iteratively adapts itself to a set of training vectors which may either represent selected tissues (supervised learning (83)) or the whole data volume (unsupervised learning (74)). Finally, the map develops several relatively homogeneous regions, which correspond to different tissues or organs in the original data. Performance of the topological map for 3-D MRI data seems to be generally equivalent to pattern recognition methods (74,83).

Edge-Based Segmentation

The aim of edge-based segmentation methods is to detect intensity discontinuities in a gray level volume. These edges (in 3-D, they are actually surfaces; however, it is common to speak about edges) are assumed to represent the borders between different organs or tissues. Regions are subsequently defined as the enclosed areas.

A common strategy for edge detection is to locate the maxima of the first derivative of the 3-D intensity function. A method which very accurately locates the edges was developed by Canny (84). All algorithms using the first derivative however have the drawback that the detected contours are usually not closed (i.e., they do not properly separate different regions). To repair broken edges, combinations with region-based methods are currently being investigated (85).

An alternative approach is to detect zero-crossings of the second derivative. The Marr-Hildreth operator convolves the input data with the Laplacian of a Gaussian; the resulting contour volume describes the locations of the edges (86). With a 3-D extension of this operator, the complete human brain could be segmented and visualized from MRI for the first time (87,88). Similar approaches were developed by other groups (89). Occasionally, however, this operator creates erroneous ''bridges'' between different materials which have to be interactively removed. Furthermore, curved edges are dislocated outward. A method to correct this error, based on morphological filters (90), is presented elsewhere (88).

Region-Based Segmentation

Region-based segmentation methods consider whole regions instead of individual voxels or contours. Since we are actually interested in regions, this approach appears to be the most natural. Properties of a region includes its size, shape, location, variance of gray levels, and its spatial relation to other regions.

A typical application of region-based methods is to postprocess the results of a previous point-based segmentation step. A *connected component analysis* is applied to determine whether the voxels which have been classified as belonging to the same class are part of the same (connected) region. If not, the voxels in the smaller regions are often

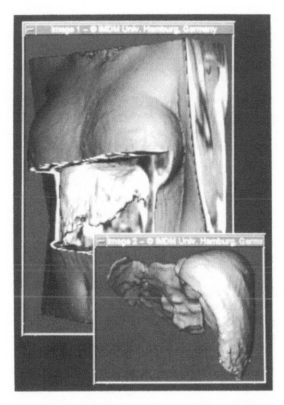

FIGURE 8   3-D image of a liver within its anatomical surroundings and a dorsal view or the excised liver from MRI. The liver was interactively segmented using morphological operations.

wrongly classified. On the other hand, *region growing* algorithms can be used to split and merge greater regions, according to certain criteria (10).

Region-based methods often combine segmentation and interpretation steps into a single algorithm. The knowledge required may be provided interactively by a human user, or automatically by a model. Cline et al. have developed an algorithm which grows a region from a user-selected seed voxel (91). Höhne and Hanson (92) propose an interactive segmentation system based on *mathematical morphology* (90). Regions are initially defined with thresholds; the user can subsequently apply operations such as "erosion" (to remove small "bridges" between erroneously connected parts), "dilation" (to close small gaps), region fill, or Boolean set operations. After each step, segmentation results are instantaneously inspected on a 3-D image (Fig. 8).

A different interactive method developed by Pizer et al. first creates a multiscale hierarchy of volume representations, based on higher-order features such as symmetry axes (93,94). Finally, the user can interactively select, add or subtract regions, or move to larger "parent" or smaller "child" regions in the hierarchy.

A number of automatic systems for region-based segmentation and interpretation also exist. Raya and Udupa use a rule-based system to successively generate a set of thresholds (95). Brummer et al. encode the knowledge required to detect brain contours in a fixed sequence of morphological operations (96). Bomans generates a set of hypotheses for every voxel, depending on its gray value (97). Location, surface-volume ratio, etc. of the resulting regions are compared to some predefined values, and the regions are modified accordingly (Fig. 9 - see color plate). Menhardt uses a rule-based system which models the anatomy with relations such as ''brain is inside skull'' (98). Regions are defined as fuzzy subsets of the volume, and the segmentation process is based on fuzzy logic and fuzzy topology.

The problem with automatic segmentation and interpretation systems is of course that the results may be wrong if the underlying model does not properly represent the data. The models used so far are not yet adequate to handle, for example, various pathologies.

Multimodality Matching

It is often desirable to combine information from different imaging modalities to improve the information available to the clinician. For example, PET images show only physiological aspects; for their interpretation, it is necessary also to know the anatomy, as shown in MRI.

In general, different data sets do not match geometrically. It is therefore required to *register* the volumes in relation to each other. This is quite a difficult task; to make it somewhat easier, external markers can be attached to the patient which will be visible on the different modalities. Their positions in the respective volumes are defining the geometric transformation. Without this additional information, it is necessary to define corresponding features in both data sets. A very robust method which registers the 3-D skin surface of the patient has been developed by Levin and others (99, 100), a result is shown in Figure 10. Other approaches use corresponding landmarks, which are, e.g., interactively defined on 3-D images (101).

Manipulation

So far, focus has been on mere visualization of the data. Taking one a step further the data are manipulated at the computer to simulate surgery (102–104). These techniques are especially useful for craniofacial surgery where a skull is dissected into small pieces, and then rearranged to achieve a desirable shape. In the system developed by Yasuda et al. (104), a cut is defined by interactively drawing a closed contour onto a 3-D image (Fig. 11). The resulting segments can be inspected from other view directions, and individually moved and rearranged in 3-D space. The system can even roughly predict the resulting face.

Image Fidelity

For clinical applications, it is of course important to assure that the resulting 3-D images really show the true anatomical situation, or at least to know about their limitations. A common approach is to compare 3-D images rendered by means of different algorithms (105). This method however is of limited value since the ''truth'' usually is not known.

A different approach to investigate image fidelity is to apply 3-D imaging techniques to simulated data (51,52,68,106), and to data acquired from cadavers (107–109). In both cases, the actual situation is available for comparison. Using the first technique, the accuracy, for instance of different shading algorithms, could be shown. Among the results of the latter studies are visibility of sutures or fracture gaps as a function of ac-

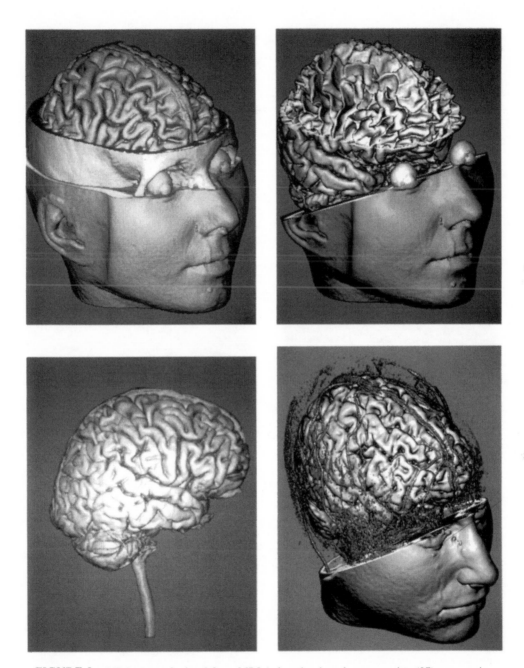

FIGURE 9   3-D images of a head from MRI (relaxation-based segmentation (97), ray casting, gray level gradient shading). (Top left) Brain and bone. (Top right) white matter unveiled. (Bottom left) Brain in a lateral view. (Bottom right) Combined display of brain from MRI with blood vessels from MR angiography.

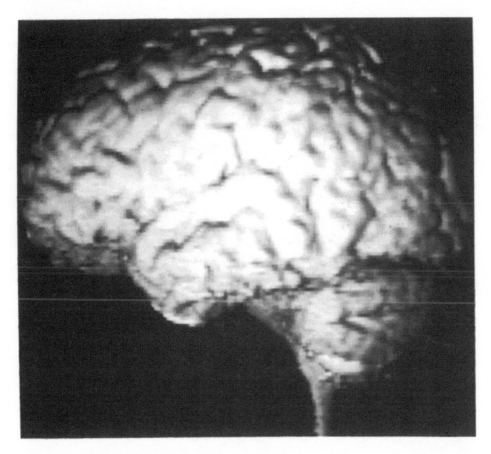

FIGURE 10 Integrated 3-D image of brain anatomy and physiology, obtained by fusing MRI and PET data. A hypometabolic lesion (dark, at center) appears in the left temporal lobe (courtesy of D. Levin, Dept. of Radiology, University of Chicago).

quisition parameters and object size. Diagnostic performance of 3-D imaging and conventional radiographs has been compared using the *receiver operator characteristic* (ROC) analysis (110).

Implementation Aspects

Acceptance of volume visualization systems in a clinical environment strongly depends on both computing times used and the availability of user-friendly interfaces. In order to speed up image generation, a number of dedicated hardware systems have been developed which allow near-real-time applications even for volume data (e.g., Voxel Processor by Goldwasser et al. (111), Cube by Kaufman and Bakalash (112), or Pixel-Planes 5 by Fuchs et al. (113,114)). A key idea of these systems is to support massively parallel operation. A survey of major systems, both research and commercial, is presented by Kaufman et al. (115).

While dedicated hardware systems are not yet used in large numbers, a number of software packages have been developed which run directly on scanner or general-purpose

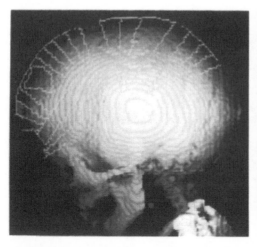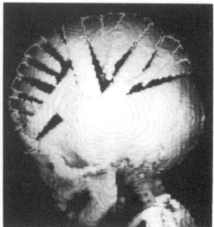

FIGURE 11   Surgical simulation. (Left) Preoperative skull with cutting lines. (Right) Result after rearrangement of the cut pieces (courtesy of T. Yasuda, Dept. of Information Engineering, University of Nagoya).

workstations (e.g., Voxel-Man (58), AVS (72), ANALYZE (73), 3D98 (116)). While the use of advanced window and menu techniques is already widespread, handling of the whole process from data conversion to 3-D imaging is still too complicated for the nontechnical user.

APPLICATIONS

At first glance, one might expect diagnostic radiology to be the major field of application for 3-D imaging. This is not the case. One reason is that clearly radiologists are especially skilled in reading cross-sectional images. Another reason is that many diagnostic tasks such as tumor detection and classification can well be done from tomographic images. Furthermore, 3-D visualization of these objects from MRI requires robust segmentation algorithms which are not yet available.

The situation is generally different in all fields where therapeutical decisions have to be made by nonradiologists on the basis of radiological images (117). A major field of application for 3-D imaging methods is *craniofacial surgery* (42,118–120). A typical case is shown in Figure 5.

Another important field of application is *traumatology*. Due to the emergency situation, planning times are usually very short. With new faster imaging modalities available and computing power ever increasing, 3-D imaging techniques are being introduced in the treatment of difficult cases. Especially in pelvic surgery where the morphology is difficult to assess, 3-D imaging is considered a great help (Fig. 12) (121,122).

An application that becomes more and more attractive with the increasing resolution and specificity of MRI is *neurosurgery planning*. Here the problem is to choose a proper access path to a lesion. Three-dimensional visualization of brain tissue from MRI and blood vessels from MR angiography before surgical intervention allows the surgeon

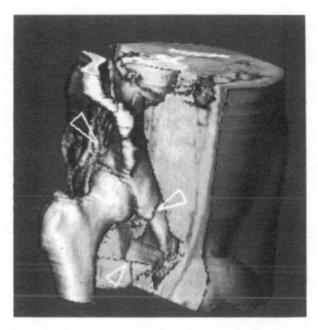

FIGURE 12 Pelvis with multiple fractures (arrows) from CT.

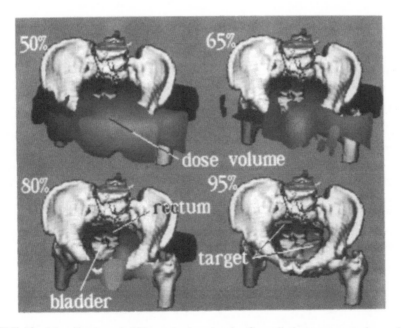

FIGURE 13 Visualization of different isodose levels of a radiation treatment plan, calculated from CT volume data. The study shows how the dose volume covers target (prostate) and organs at risk (rectum and bladder). The latter regions have been outlined by a radiologist.

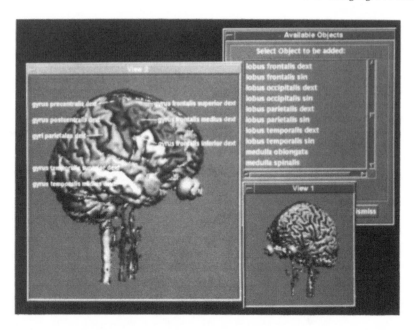

FIGURE 14   Anatomy teaching by dissection at the computer. The volume may be arbitrarily rotated and cut. By pointing to the visible surface, the selected region is highlighted and automatically annotated. The other way round, objects to be displayed can be selected from an alphabetical list.

to find a path with minimal risk in advance (Fig. 9) (58,123). In combination with a 3-D coordinate digitizer, the acquired information can even be used to guide the surgeon during the intervention (124). In conjunction with functional information from PET images, localization of a lesion is facilitated (Fig. 10) (100).

Another potential application that reduces the risk of therapeutic intervention is radiotherapy planning. Here, the objective is to focus the radiation to the target volume while avoiding radiation on healthy organs. Three-dimensional visualization of target volume, organs at risk and simulated radiation dose allows the realistic rehearsal of the treatment procedure (Fig. 13). Work in this field is done at several places (125,126).

Applications apart from clinical work include medical research and education (127,128). The 3-D brain atlas shown in Figure 14 is based on a high-quality MRI data set where every voxel has interactively been marked with a label, describing its membership to an anatomical or functional constituent of the brain (129). On the basis of the thus acquired description, various teaching programs can be written that allow dissection and surgical training at the computer screen.

CONCLUSIONS

Three-dimensional imaging in medicine has come a long way from the first experiments to the current, highly detailed renderings. As the rendering algorithms are improved and the fidelity of the resulting images is investigated, 3-D images are not mere pretty pictures, but a powerful source of information to the clinician. In certain areas such as craniofacial surgery or traumatology, 3-D imaging is increasingly becoming part of the standard preoperative procedures.

A number of problems still hinder an even broader use of 3-D imaging methods. First, current workstations are not yet able to deliver 3-D images fast enough. For the future, it is certainly desirable to be able to interact with the workstation in real time, instead of just looking at static images or precalculated movies. With further increase of computing power, this problem will be overcome in a few years.

The second major problem is the design of a user interface which is suitable for the clinician. Currently, there are still a large number of rather technical parameters to be met (e.g., for control of segmentation and shading). Acceptance in the medical community certainly will depend heavily on progress in this field.

A third problem is the segmentation of a volume into meaningful parts, representing different objects. To date, there are no robust methods which perform well in every case; especially for MRI. As has been shown, there is research in different directions going on which might eventually succeed.

In the near future, 3-D imaging is likely to see the surface-based rendering methods widely replaced by the much more powerful and flexible voxel-based rendering methods. Furthermore, a number of applications beyond mere visualization will become operational (e.g., surgical simulation systems and educational systems). In all these cases, experimental setups already are available.

The more distant future may see incorporation of functional information (e.g., of motion, force, etc.), even dynamically changing over time (4-D imaging). Another intriguing idea is to combine 3-D imaging with current efforts in *virtual reality* systems, which will enable the clinician to walk around or even fly through a virtual patient (114). The future will show which of these new techniques are really useful for clinical work.

ACKNOWLEDGMENTS

The authors thank B. Pflesser, T. Schiemann (both IMDM), and Dr. D. Friboulet (Institut National des Sciences Appliquées, Lyon) for many discussions and practical assistance. We also thank I. Gulens for her help in preparing the manuscript.

Figures are courtesy of Prof. G. T. Herman (Fig. 3), Dr. E. K. Fishman (Fig. 6), Prof. D. Levin (Fig. 10), and Dr. T. Yasuda (Fig. 11). All other 3-D images were produced with the program Voxel-Man developed at our institute. Tomographic raw data were kindly provided by Dr. F. Hottier, Philips Paris (Fig. 7), Dr. J. P. Mugler, University of Virginia (Fig. 8), and Siemens, Erlangen (Figs. 9, 14). Applications are in cooperation with Prof. W. -J. Höltje, Department of Craniofacial Surgery (Fig. 5), Dr. A. Wening, Department of Traumatology (Fig. 12), Dr. R. Schmidt, Department of Radiotherapy (Fig. 13), and Prof. W. Lierse, Department of Anatomy (Fig. 14).

Work at the IMDM is supported in part by the Werner Otto Foundation, Hamburg.

REFERENCES

1. Herman, G. T., and Liu, H. K., Display of Three-Dimensional Information in Computed Tomography, *J. Comput. Assist. Tomogr.*, 1 (1): 155–160 (1977).

2. Sunguroff, A., and Greenberg, D., Computer Generated Images for Medical Applications, *Comput. Graph*, 12 (3): 196–202, (1978).

3. Herman G. T., and Liu, H. K., Three-Dimensional Display of Human Organs from Computed Tomograms, *Comput. Graphics Image Process.*, 9: 1–21 (1979).

4. Hemmy, D. C., David, D. J., and Herman, G. T., Three-Dimensional Reconstruction of Craniofacial Deformity Using Computed Tomography, *Neurosurgery*, 13: 534–541 (1983).

5. Herman, G. T., Udupa, J. K., Display of 3-D Digital Images: Computational Foundations and Medical Applications, *IEEE Comput. Graph Appl.*, 3 (5): 39–46 (1983).

6. Vannier, M. W., Marsh, J. L., and Warren, J. O., Three Dimensional Computer Graphics for Craniofacial Surgical Planning and Evaluation, *Comput. Graph*, 17 (3): 263–273 (1983).

7. Templeton, A. W., Johnson, J. A., and Anderson, W. H., Computer Graphics for Digitally Formatted Images, *Radiology*, 152: 527–528 (1985).

8. Kaufman, A. (ed)., *Volume Visualization*, IEEE Computer Society Press, Los Alamitos, CA; 1991.

9. Rosenfeld, A., and Kak, A. C., *Digital Picture Processing*, 2nd ed. Academic Press, New York, 1982.

10. Ballard, D. H., and Brown, C. M., *Computer Vision*, Prentice-Hall Inc., Englewood Cliffs, NJ, 1982.

11. Tanimoto, S. L., *The Elements of Artificial Intelligence*, Computer Science Press, Rockville, MD, 1987.

12. Schwartz, W. B., Patil, R. S., and Szolovits, P., Artificial Intelligence in Medicine: Where Do We Stand?, *N. Engl. J. Med.*, 316 (11): 685–688 (1987).

13. Foley, J. D., van Dam, A., Feiner, S. K., and Hughes, J. F., *Computer Graphics: Principles and Practice*, 2nd ed., Addison-Wesley, Reading, MA, 1990.

14. Watt, A., *Three-Dimensional Computer Graphics*, Addison Wesley, Wokingham, 1989.

15. Upson, C., (ed.), *Proc. Chapel Hill Workshop on Volume Visualization*, Dept. of Computer Science, University of North Carolina, Chapel Hill, NC, 1989.

16. *Proc. First Conference on Visualization in Biomedical Computing, VBC '90*. IEEE Computer Society Press, Los Alamitos, CA, 1990.

17. Höhne, K. H., Fuchs, H., and Pizer, S. M. (eds.), *3D-Imaging in Medicine: Algorithms, Systems, Applications*, vol. 60, *NATO ASI Series F*, Springer-Verlag, Berlin, 1990.

18. Proc. San Diego workshop on volume visualization, *Comput. Graph.*, 24 (5): (1990).

19. Udupa, J. K., and Herman, G. T. (eds.), *3D Imaging in Medicine*, CRC Press, Boca Raton, FL, 1991.

20. Rhodes, M. L. (guest ed.) *IEEE Comput. Graph. Appl.*, 9 (2/3): (1990). Special issue on computer graphics in medicine.

21. Kaufman, A. (guest ed.), *Visual Comput.*, 6 (1): (1990). Special issue on volume visualization.

22. Coatrieux, J. L. (guest ed.), *IEEE Eng. Med. Biol. Magazine*, 9 (4): (1990). Special issue on 3D computer medical imaging.

23. Kak, A. C., and Slaney, M., *Principles of Computerized Tomographic Imaging*, IEEE Press Inc., New York, 1988.

24. Lee, J. K. T., Sagel, S. S., and Stanley, R. J. (eds.), *Computed Body Tomography with MRI Correlation*, 2nd ed., Raven Press, New York, 1989.

25. Stark, D. D., and Bradley, W.G., *Magnetic Resonance Imaging*. C. V. Mosby, St. Louis, MO, 1988.

26. Wells, P. N. T., *Biomedical Ultrasonics*. Academic Press, New York, 1977.

27. Hottier, F., and Collet Billon, A., 3D Echography: Status and Perspective. In: *3D-Imaging in Medicine: Algorithms, Systems, Applications* (K. H. Höhne, H. Fuchs, and S. M. Pizer, eds.), vol. 60, *NATO ASI Series F*, Springer-Verlag, Berlin, 1990, pp. 21–41.

28. Bernier, D. R., Christian, P. E., Langman, J. K., and Wells, L. D., *Nuclear Medicine: Technology and Techniques*, C. V. Mosby Co., St. Louis, MO, 1989.

29. Perona, P., and Malik, J., Scale Space and Edge Detection Using Anisotropic Diffusion. *Proc. IEEE Workshop on Computer Vision, (Miami)*, 1987, pp. 16–22.

30. Parker, J. A., Kenyon, R. V., and Troxel, D. E., A Comparison of Interpolating Methods for Image Resampling, *IEEE Trans. Med. Imaging*, MI-2 (1): 31–39 (1983).

31. Raya, S. P., and Udupa, J. K., Shape-Based Interpolation of Multidimensional Objects, *IEEE Trans. Med. Imaging*, MI-9 (1): 32–42 (1990).

32. Meagher, D. J., Geometric Modeling Using Octree Encoding, *Comput. Graph. Image Process.*, 19 (2): 129–147 (1982).

33. Höhne, K. H., Bomans, M., Tiede, U., and Riemer, M., Display of Multiple 3D-Objects Using the Generalized Voxel-Model. In *Proc. SPIE 914: Medical Imaging II, Part B* (R. H. Schneider and S. J. Dwyer, eds.), Newport Beach, 1988, pp. 850–854.

34. Drebin, R. A., Carpenter, L., and Hanrahan, P., Volume rendering, *Comput. Graph.*, 22 (4): 65–74 (1988).

35. Tessier, P., and Hemmy, D., Three Dimensional Imaging in Medicine: A Critique by Surgeons, *Scand. J. Plast. Reconstr. Surg.*, 20, 3–11 (1986).

36. Keppel, E., Approximating Complex Surfaces by Triangulation of Contour Lines, *IBM J. Res. Dev.*, 19 (1): 2–11 (1975).

37. Fuchs, H., Kedem, Z. M., and Uselton, S. P., Optimal Surface Reconstruction from Planar Contours, *Commun. ACM*, 20 (10): 693–702 (1977).

38. Boissonnat, J. D., Shape Reconstruction from Planar Cross Sections, *Comput. Vision Graph. Image Process.*, 44 (1): 1–29 (1988).

39. Chen, S.-Y., Lin, W. C., Liang, C.-C., and Chen, C. T., Improvement on Dynamic Elastic Interpolation Technique for Reconstructing 3-D Objects from Serial Cross Sections, *IEEE Trans. Med. Imaging* MI-9 (1): 71–83 (1990).

40. Artzy, E., Frieder, G., and Herman, G. T., The Theory, Design, Implementation and Evaluation of a Three-Dimensional Surface Detection Algorithm, *Comput. Graph. Image Process.*, 15 (1): 1–24 (1981).

41. Chen, L. S., Herman, G. T., Reynolds, R. A., and Udupa, J. K., Surface Shading in the Cuberille Environment, *IEEE Comput. Graph. Appl.*, 5 (12): 33–43 (1985).

42. David, D. J., Hemmy, D. C., and Cooter, R. D., *Craniofacial Deformities: Atlas of Three-Dimensional Reconstruction from Computed Tomography*, Springer-Verlag, New York, 1990.

43. Lorensen, W. E., and Cline, H. E., Marching Cubes: A High Resolution 3D Surface Construction Algorithm, *Comput. Graph.*, 21 (4): 163–169 (1987).

44. Cline, H. E., Lorensen, W. E., Ludke, S., Crawford, C. R., and Teeter, B. C., Two Algorithms for Three-Dimensional Reconstruction of Tomograms, *Med. Phys.*, 15 (3): 320–327 (1988).

45. Baker, H. H., Building Surfaces of Evolution: The Weaving Wall, *Comput. Vis.*, 3: 51–71 (1989).

46. Wilhelms, J., and van Gelder, A., Topological Considerations in Isosurface Generation, *Comput. Graph.*, 24 (5): 79–86 (1990).

47. Kaufman, A., Cohen, D., and Yagel, R., Volumetric Shading Techniques. In *Volume Visualization* (A. Kaufman, ed.), IEEE Computer Society Press, Los Alamitos, CA., 1991, pp. 169–173.

48. Hall, R., A Characterization of Illumination Models and Shading Techniques, *Visual Comput.*, 2: 268–277 (1986).

49. Herman, G. T., and Udupa, J. K., Display of Three-Dimensional Discrete Surfaces, *Proc. SPIE 283*, 90–97 (1981).

50. Gordon, D., and Reynolds, R. A., Image Space Shading of 3-Dimensional Objects, *Comput. Vision Graph. Image Process.*, 29: 361–376 (1985).

51. Tiede, U., Höhne, K. H., Bomans, M., Pommert, A., Riemer, M., and Wiebecke, G., Investigation of Medical 3D-Rendering Algorithms, *IEEE Comput. Graph. Appl.*, 10 (2): 41–53 (1990).

52. Pommert, A., Tiede, U., Wiebecke, G., and Höhne, K. H., Surface Shading in Tomographic Volume Visualization: A Comparative Study. In *Proc. First Conference on Visualization in Biomedical Computing*, *VBC '90*, IEEE Computer Society Press, Los Alamitos, CA, 1990, pp. 19–26.

53. Oswald, H., Kropatsch, W., and Leberl, F., A Perspective Projection Algorithm with Fast Evaluation of Visibility for Discrete Three-Dimensional Scenes. In *Proc. ISMIII '82, International Symposium on Medical Imaging and Image Interpretation*, IEEE Computer Society Press, Silver Spring, MD, 1982, pp. 464–468.

54. Tuy, H. K., and Tuy, L. T., Direct 2-D Display of 3-D Objects, *IEEE Comput. Graph. Appl.*, 4 (10): 29–33 (1984).

55. Lenz, R., Danielsson, P. E., Cronström, S., and Gudmundsson, B., Presentation and Perception of 3-D Images. In *Pictorial Information Systems in Medicine* (K. H. Höhne, ed.), vol. 19, *NATO ASI Series F*, Springer-Verlag, Berlin, 1986, pp. 459–468.

56. Höhne, K. H., DeLaPaz, R. L., Bernstein, R., and Taylor, R. C., Combined Surface Display and Reformatting for the 3D-Analysis of Tomographic Data, *Invest. Radiol.*, 22: 658–664 (1987).

57. Höhne, K. H., Riemer, M., and Tiede, U., Viewing Operations for 3D-Tomographic Gray Level Data. In: *Computer Assisted Radiology*, *Proc. CAR '87* (H. U. Lemke, M. L. Rhodes, C. C. Jaffe, and R. Felix, eds.), Springer-Verlag, Berlin, 1987, pp. 599–609.

58. Höhne, K. H., Bomans, M., Pommert, A., Riemer, M., Schiers, C., Tiede, U., and Wiebecke, G., 3D-Visualization of Tomographic Volume Data Using the Generalized Voxel-Model, *Visual Comput.*, 6 (1): 28–36 (1990).

59. Levoy, M., A Hybrid Ray Tracer for Rendering Polygon and Volume data, *IEEE Comput. Graph. Appl.*, 10: 33–40 (1990).

60. Kaufman, A., Yagel, R., and Cohen, D., Intermixing Surface and Volume Rendering. In: 3D-Imaging in Medicine: Algorithms, Systems, Applications (K. H. Höhne, H. Fuchs, and S. M. Pizer, eds.), vol. 60, *NATO ASI Series F*, Springer-Verlag, Berlin, 1990, pp. 217–227.

61. Levoy, M., Volume Rendering by Adaptive Refinement, *Visual Comput.*, 6 (1): 2–7 (1990).

62. Frieder, G., Gordon, D., and Reynolds, R. A., Back-to-Front Display of Voxel-Based Objects, *IEEE Comput. Graph. Appl.*, 5 (1): 52–59 (1985).

63. Westover, L., Footprint Evaluation for Volume Rendering, *Comput. Graph.*, 24 (4): 367–376 (1990).

64. Höhne, K. H., and Bernstein, R., Shading 3D-Images from CT Using Gray Level Gradients, *IEEE Trans. Med. Imaging*, MI-5 (1): 45–47 (1986).

65. Barillot, C., Gilbaud, B., Luo, L. M., and Scarabin, J. M., 3-D Representation of Anatomic Structures from CT Examinations, *Proc. SPIE 602: Biostereometrics '85*, 1985, pp. 307–314.

66. Tiede, U., Riemer, M., Bomans, M., and Höhne, K. H., Display Techniques for 3D-Tomographic Volume Data, *Proc. NCGA '88*, (Anaheim), 3: 188–197 (1988).

67. Zucker, S. W., and Hummel, R. A., A Three-Dimensional Edge Detector, *IEEE Trans. Pattern Anal. Machine Intell.*, PAMI-3 (3): 324–331 (1981).

68. Pommert, A., Tiede, U., Wiebecke, G., and Höhne, K. H., Image Quality in Voxel-Based Surface Shading. In: *Computer Assisted Radiology*, *Proc. CAR '89* (H. U. Lemke, M. L. Rhodes, C. C. Jaffe, and R. Felix, eds.), Springer-Verlag, Berlin, 1989, pp. 737–741.

69. Ehricke, H. H., and Laub, G., Combined 3D-Display of Cerebral Vasculature and Neuroanatomic Structures in MRI. In: *3D-Imaging in Medicine: Algorithms, Systems, Applications* (K. H. Höhne, H. Fuchs, and S. M. Pizer, eds.), vol. 60, *NATO ASI Series F: Computer and Systems Sciences*, Springer-Verlag, Berlin, 1990, pp. 229–239.

70. Levoy, M., Display of Surfaces from Volume Data, *IEEE Comput. Graph. Appl.*, 8 (3): 29–37 (1988).

71. Sabella, P., A Rendering Algorithm for 3D Scalar Fields, *Comput. Graph.*, 22 (4): 51–58 (1988).

72. Upson, C., and Keeler, M., V-BUFFER: Visible Volume Rendering, *Comput. Graph.*, 22 (4): 59–64 (1988).

73. Robb, R. A., and Barillot, C., Interactive Display and Analysis of 3-D Medical Images, *IEEE Trans. Med. Imaging*, MI-8 (3): 217–226 (1989).

74. Meinzer, H. P., Engelmann, U., Scheppelmann, D., and Schäfer, R., Volume Visualization of 3D Tomographies. In *3D-Imaging in Medicine: Algorithms, Systems, Applications* (K. H. Höhne, H. Fuchs, and S. M. Pizer, eds.), vol. 60, *NATO ASI Series F*, Springer-Verlag, Berlin, 1990, pp. 253–259.

75. Laur, D., and Hanrahan, P., Hierarchical Splatting: A Progressive Refinement Algorithm for Volume Rendering, *Comput. Graph.*, 25 (4): 285–288 (1991).

76. Blinn, J. F., Light Reflection Functions for Simulation of Clouds and Dusty Surfaces, *Comput. Graph.*, 16 (3): 21–29 (1982).

77. Duda, R. O., and Hart, P. E., *Pattern Classification and Scene Analysis*, John Wiley and Sons, New York, 1973.

78. Vannier, M. W., Speidel, C. M., Rickman, D. L., Schertz, L. D., Baker, L. R., Hildeboldt, C. F., Offutt, C. J., Balko, J. A., Butterfield, R. L., and Gado, M. H., Multispectral Analysis of Magnetic Resonance Images. In: *Proc. 9th International Conference on Pattern Recognition, ICPR '88*, IEEE Computer Society Press, Washington, DC, 1988, vol. 2, pp. 1182–1186.

79. Cline, H. E., Lorensen, W. E., Kikinis, R., and Jolesz, F., Three-dimensional Segmentation of MR Images of the Head Using Probability and Connectivity, *J. Comput. Assist. Tomogr.*, 14 (6): 1037–1045 (1990).

80. Merickel, M. B., Jackson, T., Carman, C., Brookeman, J. R., and Ayers, C. R., A Multispectral Pattern Recognition System for the Noninvasive Evaluation of Atherosclerosis Utilizing MRI. In: *3D-Imaging in Medicine: Algorithms, Systems, Applications* (K. H. Höhne, H. Fuchs, and S. M. Pizer, eds.), vol. 60, *NATO ASI Series F: Computer and Systems Sciences*, Springer-Verlag, Berlin, 1990, pp. 133–146.

81. Gerig, G., Martin, J., Kikinis, R., Kübler, O., Shenton, M., and Jolesz, F. A., Automating Segmentation of Dual-Echo MR Head Data. In: *Information Processing in Medical Imaging, Proc. IPMI '91* (A. C. F. Colchester and D. Hawkes, eds.), vol. 511, *Lecture Notes in Computer Science*, Springer-Verlag, Berlin, 1991, pp. 175–187.

82. Kohonen, T., *Self-Organisation and Associative Memory*, 2nd ed., Springer, Berlin, 1988.

83. Vaske, E., Segmentation of MRI Volume Data with the Topological Map for 3D Visualization, IMDM Technical Report 91/1, Institute of Mathematics and Computer Science in Medicine, University of Hamburg, 1991.

84. Canny, J., A Computational Approach to Edge Detection, *IEEE Trans. Pattern Anal. Machine Intell.*, PAMI-8 (6): 679–698 (1985).

85. Brelstaff, G. J., Ibison, M. C., and Eliot, P. J., Edge-Region Integration for Segmentation of MR Images. In: *Proc. British Machine Vision Conference, BMVC '90*, 1990, pp. 139–144.

86. Marr, D., and Hildreth, E., Theory of Edge Detection, *Proc R. Soc. Lond.*, B 207: 187–217 (1980).

87. Bomans, M., Riemer, M., Tiede, U., and Höhne, K. H., 3D- Segmentation von Kernspin-Tomogrammen. In: *Mustererkennung 1987, Proc. 9. DAGM-Symposium* (E. Paulus, ed.), Vol. 149, *Informatik-Fachberichte*, Springer-Verlag, Berlin, 1987, pp. 231–235.

88. Bomans, M., Höhne, K. H., Tiede, U., and Riemer, M., 3D-Segmentation of MR-Images of the Head for 3D-Display, *IEEE Trans. Med. Imaging*, MI-9 (2): 177–183 (1990).

89. Kübler, O., Ylä-Jääski, J., and Hiltebrand, E., 3-D Segmentation and Real Time Display of Medical Volume Images. In *Computer Assisted Radiology, Proc. CAR '87* (H. U. Lemke, M. L. Rhodes, C. C. Jaffee, and R. Felix, eds.), Springer-Verlag, Berlin, 1987, pp. 637–641.

90. Serra, J., *Image Analysis and Mathematical Morphology*, Academic Press, New York, 1982.

91. Cline, H. E., Dumoulin, C. L., Hart, H. R., Lorensen, W. E., and Ludke, S., 3D Reconstruction of the Brain from Magnetic Resonance Images Using a Connectivity Algorithm, *Magn. Reson. Imaging*, 5: 345–352 (1987).

92. Höhne, K. H., and Hanson, W. A., Interactive 3D-Segmentation of MRI and CT Volumes Using Morphological Operations, *J. Comput. Assist. Tomogr.*, 16(2): 285–294 (1992).

93. Pizer, S. M., Fuchs, H., Levoy, M., Roseman, J., Davis, R. E., and Renner, J. B., 3D Display with Minimal Predefinition. In: *Computer Assisted Radiology, Proc. CAR '89* (H. U. Lemke, M. L. Rhodes, C. C. Jaffe, and R. Felix, eds.) Springer-Verlag, Berlin, 1989, pp. 723–736.

94. Pizer, S. M., Cullip, T. J., and Fredericksen, R.E., Toward Interactive Object Definition in 3D Scalar Images. In: *3D-Imaging in Medicine: Algorithms, Systems, Applications* (K. H. Höhne, H. Fuchs, and S. M. Pizer, eds.), vol. 60, *NATO ASI Series F*, Springer-Verlag, Berlin, 1990, pp. 83–105.

95. Raya, S. P., and Udupa, J. K., Low-Level Segmentation of 3-D Magnetic Resonance Brain Images—A Rule-Based System, *IEEE Trans. Med. Imaging*, MI-9 (3): 327–337 (1990).

96. Brummer, M. E., Mersereau, R. M., Eisner, R. L., and Lewine, R. R. J., Automatic Detection of Brain Contours in MRI Data Sets. In: *Information Processing in Medical Imaging, Proc. IPMI '91* (A. C. F. Colchester and D. J. Hawkes, eds.), vol. 511, *Lecture Notes in Computer Science*, Springer-Verlag, Berlin, 1991, pp. 188–204.

97. Bomans, M., Vergleich verschiedener Verfahren und Entwicklung eines kombinierten Verfahrens zur Segmentation von Kernspintomogrammen des Kopfes, Ph. D. thesis, Dept. of Computer Science, University of Hamburg (in preparation).

98. Menhardt, W., Image Analysis Using Iconic Fuzzy Sets. In *European Conference on Artificial Intelligence, Proc. ECAI'88*, Pitman Publ., London, 1988, pp. 672–674.

99. Pelizzari, C. A., Chen, G. T. Y., Spelbring, D. R., Weichselbaum, R. R., and Chen, C., Accurate Three-Dimensional Registration of CT, PET, and/or MR Images of the Brain, *J. Comput. Assist. Tomogr.*, 13 (1): 20–26 (1989).

100. Hu, X., Tan, K. K., Levin, D. N., Pelizzari, C. A., and Chen G. T. Y., A Volume-Rendering Technique for Integrated Three-Dimensional Display of MR and PET Data. In: *3D-Imaging in Medicine: Algorithms, Systems, Applications* (K. H. Höhne, H. Fuchs, and S. M. Pizer, eds.), vol. 60, *NATO ASI Series F*, Springer-Verlag, Berlin, 1990, pp. 379–397.

101. Schiers, C., Tiede, U., and Höhne, K. H., Interactive 3D-Registration of Image Volumes from Different Sources. In: *Computer Assisted Radiology, Proc. CAR '89* (H. U. Lemke, M. L. Rhodes, C. C. Jaffe, and R. Felix, eds.), Springer-Verlag, Berlin, 1989, pp. 666–670.

102. Brewster, L. J., Trivedi, S. S., Tuy, H. K., and Udupa, J. K., Interactive Surgical Planning, *IEEE Comput. Graph. Appl.*, 4 (3): 31–40 (1984).

103. Arridge, S. R., Manipulation of Volume Data for Surgical Simulation. In: *3D-Imaging in Medicine: Algorithms, Systems, Applications* (K. H. Höhne, H. Fuchs, and S. M. Pizer, eds.), vol. 60, *NATO ASI Series F*, Springer-Verlag, 1990, pp. 289–300.

104. Yasuda, T., Hashimoto, Y., Yokoi, S., and Toriwaki, J.-I., Computer System for Craniofacial Surgical Planning Based on CT Images, *IEEE Trans. Med. Imaging*, MI-9 (3): 270–280 (1990).

105. Udupa, J. K., and Hung, H.-M., Surface Versus Volume Rendering: A Comparative Assessment. In: *Proc. First Conference on Visualization in Biomedical Computing, VBC '90*, IEEE Computer Society Press, Los Alamitos, CA, 1990, pp. 83–91.

106. Magnusson, M., Lenz, R., and Danielsson, P. E., Evaluation of Methods for Shaded Surface Display of CT-Volumes. In: *Proc. 9th International Conference on Pattern Recognition, ICPR '88*, IEEE Computer Society Press, Washington, DC, 1988, vol. 2, pp. 1287–1294.

107. Hemmy, D. C., and Tessier, P. L., CT of Dry Skulls with Craniofacial Deformities: Accuracy of Three-Dimensional Reconstruction, *Radiology*, 157 (1): 113–116 (1985).

108. Drebin, R. A., Magid, D., Robertson, D. D., and Fishman, E. K., Fidelity of Three-

Dimensional CT Imaging for Detecting Fracture Gaps, *J. Comput. Assist. Tomogr.*, 13 (3): 487–489 (1989).

109. Pommert, A., Höltje, W. J., Holzknecht, N., Tiede, U., and Höhne, K. H., Accuracy of Images and Measurements in 3D Bone Imaging. In: *Computer Assisted Radiology, Proc. CAR '91* (H. U. Lemke, M. L. Rhodes, C. C. Jaffe, and R. Felix, eds.), Springer-Verlag, Berlin, 1991, pp. 209–215.

110. Vannier, M. W., Pilgram, T. K., Hildebolt, C. F., and Marsh, J. L., Diagnostic Evaluation of Three-Dimensional CT Reconstruction Methods. In: *Computer Assisted Radiology, Proc. CAR '89* (H. U. Lemke, M. L. Rhodes, C. C. Jaffe, and R. Felix, eds.), Springer-Verlag, Berlin, 1989, pp. 87–91.

111. Goldwasser, S. M., Reynolds, R. A., Bapty, T., Baraff, D., Summers, J., Talton, D. A., and Walsh, E., Physicians Workstation with Real Time Performance, *IEEE Comput. Graph. Appl.*, 5: 44–57 (1985).

112. Kaufman, A., and Bakalash, R., Memory and Processing Architecture for 3D Voxel-Based Imagery, *IEEE Comput Graph. Appl.*, 8 (11): 10–23 (1988).

113. Levoy, M., Design for a Real-Time High-Quality Volume Rendering Workstation. In: *Proc. Chapel Hill Workshop on Volume Visualization* (C. Upson, ed.), Department of Computer Science, University of North Carolina, 1989, pp. 85–92.

114. Fuchs, H., Systems for Display of Three-Dimensional Medical Image Data, In: *3D-Imaging in Medicine: Algorithms, Systems, Applications* (K. H. Höhne, H. Fuchs, and S. M. Pizer, eds.), vol. 60, *NATO ASI Series F*, Springer-Verlag, Berlin, 1990, pp. 315–331.

115. Kaufman, A., Bakalash, R., Cohen, D., and Yagel, R., Architectures for Volume Rendering. In: *Volume Visualization* (A. Kaufman, ed.), IEEE Computer Society Press, Los Alamitos, CA, 1991, pp. 311–320.

116. Udupa, J. K., Herman, T., Chen, L. S., Margasahayam, P. S., and Meyer, C. R., 3D98: A Turnkey System for 3D Display and Analysis of Medical Objects in CT Data, *Proc. SPIE* 671: 154–168 (1986).

117. Höhne, K. H., Bomans, M., Pflesser, B., Pommert, A., Riemer, M., Schiemann, T., and Tiede, U., Anatomic Realism Comes to Diagnostic Imaging. *Diagn. Imaging*, 1: 115–121 (1992).

118. Vannier, M. W., Despite Its Limitations, 3-D Imaging Here to Stay, *Diagn. Imaging*, 9 (11): 206–210 (1987).

119. Marchac, D. (ed.), *Craniofacial Surgery: Proc. of the First International Congress of the International Society of Cranio-Maxillo-Facial Surgery*. Springer-Verlag, Berlin, 1987.

120. Zonneveld, F. W., Lobregt, S., van der Meulen, J. C. H., and Vaandrager, J. M., Three-Dimensional Imaging in Craniofacial Surgery, *World J. Surg.*, 13: 328–342 (1989).

121. Ney, D., Fishman, E. K., Magid, D., and Drebin, R. A., Volumetric Rendering of Computed Tomography Data: Principles and Techniques, *IEEE Comput. Graph. Appl.*, 10: 24–32 (1990).

122. Fishman, E. K., Ney, D. R., and Magid, D., Three-Dimensional Imaging: Clinical Applications in Orthopedics. In: *3D-Imaging in Medicine: Algorithms, Systems, Applications* (K. H. Höhne, H. Fuchs, and S. M. Pizer, eds.), vol. 60, *NATO ASI Series F*, Springer-Verlag, Berlin, 1990, pp. 425–440.

123. Cline, H. E., Lorensen, W. E., Souza, S. P., Jolesz, F. A., Kikinis, R., Gerig, G., and Kennedy, T. E., 3D Surface Rendered MR Images of the Brains and Its Vasculature, *J. Comput. Assist. Tomogr.*, 15 (2): 344–351 (1991).

124. Adams, L., Krybus, W., Meyer-Ebrecht, D., Rueger, R., Gilsbach, J. M., Moesges, R., and Schloendorff, G., Computer Assisted Surgery, *IEEE Comput. Graph. Appl.*, 10 (3): 43–51 (1990).

125. Schlegel, W., Computer Assisted Radiation Therapy Planning. In: *3D-Imaging in Medicine: Algorithms, Systems, Applications* (K. H. Höhne, H. Fuchs, and S. M. Pizer, eds.), vol. 60 *NATO ASI Series F*, Springer-Verlag, Berlin, 1990, pp. 399–410.

126. Schmidt, R., Schiemann, T., Höhne, K. H., and Hübener, K. H., 3-D Treatment Planning for Fast Neutrons. In: Tumor Response Monitoring and Treatment Planning, A. Breit (ed.), Springer-Verlag, Berlin, 1992.

127. Toga, A. W., (ed.), *Three-Dimensional Neuroimaging*, Raven Press, New York: 1990.

128. Mano, I., Suto, Y., Suzuki, M., and Iio, M., Computerized Three-Dimensional Normal Atlas, *Radiat. Med.*, 8 (2): 50–54 (1990).

129. Höhne, K. H., Bomanc, M., Riemer, M., Schubert, R., Tiede, U., and Lierse, W., A 3D Anatomical Atlas Based on a Volume Model, *IEEE Comput. Graphics Appl.* 12 (4): 72–78 (1992).

ANDREAS POMMERT
MICHAEL BOMANS
MARTIN RIEMER
ULF TIEDE
KARL HEINZ HÖHNE

TREE STRUCTURES

INTRODUCTION

Trees are defined in graph theory as connected acyclic graphs. Therefore any two tree nodes are connected by a unique path (1). According to another definition, a tree is a set of nodes connected with edges. One node, called the *root*, has no incoming edges and one or more outgoing edges. The remaining nodes are partitioned in independent sets, each one being another tree. This recursive definition shows that recursion techniques may be widely used in tree processing. There are several graphical tree representations, the most familiar one illustrates the structure in the opposite way from what happens in nature: the root of the tree lies at the top and the remaining nodes lie below. A set of trees is called a *forest*.

The following terminology, which can be found in any textbook on data structures (2,3), is necessary. Nodes with incoming edges from another node are called *children* of the edge source, which in an analogous manner is called the father or parent node. With a similar reasoning the terms ancestor, descendant, grandparent, brother node, etc. are produced. The number of children of a node is the *node degree*. The maximum node degree is the *tree degree*. In this respect the most interesting ones are the binary trees, quadtrees, octrees, and multiway trees.

A node with no children is called a *leaf*, *external*, or *terminal* node. The remaining nodes are called *branch*, *internal*, or *nonterminal* nodes. The path length of a node is the number of its ancestor nodes. *Internal path length*, I, of a tree is the sum of all the node path lengths. Special extra external nodes are added so that all node degrees are equal to the tree degree. *External path length*, E, of a tree is the sum of all the external nodes path lengths. The relation: $E = I + 2n$ holds, where n is the number of tree nodes. Level of a node, 1, is the path length plus one. The maximum level of the nodes of a tree is the tree *height or depth*, h or d, respectively.

The rest of the lemma is structured as follows. In the next two sections tree structures for main memory and secondary storage, respectively, are examined. Definitions, maintenance algorithms, performance measures, and applications areas are reported. This is followed by a section on tree structures for secondary key retrieval. In the last section some recent and important research topics are described. References and bibliography for further reading are included.

TREES STORED IN MAIN MEMORY

Binary trees are the most basic tree structure. A binary tree node consists of three, four, or even five fields, depending on the variation implemented. Certainly two of the fields must be the left and right pointers. The pointers may be either static ones as in Fortran and Basic or dynamic ones as in Pascal and the C language. Usually a field is also dedicated as the parent pointer, a field pointing to the parent of the node.

There are three methods for visiting all the nodes of a binary tree by following the appropriate pointers and may be implemented either recursively or by means of a stack. These methods are called preorder, inorder, and postorder traversals and are used for arithmetic expression evaluation, for information retrieval applications, etc. According to the preorder (or depth-first order) traversal every node is visited before its left descendants and its right descendants. According to the inorder (symmetric order), traversal every node is visited after its left descendants and before its right descendants. According to the postorder traversal, every node is visited after its left descendants and its right descendants. If the inorder and one of the preorder or postorder traversals are given, then the initial tree may be reconstructed in $O(n)$ time and space (4).

Leaf pointers have nil values and may be considered as wasted space. A nil right pointer may be forced to point to the successor node according to the inorder traversal. Thus this kind of traversal is more efficient and easier to perform. These pointers are called *threads* and the corresponding tree is the *right inthreaded binary tree*. This implementation requires one more boolean field to show if the right pointer is a thread or not. In the same way, at the cost of one additional boolean field, *left prethreaded binary trees* may be constructed to facilitate preorder traversal. By using two additional boolean fields it is possible to combine both methods and construct the so-called *threaded binary trees*. Experimental results have shown that traversing threaded binary trees, although qualitatively having the same $O(n)$ complexity, is almost twice as fast as traversing unthreaded binary trees (5).

If binary tree nodes are ordered in such a way that every node value is greater than the values of its left descendants and smaller than the values of its right descendants then we have a *binary search tree*. A binary search tree has at most $2^h + 1$ nodes. In this case it is called a *complete binary tree*. Almost complete binary tree of height h is the one with leaves only at the $(h-1)$-th and h-th level. *Descending heap* (or max heap or descending partially ordered tree) is an almost complete binary tree such that the key value of every node is less than or equal to the key value of its parent. Analogous is the definition of the ascending or min heap. Heaps are the basis of an efficient sorting method, the heapsort algorithm.

The search procedure for binary search trees is based on the divide and conquer technique; therefore it is recursive and straightforward. Given a key value to be searched, this value is compared with the value of the root node. In case of equality successful search is terminated. In case of inequality, if the given key has a value smaller or greater than the key of the root then the left or the right pointer, respectively, is followed. From there on, the comparisons continue at the next lower tree level in a recursive manner. If a nil pointer is met then the search terminates unsuccessfully.

Insertion is also simple. First, a search for the key value to be inserted is performed. If this value exists already, then the procedure terminates unsuccessfully. If the value does not exist, then a new node with this value is created and linked from a leaf node by changing the corresponding nil pointer to the new address.

The deletion procedure is more complicated. Given a key value to be deleted the procedure begins again by searching for it. If this values does not exist, then the deletion terminates unsuccessfully. If the key is found then three cases have to be considered. First, the case that the key is stored in a leaf node is simple. Second, if the node has only one child, then this child is connected to the father node of the node to be deleted. If the node under deletion has two children then the tree is traversed down to the leaf nodes and the greatest key value of left subtree is deleted from its current position and is stored in place of the node under deletion.

The height of a tree with n nodes may vary from log$n$ to n levels. Therefore, the search complexity in the worst case is $O(n)$, in the best case is $O(\log n)$ and in the average case it is $O(\log n)$. This property makes trees very efficient structures for database applications. As for nonequiprobable keys, if the key value set is static then it is possible to construct an *optimal binary search tree* in $O(\log^2 n)$ with guaranteed $O(\log n)$ search performance. However, if insertions and deletions with random key values arrive, then it is necessary to prevent the degeneration of the optimal tree to a linked list with $O(n)$ search complexity.

An implicit working assumption of the previous paragraphs is that all keys may be searched, inserted or deleted equiprobably. This is not always the case. In order to reduce the average search length in binary search trees with nodes having unequal probabilities to be accessed, more frequently accessed nodes should be closer to the root. There are various techniques, which are applied when the probabilities are known in advance. *Frequency ordered binary search trees* are built in $O(n^2)$ time by sorting the keys first according to decreasing frequency before insertion (6). *Median trees* choose as discriminator at every node a key so that the total accessing probabilities of the left and right subtrees are equal (7). *Median split trees* have nodes that contain the most frequent key of the corresponding subtree together with the lexical median key of the subtree keys for comparison and branching reasons (8). This version is built in $O(n\log n)$ time and has search performance bounded by $O(\log n)$ time. Improving versions have been reported in (9–11). *Greedy trees* are constructed in a bottom-up manner by combining at each step at each level two nodes with the lowest access probabilities to form a node in the upper level (12). *Huffman trees*, which are based on this technique, are used for constructing codes with minimum redundancy (13,14). However these structures are suitable for static and known in advance key sets and may degenerate to linked lists.

If the keys are not equiprobable and their access probabilities are not known in advance, then first a random binary search tree is constructed and then some heuristics are applied to improve the search performance (15). These heuristics are similar to the techniques of the self-organizing linked lists (16). For example, whenever a node is accessed then it may be exchanged with his parent by performing a single rotation or it may take the root position by performing several single rotations. Therefore, it is expected that asymptotically a near optimal tree is produced. The last method is the basis of the *splay trees*, which were introduced by Tarjan in 1985 (17).

There are many structures and algorithms aimed at keeping trees as balanced as possible. The interested reader may refer to the key paper (18). The first ones in chronological appearance are the *height balanced search trees* or *AVL trees* proposed by the two Russians Adelson-Velskii and Landis in 1962 (19), which have worst case height equal to $1.44\log(n + 2) - 0.328$. In an AVL tree the left and right subtree heights of all nodes may differ at most by one level. This is achieved by embedding one more field in the node, the *balance factor* which may take only three values: -1, 0, or 1.

Suppose that at a point in time a tree is balanced according to the above rule. If the rule is broken by an insertion, then a *rotation* has to take place in order to make the tree balanced again. The *critical node* is the node which lies closer to the insertion point on the path from the root and has a balance factor value not belonging in the set $\{-1, 0, 1\}$. The rotation is a computationally inexpensive procedure which takes place at the critical node and may be left or right. Consider a left rotation. It will be a single or a double one if the insertion is directed in the right or the left subtree, respectively, of the right child of the critical node. Similar is the right rotation, either single or double. It has been proven that after an insertion only one rotation is sufficient to rebalance the tree. Experiments have shown that for approximately every two insertions one rotation is required.

A deletion may also cause a balanced tree to become unbalanced and therefore an analogous processing is required. However, in this case, one rotation is not sufficient to rebalance the tree as rotations may propagate up to the root. Experimental results have shown that for approximately every five deletions one rotation will have to take place making the total rotation cost per deletion comparable to the rotation cost per insertion.

In the literature there have appeared many variations of the AVL trees relaxing or strengthening the constraints. One-sided height balanced (OSHB) trees have nodes with both subtrees of the same height or the right subtree is taller than the left subtree by one level (20). The balance factor in OSHB trees has only two choices which means a saving of one bit per node. The savings in space is negligible compared with the savings in search time which is bounded by an $O(\log n)$ complexity. However, this structure which does not perform much better than AVL trees has relatively more expensive maintenance than AVL trees since they need rotations due to insertions or deletions more frequently. Another variation is the k-height balanced tree (HB[k]) which allows, for every node, the subtree heights to differ at most by k levels instead of one as in AVL trees. Insert and delete operations require fewer rotations than their ancestor structure at the cost of worst search performance which is also bounded by $O(\log n)$ time (21). One-sided k-height balanced search trees with obvious properties have also been proposed and examined (22). Other tree structures falling in this category are the power trees (23), red-black trees (24), the half balanced trees (25), the i-level rotation/reorganization tree (iR tree) (26), and the balanced binary trees by Tarjan (27).

The balancing measure in AVL trees and its variations is the subtree height. Weighted balance or bounded balance trees is another version of balanced binary trees introduced by Nievergelt et al. in 1973 (28). Their balancing measure is the number of nodes of a subtree. The balance factor of a node t of such a tree, $b(t)$, is the ratio of the number of nodes of the left subtree of the node t plus one divided by the number of nodes of the tree with node t as a root plus one. A weighted or bounded balanced tree belongs in the class WB[a] or BB[a] if for every node holds the relation $a \le b(t) \le 1 - a$. Evidently the relations $0 \le b(t) < 1$ and $0 \le a \le 1/2$ are true. Any binary tree belongs in the class BB[0], while complete trees belong in the class BB[1/2]. Therefore, as parameter a tends to 1/2, trees become more balanced. The interesting range of parameter a is from 2/11 to $1 - \sqrt{2}/2$ because trees belonging in these classes may be rebalanced with one rotation per level after an insertion or deletion. The performance of weighted balance trees generally is similar to that of height balanced trees, however for $a = 1 - \sqrt{2}/2$ they outperform AVL trees.

Finally, another version of weighted balanced binary trees is the internal path reduction (IPR) trees, or path trees which have been proposed by Gonnet in 1983 (29). Evidently, the tree balancing objective is to reduce the internal path of every subtree but finally only the number of nodes of the subtree is required instead of computing or storing the internal path in every node. These trees have better search performance than their predecessors at the cost of performing more rotations due to insertions and deletions. Weighted balanced trees may be extended so that every node may have its own weight; height balanced trees may not be extended in this respect. In general the problem of balancing binary search trees has attracted even recently special interest (30, 31).

Quadtrees proposed by Finkel and Bentley in 1973 (32) are structures suitable for representing data from planar bodies such as maps, graphics, images, etc. Suppose that a colored image has to be stored as a quadtree. The image will be decomposed in four quadrants recursively until all leaf quadrants are entirely of one color. Quadtree nodes have up to four children and consequently have many nil pointers in leaf nodes. Average search time performance of a quadtree is $1.2 \log_4 n$. A generalization of quadtrees is the octree which has up to eight children per node and is used for storing and processing space bodies. Therefore, octrees are much more expensive than quadtrees in storage and maintenance. Quadtrees and octrees are some instances of the so called hierarchical structures which, for the lack of more efficient structures, have been established (mainly due to Samet's in depth work, see key papers [33–35]) as a very important tool used in computer vision, image processing, geographic information systems and related applications (36,37).

If a binary search tree becomes too large due to successive insertions, then the performance deteriorates. For example, a tree with 1000 keys requires approximately 10 key comparisons on the average for a random search. Multiway search trees may have many keys in a node. Therefore they "divide" the initial key set in many smaller ones instead of two and "conquer" the desired key much easier.

The most important type of multiway search trees is the B-tree. It is assumed that the tree's name comes from Bayer who proposed the structure in 1972 (38), or that it comes from Boeing where Bayer was working by that time or even that it comes from the words balanced or bushy. In any case, it is certain that it does not come from the word binary. Two definitions of the B-trees coexist in the literature. According to the first definition a B-tree of order m is an m-way search tree with the following properties:

(a) The root may have from 2 to m children
(b) All other nodes may have from ceil [m/2] to m keys
(c) A node with k children has $k - 1$ keys, $2 \leq k \leq m$
(d) Leaf nodes are at the same level

According to the second one a B-tree of degree *d* has the following properties:

(a) The root may have from 1 to 2d keys
(b) All other nodes may have form d to 2d keys
(c) A node with k keys has $k + 1$ children, $1 \leq k \leq 2d$
(d) Leaf nodes are at the same level

These definitions are not absolutely identical. For the moment we adopt the second definition.

Searching for a key *x* in a B-tree is a straightforward procedure. A node with k keys (key_1, key_2, . . . , key_k) has $k + 1$ pointers (p_0, p_1, . . . , p_k). First, comparisons of the key x to the keys key_i of the root node, $1 \leq i \leq k$, are performed sequentially. In case of equality the search terminates successfully. If $key_r < x < key_{r+1}$ then pointer p_r is followed to access a new node. The search continues recursively until either the key x is found or a nil pointer at the leaf level is met. The latter is the case of unsuccessful search.

Insertions are directed in leaf nodes as in binary search trees. If the accessed node is not full then the key to be inserted takes its place among the keys of the node in sorted order. If the accessed node contains already 2d keys then it splits. The $2d + 1$ keys are distributed in this node and a new one taken from the memory pool. Each node receives d keys, the smaller and the larger key values, respectively, while the middle one is posted to the parent node. If this parent node contains less than 2d keys then insertion terminates at this point. If the parent node is full then this node splits too and another key ascends one level on the path towards the root. It is evident that an insertion may cause successive splits on the path from the leaf node up to the root. Therefore, it seems that B-trees do not grow in a top-down way as binary search trees do but in a bottom-up way.

During deletion two cases may arrive: the key to be deleted is stored in an internal node or a leaf node. In the former case the tree is traversed down to the leaf nodes and the previous (or successor) key in lexicographical order takes the position of the key to be deleted. Therefore, this case is transformed to the latter one: deletion from a leaf node which has to be considered as three distinct possibilities. First, if the leaf node contains more than d keys, then the deletion procedure is straightforward. In the opposite case, the left and the right brother nodes are examined whether they have more than d keys. In this second case the sum of keys is equally distributed between the two nodes with an analogous maintenance of the comparison key at the upper level. In the third case, if both brother nodes have d keys then merging takes place with the left or right node and the comparison key of the parent node. Finally one node is freed and returned to the memory pool. (Note that first the left node is checked either for redistributing or merging.) If the parent node has exactly d keys and loses the comparison key to the lower level, a new redistribution or merging phase has to take place. These possibilities may propagate up the root, and at the extreme case, if the root contains only one key the tree may shrink by one level.

B-trees have very good search performance, that is $O(\log_d n)$. In other words a B-tree of order $d = 50$ with $n = 1000000$ keys in the worst case requires four node comparisons for a successful search. On the other hand, although insertion and deletion costs are increased due to splittings and mergings, both operations are $O(\log h)$. Another advantage of B-trees is that sequential or range searching is efficient in contrast to the hash-based structures. By definition the minimum node occupancy is approximately 50% but in practice the average occupancy is 69%.

B-trees may be implemented in secondary storage equally well. Many variations of the B-trees have been proposed for exclusive use in main memory storage. For example, 2-3 trees are a special case of B trees when $d = 1$ (39). The two or three brother trees are 2–3 trees have the extra constraint that a binary node has to have a ternary brother (40). The 2–3 right brother trees have the extra constraint that each binary node has to have a right ternary brother (41). In an analogous manner, 1–2 trees and 1–2 brother trees with zero or one key per node are defined, as well as 1–2 son trees and 1–2 neighbor trees which also fall into this category (42,43). Symmetric binary B-trees, which is a combination of binary trees and 2–3 trees, may have horizontal and vertical pointers. The restriction is that all nodes except the leaves have two descendants but there are no two consecutive horizontal pointers in any path (44). Apparently all these tree structures do not differ much from each other but mainly they have proved to be algorithmic and mathematical exercises solved by the academic community while searching for a more powerful structure.

TREES FOR SECONDARY STORAGE

Secondary storage is three orders of magnitude slower than primary storage. The interest reader may refer to (45, 46) which is a sample of many excellent textbooks on file organizations. It is evident that binary search trees implemented in disks have unacceptable performance. The term tree structured file is almost synonymous to B trees and other related variations which constitute a very good choice for materialization of disk files. The material about B-trees of the previous section holds in this section too. In the sequel some important variations of the B-tree are going to be introduced. The interested reader may refer to the key paper (47).

Chained B-trees (or simply CB-trees) has a basic difference from B-trees (48). Leaf nodes are at the same level but they may belong to two types, which are called simple and compound nodes. Compound nodes have double size than the simple ones and contain from $2n + 1$ to 4n keys or records. Evidently they reside in two pages which are chained and are referred as main and twin page. This technique postpones splitting of a simple node due to overflows unless it is a compound node and results in better storage utilization.

Given a set of keys many B-tree structures may be generated with different storage utilization and search performance. The compact B-trees, which have their nodes near the leaf level as full as possible, are space optimal. Space optimal trees are nearly time optimal but time optimal trees are nearly space pessimal (49). However, it is difficult to maintain a compact B-tree since its performance degrades rapidly after a few insertions. Huang proposed the H tree, a B-tree variation, which is parametrized in order to balance all performance measures: storage, searching, and updates (50).

The average node occupancy of B-trees is improved in B#trees, a variation with modified complicated insertion and deletion procedures. For example, when a B-tree node splits, the occupancy of each new one is exactly 50%. in B#trees when a node overflows (except the root), splitting is postponed by redistributing its keys with the keys of a sibling node with free space (first the left brother is checked). In case there is no free space in the sibling nodes, then the keys of the overflowing node together with the keys of a sibling one and the comparison key of the upper level are redistributed among these two nodes and a new one. When the root overflows the splitting procedure is identical to that of a B tree. Deletion in B#trees is different than deletion in B trees so that the minimum node occupancy is 2/3 approximately. Since due to better space utilization B# trees are shallower than B-trees, at the same time they have better search performance.

B* trees, another variation of B trees, are almost the same as B# trees as far as the insertion technique is concerned. They differ only in the fact that the root node is greater than the other nodes. More specifically in B* trees the nonroot nodes are at least 2/3 full, while the root node has as maximum capacity twice this quantity.

All the variations of the B tree family examined so far may be used either as main files or as secondary indexes to a main file. In either case all tree nodes contain one type of records or one type of keys, respectively. B+trees, another variation of the B tree family, contains entities of two different types and consists of two distinct parts. All upper levels contain only keys and forms a separate index or directory structure, while data records are stored only in leaf nodes which are called the sequence set. The index part obeys the B-tree definition rules, while leaf nodes are linked sequentially and have to be at least 50% full just like the upper level nodes.

In practice B+trees are perhaps the most popular structure in database management systems, as in DB2, Ingres etc. Also, IBM's access method VSAM is a B+ tree implementation. For this reason some more details for the maintenance of B+ trees follow. The greatest keys of the data nodes of the sequence set are stored in the lower level of the index so that branching may be performed. From this level up the structure is identical to a B tree.

Insertion of a record in the sequence set may is easy when the data node is not full. In the full node case, the result is a data node splitting, perhaps an index node splitting and at the extreme case a new root node creation. Suppose that a record from a leaf node is to be deleted. If the occupancy is greater than the minimum capacity, then the procedure terminates even if the key of this record appears in an any level of the index. In case the occupancy falls below the minimum limit, then record redistribution or data node merging at the sequence set level and reorganization of the relevant index nodes takes place.

The advantages of this structure are evident. First, nodes of the upper levels have great capacities and big fan-out ratios. Therefore, path length are shortened and searching performance is improved. It should be reminded that after file opening if the index part of the B+tree fits in main memory, then only one access to secondary storage is required. However, most often only the upper part may fit in main memory and therefore two physical page accesses are required. Second, sequential processing or range searching is very efficient since no inorder traversal is required but list processing is performed after the first relevant leaf node is located.

Another interesting variation is the Prefix B+-tree which uses compression and reduces space and time requirements (51). Since it is expected that index entries in a B+tree have common prefixes, instead of the whole key only the prefix distinguishing the successive index entries could be stored. In this way keys in the index may have variable length and processing for keeping the tree height as small as possible is difficult in a dynamic environment. B* tree with variable length records is an effort in this direction (52). Recently, more sophisticated algorithms are given for finding the optimal pagination so that a minimum depth B-tree with variable length records is achieved. These algorithms reported in (53) and (54) have $O(n\log n)$ and $O(n)$ complexity, respectively.

In practice many independent queries may be posed for answering from a file. The response time to satisfy these queries will be reduced if they are considered as a batch instead of being satisfied on a first-come-first-served basis (55). This is due to the fact that the computer resources are utilized more efficiently. The technique of batching has been examined for various files and in various environments, even in multiprocessor computer systems (56), and until recently more attention was attracted and elaborate analytic expressions were appearing in the literature (57–59). In addition, batched insertions in a tree structured file have been examined and analyzed as a mechanism to decrease the total processing time (60).

TREES FOR SECONDARY KEY RETRIEVAL

Secondary key retrieval may be performed by various access methods either in main memory or in backing storage. For example, multilists and inverted files are two traditional access methods specially designed for secondary key retrieval, the latter one being possible to be implemented as a B tree structure. The more recent grid files (61) and signature files (62) are structures performing primary as well as secondary key retrieval. Although the former has an index part, these methods are not counted as tree structures.

Combined indexes is a composite set of tree structures suitable for secondary key retrieval based on a small number of secondary keys (63). In essence, instead of keeping for any distinct key value pointers to the corresponding records of the main file as inverted files do, they keep pointers for distinct sets of key values of certain combinations of fields according to which a query may be posed. Reduced combined indexes and modified combined indexes are two variations of the basic method which improve the space and time performance (64). Disadvantage of these methods is that they require more space and update effort than an inverted index on one attribute.

Doubly chained trees (65) and the binary search trees-complex (or simply BST complex) (66) are binary trees having as basic characteristic that they use different record fields for comparison and branching at successive levels of the tree, i.e., the first field at the first level, . . , the k-th field at the k-th level, where k, a positive integer depicts the number of fields. Therefore, all these three structures have k levels. These structures also suitable for secondary key retrieval.

Quintary trees generalizes the two previous structures (67). Each node of a quintary tree in level i represents a subfile in $(k\text{-}i)$-dimensional space and has two subfiles in $(k\text{-}i)$-dimensional space that lie to the left and right of the node. This is a skeleton of the quintary tree resembling to a binary search tree. In addition, this node has three subfiles in $(k\text{-}i\text{-}1)$-dimensional space at level $i + 1$. Therefore, quintary trees have five subtrees per node and therefore they are a complex and space expensive structure. It is a structure suitable for exact match, partial match, range and partial range retrieval. Reported time complexities for the above operations are $O(k + \log n)$, $O(t + 3^{k-s} (s + \log n))$, $O(t + (\log n)^k)$ and $O(t + 3^{k-s}(\log n)^s$, respectively, where s is the number of keys specified in a partial match or range retrieval query and t is the number of records retrieved by the query.

All these access methods have proven to be of small practical interest. k-Dimensional trees (68) and k-dimensional B-trees (69) (or simply k-d trees and k-d-B-trees, respectively) not only are tree structures candidate for primary and secondary key retrieval but they perform also very well in range searching and partial match retrieval. In addition they may be used either as an index to the main file or as the main structure where the entire population of records is stored.

k-d tree indexes are binary search trees exploiting further the basic idea of the double-chained trees and related structures. Every specific field is considered in a cyclic way at every level for comparison and branching, i.e., the first field at the first level, , . . . , the k-th field at the k-th level, the first field at the $(k + 1)$-th level, and so on. Entries at the leaf level partition the records in several pages stored in backing storage. Whenever a disk page overflows then a new page is created and the index is maintained appropriately (70). Therefore, the difference compared with the double-chained trees is that they do not have exactly k levels but they may have more or less levels. It should be noted also that since range searching or partial match retrieval is possible, then many search paths may have to be followed instead of one. k–d tree indexes are useful when $n > 2^{2k}$ and their expected exact and partial match retrieval performance is $O(\log n)$ and $O(n^{1-1/k})$, respectively.

k-d tree search performance may degenerate because attributes, which are relevant according to some frequent access patterns, may be stored in separate physical pages. An important problem examined by physical database designers is clustering, that is to assign records to pages so that the total number of pages accesses, in response to a set of queries, is minimized. An effort in this direction are the generalized k-dimensional trees (or simply g-k-d trees) (71). Functioning in a bottom-up way at each level of the g-k-d tree as discriminator value is not chosen to be the median value of the corresponding key space but the value which minimizes the average number of page accesses per query. Recently, more elaborate algorithms were reported and the modified g-k-d tree

is proposed, which is built so that the sum of the cost of page accesses and index searching is minimized (72). Another two recent variations of the k-d tree index are the spatial
k-dimensional tree (or simply skd-tree) for special use in spatial databases (73) and the
holey-brick B-tree (or simply hB-tree) with index based on k-d trees and data organized
in a B+ tree like structure (74).

Random k-d trees for use in one level store (i.e., not used for indexing) have the
same performance characteristics with simple binary search trees when searching for single values. It was considered that an optimal k-d tree may be constructed in O(nlogn)
complexity time but there is no efficient algorithm to keep such a tree balanced after insertions and deletions, as happens with many version binary search trees. However, by
generalizing the concept of AVL trees it has been proven that k-d height balanced trees
may be maintained having a worst case height of $1.44\log(n + 2) + 2k - 2.3277$ (75).
Recently in another report (76) having as basic structure the balanced binary trees by
Tarjan (27), it was proved that k-d balanced binary trees guarantee access, insertion and
deletion in $O(\log n + k)$ time and require $O(k)$ single rotations for each insertion or
deletion.

k-d B trees have similarities with B-trees; in other words, tree nodes do not contain
necessarily only one record. In addition, in an analogous manner with k-d trees branching
at every level is performed by considering all the fields of the record in a cyclic way.
Being also dynamic structures they allow split and merge operations during insertions
and deletions which are performed in logarithmic time in the worst case. Experiments
have shown that the space utilization is 50–70%. B#trees, B* trees and B+ trees may be
generalized in this respect as multidimensional access methods. A more elaborate structure is the k-d B-tree with optimal branching factors per level so that partial match queries on the same attributes are answered more efficiently (77).

RECENT DEVELOPMENTS

Ordinary data structures change with time due to insertions, deletions and updates and in
this way old data are lost. A new research area is the notion of persistency. A structure
is called persistent if old data are kept so that searching in the past is possible. More
specifically, a data structure is called fully or partially persistent if any version or only the
last version of the structure may be modified respectively. See Ref. (78) for a brief introduction on the theory of persistency which has been examined on many data structures
such as stacks, queues, lists and trees and various applications such as computational
geometry (79). The term persistency has attracted mainly the interest of academics.

Another problem area similar to the persistency research area but from a different
point of view with increasing interest from industry is the area of tree structures for optical disks. Commercial optical disks at present are write-once-read-many media. Therefore insertion and deletion algorithms of any B-tree family structure cannot be applied in
this environment because the whole path from root to leaves may have to be copied.
However, some recent database applications, such as temporal databases and CAD/CAM
databases, require the storage of many versions and may be implemented only by means
of optical disks. The works by Burton and Kollias (80), Christodoulakis (81), Easton
(82), and Lomet (83) follow this direction.

Easton proposed the Write-once-B tree (WOBT) structure, which is a B+tree variation and may be entirely stored in an optical as well as in a magnetic disk. In WOBTs

no updates or deletions are performed but only insertions. All insertions are stored in the free space of the appropriate node in no particular order. If there is no free space then two new nodes are created, two keys are posted to upper index node and old versions of the same data item are not copied in the new nodes. Timestamps are a special field in each data or index record making searching possible.

An improvement of WOBT is the Time-Split B-tree (TSBT) by Lomet et al., which is stored partly in magnetic and partly in optical storage. The advantage of TSBT is that at node splitting time historic nodes are written on optical storage and new nodes are written on magnetic storage. In addition, record or key distribution may be tuned so that some past data are stored on magnetic disk.

Burton and Kollias (80) proposed the overlapping B-tree, which may be stored entirely in a magnetic as well as in an optical disk. Overlapping B-trees keep past data unchanged and copy some subtrees to represent new data due to insertions, deletions or updates (or any batched set of these operations). Evidently this structure has many root nodes making search for a specific time instance very efficient. Overlapping B+trees combine the notion of overlapping with the B+tree and as a consequence have all the B+tree advantages (84).

Balanced implicit multiway tree (BIM tree) by Christodoulakis does not look like a B-tree. Initially this structure is stored in the magnetic disk but periodically the upper tree levels (be they 100% full) are flashed to the optical disk and written sequentially one after the other on the spiral track of a CLV disk. This is the reason why no pointers are required. This structure exploits the system characteristics and therefore has improved capabilities. These four structures have advantages and disadvantages depending on the specific application and environment. Analytic or simulation results comparing all of them are not yet known.

A recent research effort is directed towards the use of elastic buckets as nodes of a tree structure. It should be remembered that the page is the smallest physical unit of storage allocation on the disk, while a bucket is a logically contiguous set of pages. When a node overflows due to insertions, two known techniques which may be used are: record redistribution with the neighbor nodes or node splitting. Another technique is to use elastic buckets, i.e. buckets of variable number of pages by means of complicated procedures of the file system. In the past elastic buckets have been applied in dynamic hashed files as in linear hashing with partial expansions by Larson (85).

Bounded disorder files by Litwin and Lomet (86, 87) and B trees with partial expansions by Lomet (88) are recent structures which combine B-trees indexes with elastic buckets as leaf nodes. These methods expand the technique of CB-trees which may have leaf nodes of only two sizes. Bounded disorder files have an B+tree index part which fits in main memory. The lowest level of this index contains three components: a comparison value, a pointer to a leaf and an extra number designating the number of pages per bucket. Pointers refer to leafs which consist of a number of contiguously stored main buckets plus one overflow bucket. After the index is traversed and the leaf is located, hashing is used to derive the appropriate bucket to be accessed. A record having to be inserted in a full main bucket is directed to the overflow bucket. If this bucket is full too, then the leaf is copied but now the number of pages per bucket is increased by one. When these elastic buckets have reached their maximum allowable size, then splitting to two elastic buckets with the minimum allowable size occurs with appropriate maintenance of the index. Bounded disorder files like B+ trees are efficient for range searching and like hashed based files require about one page access for a single retrieval. Similar is the structure of B+trees with partial expansions except that no hashing is used to locate the leaf nodes which is an elastic bucket. For a detailed analysis on this structure see reference (89) by Baeza-Yates.

It is known that quadtrees and octrees represent two-dimensional and three-dimensional data, respectively. R-tree is another hierarchical structure suitable for representing multidimensional data (90). They are a derivation of B trees since they have common properties. For example, space utilization is 50% at minimum and all leaf nodes are at the same level. Leaf nodes contain the coordinates which spatially contain a multidimensional object and a pointer to this object. Coordinates of objects at close distances are grouped in a node. In addition, every parent node contains the smallest coordinates that spatially contain all the coordinates of the objects stored in the children and the corresponding pointers to these children. Therefore, by branching through the tree levels smaller multidimensional areas are focused. Since neighbor objects may overlap in space, it is possible that when searching even for a single point many paths may have to be active. Insertions and deletions with overflows and underflows are performed with non trivial algorithms. Many variations of the R-trees have already appeared, such as packed R-trees (91), R+trees (92), and R*trees (93), which improve time and space demands. R tree family is the best representative of a newly emerging area called spatial access methods, which are a strong demand of engineering database researchers and practitioners.

EPILOG

Trees were proposed a long time ago as a powerful method for storing and accessing data. They have undergone thorough investigation for many years, but new research problems still appear, while many cases arise for practical use in a number of development efforts. Present trends in hardware and software endow the notion of tree structures with a new impulse for research and development.

REFERENCES

1. Korfhage, R.R., *Discrete Computational Structures*, Academic Press, New York, 1984, pp. 102–124.
2. Horowitz, E., and Sahni, S., *Fundamentals of Data Structures in Pascal*, 3rd ed., Computer Science Press, New York, 1990, pp. 254–335.
3. Tenenbaum, A.M., and Augenstein, M.J., *Data Structures Using Pascal*, 2nd ed., Prentice Hall, Englewood Cliffs, NJ, 1986, pp. 277–365.
4. Makinen, E., Constructing a Binary Tree from Its Traversals, *BIT*, 29:572–575 (1989).
5. Brinck, K., The Expected Performance of Traversal Algorithms in Binary Trees, *Computer J.*, 28(4):426–432 (1985).
6. Knuth, D.E., *The Art of Computer Programming, Fundamental Algorithms*, 2nd ed., Addison-Wesley, Reading, MA, 1973, pp. 305–405.
7. Gonnet, G.H., *Handbook of Algorithms and Data Structures*, Addison-Wesley, Reading, MA, 1984, pp. 69–117.
8. Sheil, B.A., Median Split Trees: A Fast Lookup Technique for Frequently Occurring Keys, *Commun. ACM*, 21(11):947–958 (1978).
9. Dobosiewicz, W., Optimal Binary Search Trees, *Intl. J Comput. Math.*, 19:135–151 (1986).

10. Huang, S., and Wong, C.K., Optimal Binary Split Trees, *J. Algorithms*, 5:69–79 (1984).

11. Huang, S., and Wong, C.K., Generalized Binary Split Trees, *Acta Informatica*, 21:113–123 (1984).

12. Korsh, J.F., Greedy Optimal Binary Search Trees, *Inform. Proc. Letters*, 14(3):139–143 (1981).

13. Huffman, D., A Method for the Construction of Minimum Redundance Codes, *Proceedings IRE*, 40 (1952).

14. Hu, T.C., and Tucker, A.C., Optimal Computer Search Trees and Variable Length Alphabetic Codes, *SIAM J. Appl. Math.*, 21(4):514–532 (1971).

15. Allen, B., and Munro, J.I., Self-Organizing Search Trees, *ACM J.*, 25(4):526–535 (1978).

16. Hester, J.H., and Hirchberg, D.S., Self-Organizing Linear Search, *ACM Comput. Surv.*, 17(3):295–312 (1985).

17. Sleator, D.D. and Tarjan, R.E., Self-Adjusting Binary Search Trees, *ACM J.*, 32:652–686 (1985).

18. Nievergelt, J., Binary Search Trees and File Organization, *ACM Comput. Surv.*, 6(3):195–207 (1974).

19. Adelson-Velskii, G.M., and Landis, E.M., An Algorithm for the Organization of Information, *Soviet Math*, 3:1259–1263 (1962).

20. Hirchberg, D.S., An Insertion Technique for One-Sided Height Balanced Trees, *Commun. ACM*, 19(8):471–473 (1976).

21. Foster, C.C., A Generalization of AVL trees, *Commun. ACM* 16(8):513–517 (1973).

22. Ottmann, T.S., Six, H.W., and Wood, D., One Sided k-Height Balanced Trees, *Computing*, 22(4):283–290 (1978).

23. Luccio, F., and Pagli, L., Power Trees, *Commun. ACM*, 21(11):941–947 (1978).

24. Guibas, L.J., and Sedgewick, R., A Dichromatic Framework for Balanced Trees. In: *Proc. of the 19th IEEE Symposium on Foundations of Computer Science*, 1978, pp. 8–21.

25. Olivie, H.J., A New Class of Balanced Search Trees: Half Balanced Binary Search Trees, *RAIRO Informatique Theorique*, 16(1):51–71 (1982).

26. Huang, S., and Wong, C.K., Binary Search Trees with Limited Rotations, *BIT*, 23:436–455 (1983).

27. Tarjan, R.E., Updating a Balanced Search Tree in O(1) Rotations, *Inform. Proc. Lett.*, 16:253–257 (1983).

28. Nievergelt, J., and Reingold, E.M., Binary Search Trees of Bounded Balance, *SIAM J. Computing*, 2(1):33–43 (1973).

29. Gonnet, G.H., Balancing Binary Trees by Internal Path Reduction, *Commun. ACM*, 26(12):1074–1081 (1983).

30. Chang, H., and Iyengar, S.S., Efficient Algorithms to Globally Balance a Binary Search Trees, *Commun. ACM*, 27(7):695–702 (1984).

31. Stout, Q.F., and Warren, B.L., Tree Rebalancing in Optimal Time and Space, *Commun. ACM*, 29(9):902–908 (1986).

32. Finkel, R.A., and Bentley, J.L., Quad Trees: A Data Structure for Retrieval on Composite Keys, *Acta Informatica*, 4(1):1–9 (1975).

33. Samet, H., The Quadtree and Related Hierarchical Data Structures, *ACM Comput. Surv.*, 16(2):187–260 (1984).

34. Samet, H., and Webber, R.E., Hierarchical Data Structures and Algorithms for Computer Graphics, Part I: Fundamentals, *IEEE Comput. Graph. Appl.*, 8(3):48–68 (1988).

35. Samet, H., and Webber, R.E., Hierarchical Data Structures and Algorithms for Computer Graphics, Part II: Applications, *IEEE Computer Graph. Appl.*, 8(4):59–75 (1988).

36. Samet, H., *The Design and Analysis of Spatial Data Structures*, Addison-Wesley, Reading, MA, 1990.

37. Samet, H., *Applications of Spatial Data Structures*, Addison-Wesley, Reading, MA, 1990.

38. Bayer, R., and McCreight, C., Organization and Maintenance of Large Ordered Indexes, *Acta Informatica*, 1(2):173–189 (1972).

39. Yao, A.C.C., On Random 2–3 Trees, *Acta Informatica*, 9(2):159–170 (1978).

40. Kriegel, H.P., Vaishnavi, V.K., and Wood, D., 2–3 Brother Trees, *BIT* 18(4):425–435 (1978).

41. Ottmann, T.S., Six H.W., and Wood, D., Right Brother Trees, *Commun. ACM*, 21(9):769–776 (1978).

42. Olivie, H.J., On the Relationship Between Son-Trees and Symmetric Binary B-trees, *Inform. Proc. Lett.*, 10(1):8 (1980).

43. Ottmann, T.S., and Wood, D., 1–2 Brother Trees or AVL Trees Revisited, *Computer J.*, 23(3):248–255 (1980).

44. Bayer, R., Symmetric Binary B-trees: Data Structure and Maintenance Algorithms, *Acta Informatica*, 1(4):290–306 (1972).

45. Saltzberg, B., *File Structures: An Analytic Approach*, Prentice Hall, Englewood Cliffs, NJ 1988, pp. 139–201.

46. Wiederhold, G., *File Organization for Database Design*, McGraw-Hill, New York, 1987, pp. 131–172, 259–326.

47. Comer, D., The Ubiquitous B-tree, *ACM Comput. Surv.*, 11(2):121–137 (1979).

48. Prabhakar, T.V., and Sahasrabuddhe, H.V., Towards an Optimal Data Structure: CB-Trees, *Proc. 10th International Conference on VLDB*, 1984, pp. 235–244.

49. Rosenberg, A.L., and Snyder, L., Time and Space Optimality in B-trees, *ACM Transact. Database Sys.*, 6(1):174–183 (1981).

50. Huang, S., Height Balanced Trees of Order (β, γ, δ), *ACM Transact. Database Sys.*, 10(2):261–284 (1985).

51. Bayer, R., and Unteraurer, K., Prefix B-trees, *ACM Transac. Database Sys.*, 2(1):11–26 (1977).

52. McCreight, E.M., Pagination of B-trees with Variable Length Records, *Commun. ACM*, 20(6):670–674 (1977).

53. Diehr, G., and Faaland, B., Optimal Pagination of B-trees with Variable Length Items, *Commun. ACM*, 27(3):241–247 (1984).

54. Larmore, L.L., and Hirchberg, D.S., Efficient Optimal Pagination of Scrolls, *Commun. ACM*, 28(8):854–856 (1985).

55. Shneiderman, B., and Goodman, V., Batched Searching of Sequential and Tree-Structured Files, *ACM Transact. Database Sys.*, 1(3):268–275 (1976).

56. Hwang, K., and Yao, S.B., Optimal Batched Searching of Tree-structured Files in Multiprocessor Computer Systems, *ACM J.*, 24(3):441–454 (1977).

57. Manolopoulos, Y., and Kollias, J.G., Expressions for Completely and Partly Unsuccessful Batched Search of Sequential and Tree-Structured Files, *IEEE Transact. Software Eng.*, 15(6):794–799 (1989).

58. Lang, S.D., Driscoll, J.R., and Jou, J.H., A Unified Analysis of Batched Searching of Sequential and Tree-Structured Files, *ACM Transact. Database Sys.*, 14(4):604–618 (1989).

59. Lang, S.D., and Manolopoulos, Y., Efficient Expressions for Completely and Partly Unsuccessful Batched Search of tree-structured Files, *IEEE Transact. Software Eng.*, 16(12):1433–1435 (1990).

60. Lang, S.D., Driscoll, J.R., and Jou, J.H., Batch Insertions for Tree Structured File Organizations—Improving Differential Database Representation, *Inform. Sys.*, 11(2):167–175 (1986).

61. Nievergelt, J., Hinterberger, H., and Sevcik, K.C., The Grid File: An Adaptable, Symmetric, Multikey File Structure, *ACM Transact. Database Structures*, 9(1):38–71 (1984).

62. Faloutsos, C., and Christodoulakis, S., Signature Files: An Access Method for Documents and Its Analytical Performance Evaluation, *ACM Transact. Office Inform. Sys.*, 2(4):267–288 (1984).

63. Lum, V.T., Multiattribute Retrieval with Combined Indexes, *Commun. ACM*, 13(11):660–665 (1970).

64. Shneiderman, B., Reduced Combined Indexes for Efficient Multiple Attribute Retrieval, *Inform. Sys.*, 2:149–154 (1977).

65. Cardenas, A.F., and Sagamang, J.P., Doubly Chained Tree Database Organization—Analysis and Design Strategies, *Computer J.*, 20:15–26 (1977).

66. Lien, Y.E., Taylor, C.E., and Driscoll, J.R., A Design and Implementation of a Relational Database, *Proc. 1st International Conference on VLDB*, 1975, pp. 507–518.

67. Lee, D.T., and Wong, C.K., Quintary Trees: A File Structure of Multidimensional Database Systems, *ACM Transact. Database Sys.*, 5(3):339–353 (1980).

68. Bentley, J.L., Multidimensional Binary Search Trees Used for Associative Searching, *Commun. ACM*, 18(9):509–517 (1975).

69. Robinson, J.T., The k–d–B Tree: A Search Structure for Large Multidimensional Dynamic Indexes, *Proc. ACM SIGMOD 81 Conference*, 1981, pp. 10–18.

70. Chang, J.M., and Fu, K.S., Extended k–d Tree Database Organization: A Dynamic Multi-attribute Clustering Method, IEEE *Transact. Software Eng.*, 7(3):284–290 (1981).

71. Fushimi, S., Kitsuregawa, M., Nakayama, M., Tanaka, H., and Moto-Oka, T., Algorithm and Performance Evaluation of Adaptive Multidimensional Clustering Technique, *Proc. ACM SIGMOD 85 Conference*, 1985, pp. 308–318.

72. Yu, C.T., and Jiang, T.M., Adaptive Algorithms for Balanced Multidimensional Clustering, *Proc. 4th IEEE Data Engineering International Conferenced*, 1988, pp. 386–393.

73. Ooi, B.C., Saks-Davis, R., and McDonell, K.J., Extending a DBMS for Geographic Applications, *Proc. 5th IEEE Data Eng. International Conference*, 1989, pp. 590–597.

74. Lomet, D., and Saltzberg, D., A Robust Multiattribute Search Structure, *Proc. 5th IEEE Data Engineering International Conference*, 1989, pp. 296–304.

75. Vaishnavi, V.K., On the Height of Multidimensional Height-Balanced Trees, *IEEE Transact. Computers*, 35(9):773–780 (1986).

76. Vaishnavi, V.K., Multidimensional Balanced Binary Trees, *IEEE Transact. Computers*, 38(7):968–985 (1989).

77. Sharma, K.D., and Rani, R., Choosing Optimal Branching Factors for k–d–B-trees, *Inform. Sys.*, 10(1):127–134 (1985).

78. Mehlhorn, K., and Tsakalidis, A., Data Structures. In: *Handbook of Theoretical Computer Science*, Elsevier Science Pub., New York, 1990.

79. Sarnak, N., and Tarjan, R.E., Planar Point Location using Persistent Search Trees, *Commun. ACM*, 29(7):669–679 (1986).

80. Burton, F.W., Kollias, J.G., Kollias, V.G., and Matsakis, D.G., Implementation of Overlapping B-Trees for Time and Space Efficient Representation of Collection of Similar Files, *Computer J.*, 33(3):279–280 (1990).

81. Christodoulakis, S., and Ford, A.D., File Organization and Access Methods for CLV Optical Disks, *Proc. ACM SIGIR 89 Conference*, 1989, pp. 152–159.

82. Easton, M.C., Key-Sequence Data Sets on Indelible Storage, *IBM J. Res. Dev.*, 30(3):230–241 (1986).

83. Lomet, D., and Saltzberg, D., Access Methods for Multiversion Data, *Proc. ACM SIGMOD 89 Conference*, 1989, pp. 315–324.

89. Manolopoulos, Y., and Kapetanakis, G., Overlapping B+-trees for Temporal Data, *Proc. JCIT 90 Conference*, 1990, p. 491–498.

85. Larson, P.A., Performance Analysis of Linear Hashing with Partial Expansions, *ACM Transact. Database Sys.*, 7(4):566–587 (1982).

86. Litwin, W., and Lomet, D., The Bounded Disorder Access Method, *Proc. 2nd IEEE Data Engineering International Conference*, 1986, pp. 38–48.

87. Litwin, W., and Lomet, D., A New Method for Fast Data Searches with Keys, *IEEE Software*, 4(2):16–24 (1987).

88. Lomet, D., Partial Expansions for File Organizations with an Index, *ACM Transact. Database Sys.*, 12(1):65–84 (1987).

89. Baeza-Yates, R.A., and Larson, P.A., Performance of B+-trees with Partial Expansions, *IEEE Transact. Knowledge and Data Eng.*, 1(2):248–257 (1989).

90. Guttman, A., R-trees: A Dynamic Index Structure for Spatial Searching, *Proc. ACM SIG-MOD 84 Conference*, 1984, pp. 47–57.

91. Roussopoulos, N., and Leifker, D., Direct Spatial Search on Pictorial Databases using Packed R-trees, *Proc. ACM SIGMOD 85 Conference*, 1985, pp. 17–31.

92. Sellis, T., Roussopoulos, N., and Faloutsos, C., The R+-tree: A Dynamic Index for Multi-dimensional Objects, Proc. 13th International Conference on VLDB, 1987, pp. 507–518.

93. Beckmann, N., Kriegel, H.P., Schneider, R., and Seeger, B., The R*-tree: An Efficient and Robust Access Method for Points and Rectangles, *Proc. ACM SIGMOD 90 Conference*, 1990, pp. 322–331.

YANNIS MANOLOPOULOS

ERRATUM

The following is a corrected version of an article that appeared in Volume 25.

FINITE-STATE MACHINES

INTRODUCTION

In order to qualify as a scientific discipline, computer science needs to have formal models of its subject matter: computation. Indeed, various such models exist, each abstracting some of the properties of real computation and modelling others. The most famous and useful model is also one of the earliest: Turing machines, proposed by Alan Turing in 1936 [1]. Turing's intention was to investigate the question of which functions cannot be computed *in principle*. Therefore, his model of computation is very strong. There is a large body of evidence suggesting that, in fact, Turing machines are the strongest possible model of real computation in the sense that any function which is not computable by a Turing machine is, in principle, not computable by any physical computer, past, present, or future (this is known as the Church/Turing thesis). Based on this thesis, computability in general is identified with computability by Turing machines. For example, a decision problem that cannot be solved by a Turing machine is called *undecidable*.

Near the other end of the spectrum is the model of *finite-state machines* (FSMs), whose origins appeared in Ref. 2. This model views a system (hardware, software, or other) as a black box with a number of input and output ports. The actions of the system are assumed to occur at discrete instants of time, so that the inputs, if continuous, are only sampled on a signal from some synchronizing source (such as a clock). Further, the system is assumed to be finite, with a bounded number of possible internal states. Another assumption is that the system is sequential—this is not intended to be a model of (asynchronous) parallel computation. Natural examples of discrete, finite, sequential systems are switching circuits (one of the early motivations for the development of this model), mechanical and electromechanical systems such as elevator control units, hydraulic and pneumatic systems, and communication systems. In particular, finite-state machines are often used for the description of communication protocols.

As an example, Figure 1 shows a finite-state model of a simple digital watch with three control buttons which will be labeled *a, b,* and *c.* The inputs to the watch consist of the events of pushing one of those buttons. In order to keep the example small, many of the details of the operation of the watch have been ignored. A more detailed description is presented later.

The FSM model is a very weak model of computation: for example, it is impossible to describe a general multiplier for arbitrary-length multiplicands using a finite-state machine. However, it is very useful and appropriate for the description of the kind of systems mentioned above, and has theoretical significance through its intimate relationship with regular languages and grammars, and by virtue of the fact that the control modules for stronger kinds of models (including Turing machines) are really just finite-state machines.

The motivation for the development of the finite-state machine model originally came from three directions: the study of neuron nets, the synthesis and analysis of switching circuits, and the theory of regular languages, for which finite-state machines serve as recognizers. Finite-state machines are still used in the design of very large-scale integrated

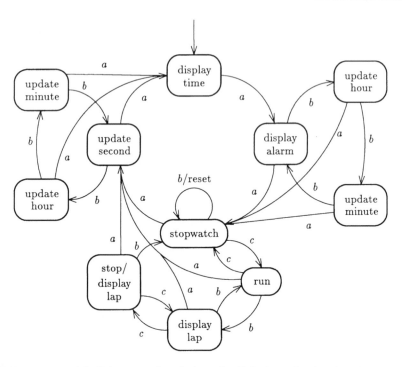

FIGURE 1   A (partial) finite-state description of a digital watch. The three buttons of the watch are labeled *a, b,* and *c.*

(VLSI) circuits, especially program logic arrays (PLAs). More recently, generalizations of the finite-state model are being applied to the design of potentially distributed control systems.

BASIC DEFINITIONS

An essential part of the FSM model is the finiteness assumption. In terms of the inputs of the system, this assumption implies that each input can only assume a finite number of possible values. Therefore, there is only a finite number of possible inputs at each input port at a given time instant. Since the inputs are assumed to be synchronized, all inputs received at the same unit can be represented by a single symbol that has a component for each port. For example, it is natural to view four inputs each of which can be 0 or 1 as a binary number between 0 and 15. Similar considerations apply to the outputs of the system, and therefore the formal model assumes with no loss of generality that the system has a single input stream and a single output stream. The set of symbols that the input can have at any time instant (the *input alphabet*) is denoted by Σ, and the set of output symbols (the *output alphabet*) is denoted by Δ. The set of internal states the machine can have will be denoted by Q.

The only information available to the machine at any time instant is its internal state and the input symbol presented to it. The function δ that gives the next state as a function of the current state and input is thus defined to transform a pair consisting of a state and an input symbol into a state. Symbolically, $\delta : Q \times \Sigma \rightarrow Q$.

Finite-State Machines with Output

In modeling sequential switching circuits it is natural to talk about the outputs of the circuit at each time instant. The outputs may be modeled as being generated between transitions or, alternatively, during the transitions. The first view gives rise to *state-assigned*, or *Moore* machines [3]. These include a function $\lambda : Q \to \Delta$ which gives the output as a function of the state. Formally, then, a state-assigned machine is a six-tuple $M = (Q,\Sigma,\Delta,\delta,\lambda,q_0)$ where q_0 is the initial state of the machine, the one it is in before any input has been received.

The computation performed by this machine on an input sequence $a_1 a_2 ... a_n$ is described by the sequence of states $q_0, q_1,..., q_n$ that the machine goes through, characterized by the equation $q_i = \delta(q_{i-1},a_i)$, and the sequence of outputs.

$$M(a_1 a_2 \cdots a_n) = \lambda(q_0)\lambda(q_1) \cdots \lambda(q_n).$$

Considering outputs to be a function of the transition instead of the state gives rise to *transition-assigned*, or *Mealy* machines [4]. These are described by the same six-tuple as state-assigned machines, except that λ maps $Q \times \Sigma$ to Δ. The sequence of states this machine goes through is defined exactly as in the case of a state-assigned machine; however, the output sequence is

$$M(a_1 a_2 \cdots a_n) = \lambda(q_0, a_1)\lambda(q_1, a_2) \cdots \lambda(q_{n-1}, a_n).$$

Finite-State Machines as Acceptors

In the context of formal languages, finite-state machines are used as decision procedures for deciding whether a given string belongs to a certain language or not. The set of all finite strings of letters from an alphabet Σ is denoted by Σ^*. A language over Σ is a subset of Σ^*. An *acceptor* (or *recognizer*) for a language is a procedure that can be given a string in S^* and determines whether or not the string is in the language. In the former case, it is said to *accept* the string, and in the latter case it is said to *reject* it. Finite-state machines can function as recognizers by providing them with a criterion (the *acceptance condition*) to determine whether the input string is accepted or rejected based on the behavior of the machine during the computation.

One possible model uses state-assigned machines with an output alphabet restricted to the two symbols 0 and 1. The acceptance condition states that a string is accepted by the machine if and only if the last symbol of the output is 1. An equivalent but more appealing characterization does not use outputs but instead designates a special subset of states as *accepting states*. Such a machine is usually called a *finite automaton* (FA). A string is accepted by the automaton if and only if the automaton halts in an accepting state after reading the string. The set of accepting states is denoted by F, and the correspondence between the two models is given by $F = \{q \in Q | \lambda(q) = 1\}$. Thus a finite automaton is formally defined as a 5-tuple (Q,Σ,δ,q_0,F).

Relationships Between the Models

As mentioned above, finite automata can be trivially viewed as a special case of state-assigned machines. There is a minor difference between state-assigned and transition-assigned machines, however, since the former always produce an output sequence whose length is one greater than the length of the input sequence, whereas for the latter the length of the output is equal to the length of the input. In particular, for an empty input (a sequence of length zero), a state-assigned machine will produce the output symbol associated with the starting state q_0, whereas a transition-assigned machine will produce an empty output. However, the first symbol of the output of any given state-assigned machine is always the same, and if we ignore it we can show that the state-assigned and transition-assigned models are equivalent [5].

Formally, if $M_1 = (Q, \Sigma, \Delta, \delta, \lambda, q_0)$ is a state-assigned machine where $\lambda(q_0) = b_0$ then there is a transition-assigned machine M_2 such that for any input sequence $a_1 a_2 \ldots a_n$ the outputs obey the equation $M_1(a_1 a_2 \ldots a_n) = b_0 M_2(a_1 a_2 \ldots a_n)$. (Concatenation of the sequences x and y is denoted by xy.) The construction is very simple: M_2 is identical to M_1 except for its output function λ' which is defined by $\lambda'(q, a) = \lambda(\delta(q, a))$. That is, the output produced by M_2 on any transition is the output M_1 would produce in the target state of the same transition.

Conversely, given a transition-assigned machine M_2 it is possible to build a state-assigned machine M_1 such that $M_1(a_1 a_2 \ldots a_n) = b_0 M_2(a_1 a_2 \ldots a_n)$ holds for every input sequence and some arbitrary output symbol b_0. This construction, however, is not as trivial. Since there may be a number of transitions (possibly with different outputs) leading to the same state of M_2, the target state of a transition of M_1 needs to contain an encoding of the output of that transition. The states of M_1 will therefore consist of pairs $[q, b]$ for a state q and output symbol b. The transitions of M_1 are determined by the first component of the state pair in the same way that M_2 operates. The second component of the final state is determined by the output of M_2 for the corresponding transition, and the output of a state pair $[q, b]$ of M_1 is simply b. Formally, if $M_2 = (Q, \Sigma, \Delta, \delta, \lambda, q_0)$ then $M_1 = (Q, \Sigma, \Delta, \delta', \lambda', [q_0, b_0])$ where $\delta'([q, b], a) = [\delta(q, a), \lambda(q, a)]$ and $\lambda'([q, b]) = b$.

REPRESENTATIONS OF FINITE-STATE MACHINES

Finite-state machines can be represented in various ways, each of which is useful for different purposes. The formal definition given in the previous section uses mathematical functions on the states and inputs. These can be naturally represented by *transition tables*, whose rows correspond to states of the machine and whose columns correspond to possible input symbols. The entries of the table specify the state entered when the machine is in a given state and receives a given input. For transition-assigned machines, the output symbol corresponding to the transition is also shown in the table.

While the representation by transition tables is useful for many algorithms operating on finite-state machines, the more human-oriented representation is visual, and depicts machines as labeled graphs, called *transition diagrams*. The nodes of the graph are the states, and the arcs correspond to transitions. Each arc is labeled with the input symbol(s) that causes the transition. For transition-assigned machines, arcs are also labeled with the output symbol produced by the transition, in the form a/b where a is the input symbol causing the transition and b is the output symbol produced by it. A special arc with no origin indicates the start state.

For example, part (a) of Figure 2 shows a state-assigned machine that acts as a modulo-4 counter. The input alphabet is $\{0, 1\}$, and the output alphabet is $\{0, 1, 2, 3\}$. The output is the number of 1's seen in the input so far, modulo-4. Part (b) of the same figure is the corresponding transition-assigned machine, whose transition table appears in part (c).

Finite automata have similar descriptions, except that instead of indications of the outputs they contain double circles representing the accepting states. For example, the

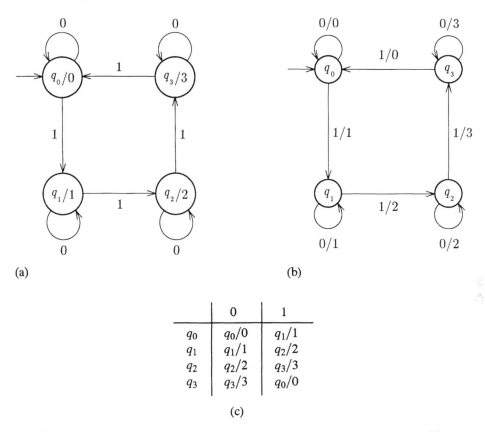

(a)

(b)

	0	1
q_0	$q_0/0$	$q_1/1$
q_1	$q_1/1$	$q_2/2$
q_2	$q_2/2$	$q_3/3$
q_3	$q_3/3$	$q_0/0$

(c)

FIGURE 2 A modulo-4 counter: (a) state-assigned (Moore) machine; (b) transition-assigned (Mealy) machine; (c) transition table for Mealy machine.

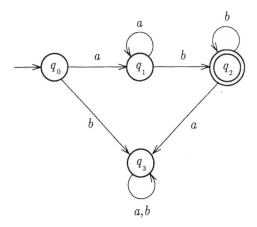

FIGURE 3 A finite automaton accepting strings consisting of one or more a's followed by one or more b's.

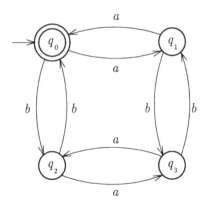

FIGURE 4 A finite automaton accepting strings with an even number of a's and an even number of b's.

automaton shown in Figure 3 recognizes the language over the alphabet $\{a,b\}$ whose strings begin with one or more as followed by one or more bs. To see that, notice that state q_1 is entered after one a is seen. Subsequent as leave the machine in the same state, which is exited when the first b is seen. When the machine is in q_2, the only accepting state, the input has consisted of one or more as followed by one or more bs, as required. If the end of the input is reached while the machine is in q_2, it has the right form and is accepted. Otherwise, the machine will terminate in one of the other states and the input will not be accepted. Note that once the automaton gets into state q_3 it will never leave it. A nonaccepting state with this property is usually called a *sink*, and is used whenever it is possible to show that a given string cannot be a prefix of any string in the language. In this example, such strings are b,aba, etc.

A further example is the automaton shown in Figure 4. An input of a will cause the machine to switch between the right and left parts, and an input of b will make it switch between top and bottom. Each state of this machine can therefore be characterized by the parity of the input letters in inputs that bring the machine to it. When the input contains an even number of bs, the machine will be in one of the two top states, q_0 or q_1, otherwise it will be in bottom state q_3 or q_4. Similarly, the left states correspond to an even number of as and the right states correspond to an odd number of as. Since q_0 is the only accepting state, it follows that the strings in the language recognized by this automaton are exactly those having an even number of as as well as an even number of bs.

A subject not treated here is the algebraic theory of finite automata; for a comprehensive treatment see the volumes by Eilenberg cited in the bibliography.

EXTENSIONS OF THE BASIC FORMALISM

The finite automata defined earlier can be extended in various ways. The power of a given extension can be measured in terms of the languages it enables the model to recognize, as well as in terms of complexity: the size of machine required to recognize a given language. The first measures the expressive power of the model, and the second measures its succinctness.

While some extensions increase the expressive power of the model, others do not. Generally speaking, removing the finiteness assumption by stipulating potentially infinite storage results in more powerful machines, from the stronger push-down automata that have an unbounded stack, to Turing machines that use an unbounded random–access memory and which according to the Church/Turing thesis are of maximal power. On the other hand, increasing the flexibility of the control unit without removing the finiteness assumption usually does not increase the expressive power of the model. However, there may be significant differences in succinctness. Such models are therefore very useful for the synthesis of finite automata, which can be first specified using a more flexible and succinct model and then mechanically translated to the basic model defined above. The following sections discuss several such extensions.

Nondeterministic Finite Automata

Consider first the case of nondeterministic finite automata (NFA) [6]. In contrast with the deterministic finite automata (DFA) described above, whose behavior is fully determined by their input sequence, nondeterministic machines may have more than one possible computation corresponding to a single input sequence.

The basic model is extended by allowing any number of transitions from a given state to be labeled with the same input symbol (including none at all). The transition function δ in this case maps $Q \times \Sigma$ to 2^Q. The value of $\delta(q,a)$ is now a subset of Q, denoting all the states in which the automaton may be after receiving the input a in state q. This set may be empty, which means that there is *no* legal transition in that case.* A string x is considered to be in the language $L(M)$ defined by the nondeterministic automaton M if there is *some* valid computation of M which accepts x (i.e., a sequence of transitions allowed by the transition function which leaves the machine in an accepting state). Note that a DFA is a special case of an NFA in which $\delta(q,a)$ is always a singleton set.

Another way to view the computation of a nondeterministic automaton is to say that whenever a choice point is reached, the automaton spawns copies of itself, each copy pursuing one alternative. A copy that has *no* possible transitions simply disappears. An accepting computation is one in which at least one of the copies resides in an accepting state when the entire input has been scanned. (This implies that if no copy remains, the input is not accepted.) This view attributes to the NFA model a limited kind of unbounded concurrency. (It is unbounded since the number of copies, or processes, can grow at each step and has no fixed bound.)

For example, suppose it is desired to build an automaton to recognize the following language L over the alphabet $\{a,b\}$. The strings in L are precisely those whose last letter has appeared previously in the string. For example, *baaaab* and *aabaab* are in L, while *aaaab* is not.

A nondeterministic finite automaton M_1 recognizing this language is shown in Figure 5a. This automaton is nondeterministic since, for example, state q_0 has two a transitions leaving it while state q_3 has no transitions leaving it at all. The automaton first skips some portion of the input sequence while remaining in state q_0. At some point it "guesses" that the next symbol is the one occurring at the end of the input and switches to either of q_1 or q_2 depending on whether that symbol is a or b, respectively. It remains in that state until it nondeterministically guesses that the last input symbol is about to appear, at which point it switches to q_3 and accepts the input.

---

*This extension is trivial, and can be replaced by a special "sink" state with a self-loop for each input symbol.

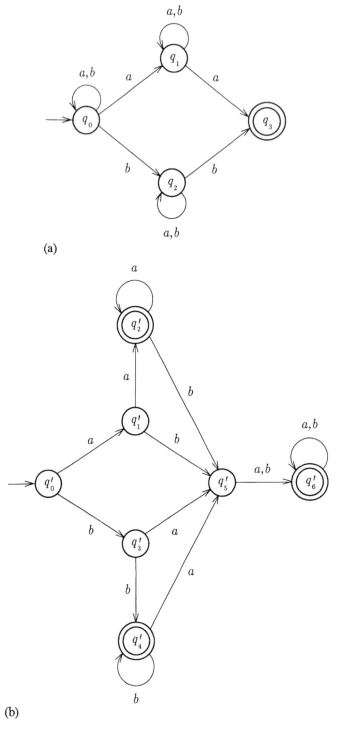

(a)

(b)

FIGURE 5   Finite automata accepting strings over $\{a,b\}$ whose last letter also appears previously in the string: (a) a nondeterministic automaton; (b) a deterministic automaton; (c) the correspondence between them.

q_0'	$\{q_0\}$	q_4'	$\{q_0, q_2, q_3\}$
q_1'	$\{q_0, q_1\}$	q_5'	$\{q_0, q_1, q_2\}$
q_2'	$\{q_0, q_1, q_3\}$	q_6'	$\{q_0, q_1, q_2, q_3\}$
q_3'	$\{q_0, q_2\}$		

(c)

FIGURE 5 (Continued)

It is now easy to see that for any string in L there is at least one accepting computation of M_1, namely the computation in which the guesses all turn out to be correct. Strings not in L will have no accepting computation, and are thus not accepted by M_1.

A deterministic automaton M_2 which recognizes the same language is shown in Figure 5b. Figure 5c gives the correspondence between the states of M_1 and M_2. For example, the input strings that leave M_2 in state q_5' may leave M_1 in either of the states q_0, q_1, or q_2.

In general, given any NFA $M = (Q, \Sigma, \delta, q_0, F)$, it is possible to construct a DFA $M' = (Q', \Sigma, \delta', q_0', F')$ which accepts the same language [6]. (In that case, M and M' are said to be *equivalent*.) The states of M' correspond to *sets* of states of M, as in the previous example, so that $Q' = 2^Q$. The transitions of M' are defined by the equation

$$\delta'(p, a) = \{\delta(q, a) \mid q \in p\}.$$

In the example above, the input a would move M_1 from q_0 to itself or to q_1, and from q_1 to itself or to q_3. The corresponding transition of M_2 therefore takes it from $q_1' = \{q_0, q_1\}$ to $q_2' = \{q_0, q_1, q_3\}$. The initial state is simply $q_0' = \{q_0\}$, and the accepting states of M' are those containing any of the accepting states of M, i.e., $F' = \left\{ p \in 2^Q \mid p \cap F \neq \emptyset \right\}$.

Thus, in the case of finite automata, nondeterminism does not increase the power of the model in terms of the languages it can recognize, since any NFA has an equivalent DFA, as shown above. However, the size of a deterministic automaton may be exponentially larger than the size of an equivalent nondeterministic automaton [7]. To see this, consider the example of Figure 5. It can be generalized to a language over an alphabet containing n different symbols which contains those strings whose last symbol also appears in some other position of the string. A nondeterministic acceptor for this language, generalizing Figure 5a, would have $n + 2$ states. A deterministic acceptor for the same language would have to remember in its states all letters which have previously appeared, and would therefore require at least 2^n states.

The construction of a deterministic automaton from a nondeterministic one gives an exponential upper bound on the size of the deterministic automaton; therefore this is a tight bound. However, this is only a worst-case bound; in practice, many of the states of the deterministic automaton may turn out to be inaccessible or redundant and may be eliminated using the techniques presented in the section Minimization of Deterministic Machines. Moreover, the inaccessible states need never be explicitly constructed.

Finite Automata with ϵ Moves

The model can be extended to allow the automata to make more than one move per input symbol. This can be modeled by allowing transitions that do not involve reading any input

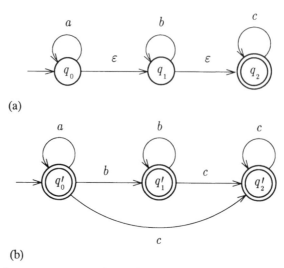

(a)

(b)

FIGURE 6   Finite automata accepting strings consisting of zero or more *a*s followed by zero or more *b*s followed by zero or more *c*s: (a) an NFA with ϵ-moves; (b) an NFA without ϵ moves.

symbol. Such transitions will be labeled with ϵ, which stands for the empty sequence. Formally, the only difference between a DFA with ϵ moves and a basic DFA is that the transition function of the former maps $Q \times (\Sigma \cup \{\epsilon\})$ to Q. Similarly, the transition function of an NFA with ϵ moves maps $Q \times (\Sigma \cup \{\epsilon\})$ to 2^Q. Again, a string is considered to be accepted by such an automaton if there is some computation, possibly including ϵ transitions, which halts in an accepting state.

For example, the automaton shown in Figure 6a recognizes the language over the alphabet $\{a,b,c\}$ whose strings are alphabetically ordered, that is, all *a*s precede all *b*s which precede all *c*s. The automaton "guesses" nondeterministically when the sequence of *a*s ends and uses the ϵ transition to switch to q_1. Similarly, it uses the second ϵ transition to switch to q_2 when the *b*s have ended.

It is straightforward to replace the ϵ transitions of a finite automaton by other (nondeterministic) transitions which are labeled with input symbols. For example, Figure 6b shows an NFA which recognizes the same language as the automaton of Figure 6a. In general, all that needs to be done is to simulate the actions of the automaton for every input symbol and any number of ϵ transitions and to add a corresponding transition. The new automaton will be in an accepting state if there is a sequence of ϵ transitions which leads from it to some accepting state in the original automaton. The new automaton will have the same number of states as the original. It follows that in the nondeterministic case, ϵ moves do not increase the expressive power of the model nor its succinctness.

In the deterministic case, the expressive power is of course the same. However, DFA with ϵ moves can be exponentially more succinct than those without. This can be shown by adapting the example in Fig. 5 to build a DFA with ϵ moves containing $2n + 3$ states to recognize the language that can only be accepted by a DFA with at least 2^n states. The construction uses ϵ moves for the nondeterministic choices and deterministically verifies that they guessed correctly, moving into a sink state otherwise. The same technique can be applied to convert any NFA with n states into a DFA with ϵ moves the number of whose states is

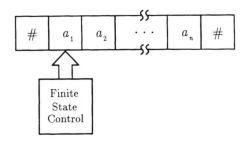

FIGURE 7   A two-way automaton with endmarkers.

bounded by n times the nondeterministic branching factor of the original NFA,[*] and thus by n^2. Thus the addition of ϵ moves to the DFA model brings its succinctness close to that of the NFA model.

Two-Way Automata

Another possible extension to the finite automata model is to endow it with a limited read-only memory: the ability to remember the whole sequence of inputs. Instead of assuming that the input is presented symbol by symbol in a temporal sequence, assume that the input sequence is given on a tape which the machine can inspect at its leisure but not modify. A two-way finite automaton (2FA) [6,8] is thus endowed with a "reading head" which can move in both directions along its input tape, as shown in Figure 7. The input sequence will be surrounded on both sides by a special *endmarker* #, which does not belong to the input alphabet; the head is initially positioned at the first (leftmost) input symbol.

The transition function of a 2FA needs to specify for every state and symbol scanned by its head the state it enters and the direction the head moves in. A deterministic two-way finite automaton (2DFA) is formally defined as a 5-tuple (Q,Σ,δ,q_0,F) just like a DFA, except that δ maps $Q \times (\Sigma \cup \{\#\})$ to $Q \times \{-1,0,+1\}$ where -1 signifies backward (or left) movement, $+1$ signifies forward (or right) movement, and 0 denotes no movement. Similarly, the transition function of a nondeterministic two-way finite automaton (2NFA) maps $Q \times (\Sigma \cup \{\#\})$ to $2^{Q \times \{-1,0,+1\}}$, allowing more (or less) than one move per state and input symbol scanned. A string is accepted by a 2DFA if it enters an accepting state at any time during its computation. If it loops indefinitely without entering an accepting state or moves past the endmarkers, the string is not accepted. A 2NFA accepts a string if it has at least one accepting computation.

The basic model can be seen to be a special case of the two-way model in which only forward movement is allowed (with a slight change in the meaning of accepting states).

A two-way automaton equivalent to the DFA of Figure 4 is shown in Figure 8. Strings in the language recognized by these automata have an even number of as as well as an even number of bs. The two-way automaton scans the input twice, first checking the parity of the as, and then checking the parity of bs. In this case, the two-way automaton has one more state than the one-way automaton. However, if this example is generalized to an input al-

---

[*]This is the maximal number of different transitions labeled with the same input symbol emanating from any state of the NFA.

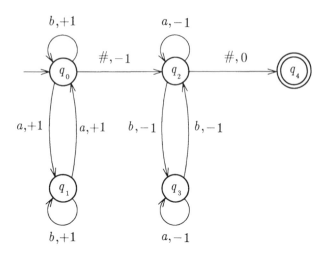

FIGURE 8   A two-way automaton accepting strings with an even number of *a*s and an even number of *b*s (cf. Fig. 4).

phabet containing n symbols, a two-way recognizer for the language of strings with even parities of all symbols would require $2n + 1$ states, while a one-way automaton would require at least 2^n states. The economy in states comes at the expense of increased computation time, which is n times longer for the two-way machine. This demonstrates that a one-way automaton may require exponentially more states than a two-way machine that recognizes the same language. (An n^n lower bound is established in Ref. 7.)

Two-way automata, however, recognize the same languages as one-way automata, and so the expressive power of the model is not changed even by this extension. This is due to the fact that while the tape can be arbitrarily long, the machine can record in its states only a bounded number of different "observations" about any input position. This point can be formalized as follows. Consider the boundary between any two symbols on the input tape of a 2DFA M with n states. When M crosses that boundary it can be in one of its n states and going in one of two directions. If that boundary is crossed more than $2n$ times, at least two of these crossings must have the same state and direction. Since the input tape is fixed and M is deterministic, it must therefore be in a loop, and the input is not accepted. Therefore accepting computations have a finite number of crossing patterns at each symbol boundary, and these can be used to build a one-way automaton which collapses all the moves of the 2DFA into one scan of the input. A one-way automaton M' which simulates M would need to remember for each move of M across that boundary from right to left whether it ever returns across the same boundary and in what state. Thus, states of M' need to contain a representation of the behavior of M on crossing the boundary from right to left in all possible states. Since this information for any boundary can be computed from the input symbol scanned and the corresponding information for the previous boundary, it is in fact possible to construct the machine M'.

The above observation is generalized to nondeterministic machines by noting that if a 2NFA passes the same boundary in the same direction at the same state then all the computation it carried out between those crossings was redundant. While this does not imply that the machine is in a loop, it does show that if there is *any* accepting computation then there is one which does not contain duplicate crossings, and the same argument therefore applies.

EQUIVALENCE AND MINIMIZATION

A natural question to ask about finite-state machines is whether it is possible to find the minimal machine (i.e., having the minimal number of states) which realizes a particular input–output relationship. This *minimization problem* is particularly interesting in the context of sequential switching circuit design, since an automaton with fewer states will presumably yield a circuit using fewer memory elements, which are usually more expensive then memoryless combinational logic.

A closely related problem is to tell whether two given machines compute the same function; this is called the *equivalence problem*. It turns out that the equivalence problem is undecidable for the next class of models—push-down automata. However, for finite-state machines the equivalence and the minimization problems are both computable [3,9].

The following discussion is limited to deterministic machines, for which these problems are actually computable in polynomial time. The nondeterministic case, where the problems are much more difficult, will be described later.

Minimization of Deterministic Machines

There are two classes of redundant states in a deterministic finite-state machine. *Inaccessible states* are those which do not participate in any computation of the machine. Formally, a state q is inaccessible if there is no input sequence x which will leave the machine in q when started on x in the initial state q_0. A machine that does not contain inaccessible states is *connected*. Inaccessible states can easily be identified in a DFA by checking whether there is some directed path leading to them from the initial state.

The second kind of redundant states are those that are equivalent to some other states. Two states p and q in a machine (Q,Σ,δ,q_0,F) are defined to be equivalent if they cannot be distinguished by any input sequence. In other words, for every input sequence the two machines (Q,Σ,δ,p,F) and (Q,Σ,δ,q,F) yield the same output sequence.

It is easy to see that this relation is an equivalence relation, and therefore partitions the states of the machine into disjoint equivalence classes. If two states are not equivalent, then there is an input sequence that can distinguish between them. If two states *are* equivalent then one of them is redundant, since all transitions leading into it may be channeled into the other without changing the input–output behavior of the machine. A machine that does not contain any equivalent states is *reduced*.

As will be shown below, for deterministic machines the minimal equivalent machine is unique up to a renaming of the states. Furthermore, this machine may be constructed from any connected equivalent machine by an iterative process of identifying equivalent states. A connected and reduced machine, in which no two states are equivalent, is therefore minimal.

The algorithm for identifying equivalent states is based on an incremental notion of equivalence, called *k-equivalence*. Two states are k-equivalent if they cannot be distinguished by input sequences of length at most k. This is also an equivalence relation, and therefore partitions the states of the machine into disjoint equivalence classes such that all states in the same class are k-equivalent and any two states in different classes are k-distinguishable, that is, they can be distinguished by an input sequence of length at most k. This partition is denoted by P_k. Since any $(k + 1)$-equivalent states are also k-equivalent, the partition P_{k+1} is a refinement of P_k in the sense that the classes of P_{k+1} are subclasses of those of P_k.

Two states p and q are $(k + 1)$-equivalent if and only if for every input symbol a the states $\delta(p,a)$ and $\delta(q,a)$ are k-equivalent and the same output is produced. Therefore, the partition P_{k+1} can be computed from the partition P_k as follows. Every two elements p and q in any class of the partition P_k need to be compared with respect to every input symbol. The states p and q are also $(k + 1)$-equivalent if in each case the transitions produce the same output and their target states are k-equivalent (as given by P_k).

If at any stage P_{m+1} turns out to be equal to P_m, there can be no change in any of the following steps, since the procedure is the same. Therefore, the last partition P_m defines k equivalence for all $k > m$, which is the same as full equivalence. This must happen after no more than n steps where n is the number of states of the original machine. To see this, consider the change in the number of equivalence classes between two steps. If the number does not change, the algorithm terminates. Otherwise, it must increase by at least 1. Since there can be no more classes than states, there can be no more than n steps.

Equivalence can be defined between the states of two different machines in exactly the same way, and the above procedure can be used to find such states. The only change to the procedure is to start it on the union of the state sets of both machines. The concept of equivalence can be extended to machines by defining two machines to be equivalent if every state of each machine has an equivalent state in the other machine. (The concept of *machine containment* is defined similarly, except that the condition only goes one way.)

Two equivalent machines whose initial states are equivalent necessarily compute the same input–output function. Of course, two nonequivalent machines may still compute the same input–output function. However, two connected and reduced machines compute the same function if and only if they are equivalent; furthermore, they need to be isomorphic, in the sense that they have exactly the same structure except for a possible renaming of states. This can be determined by simulating the procedure for determining equivalence between the two machines and showing that each equivalence class of the final partition contains exactly one state from each machine. This partition then provides the isomorphism function

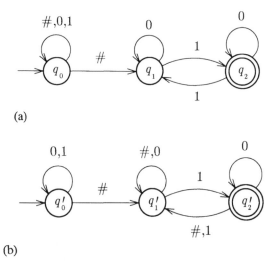

(a)

(b)

FIGURE 9 Two minimal and equivalent NFAs which are incomparable.

between the two machines.

Since the minimal machine is unique up to isomorphism, the above procedure can be used to compute the minimal machine for any given deterministic finite-state machine.

A more algebraic method for minimization is based on the Myhill-Nerode theorem [10,11]. For more detail see the texts cited in the bibliography.

Minimization of Nondeterministic Machines

The equivalence problem for deterministic finite-state machines is decidable by reduction to the deterministic versions. However, this procedure may be exponential in the worst case, since the size of the corresponding deterministic machine may be exponential. It can be shown using the techniques of Meyer and Stockmeyer [12] that the equivalence and minimization problems for nondeterministic machines are both PSPACE complete.* In fact, the minimal NFA computing a given function is not always unique. For example, the two NFAs shown in Figure 9 recognize the same language,† cannot be further reduced, and yet are nonisomorphic.

In the context motivating this investigation, the design of sequential switching circuits, these limitations are not problematic, since minimization would normally be done on the deterministic version anyway.

REGULAR EXPRESSIONS

A formalism for describing certain kinds of languages, which should be familiar to users of modern operating systems, editors, and compiler-building tools, is that of *regular expressions* [13]. Given some finite alphabet Σ, regular expressions are algebraic expressions over the symbols of Σ and the symbols ϵ and ϕ using the operations of concatenation, union, and repetition (the latter is also called Kleene's closure).

The definition of the form and meaning of regular expressions (i.e., the sets they denote) is as follows. Let a be a symbol in Σ, and let r and s be, inductively, regular expressions denoting the sets R and S, respectively. Then the following are also regular expressions:

ϕ, which denotes the empty set
ϵ, which denotes the set $\{\epsilon\}$
a, which denotes the set $\{a\}$
(rs), which denotes the set $RS = \{xy \mid x \in R, y \in S\}$
$(r + s)$, which denotes the set $R \cup S$
$(r*)$, which denotes the set $R* = \{x_1..x_n \mid x_1, ..., x_n \in R, n \geq 0\}$

Parentheses may be omitted, based on the rule that * (repetition) has the highest precedence, concatenation the next highest, and + (union) the lowest. Note that $r*$ always contains the empty string ϵ.

Languages that can be described by regular expressions are called *regular languages*.

---

*PSPACE-complete problems are the hardest problems requiring polynomial space for their solution, and are strongly conjectured to require exponential time.
†This language contains the strings over {0,1,#} which contain at least one # and an odd number of 1's after the last # sign.

Examples

The regular expression $(a + b)^*$ denotes the set of all strings over the alphabet $\Sigma = \{a,b\}$. The set of strings composed of alternating as and bs that start and end with a can be described by the two regular expressions $a(ba)^*$ and $(ab)^*a$ (as well as by infinitely many others).

Consider now the set of strings which only contain even blocks of as, which is denoted by $(aa + b)^*$. A regular expression describing the set of strings with an even number of as is $(b^*ab^*a)^*b^*$.

The last two examples can be generalized to give a regular expression describing the language L whose strings contain an even number of as as well as an even number of bs. (A finite automaton which recognizes this language was presented in Figure 4.) First, let r be the regular expression $((bb)^*a(bb)^*a)^*(bb)^*$. This expression describes all strings with an even number of as in which bs only occur in blocks of even size. The language L can now be described by

$$(r^*b(bb)^*r^*b(bb)^*)^*r^*.$$

A string in L can be matched with this expression by matching odd blocks of bs with the $b(bb)^*$ subexpressions inside the topmost repetition operator. Blocks with an even number of bs occurring among those with an odd number will match the $(bb)^*$ subexpressions of r.

Consider the language recognized by the automata of Figure 6; this is the language of all strings over $\{a,b,c\}$ which are alphabetically ordered. A regular expression describing the same language is $a^*b^*c^*$. Finally, the language recognized by the automata of Figure 9 is denoted by the regular expression

$$(0 + 1 + \#^* \#(0^*10^*1)^*10^*.$$

Relationship to Finite-State Automata

Regular expressions turn out to have the same expressive power as finite-state automata in the sense that the set of languages recognized by finite automata is exactly the set of regular languages. [This result is called *Kleene's theorem (13,14)*.] Thus there are two different characterizations of the class of regular languages. This is very useful, since each characterization may be amenable to different proof techniques, and a proof which is difficult using one formalism may be easy using the other.

Kleene's theorem can be proved by showing that for any regular expression it is possible to construct a finite automaton that recognizes the same language and vice versa. In the first direction, it is advantageous to use a strong model of finite automata, in this case NFA with ϵ moves. In order to be able to combine the automata corresponding to subexpressions easily, this proof uses only automata with a single accepting state with no exiting transitions.* The proof proceeds by induction on the structure of the regular expression, according to the definition given above. The three base cases of the proof are depicted graphically in Figure 10, and the inductive cases are shown in Figure 11.

---

*Note that any NFA can be transformed into this form by adding a new unique accepting state, and using ϵ moves to connect all old accepting states to the new one.

FIGURE 10   Translating regular expressions into NFAs: the base cases: (a) ϵ; (b) ϕ; (c) a.

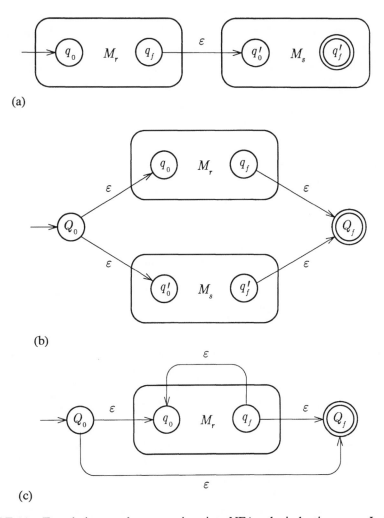

FIGURE 11   Translating regular expressions into NFAs: the inductive cases. Let M_r and M_s be restricted NFA with ϵ moves (see text) corresponding to the regular expressions r and s, respectively. The constructions in this figure correspond to the regular expressions (a) rs, (b) $r + s$, and (c) $r^\star$.

In the opposite direction, it is necessary to exhibit a regular expression for the language recognized by a given finite automaton. In this case it is best to use the most restrictive, deterministic, model. Given a DFA

$$M = (\{q_0, \ldots, q_{n-1}\}, \Sigma, \delta, q_0, F),$$

define the set R_{ij}^k to contain those strings that take M from q_i to q_j without passing through any state q_ℓ such that $\ell \geq k$. In particular, the set R_{ij}^0 is the set of all strings that take M from q_i to q_j without passing through *any* other state. Therefore R_{ij}^0 consists of strings of length one that label transitions from q_i to q_j, and if $i = j$ also the empty string ϵ. Since R_{ij}^0 is a finite set, it is always possible to construct a regular expression r_{ij}^0 for it having one of the forms ϕ, ϵ, $a_1 + \ldots + a_m$, or $a_1 + \ldots + a_m + \epsilon$.

Strings in the set R_{ij}^k can be recursively characterized as follows: first, they might belong to R_{ij}^{k-1}, in which case they don't lead the machine through q_k at all. Otherwise, they have an initial prefix in R_{ik}^{k-1} that takes the machine to q_k for the first time. Following this, there is a (possibly empty) number of substrings in R_{kk}^{k-1} which lead from q_k back to itself. Finally, the suffix is in R_{kj}^{k-1} and leads from q_k to q_j. Thus, a regular expression r_{ij}^k denoting the set R_{ij}^k is

$$r_{ij}^{k-1} + r_{ik}^{k-1}(r_{kk}^{k-1})^* \, r_{kj}^{k-1}.$$

Finally, if the accepting states of M are $q_{i_1}, \ldots, q_{i_m}$, the regular expression denoting the set recognized by M is $r_{0i_1}^n + \cdots + r_{0i_m}^n$.

Complexity

As mentioned earlier, nondeterministic automata are exponentially more succinct than deterministic automata. The relationship between deterministic automata and regular expressions is more complicated. Each description can be exponentially more succinct than the other for certain languages. An exponential lower bound on the transformation from deterministic automata to regular expression is (implicitly) given by Ehrenfeucht and Zeiger [*15*]. The corresponding upper bound is established by the construction given above, which produces expressions whose size is at most exponential in the size of the original automaton. Note that even though the transformations from NFA to DFA and from DFA to regular expressions may each increase the size of the representation exponentially, the same construction as above yields a (single) exponential upper bound on the transformation from NFA to regular expressions. Abstractly, the reason is that regular expressions and NFA both employ the same kind of nondeterminism, which may be called *existential nondeterminism*, and therefore there is no extra gain.

A worst-case exponential lower bound on the transformation from regular expressions to deterministic automata is given by the following example (which can also serve to show the corresponding result for the transformation from NFA to DFA). Define the language L_n to consist of all strings of length exactly $2n$ over the alphabet $\{0,1\}$ whose second half is not identical to the first. A regular expression describing this language consists of the union of all expressions of the form*

$$\Sigma^i 0 \Sigma^{n-1} 1 \Sigma^{n-i-1} + \Sigma^i 1 \Sigma^{n-1} 0 \Sigma^{n-i-1}$$

for all i between 0 and $n - 1$, where Σ stands for the regular expression $(\mathbf{0} + \mathbf{1})$. Each such expression describes a string whose first part does not match its second part in the i-th position. The size of this expression is proportional to n^2. A corresponding DFA would need to remember the complete first half of the string and would therefore require at least 2^n states.

Again, the upper bound in this case is given by the procedure presented above for transforming a regular expression into a linear-size NFA, which can then be turned into a DFA of at most exponential size.

While the transformation from regular expressions to NFA is linear, the opposite direction may require an exponential blowup. This also follows from Theorem 4.1 of Ref. *15*, since the complete graph used there can be viewed as a minimal NFA.

Similar questions arise regarding the succinctness of various extensions to the syntax of regular expression, such as adding intersection, complement, and/or difference, which have not been fully investigated.

REGULAR GRAMMARS

Another mechanism for describing languages which should be familiar to any one who has seen a formal definition of any programming language is that of *formal grammars* [*16–19*]. Four general classes of grammars correspond to the limitations placed on the possible production rules. The most familiar kind are *context-free grammars*, a variant of which is the well-known Backus-Naur Form (BNF). The grammars related to finite automata are a special case of context-free grammars, and are called *regular* (or *right-linear*) *grammars*.

Formally, a grammar consists of a set P of production rules over some alphabet Σ whose elements are called *terminal symbols* and another alphabet N of *nonterminal symbols* which name larger syntactic units. Production rules have the form $\alpha \to \beta$ for strings α and β from $(N \cup \Sigma)^*$. Additionally, a special symbol $S \in N$ is designated as the *start symbol* of the grammar. A grammar is thus defined as the 4-tuple (N, Σ, P, S).

The operational meaning of a production rule $\alpha \to \beta$ is that the substring α may be replaced by β in any string derived by the grammar. A string which contains no nonterminals is in the language defined by the grammar if there is a sequence of such substitutions which begins with the start symbol and ends with that string.

Formally, a string τ over the alphabet $N \cup \Sigma$ can be derived from the string σ in a grammar G (denoted by $\sigma \Rightarrow \tau$) if σ has the form $\phi \alpha \psi$ and τ has the form $\phi \beta \psi$, and G contains a production rule $\alpha \to \beta$. In other words, a substring α of σ may be changed to β by an application of the rule $\alpha \to \beta$. A string over the alphabet Σ is in the language $L(G)$ defined by the grammar G if it can be derived by a finite number of applications of rules of G from the start symbol S.

Context-free grammars (including the BNF variant) obey the restriction that the left-hand side of any production rule is a single nonterminal symbol. Regular grammars are further restricted and must have one of the forms $A \to aB$ or $A \to a$ for $A, B \in N, a \in \Sigma$. Since using these forms only the language will never contain the empty string, a rule of the form $S \to \epsilon$ is also allowed in a regular grammar whose start symbol is S.

For example, a regular grammar that defines the same language recognized by the automata of Figure 5 is

---

*The meta-notation r^i denotes the expression r repeated i times, and is not part of the syntax of regular expressions.

$$G = (\{S,A,B,C\},\{a,b\},P,S)$$

where P contains the following rules:

$$S \rightarrow aS \qquad S \rightarrow bS \qquad S \rightarrow aA \qquad S \rightarrow bB$$

$$A \rightarrow aA \qquad A \rightarrow bA \qquad A \rightarrow a$$

$$B \rightarrow aB \qquad B \rightarrow bB \qquad B \rightarrow b$$

A derivation of the string $abbaba \in L(G)$ can be described by the following chain of rule applications:

$$S \Rightarrow aS \Rightarrow abS \Rightarrow abbS \Rightarrow abbaA \Rightarrow abbabA \Rightarrow abbaba$$

(An alternative possible derivation has $S \Rightarrow aA$ as the first step.)

There is a very strong correspondence between regular grammars and nondeterministic acceptors [*17*]. Each can be directly transformed into the other, with the states of the NFA corresponding to the nonterminal symbols of the grammar. The automaton may have a single additional accepting state that corresponds to production rules of the second form ($A \rightarrow a$); this state may be thought of as corresponding to a missing nonterminal, or ϵ. In the previous example, the correspondence between the grammar G and the NFA of Figure 5a is given by:

$$q_0 \leftrightarrow S \qquad q_1 \leftrightarrow A \qquad q_2 \leftrightarrow B \qquad q_3 \leftrightarrow \epsilon$$

In general, a given grammar (N,Σ,P,S) can be transformed into an NFA $(N\cup\{\epsilon\},\Sigma,\delta,S,\{\epsilon\})$ which has a transition from A to B labeled a for every production rule $A \rightarrow aB$ of P and a transition from A to ϵ labeled a for every production $A \rightarrow a$.

Conversely, given an NFA (Q,Σ,δ,q_0,F) it is possible to construct a grammar (Q,Σ,P,q_0), which has a production rule $q_i \rightarrow aq_j$ for every transition from q_i to q_j in δ which is labeled by a. Additionally, if $q_j \in F$, the production rule $q_i \rightarrow a$ is also in P.

In both cases, the language recognized by the NFA is the same as the language defined by the grammar. It follows that the languages definable by regular grammars are exactly the regular languages. Furthermore, the complexity results presented above for nondeterministic automata apply also to regular grammars.

LIMITATIONS OF THE FINITE-STATE MODEL

The power of a particular model of computation is measured in terms of the decision problems it can solve or the functions it can compute. The first characterization is appropriate for acceptors, while the second is appropriate for machines with output.

Limitations of Finite-State Acceptors

The limitations of finite automata can be studied through the class of languages they can recognize: the regular languages. If a certain language L can be shown to be nonregular, it follows that it cannot be recognized by any finite automaton, and therefore the problem of deciding for a given string x whether $x \in L$ is not solvable in the finite-state model.

One of the simplest examples of a nonregular language is the language $L = \{a^i b^i \mid i \geq 0\}$ consisting of some number of as followed by the same number of bs. If this language were regular, it could be recognized by some DFA M. Let n be the number of states of M. Consider the sequence of states $q_{i_0}, \ldots, q_{i_n}$ that M goes through during its processing of the input string a^n. The automaton starts in the initial state $q_{i_0} = q_0$. After reading all the as, it has gone through n transitions and $n + 1$ states. Since M has only n states, it must have gone through some state q_{i_k} at least twice (this argument is the *pigeon-hole principle*). Suppose $q_{i_k} = q_{i_{k+\ell}}$ for some $\ell > 0$. If the substring a^ℓ is removed from the input string, the loop in the sequence of states would be removed, but the automaton would end up in the same state q_{i_n}, since its behavior is exclusively determined by the current state and the unseen portion of the input. For the same reason, if the string b^n is added to a^n or to $a^{n-\ell}$ the final state would be the same, and therefore M will either accept both $a^n b^n$ and $a^{n-\ell} b^n$ or reject them both. Therefore M cannot recognize the language L, and the language is not regular.

The proof above can be generalized to show the following property, called the *pumping lemma* for regular languages [6,20], which is a very useful tool for proving nonregularity of formal languages:

> For every regular language L there is a constant n such that any string $z \in L$ whose length is greater than n can be decomposed into three parts $z = uvw$ with the following properties: (1) v is nonempty; (2) the length of uv together is at most n; and (3) $uv^i w \in L$ holds for all $i \geq 0$.   The number n is no greater than the number of states of the minimal DFA which recognizes L.

For example, it is easy to use the pumping lemma to show that the language $\{a^{i^2} \mid i \geq 1\}$ of strings of as whose length is a perfect square is not regular. Suppose this language were regular, and let n be the constant in the pumping lemma. The string $z = a^{n^2}$ is in the language and can therefore be decomposed into three parts $u = a^k$, $v = a^\ell$, and $w = a^m$ such that $\ell > 0$, $k + \ell \leq n$, and $k + \ell + m + = n^2$. By the pumping lemma, the string $uv^2 w = a^{k+2\ell+m}$ must also be in the language. However, $k + 2\ell + m$ cannot be a perfect square, since $n^2 = k + \ell + m < k + 2\ell + m \leq n^2 + n < (n + 1)^2$ by the properties above. Therefore the language is not regular.

Many other languages can be proved nonregular by this method, including the language of palindromes (strings that read the same forward and backward), the language of balanced parentheses (and, more generally, languages containing mathematical expressions with balanced parentheses), the set of all strings with an equal number of as and bs, and the set of all binary representations of primes. Intuitively, what is common to all these examples is the necessity of counting unbounded numbers.

Limitations of Finite-State Transducers

Machines with outputs can be thought of as defining a function, or transduction, from sequences of inputs to sequences of outputs. For example, if the input alphabet consists of all pairs $[ij]$ of binary digits i and j and the output alphabet is $\{0,1\}$, it is natural to think of the input sequence as two binary numbers and the output sequence as a single binary number. It is natural to assume that the numbers are presented and produced starting with the least significant bit. A finite-state machine that computes the sum of two numbers is presented in Figure 12. Clearly the only thing that needs to be remembered is the carry, and indeed q_0 corresponds to carry 0, and q_1 corresponds to carry of 1.

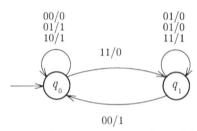

FIGURE 12   A Mealy machine that performs binary addition.

Since multiplication is repetitive addition, it might be expected that multiplication is also possible using finite-state machines. However, this is not the case. Suppose M is an FSM with n states that performs multiplication. Consider the multiplication of 2^m by itself for some $m > n$. This corresponds to the input sequence $[00]^m[11][00]^m$ and should result in the output sequence $0^{2m}1$. In the sequence of states that M goes through when reading the first n [00] pairs following the pair [11] there must be a duplication. Since the rest of the input sequence is a repetition of the same symbol, M must keep being on the same loop thereafter, and since it must produce outputs of 0 on the loop, it must go on producing 0s and cannot produce the required 1.

In general, if the input to an FSM is unrestricted, then so is the output. For example, a machine with a single state whose output symbol is identical to the input will reproduce any input string exactly. However, restrictions on the class of inputs do result in restrictions on the class of outputs. This translates into a restriction on the functions computable by FSM, and is thus a reflection on the power of the model.

One possible restriction is to have an input alphabet consisting of a single symbol, so that inputs are finite sequences of the same symbol. In effect, the particular symbol becomes irrelevant, and the machine can be thought of as an autonomous generator of outputs. A finite-state generator has a set of accepting states, and defines the language of strings produced by some path from the initial state to some accepting state. Such a generator can be reinterpreted as an acceptor, and therefore the languages that can be generated by finite-state machines are exactly the regular languages.

The function defined by an FSM M can be generalized to map a given language L to the set $M(L)$ of all output strings corresponding to inputs from L. When L is a regular language, so is $M(L)$. This can be shown by building a generator for L and directing its output to M, resulting in a generator for $M(L)$.

A different generalization of the constant input case is the requirement that the input be periodic, or even ultimately periodic. An *ultimately periodic* input is one that becomes periodic after a certain nonperiodic prefix, and has the form $uvv...v...$. An *ultimately periodic language* is a set of prefixes of an ultimately periodic string which terminate at specified positions in the strings u and v. Formally, let U be a finite set of prefixes of u and V a finite set of prefixes of v. Then the set $U \cup uv^*V$ is ultimately periodic.

It is easy to see that any ultimately periodic language can be generated by a finite-state generator. In fact, the structure of this generator is very simple: it consists of some sequence of states followed by a single loop (such generators are called *deterministic*). The converse is also true: any language defined by a deterministic finite-state generator is ultimately periodic.

It follows from the first property mentioned above that ultimately periodic languages are also regular. By linking a generator and a transducer it is possible to show that the transduction of an ultimately periodic language by a finite-state machine is also ultimately periodic.

Not every regular language is also ultimately periodic; however, regular languages over an alphabet consisting of a single symbol must be ultimately periodic. (The proof is based on the pumping lemma.) In that case, the language can be identified with the set of lengths of strings in it. A set X of integers is said to be ultimately periodic if there are numbers N and d such that for all $k > N$ the numbers k and $k + d$ are either both in X or both not in X. It is easy to see that this definition is consistent with the previous one.

This gives rise to the following construction: build a transducer C consisting of a single state which produces the output symbol 1 regardless of its input. For every regular language L, the transduction set $C(L)$ contains a string 1^k if and only if L contains a string of length k. Since $C(L)$ is regular and built out of a single symbol, it must also be ultimately periodic. This provides a tool for proving nonregularity of languages based on the lengths of their strings. For example, it follows that the language

$$L_1 = \{a^{n-1}b^1 a^{n-2}b^2 \ldots a^{n-i}b^i \ldots a^1 b^{n-1} \mid n \geq 1\}$$

is nonregular, since $C(L)$ is the set of all strings of 1s whose length is a perfect square, and the set of all squares is not ultimately periodic.

Computers as Finite-State Machines

Since the memory of any computer, including auxiliary storage, is finite, it follows that every computer can be viewed as a finite-state machine. In fact, it is true that no computer can multiply arbitrary-length numbers, since for every computer there are numbers too large for its total storage capacity. However, this is not a satisfactory way of modeling computation in general, since it is so limited. Instead, stronger models do assume some kind of unbounded memory and investigate the limitations of computation under those stronger assumptions.

In this context, it is also relevant to consider the number of states required for representing the memory of a computer. If the memory contains n bits, there are 2^n different possibilities for the contents of that memory, and therefore an exponential number of states is required to represent it as a finite-state machine. Given that the number of bits accessible to a large modern computer (disregarding the existence of computer networks) is on the order of 10^{10}, a finite-state representation would require $2^{(10^{10})}$ states. Again, this is not a satisfactory model, and a model with a more structured representation for memory is required for this purpose.

PROPERTIES OF REGULAR LANGUAGES

Closure Properties

One of the most important properties of regular languages, the pumping lemma, was presented in the previous section. The pumping lemma is mostly used to show that certain languages are not regular, and thus are not definable by any of the formalisms discussed above. Showing that a language *is* regular can of course be done by exhibiting a representation of it in one of those formalisms (of course, the more permissive formalisms are easier to use for this purpose). A different approach is to construct the language compositionally from other regular languages. This raises the question of which operations on languages preserve regularity.

An operator F is said to *preserve regularity* if it yields a regular language when applied to regular languages. The same property is often expressed by saying that the class of regular languages is *closed under the operation F*.

The regular languages are closed under many operators. In particular, the following operators preserve regularity: union, intersection, complementation, difference, concatenation, repetition, reversal, closure under prefix, and homomorphisms [6,13,20,21; see also 22,23 for further results]. These will now be discussed in turn.

For the following discussion, assume that L_1 and L_2 are regular languages recognized by the DFA M_1 and M_2 and denoted by the regular expressions r_1 and r_2, respectively. Each representation is more useful than the other for proving certain closure properties. However, a construction that is easy to describe may have bad complexity properties, and usually the DFA representation is more compact.

To show that the union $L_1 \cup L_2$ is regular, note that it can be denoted by the regular expression $r_1 + r_2$. A more complex proof using automata constructs the *product automaton* whose states are pairs containing a state of M_1 and a state of M_2 which simulates the parallel execution of both machines at once. The initial state of this automaton is the pair consisting of the initial states of the original machines, and the accepting states are those pairs which contain at least one accepting state from either machine.

The same construction of the product automaton with a different set of accepting states can be used to prove that the intersection $L_1 \cap L_2$ is regular. In this case, both components of the accepting states of the product automaton need to be accepting states of their respective automata.

The DFA M_1 can be transformed into a DFA which accepts the complement $\overline{L_1}$ of L_1 by changing accepting states to nonaccepting and vice versa. Incidentally, this provides an alternative proof for closure under intersection, which can be represented using De Morgan's law as

$$L_1 \cap L_2 = \overline{\overline{L_1} \cup \overline{L_2}}.$$

The concatenation and repetition languages $L_1 L_2$ and L_1^* are easily seen to be regular since they can be represented by the regular expressions $r_1 r_2$ and r_1^*, respectively.

The reversal x^R of a word $x = a_1 \ldots a_n$ is the word $a_n \ldots a_1$. The reversal of the language is L_1 is $L_1^R = \{x^R \mid x \in L_1\}$. A regular expression r_1^R representing this language can be obtained from r_1 by reversing all concatenations in r_1 and leaving all other operators intact. Thus this language is also regular. An alternative construction takes an automaton recognizing L_1 and builds an NFA that recognizes L_1^R by reversing the direction of transitions and exchanging initial states with accepting states.

The closure under prefix of L_1, denoted by prefix(L_1), is the set of all prefixes of strings in L_1. Formally

$$\text{prefix}(L_1) = \{x \mid xy \in L_1 \text{ for some } y \in \Sigma^*\}.$$

A DFA that recognizes this set can be built from M_1 by making any state from which *some* accepting state of M_1 is reachable into an accepting state.

Finally, a homomorphism is a mapping which assigns to every symbol in the input alphabet Σ a string over some alphabet Δ. A homomorphism $h : \Sigma \to \Delta^*$ can be extended to strings as follows:

$$h(a_1 \ldots a_n) = h(a_1) \ldots h(a_n).$$

Now h can be extended to languages by defining

$$h(L) = \{h(x) \mid x \in L\}.$$

The language $h(L_1)$ can be shown to be regular by transforming r_1 (over Σ) into a regular expression over Δ which denotes it. This is done by replacing every occurrence of each symbol a in r_1 by $h(a)$.

For example, assume the input alphabet $\Sigma = \{a,b,c,d\}$. The set of strings which contain at least one occurrence of the string aa is the concatenation of Σ^*, $\{aa\}$, and Σ^*, and is therefore regular. Its complement is the regular set L_a whose strings contain *no* occurrence of aa, i.e., where every a is isolated from other as. The sets L_b, L_c, and L_d defined similarly are also regular. Their intersection is the set L' of strings all of whose letters are isolated, and is also regular. Applying the homomorphism h defined by $h(a) = aa$, $h(b) = bb$, $h(c) = cc$, and $h(d) = dd$ to L' yields the regular language $h(L')$; letters in the strings of this language always appear in pairs.

It is important to note that all the proofs above are constructive: they provide a method for building a representation of the language resulting from an application of the operation from representations of the parts. Thus, all the closure results presented above are *effective*: they can be carried out by a computer by manipulating representations of the languages.

Decision Procedures

Many interesting questions can be asked about formal languages. Examples are: Is a language empty? Is it finite? Infinite? Universal (equal to Σ^*)? Are two languages equal? Is one language a subset of another? Are two languages disjoint?

For context-free languages, for example, many of these questions are undecidable; that is, they are not solvable in principle. For example, the problems of deciding whether two context-free languages are disjoint or whether two context-free grammars generate the same language are unsolvable. However, for regular languages all the above problems are in fact decidable [3,6].

Abstractly, the first four problems are solved by the following theorem, which follows directly from the pumping lemma:

> A regular language recognized by a DFA with n states is empty if and only if it contains no strings of length less than n; the language is infinite if and only if it contains strings of length at least n but less than $2n$.

Thus to check whether the language is empty it is only necessary to check whether one of the finite set of words of length less than n is accepted by the automaton. To check whether the language is infinite or finite it is only necessary to check whether some word of length between n and $2n$ is accepted or not. To see whether the language is Σ^*, check whether its complement is empty.

Of course, these methods are highly inefficient. In practice, these questions can be answered directly by inspecting the DFA. The language it recognizes is empty if and only if no accepting state is reachable from the initial state. The language is universal if all reachable states are accepting. It is infinite if there is at least one reachable cycle containing an accepting state.

Deciding whether two languages are equal can be performed by building DFAs for them and testing whether these are equivalent, as discussed previously. Containment of one language by another can be decided using the same methods. Alternatively, to decide whether $L_1 \subseteq L_2$, it is enough to test whether L_1 and $\overline{L_2}$ are disjoint. Two languages are disjoint if their intersection is empty; the product automaton which recognizes the intersection can be built by the methods described in the previous section and then tested for emptiness as described above.

GENERALIZATIONS OF THE FINITE-STATE MODEL

Besides the stronger computational models such as push-down automata and Turing machines mentioned above, there are other generalizations of the finite-state model. Three of these will be discussed here. The first is the use of finite-state machines to describe sets of infinite strings, the second is the addition of chance to the behavior of finite-state machines, and the third is the addition of hierarchy, bounded concurrency, and communication, which result in representations exponentially more succinct than the finite-state ones.

Languages with Infinite Strings

When modeling certain kinds of computational systems it is natural to think in terms of nonterminating computations. Such systems include telephone switching networks, air-traffic control systems, computer operating systems, and satellite control systems. The behavior of these systems can be modeled using infinite streams of inputs, states, and actions.

There are a number of characterizations of sets of infinite strings which use a finite-state machine as the basic model [24–26]. The criteria for acceptance are different, but are all based on the notion of the set of states through which the automaton passes an infinite number of times during its processing of the input string. For a given FSM M and (infinite) input string σ, this set is denoted by $\mathrm{Inf}(M,\sigma)$.

A *Büchi automaton* [24] is an FSM M with a set F of accepting states. The automaton accepts a string σ if $\mathrm{Inf}(M,\sigma) \cap F \neq \phi$. In other words, M needs to pass through some accepting state infinitely often. For example, suppose a denotes a request by a process for some resource and b denotes the granting of such a request. The requirement (called a *fairness condition*) that every request is eventually granted is given by the Büchi automaton of Figure 13. Accepting computations of this automaton pass through q_0 infinitely often; in other words, they do not stay indefinitely at q_1, which would signify an unsatisfied request.

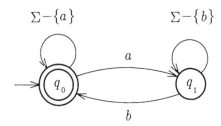

FIGURE 13   A Büchi automaton accepting infinite sequences in which every a (request) is followed by a b (service).

Muller automata [26] use a more general acceptance criterion. Instead of a set of accepting states they use a collection $\mathbf{F}$ of sets of states. A string σ is accepted by the automaton if and only if $\text{Inf}(M,\sigma) \in \mathbf{F}$. A Büchi automaton is a special case of a Muller automaton defined by $\mathbf{F} = \{I \subseteq Q \mid I \cap F \neq \phi\}$.

It turns out that the class of infinitary languages defined by deterministic or nondeterministic Muller automata is the same class defined by nondeterministic Büchi automata (as well as by various other models). These languages are called the *ω-regular languages*.

The ω-regular languages can be shown to be closed under union, intersection, and complementation. For further details see Thomas [27].

Probabilistic Automata

Physical systems contain an element of chance: it is impossible to predict their behavior with absolute confidence. An extension to the basic finite-state formalism which models probabilistic behavior is useful for studying the effects of errors on otherwise deterministic systems as well as for studying inherently probabilistic systems. Applications include the study of communication channels, the synthesis of reliable networks from unreliable components, learning, and pattern recognition.

A probabilistic finite-state machine is different from an FSM in that there is a probability associated with each transition subject to the condition that the probabilities of all transitions from a given state labeled with a given input symbol sum to one. There are state-assigned and transition-assigned probabilistic machines, as well as probabilistic acceptors.

A probabilistic finite-state machine defines a probability measure on the possible outputs for every input sequence. A probabilistic automaton P can be viewed as defining sets of strings by adding a parameter λ, called a *cut-point*, in the range $0 \leq \lambda < 1$ and considering the set $P(\lambda)$ of all inputs that are accepted with probability greater than λ. It turns out that probabilistic automata can define nonregular sets, and therefore have greater expressive power than finite automata. However, the set is always regular if λ is rational.

Probabilistic automata can be arbitrarily more succinct than finite automata. In particular, there is a probabilistic automaton P with just two states such that for every n there is a cut-point λ_n such that the set $P(\lambda_n)$ can be recognized by a DFA with no less than n states.

For further details on this subject see Paz [28].

Communication and Hierarchy

When attempting to describe a complex system using the finite-state formalism, a major difficulty is the blowup in the size of the description as more or less orthogonal components are added. For example, suppose a certain system is functionally composed of four parts, each of which is described by a finite-state machine having ten states. The combined representation would include 10,000 states. An extreme example of that was given in "Computers as Finite-State Machines," where it was pointed out that a computer with a memory of n bits requires a finite-state machine with at least 2^n states for its description. Of course, if the parts of the system are fully independent, there is no need to combine the descriptions at all. Typically, however, there are some interactions between the components of the system, and these can only be described in a joint representation. A further disadvantage of the joint finite-state description is that it is difficult to understand since the distinctions between the components are no longer present.

A number of generalizations of the basic finite-state representation attempt to rectify these problems [e.g., *29,30*]. They use communication and, to a lesser extent, a hierarchy of states , to solve the exponential blowup problem. A direct and comprehensive extension, the statechart formalism [*31,32*], is described below.

The statechart formalism enables the natural and economical description of hierarchical systems. States in this formalism have a rich internal structure. They come in two flavors: AND states and OR states. For an example of the former, consider the three update states at the left of Figure 1. Pressing the *a* button n each of them causes a transfer to the "display time" state. They can therefore profitably be grouped into one superstate, and the three *a* transitions can be replaced by a single one exiting from that state. By inspecting Figure 1 it can be seen that another two such groups can profitably be created. This has been done in Figure 14, which contains a statechart representation of the same watch.

Figure 14 contains much more detail than the finite-state machine of Figure 1. In particular, notice the additional orthogonal components labeled "light" and "beep" in the "operating" state. These are examples of AND-decomposition; in this case it means, for example, that whatever other function the *b* button has, the light goes on when it is pressed and off when it is released. In general, AND-decomposition can be used to describe concurrent processes, where the number of processes is bounded by the design.

Transitions in a statechart can trigger new events, which can be sensed throughout the statechart. Additionally, transitions may have enabling conditions on them that refer to states inside other orthogonal components. These two mechanisms allow the modelling of broadcast communication between parallel processes.

In a very strong sense, these features, collectively labeled *bounded cooperative concurrency* [*33*], provide for an exponential succinctness of description. Furthermore, this is orthogonal to the savings made possible by other extensions, such as nondeterminism. For example, combining bounded cooperative concurrency and nondeterminism is exponentially more succinct than either alone and double exponentially more succinct than the finite-state model. These bounds are tight: there are examples where each is achieved, and no higher savings can be realized.

SUMMARY

The finite-state machine model is based on the assumptions of discreteness of time as well as inputs and outputs, finiteness of the control mechanism, and sequential action. It is a weak model of computation in general, and the computations it can describe have many limitations. In particular, the class of languages it can recognize consists of the regular languages, which have very simple structure.

The weakness of this model is also its chief strength: since it is so simple, its properties are well-known and amenable to computation. As shown in Properties of Regular Languages all the reasonable questions and constructions pertaining to this model are decidable and effective. This is not the case even for the slightly more powerful context-free languages and their representation by means of push-down automata. Moreover, the variety of different formalisms with the same expressive power but different complexity and compositionality characteristics is very useful since it is possible to choose the most appropriate representation for a given task.

The practical importance of the model stems from the fact that many systems can be naturally described as finite-state machines. The results and techniques described above are therefore applicable in many cases. Even when the model is found lacking, it is many times possible to use a more general representation which contains finite-state machines as components.

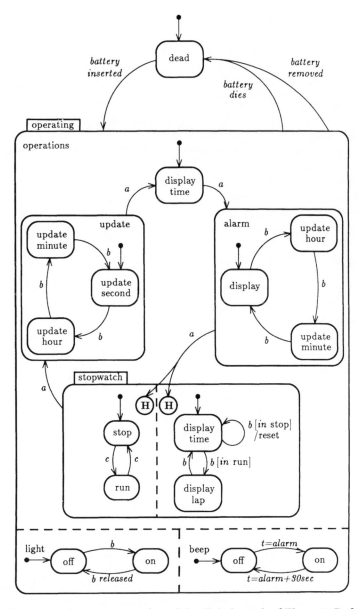

FIGURE 14   A statechart representation of the digital watch of Figure 1. Default arrows start with small circles; AND decomposition of a state is denoted by dashed lines; circled H's stand for history return (return to the configuration that existed in the previous visit of the state).

ACKNOWLEDGMENTS

D. Harel, O. Maler, Y. Moses, D. Peleg, S. Safra, and M. Tennenholz have provided helpful comments.

REFERENCES

1. A. M. Turing, "On Computable Numbers with an Application to the Entsceidungs-problem," *Proc. London Math. Soc., 2–42,* 230-265 (1936). Correction, *ibid., 2–43,* 544-546.
2. W. S. McCulloch and W. Pitts, "A Logical Calculus of the Ideas Immanent in Nervous Activity," *Bull. Math. Biophys., 5,* 115-133 (1943).
3. E. F. Moore, "Gedanken Experiments on Sequential Machines," in *Automata Studies,* C. E. Shannon and J. McCarthy (eds.), Princeton University Press, Princeton, 1956, pp. 129-153.
4. G. H. Mealy, "A Method for Synthesizing Sequential Circuits," *Bell System Tech. J., 34*(5), 1045-1079 (1955).
5. O. Ibarra, "On the Equivalence of Finite-State Sequential Machine Models," *IEEE Trans. Electr. Comp., EC–16,* 88-90 (1967).
6. M. O. Rabin and D. Scott, "Finite Automata and Their Decision Problems," *IBM J. Res., 3*(2), 115-125 (1959).
7. A. R. Meyer and M. J. Fischer, "Economy of Description by Automata, Grammars, and Formal Systems," in *IEEE Conf. Record 12th Ann. Symp. Switching and Automata Theory,* 1971, pp. 188-191.
8. J. C. Shepherdson, "The Reduction of Two-Way Automata to One-Way Automata," *IBM J. Res., 3*(2), 198-200 (1959).
9. D. A. Huffman, "The Synthesis of Sequential Switching Circuits," *J. Franklin Inst., 257*(3-4), 161-190, 275-303 (1954).
10. J. Myhill, *Finite Automata and the Representation of Events,* Technical Report 57-624, Wright Air Development Command, Wright-Patterson Air Force Base, OH, 1957.
11. A. Nerode, "Linear Automaton Transformations," *Proc. Am. Math. Soc., 9,* 541-544 (1958).
12. A. R. Meyer and L. J. Stockmeyer, "The Equivalence Problem for Regular Expressions with Squaring Requires Exponential Space," in *IEEE Conf. Record 13th Ann. Symp. Switching and Automata Theory,* 1972, pp. 125-129.
13. S. C. Kleene, "Representation of Events in Nerve Nets and Finite Automata," in *Automata Studies,* C. E. Shannon and J. McCarthy (eds.), Princeton University Press, Princeton, 1956, pp. 3-42.
14. R. McNaughton and H. Yamada, "Regular Expressions and State Graphs for Automata," *IRE Trans. Electr. Comp., EC-9,* 39-57 (1960).
15. A. Ehrenfeucht and P. Zeiger, "Complexity Measures for Regular Expressions," *J. Comp. Sys. Sci., 12*(2), 134-146 (1976).
16. N. Chomsky, "Three Models for the Description of Language," *IEEE Trans. Inform. Theory, 2*(3), 113-124 (1956).
17. N. Chomsky and G. A. Miller, "Finite State Languages," *Inform. Control, 1*(2), 91-112 (1958).
18. N. Chomsky, "On Certain Formal Properties of Grammars," *Inform. Control, 2*(2), 137-167 (1959).

19. Y. Bar-Hillel, C. Gaifman, and E. Shamir, "On Categorical and Phrase-Structure Grammars," *Bull. Res. Council Israel, 9F*, 155–166 (1960).

20. Y. Bar-Hillel, M. Perles, and E. Shamir, "On Formal Properties of Simple Phrase Structure Grammars," *Z. Phonetik. Sprach. Kommunikationsforsch., 14*, 143–172 (1961).

21. S. Ginsburg and G. F. Rose, "Operations Which Preserve Definability in Languages," *J. ACM, 10*(2), 175–195 (1963).

22. S. Ginsburg and E. H. Spenier, "Quotients of Context-Free Languages," *J. ACM, 10*(4), 487–492 (1963).

23. S. Ginsburg and G. F. Rose, "Preservation of Languages by Transducers," *Inform. Control, 9*, 153–176 (1966).

24. J. Büchi, "On a Decision Method in Restricted Second Order Arithmetics," in *Proc. Intl. Congr. on Logic, Method. and Phil. of Sci., 1960*, E. Nagel et al. (eds.), Stanford University Press, Stanford, 1962, pp. 1–12.

25. R. McNaughton, "Testing and Generating Infinite Sequences by a Finite Automaton," *Inform. Control, 9*, 521–530 (1966).

26. D. Muller, "Infinite Sequenes and Finite Machines," in *Proc. 4th IEEE Symp. on Switching Circuit Theory and Logical Design*, 1963, pp. 3–16.

27. W. Thomas, "Automata on Infinite Objects," in *Handbook of Theoretical Computer Science*, J. Van Leeuwen (ed.), North-Holland, Amsterdam, 1989.

28. A. Paz, *Introduction to Probabilistic Automata*, Academic Press, New York, 1971.

29. *Functional Specification and Description Language (SDL)*, Recommendations Z.101–Z.104, Vol. VI, Fasc. VI.7, CCITT (International Communication Union), Geneva, 1981.

30. P. T. Ward, "The Transformation Scheme: An Extension of the Data Flow Diagram to Represent Control and Timing," *IEEE Trans. Software Eng., 12*, 198–210 (1986).

31. D. Harel, "Statecharts: A Visual Formalism for Complex Systems," *Sci. Computer Progr., 8*, 231–274 (1987).

32. D. Harel, "On Visual Formalisms," *Comm. ACM, 31*, 514–530 (1987).

33. D. Harel, "A Thesis for Bounded Concurrency," in *Proceedings Symposium on Mathematical Foundations of Computer Science* (Rytro, Poland), Springer Verlag, New York, 1989.

ANNOTATED BIBLIOGRAPHY

General introductions to the range of computational models from finite-state machines to Turing machines and their uses in the theories of formal languages, computability, and complexity:

Denning, P. J., J. B. Dennis, and J. E. Qualitz, *Machines, Languages, and Computation*, Prentice-Hall, Englewood Cliffs, NJ, 1978.

Hopcroft, J. E. and J. D. Ullman, *Introduction to Automata Theory, Languages, and Computation*, Addison-Wesley, Reading, MA, 1979.

The definitive presentation of the algebraic theory of finite automata:

Eilenberg, S., *Automata, Languages, and Machines*, Vols. A and B, Academic Press, New York, 1974.

Descriptions of finite-state machines from the point of view of the design of switching circuits:

Harrison, M. A., *Introduction to Switching and Automata Theory*, McGraw-Hill, New York, 1965.

Hennie, F. C., *Finite-State Models for Logical Machines*, John Wiley, New York, 1968.

Formal mathematical treatments of finite-state machines:

Gill, A., *Introduction to the Theory of Finite-State Machines,* McGraw-Hill, New York, 1962.

Ginsburg, S., *An Introduction to Mathematical Machine Theory*, Addison-Wesley, Reading, MA, 1962.

YISHAI A. FELDMAN

Printed and bound by CPI Group (UK) Ltd, Croydon, CR0 4YY

22/10/2024

01777327-0001